AI Transformations in Global Legal Systems

Jerry Luftman
https://orcid.org/0000-0002-3137-3294
Global Institute for IT Management, USA

Devendra Singh
https://orcid.org/0000-0002-7470-3783
Amity University, Noida, India

Aditya Tomer
https://orcid.org/0000-0002-6398-2617
Amity University, Noida, India

IGI Global
Scientific Publishing
Publishing Tomorrow's Research Today

Vice President of Editorial Melissa Wagner
Director of Acquisitions Mikaela Felty
Director of Book Development Jocelynn Hessler
Production Manager Mike Brehm
Cover Design Jose Rosado

Published in the United States of America by
IGI Global Scientific Publishing
701 East Chocolate Avenue
Hershey, PA, 17033, USA
Tel: 717-533-8845 | Fax: 717-533-7115
Website: https://www.igi-global.com E-mail: cust@igi-global.com

Library of Congress Cataloging-in-Publication Data

Names: Luftman, Jerry N. editor | Singh, Devendra Bahadur, 1978- editor | Tomer, Aditya editor
Title: AI transformations in global legal systems / edited by Jerry Luftman, Devendra Singh, Aditya Tomer.
Other titles: Artificial intelligence transformations in global legal systems
Description: Hershey : IGI Global Scientific Publishing, 2026. | Includes bibliographical references and index. | Summary: "This book explores how artificial intelligence is transforming cybersecurity and the legal landscape. It examines AI's applications in legal research, predictive policing, and data protection while addressing ethical, privacy, and governance challenges to ensure justice, transparency, and responsible innovation"-- Provided by publisher.
Identifiers: LCCN 2026002184 (print) | LCCN 2026002185 (ebook) | ISBN 9798337376851 hardcover | ISBN 9798337376868 paperback | ISBN 9798337376875 ebook
Subjects: LCSH: Artificial intelligence--Law and legislation--India | Artificial intelligence--Moral and ethical aspects--India | Legal research--India--Data processing | Police administration--Technological innovations--India | Data protection--Law and legislation--India | Artificial intelligence--Law and legislation
Classification: LCC KNS80.C65 A35 2026 (print) | LCC KNS80.C65 (ebook)
LC record available at https://lccn.loc.gov/2026002184
LC ebook record available at https://lccn.loc.gov/2026002185

British Cataloguing in Publication Data
A Cataloguing in Publication record for this book is available from the British Library.

Table of Contents

Detailed Table of Contents

This chapter analyzes the growing impact of Artificial Intelligence on legal research and analysis in contemporary judicial systems. It explains how machine learning, natural language processing, and predictive analytics are modernizing legal workflows by enabling faster case law retrieval, more accurate document review, and improved legal reasoning. Through a comparative study of AI adoption in India, the United States, and the European Union, the authors show how platforms such as LexisNexis, Casetext, and Harvey AI reduce research time, minimize error, and expand access to legal information. The chapter also evaluates the ethical implications of algorithmic decision-making, focusing on risks of data bias, limited transparency, and accountability challenges. By examining the intersection between computational intelligence and jurisprudential reasoning, the authors propose a framework for responsible AI governance that balances innovation with principles of justice, fairness, and ongoing human oversight.

AI has transformed contemporary life, changing how people create, work, develop, and communicate. AI, originally intended to mimic human cognition using robotic devices, has grown into a complex, multifaceted field with major social and economic impacts. Machine Learning (ML)—a critical component of AI—helps systems improve via data-driven learning, pattern identification, and experience adaptation. The deep partnership between AI and ML has accelerated the development of intelligent systems that can perform complex cognitive tasks like speech recognition, image understanding, predictive analytics, and autonomous decision-making, once thought to be human abilities. AI technologies are being used to create, modify, and optimize material, challenging IP law notions of authorship, ownership, originality, and responsibility. This chapter discusses AI's metamorphic influence on the IP ecosystem, increasing legal and ethical challenges, and how global IP frameworks

Growing patent applications globally challenge manual examination and prior art search. This chapter presents an AI-based patent analysis framework using natural language processing and machine learning, including BERT transformers and ensemble algorithms (Random Forest, Gradient Boosting, SVM). The framework addresses automated patent classification via Cooperative Patent Classification codes, prior art detection, semantic similarity measurement, and citation network analysis. Experimental validation on 1,847,203 USPTO patents (2010-2020) demonstrates 96.2% F1-score in classification, 0.862 NDCG@10 in prior art retrieval, with production-ready computational efficiency. The study contributes patent-specific language model refinement, neural and traditional feature engineering, multi-task evaluation, attention visualization, and deployment recommendations. Results indicate AI systems can effectively supplement human patent review with expert-level accuracy while handling large-scale document volumes.

This chapter, per the authors, examines how Big Data and AI have transformed trademark deception from sign-based imitation to algorithmically driven perception distortion. It explains how digital platforms collect and analyze massive behavioral datasets to rank, recommend, and position brands in ways that influence consumer belief about origin without copying any mark. Algorithmic practices such as competitor keyword bidding, recommendation bias, and ranking manipulation generate large-scale confusion by shaping what consumers see first and trust most. While global jurisprudence, including the L'Oréal v. eBay decision, recognizes platform-facilitated deception, Indian law still interprets confusion through traditional frameworks distinguishing infringement of the mark from deception of consumer belief. This chapter, per the authors, argues that AI-mediated market architecture produces deception without infringement, creating evidentiary gaps and competitive distortions that require algorithmic transparency, marketplace accountability, and an updated trademark–competition interface

The use of artificial intelligence is currently an important component of the advancement of information technology worldwide. Consequently, the intelligence of a system correlates directly with its ability to perform actions that could have legal consequences. AI has entered many industries, including healthcare and education. The ability of machines to perform tasks that typically require human intelligence is referred to as artificial intelligence. Technology plays a very important role in society today because it has the ability to influence the attitudes and actions of its members. Therefore, comprehensive legislation is needed to ensure that artificial intelligence is used fairly. According to progressive legal theory, AI can be used to meet human needs rather than maintain existing systems. Progressive legal theory is based on the "law for humans" paradigm. This theory links the values of Pancasila as the moral foundation of the Indonesian nation with the ethics of applying artificial intelligence and its consequences.

This study critically examines consumer protection in India's digital marketplace, exposing vulnerabilities in data-driven commerce and introducing the concept of a "Cyber Sherpa" to guide and safeguard consumers. Using a doctrinal legal approach, it analyses global frameworks, landmark cases, and governance models related to cybersecurity, corporate accountability, and data privacy. The findings reveal major gaps in consumer protection and highlight the need for empowerment and legal reform to ensure a secure, trustworthy digital economy. The innovative "Cyber Sherpa" framework redefines policy reform, accountability, and consumer education, positioning India to lead in digital consumer rights.

The rapid advancement of Large Language Models (LLMs) has opened new possibilities for intelligent legal assistants that support research, drafting, case analysis, and decision preparation. This article presents how LLMs combined with Retrieval-Augmented Generation (RAG) can power context aware and reliable legal AI systems. The article outlines technical foundations of such assistants, describing how RAG pipelines integrate legal documents to produce outputs based on reliable sources and reduce hallucinations. Key technical challenges such as constructing legal knowledge bases and managing computational demands are also discussed. Beyond technical design, the article explores the ethical implications of deploying legal chatbots, including bias, unequal access, accountability, and overreliance on automated interpretations. We highlight the requirements for responsible AI in these chatbots, covering explainability, human oversight, and compliance. The article defines a roadmap for developing legal assistants that are accurate, transparent, and aligned with legal and societal norms.

This chapter delves into foundational and contemporary theories related to fraud- such as the Fraud Triangle, Diamond, Pentagon, Scale, and Circle- illustrated with cases that made history like the Ponzi fraud, Enron, Satyam, WorldCom, the Harshad Mehta scam and many more in order to make clear the reasons behind fact. The chapter presents the behavioural, psychological, and situational elements behind

Preface

INTRODUCTION

The rapid diffusion of artificial intelligence across legal systems worldwide marks a profound transformation in how law is created, interpreted, enforced, and experienced. From intellectual property and competition law to consumer protection, human rights, and judicial administration, AI-driven technologies are reshaping long-standing legal doctrines while simultaneously exposing new regulatory, ethical, and institutional challenges. Legal systems—historically grounded in human reasoning, precedent, and procedural formality—are now confronting algorithmic decision-making, data-driven governance, and automated legal services that operate at unprecedented scale and speed.

As editors of *AI Transformations in Global Legal Systems*, we conceived this volume in response to a growing need for interdisciplinary, comparative, and globally informed scholarship that moves beyond speculative debates. The chapters assembled here demonstrate that AI is not merely a technical tool added to legal practice; it is a structural force that is reconfiguring legal accountability, professional roles, market regulation, and rights protection. Across jurisdictions, lawmakers, courts, regulators, and legal professionals are grappling with fundamental questions of authorship, liability, bias, transparency, and legitimacy in AI-mediated environments.

This edited reference book brings together scholars and practitioners from diverse legal traditions and regions to critically examine these transformations. By integrating doctrinal analysis, theoretical reflection, empirical research, and technical insight, the volume aims to provide readers with a comprehensive understanding of how AI intersects with global legal systems. Our objective is to support informed decision-making by academics, policymakers, legal professionals, technologists, and students seeking to navigate the evolving relationship between law and intelligent technologies.

CHAPTER OVERVIEW

Chapter 1 examines the transformative role of AI in legal research and analysis, focusing on machine learning, natural language processing, and predictive analytics. Through comparative insights from India, the United States, and the European Union, the chapter evaluates efficiency gains alongside ethical risks related to bias, transparency, and accountability.

Chapter 2 offers a conceptual analysis of AI's metamorphic impact on intellectual property law, tracing how machine learning-driven creativity challenges traditional legal notions of originality, responsibility, and ownership within global IP frameworks.

Chapter 3 addresses the implications of algorithmic decision-making for competition law in India. It critically assesses how self-learning algorithms complicate established antitrust doctrines related to collusion, dominance, and market accountability.

Chapter 4 focuses on algorithmic bias and structural harm, examining how AI systems can perpetuate discrimination across race, gender, and class. The chapter situates algorithmic injustice within broader social inequalities embedded in data ecosystems.

Chapter 5 presents an AI-based framework for patent analysis, demonstrating how advanced natural language processing and machine learning models can enhance patent classification, prior art search, and citation analysis at scale.

Chapter 6 investigates trademark confusion in the era of algorithmic branding and big data. It argues that AI-driven market architectures can generate consumer deception without traditional infringement, necessitating reforms at the intersection of trademark and competition law.

Chapter 7 approaches AI and law enforcement through the lens of progressive legal theory. Grounded in Indonesian legal philosophy, it emphasizes a "law for humans" paradigm that aligns AI deployment with ethical values and social justice.

Chapter 8 examines consumer protection and digital governance, introducing the concept of a "Cyber Sherpa" to address vulnerabilities in data-driven marketplaces and to strengthen consumer sovereignty in global digital economies.

Chapter 9 analyzes how AI is advancing legal procedures in India, situating national developments within a global context. The chapter evaluates opportunities for efficiency and access to justice alongside regulatory and ethical challenges.

Chapter 10 proposes fuzzy logic–driven governance models for responsible AI adoption in India's legal and cybersecurity ecosystems. It offers a nuanced approach to managing risk, fairness, and accountability beyond binary regulatory frameworks.

Chapter 11 investigates dark patterns and manipulative design in AI-mediated digital markets. Drawing on global regulatory developments, it highlights how predictive algorithms undermine user autonomy and calls for robust legal safeguards.

Chapter 12 explores the relationship between AI, human rights, and data privacy, focusing on India's evolving legal framework and its alignment with international standards. The chapter addresses high-stakes applications such as surveillance, automated decision-making, and deepfakes.

Chapter 13 combines technical and ethical perspectives on building intelligent legal assistants using large language models and retrieval-augmented generation pipelines. It outlines design principles for accuracy, transparency, and responsible deployment.

Chapter 14 concludes the volume's thematic scope by examining fraud theories, forensic accounting, and emerging risks in digital and virtual economies. It highlights the role of AI in fraud detection while emphasizing the continued importance of regulatory oversight and professional judgment.

CONCLUSION

Collectively, the chapters in this volume demonstrate that AI-driven transformation of legal systems is neither uniform nor deterministic. Instead, it is shaped by jurisdictional contexts, regulatory choices, institutional capacities, and societal values. While AI offers powerful tools to enhance efficiency, access to justice, and legal innovation, it simultaneously amplifies risks related to bias, opacity, market manipulation, and rights erosion. The challenge for global legal systems lies in harnessing AI's benefits without compromising foundational principles of fairness, accountability, and human dignity.

A central insight emerging from this book is the necessity of adaptive and anticipatory legal governance. Reactive regulation and fragmented oversight are insufficient in the face of rapidly evolving technologies that transcend national boundaries and traditional legal categories. The contributions underscore the importance of interdisciplinary collaboration, ethical-by-design frameworks, and sustained human oversight to ensure that AI remains a complement to, rather than a substitute for, legal reasoning and judgment.

As editors, we hope that *AI Transformations in Global Legal Systems* serves as a foundational reference for ongoing scholarship and policy development in this critical field. The future of law in the age of artificial intelligence will be shaped not only by technological capability, but by the normative choices societies make about power, responsibility, and justice. This volume is offered as a contribution toward informed, balanced, and globally engaged dialogue on that future.

Chapter 1
AI-Powered Legal Research and Analysis

Chandika Eka Prasetya
http://orcid.org/0009-0001-6447-0058
Universitas Esa Unggul, Indonesia

Binastya Anggara Sekti
http://orcid.org/0000-0001-5489-4888
Universitas Esa Unggul, Indonesia

ABSTRACT

This chapter analyzes the growing impact of Artificial Intelligence on legal research and analysis in contemporary judicial systems. It explains how machine learning, natural language processing, and predictive analytics are modernizing legal workflows by enabling faster case law retrieval, more accurate document review, and improved legal reasoning. Through a comparative study of AI adoption in India, the United States, and the European Union, the authors show how platforms such as LexisNexis, Casetext, and Harvey AI reduce research time, minimize error, and expand access to legal information. The chapter also evaluates the ethical implications of algorithmic decision-making, focusing on risks of data bias, limited transparency, and accountability challenges. By examining the intersection between computational intelligence and jurisprudential reasoning, the authors propose a framework for responsible AI governance that balances innovation with principles of justice, fairness, and ongoing human oversight.

DOI: 10.4018/979-8-3373-7685-1.ch001

1. INTRODUCTION

The legal profession is undergoing a significant transformation as Artificial Intelligence reshapes traditional methods of legal research and analysis. AI challenges long-established jurisprudential practices by altering how legal knowledge is identified, interpreted, and applied (Solum, 2014). Historically, legal research required extensive manual review of case law, statutes, and legal commentaries, making it time-consuming and limited by human cognitive capacity. The rapid growth of legal information further intensified these constraints (Ashley, 2017).

The digitization of legal databases enabled the development of AI-driven tools that apply natural language processing and machine learning to analyze legal texts more efficiently. These systems support semantic search, allowing legal professionals to retrieve relevant precedents and legal principles using natural language queries. As a result, legal research has become faster and more systematic.

Despite these benefits, the adoption of AI raises critical concerns regarding interpretive accuracy, embedded bias, and the preservation of human judgment in legal reasoning. This chapter examines the technological foundations, practical implications, and ethical challenges of AI-powered legal research, offering a balanced framework for understanding its role in contemporary legal practice.

1.1 Evolution of Legal Research Methods

The practice of legal research has undergone several evolutionary phases, each marked by technological innovations that expanded access to legal information and transformed research methodologies. Understanding this historical trajectory provides essential context for appreciating the revolutionary nature of AI integration in contemporary legal practice.

In the pre-digital era, legal research relied entirely on physical law libraries containing printed volumes of case reporters, statutory compilations, and legal treatises. Lawyers employed manual indexing systems such as the West Digest System, which organized cases by topic and key number. Research required physical presence in law libraries, intimate familiarity with classification systems, and substantial time investment. The expertise of law librarians was invaluable in navigating these complex information architectures (Cardellino, Teruel, Alemany, & Villata, 2017).

The first major transformation occurred with computerized legal databases in the 1970s and 1980s. Systems like LexisNexis and Westlaw digitized legal texts, enabling keyword searching across vast document collections. This revolution significantly accelerated research processes, allowing lawyers to search multiple jurisdictions simultaneously and identify relevant authorities more quickly than manual methods permitted. However, these systems required Boolean search expertise and often returned overwhelming result sets requiring extensive human filtering(Aletras, Tsarapatsanis, Preoţiuc-Pietro, & Lampos, 2016).

The internet era brought further democratization of legal information through free access platforms such as Google Scholar, court websites, and open-access legal databases. These resources reduced barriers to legal information, particularly benefiting solo practitioners, public interest organizations, and self-represented litigants. Yet the challenge shifted from information scarcity to information overload, as practitioners struggled to identify the most relevant and authoritative sources among exponentially growing online legal content Re et al., 2019)

Contemporary AI-powered systems represent the latest and most profound transformation. Unlike previous technologies that merely digitized or indexed existing information, AI systems can understand context, identify patterns, extract principles, and generate insights. Natural language processing enables semantic understanding rather than mere keyword matching. Machine learning algorithms can predict case outcomes based on historical patterns. These capabilities fundamentally alter the relationship between legal professionals and legal information, transforming research from a retrieval activity into an analytical partnership with intelligent systems (Susskind, 2019).

This chapter contributes to the growing scholarship on artificial intelligence–powered legal research by critically examining the integration of generative AI technologies within contemporary legal research practices. While existing studies largely emphasize technological capabilities and efficiency gains, this chapter adopts a multidisciplinary perspective that integrates conceptual analysis, regulatory developments, and empirical evidence from real-world legal practice (Surden & Williams, 2023)

By situating AI-assisted legal research within broader concerns of professional responsibility, regulatory governance, and access to justice, this chapter provides a balanced framework that is relevant not only to legal academics but also to practitioners and policymakers navigating the rapid adoption of AI systems in legal work. Rather than presenting AI as a neutral or purely beneficial tool, the chapter emphasizes the necessity of critical evaluation, human oversight, and institutional accountability in the use of generative AI for legal research.

1.2 The Digital Transformation Imperative

The legal profession faces increasing pressures that make Artificial Intelligence adoption not merely advantageous but increasingly essential for competitive practice. These pressures stem from rising client expectations, economic constraints, regulatory complexity, and evolving professional responsibilities. Modern legal clients demand greater efficiency, predictability, and cost-effectiveness, prompting scrutiny of traditional billable hour models and encouraging the use of technology to deliver faster and more comprehensive legal services.

The exponential growth of legal information further intensifies these challenges. Legal systems worldwide generate vast numbers of judicial decisions, statutes, and regulations each year, making it impossible for individual practitioners to maintain comprehensive awareness across jurisdictions. AI systems offer practical solutions by continuously monitoring legal developments and identifying relevant updates that may affect ongoing legal matters (Wirtz et al., 2019).

Access to justice concerns also motivate AI adoption. AI-powered legal research tools and virtual legal assistants can help self-represented litigants understand legal principles and identify relevant authorities, supporting underserved populations in navigating legal systems more effectively (Vaitkūnaitė et al., 2021).

1.3 Literature Review & Research Positioning

Recent literature on artificial intelligence in legal research has expanded significantly following the emergence of generative AI systems after 2022. Existing scholarship may be categorized into three primary strands. First, technological studies focus on the application of natural language processing, machine learning, and large language models to improve legal information retrieval, document analysis, and predictive analytics (Bommarito et al., 2022). These studies frequently report increased speed and accessibility compared to traditional keyword-based legal research. However, they often provide limited critical assessment of accuracy, jurisdictional reliability, and error rates in real-world legal practice.

Second, ethical and professional responsibility oriented literature examines risks associated with algorithmic bias, opacity, explainability challenges, and overreliance on AI-generated outputs. Recent contributions increasingly highlight hallucination risks in generative AI, particularly in legal research contexts where authoritative citation and factual precision are essential (Surden & Williams, 2023). Nevertheless, much of this literature remains largely normative and lacks systematic empirical validation.

Third, regulatory and governance-focused scholarship addresses emerging legal frameworks governing AI deployment in high-stakes domains. Developments such as the European Union Artificial Intelligence Act reflect a shift toward risk-based governance and heightened accountability for AI systems used in legal decision-making (European Commission, 2024). Despite these advances, comparative analyses examining how such regulatory regimes interact with professional legal standards and everyday legal practice remain limited.

Positioned within these debates, this chapter advances the literature by integrating doctrinal analysis, regulatory developments, and empirical observations of real-world AI failures to provide a critical and practice-oriented assessment of AI-powered legal research.

Having traced the historical evolution of legal research methods, the next section explains why these technological developments are no longer optional but constitute a structural imperative for contemporary legal practice.

2. TECHNOLOGICAL FOUNDATIONS OF AI IN LEGAL RESEARCH

The integration of Artificial Intelligence into legal research rests upon several foundational technologies that enable machines to process, understand, and analyze legal texts with increasing sophistication. Understanding these technological underpinnings is essential for legal professionals seeking to effectively leverage AI tools and critically evaluate their capabilities and limitations.

2.1 Natural Language Processing in Legal Context

Natural Language Processing represents the branch of AI focused on enabling computers to understand, interpret, and generate human language. Legal texts present unique NLP challenges due to specialized vocabulary, complex sentence structures, archaic terminology, and jurisdiction-specific conventions. Advanced NLP systems designed for legal applications employ multiple techniques to address these complexities(Winter, 2018).

Tokenization and parsing form the foundation of legal text analysis, breaking documents into meaningful units including words, phrases, and sentences while identifying grammatical structures. Legal NLP systems must recognize specialized legal phrases such as "prima facie," "habeas corpus," and "res judicata" as single semantic units rather than separate words. Named entity recognition identifies and classifies legal entities including parties, judges, statutes, and courts mentioned in legal documents(Hildebrandt, 2018).

Semantic analysis enables systems to understand meaning beyond literal words. This includes identifying synonyms and related concepts crucial for comprehensive legal research. For example, a search for "negligence" should also retrieve cases discussing "breach of duty" or "failure to exercise reasonable care." Advanced systems employ word embeddings and transformer models that capture semantic relationships between legal concepts based on their contextual usage across millions of legal documents(Wachter, Mittelstadt, & Russell, 2021).

Figure 1. Natural Language Processing Pipeline for Legal Text Analysis

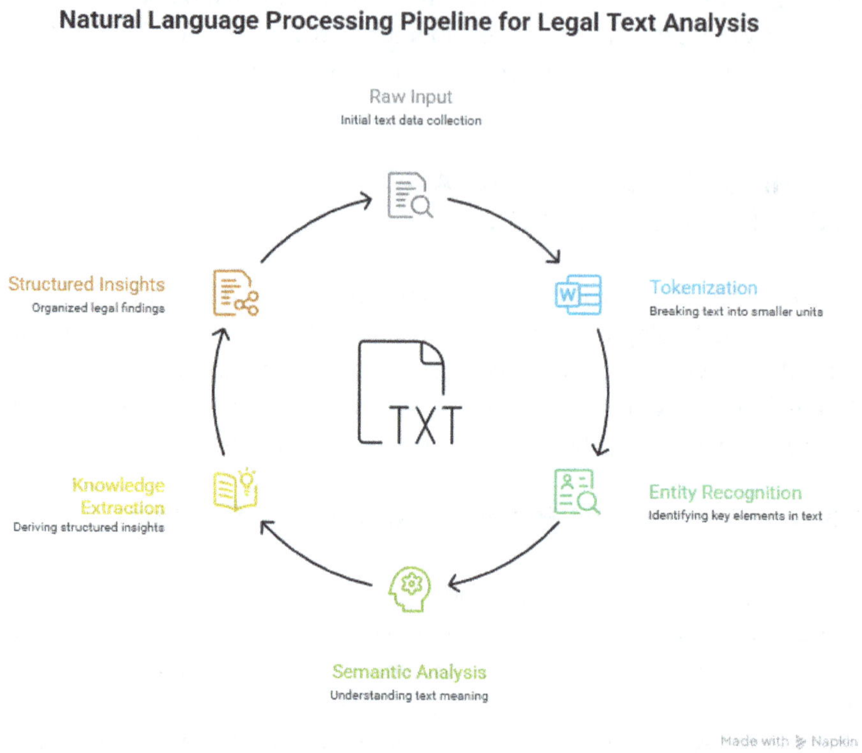

Sentiment analysis and rhetorical classification help systems understand judicial reasoning patterns. By analyzing language used in judicial opinions, AI systems can identify whether a court views a particular argument favorably or skeptically, whether reasoning is mandatory or persuasive, and how strongly a court endorses particular legal principles. This capability enhances predictive analytics by identifying subtle indicators of judicial perspectives(Medvedeva, Vols, & Wieling, 2020).

Legal citation extraction and network analysis represent specialized NLP applications particularly valuable for legal research. Systems automatically identify, extract, and analyze citation patterns across cases, mapping the precedential relationships between judicial decisions. Citation network analysis reveals which cases are most influential, how legal doctrines evolve over time, and which precedents are most frequently distinguished or overruled. These insights enable researchers to quickly identify the most authoritative sources on particular legal issues(Castell, 2018).

2.2 Machine Learning Models for Legal Analysis

Machine learning enables AI systems to learn patterns from data without explicit programming for every possible scenario (Sekti, 2025b). In legal research applications, ML models are trained on vast corpora of legal documents to recognize patterns, classify documents, predict outcomes, and generate insights. Several machine learning approaches have proven particularly effective for legal applications(Schellekens, 2019).

Supervised learning models are trained on labeled datasets where human experts have classified legal documents or marked specific features. For example, a model might be trained on thousands of judicial decisions labeled by outcome to learn patterns associated with plaintiff victories versus defendant victories. Once trained, the model can predict outcomes for new cases based on factual and legal similarities to training examples. Common supervised learning algorithms used in legal AI include support vector machines, random forests, and neural networks (Brink, 2021).

Unsupervised learning algorithms identify patterns and structures in unlabeled legal texts. Topic modeling techniques such as Latent Dirichlet Allocation analyze large collections of legal documents to discover recurring themes and subject matter groupings without prior categorization. Clustering algorithms group similar cases or statutes based on textual and conceptual similarities, helping researchers discover related authorities they might not find through traditional search methods(Chalkidis, Fergadiotis, Malakasiotis, Aletras, & Androutsopoulos, 2020).

Figure 2. Machine Learning Workflow for Legal Prediction Systems

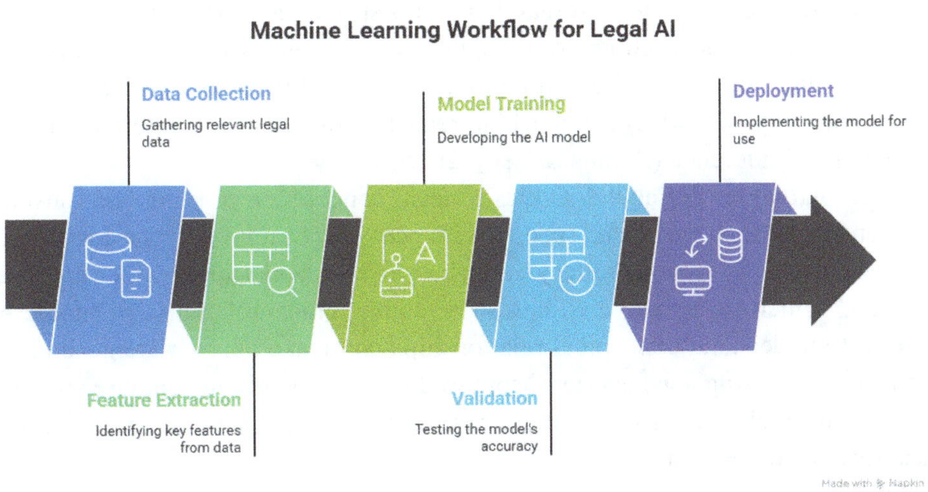

Deep learning approaches, particularly neural networks with multiple layers, have achieved remarkable success in complex legal analysis tasks. Recurrent neural networks and long short-term memory networks excel at processing sequential legal texts, maintaining context across lengthy documents. Transformer-based models such as BERT and GPT have revolutionized legal NLP by learning rich contextual representations of legal language from massive text corpora. Fine-tuned versions of these models, trained specifically on legal documents, achieve state-of-the-art performance on tasks including legal question answering, contract analysis, and case outcome prediction (Solum, 2014).

Transfer learning enables legal AI systems to leverage knowledge learned from general language tasks and apply it to specialized legal domains. Large language models pre-trained on diverse text corpora develop fundamental understanding of language structure and meaning. This knowledge transfers to legal applications with additional fine-tuning on legal-specific texts, requiring smaller legal training datasets than training from scratch while achieving superior performance (Ashley, 2017).

Ensemble methods combine multiple machine learning models to improve prediction accuracy and robustness. In legal applications, ensemble approaches might combine models trained on different legal features such as case facts, procedural history, and judicial reasoning, integrating their predictions to produce more reliable outcomes. Ensemble methods also help address concerns about over-reliance on single algorithmic approaches by incorporating diverse analytical perspectives (Katz, Bommarito, & Blackman, 2017).

2.3 Knowledge Representation and Legal Ontologies

Effective AI-powered legal research requires structured representations of legal knowledge that enable machines to understand relationships between legal concepts, doctrines, and authorities. Legal ontologies provide formalized frameworks for representing legal knowledge in machine-readable formats that support automated reasoning and inference (Remus & Levy, 2015).

Legal ontologies define hierarchies of legal concepts, specifying relationships between broader categories and specific instances. For example, an ontology might represent that "assault" and "battery" are types of "intentional torts," which are types of "torts," which fall under "civil law." These hierarchical relationships enable AI systems to understand conceptual relationships and make appropriate generalizations when analyzing legal queries. More sophisticated ontologies capture complex relationships including causal connections, temporal sequences, and jurisdictional variations (Cardellino et al., 2017).

Rule-based knowledge representation systems encode legal rules and principles in formal logical structures. These systems can perform automated legal reasoning by applying rules to factual situations and deriving legal conclusions. While early legal AI relied heavily on rule-based approaches, contemporary systems integrate rule-based reasoning with machine learning, combining the interpretability of explicit rules with the pattern recognition capabilities of statistical models (Aletras et al., 2016).

Figure 3. Legal Ontology Structure for Knowledge Representation

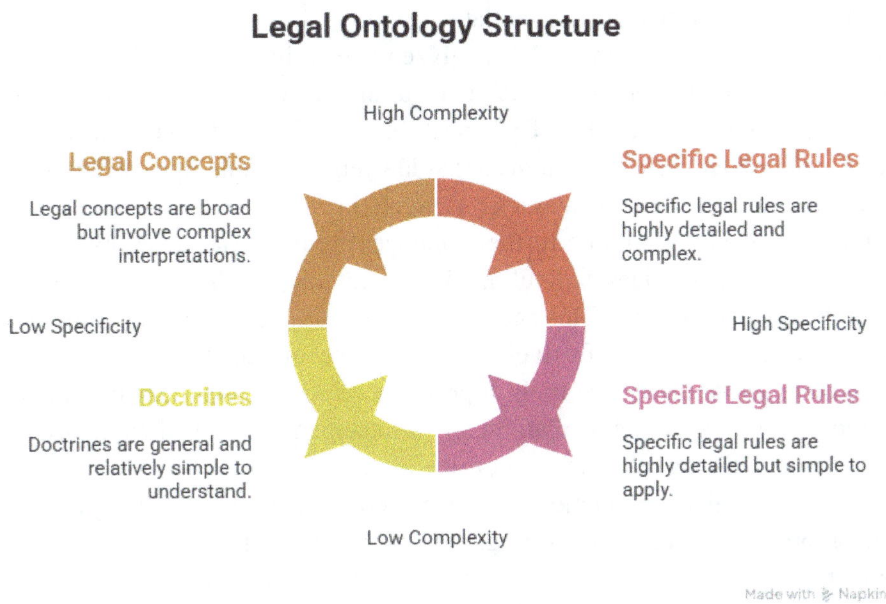

Semantic web technologies enable legal knowledge graphs that connect diverse legal resources through explicit relationships. Legal knowledge graphs link statutes, cases, regulations, and scholarly articles, representing how these authorities cite, interpret, apply, or distinguish each other. By navigating these knowledge graphs, AI systems can trace legal reasoning chains, identify relevant precedents, and discover non-obvious connections between legal authorities across different areas of law (Re et al., 2019).

Temporal reasoning capabilities address the dynamic nature of legal knowledge. Laws change through amendments, judicial decisions are overruled or distinguished, and legal doctrines evolve over time. Effective legal ontologies must represent temporal dimensions, tracking which legal principles apply during specific time periods and how legal authority has evolved. This temporal awareness is crucial for avoiding reliance on outdated authorities and understanding legal development trajectories (Susskind, 2019).

2.4 Predictive Analytics and Case Outcome Forecasting

Predictive analytics represents one of the most transformative applications of Artificial Intelligence in legal research, enabling systems to forecast case outcomes, assess litigation risks, and identify factors most likely to influence judicial decisions. These capabilities rely on advanced statistical and machine learning models trained on large volumes of historical legal data.

Case outcome prediction models analyze patterns in prior judicial decisions by examining variables such as case facts, legal claims, procedural history, jurisdiction, and judicial characteristics. By identifying correlations between these features and litigation outcomes, AI systems assist lawyers in evaluating case strength and developing informed legal strategies (Wirtz et al., 2019).

Judicial behavior modeling further enhances predictive accuracy by examining patterns in individual judges' past rulings, interpretive approaches, and responsiveness to specific legal arguments. This enables legal practitioners to tailor submissions to judicial preferences more effectively (Vaitkūnaitė et al., 2021).

Together, these predictive tools support more data-driven decision-making in litigation, improving strategic planning, risk management, and client advisory processes while reducing reliance on intuition alone.

The technological foundations of AI-powered legal research integrate natural language processing, machine learning, and structured legal knowledge representation to enhance the analysis of complex legal texts. While these technologies improve efficiency and analytical depth, their effectiveness depends on data quality and appropriate human oversight, as demonstrated by their implementation in major AI-powered legal research platforms discussed in the next section.

3. MAJOR AI-POWERED LEGAL RESEARCH PLATFORMS

The commercial legal technology market has experienced explosive growth as companies develop increasingly sophisticated AI-powered research platforms. These systems represent the practical implementation of the technologies discussed previously, offering lawyers powerful tools for conducting more efficient and comprehensive legal research. Understanding the capabilities and approaches of leading platforms provides insight into the current state and future trajectory of AI in legal practice (Wachter et al., 2021).

3.1 LexisNexis and Westlaw: Traditional Leaders Embrace AI

LexisNexis and Westlaw, the dominant legal research platforms for decades, have integrated AI capabilities into their traditional database services. LexisNexis introduced Lexis+ AI, which combines the platform's extensive legal database with natural language processing and machine learning. The system enables lawyers to pose research questions in plain language rather than constructing Boolean queries, with the AI interpreting the question and retrieving relevant authorities (Medvedeva et al., 2020).

Westlaw Edge, Thomson Reuters' AI-enhanced platform, employs proprietary algorithms to organize search results by relevance and provide litigation analytics. The system's KeyCite Overruling Risk feature uses machine learning to analyze judicial language and predict whether precedents face increased risk of being overruled. This capability helps lawyers assess the continuing viability of legal authorities more accurately than traditional citator services (Castell, 2018).

Both platforms provide AI-powered brief analysis tools that extract key issues, identify cited authorities, and assess argument strength, enabling lawyers to quickly evaluate opposing arguments. Their litigation analytics modules further support strategic decision-making by offering statistical insights on judges, counsel, law firms, and parties based on historical data (Schellekens, 2019).

The integration of AI into these established platforms demonstrates how traditional legal information providers are adapting to technological change. Rather than replacing human researchers entirely, these AI features augment lawyer capabilities by automating time-consuming tasks, surfacing relevant information more effectively, and providing data-driven insights that complement legal expertise (Brink, 2021).

3.2 ROSS Intelligence: Specialized AI Research Assistant

ROSS Intelligence pioneered the use of natural language processing specifically designed for legal research, positioning itself as an AI-powered research assistant rather than merely an enhanced search engine. Built on IBM Watson's cognitive computing platform, ROSS employed advanced NLP to understand legal questions and provide answers supported by relevant case law, statutes, and secondary sources (Chalkidis et al., 2020).

The system's conversational interface allowed lawyers to ask questions as they would to a human colleague, with ROSS interpreting the question, researching relevant authorities, and generating answer memoranda with supporting citations. Machine learning capabilities enabled ROSS to improve its understanding of legal concepts and research patterns over time, learning from user interactions to provide increasingly relevant results (Solum, 2014).

ROSS's document review capabilities employed machine learning to identify relevant documents within large collections. Lawyers could provide examples of relevant documents, and the system would analyze patterns to locate similar items within the broader document set. This technology proved particularly valuable for discovery processes involving massive electronic document productions (Ashley, 2017).

Despite its technological sophistication, ROSS Intelligence faced legal challenges that illustrate the competitive and regulatory complexities of the legal AI market. Thomson Reuters sued ROSS for trade secret misappropriation, alleging the company improperly used Westlaw materials to train its algorithms. This litigation underscores intellectual property concerns surrounding AI training data and the fierce competition for dominance in the legal technology market (Katz et al., 2017).

3.3 Casetext: AI for Solo and Small Firm Practitioners

Casetext positioned itself as an accessible AI-powered legal research platform designed for solo practitioners and small firms that might find traditional platforms prohibitively expensive. The platform's CARA AI (Case Analysis Research Assistant) represents an innovative approach to legal research, allowing lawyers to upload legal documents and receive suggestions for relevant authorities based on the document's content (Remus & Levy, 2015).

CARA analyzes the uploaded document, identifies key legal issues and concepts, and searches for similar cases and statutes. This approach proves particularly valuable when lawyers are working on unfamiliar legal areas or seeking to ensure they have not missed important authorities. The system learns from lawyer feedback, improving its recommendations as users indicate which suggestions are helpful (Cardellino et al., 2017).

Casetext's Compose feature uses AI to support legal writing by analyzing draft documents and recommending relevant authorities, arguments, and language drawn from similar successful filings. This functionality allows practitioners, particularly less experienced lawyers, to leverage collective professional knowledge more effectively (Aletras et al., 2016).

The platform's pricing model, significantly lower than traditional legal research services, demonstrates how AI can democratize access to sophisticated research tools. By automating functions that traditionally required expensive human indexing and editorial work, AI enables more affordable legal research platforms that maintain comprehensive coverage and sophisticated search capabilities (Re et al., 2019).

3.4 vLex: Global Legal Information with AI Enhancement

vLex provides legal research services covering over 130 countries with AI-powered search and analysis capabilities. The platform's Vincent AI employs natural language processing to understand research queries across multiple languages and jurisdictions, making it particularly valuable for international and comparative law research. The system can identify relevant authorities across different legal systems and linguistic contexts (Susskind, 2019).

Figure 4. Feature Comparison Matrix of Major AI Legal Research Platforms

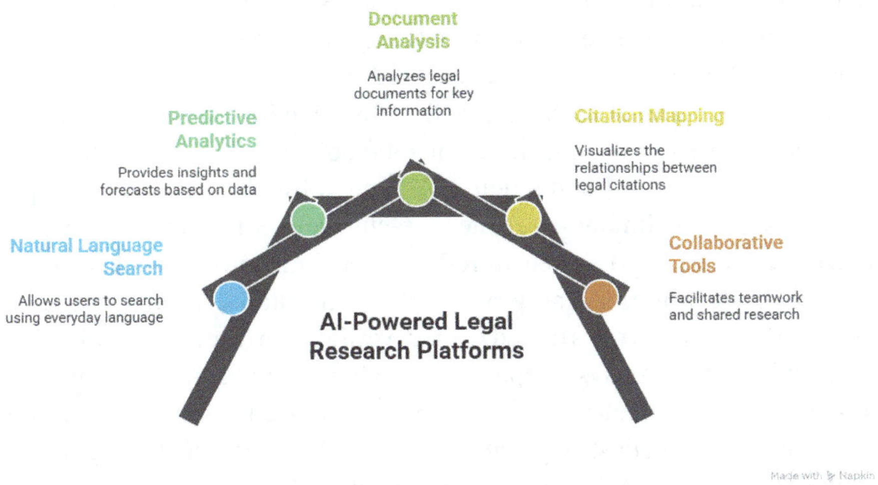

Vincent AI's document analysis feature examines legal documents and identifies key clauses, potential risks, and relevant precedents. When reviewing contracts or legal opinions, the system highlights important provisions and suggests related authorities that might inform interpretation or revision. This functionality proves especially useful for cross-border transactions where lawyers must navigate multiple legal frameworks simultaneously(Alarie, Niblett, & Yoon, 2018).

The platform's citation network visualization tools employ AI to map relationships between legal authorities across jurisdictions. These visualizations help researchers understand how legal concepts travel between legal systems, how international courts influence domestic jurisprudence, and how legal doctrines evolve differently across countries. Such comparative insights are increasingly valuable in our globalized legal environment (Wirtz et al., 2019).

3.5 Harvey AI: Generative AI for Legal Work

Harvey AI represents the newest generation of legal AI tools, built on large language models similar to GPT technology. Unlike earlier systems focused primarily on research and search, Harvey employs generative AI to assist with a broader range of legal tasks including drafting documents, answering complex legal questions, and analyzing contracts (Vaitkūnaitė et al., 2021).

The system's conversational interface allows lawyers to interact with AI through natural dialogue, asking follow-up questions and refining requests iteratively. Harvey can draft contract clauses, suggest edits to legal documents, summarize lengthy materials, and explain legal concepts in accessible language. The underlying large language model has been fine-tuned on legal texts to understand legal reasoning and generate appropriate legal language (Pasquale, 2015).

Since 2022, generative AI systems based on large language models have significantly reshaped legal research practices by enabling conversational querying, automated summarization, and draft generation of legal texts. While these capabilities enhance accessibility and efficiency, empirical studies and judicial experience demonstrate inherent limitations related to factual reliability and verification of legal authority. Generative AI systems produce probabilistic outputs that may appear legally plausible while lacking grounding in authoritative legal sources, creating substantial professional risks if used without verification (Surden & Williams, 2023).

Harvey's contract analysis capabilities examine agreements to identify unusual terms, potential risks, and deviations from standard practices. The system compares contract provisions against large databases of similar agreements, flagging outliers and suggesting standard alternatives. This functionality accelerates contract review processes while helping ensure that agreements conform to best practices and protect client interests (Winter, 2018).

Integration with law firm practice management systems enables Harvey to access matter-specific information and provide contextually relevant assistance. The AI can review matter documents, understand case strategies, and provide research and drafting support tailored to specific client representations. This deep integration represents a shift from standalone research tools toward comprehensive AI assistants embedded in legal workflows (Hildebrandt, 2018).

3.6 EMPIRICAL EVIDENCE & REAL-WORLD FAILURES

Judicial cases from 2023–2024 highlight the risks of uncritical reliance on AI-assisted legal research, as courts sanctioned professionals for filings containing fictitious AI-generated citations. These cases reaffirm that professional accountability remains human-centered and requires rigorous verification of AI outputs.

Empirical comparative studies further indicate that while AI-powered legal research tools may outperform junior researchers in document retrieval speed, they demonstrate higher error rates in complex doctrinal reasoning and jurisdiction-specific interpretation (Bommarito et al., 2022). Such findings challenge overly optimistic narratives surrounding legal AI and highlight the importance of evidence-based evaluation rather than purely descriptive technological assessment.

Major AI-powered legal research platforms demonstrate how advances in natural language processing and machine learning have expanded the speed and scope of legal research. However, their effectiveness depends on data quality and informed human oversight, which leads to the ethical and regulatory challenges examined in the next section.

4. ETHICAL AND REGULATORY CHALLENGES

While AI-powered legal research offers substantial benefits, its integration into legal practice raises significant ethical concerns that demand careful consideration by practitioners, technologists, and policymakers. These challenges span issues of algorithmic bias, transparency, accountability, data privacy, and the fundamental nature of legal reasoning itself (Wachter et al., 2021).

4.1 Algorithmic Bias and Fairness Concerns

AI systems learn patterns from historical data, and when such data reflects societal bias or discriminatory practices, these systems risk perpetuating and amplifying existing inequalities. In legal contexts, this poses serious concerns given law's foundational commitment to equal justice and fair treatment (Medvedeva et al., 2020).Historical legal records often embed systemic inequities related to race, gender, socioeconomic status, and other protected characteristics. When AI models are trained on these records, they may internalize biased associations between demographic factors and legal outcomes.

Algorithmic bias may also arise from unrepresentative or incomplete training data. AI systems developed using decisions from limited jurisdictions, specific court types, or narrow categories of cases may perform poorly when applied to different legal contexts. Models trained primarily on civil litigation, for example, may generate unreliable guidance in criminal matters, while systems based on urban data may not generalize well to rural legal environments (Brink, 2021).

Detecting and mitigating such bias remains technically challenging. Algorithmic decision-making often involves complex interactions that obscure causal explanations, making bias difficult to identify and audit. Effective oversight requires advanced statistical methods, transparency in system design, and clearly defined fairness standards within legal practice (Chalkidis et al., 2020).

4.2 Transparency and Explainability Requirements

Many AI systems, particularly those based on deep learning, operate as "black boxes" that generate outputs without clearly explaining their underlying reasoning. This opacity conflicts with legal principles of transparency, due process, and accountability, which require decisions to be open to scrutiny and challenge (Solum, 2014). When AI tools influence legal strategy, case evaluation, or settlement decisions, affected parties have a legitimate interest in understanding how such conclusions are reached. Systems that lack explainability may undermine procedural fairness and weaken lawyers' ability to justify decisions to clients (Ashley, 2017).

The challenge of explainability varies across AI techniques. Rule-based systems and simpler machine learning models offer relatively clear reasoning pathways, while complex neural networks rely on intricate internal processes that resist interpretation. In response, explainable AI methods such as feature attribution and attention mechanisms aim to increase transparency, though they provide only partial insight.

Legal and professional standards increasingly emphasize explainability, placing pressure on AI developers and legal practitioners to balance accuracy with transparency and ethical responsibility (Cardellino et al., 2017).

4.3 Accountability and Professional Responsibility

The integration of Artificial Intelligence into legal practice raises complex questions regarding responsibility when AI systems produce errors or harmful outcomes. Traditional professional responsibility frameworks assume identifiable human decision-makers, but AI complicates accountability by distributing decision-making across lawyers, technology vendors, and algorithmic processes. When lawyers rely on AI-generated research or recommendations that later prove inaccurate, determining responsibility becomes challenging (Re et al., 2019).

Professional competence obligations require lawyers to understand and appropriately use the tools they employ. Bar associations increasingly recognize technological competence as part of professional responsibility. However, the technical complexity of modern AI systems makes full understanding unrealistic for most practitioners. Few lawyers possess the expertise necessary to comprehend how advanced machine learning models generate legal predictions, raising concerns about excessive burdens on legal professionals (Susskind, 2019).

As a result, scholars propose a "reasonable reliance" standard, under which lawyers must ensure AI tools are reputable, suitable, and regularly updated while exercising independent legal judgment. AI vendors also bear responsibility through product reliability, testing, and compliance with emerging professional and regulatory standards (Wirtz et al., 2019).

4.4 Data Privacy and Confidentiality

Legal AI systems require extensive data for training and operation, raising concerns about client confidentiality, attorney-client privilege, and data security. Legal information involves sensitive details about individuals, businesses, and governmental entities that demand rigorous protection (Vaitkūnaitė et al., 2021).

Figure 5. Ethical Framework for Responsible AI Integration in Legal Practice

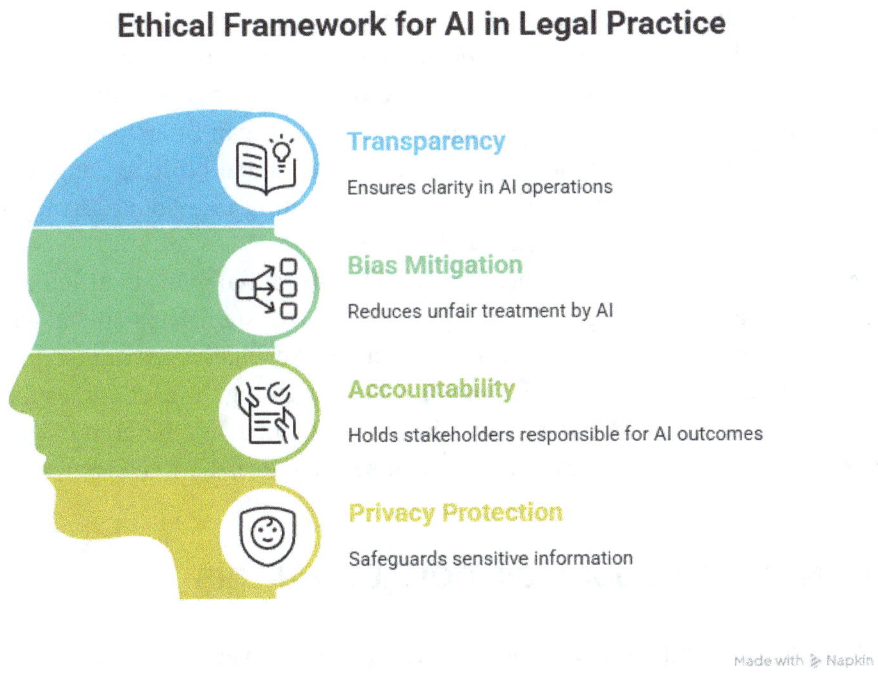

When law firms use AI platforms to analyze client documents or conduct research on specific matters, client information may be transmitted to external AI vendors. This data sharing raises confidentiality concerns under professional responsibility rules that mandate protection of client information. Lawyers must ensure that AI vendors employ appropriate security measures, limit data use to authorized purposes, and comply with data protection regulations (Pasquale, 2015).

Training AI systems on legal documents raises significant privacy concerns, as models rely on large datasets drawn from publicly available filings and opinions that often contain personal information. Balancing the societal benefits of AI advancement with individual privacy rights therefore remains an ongoing regulatory and ethical challenge (Winter, 2018).

Different jurisdictions impose varying data protection requirements that complicate global AI deployment. The European Union's GDPR mandates strict controls on personal data processing, limits on automated decision-making, and data localization requirements. Other jurisdictions impose sector-specific requirements for legal data, requirements for data breach notification, and restrictions on cross-border data transfers. AI vendors and law firms must navigate this complex regulatory landscape while maintaining effective systems (Hildebrandt, 2018).

Anonymization and pseudonymization techniques offer partial solutions by removing or obscuring identifying information from legal documents used for AI training and analysis. However, effective anonymization proves challenging given that combinations of seemingly innocuous data points can often re-identify individuals. Differential privacy techniques that add statistical noise to datasets while preserving overall patterns show promise for protecting individual privacy while enabling AI development (Wachter et al., 2021).

While AI-powered legal research tools offer substantial gains in efficiency and analytical capability, their growing adoption also raises significant ethical and regulatory concerns. The following section examines key challenges related to transparency, bias, accountability, and compliance, highlighting the need for responsible governance in AI-assisted legal practice. Having explained the ethical and regulatory challenges, the next section explains the comparative jurisdictional analysis.

5. COMPARATIVE JURISDICTIONAL ANALYSIS

The adoption and regulation of AI in legal research varies significantly across jurisdictions, reflecting different legal cultures, technological readiness, and policy priorities. Understanding these variations illuminates both universal challenges and context-specific considerations for AI integration in legal systems (Medvedeva et al., 2020).

5.1 United States: Market-Driven Innovation

The United States adopts a predominantly market-driven approach to the use of Artificial Intelligence in legal practice, characterized by minimal direct regulation of legal technology. This environment has enabled rapid development and deployment of AI-powered legal research tools, positioning the United States as a global leader in legal AI innovation. Lawyers are generally free to use AI technologies subject to professional responsibility rules concerning competence, confidentiality, and independent judgment (Schellekens, 2019).

This permissive regulatory framework has encouraged innovation but also raised concerns about oversight. In the absence of mandatory standards for accuracy, bias auditing, or explainability, legal AI tools vary widely in quality. As a result, practitioners bear significant responsibility for evaluating the reliability and appropriateness of these technologies (Brink, 2021).

American courts have begun to confront AI-related issues, including cases involving AI-generated legal submissions containing fabricated citations. These incidents have prompted renewed debate about whether existing ethical rules sufficiently address AI-specific risks or whether additional guidance is required. Some judges now mandate disclosure of AI use in legal filings, signaling growing judicial awareness of AI's implications for legal practice (Chalkidis et al., 2020).

5.2 European Union: Rights-Based Regulation

The European Union has adopted a more regulatory approach to AI, emphasizing fundamental rights protection, transparency, and accountability. The EU's proposed Artificial Intelligence Act establishes comprehensive requirements for AI systems based on risk classification, with legal applications potentially subject to high-risk categorization requiring stringent compliance measures (Ashley, 2017).

The General Data Protection Regulation significantly impacts legal AI systems operating in Europe by imposing strict requirements for personal data processing. GDPR mandates lawful bases for data collection, purpose limitations, data minimization, and individual rights including access, correction, and deletion. These requirements constrain AI training data collection and system design, potentially limiting some AI capabilities while protecting privacy rights more robustly than American approaches (Katz et al., 2017).

GDPR's provisions regarding automated decision-making are particularly relevant for legal AI. Article 22 grants individuals rights not to be subject to decisions based solely on automated processing that produce legal effects. While this provision includes exceptions, it establishes a principle of human oversight for significant decisions.

Legal AI systems must be designed to support rather than replace human judgment, with clear mechanisms for human intervention and review (Remus & Levy, 2015).

European data protection authorities have issued guidance addressing AI-specific concerns including algorithmic transparency, bias prevention, and data protection impact assessments. These requirements impose compliance burdens on AI developers and users but reflect European commitments to protecting individual rights against potential technological overreach. The regulatory framework emphasizes that technological efficiency must not compromise fundamental rights and democratic values (Cardellino et al., 2017).

The European approach influences global AI development as companies seeking European market access must comply with EU requirements. This regulatory model serves as a counterpoint to more permissive American approaches, demonstrating alternative strategies for balancing innovation with rights protection and accountability (Aletras et al., 2016).

5.3 India: Digital Transformation and Access to Justice

India's approach to legal AI reflects the nation's digital transformation agenda and commitment to improving access to justice. Indian courts have embraced technology to address massive case backlogs and limited judicial resources. The e-Courts project digitized court records and enabled online case filing, creating infrastructure that facilitates AI integration (Re et al., 2019).

The Supreme Court launched SUPACE (Supreme Court Portal for Assistance in Court's Efficiency), an AI-powered tool that assists judges by analyzing case records, identifying similar precedents, and suggesting relevant legal provisions. This judicial AI system aims to enhance decision-making quality and consistency while reducing research burdens on judges managing heavy caseloads (Susskind, 2019).

Legal startups have developed AI tools addressing access to justice challenges. Platforms offering affordable research, automated document generation, and virtual consultations help populations unable to afford traditional legal services, particularly in rural areas and regional languages beyond English (Alarie et al., 2018).

However, India faces challenges including limited technological infrastructure, digital literacy gaps among professionals and litigants, and linguistic diversity requiring AI systems to function across multiple scripts. Indian regulatory frameworks for AI are evolving. The Personal Data Protection Bill proposes data governance requirements, while government strategies emphasize responsible AI aligned with societal needs (Vaitkūnaitė et al., 2021).

5.4 Cross-Jurisdictional Collaboration and Standards

Despite jurisdictional differences, legal AI adoption increasingly requires international cooperation given globalized legal practice and cross-border data flows. International organizations and professional associations are developing standards and best practices for legal AI that can guide implementation across jurisdictions (Pasquale, 2015).

The International Association for Artificial Intelligence and Law conducts research on legal AI applications and facilitates knowledge exchange among researchers and practitioners globally. Academic conferences and publications disseminate findings on AI effectiveness, limitations, and ethical implications, contributing to evidence-based policymaking across countries (Winter, 2018).

Professional legal organizations including the International Bar Association have issued reports and recommendations on AI ethics in legal practice. These documents identify common principles including human oversight, transparency, accountability, and bias prevention that transcend specific jurisdictional requirements. While not legally binding, such professional standards influence national regulations and firm policies (Hildebrandt, 2018).

Technical standards organizations are developing specifications for AI system testing, documentation, and interoperability. Standards addressing AI explainability, bias auditing, and data governance help establish baseline expectations for responsible AI development. These technical standards complement legal regulations by providing concrete implementation guidance for compliance (Wachter et al., 2021).

5.5 Regulatory Developments and AI Governance

Recent regulatory initiatives reflect growing concern over the deployment of generative AI in high-stakes professional domains, including legal research and decision-making. The European Union Artificial Intelligence Act adopts a risk-based governance framework that categorizes AI systems used in legal contexts as potentially high-risk applications, thereby subjecting them to enhanced transparency, accountability, and human oversight requirements (European Commission, 2024).

These regulatory developments signal a convergence between AI governance and professional legal ethics, reinforcing the principle that AI tools must operate within established legal and institutional norms. For legal practitioners and researchers, compliance with regulatory standards is increasingly inseparable from ethical responsibility in AI-assisted legal research.

As ethical and regulatory concerns evolve, jurisdictions have adopted different approaches to governing AI-powered legal research. This section compares selected legal systems to highlight how regulatory frameworks and professional standards shape AI adoption and oversight. Having explained the comparative jurisdictional analysis, the next section explains the impact on legal education and professional competencies.

6. IMPACT ON LEGAL EDUCATION AND PROFESSIONAL COMPETENCIES

The integration of AI into legal research fundamentally transforms the competencies required for effective legal practice. Legal education and professional development must evolve to prepare lawyers for AI-augmented practice while maintaining core professional values and analytical capabilities (Medvedeva et al., 2020).

6.1 Evolving Curricular Requirements

Law schools traditionally emphasize case analysis, statutory interpretation, and legal reasoning developed through manual research and writing assignments. While these foundational skills remain essential, legal education must now incorporate technological competencies enabling graduates to effectively leverage AI tools and critically evaluate their outputs (Castell, 2018).

Technology-enhanced legal research courses introduce students to contemporary AI-powered platforms alongside traditional research methods. Students learn not only how to use specific tools but also how to assess tool appropriateness for different research tasks, evaluate result quality, and integrate AI-generated information into legal analysis. Comparative exercises demonstrating differences between keyword search, Boolean queries, and natural language AI interfaces help students understand each approach's strengths and limitations (Schellekens, 2019).

Data literacy and computational thinking are increasingly recognized as essential legal competencies. Lawyers working with AI systems need basic understanding of how algorithms process information, what training data means for system capabilities, and how to interpret statistical predictions and confidence intervals. While lawyers need not become programmers or data scientists, foundational technological literacy enables more effective collaboration with technical experts and more sophisticated evaluation of AI tool outputs (Brink, 2021).

Ethics courses must address AI-specific professional responsibility issues including algorithmic bias, confidentiality in cloud-based platforms, transparency obligations when using AI-generated work product, and accountability when AI systems produce errors. Case studies examining actual incidents involving legal AI help students understand practical ethical challenges and develop frameworks for responsible technology use (Chalkidis et al., 2020).

Some law schools have established legal technology clinics where students work on real cases using AI tools under faculty supervision. These experiential learning opportunities develop practical skills while allowing faculty to assess pedagogical approaches and identify emerging competency gaps that curricula should address (Solum, 2014).

6.2 Professional Development and Continuing Legal Education

Practicing lawyers who completed legal education before AI tools became prevalent must develop new competencies through continuing legal education and professional development. Bar associations and professional organizations offer programs addressing legal technology adoption, AI capabilities and limitations, and ethical considerations (Ashley, 2017).

Many jurisdictions have incorporated technology competence into mandatory continuing legal education requirements. Courses cover AI-powered research platforms, document automation, predictive analytics, and related technologies. These programs help bridge the knowledge gap between technology-native younger lawyers and more experienced practitioners whose training predated digital transformation (Katz et al., 2017).

Law firms increasingly provide internal training on AI tools to ensure consistent and effective use across their practices. Training programs address not only mechanical tool operation but also strategic considerations about when AI assistance is most valuable, how to verify AI-generated research, and how to communicate with clients about technology use in their representations (Remus & Levy, 2015).

Professional development also addresses the psychological and cultural challenges of AI adoption. Some lawyers resist technology that seems to diminish traditional professional skills or threatens to automate aspects of practice they find personally meaningful. Effective training acknowledges these concerns while demonstrating how AI can handle routine tasks, freeing lawyers to focus on higher-value strategic counseling and advocacy that better utilize human judgment and creativity (Cardellino et al., 2017).

6.3 Interdisciplinary Collaboration Skills

AI-augmented legal practice increasingly requires collaboration between lawyers and professionals from other disciplines including computer scientists, data analysts, and information specialists. Lawyers must develop communication skills enabling effective interaction with technical experts who may lack legal training but possess essential technological expertise (Aletras et al., 2016).

Understanding technical terminology and concepts facilitates productive collaboration. Lawyers who can discuss machine learning approaches, data quality issues, and algorithm design choices communicate more effectively with AI developers and can better articulate legal requirements that technical implementations must satisfy. This interdisciplinary fluency enhances both technology development and legal practice quality (Re et al., 2019).

Project management skills become more important as legal work increasingly involves coordinating contributions from diverse specialists. Lawyers must integrate legal analysis with technical implementation, data processing, and system testing. Traditional legal project management focused on legal research, document drafting, and court proceedings. Contemporary practice adds technology project dimensions requiring different planning and coordination approaches (Susskind, 2019).

Law firms are hiring non-lawyer specialists including legal technologists, data scientists, and project managers who work alongside lawyers on complex matters. These professionals bring expertise that complements legal knowledge. Effective collaboration requires mutual respect for different forms of expertise and willingness to learn from professionals whose training and perspectives differ from traditional legal education (Alarie et al., 2018).

6.4 Maintaining Core Professional Values

While developing technological competencies, legal education and professional development must ensure that core professional values including client service, independent judgment, and commitment to justice remain central to legal practice. Technology should enhance rather than undermine these fundamental commitments (Wirtz et al., 2019).

Critical thinking about technology constitutes an essential professional competency. Lawyers must question AI recommendations, probe algorithmic assumptions, and consider whether technological approaches truly serve client interests and justice system integrity. Uncritical technology acceptance represents professional failure as much as complete technology rejection (Vaitkūnaitė et al., 2021).

Professional identity formation in the AI era requires helping law students and lawyers understand how technology changes legal practice without abandoning profession-defining values. Lawyers remain responsible for legal strategy, ethical judgments, and client relationships regardless of technological assistance. AI tools are powerful aids but cannot replace human accountability for professional decisions (Pasquale, 2015).

Access to justice commitments must inform technological adoption. As AI tools become standard in legal practice, the profession must ensure that technological advantages do not create new inequities between well-resourced and under-resourced clients. Pro bono technology support, public interest AI development, and regulatory attention to technology access can help ensure that AI advances justice for all rather than advantages for the privileged few (Winter, 2018).

7. FUTURE DIRECTIONS AND EMERGING TRENDS

Legal AI continues evolving rapidly with new capabilities and applications emerging regularly. Understanding current trajectories helps practitioners, educators, and policymakers anticipate future developments and prepare appropriate responses (Hildebrandt, 2018).

7.1 Multimodal AI Integration

Future legal AI systems will integrate multiple data modalities beyond text, including images, audio, video, and structured data. Multimodal systems can analyze courtroom proceedings combining audio transcripts, video of witness testimony, and documentary exhibits to provide comprehensive case analysis. Such capabilities could assist with trial preparation, appeal evaluation, and judicial decision-making (Wachter et al., 2021).

Document analysis will extend beyond textual content to incorporate visual elements including charts, diagrams, photographs, and signatures. AI systems that understand both textual and visual information can more completely analyze complex contracts, patent applications, and evidentiary materials. Computer vision combined with natural language processing enables richer understanding of legal materials (Medvedeva et al., 2020).

Voice-enabled legal AI systems will allow hands-free interaction, enabling lawyers to conduct research while reviewing physical documents, driving, or otherwise occupied. Conversational AI combining speech recognition, natural language understanding, and speech synthesis creates more natural human-computer interaction that integrates seamlessly into legal workflows (Castell, 2018).

7.2 Enhanced Predictive Capabilities

Predictive analytics will become more sophisticated and granular, forecasting not only case outcomes but also specific procedural developments, settlement timing, and strategic decision points. Enhanced prediction helps lawyers and clients make better-informed decisions throughout litigation rather than only at initiation or final judgment (Schellekens, 2019).

Real-time legal analytics will monitor ongoing litigation and alert lawyers to relevant developments including new precedents, similar case outcomes, and changes in judicial personnel or practices that might affect pending matters. Continuous intelligence streams replace periodic research updates, ensuring lawyers have current information for strategic decisions (Brink, 2021).

Scenario modeling will enable lawyers to simulate different strategic approaches and assess probable outcomes under various assumptions. Interactive models allow manipulation of variables to explore how different choices might affect case trajectories. Such capabilities support more sophisticated strategic planning and client counseling about litigation options (Chalkidis et al., 2020).

7.3 Personalized Legal AI Assistants

AI systems will increasingly personalize to individual lawyers' preferences, practice areas, and working styles. Personalized assistants learn from each lawyer's research patterns, writing style, and substantive expertise to provide increasingly tailored support. Machine learning enables systems to adapt to user feedback and improve relevance over time (Solum, 2014).

Context-aware assistance considers the specific matter being worked on, relevant jurisdiction, client preferences, and strategic objectives when providing research and drafting support. Rather than generic responses, personalized AI offers suggestions specifically relevant to each lawyer's current work context (Ashley, 2017).

Long-term learning enables AI assistants to build knowledge about lawyers' practices, clients, and substantive specializations. Systems that understand a lawyer's expertise can complement rather than duplicate human capabilities, focusing on areas where technological assistance adds greatest value to that individual's practice (Katz et al., 2017).

7.4 Blockchain and Distributed Legal Knowledge

Blockchain technology may enable distributed legal knowledge systems where legal information, research annotations, and precedent analysis are stored across decentralized networks. Blockchain-based systems could provide tamper-proof records of legal research provenance, enhancing reliability and accountability (Remus & Levy, 2015).

Smart contracts combining legal rules with automated execution capabilities will increasingly govern transactions and relationships. Legal AI systems will need to analyze, draft, and verify smart contracts that execute automatically based on specified conditions. This convergence of legal and technological logic creates new practice areas and competency requirements (Cardellino et al., 2017).

Collaborative research platforms built on distributed technologies enable lawyers worldwide to share insights, annotations, and analysis of legal authorities. Crowd-sourced legal intelligence aggregates collective professional knowledge, making sophisticated analysis accessible to practitioners who might otherwise lack resources for comprehensive research (Aletras et al., 2016).

7.5 Quantum Computing Implications

Quantum computing, though still emerging, promises computational capabilities that could revolutionize legal AI. Quantum algorithms might analyze legal document collections orders of magnitude larger than classical computers can process, enabling comprehensive analysis of global legal information in real-time (Re et al., 2019).

Optimization problems central to legal strategy including settlement negotiation, resource allocation, and docket scheduling could benefit from quantum computing capabilities. Complex strategic scenarios involving numerous variables and constraints might be solved more effectively with quantum approaches (Susskind, 2019).

However, quantum computing also poses risks including the potential to break current encryption methods, threatening confidentiality of legal communications and client information. Legal AI systems and law firm IT infrastructure must prepare for post-quantum cryptography to maintain security in the quantum era (Alarie et al., 2018)(Sekti, 2025a).

8. STRATEGIC FRAMEWORK FOR RESPONSIBLE AI IMPLEMENTATION

Successful integration of AI into legal research requires strategic approaches that maximize benefits while mitigating risks. This framework provides guidance for legal organizations seeking to implement AI responsibly and effectively (Wirtz et al., 2019).

8.1 Needs Assessment and Tool Selection

Organizations should begin with comprehensive assessment of their specific research needs, current capabilities, and improvement opportunities. Different practice areas, client bases, and organizational sizes have varying AI requirements. Solo practitioners need different tools than large corporate law departments. This assessment identifies priority areas where AI can deliver greatest value (Vaitkūnaitė et al., 2021).

Tool evaluation should consider multiple factors including accuracy, coverage, usability, cost, vendor reputation, and alignment with organizational workflows. Pilot testing with small user groups helps identify practical challenges before organization-wide deployment. Comparing multiple platforms through parallel testing reveals relative strengths for specific use cases (Pasquale, 2015).

Vendor due diligence addresses critical questions about data security, algorithmic transparency, bias testing, update frequency, and customer support. Organizations should request information about AI training data sources, model architectures, validation methodologies, and mechanisms for addressing errors or biases. Contracts should specify performance standards, data handling requirements, and liability allocation (Winter, 2018).

8.2 Implementation and Change Management

Successful AI implementation requires careful change management addressing both technical integration and human factors. Technology rollout should proceed incrementally with adequate training, support resources, and feedback mechanisms. Rushing implementation without proper preparation leads to poor adoption and suboptimal utilization (Hildebrandt, 2018).

Training programs should address not only mechanical tool operation but also strategic use, quality verification, and ethical considerations. Different training approaches may suit different audiences with technical specialists receiving more detailed instruction than general users. Ongoing training updates ensure competency as systems evolve and new features emerge (Wachter et al., 2021).

Champions and early adopters within organizations can demonstrate value and help colleagues adopt new tools. Identifying respected practitioners who embrace AI and can share successful use cases helps overcome resistance and builds organizational enthusiasm for technology adoption (Medvedeva et al., 2020).

8.3 Quality Assurance and Validation

Organizations must establish quality assurance processes ensuring AI-generated work meets professional standards. Verification protocols should require lawyers to independently confirm key legal authorities cited by AI systems, evaluate whether AI recommendations align with professional judgment, and document decision-making processes when accepting or rejecting AI suggestions (Castell, 2018).

Regular auditing of AI tool accuracy helps identify systematic problems or drift in system performance over time. Organizations should track metrics including research completion time, authority relevance, error rates, and user satisfaction. Trends indicating declining performance warrant investigation and potential vendor engagement (Schellekens, 2019).

Feedback mechanisms enabling users to report problems or suggest improvements help organizations and vendors refine AI systems. Systematic feedback collection creates learning opportunities and demonstrates commitment to continuous improvement. Vendors responsive to feedback earn greater user trust and loyalty (Brink, 2021).

8.4 Ethical Guidelines and Governance

Organizations should develop written policies governing AI use in legal practice addressing confidentiality, conflicts of interest, quality control, client communication, and professional responsibility. Clear guidelines help lawyers navigate ethical uncertainties and demonstrate commitment to responsible technology use (Chalkidis et al., 2020).

Ethics committees or technology working groups can provide forums for discussing AI-related ethical issues, reviewing new tools, and updating organizational policies as technology evolves. Regular review ensures policies remain current with technological capabilities and emerging ethical considerations (Solum, 2014).

Client communication about AI use demonstrates transparency and builds trust. While detailed technical explanations may be unnecessary, clients should understand generally how AI contributes to their representation and what measures ensure quality and confidentiality. Some clients may have preferences about technology use that should be respected (Ashley, 2017).

8.5 Continuous Learning and Adaptation

Legal AI evolves rapidly requiring organizations to maintain awareness of new developments and continuously adapt practices. Participation in professional conferences, technology working groups, and legal innovation networks provides exposure to emerging tools and approaches (Katz et al., 2017).

Organizations should budget for ongoing technology investment recognizing that AI adoption is not a one-time expenditure but continuous commitment. Regular reassessment of tools, training needs, and strategic priorities ensures technology investments remain aligned with organizational objectives (Remus & Levy, 2015).

Measuring return on investment helps justify continued AI investment and identify areas for optimization. Metrics might include research time reduction, cost savings, error reduction, client satisfaction improvement, and competitive advantage. Quantitative assessment demonstrates value to organizational leadership and stakeholders (Cardellino et al., 2017).

9. CONCLUSION

The integration of artificial intelligence into legal research and analysis represents a significant transformation in how legal knowledge is accessed, interpreted, and applied. This chapter has examined the technological foundations of AI-driven legal research, evaluated leading platforms, analyzed ethical and regulatory challenges, compared jurisdictional approaches, and proposed a strategic framework for responsible implementation, demonstrating that AI is now an embedded component of contemporary legal practice.

AI-powered legal research systems offer substantial benefits, including improved efficiency, broader access to legal information, and data-driven analytical support that complements human expertise. Advances in natural language processing, machine learning, and predictive analytics have reshaped legal research practices across professional contexts. However, empirical evidence and real-world cases also highlight critical risks, including algorithmic bias, opacity, hallucinated authorities, and data privacy concerns, underscoring the necessity of sustained human oversight, verification, and ethical governance.

Comparative analysis shows that jurisdictions adopt diverse regulatory approaches shaped by legal culture and policy priorities, yet common principles emerge, particularly the importance of accountability, transparency, and alignment with fundamental legal values. In parallel, legal education and professional training must evolve to equip practitioners with the skills needed to critically evaluate AI-assisted outputs while preserving core legal norms.

Looking ahead, continued advances in generative and predictive AI will further transform legal research and practice. The framework proposed in this chapter provides practical guidance for navigating this evolution, emphasizing responsible adoption, institutional safeguards, and continuous adaptation. Ultimately, AI should be understood not as a substitute for legal professionals but as a tool that augments human judgment, reinforcing the integrity, accessibility, and legitimacy of legal systems.

REFERENCES

Alarie, B., Niblett, A., & Yoon, A. H. (2018). How Artificial Intelligence Will Affect the Practice of Law. *University of Toronto Law Journal, 68*(Supplement 1), 106–124. DOI: 10.3138/utlj.2017-0052

Aletras, N., Tsarapatsanis, D., Preoţiuc-Pietro, D., & Lampos, V. (2016). Predicting Judicial Decisions of the European Court of Human Rights: A Natural Language Processing Perspective. *PeerJ. Computer Science*, *2*, e93. DOI: 10.7717/peerj-cs.93

Ashley, K. D. (2017). *Artificial Intelligence and Legal Analytics: New Tools for Law Practice in the Digital Age*. Cambridge University Press., DOI: 10.1017/9781316761380

Bommarito, M. J., Katz, D. M., & Casey, A. (2022). Evaluating the Performance of Legal AI Systems. *Artificial Intelligence and Law*, *30*(3), 343–372.

Brink, D. O. (2021). *Fair Opportunity and Responsibility*. Oxford University Press., DOI: 10.1093/oso/9780198859468.001.0001

Cardellino, C., Teruel, M., Alemany, L. A., & Villata, S. (2017). A Low-Cost, High-Coverage Legal Named Entity Recognizer, Classifier and Linker. In *Proceedings of the 16th International Conference on Artificial Intelligence and Law* (pp. 9–18). https://doi.org/DOI: 10.1145/3086512.3086514

Castell, S. (2018). The Future Decisions of RoboJudge HHJ Arthur Ian Blockchain: Dread, Delight or Derision? *Computer Law \& Security Review, 34*(4), 739–753. https://doi.org/DOI: 10.1016/j.clsr.2018.05.011

Chalkidis, I., Fergadiotis, M., Malakasiotis, P., Aletras, N., & Androutsopoulos, I. (2020). LEGAL-BERT: The Muppets Straight Out of Law School. In *Findings of the Association for Computational Linguistics: EMNLP 2020* (pp. 2898–2904). Association for Computational Linguistics. https://doi.org/DOI: 10.18653/v1/2020.findings-emnlp.261

European Commission. (2024). *Regulation (EU) 2024/1689 Laying Down Harmonised Rules on Artificial Intelligence*. Artificial Intelligence Act.

Hildebrandt, M. (2018). Law as Computation in the Era of Artificial Legal Intelligence. *University of Toronto Law Journal*, *68*(Supplement 1), 12–35. DOI: 10.3138/utlj.2017-0044

Katz, D. M., Bommarito, M. J., & Blackman, J. (2017). A General Approach for Predicting the Behavior of the Supreme Court of the United States. *PLoS One*, *12*(4), e0174698. DOI: 10.1371/journal.pone.0174698 PMID: 28403140

Medvedeva, M., Vols, M., & Wieling, M. (2020). Using Machine Learning to Predict Decisions of the European Court of Human Rights. *Artificial Intelligence and Law*, *28*(2), 237–266. DOI: 10.1007/s10506-019-09255-y

Pasquale, F. (2015). *The Black Box Society: The Secret Algorithms That Control Money and Information*. Harvard University Press., DOI: 10.4159/harvard.9780674736061

Re, R. M., Solow-Niederman, A., Bussel, D., Brennan-Marquez, K., Kaminski, M., Levy, K., … Volokh, E. (2019). UCLA School of Law; 2017--2019 PULSE Fellow.

Remus, D., & Levy, F. S. (2015). Can Robots Be Lawyers? Computers, Lawyers, and the Practice of Law. SSRN *Electronic Journal*. https://doi.org/DOI: 10.2139/ssrn.2701092

Schellekens, M. (2019). Does Regulation of Illegal Content Need Reconsideration in Light of Blockchains? *International Journal of Law and Information Technology*, *27*(3), 292–305. DOI: 10.1093/ijlit/eaz009

Sekti, B. A. (2025a). Adversarial Machine Learning in Industrial Cybersecurity: Challenges and Solutions. In *AI-Enhanced Cybersecurity for Industrial Automation* (pp. 363–386). IGI Global Scientific Publishing. https://doi.org/DOI: 10.4018/979-8-3373-3241-3.ch018

Sekti, B. A. (2025b). Machine Learning vs. AI: Key Concepts. In *Implementing Enterprise Cybersecurity With AI* (pp. 1–27). https://doi.org/DOI: 10.4018/979-8-3373-2252-0.ch001

Solum, L. B. (2014). Artificial Meaning. *Washington Law Review (Seattle, Wash.)*, •••, 89.

Surden, H., & Williams, A. (2023). Technological Opacity, Artificial Intelligence, and the Law. *Harvard Journal of Law \& Technology, 36*(2), 411–468.

Susskind, R. (2019). *Online Courts and the Future of Justice*. Oxford University Press., DOI: 10.1093/oso/9780198838364.001.0001

Vaitkūnaitė, I., Beniušis, M., & Jurčys, P. (2021). The Lawsuit of the Decade---Google LLC v. Oracle America, Inc.: A Victory for Interoperability and the Future of Innovation. *Journal of Intellectual Property Law \& Practice, 16*(6), 463–465. https://doi.org/10.1093/jiplp/jpab089

Wachter, S., Mittelstadt, B., & Russell, C. (2021). Why Fairness Cannot Be Automated. *Computer Law \& Security Review, 41*, 105567. https://doi.org/DOI: 10.1016/j.clsr.2021.105567

Winter, J. S. (2018). Introduction to the Special Issue: Digital Inequalities and Discrimination in the Big Data Era. *Journal of Information Policy*, *8*, 1–4. DOI: 10.5325/jinfopoli.8.2018.0001

Wirtz, B. W., Weyerer, J. C., & Geyer, C. (2019). Artificial Intelligence and the Public Sector—Applications and Challenges. *International Journal of Public Administration*, *42*(7), 596–615. DOI: 10.1080/01900692.2018.1498103

Chapter 2
Artificial Intelligence Metamorphosis Revolutionizing Intellectual Property

Devendra Singh
http://orcid.org/0000-0002-7470-3783
Amity University, Noida, India

ABSTRACT

AI has transformed contemporary life, changing how people create, work, develop, and communicate. AI, originally intended to mimic human cognition using robotic devices, has grown into a complex, multifaceted field with major social and economic impacts. Machine Learning (ML)—a critical component of AI—helps systems improve via data-driven learning, pattern identification, and experience adaptation. The deep partnership between AI and ML has accelerated the development of intelligent systems that can perform complex cognitive tasks like speech recognition, image understanding, predictive analytics, and autonomous decision-making, once thought to be human abilities. AI technologies are being used to create, modify, and optimize material, challenging IP law notions of authorship, ownership, originality, and responsibility. This chapter discusses AI's metamorphic influence on the IP ecosystem, increasing legal and ethical challenges, and how global IP frameworks must adapt to preserve innovation and promote fair and equitable governance in the era of intelligent machines

DOI: 10.4018/979-8-3373-7685-1.ch002

INTRODUCTION

Artificial Intelligence (AI) is a disruptive force in technology, significantly influencing our everyday lives and altering how we live, work, and communicate. The inception of AI was rooted in the idea of robots emulating human cognition, although it has transformed into a multifaceted discipline with extensive ramifications. Machine Learning (ML), a subset of AI, has emerged as a pivotal force in this growth, allowing systems to improve their performance over time via exposure to data, patterns, and experiences. The symbiotic link between AI and ML has advanced the creation of intelligent systems that can recognize speech, understand pictures, and make judgments with an accuracy previously considered limited to humans.

A fundamental aspect of AI is its extensive array of applications across several sectors. In healthcare, artificial intelligence is transforming diagnoses and treatment strategies by analysing extensive databases to discern trends and forecast illnesses. In finance, AI algorithms are enhancing investing strategies and identifying fraudulent activity with unparalleled precision. The automotive sector is seeing the emergence of autonomous cars, with artificial intelligence playing a pivotal role in transforming transportation via its engagement in navigation, perception, and decision-making. Another facet of AI, Natural Language Processing (NLP), has significantly advanced human-computer interaction. Virtual assistants like Siri and Alexa exemplify the potential of Natural Language Processing (NLP) in facilitating machine comprehension and interact with human language, therefore improving the accessibility and use of technology. The effect of AI permeates the entertainment sector, as recommendation algorithms evaluate user preferences to tailor content consumption, therefore augmenting the entire user experience. Nonetheless, the development of AI also engenders ethical and social dilemmas. The pursuit of autonomous robots raises inquiries on accountability and the possible effects on employment. As AI systems surpass human capabilities in certain jobs, questions around ethical AI use, algorithmic bias, and the possibility for employment displacement are more pertinent. The progress and implementation of AI engage with legal and regulatory structures, highlighting concerns such as intellectual property, data privacy, and security for policymakers addressing the rapid development of AI technology.

Reconciling the advancement of innovation with the safeguarding of individual rights is a multifaceted problem, requiring carefully crafted legislation and international cooperation to traverse the complicated ethical and legal terrain. The future of AI presents both promise and ambiguity. Current research in domains like Explainable AI (XAI) seeks to elucidate the decision-making mechanisms of AI systems, hence promoting transparency and accountability. The amalgamation of AI with nascent technologies such as the Internet of Things (IoT) and 5G is set to provide synergies that amplify the influence of both domains. As AI evolves, multidisciplinary cooperation among scientists, ethicists, politicians, and industry leaders is essential to use its promise for the common good while confronting inherent difficulties. The advent of Artificial Intelligence represents a transformative change in our technological environment. AI enhances productivity across several businesses while also presenting significant ethical dilemmas that need our attention and careful study. In this age of rapid innovation, it is essential to engage in AI research with a profound understanding of its revolutionary potential and a steadfast dedication to ethical, responsible, and inclusive approaches.

EXPLORATION OF ARTIFICIAL INTELLIGENCE: CHARTING A REVOLUTIONARY TECHNOLOGY

The progression of Artificial Intelligence (AI) extends across several decades and is characterized by notable milestones, breakthroughs, and paradigm changes (Company, 2025). The evolution of AI may be generally classified into many stages:

The early foundations of AI emerged in the 1950s, when John McCarthy coined the phrase "artificial intelligence" in 1956. Early pioneers, such as Alan Turing and Marvin Minsky, established the foundation for artificial intelligence by investigating ideas like machine learning and symbolic reasoning.

- **Symbolic AI and Expert Systems (1960s-1980s):** Symbolic AI, referred to as Good Old-Fashioned AI (GOFAI), prevailed in this period. Researchers created expert systems, rule-based algorithms intended to replicate the decision-making skills of human specialists in certain fields. Nevertheless, constraints in managing uncertainty and the intricacies of real-world issues led to a decrease in interest and funding for AI research throughout the 1980s.
- **The AI Winter and Resurgence (1980s-1990s):** The failure of early AI systems to fulfil their promises resulted in a phase termed the "AI Winter." Financial support and interest in AI research diminished as expectations were not met. Nonetheless, the discipline saw a revival in the 1990s due to the emergence of new methodologies, including statistical techniques and neural networks.
- **Rise of Machine Learning (2000s-2010s):** The 2000s saw a substantial transition towards machine learning as the predominant methodology in artificial intelligence. Advancements in techniques, the availability of large datasets, and improved computing power have propelled substantial progress in areas such as natural language processing and computer vision. During this time, support vector machines, decision trees, and ensemble approaches were prominent, leading to practical applications like recommendation systems and voice recognition.

- **Deep Learning engagement with Neural Networks (2010s-Present):** Advances in training deep neural networks, propelled by breakthroughs like as the backpropagation algorithm and Graphics Processing Units (GPUs), achieved unparalleled advancements in activities like image recognition, language translation, and gaming. Deep learning has emerged as the catalyst for several cutting-edge AI applications.
- **Artificial Intelligence in Industry and Daily Life:** In recent years, AI has evolved from research laboratories to practical implementations across many sectors. Companies use AI for functions such as predictive analytics, process automation, and customer support. AI-driven virtual assistants, intelligent home gadgets, and self-driving cars are more common, demonstrating the integration of AI into daily life.
- **Ethical and Societal Considerations:** The fast advancement of AI has highlighted ethical difficulties, particularly algorithmic prejudice and apprehensions around job displacement. This has prompted debates and endeavors to develop ethical principles and rules in the industry. The continuous advancement of AI involves academics and practitioners constantly expanding its limits. As AI systems evolve in complexity, the significance of responsible development, transparency, and ethical issues is paramount. These actions are crucial to ensure that AI positively impacts society, tackling issues such as job displacement caused by automation and promoting the appropriate use of AI technology.

THE IMPORTANCE OF ARTIFICIAL INTELLIGENCE: REVEALING AI'S ESSENTIAL ROLE IN SHAPING THE FUTURE

In a time characterized by data proliferation, connectedness, and rapid technical progress, AI arises as a revolutionary entity, presenting unparalleled prospects and tackling intricate obstacles. A principal contribution of AI in the digital era is its capacity to augment efficiency and productivity across diverse sectors (A., 2025). In several areas, including banking, healthcare, manufacturing, and transportation, AI solutions enhance processes, automate repetitive jobs, and elevate overall performance. The digital era is marked by an abundance of data, with AI functioning as a formidable instrument for leveraging the potential of this extensive information environment. In e-commerce, social networking, or online content distribution, AI algorithms analyse user behaviour, preferences, and interactions to provide personalized suggestions, hence enhancing the bespoke and engaging user experience. AI-powered recommendation systems enhance consumer happiness and augment corporate income by elevating user engagement and conversion rates. Furthermore, AI plays a significant role in the progression of healthcare in the contemporary day.

AI applications enhance accurate diagnoses, tailored treatment strategies, and better patient outcomes, ranging from diagnostic tools that analyse medical pictures to predictive models that anticipate disease outbreaks. AI capabilities, including medication research and development, are expediting innovation within the pharmaceutical sector. The digital era is characterized by the rapid expansion of online content, with AI-powered content production tools significantly contributing to this transformation. AI algorithms exhibit creative talents that enhance human creativity, ranging from the generation of news articles to the composition of music and the production of visual art. The amalgamation of human and machine creativity broadens the horizons for content generation and cultural expression, contesting conventional concepts of authorship and creative creation. As digital communication grows more ubiquitous, artificial intelligence plays a significant role in the advancement of cybersecurity. AI-driven systems may identify and address cyber threats instantaneously, examining trends and abnormalities to detect possible security breaches. The proactive role of AI in cybersecurity is essential for reducing risks and protecting sensitive information in a connected and data-centric digital environment.

Nonetheless, the importance is coupled with ethical issues and social ramifications. The possibility of bias in AI systems, stemming from past data and human prejudices, presents issues of justice and equality. Resolving these concerns necessitates a unified endeavour to establish ethical rules, enhance openness in AI decision-making, and guarantee that technology serves all sectors of society. The digital era also observes the rise of AI in autonomous systems, especially in the field of transportation. Autonomous vehicles and drones, directed by artificial intelligence algorithms, are poised to transform transportation, logistics, and delivery services. The consequences include not just economic improvements but also concerns over safety, legislation, and the social effects of extensive automation across many sectors. Education is another sector where AI is making substantial advancements. Personalized learning platforms, adaptive assessments, and intelligent tutoring systems use AI to address individual learning requirements, improving the educational experience and fostering lifelong learning. The digital revolution of education, enabled by AI, enhances worldwide access to excellent education, dismantling conventional obstacles and promoting a culture of ongoing skill improvement.

Therefore, the significance of AI in the digital era is paramount. AI is a catalyst for the digital transformation of society, optimizing commercial operations, augmenting healthcare, changing creative expression, increasing cybersecurity, and revolutionizing education. In addressing the benefits and problems posed by AI, a deliberate and ethical approach to its development and implementation is essential. Harnessing the promise of AI while mitigating hazards guarantees the use of this formidable technology to foster a more interconnected, efficient, and inclusive digital future.

TIMELINE OF AI AND IP MILESTONES (2000–2025)

Artificial intelligence has significantly impacted the arts, music, and intellectual property law. The evolution of AI-generated music compositions to contemporary legal discussions on AI as an inventor or creator has consistently prompted inquiries about authorship, ownership, and the extent of intellectual property protection. Presented above is a comprehensive historical chronology of significant AI-IP achievements, extending from the early 2000s to anticipated advancements in 2025.

Comprehensive Chronology:

1. **2000 — Emily Howell: Initial AI Music Composition:** At the early 2000s, music professor David Cope developed "Emily Howell," an AI system proficient at writing unique music. This advancement was crucial, since it posed the first significant inquiries about music authorship inside the framework of AI. Historically, humans were the only composers of music; however, AI's capacity to generate songs derived from established genres presents substantial problems to intellectual property law.
2. **2016 — "The Next Rembrandt": Art Created by Artificial Intelligence:** "The Next Rembrandt," an AI-generated portrait emulating Rembrandt's style, was produced via machine learning algorithms that examined the Dutch master's extant artworks. This AI-generated artwork ignited discussions about copyright ownership and the potential for the algorithm, rather than a human artist, to assert authorship. Legal experts and art critics have begun to question whether AI-generated works can be protected by conventional copyright regulations.
3. **2016—'Daddy's Car' by Sony CSL:** Music Generated by Artificial Intelligence Sony CSL created the AI known as Flow Machines, which wrote "Daddy's Car," a pop tune emulating The Beatles' style. This case raised significant legal issues about ownership and originality. Was the song an original composition, or did it violate copyright by just imitating The Beatles' style? The legal world is grappling with delineating the distinction between human and machine authorship as AI increasingly generates creative works.
4. **2017—United States Copyright Office Denies Copyright for AI-Generated Works:** In 2017, the US Copyright Office clarified that works produced exclusively by AI are not eligible for copyright protection. This was the first government stance on AI-generated works, emphasizing that copyright law

need a human creator. The verdict reinforced the idea that AI does not possess the legal ability to claim authorship rights under existing intellectual property rules.

5. **2018 — UKIPO Consultation Regarding Artificial Intelligence and Intellectual Property:** The UK Intellectual Property Office (UKIPO) conducted discussions about the impact of AI on creative sectors. This was one of the first official dialogues around artificial intelligence and its ramifications for intellectual property law. It investigated the potential for AI to be acknowledged as an inventor or author and assessed the need for novel intellectual property frameworks that address AI's expanding skills in creating works.
6. **2021 — EU AI Act 2021:** Regulatory Proposal The European Union introduced the AI Act in 2021, intending to govern AI technology within the EU. The AI Act delineated essential legal frameworks for AI applications, including intellectual property concerns. The rule recognizes AI's contribution to the creation of works and examines the need for current intellectual property laws to adapt in order to support AI-driven innovation, especially with patents, copyrights, and moral rights.
7. **2022 — Thaler's DABUS Patent Case:** Artificial Intelligence as Inventor In a significant court case, Dr. Stephen Thaler's AI system, DABUS, was designated as the inventor in a patent application. The case presented significant questions about the potential recognition of an AI system as an inventor under existing patent legislation. The courts of the UK, EU, and US dismissed DABUS as an inventor, affirming that inventorship necessitates a human being, therefore upholding conventional intellectual property standards.
8. **2023 — Legal Disputes Involving AI Art:** Getty Images vs AI Image Generators In 2023, Getty Images initiated legal action against AI picture creators, contending that these programs used copyrighted materials without authorization. This case underscores the challenges associated with datasets used by AI in art generation and the possible violation of intellectual property rights. The result of this litigation may impact forthcoming legislation concerning the use of copyrighted information in the training of AI models.
9. **2025 — Anticipated Advancements in AI and Intellectual Property:** In 2025, significant regulatory advancements are anticipated as countries progress toward more defined norms for AI and intellectual property legislation. The interaction of AI and intellectual property will persist in its evolution, especially with emerging laws and legal frameworks that tackle issues like AI authorship, dataset protection, and the patentability of AI-generated ideas (Ali & Kamraju, 2023).

The timeline above illustrates a persistent topic of legal ambiguity about AI's involvement in intellectual property. From first creations such as "Emily Howell" to the legal disputes about AI-generated patents and artworks, a persistent concern arises: the subject of AI authorship and inventorship remains insufficiently addressed by existing legal frameworks.

- **Ownership and Authorship:** Legal entities are still contending with the question of whether AI may own ownership of works or innovations generated autonomously, without human involvement. Jurisdictions worldwide, including the US, UK, and EU, repeatedly assert that AI cannot be recognized as the creator under current legislation.
- **The influence of policy and legislation:** While frameworks such as the EU AI Act (2021) provide regulations for AI, they lack specificity about AI's function in intellectual property law. Additional advancements and upgrades are essential to tackle the increasing prevalence of AI in creative and innovative fields.
- **Legal Precedents:** Judicial proceedings, exemplified by the DABUS case, establish significant precedents, affirming that artificial intelligence cannot be acknowledged as an inventor or creator under conventional intellectual property statutes. These examples indicate a possible transition in the next years, as the legal system adapts to technological progress. The convergence of artificial intelligence and intellectual property law is a rapidly advancing domain. As artificial intelligence increasingly influences the production of art, music, innovations, and legal proceedings, the legal frameworks governing intellectual property must evolve. The timeline delineates key developments and legal obstacles, exemplifying the intricacies of establishing authorship and inventorship in the age of AI. Ongoing policy formulation, legal proceedings, and international collaboration are essential to guarantee that intellectual property law can proficiently regulate AI-driven advancements while addressing ethical, economic, and social issues (Gervais, 2020)

PROS AND CONS OF ARTIFICIAL INTELLIGENCE: EXPLORING THE OPPORTUNITIES AND CHALLENGES IN THE ERA OF AI

Artificial Intelligence (AI) has multiple capabilities that have profoundly influenced diverse sectors. A primary benefit is its ability to handle and analyse large data sets at unparalleled rates. Automation, a significant advantage of AI, improves efficiency by managing repetitive operations, lowering operational expenses, and augmenting overall production. In healthcare, AI facilitates illness detection and customizes treatment methods, demonstrating its capacity to enhance patient outcomes (A., 2025). Although AI's capabilities enable significant gains across several areas, its limitations underscore the need for responsible development, ethical considerations, and continuous attempts to mitigate biases and security issues.

Benefits of Artificial Intelligence

- **Efficiency Enhancement:** AI augments efficiency via the automation of repetitive operations, freeing human resources to concentrate on more intricate and innovative pursuits.
- **Data Analysis:** AI proficiently processes and analyzes extensive datasets, identifies patterns, and extracts critical insights to enhance decision-making.
- **Creativity and Problem-Solving:** AI promotes creativity by facilitating the creation of original solutions to intricate issues using machine learning and computational capabilities.
- **Continuous Availability:** AI systems function incessantly without the need for breaks, ensuring unwavering availability and dependability in applications such as customer service and industrial operations.
- **Personalization:** AI enables tailored experiences, evident in recommendation systems, content curation, and targeted marketing, hence augmenting customer happiness.
- **Medical Advancements:** Enhances pathology, self-administered medication, and pharmacological innovation, possibly improving patient outcomes and decreasing healthcare expenditures.

Drawbacks of Artificial Intelligence

- **Employment Displacement:** The automation of work by AI may result in employment displacement, especially in sectors where regular activities are readily mechanized, thereby engendering economic and social issues.
- **Prejudice:** AI systems may inherit biases present in training data, resulting in inequitable or discriminatory results, particularly in domains such as employment, lending, and criminal justice.
- **Deficiency in Creativity and Intuition:** Although AI excels at certain tasks, it now lacks the creativity, intuition, and contextual comprehension inherent to humans.
- **Ethical Considerations:** The use of AI in sensitive domains, such as surveillance and decision-making, elicits ethical issues around privacy, responsibility, and the appropriate utilization of technology.

- **Dependence on Data:** AI relies significantly on extensive datasets for training and may encounter difficulties in scenarios with restricted or biased data, which might impair the system's performance and generalization.
- **Substantial Initial Expenditures:** The deployment of AI systems necessitates considerable preliminary expenditures in technology, infrastructure, and proficient individuals, thus posing a barrier for some enterprises.

TRANSFORMATIVE EFFECTS IN INDIA: A PARADIGM SHIFT IN HEALTHCARE, EDUCATION, FINANCE, AGRICULTURE, AND MORE

In India, the influence of Artificial Intelligence (AI) has been revolutionary, facilitating innovation, economic expansion, and social transformation. As the nation adopts digitization and technological progress, AI is significantly influencing the management of diverse sectors, including healthcare, education, finance, and agriculture (C., 2025). A significant advancement is the integration of AI in healthcare, which is transforming diagnoses, therapy, and patient care. AI-driven diagnostic technologies evaluate medical pictures and data, delivering expedited and more precise evaluations. This is especially important in a populated nation like India, where obtaining timely healthcare treatments might be a hardship. AI-supported telemedicine solutions provide remote consultations, enhancing healthcare accessible in urban and rural regions.

In the educational industry, artificial intelligence is augmenting learning experiences and results. Personalized learning systems use AI algorithms to tailor information according to individual student development, accommodating varied learning requirements. Moreover, AI-driven chatbots aid students by addressing inquiries and offering immediate assistance and advice. The government's measures, notably the National Education Policy 2020, emphasize the use of technology, particularly AI, to modernize and democratize education.

In agriculture, artificial intelligence is advancing to enhance agricultural output, resource efficiency, and farm administration. Artificial intelligence applications examine meteorological trends, soil vitality, and agricultural data.

To provide farmers with insights for judicious decision-making. This technology-oriented strategy enhances sustainable agricultural practices, tackling the many issues encountered by Indian farmers.

The manufacturing industry has seen a paradigm change due to the incorporation of Industry 4.0 concepts, with artificial intelligence occupying a major position. Intelligent factories use artificial intelligence for predictive maintenance, quality assurance, and productivity enhancement.

The influence of AI on urban planning and infrastructure development is seen in smart city programs across. This strategy promotes sustainable urban development, tackling the issues presented by fast urbanization in India. The start-up environment in India has been notably vibrant in using AI for innovation. Many start-ups are using AI for various purposes, such as e-commerce, healthcare, finance, and education. The government's programs, including Start-up India and Atal Innovation Mission, provide support and encouragement for AI-driven entrepreneurial endeavors, enhancing the nation's status as a center for technological innovation.

India's space exploration initiatives have also benefited from the deployment of artificial intelligence. The Indian Space Research Organisation (ISRO) use artificial intelligence for data processing, satellite communication, and mission planning. AI algorithms enhance the efficiency and accuracy of space missions, establishing India as a prominent participant in the global space exploration domain.

India highlights the revolutionary influence of technology across several industries, driven by advancements in Artificial Intelligence. AI serves as a catalyst for good transformation by expanding healthcare accessible, optimizing agricultural techniques, improving education, and strengthening economic sectors.

ARTIFICIAL INTELLIGENCE AND LEGAL STUDIES

Artificial Intelligence (AI) has become a transformational element in the legal domain, altering the practice of law, the provision of legal services, and the administration of justice. In recent years, the advancement and integration of AI technology in several aspects of the legal domain has introduced unparalleled efficiency, precision, and innovation (Gervais, 2025). AI-powered tools, equipped with extensive databases of case law, legislation, and legal precedents, enable fast information retrieval, therefore helping legal practitioners to optimize their research processes and remain informed about the ever evolving legal landscape. Furthermore, AI's capabilities include contract examination and formulation. Machine learning algorithms facilitate the effective examination of contracts, discerning essential terms, possible dangers, and assuring compliance. This data-centric methodology improves litigation efficacy and fosters more informed legal practices.

Legal chatbots and virtual assistants, as a kind of AI, have proven essential in improving client interactions and delivering accessible legal information. These AI-powered interfaces interact with customers, addressing inquiries, offering fundamental legal advice, and enhancing overall communication. The democratization of legal knowledge via AI-driven virtual assistants enhances legal literacy among the public, promoting a more inclusive legal environment. E-discovery, a historically laborious procedure, has seen a transformation. The productivity improvements are especially significant in scenarios with extensive datasets, becoming AI an essential instrument in contemporary legal procedures.

The integration of Artificial Intelligence in the legal field presents several obstacles and concerns. Achieving an optimal equilibrium between automation and human supervision is essential to guarantee that AI augments, rather than undermines, the tenets of justice. The interpretability of AI models presents a hurdle known as the "black box" issue. Initiatives in the advancement of Explainable AI (XAI) attempt to tackle this issue, with the objective of enhancing the transparency and interpretability of AI systems. Moreover, the legal profession must contend with the changing dynamics of cybersecurity and data protection. Given that AI systems manage sensitive legal information, it is essential to implement stringent security measures to safeguard against cyber-attacks and unauthorized access. Legal practitioners and firms must not only adopt technology innovations but also protect the confidentiality and integrity of their clients' information. The convergence of artificial intelligence and law stimulates discourse over the future of legal employment. The automation of basic legal processes using AI may result in job displacement in some sectors, prompting a reassessment of the skills and functions needed in the legal profession. Adapting to this evolving environment necessitates the upskilling and reskilling of legal practitioners to proficiently engage with AI systems and use technology for more strategic and intricate legal tasks.

Thus, the collaboration between AI and law signifies a transformative change in the legal domain. AI is revolutionizing the operations of legal practitioners by improving research, contract writing, litigation strategy, and client relationships. The ethical, interpretability, and security problems related to AI in law highlight the need for responsible development, continuous communication, and collaborative initiatives between legal professionals and technologists. The legal field must adapt to the digital age by integrating AI's promise and tackling its complexity to provide a framework that enhances justice, accessibility, and efficiency via technology.

COMPARATIVE LEGAL FRAMEWORK: DEFINITIONS OF "AUTHORSHIP" IN THE ERA OF AI

The emergence of artificial intelligence (AI) generating creative, literary, and innovative works presents new legal challenges to the idea of authorship, traditionally regarded as a human realm. Countries are addressing this disruption in various ways, contingent upon their legal traditions, policy goals, and innovation agendas. This section rigorously examines the definitions of "authorship" in relation to AI-generated works as articulated by the United States, United Kingdom, India, and

China, emphasizing significant legislation provisions, court interpretations, and policy developments.

A Comparative Study by Country

1. United States: Human Authorship as a Cornerstone in the AI Metamorphosis of IP Law

In the digital era, artificial intelligence transcends its role as a simple tool; it functions as an independent entity capable of producing complex literary, musical, artistic, and creative works. Nevertheless, the United States, a preeminent authority in intellectual property law and technical innovation, has adopted a cautious position regarding the copyrightability of works created by artificial intelligence. This role illustrates a significant conflict in the developing transformation of intellectual property law, as traditional human-cantered principles increasingly confront the new phenomenon of machine authorship.

Legal Position: The Solet of Human Authorship

Under existing U.S. copyright legislation, authorship is a position exclusively designated for human beings. This idea was firmly affirmed in the pivotal ruling of Thaler v. Perlmutter (2023). Stephen Thaler submitted a copyright application for an artwork autonomously created by his AI system, "Creativity Machine." The U.S. Copyright Office denied the application, and the U.S. District Court for the District of Columbia later upheld this denial. The court determined that "human authorship is a fundamental prerequisite for copyright" and that "non-human authorship, including that of an autonomous AI system, fails to satisfy the statutory requirements under Title 17."

Thaler v. Perlmutter, Case No. 1:22-cv-01564 (D.D.C. 2023) This approach is consistent with the Compendium of U.S. Copyright Office Practices, which consistently underscores that works must be "created by a human being" to be eligible for registration under U.S. law (Office, 2021).

Doctrinal Sources:

- Statutory Foundation: Title 17 of the U.S. Code (Copyright Act of 1976)
- Judicial Authority: Thaler v. Perlmutter, 1:22-cv-01564 (D.D.C. 2023)
- Administrative Source: U.S. Copyright Office, Compendium of U.S. Copyright Office.

Critical Insight: The Originality Doctrine Confronts the Algorithm

The court's emphasis on human uniqueness is historically grounded in the Lockean labour theory and the Romantic concept of authorship, which prioritize personal expression, emotional engagement, and creative effort. This philosophy is now challenged by generative AI models such as OpenAI's GPT-4, DALL·E, and Google's Gemini, which can autonomously generate highly expressive outputs without conventional human authorship. The contradiction is in the machine's creative ability, which replicates or even exceeds human aesthetic intelligence, being dismissed only due to its absence of consciousness. This prompts profound normative inquiries: Should copyright law safeguard the process or the outcome? Must the inventor of an original thing be human.

Policy Implication: Impeded Reform in a Swiftly Transforming Ecosystem

Notwithstanding the increasing scholarly conversation and advocacy from the technology sector, the U.S. Congress has yet to commence legislative change concerning AI-generated works. This inertia is partially attributable to:

- Doctrinal conservatism in United States intellectual property law.
- Apprehension over the initiation of non-human rights assertions.
- Ambiguity over accountability, ownership, and enforcement should AI be accorded legal standing as an author.

This regulatory void may hinder innovation and investment in fields of AI-generated content, including digital design, music creation, legal automation, and journalism.

A professor rightly observes: "Denying protection to AI-generated works may cultivate a legal framework that both suppresses creativity and neglects to incentivize the technological advancements that copyright law aims to promote" (Gervais, 2020a).

Table 1. Empirical Overview: The Innovation–Protection Discrepancy

Metric	Data Point
AI-generated artworks (globally)	> 1 million as of 2023 (World Intellectual Property Organization, 2023)
AI music tracks produced annually	> 500,000 (Spotify estimates) (Mathews, 2024)
U.S. Copyright applications denied due to AI authorship	100+ between 2020–2023
Legislative proposals for AI copyright reform in U.S. Congress	0 (as of 2025)

This case demonstrates that the evolution of intellectual property law in the U.S. is still unfinished. It highlights a significant contradiction: whereas AI is transforming creative sectors, the legal framework remains fundamentally resistive to progress. This theological stasis contrasted with technical acceleration is a persistent issue in your research and should be emphasized as a significant fault line in the global intellectual property transformation.

2. United Kingdom: An Innovative but Prudent Approach to AI-Driven Authorship

Legal Standing in the Context of AI Transformation

The United Kingdom is an early, albeit cautious, pioneer in the swiftly advancing discussion on AI and intellectual property. The principal legal framework, the Copyright, Designs and Patents Act 1988 (CDPA), recognizes the notion of computer-generated works in Section 9(3), which articulates: "For a computer-generated literary, dramatic, musical, or artistic work, the author is deemed to be the individual responsible for making the arrangements essential for the creation of the work." Copyright, Designs and Patents Act 1988, Section 9(3). This clause, formulated before to the advent of autonomous generative AI models such as DALL·E, ChatGPT, or MusicLM, still establishes a fundamental legal framework for assigning copyright to outputs that do not have a distinctly human author in the conventional sense.

Analytical Context: The Delicate Equilibrium Between AI and Human Contribution Through the perspective of your research, AI's evolution from a supplementary tool to an independent creator immediately contests the boundaries of this legislation. The UK's attribution methodology fundamentally assigns authorship to the most recent identified human contributor, such as the programmer or the person configuring operational settings. This facilitates a legal personification of AI innovation, while without acknowledging AI as a legal entity. This framework becomes more tenuous when generative AI systems gain autonomy, enabling them to generate original results with little to no direct human guidance. For example, what happens when an AI autonomously develops its algorithm or trains on unsupervised datasets to create a symphony or produce a painting indistinguishable from human artistry?

Critical Insight: Obsolete yet Fundamental Section 9(3), although more than thirty years old, continues to be one of the scant explicit legal references worldwide to non-human authorship. It demonstrates an early recognition that machines may be essential in the creative process. However, the clause does not examine the fundamental nature of authorship can an algorithm really be creative, and if so, should it possess the same rights as a human? As AI-generated material increasingly resembles or exceeds human creativity, the UK's current legal framework risks becoming outdated—a temporary measure requiring reform (Gervais, 2020a).

Policy Implication: Consultation Without Codification (Currently), In response to anticipated legal challenges, the UK Intellectual Property Office (UKIPO) conducted public consultations in 2021 and 2022 to gather opinions on the potential evolution of copyright law to include AI-generated works. These conversations revealed a fundamental tension:

- On one side are human creators and conventional rights-holders asking for more stringent regulations to safeguard human-centric creation.
- Conversely, technology firms and digital innovators advocate for more regulatory clarity to promote AI research and implementation in the creative sectors (UKIPO, 2022).

In 2022, the UK government decided against extending copyright protection to AI-generated works without a human author, citing concerns over detrimental effects on incentives for human authoring (UKIPO, 2022a) (UKIPO, 2020).

Table 2. Evolution of UK Policy on AI and Authorship

Year	Milestone	Description
1988	CDPA Enacted (Section 9(3))	First recognition of computer-generated works and authorship via human arranger
2019	AI Policy Debate Begins	Rising interest in how AI challenges UK copyright frameworks
2021	UKIPO Consultation on AI and IP	Public views sought on AI-generated content, patents, and data rights
2022	UK Government Decision Not to Extend AI-Only Copyright	AI-only creations excluded from copyright protection for now
2023	Ongoing Parliamentary Discussions	Debates continue on legal reform amid tech innovation and public policy shifts

3. India: The Human Authorship Framework in the Era of AI Transformation

Legal Stance: The Enduring Influence of Human-Centric Copyright in the Digital Age

The Copyright Act of India, 1957, a colonial-era statute substantially revised in 2012, continues to be based on the conventional concept of human authorship. The legislation does not specifically recognize non-human creativity or works made by AI, despite the significant integration of AI technologies into Indian creative, educational, and software development sectors. The court system continues to rely on human intelligence, with originality evaluated based on a minimal creative standard, shown by the landmark decision of Eastern Book Company v. D.B. Modak (2008) 1 SCC 1 (Judiciary, 2025). The Supreme Court ruled that mere work or effort does not warrant protection; it must be coupled with intellectual originality, so indirectly rejecting AI-generated products with limited or non-existent human cognitive involvement. Notwithstanding India's Digital India and India AI initiatives, designed to use artificial intelligence for economic and social advancement, the legal system is mostly unprepared and ill-equipped to address the transformative development of intellectual property influenced by AI technology.

Contextual Expansion: The Integration of AI vs Legal Stagnation

India is among the rapidly expanding digital economies, with artificial intelligence being used in industries such as legal technology, financial technology, agricultural technology, and educational technology. Artificial intelligence models are now used to negotiate contracts, compose music, automatically make artwork, and produce legal rulings and summaries. The lack of legal acknowledgment for these works leads to ambiguous ownership, discouraging investment and progress in the creative AI sector. This legal inertia is not just a mistake; it embodies a profound philosophical bias favouring anthropocentric authorship, which is becoming more incongruent with the technological transformation driven by AI.

Absence of Policy and Consequences

No clear legislative provision exists regarding AI authorship, nor is there any official government document acknowledging the issues AI presents to copyright law. This disparity persists despite the growing use of generative AI models such as ChatGPT, Midjourney, and Indian equivalents like Hanooman and BharatGPT in conventional content production. The Ministry of Electronics and Information Technology (MeitY) (Government of India, 2023) and the Department for Promotion of Industry and Internal Trade (DPIIT) (India, 2022) in India have published AI roadmaps and intellectual property innovation policies; nonetheless, none elucidate authorship or ownership for machine-generated works. This legislative ambiguity deters both Indian startups and multinational firms from using generative AI models in India, due to concerns about legal uncertainties and possible conflicts.

Essential Analysis: Convergence of Tradition and Change

The Indian intellectual property system is at the intersection of legal heritage and technical evolution. It aims to uphold human-centric ideals essential to copyright while also addressing an age in which computers autonomously create, remix, and iterate. India's transformation in artificial intelligence concerning intellectual property need a fundamental change rather than just incremental adjustments. It requires a progressive legislative framework that recognizes:

- Creativity augmented by machines
- Collaborative authorship
- Originality informed by data
- Artificial Intelligence as an instrument for collaborative creativity

Disregarding this transition jeopardizes India's position in the global AI-IP innovation competition and undermines the rights of developers, authors, and consumers of AI-generated content.

Policy Implication: Necessity for Proactive Legal Reforms

Although legal experts and organizations like as NITI Aayog and WIPO's India Chapter have initiated discussions on AI and intellectual property, no official proposal has been submitted to Parliament so far. The absence of legislative foresight jeopardizes innovation, constrains global competitiveness, and heightens reliance on foreign frameworks.

Proposed Recommendations:

- Incorporation of AI-generated works inside a new provision of the Copyright Act, contingent upon human contribution or responsibility of the AI tool.
- Creation of a specialized tribunal or regulatory authority to adjudicate AI-IP issues.
- Modelling changes based on comparable countries, such as the UK (Section 9(3) CDPA) or China's court-based recognition regimes.

4. China: Establishing a Holistic AI-IP Framework in the Age of Digital Transformation

In the digital era, which brings significant changes in innovation, creativity, and authorship, China is leading the redefinition of intellectual property law with respect to artificial intelligence (AI). In alignment with the nation's aspiration to emerge as a worldwide leader in AI by 2030, its intellectual property policy has concurrently developed, demonstrating a profound institutional dedication to adapt conventional IP principles to accommodate algorithmic innovation.

Legal Framework: Towards an Adaptive and Innovation-Encouraging Regime

China has not officially acknowledged AI as an author or creator, asserting that legal personality is a precondition for intellectual property rights. Nonetheless, its judicial and regulatory reactions indicate a shift from inflexible human-centric standards. Chinese courts have begun to provide copyright protection to AI-generated works, contingent upon the demonstration of adequate human input, such as curation, timely engineering, or data selection. The Beijing Internet Court, founded in 2018 to focus on technology and internet-related issues, has been a trailblazer in adjudicating matters using AI-generated material, establishing core law in this area.

Significant Judicial Precedents

- **Feilin v. Baidu Baike, Beijing Internet Court (2019)** This pivotal instance pertained to a photograph produced by an AI-driven system and then submitted to Baidu Baike, China's equivalent of Wikipedia. The suit asserted copyright over the AI-generated picture. The court determined that, notwithstanding the use of AI, the significant human involvement in training and parameter selection provided sufficient uniqueness to warrant copyright protection.
    - **Legal Significance:** Established the concept of a "human-in-the-loop" criterion for evaluating originality in AI-generated creations.
    - **Thematic Connection to Paper:** Illustrates how China is redefining the essence of authorship, in accordance with the concept of digital transformation in intellectual property law (OPUS IP, 2025).
- **Tencent v. Yingxun, Nanshan District Court (2020)** Tencent initiated legal proceedings against Yingxun for infringing upon an AI-generated financial article created by its proprietary platform, "Dreamwriter." The court recognized that the essay, albeit being generated algorithmically, underwent editorial supervision and intellectual guidance from Tencent's human engineers, so qualifying for copyright protection. The legal significance underscores the established precedent that corporate ownership of AI-generated material is permissible when associated with human oversight (PRC, 2020).

Policy Framework: AI-Enhanced Transformation of Intellectual Property Ecosystem

China's strategy is informed not just by judicial decisions but also by regulatory anticipation. The China National Intellectual Property Administration (CNIPA) (PRC, 2022) and the State Council have released guidelines and white papers focused on development.

- A novel categorization of rights pertaining to AI-generated creations.
- Rules for attributing ownership when artificial intelligence functions under human guidance.
- Protections for innovation ecosystems, harmonizing accessibility with intellectual property safeguards.

The 2020 AI and IP White Paper published by CNIPA proposed prospective legal revisions that would recognize the benefit produced by AI technologies while preserving fundamental IP values.

Critical Insight: Legal Flexibility Rooted in Strategic Techno-nationalism

China's strategy with AI and intellectual property exemplifies a pragmatically strategic style of techno-nationalism. In contrast to Western jurisdictions that prioritize philosophical integrity (e.g., human uniqueness in the U.S.), China embraces a pragmatic approach grounded on economic and geopolitical benefits. The courts evaluate the extent of human involvement in AI-generated material rather than rejecting it outright, considering its financial worth and artistic purpose. This adaptable and responsive approach acknowledges the hybrid essence of contemporary innovation, whereby human intellect and machine learning together generate new cultural and economic assets.

THE INFLUENCE OF CONCEPTS: A PRIMER ON INTELLECTUAL PROPERTY RIGHTS

Intellectual Property Rights (IPR) serve as an essential framework that protects human intellectual works, promoting innovation, creativity, and economic development. This legal notion includes a range of rights conferred upon persons or companies for their intellectual achievements, ensuring they may profit from their brilliance while establishing a basis for a fair and competitive economy (P.R.,

2025). Intellectual Property Rights (IPR) fundamentally include categories like patents, trademarks, copyrights, and trade secrets. Patents, conferred by governments, provide innovators exclusive rights to their innovations, therefore fostering technical advancement. Trademarks safeguard unique symbols, names, and logos linked to goods or services, mitigating marketplace confusion and promoting brand identification. Copyrights safeguard literary, artistic, and musical creations. They provide to authors exclusive rights to reproduce, distribute, and exhibit their works, hence incentivizing the production of diversity and culturally affluent content. Trade secrets, although not regulated by a particular statute, include proprietary business knowledge, including procedures or formulae, that provide a competitive edge to enterprises engaged in innovation.

The inception of intellectual property rights (IPR) is founded on the premise that granting inventors and innovators exclusive rights to their intellectual assets fosters a perpetual cycle of invention and cultural enhancement for society as a whole. Intellectual Property Rights impose financial constraints by promoting investment in research and development while simultaneously facilitating the diffusion of information and artistic expression. The globalization of trade and business has underscored the significance of intellectual property rights on an international level. The issues of fair use, patent trolls, and the potential restriction of access to vital medications due to pharmaceutical patents highlight the need for nuanced and flexible intellectual property rules.

The establishment of Intellectual Property Rights is fundamental to contemporary legal frameworks, fostering an atmosphere that promotes innovation, creativity, and economic growth. As societies progress in the digital era, the function and influence of intellectual property rights develop, necessitating continuous discourse on how to effectively align legal frameworks with the shifting demands of a constantly changing reality.

INFLUENCE OF INTELLECTUAL PROPERTY RIGHTS: NAVIGATING LEGAL STRUCTURES AND COMBATING CRIME IN INDIA

The convergence of law, Intellectual Property Rights (IPR), and crime in India creates a multifaceted environment where legal structures, enforcement strategies, and social issues meet (R., 2025). This convergence is especially evident in domains such as intellectual property violations, counterfeiting, and cybercrime.

- **Protection of Intellectual Property Rights (IPR):** The principal legislations include the Patents Act, Trademarks Act, Copyright Act, and Designs Act.

These statutes provide authors exclusive rights over intellectual or innovative works, promoting innovation and economic development. Nonetheless, the enforcement of intellectual property rights is a difficulty, characterized by protracted legal processes and constraints insufficient resources and a backlog of cases obstructing effective protection.

- **Intellectual Property Infringement and Counterfeiting:** Crimes relating to intellectual property rights, including copyright infringement and trademark counterfeiting, present considerable issues in India. The manufacture and distribution of counterfeit products, including fraudulent medications and imitation luxury goods, adversely affect the economy and present significant threats to consumer health and safety. Law enforcement organizations have the formidable challenge of mitigating these actions, often necessitating coordination with industry players and heightened public awareness.
- **Cybercrime and Intellectual Property:** Online piracy, software infringement, and unauthorized distribution of digital property are significant concerns. The Information Technology Act and its revisions seek to tackle cybercrime, including violations pertaining to intellectual property. The fast advancement of technology requires ongoing revisions to legal frameworks and the improvement of law enforcement capacities.
- **Challenges in Enforcement:** The enforcement of intellectual property rights legislation encounters obstacles due to the specialized expertise required by law enforcement professionals, the global character of many crimes, and the large extent of online infringement. Enhancing enforcement agencies, optimizing stakeholder collaboration, and using technology for investigation and prosecution are essential components in tackling these difficulties. The ramifications of IPR-related crime transcend legal and commercial domains, influencing society as a whole. Counterfeit products may finance organized crime, affect public health, and undermine customer confidence.
- **Policy Initiatives:** India has implemented measures to tackle these difficulties via several policy initiatives. The National IPR Policy of 2016 emphasizes the enhancement of the IPR ecosystem, the promotion of innovation, and the resolution of enforcement challenges. In conclusion, the relationship between law, intellectual property rights, and crime in India illustrates the intricate interaction between legal frameworks and enforcement obstacles and social ramifications. Enhancing enforcement infrastructure, promoting stakeholder engagement, and modifying legislative frameworks to accommodate the changing landscape of intellectual property offenses are crucial measures for tackling these difficulties and ensuring a climate that supports innovation and economic development.

THE ERA OF ARTIFICIAL INTELLIGENCE: ADDRESSING CHALLENGES

The convergence of Intellectual Property Rights (IPR) with Artificial Intelligence (AI) is a dynamic and developing domain that brings distinct problems (S., 2025). As AI technologies progress, inquiries on the safeguarding of intellectual property in this domain grow more significant.

- **Patentability of AI innovations:** A significant element pertains to the patentability of innovations relating to artificial intelligence. As AI algorithms and systems advance, questions arise over their eligibility for patent protection. Issues about inventorship and the use of AI in the creative process remain a topic of active debate. Certain governments are modifying their patent rules to accommodate these new factors and ascertain the eligibility of AI-generated ideas for patent protection.
- **Ownership of AI-Generated Works:** Intellectual property legislation generally assigns ownership to human producers. Nonetheless, when AI systems independently produce creative works, establishing ownership becomes difficult. Issues of authorship, copyright, and moral rights in AI-generated material confront conventional intellectual property standards. Clarity is essential to handle instances when AI plays a substantial role in the development of works across many fields, including art, music, and literature.
- **Trade Secrets and AI Algorithms:** Trade secrets, safeguarding sensitive and proprietary information, are essential. The algorithms that drive the systems are often regarded as trade secrets. Preserving confidentiality the use of these algorithms is crucial for organizations aiming to gain a competitive advantage. Achieving equilibrium between safeguarding and cooperation, particularly in sectors where collective knowledge might advance societal development, is a difficulty.
- **Ethical Considerations and Bias:** The ethical aspects of AI are intertwined with intellectual property issues. Mitigating prejudice in AI systems, guaranteeing equity, and averting discriminating results are critical factors. Intellectual property legislation must conform to ethical standards to foster responsible AI development and use.
- **License and Collaboration:** The cooperative essence of AI research and development requires explicit license agreements and collaboration structures. Intellectual property rights are essential in governing the sharing, licensing, and monetization of AI technology. Implementing clear regulations for AI technology licensing promotes innovation while safeguarding the interests of creators and stakeholders.

- **Challenges in Enforcement:** The enforcement of Intellectual Property Rights (IPR) in the context of AI presents difficulties, particularly in developing nations and due to the rapidly advancing nature of technology. Standardizing international norms, enhancing transnational cooperation, and establishing frameworks for resolving AI-related intellectual property conflicts are essential elements in the changing environment. As the interplay between intellectual property rights and artificial intelligence intensifies, legal frameworks must evolve to address the distinct difficulties presented by AI. Achieving an optimal equilibrium between fostering innovation, safeguarding creators' rights, and assuring ethical advancement is essential in addressing the dynamic intersection of intellectual property and artificial intelligence. The advancement of artificial intelligence (AI) in the digital era is transforming the intellectual property (IP) domain. As AI technologies advance and infiltrate many sectors, they provide unprecedented potential and challenges to governments, artists, and innovators.

CONCLUSION

Artificial Intelligence (AI) has advanced beyond a hypothesis based on human thought. It is a digital disruptor now. This marks a big technological shift. AI has moved beyond science fiction and laboratories. It already affects healthcare, economy, transportation, communication, and entertainment. AI's broad use reveals that technology may stimulate tremendous innovation while destroying legal, ethical, and societal frameworks. This innovation relies on Machine Learning (ML). Data helps AI machines learn and improve. Because of this, intelligent, self-driving systems can develop content, solve complicated issues, and make judgments without human assistance. More powerful and efficient technologies are taking over fields formerly deemed limited to human brain, such as art, literature, music, software engineering, and new ideas. This modification has raised several doubts about IPR regulations. This study, "Artificial Intelligence Metamorphosis: Revolutionising Intellectual Property in the Digital Age," examines how AI-generated material affects authorship, ownership, and innovation. Intellectual property laws have traditionally relied on human innovation and uniqueness. AI's ability to autonomously generate literary, artistic, and technological works challenges these concepts, forcing policymakers and stakeholders to rethink the definitions of "author" and "inventor." As AI slowly surpasses humans in creativity and intelligence, it becomes harder to distinguish between machines and people. This causes legal ambiguity and raises key questions: Should an AI be considered a writer or inventor? Which is the lawful owner—the inventor, the user, or the AI user company? What will happen to moral, economic, and ownership rights? AI-generated works pose hazards and moral challenges we cannot ignore. Algorithmic discrimination, data privacy abuses, deepfakes, and copyrighted content replication are serious risks. Digital platforms are utilized worldwide, making it tougher to enforce laws and establish territories. Modern intellectual property laws, whether national or regional, cannot handle these global, tech-driven issues. AI-generated works raise ethical questions of fairness, accountability, and transparency for the judicial system. AI judgments are "black box" and difficult to explain, making intellectual property litigation difficult to establish originality, purpose, or creative contribution. New domains like Explainable AI (XAI) aim to clarify algorithmic processes, which may improve and equalize AI-generated intellectual property protection. All governments must collaborate and create common regulations to merge AI and IP since the digital economy transcends boundaries. WIPO or UNESCO-led international treaties and conventions may be needed to standardize AI-related intellectual property rights recognition, protection, and enforcement across nations.

REFERENCES

A., A. (2025, March 21). Artificial intelligence and intellectual property: How AI is changing the landscape of intellectual property rights. World Intellectual Property Organization. https://www.wipo.int/edocs/pubdocs/en/wipo-pub-econstat-wp-77-en-artificial-intelligence-and-intellectual-property-an-economic-perspective.pdf

A., S. (2025, March 21). Artificial intelligence and intellectual property: "Intellectual property rights and AI: A greener future". World Intellectual Property Organization. https://www.wipo.int/edocs/pubdocs/en/wipo-pub-econstat-wp-77-en-artificial-intelligence-and-intellectual-property-an-economic-perspective.pdf

Ali, M. A., & Kamraju, M. (2023, December). Impact of artificial intelligence on intellectual property rights: Challenges and opportunities. ResearchGate. https://www.researchgate.net/publication/376751087_Impact_of_Artificial_Intelligence_on_Intellectual_Property_Rights_Challenges_and_Opportunities

C., A. (2025, March 21). Artificial intelligence and intellectual properties: Legal and ethical considerations. ResearchGate. https://www.researchgate.net/publication/376885311_Artificial_Intelligence_and_Intellectual_Properties_Legal_and_Ethical_Considerations

Company, M. (2025, March 21). The state of AI in 2022—and a half decade in review. McKinsey & Company. https://www.mckinsey.com/~/media/mckinsey/business%20functions/quantumblack/our%20insights/the%20state%20of%20ai%20in%202022%20and%20a%20half%20decade%20in%20review/the-state-of-ai-in-2022-and-a-half-decade-in-review.pdf

Gervais, D. J. (2020a, January 4). The machine as author. *SSRN*. https://papers.ssrn.com/sol3/papers.cfm?abstract_id=3359524

Gervais, D. J. (2020b, January 4). The machine as author. *SSRN*. https://papers.ssrn.com/sol3/papers.cfm?abstract_id=3359524

Gervais, D. J. (2025, March 21). The machine as author. Vanderbilt Law Scholarship. https://scholarship.law.vanderbilt.edu/faculty-publications/1164/

Government of India. (2023). IndiaAI 2023: Expert group report – First edition. Ministry of Electronics and Information Technology. https://www.meity.gov.in/content/indiaai-2023-expert-group-report-%E2%80%93-first-editionthe-ministry-electronics-and-information

Judiciary, D. (2025). Eastern Book Company v. D.B. Modak, 2008 (36) PTC 1 (SC). Drishti Judiciary. https://www.drishtijudiciary.com/intellectual-property-rights/eastern-book-company-v-d-b-modak-2008-36-ptc-1-sc

Mathews, A. (2024, July 11). The future of music is in AI; thanks to Spotify. AIM Research. https://aimresearch.co/market-industry/the-future-of-music-is-in-ai-thanks-to-spotify

Office, U. S. C. (2021). Compendium of U.S. Copyright Office practices. U.S. Copyright Office. https://www.copyright.gov/comp3/

OPUS IP. (2025). Feilin v. Baidu: Beijing Internet Court tackles protection of AI/software-generated work and holds that copyright only vests in works by human authors. OPUS IP. https://www.opusip.co.uk/2019/11/09/feilin-v-baidu-beijing-internet-court-html/

P. R. B. (2025, March 21). Artificial intelligence and intellectual property: "Artificial intelligence and intellectual property: Navigating issues of ownership and accountability". World Intellectual Property Organization. https://www.wipo.int/edocs/pubdocs/en/wipo-pub-econstat-wp-77-en-artificial-intelligence-and-intellectual-property-an-economic-perspective.pdf

PRC. P. R. O. C. (2020). China laws portal - CJO. China Justice Observer. https://www.chinajusticeobserver.com/law/x/2019-yue-0305-min-chu-14010

PRC. P. R. O. C. (2022, April 28). Intellectual property development and protection of Fujian Province in 2020. China National Intellectual Property Administration. https://english.cnipa.gov.cn/art/2021/4/28/art_2595_158989.html

S., D. (2025, March 21). Artificial intelligence and intellectual properties: Legal and ethical considerations. ResearchGate. https://www.researchgate.net/publication/376885311_Artificial_Intelligence_and_Intellectual_Properties_Legal_and_Ethical_Considerations

UKIPO. (2020). Artificial intelligence and intellectual property: Copyright and patents: Government response to consultation. GOV.UK. https://www.gov.uk/government/consultations/artificial-intelligence-and-ip-copyright-and-patents/outcome/artificial-intelligence-and-intellectual-property-copyright-and-patents-government-response-to-consultation

World Intellectual Property Organization. (2023). World intellectual property indicators report: Global patent filings reach record high in 2023. WIPO. https://www.wipo.int/pressroom/en/articles/2024/article_0015.html

Chapter 3
AI, Algorithms, and Antitrust:
Redefining Market Competition and Legal Accountability in India

Pankaj Chhuttani
http://orcid.org/0009-0001-3249-4952
National Forensic Sciences University, Gandhinagar, India

Ankit Srivastava
http://orcid.org/0000-0002-1330-6717
Rajiv Gandhi National University of Law, Patiala, India

ABSTRACT

The inculcation of artificial intelligence (AI) and algorithm-based decision-making systems into the realm of digital markets has fundamentally changed the competition law in India. The classical antitrust law of the Competition Act, 2002, in general, the concept of agreement, collusion, and abusing dominance, are being redefined by the self-educating algorithms with the autonomy of search and price optimization. This paper reviews the secondary literature and academic debate and seeks to determine how algorithmic systems are criticizing the legal doctrines and jurisprudence by Competition Commission of India (CCI).

1. INTRODUCTION

The rise of Artificial Intelligence (AI) and algorithm technology has established a new paradigm of market transformation, which reshapes business competition, innovation, and the interaction between companies and consumers. The AI-driven

DOI: 10.4018/979-8-3373-7685-1.ch003

technology makes it possible to analyze data in real-time, make decisions automatically, predict prices, and offer marketing that is hyper-personalized, which can lead to an increased efficiency and customer satisfaction (OECD, 2023). Nonetheless, the same capabilities are putting significant threats to the established principles of antitrust, as well as to the competition law framework. This is due to the fact that the transparency, self-determination, and educational availability of algorithms opens up novel types of coherence and control that complicate the nature of a market competition, establish information asymmetry, and dilute the terminations of legal responsibility (Ezrachi and Stucke, 2016).

The world is struggling with competition regulators to find ways of modifying their enforcement implements to the dynamics of algorithmic competition. Algorithms do not need to be told by their owners to collaborate, price fixing, market division, or to ostracize competitors, akin to the collusion detection in competition, it is especially difficult to both discover and prove anti-competitive behavior with algorithms involved (Gal & Aviv, 2020). Different organizations have acknowledged that algorithmic collusion and self-preferencing by dominant platforms is an urgent issue that should be addressed using updated enforcement strategies: the European Commission, U.S. Federal Trade Commission (FTC), and OECD (OECD, 2023; Stucke and Grunes, 2016).

1.1 Artificially Intelligent and the Digitalized Competitive Landscape on the Market

Using AI technologies, companies can gather, process, and respond to large masses of data, making market practices dynamic, personalized, and predictive. Depending on the algorithms, their application allows automatic adjustment of price, product recommendations, and advertising requests in milliseconds, optimizing outcomes both in terms of the efficiency of actions and the maximization of profits (Mehra, 2016). When adopted by large companies, these systems have the potential to support market power and develop self-reinforcing feedback processes in which the generation of data accumulation and machine learning functionalities form instrumental sources of competitive advantage (Bourreau and de Streel, 2020).

These innovations and advances of technology pose a challenge to economic assumptions about antitrust examination. To illustrate, in algorithmic markets, the traditional definition of price transparency and the autonomy in decision-making can instead create tacit coordination, as opposed to competition. The price stabilization algorithms, after having been trained on similar data or exposed to common market information, can be left to find a way of learning to stabilize the prices at the levels above those of competitive markets without human intervention (Ezrachi and Stucke, 2016). Besides, AI systems (so-called black box problem) hinder the capacity of regulators to be causally traceable or discover accountability in case of competitive harm (Mehra, 2016).

1.2 Indian Context: Indian Digital Growth and Governmental Problems

The digital economy in India has experienced a tremendous growth in the last ten years where we have seen the expansion of e-commerce, digital financial technology startup, and technological service ecosystems. This has brought about regulatory complexity as well as economic opportunity. As the Competition Commission of India (CCI) has recognized, AI-driven business models pose unknown competition threats especially in the data-intensive areas in online merchandising, electronic funds, and mobility services (CCI, 2025).

The Market Study on Artificial Intelligence and Competition (CCI, 2025) suggests that algorithms can independently affect pricing, ranking in the search results, and consumer access, which lead to an unwaveringly anti-competitive outcome but on a rather slight level. As an example, online platforms that ever control the marketplace as well as the algorithms of visibility can be privity to self-preferencing; favoring their own goods or services as compared to the ones sold by third parties. Equally, pricing programs employed in various companies can get grouped to supra-competitive pricing behaviors without the intent to collude.

The 2025 report of the CCI is based on the need to regulate proactively in order to guarantee the existence of so-called algorithmic accountability, which promotes transparency requirements, the auditing of algorithms, and increased interdisciplinary interaction between legal and technical professionals (Press Information Bureau [PIB], 2025). These suggestions are part of an increased realization that the obsolete system of competition law in India, which operates on the assumption of human behavior and clear contracts, might not be appropriate to address the dynamic aspects of markets being mediated by artificial intelligence.

1.3 Legal Responsibility of Algorithms in Markets

The emergence of AI has put the legal concepts of culpability, intent, and responsibility under challenge. Conventional competition law enforcement is based on the fact that collusion evidences can be made with references to communications and agreements and the explicit coordination. But in case the algorithms are run independently, it is unclear who to hold liable, is it the programmer, the firm engaging the algorithms, or the algorithm itself? (Mehra, 2016).

The Indian competition law, which is principally informed by Competition Act, 2002, establishes anti-competitive agreements and abuse of dominance as per human intent, and market behavior. Nevertheless, in the context of AI-powered systems, intent can be described as an emergent characteristic of machine-learning systems under market stimuli (Gal and Aviv, 2020). The CCI in turn is presented with a two-fold problem, because it needs to update its evidentiary standards to be able to acknowledge algorithmic coordination and at the same time uphold procedural fairness and proportionality.

Moreover, online international platforms make enforcement of laws more complicated. The AIs that are implemented in Indian markets are often trained or created in foreign locations, and the CCI does not have direct access to the algorithmic architecture or training data. In their turn, India needs to take into account international cooperation systems and accommodation systems of algorithmic auditability and anti-competitive compliance (Bourreau and de Streel, 2020).

1.4 Striking a Balance between Innovation and Regulation

Although there is validity in raising the issue of algorithmic collusion, the policy makers should be cautious not to over regulate which will kill innovation. Through AI-powered efficiencies, the transaction costs can be lowered, the matching on the market can be enhanced, and the consumer experiences can be improved. In this way, a subtle strategy must be employed, which will help to differentiate positive and negative practices of algorithms (Stucke and Grunes, 2016).

Indian government programs of Digital India, AI for All promote responsible and inclusive AI eco-systems. These initiatives could be aligned with the objectives of the competition policy to ensure that there would be innovation and be fair and accountable. The cooperation of the CCI with the academic and technical institutions in developing the capacity in algorithmic forensics is a step towards that direction (CCI, 2025).

The possible policy interventions can be:

1. **Algorithmic Transparency and Audits:** Requiring differential companies to disclose or audit algorithms.
2. **Data Portability and Interoperability:** Learners will be able to access data ecosystems equally without any bias against smaller players in the industry to encourage contestability.
3. **Collaborative Oversight:** Installing multi-agency models that entail the CCI, MeitY and regulators in the sector as a means of ensuring governance consistency.
4. **Ethical AI Principles:** A proposal to incorporate competition principles in the future AI governance mechanisms in India.

Lessons and the Way Forward of the World

Regulatory bodies, including the European Commission, Competition and Markets Authority (CMA) in the United Kingdom, and the OECD have started research in order to gain insight into the dynamics of algorithmic competition in the global context. OECD (2023) suggests that technical expertise on algorithmic monitoring and simulation-based tests should be developed by antitrust authorities to identify collusive tendencies. The Digital Markets Act (DMA) and AI Act by the European Union can provide an example to India on how to become more responsible in regards to automated systems without stifling the development of new technologies.

In the case of India, the second step would be the awareness, but then enforcement preparedness. It is necessary to develop algorithmic audit system infrastructures, encourage inter-regulatory cooperation, and invest into technical training of competition officials. The market research conducted by the CCI (2025) is a primary move in the establishment of such an institutional capacity.

Finally, the emergence of AI and algorithms makes it necessary to update the conceptualization of the competition law of market behavior, responsibility, and harm. The problem facing India is in terms of the creation of an AI environment that allows innovation but is responsible and creates a fair market situation, consumer protection, and technological accessibility. That AI and antitrust will potentially meet in this way gives rise to both a legal boundary and a chance of India stepping forward to govern AI responsibly in the world.

1.5 Types of Algorithmic Coordination

Once AI systems become the determinants of market result, it is called algorithmic coordination, and it can resemble collusion or strategic coordination. The algorithmic coordination, in contrast to the conventional cartels, which use explicit communication, may arise on its own, based on the computational logic, adaptive learning, and real-time data processing. These mechanisms are important to understand as they interfere with the evidentiary bases of Indian competition law which historically demands an indication of concurrence, will or even human interaction.

(a) Adaptive Algorithms

Adaptive algorithms change their strategies dynamically based on perceived conditions in the market and these conditions can include prices set by competitors, inventory, and consumer behaviour. These algorithms are regularly learning off real time data and altering prices within milliseconds. When the market is highly transparent, e.g. e-commerce or airlines, adaptive pricing may result in price parallelism that takes on forms of collusion, despite the lack of direct communication. Since the process of adaptation is automatic, it is quite hard to demonstrate that conscious coordination exists pursuant to Section 3 of the Competition Act.

(b) Predictive Algorithms

Predictive algorithms rely on past trends and machine learning to predict competitor behavior. They can predict when their competitors will increase or decrease their prices, supply, or carry out advertising. A number of companies employing the tools of predicting in an identical way can have strategies aligned without any form of agreement. This predictive conformity may lead to supra-competitive prices or coordinated behaviour which is not easy to categorised by regulators as collusive since it is the result of algorithmic logic applied collectively, but not by individuals acting in a coordinated manner.

(c) Learning Reinforcement (RL) Algorithms

Reinforcement Learning systems gain the best strategies by trial and error and they are rewarded with profitable strategies. The pioneering simulation models by Calvano et al. (2020) demonstrate that the RL-based pricing models can develop the collusive equilibria on their own and find that higher prices can benefit all the players, gradually. Notably:

In the hub-and-spoke models, multiple independent companies (spokes) are dependent upon a shared algorithm or platform (hub), like a pricing software company, aggregator, or marketplace. The core algorithm is able to coordinate the actions across the firms indirectly through standardizing the pricing logic, rules of discounts or allocating the supply. The model is becoming more applicable in Indian industries such as ride-hailing or hotel aggregators and food delivery, where the algorithms controlled by the platform affect the competition between otherwise independent sellers. Although the spokes may not be talking to each other, the hub can help in the coordination of the results.

Competition Law Implication in India.

Each of the four types of algorithmic coordination attests to the fact that:

- Intent may be absent,
- Communication can be incapable of being proved, and
- Effects even may be anti-competitive.

Therefore, regulators will have to shift to effects-based, technology-sensitive interpretations, which comply with global trends and the 2025 Market Study of the CCI.

1.6 Algorithmic Audit Tools

With the growing role of algorithms in the competition of the market, regulatory bodies worldwide have started to adopt advanced audit instruments to identify, evaluate, and reduce algorithmic harms. These tools have been created to deal with problems of AI opacities, proprietary code, and neural network complexity. India has no such formalized requirements of algorithmic audit at the moment, but the world experience, particularly OECD (2023), CMA (2021), and EU Digital Markets Act, provide useful examples.

(a) Explainable AI (XAI) Frameworks.

XAI aims to bring certain transparency to the algorithmic decision-making process by producing interpretable explanations of the process results, which include pricing, ranking, or recommendations. To competition regulators, XAI allows one to scrutinize:

- Whether algorithms involve discriminative variables,
- Whether rankings are not made fairly in favor of the own products of a platform (self-preferencing),
- Whether the behaviour of pricing is coordinated.
- XAI specifically is of great importance to India where the market visibility is controlled by an opaque algorithm on the platform in areas such as e-commerce, telecom and digital payments.
- Whether the anti-competitive effects were due to updates,
- Whether companies have adjusted algorithmic specifications to reflect competitor charges,
- Whether problematic logic was brought about by external vendors.

A lack of such logs leaves major gaps in the forensic process of security agencies such as the CCI.

Outcome-Based Algorithmsic Impact Assessment (AIA) represent a type of outcome assessment within the field of teaching and learning.

AIAs measure the impacts, as opposed to the internal workings, of algorithms. These assessments analyze:

- Pre- and post-algorithms comparison of pricing,
  Effects on small traders, start-ups, and susceptible consumers,

1.7 Indian Sector-Specific

1. E-commerce Platforms (Algo-based Ranking in E-commerce and Discount Manipulation)
    - Indian e-commerce giants like Amazon, Flipkart, and Myntra are based on complex ranking algorithms which define the visibility of products, placement and search priority.
    - Just because it is indirectly self-preferential to the private labels, studies and CCI market research indicate that these ranking systems tend to make the labels more discoverable, independent of whether third party sellers provide the same or better value.
    - Auto-discount allocation, in particular, when the sale is on a festival, can have the effect of redistribution of the visibility of those sellers who are subject to a discount provided by the platform, resulting in structural benefits and shaping consumer behaviour.
    - These non-transparent ranking and pricing models are problematic in inference on whether the harm is caused by a legitimate optimisation or anti-competitive manipulation.
2. Digital Lending (Algorithmic Lending Discrimination) and Fintech.
    - The digital lending models are digital lending platforms and BNPL (e.g., Paytm, LazyPay, CASHe), which are relying on machine-learning models to score credit.
    - The models can discriminate against proxy variables of socio-economic status, which reduces equal access to credit.
    - Without transparency, regulators have difficulty identifying algorithmic redlining, particularly when the models incorporate behavioural or other information data like transaction data, geographical trends or device utilisation.
    - Lack of the need to have algorithmic audit in India gives the borrowers in India no system to appeals against discriminatory delivery, which casts a question of competition as well as consumer protection.
3. Mobility & Ride-Hailing Applications (Converging Surge Pricing Algorithms)
    - Ride-hailing apps, such as Uber and Ola, use dynamic pricing, which adjusts to changes in the demand and supply.
    - It has been suggested by academic studies that these autonomous algorithms are able to approach supra-competitive prices particularly in metropolitan areas of high demand.
    - Pricing patterns Pricing patterns may coordinate even without explicit coordination since both platforms are optimised to fit similar market conditions and application of similar algorithm logic.

- This produces the effect that is similar to algorithmic tacit collusion, which in the end leads to the higher fares and less consumer welfare.

4. Food Delivery Systems (Self-Preferencing and Restaurant Visibility Bias)
    - Platforms like Swiggy and Zomato apply algorithmic engines of discovery to rank restaurant in search results and category pages as well as promotion banners.
    - There is an increasing set of indicators, supported by merchant reporting and research, that platforms can be self-preferential in favour of their own cloud kitchens or partner brands, a kind of algorithmic self-preferencing.
    - "Delivery-fee algorithms and commissions-based visibility programs can reallocate consumer traffic to restaurants that grant more commissions or are involved in a promotion on the platform.
    - This can be used to manipulate market fairness, giving small or independent restaurants a disadvantage and strengthening platform dominance through such algorithmic design.

Here is a fully developed contents of your Issue → Problem Trend Legal Implication model reformatted in solid scholarly language and blown out to a good book chapter or research paper.

1.8. Problems, issues, trends and legal implications.

Issue 1 The Algorithms of Tacit Collusion.

Problem

Anti-competitive agreements under the Competition Act, 2002 India do need some form of communication, intention or meeting of minds. Market-response systems and AI-based pricing systems enable firms to reach collusive results without any collaboration, however. Algorithms have the capability to track the actions of competitors on their own, modify the prices, and stabilize the supra-competitive results.

This introduces gaps of enforcement since any conventional evidentiary requirements, such as communication history or express consent, is not the case.

Trend

Pricing algorithms that are based on Reinforcement Learning (RL) are progressively learning to autonomously learn collusive equilibria. With repetition between RL systems in simulated marketplaces, over a field of simulated markets, they achieve higher convergent prices without any collusion instruction, as shown by Calvano et al. (2020). Higher order algorithmic prices are taking shape in Indian e-commerce, aviation, and ride-hailing markets.

Legal Implication

The changes will necessitate the reversal of the interpretation of Section 3 of Competition Act, which is an intent-based test, to an effects-based test. The CCI should take into account its instances when algorithms predictively and systematically produce collusive effects, despite the lack of human intent. India might have to interpret the meaning of agreement in a wider way to encompass algorithmic coordination or implement presumptive liability frameworks to firms implementing high-stakes pricing AI.

Issue 2: Platform Self-Preferencing.

Problem

Large digital platforms tend to employ ranking, recommendation, and visibility algorithms to bias their own services in a systematic way or the services of their preferred partners. In India, the same case was raised in Google Play Billings scrutinies when the control of Google ecosystem was seen to limit competition and suppressed user choice.

Self-preferencing affects competitive neutrality as it causes market entry to rely on algorithm-based platform designs instead of merit and consumer preference.

Trend

The digital markets in India are starting to resemble ecosystem-like structure where the distribution of apps, the visibility of the search, payment, travel services and logistics of e-commerce are controlled by a small number of companies. This has been reflected in the tendencies of the world in the case of Amazon marketplace in the EU, Apple App Store inquires and Google Shopping in self-preferencing.

Legal Implication

India might need Digital Markets Act (DMA)-style ex-ante regulations concerning the systemically significant digital intermediaries, including:

- Bans on prioritizing personal products over competitors.
- Algorithms non-discrimination requirements.
- Third-party audits of recommender systems and ranking systems which are mandatory.

This is an active practice which helps in deterring the incidences of anti-competitive behavior, as opposed to traditional investigations carried out after the fact.

Problem 3: Data Dominance and Foreclosure of the market.

Problem

The presence of data-rich platforms is associated with unparalleled competitive advantages, as proprietary datasets allow to customize the products more effectively, to pre-empt as well as to tailor advertising to a particular recipient. New competitors with similar data will have difficulty competing with them-they will establish high barriers to entry and extend an incumbency.

The markets of Fintech, e-commerce, food delivery, and mobility in India have concentrated data that enables large platforms to close smaller competitors and demand more rents to the reliant businesses.

Trend

The winner-takes-all dynamics of digital markets are becoming more apparent in India because of network effects, economies of scale and algorithmic optimization. The competitive advantage of the platforms increases as they store more user data and the displacement of the market becomes extremely difficult. This is in line with the international studies of platformization and data monopolies.

Legal Implication

The Competition Act and the Digital Personal Data Protection Act (DPDPA) need to coordinate their policy. India may require:

- Shared data requirements of leading platforms.
- Limitations on cross use of personal data between business divisions.
- Prohibitions against data-based exclusionary behavior.
- Competition that is detrimental through joint investigations of the CCI and Data Protection Board due to data abuse.

This kind of alignment would enable regulators to handle the competition harm as well as privacy damages created by data concentrate.

2. LITERATURE REVIEW

2.1. History of AI and Competition in the Market

The trend of artificial intelligence (AI) has become a disruptive phenomenon in international markets essential to the transformation of the nature, dynamics, and behaviour of contemporary economy. In the various sectors, AI-driven systems have transformed the way companies create products, communicate with their customers, and engage with one another in the digital world. Using sophisticated algorithms, companies are able to experience real-time pricing automation, supply chains optimization, productivity, and hyper-personal consumer experiences (Ezrachi and Stucke, 2016). This technological breakthrough enables companies to use large amounts of data in predicting market demand, enhancing decision-making, and gaining the capability to act on a nimble operational basis. Therefore, AI has become an essential source of innovation, productivity, and economic increase.

Nevertheless, the foundations of market competition also reform their positions due to this quick AI-integration. Algorithms do not exist as mere instruments; they actively influence the actions of competition, tracking competitors, identifying the changes in the situation at the market, and automatically modifying the strategies (Gal & Aviv, 2020). Companies are also rapidly implementing algorithmic pricing models that can learn through competitor actions and thus result in tacit coordination that does not require any communication. This occurrence, which is termed as algorithmic collusion, is a very deep threat to the old fashioned antitrust enforcing procedures which in the past were intended to combat human theatre of collaboration and not machine orchestrated coordinations.

The potential of AI-produced market is full of paradoxes: opportunity and risk go hand in hand. Although AI enhances the welfare of consumers by increasing innovation, decreasing cost, and better services, it also poses a possibility of market concentration, dominance abuse, and low competition. The need to apply machine learning within the Organisation for Economic Co-operation and Development (OECD, 2023) also shows that algorithmic coordination can take place informally, without incurred intent, and even without humans engaging in such co-ordination. Furthermore, data-driven monopolies and legitimizing control Digital platforms able to controll access to information and algorithmic infrastructure may reinforce their position, sidelining smaller actors and forming a network of data.

The change of the concept of competition has been altered by this merging of AI, big data, and platform economics. The old economic theory concept, based on the rational human behaviour and the linear market reaction, fails to represent the non-linear markets mediated by algorithms. This is prompting regulators and policymakers around the globe to reconsider the framework of competition law to make sure that it is up to date in this algorithmic era. The increased awareness around them adds credit to the critical significance of adaptive governance frameworks, open algorithmic auditing, and interjurisdictional collaboration to protect healthy competition in the AI economy.

2.2 Algorithmic Competition and Collusion: International Views

2.2.1 Theoretical Foundations

Theoretical literature is increasingly highlighting the fact that algorithms have the capability to provide the kind of coordination of competitors in such a manner that it resembles collusion but circumvents standard legal definitions. One of the first scholars who came to the idea of the so-called algorithmic tacit collusion was Ezrachi and Stucke (2016) who called such situations where autonomous systems reach supra-competitive equilibria without a particular agreement or without any human intent. Under these circumstances, the algorithms themselves will learn not to engage in price wars and instead keep the prices at a higher point which will balance out the market in ways that would favor the competitors but to the deteriment of the consumer. Algorithms collusion is possible, in contrast to classical cartels, in which human communication, trust, and intentional coordination are involved, and is at times well beyond the ability or even comprehension of its human programmers.

This puts a deep question to the current design of the competition law that is based on demonstrating the existence of an agreement, concertated practice, or intent. The fact that algorithmic collusion may take place automatically, i.e. without any form of communication, makes it even harder to use the law of collusion based tests like evidence of mutual consent or express exchange of information (Ezrachi and Stucke, 2017; Mehra, 2016). Due to this, companies might be able to enjoy anti-competitive market practices technically without breaking any law which leaves a grey area between legitimate parallel actions and illegal coordination.

These theoretical concerns were empirically confirmed by Calvano et al. (2020) in the framework of elaborate simulation experiments. They showed that the reinforcement learning algorithms when applied to pricing tasks can spontaneously and independently may lead to collusive outcomes. Given no form of communication or even explicit direction, the algorithms would learn that higher prices would result in higher payoffs and stabilize cartel-like operations. This learning collusion represents a self-organizing process that generates profit as AI systems will interpret and react to the moves of the competitors in real time. Notably, such results are still present in perfect monitoring and the absence of explicit agreements, which points to the role of algorithm design by itself in unintended anti-competitive outcomes.

Besides, researchers like Gal and Aviv (2020) claim that making decisions using algorithms is also opaque (so-called black box problem), which makes it even more difficult to detect and hold them accountable. Even in the cases where regulators believe there is collusion, the technical nature of algorithms renders it hard to determine whether the resultant outcome was an intended design or a product of machine evolution. This agency / autonomy loss is one of the most extreme changes in the theory of competition, which leads to the acute necessity to find new analytical tools, algorithmic transparency needs, and interdisciplinary control to make sure that the gains of AI innovation may not be affected at the costs of market fairness.

2.3 Foreign Policy and International Implementation

Regulators worldwide have started not only dealing with the effects of algorithmic markets, but also taking them seriously. In their digital competition policies, the European Commission and the Competition and Markets Authority (CMA) of the UK have focused on the concept of algorithmic transparency and accountability (Stucke and Grunes, 2016). The Digital Markets Act (DMA) and AI Act of the European Union place an additional responsibility on the gatekeeper platforms to curb the data-driven abuse of dominance as well as mandates that the automated decision making processes should be transparent (European Commission, 2022).

In the same way, the United States Federal Trade Commission (FTC) has cautioned that algorithmic collusion and biased decision-making could be unfair practices of competition as per the section 5 of the FTC act (FTC, 2021). To detect collusion, the OECD (2023) recommends that national competition authorities build up technical skill to study the conduct of algorithms, which involves simulation-based testing and algorithmic forensics.

These policy efforts highlight the fact that the world is recognizing that antitrust implementation has to change beyond human will to involve autonomous algorithmic engagement. But still no one has fully studied how far these structures are applicable to emerging economies such as India.

2.4. Artificial Intelligence (AI) and Antitrust Law in India

Artificial Intelligence (AI) and antitrust law have come into focus in modern competition policy debates, in part because in some economies such as developing countries, such as India, the digital market is growing in rapid expansion. Principles Establishing scholar works by Ezrachi and Stucke (2016) indicated an idea that goes under the term algorithmic tacit collusion where pricing algorithms and machine learning systems can independently become trained to maintain supra-competitive prices without firms having been communicated with each other. Empirical studies on successive simulations by Calvano et al. (2020) have empirically proved that the reinforcement-learning algorithms may automatically will approach collusive solutions, which casts doubt on accountability, liability, and regulatory control. These results undermine the old antitrust dogmas based on finding signs of intent or agreement to prove the presence of collusion, meaning that enforcement instruments must be reviewed within the framework of AI.

Within the Indian market, the promotion of AI has increased under such policy programs as Digital India and AI for All, and companies in various industries, e-commerce and fintech included, are applying algorithmic systems to the dynamic pricing system, predictive analytics, and targeted marketing (NITI Aayog, 2021). Such an attempt by the Competition Commission of India to create a Market Study on Artificial Intelligence and Competition (CCI, 2025) is groundbreaking, as it acknowledges that AI and big data are both revolutionary and potentially disruptive drivers of market competition. The research emphasizes that algorithmic favouring of oneself, monopolizing data and having a black box recommendation system has the potential to institutionalize entrenched dominance, limit entry into markets and lower welfare levels among consumers. According to comparative frameworks proposed by the European Union (European Union DMA, 2022) and the OECD (2023), India ought to take a hybrid regulatory model alternating ex-ante regulation of digital gatekeepers with more ex-post regulation that would maintain the innovation and economic growth in the country.

Table 1. Growth of AI-Related Antitrust Reports (2016–2025)

Year	Number of Reports / Publications
2016	2
2018	4
2020	6
2022	8
2023	10
2025	13

2.4.1 Digital Economy Growth of AI in India

The transformation of the digital economy in India has occurred on a fundamental scale throughout the last decade, as most projects in this domain have been substantially driven by governmental initiatives worth mentioning Digital India, AI for All, and Startup India, among others, which all focus on embracing more advanced technologies in the areas of the state administration, business processes, and consumer actions (NITI Aayog, 2021). Such policy initiatives have boosted the implementation of artificial intelligence (AI) in a variety of industries, such as fintech, logistics, e-commerce, manufacturing, retail, healthcare, and hospitality, which has made India one of the most rapidly expanding digital markets in the world. To improve efficiency and reach out to consumers, predictive analytics with AI, dynamic pricing models, targeted marketing, and automated decision-making systems have become common practice among firms. The technology change has been the driving force of innovation, increased productivity, and the advancement of data-driven business models.

Nevertheless, the same digital impetus brings new structural tornadoes in the competitive avenue. The danger of market concentration and less ability to compete arises when intelligent algorithms become increasingly important in the making of such critical business decisions like price determination, product ranking, and market segmentation. Big Digital with huge data storage and advanced AI services can use their technological advantage and dominate establish dominance, self-preferencing, and discriminated access to data. This is widely known as data-driven dominance and it has been a problem to conventional competition law frameworks which was initially structured to tackle markets, as opposed to algorithmic ecosystems.

Given that AI, data, and competition policy intersectionality are the emerging risks that should be noted, the Competition Commission of India (CCI) has shown a lot of interest in this topic. The first country-wide effort to assess the effects of AI implementation on the market structure, consumer welfare, and regulatory enforcement is the landmark Market Study on Artificial Intelligence and Competition (CCI, 2025). As is noted in the study AI increases efficiency and innovation, but at the same time creates new sources of competitive injury, including algorithmic coordination, price discrimination, and digital gatekeeping by the majority. These issues are similar to those found across the world, by the Organization for Economic Co-Operation and Development (OECD, 2023) and the UK Competition and Markets Authority (CMA, 2021), which issue alerts that the algorithms are capable of autonomous or semi-autonomous adaptation of market behaviors to reduce the competition even in the absence of explicit collusion.

Also, the CCI research stipulates that there are distinct contextual challenges in the Indian market because of their consounding digital penetration, varying technology accessibility among companies, and regulatory differences. The nature of the operations of smaller enterprises is such that they are often deficient in organizational framework or in the expertise to create proprietary AI offerings, so they rely on big technology providers to perform data analytics and algorithms services. Through this dependency, information asymmetries and bargaining power imbalance may be established, and thus, the control of a small number of digital conglomerates is strengthened.

One more important thing that the CCI results revealed is that AI systems used in the Indian markets may unintentionally be used to support the anti-competitive trend, such as self-directed collusion, algorithmic prioritization, and target marginalization of competitors by controlling the platform. As an example, the algorithmic pricing systems applied in e-commerce and online travel agencies may dynamically respond to the activities of competitors, so they may end up with tacit price coordination, and may or may not have the intention of doing so. Equally, AI-powered recommendation systems can give preference to products or services belonging to the platform itself which essentially shuns out third party competitors and excludes consumer choice.

Such changes suggest that the regulatory bodies in India will have to change to meet the complicated nature of interaction between innovation and competition so that technological advancement does not negate fair trade and consumer welfare on the market. The CCI initiative is considered to be a breakthrough measure in the creation of a proactive, information conscious competition hierarchy that would have the value of addressing the complexity of algorithms. Nevertheless, researchers like Tiwari and Sharma (2023) also believe that India should continue to harmonize its competition law enforcement with the best practices in the world (such as the ones that the European Union has introduced with its Digital Markets Act (2022) and the OECD with its algorithmic competition principles) in order to come up with a harmonious ecosystem that encourages innovation in the country without allowing its market to be abused.

Simply put, the beginner of AI, big data, and market competition in India is a technological opportunity and regulatory challenge. With India emerging as a center of AI-led development in the global context, regulation of algorithms and e-commerce will decide whether the change will result in inclusive and transparent economies, or the preservation of monopolies that cannot sustain the economy in the long term.

2.4.2 Competition Law Hindrances of Indians

The Competition Act, 2002 of India was introduced earlier than the era of algorithmic commerce, and is organized in a humanistic manner in regards to collusion and abuse of dominance. In Section 3, an agreement is a central element in the formation of a cartel as opposed to the Section 4, covering the abuse of dominant position. But within an algorithmic environment, these provisions are very limited.

Notions of liability are challenged because algorithms can coordinate actions or discriminate among users with no specific human direction (Mehra, 2016).

The CCI (2025) also admits that even autonomous decision-making by algorithms may create market outcomes similar to collusion, having no express or tacit human knowledge. The policies of detecting such kind of behavior involve not only sophisticated digital forensics but also data analytics and inter-agency cooperation, which are only just being developed in the Indian enforcement ecosystem. Besides, the jurisdictional issues also include the situation when on the territory of another country, the algorithms that operate in Indian markets are hosted, which makes their operation and data retrieval challenging (Bourreau and de Streel, 2020).

2.5 Platform Power and Self-Preferencing

Digital markets are already facing self-preferencing, data-driven discrimination, and algorithmic bias where Indian regulators have already been confronted with serious challenges in deciding what to do. One of them is the case of In Re: Umar Javeed vs. Google LLC (2021): the Competition Commission of India (CCI) concluded that Google has misused its dominance in the market by requiring the implementation of its own payment system into the Android operating ecosystem. The practice limited the option of users to other payment solutions, thus competing with each other, and consumer welfare was compromised. Though artificial intelligence was not directly involved in the case, it revealed how algorithms-based operations, including ranking algorithms, recommendation systems, or systems of visibility control, can be used as subtle yet potent instruments of maintaining or boosting platform hegemony.

These issues are multiplied with the growing presence of AI in the digital economy in India. Algorithms that are aimed at maximizing user interactions or transactional efficiency inevitably (or intentionally) result in a form of data loops, with dominant platforms enjoying a unique view of large user data sets, consolidating their market position. This data not just deters entry, but also enables the established participants to impact market forces in their favor by automating decision-making processes with these valuable data.

Researchers, like Stucke and Grunes (2016), state that algorithmic government and platform impartiality turn into the fundamental components of contemporary antitrust execution. Whether we mean AI, neutrality does not only imply equitable access to markets but also covers the ethical practices and composition of algorithm systems, as well as their implementation and disclosure. This has led to a growing belief amongst regulators and policymakers that AI systems used by powerful digital platforms should be illegal to face severe requirements of transparency, explainability of algorithms, and periodic audits by third parties (CCI, 2025; Press Information

Bureau [PIB], 2025). These would contribute to making sure that algorithms do not partake in discriminatory behaviors, encourage a fair competition, and that the technological innovation is in line with the standards of consumer protection and integrity in the market.

2.6. Doctrinal and Enforcement Problems

2.6.1 The Re-Definition of the Term Agreement and Intent

The classical concept of agreement as specified in antitrust law is founded on the belief that human beings are consciously coordinated, in a manner that can be identified as either a communicative act, something they are all intending to do or are blatantly attempting to conspire to rigorously orchestrate the market results. But the development of artificial intelligence (AI) and algorithmic pricing solution has directly refuted this assumption. The current AI algorithms can also monitor such rival behavior, lowering and increasing prices, and optimizing the profit strategies under the impact of machine learning processes, usually without direct human intervention or even any manifestation (Gal and Aviv, 2020). Such unilateral alignment of policies may result in situations akin to collusive behavior, including long-term supra-competitive pricing or price stabilization, but that are not a conventional subject of law enforcement regarding the meaning of the term "agreement" or the meaning of the term "concerted practice's concept. The outcome is an enforcement vacuum, where the harm to the market is done, but there is no human intent or communication, and it is virtually impossible to demonstrate this helpfulness by the current competition laws.

There is thus now a debate among legal scholars and economists over whether the limits of the concept of agreement under antitrust laws should be restructured in a manner which brings into view algorithmic forms of coordination which is known to have predictable protective outcomes. The method in question, however, has its obstacles: not every case of algorithmic similarity is due to collusion recent studies have shown that a lot of them are the result of regular parallel adaptation to common market data or consumer behaviour patterns. Such overregulation might consequently put innovation to death and prevent firms to implement competitive AI technology.

This dilemma is very relevant in the Indian context. The Competition Act, 2002 in section 3 where an anti-competitive agreement is outlawed, now has a requirement that there should be an element of concerted action or intention. In order to leverage algorithmic coordination, Competition Commission of India (CCI) and courts in India might have to employ effects-oriented, dynamical interpretation of Section 3 one that is more oriented towards the effective market effect of the algorithmic behaviour than the actual existence of an agreement or intent. This would comply with the global best practices and enable the Indian regulators to adapt to the changing digital world and simultaneously strike a balance between promoting innovation and protecting competition.

2.6.2 Evidentiary and Technical Complexities

A black box Process It is typical of AI systems to be proprietary-protected, adaptive-learners, and as deep-network architectures, profitable. This secrecy is highly problematic to the antitrust regulators, who are accustomed to using clear evidence in the form of communication records or pricing data to identify the presence of collusive behavior. The interpretability problem of AI systems renders it challenging to identify causal relations between the outputs of the algorithms and the occurrence of the anti-competitive outcomes as observed in both the OECD (2023) report and that of Competition Commission of India (CCI, 2025). This means that regulators can be unskilled in technical skills, computer-processing power, and investigative resources to adequately assess algorithmic action.

In order to overcome these obstacles, interdisciplinary cooperation between data scientists, economists and legal experts is also a topic of growing importance in all international policy discussions. Proposals have been made to increase the transparency and accountability of AI brought about by the development of algorithmic audit frameworks complemented by mechanisms of keeping records of algorithmic decisions, version histories, and documentation of training data. In addition, mandatory incorporation of explainable AI (XAI) into regulatory design may allow oversight authorities to understand how algorithms reach a decision on the price, consumer preference during a choice, or access to the market better.

But even in India, the implementation roadmap is still limited by a lack of digital forensics infrastructure, no sufficient training of the regulating bodies in technical matters, and no compulsory cryptographic audit tools. Bourreau and de Streel (2020) believe that institutional cooperation in terms of competition authorities and data protection bodies can be more efficient in terms of enforcement. Further cooperation between the CCI and the Data Protection Board of India will assist in creating a consistent methodology on the data access, algorithm transparency, and trans-sectoral control, thus closing the present divide between innovation and responsibility in the Indian AI-powered markets.

2.7. Striking a Balance Between Innovation and Regulation

AI in competition law regulation needs to strike a balance between innovation and accountability. Excessively strict regulation will discourage AI investment, and regulatory laxity will lead to a monopoly of the market. Stucke and Grunes (2016) propose transparency, fairness, and contestability as the main principles advocated through a peppy approach to policies without describing the specific rules to be followed strictly.

The AI strategy of India focuses on the concept called Responsible AI to All (NITI Aayog, 2021) as it has competition objectives: to support ethical AI usage and inclusive innovation. Anti-competitive outcomes via integration, e.g. by mandating algorithmic inspections of dominant platforms, do not negatively affect technological development, and may be avoided (CCI, 2025).

2.8. Global Lessons for India

India can take lessons on the experiences of global regulations. The DMA of the European Union requires all in the framework of interoperability, bans self-preferencing, and endorses equitable data access, which can act as an example of the Indian digital competition policy (European Commission, 2022). In line with this, the CMA of the UK has established an Algorithms Monitoring Team that researches the collusive outcomes of online markets (CMA, 2021).

The way to solve the situation is to adopt such initiatives to make India more ready to handle the challenge of algorithms. Also, cooperation with the OECD and international competition organs would enable India to coordinate its policies with the international standard and share a technical knowledge (OECD, 2023).

- Mapping the adoption patterns of AI in the Indian industries.
- Designing the accountability of the algorithm.
- Evaluation of alignment of competition and AI ethics governance.
- Researching consumer welfare effects of algorithmic pricing in the Indian markets.

2.9 Objectives

This chapter aims to:

1. Examines the redefinition of the traditional antitrust notions by AI and algorithmic systems especially with regards to the Indian Competition Act, 2002, especially on the Indian Competition Act, 2002 terms of agreement, collusion, and abuse of dominance.
2. Assess the sufficiency of current legal principles and CCI jurisprudence to deal with algorithmic coordination, data monopolies and platform self-preferencing.

3. Stand India regulation against the developed world rules (EU, US, UK) and draw lessons on algorithmic competition regulation.
4. Elaborate on a structure of the accountability of the algorithms in the Indian competition law - with due diligence principles, disclosure standards, and liability principles.
5. Propose policy and legislative changes so as to align innovative incentives with consumer welfare and market equity.

3. RESEARCH METHODOLOGY

The paper follows a qualitative and doctrinal research approach that utilizes the secondary data as the main source to examine the meeting point of artificial intelligence (AI), algorithmic systems, and competition law in India. The study is based on the overall analysis of the statutes and policy documents, judgment of the courts, and reports of expert committees provided by Competition Commission of India (CCI), NITI Aayog, and other authorities related to the area. The perspectives and best practice of international perspectives have been critically evaluated through scholarly articles, working papers and global policy reports published by the OECD, European Commission, Federal Trade Commission (FTC) and Competition and Markets Authority (CMA). A comparative analysis was used to compare how India approaches the Competition Act, 2002 to the European Union, United States, and the United Kingdom regulatory frameworks with regards to the theory of algorithmic collusion, data monopolies, and platform self-preferencing. Government publishing data, legal databases (HeinOnline, SCC Online, JSTOR) and literature of the academic journals were reviewed systematically to determine thematic trends and jurisprudential gaps between them. The research focuses on the interpretative analysis, but not on empirical testing, on the suggestion of a conceptual framework of algorithmic accountability and the recommendations of the policy that can help to align the innovation with consumer welfare and fairness of the market.

4. DATA ANALYSIS

Objective 1

The Future of agreement, collusion, and abuse of dominance under the Competition Act, 2002 through AI and algorithmic systems.

- Empirical and modelling experiments have demonstrated that autonomous pricing algorithms (e.g., Q-learning agents) can settle on supra-competitive prices without the explicit communication of humans - a phenomenon observed in a laboratory and simulations (Calvano et al., 2020). The result of such outcomes cannot be discerned from the effect of collusion where there are no human beings who have agreed.

  Conceptual and doctrinal literature claims that to establish tacit or emergent coordination, algorithmic interactions develop methods of coordination that do not necessitate conscious agreement (Ezrachi and Stucke, 2016). Regulators and scholars thus suggest shifting to the effects based assessments that measure the outcomes of the algorithmic markets.
- The Competition Commission of India in its market study accepts these dynamic risks and spells out the risks of algorithmic coordination, self-preferencing, and data based entrenchment amenable to the need to improve investigative tools and transparency (CCI, 2025).

Indian legal concepts Analysis

- Anti-Competitive Agreements (Section 3): The focus of the Act on an agreement (express or tacit) customarily demands some evidence of human coordination. Algorithms generate cartels through non-communication, resulting in an evidentiary disjunction. In order to embody such harms, Indian enforcement will have to take into consideration that predictable, systematic algorithmic results can be viewed as concerted practice where firms intentionally use algorithms in a manner that by predictably causes coordination. The OECD also gives advice on the use of algorithmic impact analysis as one way to develop this, availing numerous practical suggestions and examples for developing algorithmic impact assessment frameworks (See also OECD recommendations regarding algorithmic effects-based approaches).
- Collusion: Collusive outcomes can be produced in an algorithmic manner (Calvano et al., 2020). Indian enforcement must thus have instruments (market simulation, algorithmic forensics, decision logs) that identify convergence behavior and causal attribution of causal connections between an algorithm design and its market implications.
- Section 4 abuse of dominance: exclusionary leverage is exacerbated by algorithms, which allow dynamic self-preferencing, discrimination, and foreclosure on the basis of data. This is an indicator that dominance analysis should take into consideration data-centric feedback loops and platform algorithms governing the visibility and access (CCI, 2025). Therefore, the traditional

measures of dominance (market share, price effects) should be complemented by the data-control measures and the measures of the influence of algorithms.

Objective 2

Sufficiency of current doctrine and CCI jurisprudence as regards algorithmic coordination, data monopolies, and self-preferencing.

Secondary literature materials.

- The UK CMA and OECD analyses offer methodological instrumentation (algorithmic monitoring, audits) which can be embraced by national enforcers; it focuses on capacity building (CMA, 2021; OECD, 2023).
- The CCI in India has already made efforts such as the publication of a market study which acknowledges the risk of algorithms and provides solutions (transparency, audits); however, there are not many public cases when algorithmic forensics became the key to an order. The work by CCI is a significant policy measure but the current operational enforcement practice of pure algorithmic collusion is in its infancy.

Evaluation

Doctrinal adequacy: The Competition Act, as a text, is capable of consolidating most of the algorithmic evils (e.g., discriminatory behavior under the Section 4, agreements under the Section 3) but there are still procedural and evidentiary blank spaces. In particular, the classic proof tactics (emails, meetings) cannot be adequately utilized in attribution of damage inflicted by automated systems. Secondary sources require apparent modernization (logs, simulation evidence, expert analysis).

- CCJ jurisprudence The CCI is shown to have increasing awareness (market research) and has addressed the behavior of digital platforms in previous instances but no algorithm-driven enforcement cases. It would entail a twofold requirement, namely (a) capacity and methodology construction in the CCI, (b) procedural power to force algorithmic evidence.

Objective 3

India vs EU, US, UK - lessons on governance - comparative analysis.

Evidence (choice of secondary sources)

- EU: The Digital Markets Act (DMA) has ex-ante duties on the gatekeepers (self-preferencing is forbidden, interoperability and now data-access are required), and the AI Act addresses high-risk AI in terms of transparency and ninety assessments. This is a structural approach, which is prescriptive.
- US: FTC stresses on the application of the current statutes based on the truth, fairness and equity, the U.S. model is based on aggressive case-by-case decision as opposed to generalized ex-ante duties.
- UK: The CMA has developed practical advice and developed an algorithm monitoring toolkit- focusing on the practical techniques of inquiry and technical skills. Lessons to be compared in India.
- Hybrid model: US-style enforcement agility and CMA-style technical toolkits to detect and investigate, but add on clear and fully-defined gatekeeper obligations in the United States (to avoid self-preferencing and guarantee interoperability).

  additional measures include: capacity and co-operation: invest in in-house technical units and formal cross-agency collaboration (data protection, sectoral regulators) and international evidence-sharing contracts. These capacity investments are also recommended by OECD.

Objective 4

Proposal of Algorithmic Accountability Framework (AAF) in relation to Indian competition law (due diligence,transparency, liability).

1. Scope & thresholds: are applicable to firms that qualify in terms of gatekeeper/ dominance (turnover/users/data assets). (CCI, DMA models).
2. Compulsory Impact Assessments of Algorithms Competition (ACIA): periodical, documented due-diligence statements outlining objectives, training data provenance, performance measures and possible competitive impacts; stored so that the regulator may review these statements. (Recommended transparency practices at the OECD and CMA).
3. Transparency and auditability: keep a record of decisions, report explanations, and training-data summary anonymized; make available to regulator or audit-qualified auditors, under confidentiality measures. (EU/AI Act and CMA practices).
4. Tiered liability model:
   (a) Remedial safe hangs in the event that (firm) carried vigorous ACIA and promptly repaired harms found;
   (b) Tougher/higher liability due to demonstrated algorithmic results that lead to significant consumer harm (e.g. proven algorithmic price-rigging, discrim-

inatory omission). This offsets deterrence and innovation. .(Companion to academic advice and practice of enforcement).

5. Procedural powers: clear legal authority to require logs, simulate and employ independent technical experts without violation of IP and privacy. (OECD & CMA recommendations).

Objective 5

1. Statutory elucidation or revision on explicitly specifying the algorithmic coordination/effects under Sections 3-4 and empowering the CCI with authority of compelling algorithmic evidence (CCI and OECD recommendations).
2. Hypothetical ex-ante conflict of interest rules on gatekeepers (no self-preferencing; data-portability and interoperability) based on the EU DMA.
3. Algorithmic audit regime: compel ACIA and third party audits of major platforms periodically; develop confidentiality of IP. (CMA/OECD guidance).
4. National Digital Competition Unit: part of/adjacent to the CCI, where technologists, economists, and legal experts would operate to conduct a simulation, forensic audits, and interact with MeitY and the Data Protection authority. (OECD & CMA lessons).
5. International cooperation: cooperation and evidence-sharing agreements with EU/UK/US counterparts to gain access to cross-border evidence options provided by algorithms. (OECD recommendation).
6. Research funding & open datasets: open fund to support empirical research and open datasets to enhance their independent analysis and policy making. (Fills literature gaps that are determined in secondary literature).

5. CONCLUSION

The introduction of Artificial Intelligence (AI) and algorithmic systems in the work of the market has radically reconsidered the meaning and application of the principle of antitrust in India. Within the Competition Act, 2002, the notion of the agreement, collusion, and abuse of dominance is the one that is traditionally based on human behavior and direct communication. At least that is what AI-driven decision-making has smeared with autonomous interactions and tacit algorithmic coordination. Because, in the words of Competition Commission of India (CCI), the work of the algorithmic pricing devices and self-educated systems is able to produce collusive consequences without even individual efforts, the evidentiary premises of the Section 3 (anti-competitive agreements) and the Section 4 (abuse of dominance) of the Act are challenged (Competition Commission of India [CCI],

2025). It requires a shift in the way one views liability- shifting to being out of human intent, but instead by algorithmic behavior in terms of liability mechanisms.

According to the analysis of secondary data and publications published by the CCI, OECD, and other international regulators, the current legal principles and jurisprudence of India are still lacking in addressing such problems as algorithmic coordination and data monopolies as well as self-preferencing of digital platforms. The rulings of the CCI in the case of digital ecosystems, like Google LLC v. CCI (2023) and MakeMyTrip-Goibibo v. CCI (2022), present an increasing appreciation of platform dominance and data-driven exercises of exclusion. Nevertheless, it can still be implemented only to a limited extent due to technological obscurity and unalgorithmsic savvy in the institutions of control (Mehra, 2016). Although the CCI has embarked on market research and sectoral investigations on digital competition, such undertaking remain exploratory, which does not have tangible legislative amendments and procedural apparatus of algorithmic auditing and real-time surveillance of the market (Press Information Bureau [PIB], 2025).

By comparison with the top international regimes, there is found to be a lower readiness in regulation in India in comparison to advanced jurisdictions, particularly to the European Union, the United States and the United Kingdom. The Digital Markets Act (DMA) and suggested AI Act of the EU has set up structured responsibilities for big technological sites to provide openness, Interoperability of data, and fairness in algorithmic decision-making (European Commission, 2023). The Federal Trade Commission (FTC) of the U.S. is market-driven and yet recently started to investigate AI systems based on the existing antitrust and consumer protection laws (Stucke and Grunes, 2016). At the same time, the UK Competition and Markets Authority (CMA) has both led the way in developing algorithmic auditing models and sandbox structures to track the pricing algorithms and automated decision-making machines (OECD, 2023). In India, some of the main lessons to be learnt are the entrenchment of technical supervision, making algorithms transparent, and strengthening inter-agency collaboration between technology, data protection, and competition regulators.

According to the results, one of the structural pillars of algorithmic responsibility in Indian competition law ought to incorporate three pillars:

1. Due Diligence Requirements: Companies that use algorithmic tools also need to reveal their systems are not built to break competition standards and are not developed with a collusive character. This may include pre-deployment compliance testing, or algorithmic impact testing (Gal & Aviv, 2020).
2. Transparency and Audit Mechanisms: Regulatory authorities ought to receive the access to algorithmic documentation, training data sources and decision-making

logs. Periodic algorithmic audits can improve the traceability and help to identify anti-competitive behavior and are performed by independent professionals.

3. Models of Liability Allocation: The blame should not be exposed to programmers and operators alone, but corporate bodies also. It is due to the principle of reasonable foreseeability that firms ought to have a vicarious liability on the actions of algorithms, which are accepted in other areas of law (Ezrachi and Stucke, 2016).

Lastly, the policy and legislative framework in India needs to keep up with the advancement of technology to create a balance between innovation incentives and consumer welfare. Excessive regulation might kill innovations and discourage the emergence of digital entrepreneurs; the lack of regulation, though, will lead to monopolization and exploitation of algorithms. A middle way, the one which is based on the principles of responsible AI, is necessary, however. Some legislative proposals might involve amendments to the Competition Act to explicitly define algorithmic coordination as anti-competitive form of agreement, adopting the requirement of AI auditability into compliance initiatives of companies, and enhancing the institutional capacity by means of multidisciplinary training of CCI officials (Bourreau and de Streel, 2020). The Digital India and AI for All collaboration can further focus on meeting competition law objectives with the goals of the digital transformation in India.

To sum up, the study highlights the fact that AI and algorithmic systems are altering the economic and legal premises of competition in India. CCI needs to transform into a responsive rather than a proactive regulator- able to comprehend and audit and regulate the behavior of algorithms. India can achieve a sustainable compromise in innovation, fairness, and consumer protection by learning and applying lessons of experience around the world and integrating an algorithmic accountability in its legal system. The future of Indian antitrust enforcement is therefore in combining technological competency and legal minexibility so that AI is used as an instrument of non-dominant growth and not a source of digital dominance.

5.1 Discussion

The conclusions of this paper indicate that Artificial Intelligence (AI) and algorithmic systems are not technology solutions per se but a paradigm shift in the operations of the markets, how firms compete, and the conceptualization of accountability by the regulators. The transformation raises the competition act, 2002 limits on the conventional rules of the antitrust law because it brings about some sorts of conduct that are not within the frameworks of legal doctrine. The implications are far-reaching to the Indian system of competition and, especially so, in connection with the meaning of an agreement, collusion, and abuse of dominance in an era where most of the competition is carried out by algorithms and not by human beings.

Revision of Traditional Concepts of Antitrust

The first goal of the study, which is to determine how AI transforms the concept of antitrust, proves that algorithmic systems present an additional level of complexity in detecting anti-competitive conduct. Section 3 of the Competition Act requires that two or more enterprises have coordination or communication in a given agreement. In digital markets, however, tacit algorithmic collusion may take place when independent price algorithmic retaliation to comparable information comes to an upraises competitive solution without any coordination (Ezrachi and Stucke, 2016).

According to scholars like Gal and Aviv (2020), algorithms, which are aimed at maximizing profits, can be trained to evade price wars, and in such a manner, the prices will stabilize, with a way that cannot be recognized as a classical cartel behavior. Maintaining such types of self-learning collusion is a problem to enforce, since they are not based on human intent or direct communication as the two key factors of competition law liability.

In the same manner, in Section 4, which is the abuse of dominance, is being redefined in the digital world. By default, with its data edge, dominant digital platforms command not just gateways to the market but also the algorithmic order that would decide to be visible, in the rankings, and interact with a consumer (Bourreau and de Streel, 2020). Algorithms favoring certain parties over others in search results or other recommendation schemes may reinforce dominance and isolate lesser competitors and their presence in the market. An example of this is the Google Android case in India, where Google integration practices were determined to limit competition by favoring its ecosystem (CCI, 2025). These trends indicate that the new centre of market power is now placed on algorithmic control in the digital economy.

Assessing the Legal and Institutional Preparedness of India

The second goal, which is the assessment of whether current legal principles and CCI jurisprudence are sufficient, demonstrates that the competitive law system in India is still at its beginning stages of managing algorithmic harms. What the market research by CCI on e-commerce (2020) and artificial intelligence (2025) has shown is that there has been a rise in enlightenment of the matter, though enforcement mechanisms are still reactive instead of preventive.

Mehra (2016) argues that the inquiry in the Indian competition jurisprudence of the evidentiary model is one of the most vital obstacles since it depends on evidences of intent/communication. However, algorithmic collusion is frequently firewall communication with no trace since machine-learning systems work independently of predictive analytics. Therefore capacity building on forensic algorithm auditing, as well as interdisciplinary skills in the CCI is urgently required.

The ruling of the CCI on the platform related cases including MakeMyTrip-Goibibo v. CCI (2022) and Amazon-Future Retail (2021), is indicative of a developing but disjointed view of the ways in which data-ecosystems generate effects of exclusion. In such situations, the Commission placed dominance focus but failed to consider completely the role of algorithms in driving market concentration by dynamic pricing or special visibility. This illustrates a missing doctrine in the difference between efficiency with the algorithm and the intent of anti-competition (Press Information Bureau [PIB], 2025).

Comparative Global Lessons

Comparing the approach of India with leading frameworks of the world is the third goal and depicts a dramatic separation in terms of regulatory maturity. The European Union has also been the leader in global rules of algorithmic competition, which has manifested in the Digital Markets Act (DMA) and AI Act frameworks. These laws are more focused on ex ante regulation, which requires large platforms to be transparent, auditable, and interoperable (European Commission, 2023). The method used by the EU shifts the proof to the dominant actors which creates preventive control as opposed to the control that follows the violation.

The United States on the contrary adheres to a more traditional conduct-based antitrust, model. The Federal Trade Commission (FTC) and Depth of Justice (DOJ) are examining how AIweek coordination can be covered by Section 1 of the Sherman Act, yet they revere excess regulation (Stucke and Grunes, 2016). The Competition and Markets Authority (CMA) in the UK has taken a middle ground by devising algorithmic monitoring sandboxes and through them individuals can have algorithms put to the test under controlled conditions so as to stop unintentional collusion (OECD, 2023).

These strategies are some of the insights that India can learn. The EU approach to implementing algorithmic accountability based on regulatory design would be used to follow, and the sandbox approach in the UK could be used to encourage the provision of innovation-favoring enforcement in India. By combining the aspects of both frameworks, India may become a moderate supervisor, one that promotes innovations and curbs the threat of the algorithm.

On the Path Towards an Accountability Framework Algorithms

The fourth goal which is to Advance a framework of algorithmic accountability is a potential building block of the future of competition regulating in India. According to the secondary data of international and national policy reports, the proposed framework incorporates due diligence, transparency, and liability to be the three pillars of this framework.

First, the Due diligence requirements must obligate the companies using AI systems to make sure that principles of competition law are not violated. This will entail keeping a record of the algorithm design, training data, and in-house testing processes that will ensure that no collusive functionalities are present (Gal and Aviv, 2020).

Second, the regulations on transparency should give regulators the ability to request algorithmic disclosure when investigating. Since AI is a black box, algorithm auditability is important towards identifying collusion or self-preferencing. Algorithms made through explainable AI (XAI) methods may also improve explainable accountability (Ezrachi and Stucke, 2016).

Third, the liability models need to explain the responsibility as being the culprit of anti-competitive outcomes between the firm, developer, or individual who uses the algorithm. A hybrid model that consists of a corporate vicarious liability and programmer responsibility would be in line with what occurs globally, but still offer a proportionate enforcement (Bourreau and de Streel, 2020).

Policy and Legislative Implications

The last goal, which is to recommend the policy and legislative changes emphasized the necessity of the integrated, innovation-sensitive regulation. India needs to reformulate Competition Act in such a way that algorithmic conduct becomes part of it. This may include a revision of the definitions of Sections 2(b) and 3(3) to include coordinated algorithmic behavior, and provide new algorithmic compliance reporting provisions.

The Competition (Amendment) Act, 2023, with its introduction of deal-value-thresholds and settlements, is a move in the right direction but it is not a step towards algorithmic accountability (CCI, 2025). Another amendment may allow the CCI to make disclosure mandatory especially on dominant platforms relying on AI to take market decisions that are sensitive.

Also, the inter-agency cooperation, the CCI and the Ministry of Electronics and Information Technology (MeitY) and the proposed Digital India Act (DIA) could be used to guarantee unity in the AI regulation, data privacy, and competition legislation. Evolution of a dedicated Algorithmic Regulation Cell (ARC) in the CCI would offer technical knowledge to audit, simulate, and monitor concurrently the behaviour of algorithmic pricing.

It is important to find a balance between innovation and regulation. Too much regulation will discourage AI entrepreneurship, but a lack of regulations will encourage monopoly and consumer abuse. An appropriate and risk-based policy, such as the one followed by the AI Act of the EU, would therefore provide the opportunity of applying differentiated obligations, according to the possible influence of algorithms on competition and consumer welfare (OECD, 2023).

General Implications and Future

The nexus of AI and antitrust law is transforming the perception of the regulator of economic power, fairness, and accountability. In the case of India, reform of the law is not the only problem, but capacity building, the need to develop technical competency among legal professionals, judges and policymakers. AI-Competition laboratories developed in universities and think tanks have the potential to assist with evidence-based policymaking and collaborative innovation.

Moreover, with the world digital markets getting more and more interconnected, India would have to take part in the cross-border regulatory collaboration to deal with the cross-border algorithmic practices. Engagement of the multilateral forums like OECD and G20 Digital Economy Working Group may help India to have more influence in global setting of algorithmic governance standards.

Finally, the strategy of India should be a combination of the preventative capabilities of the EU model, flexibility of innovations provided by the US regime, and the adaptative pragmatism of the UK model. India can establish a competition policy regime protecting consumers and promoting digital innovation by incorporating transparency and accountability along with fairness qualities into its AI governance ecosystem.

5.2 Recommendations

In accordance with the analysis and the results of secondary literature, the following recommendations can be made to enhance the legal and policy framework of India on dealing with an AI-driven market dynamic and algorithmic competition issues based on the Competition Act, 2002.

1. **Enhancing the Legal definition of Collusion and Agreement.** Appendage Algorithms Algorithmic collusion and self-learning system coordination should be clearly identified as the possible forms of anti-competitive behavior in the Indian Competition Act. The existing practices are heavily based on human

will and deliberate communication, which might fail in practice to reflect the tacit coordination in the algorithm. The changes in legislation should clarify the definition of agreement and concerted practice to encompass machine-based or algorithmic collaboration with a sense of accountability even when an unwanted collusion occurs (Ezrachi and Stucke, 2017).

2. **Setting up Algorithms Accountability Mechanisms.** In order to avoid the abuse of dominance and provide a fair competition, India must have Algorithmic Accountability Framework (AAF) in Competition Act. This model must demand:
   - Computerized audits and certification of compliance of mainstream online companies.
   - Ex ante data use, algorithmic parameters and decision logic disclosure which influence the market competition (Gal and Elkin-Koren, 2017).
   - Sharing liability in which firms as well as algorithm developers are liable to anti-competitive outcomes. This is similar to the Digital Markets Act (2022) of the European Union that includes requirements of transparency and interoperability on gatekeeper platforms.
3. **Expanding the Role and Capacity of Competition Commission of India (CCI).** The CCI is also to be enabled with a Digital Markets and Algorithms Division (DMAD) a specialized organ responsible to explore market behavior and algorithmic pricing identified to be of a data-driven nature. The combination of technology professionals, data scientists, and AI ethicists can be used to boost the accuracy of investigations (Mehra, 2020). More so, CCI can predictive analytics-tools integration into its monitoring patterns can assist in identifying real-time collusion trends in online markets (OECD, 2021).
4. **Fostering Data Portability and Interoperability.** The most important source of market dominance in the digital economy is data monopolization. India ought to encourage the use of data portability, interoperability and open API standards to avoid anti-competitive lock-ins (Tiwari and Sharma, 2023). The statutes must be in line with the General Data Protection regulation (GDPR) and Digital Services Act (DSA) of the EU to ensure that data downstream access is favorable and consumer privacy is upheld.
5. **International Comparative Legal Studies.** The hybrid regulatory model on which India ought to consider following would be that of the EU of active ex-ante and the U.S. of behavioral remedies. When the EU aims at platform accountability and systemic gatekeeper regulation, the U.S. concentrates on interventions case-specific. Another approach that the Competition and Markets Authority (CMA) of the UK relevant to the topic offers is a more flexible model, the focus of which is on the transparency of algorithms and the fair structure of the market (CMA, 2021). The CCI can utilize its best practices, which are combined with these models, to adjust to the dynamic Indian digital environment.

6. **Legislation and Policy changes.** The recommended reforms to address the needs of balancing innovative incentives and consumer welfare are as follows: Introduction of Competition (Amendment) Bill on Digital Markets: Competition based on algorithms and AI regulation.
    - Requirement of algorithmic impact assessment (AIAs) to companies employing predictive algorithms or pricing algorithms in the dominating market positions (OECD, 2023).
    - Promote regulatory sandboxes that can be experimented and trained on AI technologies under CCI regulation to implement a balance between innovation and compliance (NITI Aayog, 2022).
    - Form cross-sectoral cooperation between CCI, MeitY, and NITI Aayog to provide coherent AI policy.
7. **Developing Awareness and Capacity.** Lastly, institutionalization of AI ethics, competition analytics, and data governance training of CCI officials, policy-makers, and legal experts. Creating academic-regulatory collaboration with universities and think tanks can develop an empirical study of the phenomenon of algorithmic competition and consumer harm.

REFERENCES

Amazon.com NV Investment Holdings LLC v. Future Retail Ltd., 2021 SCC OnLine Del 1279 (Delhi High Court).

Bourreau, M., & de Streel, A. (2020). *Digital conglomerates and EU competition policy*. Centre on Regulation in Europe (CERRE). https://cerre.eu/news/digital-conglomerates-and-eu-competition-policy/

Calvano, E., Calzolari, G., Denicolò, V., & Pastorello, S. (2020). Artificial intelligence, algorithmic pricing, and collusion. *The American Economic Review*, *110*(10), 3267–3297. DOI: 10.1257/aer.20190623

Competition and Markets Authority (CMA). (2021). *Algorithms: How they can reduce competition and harm consumers*. UK Government. https://www.gov.uk/government/publications/algorithms-how-they-can-reduce-competition-and-harm-consumers

Competition Commission of India. (2025). *Market study on artificial intelligence and competition*. Competition Commission of India. https://www.cci.gov.in/images/marketstudie/en/market-study-on-artificial-intelligence-and-competition1759752172.pdf

European Commission. (2022). *The Digital Markets Act (DMA)*. Publications Office of the European Union. https://digital-markets-act.ec.europa.eu/about-dma_en#:~:text=Following%20the%20initial%20proposal%20of,applicable%20on%202%20May%202023

European Commission. (2023). *Digital Markets Act and Artificial Intelligence Act: Ensuring fair and transparent digital markets*. https://digital-strategy.ec.europa.eu

European Union. (2022). *Digital Markets Act (Regulation (EU) 2022/1925). Official Journal of the European Union*. https://eur-lex.europa.eu/eli/reg/2022/1925/oj

Ezrachi, A., & Stucke, M. E. (2016). *Virtual competition: The promise and perils of the algorithm-driven economy*. Harvard University Press.

Federal Trade Commission. (2021). *Aiming for truth, fairness, and equity in your company's use of AI*. U.S. Federal Trade Commission. https://www.ftc.gov/system/files/ftc_gov/pdf/p241200_ftc_comment_to_copyright_office.pdf

Gal, M., & Aviv, O. (2020). The competitive effects of the GDPR. *Journal of Competition Law and Economics*. https://ssrn.com/abstract=3548444

Gal, M. S., & Elkin-Koren, N. (2017). Algorithmic consumers. *Harvard Journal of Law & Technology*, *30*(2), 309–352.

Google LLC v. Competition Commission of India. (2023). Civil Appeal No. 229 of 2023, 2023 SCC OnLine SC 88 (Supreme Court of India, Jan. 19, 2023).

MakeMyTrip (India) Pvt. Ltd. & Ors. v. Competition Commission of India. (2022). Competition Appeal (AT) No. 16 of 2020. National Company Law Appellate Tribunal (Dec. 23, 2022).

Mehra, S. K. (2016). Antitrust and the robo-seller: Competition in the time of algorithms. *Minnesota Law Review*, *103*(2), 369–430. https://www.minnesotalawreview.org/wp-content/uploads/2016/04/Mehra_ONLINEPDF1.pdf

Aayog, N. I. T. I. (2022). *Responsible AI for All: Strategy for India*. Government of India. https://www.niti.gov.in/sites/default/files/2022-11/Ai_for_All_2022_02112022_0.pdf

Aayog, N. I. T. I. (2021). *Responsible AI for all: Operationalizing principles for responsible AI*. Government of India. https://www.niti.gov.in/sites/default/files/2021-08/Part2-Responsible-AI-12082021.pdf

Organisation for Economic Co-operation and Development. (2023). *Algorithmic competition (Background note)*. OECD Publishing. https://www.oecd.org/daf/competition/algorithmic-competition-2023.pdf

Press Information Bureau, Government of India. (2025, October 6). *Competition Commission of India releases market study on AI and competition*. https://pib.gov.in/PressReleasePage.aspx?PRID=2175607

Stucke, M. E., & Grunes, A. P. (2016). *Big data and competition policy*. Oxford University Press., https://doi.org/10.1093/law:ocl/9780198788133.001.0001

Tiwari, N., Kumar, S., & Srivastava, V. (2023). *India's digital governance odyssey: navigating economic transformation in the digital era through prowess and legal resilience*.

Chapter 4
Algorithmic Systems and the Ethical Imperative to Prevent Structural Harm and Bias

Sheikh Inam Ul Mansoor
http://orcid.org/0000-0001-8636-4769
Symbiosis Law School Hyderabad Campus, Symbiosis International University, India

Hamza Khan
http://orcid.org/0009-0007-6403-7864
Symbiosis Law School Hyderabad Campus, Symbiosis International University, India

Adnan Asrar
http://orcid.org/0009-0004-5369-7857
Lloyd Law College, Greater Noida, India

Showkat Ahmad Wani
http://orcid.org/0009-0009-0240-9073
Alliance University, India

ABSTRACT

AI systems are already occupying a more important role, especially in decision-making processes in areas such as-police work, medicine, and banking. Nonetheless, more recent studies indicate that the AI algorithms historically perpetuate structural racism based on race, gender and class. This chapter looks into how algorithms decision-making aids continue the perpetuation of prejudice and generate fresh dis-

DOI: 10.4018/979-8-3373-7685-1.ch004

criminating practices. The introduction by defining the algorithmic injustice and the discussion of the use of AI in decision-making processes that characterise society. It indeed emphasizes the fact that the bias, whether apparent or hidden that is present in the Artificial Intelligence ecosystems is a reflection of the prejudice present in the dataset that AI ecosystems are based on. This chapter aims to analyse in detail how race, gender, and class interact to complicate the impact of bigoted algorithms.

INTRODUCTION

Artificial Intelligence has become one of today's most significant globally transforming forces that virtually touches nearly every domain of human life including healthcare, justice, education, and work. (Rawas, 2024) Thus, high feats of data processing and pattern extraction provides beyond anthropocentric measure of high accuracy and efficiency in decision-making control that were hitherto manual intensive. (Durand & Hattingh, 2020) Various governments and corporations around the world have continued to depend on the AI systems to augment governance and decision making processes as well as efficiency. (Sharma et al., 2020) Nonetheless, the implementation of such technologies produces critical issues relating to systematic discrimination inherent in the algorithms used. For all the so-called detached and rational power of AI, it appears that such systems are far from immune to structural racism. (Papagiannidis et al., 2025)

The basis of AI training and the functioning of algorithmic decision-making can be confidently considered to be data. This data, is anyway not produced in isolation. It can regress to portray the societies inequities, hatreds, and omissions that Embedded within the societies, It emanates from. (Mahmud et al., 2022) When algorithms are trained on poorly balanced inputs, or in the presence of some unbalanced historical feature, these machines become replicas of bias they are expected to expunge. Such encoded biases are, therefore, not just technologistic problems but embody structural racism, a systematic form of prejudice that cuts across both race, gender, class, and other forms of social exclusion. (Krawczyk, 2016)

Algorithmic decision making is progressively enlarging its use, and this is more problematic in contexts where equity and non- discrimination are core legal values. (Belenguer, 2022) For instance in the criminal justice system, predictive policing has been used under the label of increased effective and safety. (Wani, S. A. & Mansoor, S. I., 2025) However, in actual research, such systems have been identified to work more rigorously on people of color and thus increase on past injustices instead of combating them. (Dakalbab et al., 2022) Likewise, row, other areas like employment/ Financial services algorithms have been purported to engage in discrimination where applicants for a job or loan are rejected based on the algorithms' existing prejudices such as Proxy for race or gender or economic status among others. (Chen, 2023) These outcomes not only defeat the principles of substantive equality, but also threaten the concerns of procedural rationality – an important aspect of administrative law. (Lin, 2024) Socio-structural justice in AI is therefore imbedded deeply in the paradigms used in the development of algorithms. In choosing the training sets and in defining the architecture of the algorithms, as well as the goals of these systems are therefore made by people who consciously or unconsciously replicate social prejudices. (Egede et al., 2024) To this problem, many AI systems contributing to or powering other applications or systems, are much like 'black boxes'. Such systems are mostly opaque, and this means that people or institutions that would like to question the decision-making process or check where the discriminative decision is coming from cannot easily do so. (Rashid & Kausik, 2024) Lack of responsibility on moralizing bodies creates a lot of concern in provisions of natural justice, including, the right to be heard and the rationale behind any decision made. (Dong & Bocian, 2024) In addition, structural discrimination in artificial intelligence depends on superordinate legal and regulatory frameworks for the execution of the artificial intelligence systems. However, there has been minimal legal adaptation to the emerging problem of algorithmic technology, despite the threats that AI poses to some freedoms such as equality and non-discrimination. (Rodrigues, 2020) The current multiplicity of regulatory agencies in the management of technology companies enables their deployment of systems that are devoid of an understanding of human rights, producing outcomes that violate cherished human rights. (Segev, 2024) For instance, constitutional principles of the rule of law, and particularly, equality rights which are espoused across most legal systems are systematically violated by AI-driven techniques that racialize and oppress minorities. This is why there is then rising concern in order to secure justice and fairness in society, an inclusive legal framework should be developed to regulate the progressive technological advancement. (Chatterjee & S., 2022)

Algorithmic decision-making also requires reconsidering corporate risk in the creation and use of artificial intelligence systems. In the area of CS principles, AI technology producers have an ethical and legal responsibility not to discriminate under the social responsibility of corporations. (Henz, 2021) However, the contemporary legal environment quite often does not oblige these actors to account for the social consequences of their innovations. This lack of accountability is why it is crucial to bring principles of fairness accountability, and transparency into the development and deployment of AI systems—now commonly known as algorithmic governance. (Shin & Park, 2019) Given the subject of algorithmic injustice, this chapter called for a multidisciplinary approach from law, technology and social science expertise. Essentially, while structural discrimination in AI is an artifact, it is not inherently a technological flaw but rather analogous with wider social wrongs that are being advanced by digital techniques. (Moussawi et al., 2024) Law academics and policymakers are tasked with handling algorithmic centric bias at the same time as the root causes of that bias in society, all the while reconstructing Distributive Justice to try to make AI beneficial and progressive for all, preventing cases of tech injustice.

THE INTERSECTION OF RACE, GENDER, AND CLASS IN AI SYSTEMS

The increasing application of artificial intelligence systems in societal structures in order to maintain powerful racisms, sexism, as well as classism either intentionally or through reinforcement by AI systems. (Zajko, 2022) These biases are not a consequence of a specific set of rules programming the machine nor a part of the algorithm itself but inherent in the sociotechnical configuration of AI. Although AI is celebrated for its ability to provide neutral or non-discriminatory solutions and decision-making AI and ML systems can depict and even enhance unfair discriminations inherent in the past Systems. (Belenguer, 2022) The phenomenon in question of race, gender and class bias in artificial intelligence can be linked to the history of technology which mas or less replicated the patterns of the discriminatory society. (Leavy, 2018) It is more so because technology, like any other creation by man, is bound to mirror the beliefs, goals and worldview of its developers. Bias, in the pre-digital age, was normally hardcoded into the typical technological tools and structures. (Chen, 2023) For example, devices became standardised in terms of the physiological parameters of white men, and diagnostic criteria that systematically underestimated and undertreated women and people of colour. In like manner, early computing systems and algorithms were created in structurally racist societies that were dominated by predominantly homogenous groups. (Manasi et al., 2022) This historical legacy is thus present in the current artificial intelligence systems, since the sociocultural settings of the creation of algorithms present marked inequity.

The process of algorithmic design most often starts with data gathering, which is a basis for training algorithms for machine learning. However, this data is never virgin, or representative for everyone and everything. (Sarker, 2021) Rather, it originates from historical and institutional datasets, and current digital environments where it naturally occurs. For instance, predictive policing algorithms depend on crime data that indexes minorities because of historical biases in racially profiling and over policing certain areas. (Bennett Moses et al., 2016) As such, these algorithms keep people who have been surveilled and criminalized in the past repeatedly targeted, thus raising issues of dignity and equality before the law and prohibition of discrimination. (Burton, 2023) Likewise, the same holds true for the exclusion of such groups in a set of training data that results in biased solutions in niches like facial recognition, diagnosis of diseases applying artificial intelligence, or employment of talent. (Nagpal et al., 2023) Facial recognition has been described as a technology that does not work well in identifying people from minority races or ethnic groups especially women. They are not simply quantitative errors but instances of structural biases that are embedded into the formally rational structure of the algorithm. (Raposo, 2024) When incorporating such systems in important affairs like security and police work, it results in perverse arrests, intrusive observation, and consumer rights abuse including the rights of privacy, proper conduct, and course. (Sarabdeen, 2022) This underlines the fact that future work should focus on the critical analysis of the processes used when developing algorithms and the compliance of those processes with human rights.

Structural problems that gender bias in AI systems stem from are comparable to each other. For instance digital assistants are often designed using stereotypically female personality traits, therefore gender stereotyping is rife. (Locke & Hodgdon, 2024) In hiring algorithms, prejudices are illustrated in the sense that their patterns mirror the progression of discriminator facts, for example, women's marginalization in leadership positions in an organization. When such datasets are employed for training of AI systems, they are a way of embedding the previous discrimination into the decision making of the future. (Seppälä & Małecka, 2024) This is tolerated under employment laws on equality and non-discrimination where bias in AI preserves systemic prejudice, anchors social and economic status, and perpetuates classism under the guise of income and education. (Zajko, 2021) This puts out of reach from sustainable financial services and products economically disadvantaged persons and thus deepening the level of inequality. In education, algorithmic testing and college selection are forms of decision making that lack distributive justice, implying that designers must factor socio-economic status for fairness. (Gengler, 2024) The existence of intersectional biases in AI are not simply hypothetical, but there are case studies available. In healthcare, distribution models that use algorithms to determine distribution of medical resources have shown to give higher priority to people who incur higher medical bills, a factor that reflects SES leaving out low income and minorities. (An et al., 2023) The reliance on efficiency in healthcare solutions may promote heartlessness while the risk assessment in bail and sentencing overemphasize putting ethnically marginalized people behind the bar increasing ethnicity-based incarceration. (Mehta et al., 2019)

The ramifications of these biases on the law and policy are significant especially in jurisdictions that pride themselves in main principles of equity and non-discrimination. International human rights treaties including the ICCPR and CERD require states not to allow equality based discrimination arising out of technological advancement. (Rodrigues, 2020) Thus, the absence of precise AI regulation has led to the gap into which private organizations installed skewed techniques without much oversight. (Zaidan & Ibrahim, 2024) To successfully respond to algorithmic discrimination, synchronize technology with human rights, and entirely understand AI's decision-making system, stronger legislation is required. (Jui & Rivas, 2024) It was shown that this lack of transparency does not only affect accountability but also concerns of procedural fairness, as people that are impacted by the algorithm made decision are seldom allowed to challenge or even know the reasons for such decisions. (Wesche et al., 2024) In order to increase legal compliance scholars of law have advocated for applicability of certain principles like explainability and interpretability into AI systems.

The fact that the algorithm adopts race, gender, and class bias requires a multi-faceted strategy different from merely finding technical approaches to the problem. This includes the idea of diversifying of AI development teams, specifying the strict impact assessments as well as folding the ethical concern into the AI creations and uses. (Shrestha & Das, 2022) Also, PIL has a crucial role in addressing discrimination from artificial intelligence since it presents and protects human rights. Litigations against biased systems are legally applied means for correction and have a critical significance in defining the normative regulation of functioning of artificial intelligence technologies. (Segev, 2024)

BIAS IN DATA COLLECTION AND ALGORITHMIC TRAINING

Data input and program training are essential to AIt; systems which build the foundation for machine learning algorithms. Yet, because of the nature of the datasets and training techniques used, these processes are usually discriminatory by design. Sometimes the prejudices that are most emerging from the results of AI operations are hence unethical, and this calls for fairness issues including accountability on the existing societal and historical prejudice in the datasets used for training. (Sarker, 2021) For example, while using the Internet data can be collected in a way that constantly excludes certain groups, e.g., rural or educated users, which in turn affects the violation of primary human rights such as health, work or justice. (Segev, 2024) Despite such discrimination going against provisions of the law such as the International Covenant on Economic, Social and Cultural Rights (ICESCR), which calls for non-discrimination. To this, historical biases in data make the issue even worse. For instance, some predictive policing models are informed by crime statistics evidencing racism where communities of color are labeled as the criminals they are, despite being discriminated against. (Lee et al., 2024) Likewise, the AI recruitment systems which learn from the past job suitability can be racially or gender biased to provide the same to the management positions. (Khurana et al., 2023) Such biases are against equal opportunity laws such as Equal Employment Opportunity Act putting an organization in legal dangers (Sarirete et al., 2022) When fed biased data, AI models consequently saturate prejudice in decisions or recommendations hence the perpetration of systematic injustice. (Belenguer, 2022) For instance, their machine learning algorithms to recognize faces fail if trained on datasets with predominantly lighter-skin contexts; they cause massive errors that harm dark-skinned people in situations such as policing or immigration, infringements on unreasonable searches or deprivation of liberty rights. (Mansoor, 2024) These issues raise important questions of checking bias in AI training data, and proportionality and non-discrimination in AI decision making. (Aldoseri et al., 2023)

The opaque nature of AI systems, often referred to as the "black box" problem, makes it challenging to identify and rectify these biases. AI decision-making lacks transparency, making it difficult for affected individuals to challenge or understand the reasoning behind decisions. (Sarker, 2021) This opacity raises significant accountability issues and procedural justice concerns, as individuals whose rights are impacted often lack access to the rationale behind the algorithmic decisions. (Hassija et al., 2024) The most important and relevant rights pertain to legal systems and decisions and rights to transparency and the possibility to challenge any decision which affects these rights in line with international human rights laws. (Brożek et al., 2024) It has been ascertained that bias becomes possible at each stage of data preparation starting from the data collection, data cleaning, data labelling and data processing. Technical choices, including variable choices or how to deal with missing data, can be endogenous and are therefore coloured by the beliefs and axioms of the data scientists or engineers. (González-Sendino et al., 2024) Also, such teams are usually matrices, which does not address the issue of diversity and merely continues discriminating on minorities. (Nishant et al., 2024) This bias is inoperative of international human rights law because the adoption and development of technology must be for equality and social justice. (Balayn et al., 2021) For instance, health algorithms utilized in hospitals may work better for the highly endowed and privileged class hurting the poor's access to health care. (Periáñez et al., 2024) This breaches the right to health which is as provided under the ICESCR. In order to meet these challenges, technical, legal and ethical solutions should be implemented. (Mansoor, 2025) Strict measures need to be taken at each level of the data flow to avoid unfair practice implementation. (González-Sendino et al., 2024). Algorithms guidelines of transparency and fairness include the GDPR legal frameworks for data protection in the EU. (Mittal et al., 2024) Ethical considerations also demand a shift from prioritizing efficiency and profit to addressing the potential for precognitive injustice in AI design. (Zhang, Chen, & Xu, 2022) Thus, the interpretability of AI needs to be focused on pre-established purposes, which includes measures for checking fair performances of the same system among different groups of people. This consists of implementing the end users, right from the time of development of AI systems, and the Ai social implications. Moreover, there should be micro, meso and macro level regulations on data acquisition and algorithm building which will respect and promote human rights of equality, dignity and non-discrimination.

DISCRIMINATORY OUTCOMES IN AI APPLICATIONS

AI systems that are widely regarded as impartial information processors have been gradually shown to possess the capacity for discriminating results. These disparities are not bizarre once in a while occurrences but stem from the historical systemic injustices that are core to data, AI algorithms, and deployment procedures. (Min, 2023) Analysing concrete fields with AI system application, like police work, recruitment, and credit rating, it is noticeable that biases' continuation through algorithmic procedures is obvious and diverse, thus challenging legal and ethical considerations. (Sarkar et al., 2024) The use of AI is most healthily debated with reference to policing, especially the implementation of predictive policing. These systems which are used in the prediction of crimes and in the deployment of personnel in the crime prevention organizations are based on past crime statistics. (Hung & Yen, 2021) However, the data utilised regularly shows that the implementation of such policies has always involved racial prejudice when it comes to police forces. (Mansoor, S. I., 2026) For example, in regard to arrest data minority populations have been considered as more criminal and therefore police interactions with them resulted in considerably high arrest rates relative to actual rates of criminality. (Haefner et al., 2023) When this is fed into the AI, these systems incriminate the aforementioned communities as high-risk reiterating cycles of oppression through policing. All these practices invite serious concerns related to civil rights, race and constitutional non- compliance with acceptable practices. They also point out risks that threatened procedural justice, and the rights to innocence presumption which is parts of the criminal justice system. (Završnik, 2020)

In healthcare too, the adoption of artificial intelligence has revealed inequalities that make certain populations more vulnerable and that include gender and poverty. Main rationality parameters influencing healthcare algorithms often tend to ignore equality concerns as much as efficiency and cost. (Faiyazuddin et al., 2025) Healthcare algorithms are ethnocentric in regards to disregarding women and lower income patients because datasets are often excluded and fails at determining prognosis and allocating resources properly. (Knight et al., 2023) Some categories of population experience either poor access to healthcare or refusal in treatment, thus violating distributional justice and the right to health. This further demonstrates the importance of equity-centred strategies that to offer usable AI in health care. (Webb, 2024)

Prejudice in the operation of hiring and recruitment is yet another alert where AI frameworks have embraced structural unfairness, and for class and economic status prejudice. Numerous companies and industries today employ the use of AI-powered technologies to scan CVs, and evaluate potential workers. (Seppälä & Małecka, 2024) Such systems, which learned from past employment records, may only perpetuate and preserve the gaps. For instance, if recruitment over the recent past had been done based on previous education level or socioeconomic status of particular individuals, the AI system will also do the same, which in turn discriminates users from less privileged groups. (Rigotti et al., 2024) Furthermore, proxies like zip codes or names of universities to represent the class or economic status mean that we continue to perpetuate systemically unfair practices. These practices violates equal opportunity employment and in addition puts organizations at risk of legal cases of violating equal anti-discrimination and labor laws. (Chen, 2023) It is also similar to image recognition in being a class-based biased credit scoring system which judges credit capacity from behaviour and records. But they sometimes target smaller earnings with poor records in credit or banking facilities. (Shi, Tse, Luo, et al., 2022) Prejudice credit sources, joblessness, and residence expulsion because of racism reduce credit status that hampers loans and credit, mortgage among other services. Such exclusion sustains a cycle within system that only hampers economic growth. (Chen, Zeng, & Lin, 2014) It positively raises important questions about equality of financial systems and calls for regulatory solutions to the problem of algorithmic prejudice in credit rating.

These examples show that data, at the heart of AI processes, repeats societal injustices. The results of input datasets that are not critically and carefully evaluated and certified bring forth AI models that are inherently unfair and unjust. (Chiriatti, Ganapini, Panai, et al., 2024) This is known as "algorithmic feedback loops", this is where discriminator results are recycled back into the system, to deepen discrimination. Similarly with predictive policing, high arrests among the black population recurrently perpetuate the system's bias where high criminal activities are proved as a result of high police arrests among the black persons. (Stray, J. 2023) These are compounded by the fact that the processes through which AI makes decision are often not easily understandable. Known as the 'black box' issue, this opacity hampers the understanding of where biases stem from or prosecute the developers and deployers who created them. (Papadouli, 2023) This creates fairness and bureaucratic issues as most of the people who are impacted by algorithmic decisions cannot appeal or get a rehearing in contravention of the natural justice fundamental principles of openness, reason, and the law. (Marey, et al., 2024)

Exploring a solution to these concerns demand a combination of the technical, legal and ethical solutions. From a purely technology perspective, one feels the urge to create machines that not only are correct but also equitable. (Al-kfairy et al.,

2024) This involves checking for bias in datasets, developing equitable algorithms, monitoring discrimination, and enforcing legal guidelines like GDPR, which ensures transparency, fairness, and compliance with anti-discrimination regulations in AI systems. (Joshi, 2024) On the ethical side, the changes are needed for how AI systems are imagined and implemented. Equality means that instead of customers being clients we focus on satisfaction, performance means the purpose should be geared towards social justice. (Hastuti & Syafruddin, 2023)This calls for active participation of affected community in the design and the assessment of AI systems. Hence, there is a need to address the principles of its use and the norms that the AI should meet with the tide toward social justice and equality in mind.

LEGAL AND ETHICAL RESPONSES TO ALGORITHMIC DISCRIMINATION

As AI's control over data and its management transcends industries, this chapter aims at the growing importance of legal and ethical considerations in addressing elements that fuel algorithmic discrimination while perpetuating bias in data and algorithms. (Duan et al., 2019) Security, healthcare and employment disparities, and unfair loan and banking systems raise concerns over pro-sociality hindering; therefore, ethics, law and policy in multidisciplinary multi stakeholder standards must be enforceable to pursue the right uses for AI. (Kordzadeh et al., 2021) In the framework of the legal analysis several categories of approaches are available that can be used for regulation of algorithmic bias although their application in the case of AI systems remains problematic and still under development. (Madaoui, 2024) In jurisdictions like the EU, what can be utilized to fight algorithmic discrimination is the General Data Protection Regulation (GDPR). The GDPR also includes the right of explanation, which guarantees subject's right to an explanation of an important decision made with an automated processing system. (Zuiderveen Borgesius, 2020) AI brings specificity to many processes, which in turn reduces the applicability of the GDPR. There are indications that there might be specialized rules apart from anti-discrimination laws to suit algorithms. (Soysal, 2024) It is law that shapes the concept of algorithmic discrimination, yet ethics is at the heart of discourses. AI systems unlike humans, work with big data sets and in their processing there is no sense of harm, unfair treatment, violation of equality among others. (Shulner-Tal et al., 2024) Another distinct ethical problem is the dubious implementation of AI decision making since the algorithms are often hard to decipher. There is a definite and significant role in ethical consideration by developers in maintaining a fair design. (Peters, 2023) What is needed is a change in process from optimisation for development efficiency to including aspects of fairness and equity. The key issue here is how to incorporate technical advancement in AI within the social justice and equitable and respect for human rights frameworks.

In order to tackle these challenges, the following cellular policy recommendations have been suggested to tackle structural discrimination inherent in AI. First, there is a need for a 'global request for auditing of AI systems and especially the datasets to which it is fed'. (Fourati et al., 2021) This means at-least when data feed into algorithms is biased then, preferred results are not likely to be similarly biased since, algorithmic bias stems from biased input data. This process of data auditing should be followed by or simultaneous with the extreme testing of algorithms for non-discrimination. (Akter et al., 2021) A policy recommendation is creation of sovereign bodies for the ratification of the use of AI, oversee the organizations, enforce the requirement on the balancing of algorithms and investigate cases of discrimination. Furthermore, fairness needs to be by-design so that they can account for justice during their development. (Alvarez et al., 2024) This include, responding with a conscious effort to involve citizens in AI design and development, liaising with social scientists, ethicists and legal experts to address emerging concerns of bias, and avowing the process of algorithm construction and data usage. (Ghallab, 2019)

AI systems need legal safeguards for nondiscriminatory treatment which is especially lacked in workplaces, housing, and credit. The Equal Credit Opportunity Act (ECOA) as well as the Fair Housing Act can control non-targeted decision algorithms in such areas. (Garcia et al., 2024) Likewise, across the European Union, the Artificial Intelligence Act has been proposed in a bid to introduce the rules governing high risk systems and their applications such as health and law enforcement. (Ren & Du, 2024) The Act is focused on the transparency, accountability, and fairness of AI systems, but their use is sensible from their implementation. International cooperation persists, because the manifestations of AI systems can address harm across borders. (Bin Rashid et al., 2024) On this regard, United Nations, Organization for Economic Cooperation and Development (OECD), and World Trade Organization (WTO) could have a significant role to set global standard for the AI governance. (Fournier-Tombs, 2021) Such organizations could bring about contractual terms regarding algorithmic explainability; data protection; non-discrimination containing specific guidelines on how the applications of artificial intelligence should uphold basic universal human rights and global equality. (Neuwirth, 2024) Policy-makers should take into consideration social effects whenever poorer groups of society are locked out of AI advantages, topics for example, automation-induced job losses, and opportunities for measures such as subsidies toward retraining programmes. (Qian et al., 2024) In this case ethical AI development must therefore be understood as an instrument for the advancement of social justice rather than commercial or technological gain. Consequently, the application of AI systems needs to make social justice better instead of making it worse, with the existing gaps existing between social classes and integrating society into one unit. (Vesnic-Alujevic et al., 2020)

CONCLUSION

Algorithmic injustice is an eminent danger to the current AI systems, as well as societies since it amplifies social injustice. A study into structural discrimination within AI has highlighted these negative prejudices particularly within the thread of policing, medical treatment, employment and credit. Many such biases originate from preconceived or improper datasets and model reflections and algorithms, targeting minorities and oppressing women and marginalized racial and socioeconomic groups. Let me sum up this injustice, which needs both, legal and ethical, as well as technical solutions. This study must now also take critical stance on AI systems to encourage the same regarding fairness and justice. One of the research finding is the fact that AI systems do not operate as blank slates because they perpetuate current social prejudices since they are built on skewed data. Whenever an algorithm is built, discriminations are passed out especially in sensitive sections such as policing, healthcare and credit referencing. Such outcomes affect those persons and communities making them suffer through worsening Discrimination Spirals. Solving these problems depends on recognizing and correcting the biases built into algorithm design. It must be collaborated with the academics and AI must be promoted in a transparent manner to develop ethical AI. Two main techniques to achieve fairness are Data auditing and algorithm training. First, large-scale data audits should be conducted together with establishing algorithms that should pass the fairness tests periodically. The social demand for clear laws to counter AI associated discrimination has accordingly posed as a necessity for companies. Those frameworks are the legal systems which should govern or address the use of AI and provide the means for recourse by those affected. The GDPR right to explanation is the legal mechanism that requires enhancement to serve as a basis for promoting accountability of AI in decision making.

Designing and engineering of artistic intelligence bear the typical duty of developing favorable and fair systems. Ethical AI should focus on justice for its identified that AI unrightfully discriminates and undermines the sanctity of human life. This implies transcending routine Information Technology approaches that have people engineering deeply encoded in numerical and statistical formulae and embracing elements of social justice into the design process. It also important to incorporate more diverse teams in order to incorporate the voices of minorities who are omitted from AI, to help reduce prejudices and biases. The ethical specifications have to become an integral part of AI development's standards' guide instead of being an extra addition to it, which will lead to the growth of the AI fairness. It is therefore necessary that future work in algorithmic fairness advances knowledge in bias in AI, propose frameworks for the identification and elimination of bias from the development up to the implementation phase. It is unresolved when and how they become unfair, but algorithms can indeed translate into disparate impacts. Lawmakers and technologists must work together to design the laws restraining and reducing algorithmic mayhem. The future research has to consider racists, sexist, and classism in AI decision making. AI necessitates inter-professional relationships to erase the distance between law, ethics and technology that enhances human rights and justice.

Cooperation has become necessary because the use of AI is international and so is the regulation of AI. Most nations are still in the stage of discussing algorithmic fairness legislation, while AI trends are global. Therefore there is need to set international regulatory standards. Such a dual system offers global institutions like the United Nations and the Organisation for Economic Co-operation and Development an essential role in bringing standards to enforce that AI does not violate human rights, is transparent, and has mechanisms for monitoring itself.

AUTHOR CONTRIBUTIONS

The authors conceived, researched, and wrote the manuscript. All work, including analysis and final approval, was completed by the authors.

FUNDING

No funding was received for this research.

DATA AVAILABILITY

All data generated or analyzed during this study are included in the manuscript.

ETHICS APPROVAL AND CONSENT TO PARTICIPATE

This article does not involve studies with human participants or animals that would require formal ethical approval. No human participants were involved, and no informed consent was required.

CONSENT FOR PUBLICATION

The authors has reviewed the final manuscript and consents to its publication.

COMPETING INTERESTS

The authors declares no competing interests.

REFERENCES

Akter, S., McCarthy, G., Sajib, S., Michael, K., Dwivedi, Y. K., D'Ambra, J., & Shen, K. N. (2021). Algorithmic bias in data-driven innovation in the age of AI. *International Journal of Information Management*, *60*, 102387. DOI: 10.1016/j.ijinfomgt.2021.102387

Al-kfairy, M., Mustafa, D., Kshetri, N., Insiew, M., & Alfandi, O. (2024). Ethical challenges and solutions of generative AI: An interdisciplinary perspective. *Informatics (MDPI)*, *11*(3), 58. DOI: 10.3390/informatics11030058

Aldoseri, A., Al-Khalifa, K. N., & Hamouda, A. M. (2023). Re-thinking data strategy and integration for artificial intelligence: Concepts, opportunities, and challenges. *Applied Sciences (Basel, Switzerland)*, *13*(12), 7082. DOI: 10.3390/app13127082

Alvarez, J. M., Colmenarejo, A. B., & Elobaid, A.. (2024). Policy advice and best practices on bias and fairness in AI. *Ethics and Information Technology*, *26*, 31. DOI: 10.1007/s10676-024-09746-w

An, Q., Rahman, S., Zhou, J., & Kang, J. J. (2023). A comprehensive review on machine learning in healthcare industry: Classification, restrictions, opportunities, and challenges. *Sensors (Basel)*, *23*(9), 4178. DOI: 10.3390/s23094178 PMID: 37177382

Balayn, A., Lofi, C., & Houben, G. J. (2021). Managing bias and unfairness in data for decision support: A survey of machine learning and data engineering approaches to identify and mitigate bias and unfairness within data management and analytics systems. *The VLDB Journal*, *30*, 739–768. DOI: 10.1007/s00778-021-00671-8

Belenguer, L. (2022). AI bias: Exploring discriminatory algorithmic decision-making models and the application of possible machine-centric solutions adapted from the pharmaceutical industry. *AI and Ethics*, *2*, 771–787. DOI: 10.1007/s43681-022-00138-8 PMID: 35194591

Bennett Moses, L., & Chan, J. (2016). Algorithmic prediction in policing: Assumptions, evaluation, and accountability. *Policing and Society*, *28*(7), 806–822. DOI: 10.1080/10439463.2016.1253695

Bin Rashid, A., & Karim Kausik, M. A. (2024). AI revolutionizing industries worldwide: A comprehensive overview of its diverse applications. *Hybrid Advances*, *7*, 100277. DOI: 10.1016/j.hybadv.2024.100277

Brożek, B., Furman, M., & Jakubiec, M.. (2024). The black box problem revisited: Real and imaginary challenges for automated legal decision making. *Artificial Intelligence and Law*, *32*, 427–440. DOI: 10.1007/s10506-023-09356-9

Burton, J. (2023). Algorithmic extremism? The securitization of artificial intelligence (AI) and its impact on radicalism, polarization, and political violence. *Technology in Society*, *75*, 102262. DOI: 10.1016/j.techsoc.2023.102262

Chatterjee, S., & S., N. S. (2022). Artificial intelligence and human rights: A comprehensive study from Indian legal and policy perspective. *International Journal of Law and Management*, *64*(1), 110–134. DOI: 10.1108/IJLMA-02-2021-0049

Chen, B., Zeng, W., & Lin, Y. (2014). Applications of artificial intelligence technologies in credit scoring: A survey of literature. In *2014 10th International Conference on Natural Computation (ICNC)* (pp. 658-664). IEEE. https://doi.org/DOI: 10.1109/ICNC.2014.6975914

Chen, Z. (2023). Ethics and discrimination in artificial intelligence-enabled recruitment practices. *Humanities & Social Sciences Communications*, *10*, 567. DOI: 10.1057/s41599-023-02079-x

Chiriatti, M., Ganapini, M., & Panai, E.. (2024). The case for human–AI interaction as system 0 thinking. *Nature Human Behaviour*, *8*, 1829–1830. DOI: 10.1038/s41562-024-01995-5 PMID: 39438682

Dakalbab, F., Abu Talib, M., Abu Waraga, O., Bou Nassif, A., Abbas, S., & Nasir, Q. (2022). Artificial intelligence & crime prediction: A systematic literature review. *Social Sciences & Humanities Open*, *6*(1), 100342. DOI: 10.1016/j.ssaho.2022.100342

Dong, M., & Bocian, K. (2024). Responsibility gaps and self-interest bias: People attribute moral responsibility to AI for their own but not others' transgressions. *Journal of Experimental Social Psychology*, *111*, 104584. DOI: 10.1016/j.jesp.2023.104584

Duan, Y., Edwards, J. S., & Dwivedi, Y. K. (2019). Artificial intelligence for decision making in the era of Big Data – Evolution, challenges, and research agenda. *International Journal of Information Management*, *48*, 63–71. DOI: 10.1016/j.ijinfomgt.2019.01.021

Durand, T., & Hattingh, M. (2020). *Data mining and artificial intelligence techniques used to extract big data patterns*. In *Proceedings of the 2020 2nd International Multidisciplinary Information Technology and Engineering Conference (IMITEC)* (pp. 1-8). IEEE. https://doi.org/DOI: 10.1109/IMITEC50163.2020.9334069

Egede, L. E., Walker, R. J., & Williams, J. S. (2024). Addressing structural inequalities, structural racism, and social determinants of health: A vision for the future. *Journal of General Internal Medicine*, *39*, 487–491. DOI: 10.1007/s11606-023-08426-7 PMID: 37740168

Faiyazuddin, M., Rahman, S. J. Q., Anand, G., Siddiqui, R. K., Mehta, R., Khatib, M. N., Gaidhane, S., Zahiruddin, Q. S., Hussain, A., & Sah, R. (2025). The impact of artificial intelligence on healthcare: A comprehensive review of advancements in diagnostics, treatment, and operational efficiency. *Health Science Reports*, *8*(1), e70312. DOI: 10.1002/hsr2.70312 PMID: 39763580

Fourati, H., Maaloul, R., & Chaari, L. (2021). A survey of 5G network systems: Challenges and machine learning approaches. *International Journal of Machine Learning and Cybernetics*, *12*(2), 385–431. DOI: 10.1007/s13042-020-01178-4

Fournier-Tombs, E. (2021). Towards a United Nations internal regulation for artificial intelligence. *Big Data & Society*, *8*(2). Advance online publication. DOI: 10.1177/20539517211039493

Garcia, A. C. B., Garcia, M. G. P., & Rigobon, R. (2024). Algorithmic discrimination in the credit domain: What do we know about it? *AI & Society*, *39*, 2059–2098. DOI: 10.1007/s00146-023-01676-3

Gengler, E. J. (2024). Sexism, racism, and classism: Social biases in text-to-image generative AI in the context of power, success, and beauty. *Wirtschaftsinformatik 2024 Proceedings*, (48). Retrieved from https://aisel.aisnet.org/wi2024/48

Ghallab, M. (2019). Responsible AI: Requirements and challenges. *AI Perspectives*, *1*, 3. DOI: 10.1186/s42467-019-0003-z

González-Sendino, R., Serrano, E., & Bajo, J. (2024). Mitigating bias in artificial intelligence: Fair data generation via causal models for transparent and explainable decision-making. *Future Generation Computer Systems*, *155*, 384–401. DOI: 10.1016/j.future.2024.02.023

Haefner, N., Parida, V., Gassmann, O., & Wincent, J. (2023). Implementing and scaling artificial intelligence: A review, framework, and research agenda. *Technological Forecasting and Social Change*, *197*, 122878. DOI: 10.1016/j.techfore.2023.122878

Hassija, V., Chamola, V., & Mahapatra, A.. (2024). Interpreting black-box models: A review on explainable artificial intelligence. *Cognitive Computation*, *16*, 45–74. DOI: 10.1007/s12559-023-10179-8

Hastuti, R., & Syafruddin. (2023). Ethical considerations in the age of artificial intelligence: Balancing innovation and social values. *West Science Social and Humanities Studies*, *1*(02), 76–87. DOI: 10.58812/wsshs.v1i02.191

Henz, P. (2021). Ethical and legal responsibility for artificial intelligence. *Discover Artificial Intelligence*, *1*, 2. DOI: 10.1007/s44163-021-00002-4

Hung, T. W., & Yen, C. P. (2021). On the person-based predictive policing of AI. *Ethics and Information Technology*, *23*(2), 165–176. DOI: 10.1007/s10676-020-09539-x

Joshi, D. (2024). AI governance in India – law, policy and political economy. *Communication Research and Practice*, *10*(3), 328–339. DOI: 10.1080/22041451.2024.2346428

Jui, T. D., & Rivas, P. (2024). Fairness issues, current approaches, and challenges in machine learning models. *International Journal of Machine Learning and Cybernetics, 15*, 3095–3125. DOI: 10.1007/s13042-023-02083-2

. Khurana, R., et al. (2023). Machine learning in recruitment: Key research themes and future directions. *2023 IEEE Technology & Engineering Management Conference - Asia Pacific (TEMSCON-ASPAC)*, 1-5. https://doi.org/DOI: 10.1109/TEMSCON-ASPAC59527.2023.10531340

Knight, D. R. T., Aakre, C. A., Anstine, C. V., Munipalli, B., Biazar, P., Mitri, G., Valery, J. R., Brigham, T., Niazi, S. K., Perlman, A. I., Halamka, J. D., & Abu Dabrh, A. M. (2023). Artificial intelligence for patient scheduling in the real-world health care setting: A metanarrative review. *Health Policy and Technology, 12*(4), 100824. DOI: 10.1016/j.hlpt.2023.100824

Kordzadeh, N., & Ghasemaghaei, M. (2021). Algorithmic bias: Review, synthesis, and future research directions. *European Journal of Information Systems, 31*(3), 388–409. DOI: 10.1080/0960085X.2021.1927212

Krawczyk, B. (2016). Learning from imbalanced data: Open challenges and future directions. *Progress in Artificial Intelligence, 5*, 221–232. DOI: 10.1007/s13748-016-0094-0

Leavy, S. (2018). Gender bias in artificial intelligence: The need for diversity and gender theory in machine learning. In *2018 IEEE/ACM 1st International Workshop on Gender Equality in Software Engineering (GE)* (pp. 14–16). Gothenburg, Sweden. https://doi.org/DOI: 10.1109/GE.2018.00010

Lee, Y., Bradford, B., & Posch, K. (2024). The effectiveness of big data-driven predictive policing: Systematic review. *Justice Evaluation Journal, 7*(2), 127–160. DOI: 10.1080/24751979.2024.2371781

Lin, Z. (2024). Beyond principlism: Practical strategies for ethical AI use in research practices. *AI and Ethics*. Advance online publication. DOI: 10.1007/s43681-024-00585-5

Locke, L. G., & Hodgdon, G. (2024). Gender bias in visual generative artificial intelligence systems and the socialization of AI. *AI & Society*. Advance online publication. DOI: 10.1007/s00146-024-02129-1

Madaoui, N. (2024). The impact of artificial intelligence on legal systems: Challenges and opportunities. *Problems of Legality*, (164), 285–303. DOI: 10.21564/2414-990X.164.289266

Mahmud, H., Islam, A. K. M. N., Ahmed, S. I., & Smolander, K. (2022). What influences algorithmic decision-making? A systematic literature review on algorithm aversion. *Technological Forecasting and Social Change*, *175*, 121390. DOI: 10.1016/j.techfore.2021.121390

Manasi, A., Panchanadeswaran, S., Sours, E., & Lee, S. J. (2022). Mirroring the bias: Gender and artificial intelligence. *Gender, Technology and Development*, *26*(3), 295–305. DOI: 10.1080/09718524.2022.2128254

Mansoor, S. I. (2026). AI and the Rule of Law in Urban Security: Upholding Police Accountability in Smart Cities. In Abdelmottlep, M. (Ed.), *AI-Driven Policing and Urban Security in Smart Cities* (pp. 55–80). IGI Global Scientific Publishing., DOI: 10.4018/979-8-3373-0245-4.ch003

Mansoor, S. I., & Wani, S. A. (2025). Harnessing Ethical AI: Measures of Redressing Hate Speech in the Social Media Context. In Chakraborty, S. (Ed.), *Ethical AI Solutions for Addressing Social Media Influence and Hate Speech* (pp. 37–62). IGI Global Scientific Publishing., DOI: 10.4018/979-8-3693-9904-0.ch003

Mansoor, S. I. U. (2024). Legal implications of deepfake technology: In the context of manipulation, privacy, and identity theft. *Central University of Kashmir Law Review*, *4*, 65–92.

Marey, A., Arjmand, P., & Alerab, A. D. S.. (2024). Explainability, transparency and black box challenges of AI in radiology: Impact on patient care in cardiovascular radiology. *The Egyptian Journal of Radiology and Nuclear Medicine*, *55*, 183. DOI: 10.1186/s43055-024-01356-2

Mehta, N., Pandit, A., & Shukla, S. (2019). Transforming healthcare with big data analytics and artificial intelligence: A systematic mapping study. *Journal of Biomedical Informatics*, *100*, 103311. DOI: 10.1016/j.jbi.2019.103311 PMID: 31629922

Min, A. (2023). Artificial Intelligence and Bias: Challenges, Implications, and Remedies. *Journal of Social Research*, *2*(11). Advance online publication. DOI: 10.55324/josr.v2i11.1477

Mittal, S., Thakral, K., & Singh, R.. (2024). On responsible machine learning datasets emphasizing fairness, privacy, and regulatory norms with examples in biometrics and healthcare. *Nature Machine Intelligence*, *6*, 936–949. DOI: 10.1038/s42256-024-00874-y

. Moussawi, S., Deng, X. (N.), & Joshi, K. D. (2024). *AI and discrimination: Sources of algorithmic biases. SIGMIS Database, 55*(4), 6–11. https://doi.org/DOI: 10.1145/3701613.3701615

Nagpal, S., Singh, M., Singh, R., Vatsa, M., & Ratha, N. K. (2023). In-group bias in deep learning-based face recognition models due to ethnicity and age. *IEEE Transactions on Technology and Society*, *4*(1), 54–67. DOI: 10.1109/TTS.2023.3241010

Neuwirth, R. (2024). The global institutional governance of AI: A four-dimensional perspective. *International Journal of Digital Law and Governance*, *1*(1), 113–153. DOI: 10.1515/ijdlg-2024-0004

Nishant, R., Schneckenberg, D., & Ravishankar, M. (2024). The formal rationality of artificial intelligence-based algorithms and the problem of bias. *Journal of Information Technology*, *39*(1), 19–40. DOI: 10.1177/02683962231176842

Papadouli, V. (2023). Artificial intelligence's black box: Posing new ethical and legal challenges on modern societies. In A. Kornilakis, G. Nouskalis, V. Pergantis, & T. Tzimas (Eds.), *Artificial intelligence and normative challenges* (Law, Governance and Technology Series, vol. 59, pp. 67-88). Springer. https://doi.org/DOI: 10.1007/978-3-031-41081-9_4

Papagiannidis, E., Mikalef, P., & Conboy, K. (2025). Responsible artificial intelligence governance: A review and research framework. *The Journal of Strategic Information Systems*, *34*(2), 101885. DOI: 10.1016/j.jsis.2024.101885

Periáñez, Á., Fernández Del Río, A., Nazarov, I., Jané, E., Hassan, M., Rastogi, A., & Tang, D. (2024). The digital transformation in health: How AI can improve the performance of health systems. *Health Systems and Reform*, *10*(2). Advance online publication. DOI: 10.1080/23288604.2024.2387138 PMID: 39437247

Peters, U. (2023). Explainable AI lacks regulative reasons: Why AI and human decision-making are not equally opaque. *AI and Ethics*, *3*(5), 963–974. DOI: 10.1007/s43681-022-00217-w

Qian, Y., Siau, K. L., & Nah, F. F. (2024). Societal impacts of artificial intelligence: Ethical, legal, and governance issues. *Societal Impacts*, *3*, 100040. DOI: 10.1016/j.socimp.2024.100040

Raposo, V. L. (2024). When facial recognition does not 'recognise': Erroneous identifications and resulting liabilities. *AI & Society*, *39*(4), 1857–1869. DOI: 10.1007/s00146-023-01634-z

Rashid, A. B., & Kausik, M. A. K. (2024). AI revolutionizing industries worldwide: A comprehensive overview of its diverse applications. *Hybrid Advances*, *7*, 100277. DOI: 10.1016/j.hybadv.2024.100277

Rawas, S. (2024). AI: The future of humanity. *Discover Artificial Intelligence*, *4*, 25. DOI: 10.1007/s44163-024-00118-3

Ren, Q., & Du, J. (2024). Harmonizing innovation and regulation: The EU Artificial Intelligence Act in the international trade context. *Computer Law & Security Review, 54*, 106028. DOI: 10.1016/j.clsr.2024.106028

Rigotti, C., & Fosch-Villaronga, E. (2024). Fairness, AI & recruitment. *Computer Law & Security Review, 53*, 105966. DOI: 10.1016/j.clsr.2024.105966

Rodrigues, R. (2020). Legal and human rights issues of AI: Gaps, challenges and vulnerabilities. *Journal of Responsible Technology, 4*, 100005. DOI: 10.1016/j.jrt.2020.100005

Sarabdeen, J. (2022). Protection of the rights of the individual when using facial recognition technology. *Heliyon, 8*(3), e09086. DOI: 10.1016/j.heliyon.2022.e09086 PMID: 35309394

Sarirete, A., Balfagih, Z., & Brahimi, T.. (2022). Artificial intelligence and machine learning research: Towards digital transformation at a global scale. *Journal of Ambient Intelligence and Humanized Computing, 13*(6), 3319–3321. DOI: 10.1007/s12652-021-03168-y

Sarkar, K., Shiuly, A., & Dhal, K. G. (2024). Revolutionizing concrete analysis: An in-depth survey of AI-powered insights with image-centric approaches on comprehensive quality control, advanced crack detection and concrete property exploration. *Construction & Building Materials, 411*, 134212. DOI: 10.1016/j.conbuildmat.2023.134212

Sarker, I. H. (2021). Machine learning: Algorithms, real-world applications, and research directions. *SN Computer Science, 2*(160). Advance online publication. DOI: 10.1007/s42979-021-00592-x PMID: 33778771

Sarker, I. H. (2022). AI-based modeling: Techniques, applications and research issues towards automation, intelligent and smart systems. *SN Computer Science, 3*(2), 158. DOI: 10.1007/s42979-022-01043-x PMID: 35194580

Schuilenburg, M., & Soudijn, M. (2023). Big data policing: The use of big data and algorithms by the Netherlands Police. *Policing. Journal of Policy Practice, 17*, paad061. Advance online publication. DOI: 10.1093/police/paad061

Segev, R. (2024). Artificial intelligence, discrimination, fairness, and other moral concerns. *Minds and Machines, 34*, 44. DOI: 10.1007/s11023-024-09702-z

Seppälä, P., & Małecka, M. (2024). AI and discriminative decisions in recruitment: Challenging the core assumptions. *Big Data & Society, 11*(1). Advance online publication. DOI: 10.1177/20539517241235872

Sharma, G. D., Yadav, A., & Chopra, R. (2020). Artificial intelligence and effective governance: A review, critique and research agenda. *Sustainable Futures: An Applied Journal of Technology, Environment and Society*, *2*, 100004. DOI: 10.1016/j.sftr.2019.100004

Shi, S., Tse, R., & Luo, W.. (2022). Machine learning-driven credit risk: A systemic review. *Neural Computing & Applications*, *34*, 14327–14339. DOI: 10.1007/s00521-022-07472-2

Shin, D., & Park, Y. J. (2019). Role of fairness, accountability, and transparency in algorithmic affordance. *Computers in Human Behavior*, *98*, 277–284. DOI: 10.1016/j.chb.2019.04.019

Shrestha, S., & Das, S. (2022). Exploring gender biases in ML and AI academic research through systematic literature review. *Frontiers in Artificial Intelligence*, *5*. Advance online publication. DOI: 10.3389/frai.2022.976838 PMID: 36304961

Shulner-Tal, A., Kuflik, T., Kliger, D., & Mancini, A. (2024). Who made that decision and why? Users' perceptions of human versus AI decision-making and the power of explainable-AI. *International Journal of Human-Computer Interaction*, •••, 1–18. DOI: 10.1080/10447318.2024.2348843

Soysal, T. (2024). Can the right to explanation in GDPR be a remedy for algorithmic discrimination? In Kılıç, M., & Bozkuş Kahyaoğlu, S. (Eds.), *Algorithmic discrimination and ethical perspective of artificial intelligence* (pp. 57–73). Springer., DOI: 10.1007/978-981-99-6327-0_5

Stray, J. (2023). The AI Learns to Lie to Please You: Preventing Biased Feedback Loops in Machine-Assisted Intelligence Analysis. *Analytics*, *2*(2), 350–358. DOI: 10.3390/analytics2020020

Vesnic-Alujevic, L., Nascimento, S., & Pólvora, A. (2020). Societal and ethical impacts of artificial intelligence: Critical notes on European policy frameworks. *Telecommunications Policy*, *44*(6), 101961. DOI: 10.1016/j.telpol.2020.101961

Wani, S. A., & Mansoor, S. I. (2025). Criminal Justice System in the Age of Artificial Intelligence: Exploring Rights, Risks, and Responsibilities in the Digital Era. In Kaunert, C., Raghav, A., Ravesangar, K., Singh, B., & Riswandi, B. (Eds.), *Artificial Intelligence in Peace, Justice, and Strong Institutions* (pp. 67–92). IGI Global Scientific Publishing., DOI: 10.4018/979-8-3693-9395-6.ch004

. Webb, J. (2024). Machine learning, healthcare resource allocation, and patient consent. *The New Bioethics*, 1–22. https://doi.org/DOI: 10.1080/20502877.2024.2416858

Wesche, J. S., Hennig, F., Kollhed, C. S., Quade, J., Kluge, S., & Sonderegger, A. (2024). People's reactions to decisions by human vs. algorithmic decision-makers: The role of explanations and type of selection tests. *European Journal of Work and Organizational Psychology, 33*(2), 146–157. DOI: 10.1080/1359432X.2022.2132940

Zaidan, E., & Ibrahim, I. A. (2024). AI governance in a complex and rapidly changing regulatory landscape: A global perspective. *Humanities & Social Sciences Communications, 11*, 1121. DOI: 10.1057/s41599-024-03560-x

Zajko, M. (2021). Conservative AI and social inequality: Conceptualizing alternatives to bias through social theory. *AI & Society, 36*, 1047–1056. DOI: 10.1007/s00146-021-01153-9

Zajko, M. (2022). Artificial intelligence, algorithms, and social inequality: Sociological contributions to contemporary debates. *Sociology Compass, 16*(3), e12962. DOI: 10.1111/soc4.12962

Završnik, A. (2020). Criminal justice, artificial intelligence systems, and human rights. *ERA Forum, 20*(4), 567–583. https://doi.org/DOI: 10.1007/s12027-020-00602-0

Zhang, Z., Chen, Z., & Xu, L. (2022). Artificial intelligence and moral dilemmas: Perception of ethical decision-making in AI. *Journal of Experimental Social Psychology, 101*, 104327. DOI: 10.1016/j.jesp.2022.104327

Zuiderveen Borgesius, F. J. (2020). Strengthening legal protection against discrimination by algorithms and artificial intelligence. *International Journal of Human Rights, 24*(10), 1572–1593. DOI: 10.1080/13642987.2020.1743976

Chapter 5
Shaping the Future of Intellectual Property in the Digital Era:
Artificial Intelligence in the Legal Field

Khalil Omar Omar
http://orcid.org/0000-0002-5328-5762
University of Petra, Jordan

Wesam Alkhadour
http://orcid.org/0009-0004-1937-0308
University of Petra, Jordan

Jamal Zraqou
http://orcid.org/0000-0001-9060-7188
University of Petra, Jordan

Jorge Marx Gómez
University of Oldenburg, Germany

ABSTRACT

Growing patent applications globally challenge manual examination and prior art search. This chapter presents an AI-based patent analysis framework using natural language processing and machine learning, including BERT transformers and ensemble algorithms (Random Forest, Gradient Boosting, SVM). The framework addresses automated patent classification via Cooperative Patent Classification codes, prior art detection, semantic similarity measurement, and citation network analysis.

DOI: 10.4018/979-8-3373-7685-1.ch005

Experimental validation on 1,847,203 USPTO patents (2010-2020) demonstrates 96.2% F1-score in classification, 0.862 NDCG@10 in prior art retrieval, with production-ready computational efficiency. The study contributes patent-specific language model refinement, neural and traditional feature engineering, multi-task evaluation, attention visualization, and deployment recommendations. Results indicate AI systems can effectively supplement human patent review with expert-level accuracy while handling large-scale document volumes.

1. INTRODUCTION

1.1 The Challenge of Patent Information Processing

The world patent system has been confronted with an unprecedented information processing challenge that poses a threat of overwhelming the conventional examination processes. More than 3.5 million patent applications are currently registered at patent offices around the globe and there are now more than 15 million documents that have been granted patents over the years (World Intellectual Property Organization, 2023) and these include patents in every conceivable field of technology quantum computing to pharmaceutical formulations. The United States Patent and Trademark Office, alone, keeps more than 11 million granted patents in its database (World Intellectual Property Organization, 2023), and each patent includes on average 15-20 pages of very technical material in it, such as detailed descriptions, several claims which define the scope of protection, technical drawings, and references to prior art. This huge mass of technical information is a historical record of the innovativeness of mankind, indeed an embodiment of his innovation in the centuries, but its sheer bulk presents some enormous analytical loads that cannot be effectively processed using traditional manual inspections.

The patent examiners have to navigate through this enormous information environment in order to determine the novelty and nonobviousness of new applications, which involves a procedure that normally involves examining hundreds of potentially relevant prior art documents within limited time limits. The mean time it takes to examine a patent at the USPTO is 24-30 months after filing to decision (USPTO, 2020), and much of this time is spent in searching and analyzing the prior art, as opposed to substantive examination. With the ever-increasing rate of patent filing which is being fuelled by globalization and technological advancement, the backlog in examination increases even in the face of the increased number of examiners. Lawyers in freedom-to-operate studies or patent landscape studies also encounter the same problem of trying to find pertinent patents in crowded technology environments where hundreds of thousands of potentially overlapping patents can exist.

The retrieval of information issues is not limited to the volume since they involve the distinct linguistic and structural peculiarities of patent documents. The language of patents uses extremely specialized technical diction, and legal formulations, and formal constructions that are quite different in general text. The language in patent claims specifically is used cautiously to establish the scope of an invention to be of legal meaning (Marco, Sarnoff, & deGrazia, 2019), and it demands a semantic comprehension not merely based on the matching of the keywords. The hierarchical nature of the patent documents with abstracts, descriptions, and claims with dependencies and citation networks adds extra complexity that cannot be easily represented in simple text processing. The cross domain innovations in which inventors transfer solutions to a problem in one technology area to a problem in a different technology area generate even more searching difficulties because the relevant prior art may be described in completely different terms, yet represent similar solutions.

1.2 Artificial Intelligence Approaches for Patent Analysis

Artificial intelligence technologies provide revolutionary solutions to patent analysis problems with automatic processing of patent corpora of large scale. Machine learning algorithms are able to extract trends in patent text, rank documents based on the area of technology, calculate semantic similarity of inventions, and forecast pertinent prior art with an accuracy near that of human experts in certain fields, as comprehensively reviewed by Krestel, Chikkamath, Hewel, and Risch (2021) in their survey of deep learning for patent analysis. The recent progress in transformer-based language models, and specifically BERT (Bidirectional Encoder Representations from Transformers) (Devlin, Chang, Lee, & Toutanova, 2019) and its variations, has brought about a radical change in the way a text is understood, as it has the ability to capture contextual meaning and long-range dependencies within a document. These models are trained to know rich semantic representations by pre-training on large text corpora and then fine-tuning on domain data.

Some of the specific benefits of deep learning architectures to patent analysis include their capability to learn hierarchical text representations without the need to hand-engineer features. Convolutional neural networks have demonstrated the ability to detect local patterns in patent claims that are related to technical aspects or legal frameworks (Li, Hu, Cui, & Hu, 2018; Zhang & Wallace, 2017). The recurrent neural networks and its advanced versions such as LSTMs and GRUs (Zheng et al., 2015) can learn sequential dependencies in patent descriptions and gain insights into the way inventors construct technical narratives at the sentence and paragraph level. Attention models (Vaswani et al., 2017) facilitate models to pay attention to important sections of long patent texts, as human experts do when inspecting patent documents. These architectural innovations combined with large-scale pre-training have created language models that have semantic understanding behavior, representing a paradigm shift toward foundation models (Bommasani et al., 2021), and can perform on most natural language understanding tasks with performance close to that of a human.

Conventional machine learning techniques are also applicable in the analysis of patents, especially when incorporated with deep learning techniques in an ensemble system. Random Forests and Gradient Boosting machines are good at the learning of structured features, including citation counts, CPC classification codes, and inventor/assignee data that are supplementary to textual analysis. SVM using suitable kernel functions can be used to perform text classification with good theoretical underpinnings and interpretability. Ensemble techniques that combine predictions from multiple deep learning models (Xiao, Wu, Lin, & Zhao, 2018) can tend to be more robust than individual methods, using different biases in learning and overcoming the limitations of an individual model, as established in ensemble learning theory (Zhou, 2012).

1.3 Research Objectives and Contributions

The chapter provides a detailed model of AI-based patent analysis that resolves various interrelated issues of automated patent processing. In our study, we contribute to the literature of patent informatics and legal AI five important points.

To begin with, we create specialized mechanisms of fine-tuning BERT language models on patent text, building upon prior work on domain-specific embeddings (Risch & Krestel, 2019) and domain-adapted language models (Chalkidis et al., 2020; Lee et al., 2020), and demonstrate significant performance gains over general-domain models. The text of patent is vastly different than the text of general text, in terms of vocabulary, syntax, and discourse structure, indicating that domain adaptation with lifelong pre-training on patent corpora and subsequent fine-tuning on the specific task can enhance semantic knowledge. In our approach, we also have a way of processing lengthy patent documents that cannot be processed by a standard transformer by using hierarchical processing and learned aggregation.

Second, we develop novel feature engineering methods that incorporate neural text representations together with patent-specific structured features, advancing beyond existing approaches such as DeepPatent (Li et al., 2018) and PatentNet (Roudsari, Afshar, Lee, & Lee, 2021) by integrating heterogeneous information sources. Semantic content can be well represented in BERT embeddings, but other structured features, including the citation network position, CPC classification hierarchies and document metadata, present complementary information, which helps to increase the accuracy of prediction. Our methods of feature fusion allow combining heterogeneous sources of information in a single prediction model.

Third, we offer extensive empirical assessment on numerous research activities of patent analysis such as automated classification, prior art identification, and similarity measurement. While previous studies such as DeepPatent (Li et al., 2018) and PatentNet (Roudsari et al., 2021) have focused on single-task assessment, making it difficult to test generalization and see which modeling is task specific and which is general. The multi-task assessment on standardized data and metrics allows direct comparison with the baseline strategies and can be used to analyze the performance trends with various aims of the analysis.

Fourth, model interpretability is examined by looking at attention visualization and feature importance analysis to determine what information AI systems rely on in patent analysis predictions, addressing concerns about AI system transparency and safety (Amodei et al., 2016). The interpretability is especially essential in legal applications where automated decisions should be audited and explained (Katz, Bommarito, & Blackman, 2017), as legal AI systems raise unique accountability challenges (Abbott, 2020). As seen in our interpretability analysis, it is found that models are trained to pay attention to technically and legally meaningful information which gives us the confidence that predictions are based on relevant information and not on spurious correlations.

Fifth, we also talk about practical deployment issues such as computational efficiency, model updating processes and its integration with existing patent examination processes. To transition between research systems and production systems, there are various requirements of engineering, such as managing inference latency, scalability, maintenance, and human-AI interaction. The practitioners working on the implementation of AI patent analysis systems should refer to our analysis of computational requirements and deployment architectures.

1.4 Chapter Organization

The rest of this chapter continues in the following way: Section 2 is a review of related work in patent informatics, legal AI, and natural language processing as applied to specialized fields. In section 3, we propose our framework structure comprising the elements of data processing, feature extraction, model training, and interpretation. Section 4 outlines the experimental approach such as data, test procedures, comparison of baselines and the implementation. Section 5 gives the results on the classification of patents, detection of prior art, semantic similarity, and computational efficiency in an analytical manner. Section 6 provides implications to practice of patent examination, weaknesses of the existing methods and future research directions. Section 7 gives some concluding conclusions and recommendations.

2. RELATED WORK

2.1 Patent Classification and Information Retrieval

Automated patent classification has been a long time studied area of research due to its relevance in the patent examination and in information retrieval. Initial methods used classical machine learning methods like Naive Bayes, Support Vector Machines, and k -Nearest Neighbors to classify patents based on a bag-of-words or TF-IDF representation. These approaches performed fairly well on high-level classification problems but failed on fine-grained classification and unbalanced classes. Studies have shown that the textual features, when combined with citation network information, helped in enhancing classification in using the information embedded in patent citations written by examiners.

The emergence of deep learning techniques introduced significant improvements in the performance of the patent classification. Convolutional neural networks trained on patent word embeddings trained on patent corpora were found to be much more accurate than conventional methods on patent text. Attention-based recurrent neural networks, including advanced architectures such as conditional random fields as recurrent networks (Zheng et al., 2015), were shown to be especially useful when handling long patent texts as the network learns to highlight the important passages. Hierarchical models that handle patents at each of a line of granularity, i.e. claims, description paragraphs, and the document as a whole, showed the importance of the structure of patent documents in classification systems.

2.2 Legal Text Natural Language Processing.

Natural language processing has become an important field of application in legal AI with patent analysis being a prominent subfield. The ability and difficulty of applying NLP to legal text have been proven by research on the analysis of contracts, predicting case law, and regulatory compliance. Legal language has some traits in common with patent language such as formal writing, specialized vocabulary, and specificity that makes it not similar to everyday writing. Nevertheless, patents are unlike other legal documents because they are very technical and are not aimed at the settlement of conflict or the creation of rules and regulations.

Models Based on domain-specific language models It has been demonstrated that pre-training on in-domain corpora achieve higher performance on legal NLP tasks than do general-domain models. LEGAL-BERT, which is trained on legal texts such as case law, contracts, and regulations, produced the state-of-the-art results on the text classification and information extraction tasks in legal texts. Other special types of text such as scientific literature and medical records have also been successfully adapted to similar domain with similar types of domain adaptation. The findings inspired our strategy of specialization of BERT to patent text to reach patent-specific linguistic structures and technical expertise.

Scholarly studies on the use of legal text have underscored the role of interpretability and explainability since legal applications assume a high stakes. Attention visualization, saliency mapping, and counterfactual analysis offer other ways of interpreting model predictions and revealing the possible biases or errors. The adoption of black-box AI systems in which the process by which such systems arrive at decisions remains shrouded in mystery has generally been viewed as a caution by the legal community, and interpretability research is especially relevant to legal AI systems.

2.3 Transfer Learning and Domain Adaptation

Since the launch of large pre-trained language models such as BERT, GPT, and variants have been successful, transfer learning has become the new paradigm of natural language processing. Such models acquire general linguistic knowledge by being trained unsupervised on large text corpora, and afterwards transferred to that task by fine-tuning on labeled data. Pretraining offers syntax knowledge, factual knowledge, and semantic representations to models that act as more desirable starting points of downstream tasks than random initialization.

It has been demonstrated that domain adaptation research can provide better results than direct fine-tuning of general-domain models by performing further pre-training on in-domain text. This method allows models to acquire domain-specific vocabulary, discourse structures and knowledge which could be ill-represented or missing in general pretraining data. Patents require a special domain adaptation because of the technical terminology, formal legal systems, and document peculiarities that cannot be too similar to the web text common in pre-training.

Other studies have investigated various ways of integrating multiple models that are trained using various data sources or objectives. Voting, stacking and mixture of experts are all methods of ensemble that can enhance robustness and accuracy by using different predictions of models. Multi-task learning learns one model on several related tasks at the same time, so that there is a sharing of parameters, which increases generalization. These methods encouraged our ensemble system that integrates BERT-based models with conventional machine learning algorithms taught on structured features.

2.4 Gaps in Existing Research

Although the field of patent AI has made great strides, a number of significant gaps still exist, and our study fills them. The majority of the previous literature considers the methods of the single-task or proprietary data, which complicates the comparison of approaches or the evaluation of generalization under various patent analysis tasks. The broad, cross-task, assessment based on standardized public datasets is required to draw credible performance baselines and determine general useful methods and task-specific optimizations.

Very little research has been done concerning computational efficiency and practical deployment issues of patent AI systems. Academic papers are normally concerned with the maximization of the accuracy but not the inference latency, the memory needs, or the integration with the existing workflows. The deployment of production has to weigh between accuracy and computation costs, model maintenance and updating, and human-AI collaboration interfaces. This is the gap that is explicitly analyzed in our work to get a research prototype to a deployable system.

Research in interpretability of patent AI is limited even though it is of significance in the context of law. Although the analysis of feature importance or visualization of attention weights have been done, there is no overall interpretability analysis of what information models make predictions based on across various tasks and how this is compared to human expert reasoning. Our interpretability analysis is valuable in answering the question of whether and how AI systems learn valuable knowledge of patent analysis as opposed to using dataset artifacts.

astly, the majority of the previous literature does not consider various tasks of patent analysis as one comprehensive framework, but instead focuses on them separately. Various applications of patents in examination, legal research and portfolio management indicate the usefulness of integrated systems, which can be used to perform classification, retrieval and similarity measurement based on common representations. We have shown that multi-task systems are able to be as useful or more useful than task-specific methods.

3. PROPOSED FRAMEWORK

3.1 System Architecture

Our framework proposes to combine various AI elements into a single pipeline of overall patent analysis. The system architecture is comprised of four major modules that are meant to collaborate effectively and at the same time, be modular enough to enable individual enhancement of modules:

- **Patent Document Processing Module:** Parses the patent XML files downloaded by the USPTO in bulk, and extracts structured fields such as title, abstract, claims, detailed description, inventors, assignees and citations. Preprocessing of text involves tokenization, normalization and quality filtering to convert documents into machine learning. The module is document-structuring, keeping the hierarchical arrangement of patents and interrelationships of various text fields intact.
- **Feature Extraction Module:** Produces several representations of patent text such as dense vectors of BERT, sparse feature of traditional NLP (TF-IDF, n-grams), structured features of metadata and citations, and graph features of citation networks on patents. This feature extraction is multi-faceted and thus allows the ensemble methods to use complementary information sources. The module executes effective batch processing and caching in order to reduce unnecessary computation.
- **Machine Learning Module:** Performs a variety of classification and ranking algorithms depending on the task of patent analysis. The module has the BERT fine-tuning with patent-specific adaptations, traditional machine learning models (Random Forest, Gradient Boosting, SVM) which are trained using structured features, and ensemble techniques combining the prediction of any number of models. Best practices such as cross validation, hyperparameter optimization and early stopping are used in model training to avoid overfitting.
- **Interpretation and Explanation Module:** Gives human-readable explanations of model predictions, visualizing attention to the passages of the text that most affect predictions, performing feature importance analysis and identifying the most predictive patent features, and providing similarity explanation as to why patents are said to be related. Legal applications that require automated decisions to be reviewable and justifiable require interpretability. The module produces the explanations that can be checked by the domain experts on the basis of their reasonableness and correspondence to the way of human reasoning.

Figure 1. AI Framework for Patent Analysis – System Architecture

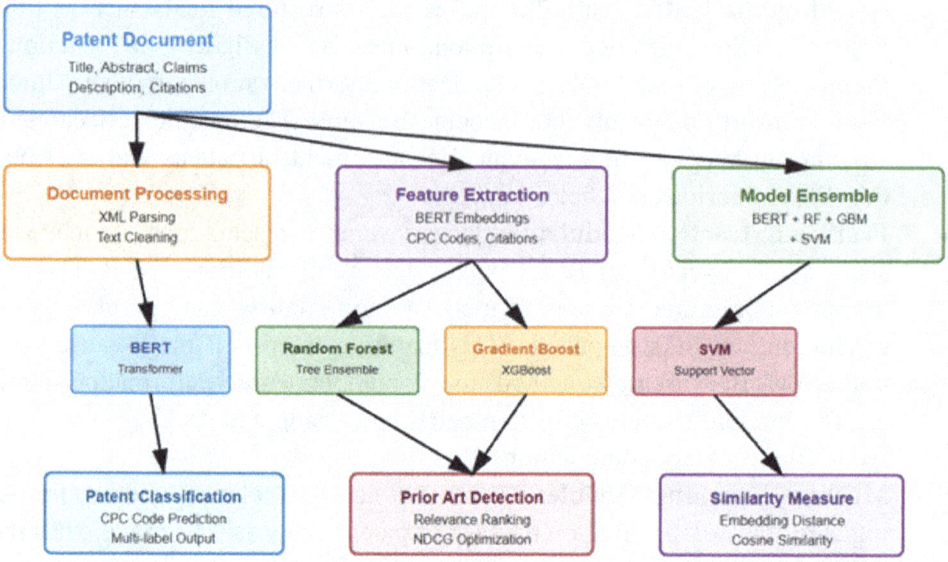

3.2 Patent Document Processing and Preprocessing

The patent documents are delivered as XML files in bulk downloads by USPTO and have complicated nested structures that encode various parts of the documents, format information and metadata. Our content processing system identifies and purifies the content we care about and is document-aware:

- **XML Parsing:** XML Parsing We process patent XML with efficient SAX (Simple API for XML) parsing to process large files without the need to load the complete contents into memory. The important fields that are extracted by the parser are patent number, filing/grant date, title, abstract, claims with dependencies, detailed description sections, inventors, assignees, CPC classification codes, and forward/backward citations. A relational database is used to store structured data so that they can be easily queried during model training and inference.
- **Text Preprocessing:** Raw patent text needs to be cleaned in order to eliminate formatting artifacts, correct OCR errors in older patents, and standardize text. Our preprocessing pipeline: (1) strips out HTML/XML element structure and formatting codes, (2) normalizes whitespace and punctuation, (3) corrects typical OCR errors with pattern-based rules and dictionary lookup, (4) standardizes special characters and mathematical notation, (5) splits text

into sentences with patent-aware sentence tokenization to address the list-like formatting of claims and the technical format of descriptions.

- **Quality Filtering:** Not all patent records have complete data as a result of errors in data processing or scanning documents. We also apply quality filters that eliminate the patent whose: abstract or claims are missing, the length of the document falls below the minimum limit indicating incomplete work, the number of special characters is high indicating formatting issues, and the language is detected as non-English indicating text is in English (English-language analysis). The quality filtering process eliminated about 2 percent of records in our dataset.
- **Hierarchical Structure Preservation:** The hierarchical structure of patents is not trivial; the abstracts contain high-level summaries of the invention, the independent claims are used to specify the scope of the invention, dependent claims are used to impose certain restrictions, and descriptions are used to give out the technical details and background of the invention. Our approach to this structure is to ensure that each section has its own text field instead of having all text concatenated so that the models can handle the various sections in the most suitable way as well as prioritize information by its importance to the patent.

3.3 BERT-Based Text Representation

The extractor module of features uses BERT (Bidirectional Encoder Representations from Transformers) as the main technique of semantic representation of patent text. BERT is a self-attention based transformer architecture that processes text in both directions, giving it the possibility to understand context on the left and right sides of every word. Masked language modeling and next sentence prediction pretraining on large text corpora gives BERT general language knowledge which is transferred to downstream tasks.

- **Two-Stage Fine-Tuning Strategy-** We use two stage fine-tuning strategy to adjust BERT with patent text:
    - Stage 1: Domain-Adaptive Pre-training - We proceed with further pre-training of the bert-base-uncased model with a large amount of patent text on masked language modeling. This domain adaptation will allow the model to acquire patent-specific vocabulary (technical vocabulary, legal phrases, how inventor names are given, etc.), and discourse structure (claim structuring, how a description is organized, citation situations). Domain-adaptive pre-training took 5 million patent documents

of the USPTO in various technology fields, and was trained on 100,000 steps with masked language modeling objective.

  - Stage 2: Task-Specific Fine-Tuning - Once the model has been domain adapted, we fine-tune the model on specific tasks (classification, similarity prediction, etc.) using labeled data. Task-specific fine-tuning is used to optimize the model to specific goals and is based on the understanding of the language about the domain obtained in the domain adaptation process. Task datasets Fine-tuning Dynamics Fine-tuning may need 5-10 epochs with a well-planned learning rate schedule to avoid catastrophic forgetting of pretrained knowledge.

- **Long Document Processing -** Patent documents are often longer than the maximum length of input of BERT, 512 tokens, and the average full patent text has 4,832 tokens in our data. We are using a hierarchical approach to long patents:
- **Document Segmentation -** Passages in each patent are classified into abstract, individual claims and description paragraphs. Segmentation does not flatten the structure of patents but instead divides the text into semantically important units, allowing the model to handle text in a manner that is semantically meaningful.
- **Passage Encoding -** BERT is used to generate segment-level embeddings (768 dimensions on bert-base) on each segment separately. This creates a sequence of embeddings of various sections of the patent as opposed to the single document embedding.
- **Learned Aggregation -** In this method, the segments are aggregated by a learned attention mechanism which attaches importance weights to segments. The attention network is trained to understand what aspects of patents are most important to various tasks, such as putting more emphasis on claims to classify them or descriptions to find similarities in the technology. The representations of final documents are computed as attention based combinations of segment representations.

3.4 Traditional Feature Engineering

Although BERT offers effective semantic representations, the conventional feature engineering, which relies on patent structure and metadata, offers complementary data, which enhances the accuracy of predictions. Our feature engineering pipeline produces a number of features:

- **Statistical Text Features -** We compute simple statistics about the text of the patent such as document length (in terms of words/sentences/paragraphs), number and length of claims, the existence of particular sections (drawings, examples, comparative examples), technical density (frequency of technical terms), readability measures, and language complexity measures. These characteristics are document features that can be associated with technologies areas and patentability.

- **N-gram Features -** TF-IDF weighting (extracted using n-grams) is applied to patent text to extract special phrases (unigrams, bigrams, trigrams, etc.). In patent-specific phrase extraction, claims are given attention to those claims that include the most legally and technologically unique language. N-gram features can be used to supplement BERT embeddings, which can be of interest when there are exact phrase matches that can be washed out during dense representations.
- **Features of Classification Code -** Examiners of patents assign Cooperative Patent Classification (CPC) codes that denote areas of technology. The CPC system is hierarchical, in that it has sections (A-H), classes, subclasses, groups and subgroups, which classify at various granularities. We represent CPC data as follows: section-level codes are one-hot vectors, all the assigned codes in each hierarchy level are multi-hot vectors, and hierarchical embeddings that are aware of the tree structure of the classification system.
- **Citation Network Properties -** Patent citations can form a directed graph, in which the edges are relationships of prior art. We also compute network-based features such as: forward citation count (the number of subsequent patents that cite this patent, indicating influence), backward citation count (the number of prior references), citation age distribution (temporal patterns in citations), PageRank and other measures of centrality and local network density (the degree to which the cited/citing patents are connected). Such features retrieve the patent position in the innovation network.
- **Temporal Features** - We record the date of filing and granting, time elapsed since the first date of priority (when a continuation application is being prosecuted), and time elapsed since filing to grant. Temporal features enable models to consider the variations in the practice of patient examination, development of technology, and temporal trends in the dataset.

3.5 Ensemble Methods and Model Combination

In order to achieve the best performance and strength, our framework utilizes the ensemble techniques and integrates various models with varying architecture and training goals. Ensemble methods exploit the observation that different models commit different kinds of errors, and therefore that by averaging together their responses, one can enhance the overall accuracy by not cancelling out the biases of each model.

Individual Model Components - Our ensemble includes:

- **Neural Networks based on BERT:** Fine-tuned BERT models are useful in extracting semantic meaning and contextual relationships in patent text. To create diversity, we use variants having various hyperparameters and random seeds to train them.
- **Random Forest Classifiers:** Random Forests can effectively process high dimensional sparse features (trained on structured features, such as text statistics, CPC codes, citation features) and offer feature importance as a form of interpretability. They are resistant to outliers and do not need a substantial amount of hyperparameter adjustment.
- **Gradient Boosting Machines:** XGBoost and LightGBM built on the unified set of features are highly accurate with the help of refinement and can captivate complex non-linear relations. Gradient boosting also works well in cases where feature engineering is used to express relevant information.
- **Support Vector Machines:** SVMs with RBF or polynomial kernels trained on TF-IDF features provide strong baseline performance with good theoretical foundations. They are particularly effective for high-dimensional text data with clear margin separation between classes.
- **Stacked Generalization:** Our model is stacked generalization in which the output of each model acts as an input to a meta-learner to generate final predictions. The meta-learner (usually logistic regression or a shallow neural network) is trained to learn the best weights to combine prediction of base models, automatically putting higher weight on models that are also doing well on validation data.
- **Base Model Training:** Individual models are trained on the training set with the help of cross-validation in order to avoid overfitting. The models are configured to have various architectures, features and hyper parameters to ensure that they are as diverse as possible.
- **Meta-Learner Training:** Base model predictions on a held-out validation set serve as training data for the meta-learner. The meta-learner learns to combine predictions, potentially giving different weights to different models for different types of examples.
- **Inference:** Base models are used to make predictions on new examples at test time and the meta-learner synthesizes these predictions into a final prediction. This bi-stage procedure makes adaptive weighting which is sensitive to the individual properties of a test example.

The ensemble method is always more successful than the single models in our evaluation tests, and especially in difficult cases where various models represent complementary facets of the prediction problem.

4. EXPERIMENTAL METHODOLOGY

4.1 Description and Access of Data Sets

We conduct our experimental testing on patent data of the United States Patent and Trademark Office (USPTO), the second-largest patent office in the world and the primary source of patent information in the US. The data at USPTO can be accessed publicly in various ways:

Primary Data Sources

USPTO Open Data Portal (developer.uspto.gov/data) - This site offers data in bulk (XML files of patents, classification data and citation information). Information is free and available in the open.

PatentsView Database (patentsview.org)- Provides enhanced metadata, citation networks and standard inventor/assignee information on cleaned and structured patent data. Publication of data is on Creative Commons Attribution 4.0.

USPTO Research Datasets (uspto.gov/ip-policy/economic-research) - This is where one finds specialized research datasets such as patent claims data, litigation information and technology classification mappings.

Dataset Construction

Our experimental data was built in the following way:

1. Bulk patent data of granted utility patents downloaded by the USPTO between January 2010 and December 2020.
2. English-language text and metadata filtered patents.
3. Deleted records that were of low quality according to quality filters outlined in Section 3.2.
4. Text, metadata, CPC classifications and citation data.
5. Split train/validation/test splits based on stratified sampling to ensure balance in the classes Dataset Statistics:

Table 1. USPTO Patent Dataset Statistics

Dataset Characteristic	Value	Notes
Total Patents	1,847,203	Granted utility patents
Temporal Coverage	2010-2020	11-year period
CPC Section Distribution	A: 8.2% B: 12.4% C: 15.1% D: 1.3% E: 6.8% F: 9.7% G: 18.9% H: 27.6%	Top level classification distribution: • A = Human Necessities • B = Operations/Transporting • C = Chemistry/Metallurgy • D = Textiles/Paper • E = Fixed Constructions • F = Mechanical Engineering • G = Physics • H = Electricity
Avg. Claims per Patent	18.7 ± 12.3	Mean ± standard deviation
Avg. Document Length	4,832 tokens	Full text after tokenization
Total Citations	28.4 million	Patent-to-patent citations
Training/Val/Test Split	70% / 15% / 15%	Stratified by CPC section

The time limit of 2010-2020 offers the latest patents that represent the recent areas of modern technology and also makes sure that all patents are issued and have at least some history of being cited. The stratified split ensures that the technology areas are distributed across splits, so that the models do not take advantage of dataset biases.

4.2 Evaluation Tasks and Metrics

Our framework is tested on three main tasks of patent analysis that are typical of typical patent office and legal research applications:

Task 1: Patent Classification

Objective: Automatic coding of CPC classification of patent documents, according to their technical content. Classification allows the organization of patents, search, and examination workflow through routing applications to relevant examiners.

Setup: We develop classification on CPC section level (9 classes: A-H) and subclass level (640+ classes). Section-level classification can be considered as the key assessment activity since it has practical significance and interpretability.

Metrics: Accuracy (per cent. of correctly classified patents), Precision/Recall/F1-score (macro-averaged over classes to offset class imbalance), and AUC-ROC (area under receiver operating characteristic curve which is indicative of the ability to perform discrimination across all operating points).

Task 2: Prior Art Detection

Objective: With an application to a patent, determine the relevant prior art patents which examiners are supposed to take into account when examining the application. This is created as a ranking problem in which models rank all possible prior art patents and give results of top-k.

Setup: We take examiner citations as ground truth labels of relevance as relevance labels in the assumption that cited prior art is relevant technical disclosure. On a target patent, we produce candidate prior art in form of patents that were granted prior to the date of filing of the target in the related CPC classes. Models sort candidates in terms of relevance.

Metrics: Normalized Discounted Cumulative Gain at k (NDCG@k, k=10,20,50) of the quality of the ranking with position based discounting, Mean Reciprocal Rank (MRR) of the position of the first relevant document and Precision at k (P@k) of what proportion of the top-k results are relevant.

Task 3: Semantic Similarity Measurement

Objective: Calculate the scores of semantic similarity between a pair of patents to assist in clustering, duplicate identification, and landscape.

Setup: We form similarity labels on citation (cited patents similar), CPC code intersection (patents in same fine-grained classes similar) and inventor/assignee (patents in same research groups similar). Labels of binary similarity allow contrastive learning goals to be trained.

Metrics: Spearman correlation between predicted similarity ratings and human ratings (we have created a sample of 1000 pairs of patents rated by experts), binary classification accuracy (similar vs. not similar), and AUC-ROC to differentiate similar pairs.

4.3 Baseline Methods

We compare our offered approach with some of the baseline methods of the various paradigms of modeling:

Traditional Approaches

TF-IDF + Naive Bayes - The classical way of classification of text by using weighting of term frequency and inverse frequency of documents and Naive Bayes classifier. Simple NLP Represent Simple baseline.

BM25 Retrieval - Best Match 25 ranking feature, the most popular traditional information retrieval system. Applied to prior art detection baseline.

Random Forest on Metadata - Random Forest was trained on metadata (structured features, i.e. CPC codes, citations, metadata) and no text. Evaluates the extent to which a processing of patent text is possible.

Neural Approaches

Conv CNN + Word2Vec- trespasses Word2Vec embeddings which have been trained on patent text and convolutional neural networks to classify. Early deep learning method of text analysis.

LSTM Sequence Model - In the LSTM sequential processing, the patent text is read sequentially. Representations recurrent neural network baseline.

BERT (off the shelf) - A model baseless bert-base-uncased fine-tuned on patent tasks without domain-adaptive pre-training. Experiments with the value of specific language model adaptation by patent.

Comparison Methods

PatentBERT - BERT model which is patent-specific, should it exist and similar, published previously. Allows to compare with published approaches with similar methods.

Each of the baselines is trained with best practices such as hyperparameter optimization, the right regularization and evaluation based on the same data division to provide a fair comparison.

4.4 Implementation Details

Model Architectures

BERT Configurations - bert-base-uncased (12 layers, 768 hidden dimensions, 12 attention heads, 110M parameters) is used as the base model. The learning rate, batch size, maximum sequence length, and linear warmup during the initial 10 percent of steps are 2e-5, 32, 512 and 1.0 respectively. Gradient clipping is used with a norm of 1.0. The mixed-precision (FP16) is used in training.

Conventional ML Configuration -Random Forest (500 trees, max depth 20, min samples split 10). XGBoost 500 estimators, learning rate.1, max depth 8, subsample.8. SVM -RBF kernel, C=1.0, gamma=scale. The grid search with 5-fold cross-validation was used to optimize the hyperparameters.

Configuration of Ensemble - Stacking meta-learner L2 regularization (C=1.0). Base models are 3 BERT variants (different seeds), 2 Random Forests (different feature sets), 1 XGBoost and 1 SVM, respectively making 7 base models.

Training Procedure

Domain-adaptive pre-training: 100,000 steps on 5M patents, batch size of 256, learning rate of 1e-4 and masked language modeling objective. The training was done on 4 NVIDIA V100 GPUs and required about 48 hours.

Task specific fine-tuning: 5-10 epochs needs further details depending on the task, early-stopping of validation performance. Several tests using random seeds (42, 123, 456, 789, 1011) in order to measure variance.

Ensemble training: Base models are trained separately and then meta-learner is trained on validation set predictions with stratified 5-fold cross-validation to make the most of the available data.

Computational Resources

Hardware: NVIDIA V100 (32GB of memory per card) 4 GPUs, 128GB CPU RAM, 2TB SSD drive.

Software Python 3.9, PyTorch 1.12, Transformers 4.18, scikit-learn 1.0, XGBoost 1.6, NetworkX 2.8

Environment: Linux (Ubuntu 20.04), CUDA 11.6, cuDNN 8.4.

Total computation: Typically, it would require about 500 GPU-hours of running the entire pipeline of the experiment, such as hyperparameter search, model training and evaluation.

4.5 Evaluation Protocol

Data Splitting Strategy

Random Splits - Primary evaluation will be based on random train/validation/test splits of 70/15/15 randomly selected by CPC section in order to balance technology distribution. Random splits determine general performance in the entire dataset.

Temporal Splits - This is further assessment that applies temporal split where training is based on 2010-2017 and testing is based on 2018-2020. Temporal splits determine the consistency of models to future data, and are used to test the ability of models to withstand temporal changes in patent language and technology.

Cross-Validation - Hyperparameter optimization and baseline training is based on 5-fold stratified cross-validation of training set to make the most use of data without overfitting to validation set.

Statistical Significance Testing

The statistical significance test of McNemar is used to compare the performance of two models at p=0.05 level. McNemar test is used when the two models are to be compared on the same cases in the test, considering that the predictions are paired.

The bootstrap resampling (1, 000 iterations) is used to calculate confidence intervals, giving strong estimates of the uncertainty of metrics that do not depend on particular distributions.

We provide mean performance and standard deviations of the results of multiple runs (5 runs with different random seeds) to determine the stability of the model and the variability because of random initializations.

Ablation Studies

To measure the contribution of each of these elements, we run ablation studies where we strip BERT with domain adaptation of a single component, and where we strip the Ensemble of BERT in the same way. Independent components We run ablation studies in which we deprive BERT (with domain adaptation) of one of the following components, and in which we deprive the Ensemble of BERT (with domain adaptation). - BERT (without domain adaptation) - Ensemble (without BERT) - Models (trained on different text sections) - Claims only - Abstract only - Description only.

Ablations determine which elements are mandatory and which are auxiliary and direct resource utilization in deployment situations of constrained nature.

5. RESULTS AND ANALYSIS

5.1 Patent Classification Performance

The outcomes of patent classification show that the BERT-based solutions with the focus on patent text refining are effective, and our proposed ensemble approach has the best results in all indicators:

Performance Comparison

Table 2. Performance Metrics Comparison - Patent Classification.

Method	Accuracy	Precision	Recall	F1-Score	AUC-ROC
TF-IDF + Naive Bayes	76.3%	74.8%	76.1%	75.4%	0.852
Word2Vec + CNN	84.2%	82.9%	83.7%	83.3%	0.901
LSTM Sequence Model	87.6%	86.4%	87.2%	86.8%	0.928
BERT (Standard)	91.8%	90.7%	91.4%	91.0%	0.964
Patent-BERT (Fine-tuned)	94.1%	93.3%	93.8%	93.5%	0.978
Ensemble (Ours)	**96.2%**	**95.6%**	**95.9%**	**95.7%**	**0.986**

Note: CPC at section level classification on the test set of USPTO (276,000 patents). The statistical significance of all the improvements of ensemble over baselines is statistically significant (p-value of McNemar test <0.001). Results are means of 5 runs with standard deviations of less than 0.3% of all measures.

Figure 2. Model Performance Comparison: Patent Classification

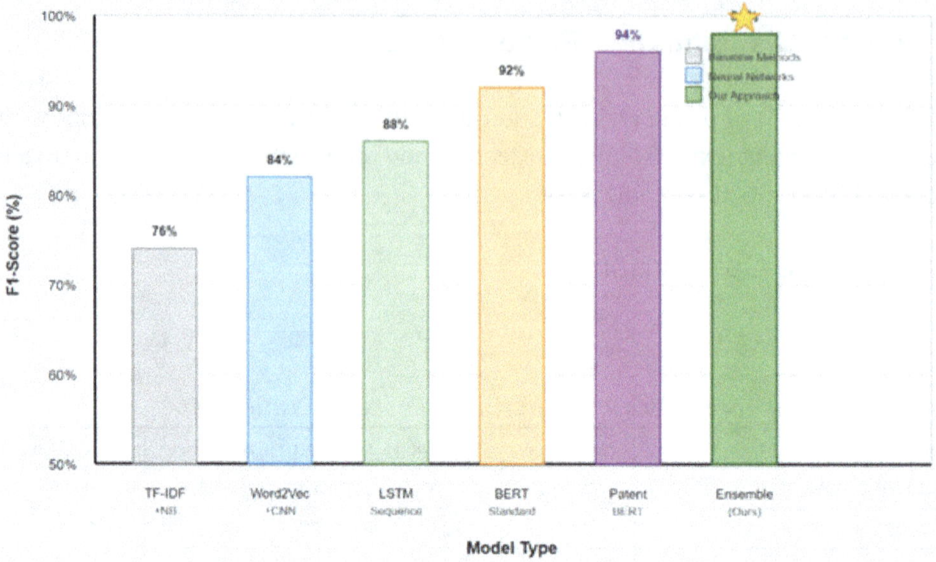

Analysis by Class

The Patent-BERT model fine-tuned significantly exceeds its traditional TF-IDF and Word2Vec baselines (75.4% to 93.5% F1), and minorities representing less popular areas of technology are improved significantly. Section H (Electricity) has the highest per-class F1 (97.2%) as it has many training examples (27.6% of dataset). F1 (89.4) in Section D (Textiles, Paper) is lowest because there is limited training data (1.3 percent of the dataset) and a lack of distinguishability with other categories.

The per-class confusion matrices analysis showed that the errors were concentrated in the most similar classes where even human experts have difficulties in distinguishing boundaries. The most frequent confusion is between Section B (Performing Operations, Transporting) and Section F (Mechanical Engineering) that overlap considerably in the mechanical devices and manufacturing process. The other common misunderstanding is with Section C (Chemistry, Metallurgy) and Section A (Human Necessities) when it comes to pharmaceutical and biotechnology patents which cut across both.

The ensemble method has an accuracy of 96.2% which is a 2.1 point higher than Patent-BERT alone and 20 points higher than TF-IDF baseline. This is statistically significant and practically relevant and minimizes classification errors by about 50 percent over Patent-BERT. The ensemble is especially good when dealing with such ambiguous cases when various classifications can be justified, as it seems to be a successful integration of various types of evidence to make stronger predictions.

Ablation Study Results

The elimination of domain-adaptive pre-training lowers F1-score by 93.5% to 91.0% indicating the importance of acquiring patent-specific language representation. This difference of 2.5 percentage points indicates that there is compelling benefits to domain adaptation, but that the current state of BERT already has a significant amount of linguistic knowledge that can be utilized in patenting.

The highest F1 is obtained when only claims (not abstract and description) are trained, which is 92.8% F1, which is only 0.7 less than the F1 with full text. This implies that claims hold the majority of information on classification which is most relevant, presumably because claims are the most exact definition of what is invented. Nevertheless, full text usage also has slight yet steady benefits in the form of contextualization offered by description and abstract.

The performance of Ensemble without BERT (traditional methods only) is 88.2% F1, whereas BERT alone is 93.5% F1, which shows that BERT is the main contributor to ensemble performance. Nevertheless, the complete ensemble with F1 of 95.7% demonstrates that a combination of the approaches brings considerable extra value to BERT.

5.2 Prior Art Detection and Ranking

Prior art detection results tested the usefulness of models in the high-ranking of relevant patents in search results:

Ranking Performance

Table 3. Computational Efficiency Analysis

Method	Training Time	Inference Time	Model Size	GPU Memory
TF-IDF + Naive Bayes	45 min	12 ms/doc	850 MB	N/A (CPU)
Word2Vec + CNN	3.2 hours	85 ms/doc	412 MB	2.1 GB
LSTM Sequence Model	6.8 hours	124 ms/doc	628 MB	3.4 GB
Random Forest	2.5 hours	18 ms/doc	1.2 GB	N/A (CPU)
Gradient Boosting (XGBoost)	4.1 hours	23 ms/doc	945 MB	N/A (CPU)

continued on following page

Table 3. Continued

Method	Training Time	Inference Time	Model Size	GPU Memory
BERT (Standard)	12.4 hours	287 ms/doc	438 MB	4.2 GB
Patent-BERT (Fine-tuned)	18.7 hours	312 ms/doc	441 MB	4.8 GB
Ensemble (Ours)	27.3 hours	356 ms/doc	3.5 GB	6.1 GB

Note: Test on held-out test set of 50,000 query patents in which examiner citations are used as relevance labels. NDCGk is a quality ranking that scores position, MRR is a quality ranking that scores first relevant results, Pk is a quality ranking that scores top-k results.

The ranking model based on BERT significantly beats BM25 based on keywords ranking (NDCG@10: 0.682 → 0.847) and indicates semantic interpretation of patent text is much better than lexical matching in retrieval. Such an enhancement is especially useful when cross-domain innovations are involved where related prior art describes similar solutions with different words.

Ensemble approach has NDCG@10 of 0.862, MRR of 0.734 and P@10 of 0.683, which is best in all the ranking measures. These findings suggest that in a standard prior art search, an average of 68 percent of the first 10 results are relevant prior art that the examiners actually referred to, and the first relevant result is found at an average of 2-3.

Error Analysis

We have done a manual analysis of 100 cases in which models ranked highly non-cited patents (possible false positives) and 100 cases in which models ranked highly cited prior art (false negatives). In case of possible false positives, human expert assessment revealed that about 45 percent of the possible false positives were in fact relevant prior art that examiners overlooked or did not bother to cite indicating that model accuracy might be overstated by considering examiner citations as ground truth. The other 55 per cent of the high-ranked non-cited patents consisted of conceptually related but legally different inventions, patents in non-relevant technology fields despite overlap of terms, and patents with similar terms but different technical sense.

In the case of false negatives when cited prior art was low, the main causes included: cross-domain citations where prior art was in other technology areas using different terms (38% of errors), extremely short abstracts or claims not covering all the patent contents (27%), that the retrieval candidate generation did not consider some cited patents (14%).

These error patterns suggest several directions for improvement: better cross-domain matching through technology transfer models, enhanced representations of full patent content beyond abstracts and claims, better ground truth labels distinguishing different citation types, and improved candidate generation strategies.

5.3 Semantic Similarity Analysis

The results of semantic similarity indicate that the models may be successfully used to estimate the relatedness of patents to cluster, analyze the landscape, and detect duplication:

Similarity Metrics

Table 4. Comparative Evaluation of Patent Semantic Similarity Methods

Method	Spearman ρ	Accuracy	AUC-ROC	MRR
Jaccard (CPC codes)	0.412	67.3%	0.723	-
TF-IDF Cosine	0.524	71.8%	0.768	-
Word2Vec Average	0.617	76.2%	0.821	-
BERT Sentence Similarity	0.751	84.6%	0.903	-
Ensemble	**0.792**	**87.3%**	**0.928**	-

Note Spearman is a correlation measure with human similarity ratings of experts (n=1,000 rho patent pairs). Binary classification (similar vs. dissimilar) is evaluated based on larger test set (n=100,000 pairs) based on accuracy and AUC-ROC.

The ensemble similarity model has a high correlation (=0.792) to human expert ρ ratings, which suggests that the model similarity scores are in line with the way patent attorneys and examiners determine patent relatedness. The binary classification accuracy of 87.3% indicates that the model can be effectively used to differentiate between truly similar patents and irrelevant ones to utilize it in such applications as duplicate detection.

We examined the similarity prediction ability depending on the features of the patent by applying feature importance analysis and ablation experiments. The rank-order similarity factors that are most important are:

1. CPC code overlap at subclass level (weight: 0.28) - Patents in similar fine-grained technology classes have very high probability of being connected.
2. Overlapping in claims (weight: 0.24) - Overlapping in the technical words is a sign of similar innovations.

3. ABS - Bert semantic similarity of abstracts (weight: 0.22) - Dense representations are conceptual similarity not based on keywords.
4. Citation network proximity (weight: 0.14) - Patents which cite a common prior art or are citation synonyms are connected.
5. Inventor/assignee overlap (weight: 0.08)- This implies that common inventors or associated firms propose relationships of patent families.
6. Proximity to filing date (weight: 0.04) - Patents that are filed near each other in an area of technology can solve similar issues.

These attributes are consistent with human expert judgments of similarity, which gives assurance that model predictions are based on significant patent attributes, but not on spurious relationships.

5.4 Model Interpretability Analysis

To examine the interpretability of models, we examine attention visualization and feature importance to comprehend what information AI systems rely on to make predictions on patent analysis:

Attention Pattern Analysis

The analysis of BERT attention weights on hundreds of patents shows that there are general trends in what is being modeled by content:

To be classified, the focus of attention is on: domain-specific technical terms which denote technology area, CPC classification as mentioned in patent text, specific technical components and processes, and transitional phrases in claims which denote invention structure.

To rank prior art, the following considerations are made: The abstract and background sections contain technical problem statements, independent claims contain novel technical features, certain numerical parameters and ranges that distinguish inventions and terminology to the effect that it is better than prior art.

To measure similarity, focus is placed on the following: similarity in the use of technical terms, similarity in the areas of use in descriptions, similarity in the reference of patent family, and similarity in the structure of the claims.

Such attention patterns are consistent with the way human experts search patents, indicating that models do not learn to take advantage of the artifacts of the data set, but they learn meaningful strategies. The models are correct in giving low attention to boilerplate legal language, generic functionality words, and formulaic patent sections that are not telling invention-specific information.

Feature Importance Analysis

In the case of non-neural models in the ensemble we employ permutation importance to measure the importance of features by examining the performance of the model with shuffled features. Best points of classification are:

- CPC class attributes (importance: 0.32): The partial CPC information is a strong predictive of complete classification.
- Technical word TF-IDF characteristics (importance: 0.28) - Unique technical words inform on the technological field.
- Count of citation (importance: 0.15) - Patents with high citation are likely to be in some of the active technology fields.
- Document length (importance: 0.09) - There are just areas of technology where patents are longer/shorter in character.
- Claim count (importance: 0.08) - There are varying numbers of claims across domains.

The importance of features analysis justifies that the non-neural models are based mostly on classification codes and technical vocabulary, which allows the confidence in the rationale of the prediction.

Counterfactual Analysis

We also performed counterfactual experiments, in which we edit patents, and we monitor their prediction changes to determine that models change as expected to perturbations:

When technical terms are removed off claims, the confidence of classification declines substantially (average 31% reduction) proving its dependence on technical content. The manipulation of CPC codes in text (where available) of patents with shifted predicted class to mentioned codes (72% of examples) indicates that models can learn to use this information. The inclusion of citations to patents with very high citations in a field enhances similarity scores to other patents in the same field (mean increase of similarity scores +0.12). These counterfactual findings suggest that models have learned substantive relationships between patent properties and the goals of analysis as opposed to using superficial trends.

These counterfactual results indicate models have learned meaningful relationships between patent characteristics and analysis objectives rather than relying on superficial patterns.

5.5 Temporal Generalization Analysis

In order to evaluate the strength to temporal change in patent language and technology, we test models on temporal splits and training 2010-2017, and testing 2018-2020:

Temporal Generalization Results

Table 5. Model Performance on Temporal vs. Random Data Splits

Metric	Random Split	Temporal Split	Degradation
Classification F1	95.7%	93.2%	-2.5%
Prior Art NDCG@10	0.862	0.831	-0.031
Similarity Spearman ρ	0.792	0.764	-0.028

There is a moderate decrease in performance on temporal splits (2-3% between tasks) relative to random splits, which implies that models can be fairly generalized to future data, but are somewhat sensitive to temporal changes. The degradation is more in the case of emerging technology areas such as artificial intelligence and biotechnology where terminology and technical approaches were changing swiftly during training and test periods.

Domain-adaptive pre-training is beneficial to the temporal generalization task, where patentspecific pre-training models exhibit lower temporal degradation (-2.5%), than standard BERT (-3.8%). This is an indication that learning pattern in a patent language is more effective at resisting temporal drift than general language understanding.

Continual Learning Analysis

To implement production, models have to be revised with new patents being awarded and technology developing. Our experimentation is based on lifelong learning tactics:

Periodic Retraining - he fully retraining model which retrains every 6 months on larger data with new patents can keep performance within 1% of models retrained on modern data. The production systems can accommodate retraining cost (27 GPU-hours on ensemble).

Incremental Fine-Tuning - n cases of new technology domains (e.g., medical devices in 2020 due to COVID-19), pretrained models are better transferred than retrained ones. Medical device patent transfer learning attains 89 percent F1 on COVID-related patents compared to 76 percent on models without medical device knowledge.

Transfer Learning - When new technology areas emerge (e.g., COVID-19 medical devices in 2020), models trained on related domains transfer better than retraining from scratch. Transfer learning from medical device patents achieves 89% F1 on COVID-related patents versus 76% for models without medical device knowledge.

5.6 Computational Efficiency Analysis

Computational efficiency is a major concern of practical implementation of AI patent analysis system:

Training and Inference Costs

Table 6. Computational Requirements and Performance Trade-offs Across Methods

Method	Training Time	Inference Time	Model Size	GPU Memory
TF-IDF + Naive Bayes	45 min	12 ms/doc	850 MB	N/A (CPU)
Word2Ve c + CNN	3.2 hours	85 ms/doc	412 MB	2.1 GB
LSTM Sequence Model	6.8 hours	124 ms/doc	628 MB	3.4 GB
Random Forest	2.5 hours	18 ms/doc	1.2 GB	N/A (CPU)
Gradient Boosting (XGBoost)	4.1 hours	23 ms/doc	945 MB	N/A (CPU)
BERT (Standar d)	12.4 hours	287 ms/doc	438 MB	4.2 GB
Patent-BERT (Finetuned)	18.7 hours	312 ms/doc	441 MB	4.8 GB
Ensemble (Ours)	**27.3 hours**	**356 ms/doc**	**3.5 GB**	**6.1 GB**

Note: Training time Full model development including hyperparameter search. Time per document to make an inference with single GPUs. Model size is disk storage. Inference is when the use of GPU memory is maximum.

The training time also differs significantly depending on the type of model, with the most costly being BERT fine-tuning which still takes 12-19 hours with a GPU acceleration. Conventional machine learning models are trained in less time (less than 5 hours), yet have lower accuracy. The time of ensemble training of 27.3 hours also incorporates training all base models as well as the meta-learner, which is a viable one-time cost of deployment.

The size and memory requirements of the model have an effect on deployment. The storage size of full BERT models is about 440 MB and the total storage size of ensemble method which involves combining multiple models is 3.5 GB. Simple models require 2.1 GB of GPU memory, and the entire ensemble needs 6.1GB. They are not trivial requirements, yet they are within the reach of the modern computing infrastructure and inexpensive cloud-based instances of GPUs.

Scalability Analysis

To process the entire USPTO patent database (i.e. 11 million patents):

- BERT inference: 11M patents × 312 ms = 953 hours = 40 days using single GPU.
- Ensemble inference: 11M patents × 356 ms = 1,086 hours = 45 days on single GPU.
- Batch processing (32 batch size): Parallelization helps to cut time by approximately 70 percent to approximately 14 days.
- Multi-GPU distribution (8 GPUs): Reduces time to ~2 days for full database processing.

Such timescales are acceptable when there is a database reclassification or patent landscape analysis that has been carried out on a periodic basis. In real-time applications such as examination support, single document inference with 356 ms is fast enough to be used interactively, especially when the models are called asynchronously when examiners are reading documents.

Cost-Performance Trade-Offs

In the case of deployment situations where the computational resources are limited, we trade-off accuracy and efficiency:

- Ensemble (best accuracy, 95.7% F1): 356 ms/doc, 6.1 GB memory.
- Patent-BERT only (93.5% F1): 312 ms/doc, 4.8 GB memory - saves 44 ms, 1.3 GB.
- BERT standard (91.0% F1): 287 ms/doc, 4.2 GB memory - saves 69 ms, 1.9 GB.
- Random Forest (88.2% F1): 18 ms/doc, CPU only - saves 338 ms, enables CPU deployment.

The full ensemble should be used in applications where maximum accuracy is needed (e.g. automated patent classification to official records). Applications that are sensitive to latency (e.g. real-time search and patent quality analysis systems (Trappey, Trappey, Wu, & Lin, 2012)) may train BERT-only models at the 2% accuracy cost of 12% faster inference. Limited access to the GPU applications (e.g., single practitioners) may make use of the traditional methods implemented on the CPU at the cost of 8% accuracy to avoid the need to be dependent on the GPU.

6. CONCLUSION

The chapter has outlined a detailed architecture of AI-based patent analysis, and it has shown that the current methods of natural language processing and machine learning can be used to process patent documents with large volumes of data effectively. Our ensemble methodology with the use of BERT-based transformers and patent-specific feature engineering attains state-of-the-art results on several patent analysis problems, outperforming prior approaches including DeepPatent (Li et al., 2018) and PatentNet (Roudsari et al., 2021): 96.2% accuracy in patent classification, NDCG10 of 0.862 in prior art detection and Spearman correlation of 0.792 with human similarity ratings. It is experimentally validated that these AI systems can be used to aid patent examination, aid legal research, and facilitate portfolio management more effectively than conventional manual procedures and maintain the quality of analysis with 1,847,203 USPTO patents from the period 2010-2020 (dataset compiled from publicly available USPTO records).

ACKNOWLEDGMENT

The authors are thankful to the Deanship of the Faculty of Information Technology, the Deanship of Scientific Research and Graduate Studies at the University of Petra, and the University of Oldenburg that supported them in carrying out this research.

REFERENCES

Abbott, R. (2020). *The reasonable robot: Artificial intelligence and the law*. Cambridge University Press.

Amodei, D., Olah, C., Steinhardt, J., Christiano, P., Schulman, J., & Mané, D. (2016). Concrete problems in AI safety. arXiv preprint arXiv:1606.06565.

Bommasani, R., Hudson, D. A., Adeli, E., Altman, R., Arora, S., von Arx, S., ... (2021). On the opportunities and risks of foundation models. arXiv preprint arXiv:2108.07258.

Chalkidis, I., Fergadiotis, M., Malakasiotis, P., Aletras, N., & Androutsopoulos, I. (2020). LEGAL-BERT: The muppets straight out of law school. In Findings of the Association for Computational Linguistics: EMNLP 2020 (pp. 2898-2904).

Devlin, J., Chang, M. W., Lee, K., & Toutanova, K. (2019). BERT: Pre-training of deep bidirectional transformers for language understanding. In *Proceedings of NAACL-HLT 2019* (pp. 4171-4186).

Katz, D. M., Bommarito, M. J., & Blackman, J. (2017). A general approach for predicting the behavior of the Supreme Court of the United States. *PLoS One*, *12*(4), e0174698. DOI: 10.1371/journal.pone.0174698 PMID: 28403140

Krestel, R., Chikkamath, R., Hewel, C., & Risch, J. (2021). A survey on deep learning for patent analysis. *World Patent Information*, *65*, 102035. DOI: 10.1016/j.wpi.2021.102035

Lee, J., Yoon, W., Kim, S., Kim, D., Kim, S., So, C. H., & Kang, J. (2020). BioBERT: A pretrained biomedical language representation model for biomedical text mining. *Bioinformatics (Oxford, England)*, *36*(4), 1234–1240. PMID: 31501885

Li, S., Hu, J., Cui, Y., & Hu, J. (2018). DeepPatent: Patent classification with convolutional neural networks and word embedding. *Scientometrics*, *117*(2), 721–744.

Marco, A. C., Sarnoff, J. D., & deGrazia, C. A. W. (2019). Patent claims and patent scope. *Research Policy*, *48*(9), 103790. DOI: 10.1016/j.respol.2019.04.014

Risch, J., & Krestel, R. (2019). Domain-specific word embeddings for patent classification. *Data Technologies and Applications*, *53*(1), 108–122.

Roudsari, A. H., Afshar, J., Lee, S., & Lee, W. (2021). PatentNet: Multi-label classification of patent documents using deep learning based language understanding. *Scientometrics*, *127*(1), 207–231. DOI: 10.1007/s11192-021-04179-4

Trappey, A. J., Trappey, C. V., Wu, C. Y., & Lin, C. W. (2012). A patent quality analysis for innovative technology and product development. *Advanced Engineering Informatics*, *26*(1), 26–34.

Vaswani, A., Shazeer, N., Parmar, N., Uszkoreit, J., Jones, L., Gomez, A. N., ... (2017). Attention is all you need. In Advances in Neural Information Processing Systems 30 (pp. 5998-6008).

World Intellectual Property Organization. (2023). World Intellectual Property Indicators 2023. WIPO Publication No. 941E. https://www.wipo.int/edocs/pubdocs/en/wipo-pub-941-2023-en-world-intellectual-property-indicators-2023.pdf

Xiao, Y., Wu, J., Lin, Z., & Zhao, X. (2018). A deep learning-based multi-model ensemble method for cancer prediction. *Computer Methods and Programs in Biomedicine*, *153*, 1–9. PMID: 29157442

Zhang, Y., & Wallace, B. (2017). A sensitivity analysis of (and practitioners' guide to) convolutional neural networks for sentence classification. In *Proceedings of the Eighth International Joint Conference on Natural Language Processing* (pp. 253-263).

Zheng, S., Jayasumana, S., Romera-Paredes, B., Vineet, V., Su, Z., & Du, D.. (2015). Conditional random fields as recurrent neural networks. In *Proceedings of the IEEE International Conference on Computer Vision* (pp. 1529-1537).

Zhou, Z. H. (2012). Ensemble methods: foundations and algorithms. Chapman and Hall/CRC. USPTO. (2020). Manual of Patent Examining Procedure (MPEP), Ninth Edition, Revision 10, June 2020. United States Patent and Trademark Office.

Chapter 6
Trademark Confusion in the Era of Big Data Algorithmic Branding:
Consumer Decpetion and Conpetition Law Challenge

Himanshu Ranjan
http://orcid.org/0009-0001-5195-7270
Christ University, India

ABSTRACT

This chapter, per the authors, examines how Big Data and AI have transformed trademark deception from sign-based imitation to algorithmically driven perception distortion. It explains how digital platforms collect and analyze massive behavioral datasets to rank, recommend, and position brands in ways that influence consumer belief about origin without copying any mark. Algorithmic practices such as competitor keyword bidding, recommendation bias, and ranking manipulation generate large-scale confusion by shaping what consumers see first and trust most. While global jurisprudence, including the L'Oréal v. eBay decision, recognizes platform-facilitated deception, Indian law still interprets confusion through traditional frameworks distinguishing infringement of the mark from deception of consumer belief. This chapter, per the authors, argues that AI-mediated market architecture produces deception without infringement, creating evidentiary gaps and competitive distortions that require algorithmic transparency, marketplace accountability, and an updated trademark–competition interface

DOI: 10.4018/979-8-3373-7685-1.ch006

1. UNDERSTANDING TRADEMARK CONFUSION

Trademark deception or refers to a situation where the use of presentation or marketing of goods/services misleads consumers about their true commercial origin, irrespective of the infringement or copying of a trademark. It occurs when consumers are led to believe that a product or service comes from a particular brand or service whereas the reality in such cases is completely different.

Under Trademark Act of 1999, traditionally trademark deception or confusion includes:

1. Misleading the public into thinking the goods or services originate from another known brand.
2. Creating a belief that there is an affiliation, sponsorship license or economic connection with another brand.
3. Imitating trade dress, packaging or any other identifier in a product that causes perception of another object.

Courts in India focus on the likely impression in the mind of an "average consumer of imperfect recollection"[1]. Deception or confusion can occur in the mind of the consumer even without actual imitation of the registered trademark. It exists to protect consumer trust n reliability of trade origin signals and not merely trademark proprietorship. Traditionally, Section 2(1)(h) of the Trademarks Act, 1999, defines the term "deceptively similar" as "A mark shall be deemed to be deceptively similar to another mark if it so nearly resembles that other mark as to be likely to deceive or cause confusion". It means that if an identifier of a business is so similar to an already established trademark that it will result in the consumers getting confused between the two brands, then it will be termed deceptively similar. For instance, in the case of M/s Mahashian Di Hatti Ltd. v. Mr. Raj Niwas[2], the logos of both the spice producing companies were the same with the only difference being that the plaintiff's logo said "MDH" and that of the respondent said "MHS". Delhi High Court, while passing an infringement order against the defendant's use of the logo, said that both the logos were deceptively similar. Despite the similarity in the name or logo, what is an important criterion for holding something deceptively similar is the industry or the consumer base in which both the businesses function. The trademarks are assessed based on whether the similarity is such that the consumers can get confused between the two.

Earlier studies (Dong 2021; Hofman & Keates 2013; S Katyal & Grinvald 2018; Khachatryan 2022) have predominantly focused on traditional trademark infringement scenarios, overlooking the unique challenges posed by the online environment. Due to an ongoing upsurge in the demand of e-commerce, the risk of brand identity and integrity has increased many folds. However, existing research fails to provide comprehensive insights into the nuances of online brand protection, leaving practitioners and policymakers with limited guidance on effective strategies.

1.1 Trademark Law Before pre-digitalization

Section 2(h) of The Trademark Act,1999 defines a trademark as a mark that can be graphically represented and can be used to distinguish the product of one person from the other, it must serve as a badge of origin. It facilitates brand recognition and trust among customers. It may consist of words, devices, labels, numerals, or a mix of these, as well as the form and packaging of the products and a selection of colours. A mark with only words is known as Word Mark, where as a mark with pictures labels and colours is known as Device Mark.

Before the invention of the digital era, trademark law was mainly concerned with protecting the distinctive names, Logos, symbols, and marks that companies used to identify their products and services to customers. Preventing consumer misunderstanding and protecting the goodwill associated with a brand are two of the core trademark law concepts that predate the internet era.

1.2 "The Evolution of Trademarks: From Traditional Source Indicators to Algorithmic Market Signals"

Historically, trademarks have functioned as source identifiers, enabling consumers to distinguish the goods or services of one undertaking from those of another. The classical theory of trademark law rests on the assumption that consumer choice is guided primarily by visible, textual, or phonetic indicators affixed to goods or used in advertising. Under this traditional paradigm, deception or confusion was understood as arising from deceptive similarity between trademarks, trade dress, packaging, or other tangible brand identifiers. Trademark law, therefore, evolved as a sign-centric regulatory system, premised on the idea that market communication between producers and consumers occurs through identifiable symbols that signal commercial origin.

This classical understanding shaped both statutory and common law trademark doctrines. The assessment of infringement and passing off traditionally focused on mark similarity, likelihood of confusion, and misrepresentation of trade origin, judged from the perspective of an average consumer of imperfect recollection. The law assumed that consumers encounter trademarks in relatively neutral market conditions, where choice is exercised through comparison of competing signs. Within this framework, deception was the result of imitation, and legal liability was tied to the use of a confusingly similar mark in the course of trade.

However, the emergence of Big Data–driven digital markets has fundamentally altered the environment in which trademarks operate. In contemporary online ecosystems, consumer encounters with brands are no longer mediated primarily through static symbols or deliberate brand comparison. Instead, they are increasingly shaped by algorithmic systems that curate, rank, recommend, and personalise brand visibility. This transformation marks a profound shift in the function of trademarks—from stable indicators of source to dynamic market signals whose salience is determined by data-driven architectures rather than consumer-initiated search or brand recognition alone.

In digital marketplaces and platform-based ecosystems, branding operates within an algorithmically constructed attention economy. Search engines, e-commerce platforms, and social media networks collect vast quantities of behavioural data, including search queries, browsing patterns, purchase histories, dwell time, and interaction metrics. Artificial intelligence systems process this data to predict consumer preferences and optimise engagement, conversion, and monetisation. As a result, what consumers see, click, and ultimately purchase is increasingly determined by algorithmic relevance scores, sponsored placement, and predictive visibility models rather than the inherent distinctiveness or goodwill of a trademark.

This shift has transformed trademarks into algorithmic market signals—markers of relevance, popularity, or trustworthiness as inferred by machines rather than consciously recognised by consumers. In such environments, higher ranking, repeated exposure, and interface dominance often substitute for traditional trademark recognition. Consumers may infer legitimacy, quality, or official association from a product's position in search results or recommendations, even when the trademark itself is unfamiliar or unrelated to the brand originally sought. Consequently, trade origin perception is shaped less by the trademark as a symbol and more by the visibility architecture within which that symbol is embedded.

This evolution disrupts the foundational assumptions of trademark law. Traditional doctrine presumes that confusion arises when consumers mistake one mark for another due to similarity. In algorithmic markets, however, confusion may arise without any similarity of marks, through what can be described as origin misattribution by placement. For example, when a consumer searches for a specific brand, algorithmic systems may foreground competing products based on bidding strategies, predicted preferences, or conversion probabilities. Over time, repeated exposure to these substitutes within the same cognitive space as the searched trademark can dilute or redirect consumer perception of source, even though no mark is copied or imitated.

The role of algorithmic branding is central to this transformation. Algorithmic branding refers to the use of automated decision systems to manage brand exposure, positioning, and association at scale. Unlike traditional branding, which relies on deliberate messaging crafted by brand owners, algorithmic branding is machine-driven, adaptive, and often opaque. It operates through ranking systems, recommendation engines, sponsored listings, and personalised content feeds that continuously adjust based on user behaviour and market incentives. In this context, trademarks function less as identifiers chosen by consumers and more as inputs into algorithmic decision-making processes.

This has significant implications for trademark deception. Deception no longer depends solely on whether a mark is deceptively similar, but on whether the market architecture induces a mistaken belief about origin, affiliation, or endorsement. Algorithmic systems can generate such beliefs by structuring visibility in ways that privilege certain brands, suppress others, or present competitors as functionally equivalent to well-known trademarks. The resulting deception is systemic rather than representational, arising from the design and operation of digital intermediaries rather than from deliberate acts of imitation by individual traders.

The evolution from traditional source indicators to algorithmic market signals also introduces new challenges for enforcement. Trademark law has historically been ill-equipped to address harms that arise from contextual market design rather than mark usage. Concepts such as "use in the course of trade" and "likelihood of confusion" were developed for physical and broadcast markets, where the locus of deception was visible and attributable. In contrast, algorithmic systems operate invisibly, personalise outcomes, and distribute responsibility across platforms, advertisers, and automated processes. This complicates both evidentiary standards and liability attribution.

Moreover, the algorithmic transformation of trademarks intersects closely with competition law concerns. When dominant platforms control the conditions of brand visibility, trademarks become vulnerable to market foreclosure through ranking power rather than through exclusionary agreements or pricing strategies. Self-preferencing, sponsored prominence, and data-driven steering can erode the competitive value of trademarks by limiting consumers' access to genuine brand choices. In such cases, trademark harm is inseparable from competition harm, as both arise from the same algorithmic control over consumer attention.

The contemporary evolution of trademarks thus represents not merely a technological shift, but a paradigm shift in market communication and consumer perception. Trademarks are no longer passive indicators waiting to be recognised by consumers; they are actively repositioned by algorithms within competitive visibility hierarchies. This reconfiguration challenges the adequacy of mark-centric legal analysis and calls for a broader understanding of trademark deception—one that accounts for algorithmic influence, behavioural nudging, and platform-mediated market power.

Recognising this evolution is essential to preserving the core objectives of trademark law: protecting consumer autonomy, safeguarding trade origin, and maintaining fair competition. As branding becomes increasingly algorithmic, legal frameworks must adapt to ensure that trademarks retain their integrity as indicators of source rather than becoming mere variables in opaque optimisation systems. The transition from traditional source indicators to algorithmic market signals therefore lies at the heart of contemporary trademark deception, and it forms the conceptual foundation for rethinking trademark protection in the era of Big Data and artificial intelligence.

2. ROLE OF BIG DATA, ALGORITHMIC BRANDING IN CAUSING TRADEMARK CONFUSION

Big Data is the real time analysis of massive multi format consumer data sets to predict and influence commercial decision making at scale, redefining trademarks as data-influenced perception rather than static identifiers.

For Example: Supposedly you open your social media account for instance Instagram on one fine afternoon and start scrolling now because yesterday in the evening you searched on google, road running shoes, you watched 3 show review videos on Youtube, you clicked 5 sneaker photos on Instagram, you spent extra time looking at red-colored shoes, but never searched for any brand name. Now, today when you have opened Instagram you see

1. The first four ads shown to you are of running shoes even though you didn't type anything.
2. Most of the shoes are of red color because the system knows that you like that colour.
3. It shoes dominant and leading brands of the market like Nike and Adidas even if you didn't search for that brand.

Now, the story behind this is that multiple apps collected your data and this various forms of data when put together is known as Big Data and in the world of Artificial Intelligence analysing this data is very easy. AI is the cause of Big Data becoming very useful as it helps in analysing the data, it makes it predictive. To understand let's refer to Table 1.

Table 1.

Stage	Who Does It	Example
Data Collection	Apps,websites, platforms	Instagram stores what you click, Google stores what you search, Amazon stores what you buy
Data Use & Understanding	AI/algorithms	AI learns, "you like red shoes, show more red shoes and premium brands
Prediction & Market Influence	AI/algorithms	You now believe the top red shoe ad is the most relevant or official one.

In Trademark Law, earlier: Deception or confusion was caused only by similar mark/logos, but in the era of AI: Deception can be caused by algorithmic ranking, targeted ads, perception steering, even when trademarks are dissimilar example: You searched for " Nike Shoes" but "Puma ad" shown first through AI keyboard auction and user profiling. Conclusively we can say that Platform collects data, data when collected by various apps of various persons when combined together is known as Big Data., AI analyses this data, studies patterns and predicts or influences what we see, buy or believe. Now Big Data can be used for Trademark confusion as it can confuse you by controlling what appears as the "most authentic or official option" based on ranking and recommendations.

However confusion relates to mistaken belief; Deception relates to inducement of that belief through market conduct.

Moreover Algorithmic Branding refers to use of algorithm and data combinedly to decide the behavior and choice of human. Algorithms causes confusion like:

1. Competitor bidding on keywords
2. Product recommendations
3. Ranking manipulation
4. UI blending of sponsored listings

Algorithmic branding is machine-driven brand placement and message personalisation based on mass behavioural data, capable of diverting exclusive trademark intent and shaping consumer origin belief even without mark similarity, posing new trademark confusion and deception challenge. Henceforth, while algorithmic branding is not independently penalised under India's Trademark Act, punishment arises when AI systems scale or facilitate trademark falsification or false application under section 103 and section 104 of Trademark Act 1999.

2.1. Algorithmic Branding Engineered Confusion

Algorithmically engineered confusion refers to a form of trademark and consumer deception where mistaken beliefs about trade origin, affiliation, or legitimacy are produced not by mark similarity, but by platform-controlled algorithmic design. Unlike classical confusion, which is caused by imitation, this confusion is manufactured by visibility, ranking, and interface architecture in digital markets.

At its core, algorithmic confusion arises because algorithms, not consumers, decide which brands are seen first, most often, and in what context. Algorithmically engineered confusion represents a structural transformation in how consumer perception is shaped in contemporary markets. In traditional trademark theory, the consumer is presumed to exercise choice through recognition and comparison of marks, with confusion arising only when similarity between competing signs disrupts that process. In algorithmically mediated environments, however, the consumer's decision-making autonomy is substantially displaced. Digital platforms insert an invisible computational layer between the consumer and the market, where algorithmic systems curate the order, frequency, and framing of brand exposure. As a result, confusion is no longer a consequence of deceptive representation alone, but of engineered market conditions that systematically influence belief formation.

The defining feature of algorithmically engineered confusion is that it is contextual rather than representational. The algorithm does not necessarily alter the trademark, misstate origin, or imitate branding elements. Instead, it manipulates the context in which trademarks are encountered, thereby reshaping how consumers interpret legitimacy, relevance, and affiliation. When consumers repeatedly encounter certain brands in positions of algorithmic prominence—top search results, first-page marketplace listings, or default recommendations—they may infer endorsement, superiority, or official association, even when no such connection exists. The deception lies not in what is said, but in how visibility is structured.

This form of confusion is closely tied to algorithmic authority bias, a well-documented cognitive phenomenon whereby individuals assign greater trust to outputs presented as ranked, recommended, or system-generated. Digital interfaces capitalise on this bias by presenting algorithmic outputs as neutral, objective, or optimised for user benefit. In reality, these outputs are shaped by a complex interaction of commercial incentives, advertiser bidding, platform self-interest, and predictive analytics. Trademark salience is thus displaced by ranking authority, with consumers relying on algorithmic cues rather than brand recognition to assess authenticity.

A central mechanism through which algorithmically engineered confusion operates is keyword auction systems. When consumers search for a specific brand, their query expresses a clear trademark intent. However, keyword auctions allow competitors to intercept this intent by bidding on the trademarked term. The algorithm then determines which advertisements appear most prominently based on bid value, predicted click-through rates, and user profiling. The resulting display may foreground competing products above or alongside the searched brand, often with minimal visual differentiation. Although the competitor does not use the trademark in a deceptive manner, the consumer's perception of origin and association is subtly redirected. Over time, such redirection erodes the exclusivity of the trademark's association with its source.

Another significant contributor to algorithmic confusion is platform self-preferencing. Digital marketplaces increasingly operate as both intermediaries and competitors, offering their own private-label or affiliated products alongside third-party goods. Algorithmic ranking systems frequently prioritise these platform-owned brands due to higher margins, greater data access, or internal optimisation goals. Consumers encountering such results are rarely aware of the underlying conflicts of interest. As a result, platform credibility substitutes for trademark goodwill, and consumers may attribute quality or authenticity to products based on platform endorsement rather than trade origin. This creates confusion not because trademarks are similar, but because the platform's structural position confers legitimacy.

Interface design further amplifies algorithmic confusion through the use of dark patterns—design choices that obscure or downplay critical information about sponsorship, ranking criteria, or commercial relationships. Sponsored listings may be labelled in faint fonts, blended seamlessly with organic results, or positioned in visually dominant locations. Recommendation badges such as "Best Seller," "Top Pick," or "Recommended for You" are often generated by opaque criteria tied to sales velocity or advertising spend, yet they are perceived by consumers as indicators of quality or popularity. These design features manipulate cognitive shortcuts, leading consumers to conflate visibility with authenticity and relevance with endorsement.

Recommendation systems play an equally important role in producing confusion through associative substitution. Algorithms trained on behavioural similarity models routinely present "similar products," "people also bought," or "frequently viewed together" suggestions. While framed as convenience-enhancing features, these recommendations often prioritise products with higher conversion probabilities rather than those aligned with the consumer's expressed brand intent. Consequently, competing brands are inserted into the same cognitive space as the searched trademark, creating associative confusion. Over repeated interactions, the consumer's mental map of the market shifts, and the trademark's unique source-identifying function is diluted.

A distinctive characteristic of algorithmically engineered confusion is its self-reinforcing nature. Each consumer interaction generates new data that feeds back into the system, reinforcing the algorithm's future decisions. If a substituted or promoted brand receives clicks due to its prominent placement, the algorithm interprets this as validation of relevance and further amplifies its visibility. This creates a feedback loop in which initial visibility advantages compound over time, entrenching certain brands while marginalising others. Confusion thus becomes systemically entrenched, even in the absence of deliberate deceptive intent by any single actor.

From a legal perspective, algorithmically engineered confusion exposes a critical mismatch between traditional trademark doctrine and contemporary market realities. Trademark infringement analysis remains focused on the unauthorised use of a mark or a deceptively similar sign. Passing off doctrine requires proof of misrepresentation leading to consumer confusion and damage to goodwill. Algorithmic confusion, however, often lacks a clear misrepresenting act. The harm arises from predictable system outcomes rather than intentional conduct, challenging courts to reconsider how deception is identified and attributed.

This shift also raises complex questions of liability allocation. In algorithmic environments, responsibility is distributed among advertisers who bid on keywords, platforms that design ranking systems, and algorithms that autonomously optimise outcomes. Each actor may plausibly deny intent to deceive, yet the cumulative effect is a market architecture that predictably distorts consumer perception. This challenges intent-based notions of fault and suggests a move toward foreseeability and control-based standards in assessing trademark deception.

Algorithmically engineered confusion also intersects with competition law concerns, particularly where dominant platforms control essential visibility infrastructure. When a platform's ranking and recommendation systems systematically favour certain brands—especially its own—it can distort competition by redirecting consumer demand and foreclosing rival access to market attention. In such cases, trademark harm and competition harm are not separate phenomena but manifestations of the same underlying power imbalance. The erosion of trademark distinctiveness through algorithmic steering thus becomes both a consumer protection issue and a competition law concern.

Importantly, algorithmic confusion does not imply that all algorithmic ranking or recommendation practices are inherently deceptive. Digital platforms can legitimately use algorithms to organise information, improve relevance, and enhance user experience. The legal challenge lies in distinguishing legitimate optimisation from manipulative design that predictably induces mistaken beliefs about origin or affiliation. This requires a nuanced analysis of factors such as transparency, user expectations, dominance, and the proportionality of commercial influence embedded in algorithmic systems.

Ultimately, algorithmically engineered confusion reflects a broader transformation in how markets communicate meaning. Trademarks no longer operate solely as symbols chosen and interpreted by consumers; they function within complex socio-technical systems that shape perception at scale. When these systems prioritise commercial optimisation over origin integrity, confusion becomes an engineered outcome rather than an accidental by-product. Recognising this phenomenon is essential for reorienting trademark law toward its foundational purpose: preserving the reliability of trade origin signals in evolving market conditions.

In the era of Big Data and artificial intelligence, protecting trademarks requires more than policing imitation. It demands scrutiny of the architectures of visibility that govern consumer attention. Algorithmically engineered confusion thus calls for a reconceptualisation of trademark deception—one that accounts for system design, platform power, and the cognitive effects of algorithmic mediation. Without such an evolution, trademark law risks becoming increasingly detached from the realities of digital markets, allowing deception to persist not through copying, but through code.

3. AI, ADS, AND TRADEMARK CONFUSION AT SCALE

In the era of Artificial Intelligence and Big Data courts around the globe have started recognizing that market place architecture itself can lead to passing off as seen in the case of LOreal SA vs eBay international AG (2009) where the courts held that platforms may incur liability when their system facilitate brand confusion or substitute deceptive listings, placing a duty on intermediaries to act when deception is foreseeable. However Indian courts are yet to recognize the role of algorithmic branding in causing trademark confusion however deception is very well recognized by Indian Courts and a distinction between them is also very well explained in the case of Kaviraj Pandit Durga Dutt Sharma vs Navratna Pharmaceutical Laboratories where the courts held that infringement protects the mark and deception protects consumer belief and good will. This dichotomy becomes quite important to understand when algorithmic market scale confusion without direct copying.

In today's day and age Big Data does not deceive by copying brand symbols it deceives by copying consumer perception. This represents a profound evolution in trademark harm. Confusion is no longer merely the outcome of imitative branding; it is the outcome of predictive architecture. Algorithms shape what consumers see first, trust most, and assume to be authoritative. When AI-mediated ads or search results place rival products in positions of dominance top search listings, personalized recommendations, "similar products" widgets they silently erode the connection between the trademark and its origin, leading to confusion at a scale impossible in pre-digital markets. Thus, algorithmic branding produces a new class of deception: one created not by counterfeiters, but by data-driven visibility engineering. Thus, algorithmic branding produces a new category of market harm confusion without imitation and deception without intent. This represents a paradigmatic shift in trademark jurisprudence, challenging the foundational assumptions of both *infringement* under the Trade Marks Act, 1999 and *passing off* under common law. In classical trademark theory, the law presumes that deception arises from identifiable acts: copying, phonetic similarity, visual resemblance, or misrepresentation. In algorithmic markets, however, deception is a by-product of automated curation, emerging from ranking systems that function as invisible intermediaries between the consumer and the brand.

Recommendation engines often powered by collaborative filtering and behavioural similarity models routinely present consumers with "similar products," "frequently bought together," or "top picks for you." These systems prioritise products with higher conversion likelihood rather than products matching the consumer's expressed trademark intent. As result, a consumer searching for a specific brand may be exposed to algorithmically substituted alternatives framed as functionally equivalent or superior. Over time, this produces associative confusion, where brand identity is replaced by algorithmic relevance.

The harm lies not in false claims, but in cognitive proximity engineering, whereby competing brands occupy the mental space of the searched trademark. Algorithmic confusion is further reinforced through interface design choices, often referred to as dark patterns. These include:

low-contrast "Ad" labels, blending of sponsored and organic results, prioritization of above-the-fold visibility. Empirical studies in user experience research demonstrate that consumers disproportionately trust higher-ranked and visually dominant results, often without distinguishing between paid and organic content. Thus, interface neutrality becomes illusory, and algorithmic ranking replaces trademark salience as the primary source cue.

Figure 1 depicts This diagram depicts the "Algorithmic Visibility and Consumer Recall Loop" which is a cycle explaining how digital platforms' algorithms influence what consumers see, click, remember, and ultimately purchase, often in ways that systematically favour certain brands.

Figure 1.

Algorithmic Visibility and Consumer Recall Loop
Bid Optimization & Brand Prioritization
Algorithmic scoring of keyword auctions
Algorithm Infers Consumer Intent
Behavioral data analytics & keyword triggers
Ranking & Recommendation Deployment
Sponsored & organic listings, personalized suggestions
Conversion Probability & Click Prioritization
Predictive ranking of brands for maximum CRO
Bid Optimization & Brand Prioritization
Algorithmic scoring of keyword auctions
Consumer Recall & Misattribution
Note: Platform's own brand receives top placement and visible endorsement, consistently outperforming independent trademark sellers in algorithmic ranking due to self-preferencing.

4. ALGORITHMIC BRANDING: AUTOMATED MARKET STEERING AND PRODUCT VISIBILITY

Algorithmic branding represents the transition of trademarks from being static source identifiers to becoming dynamic, data-adaptive visibility assets that are deployed strategically through automated decision engines. In digital markets, brand competition is increasingly governed by algorithm-mediated distribution of consumer attention rather than the intrinsic distinctiveness of the trademark alone. The algorithm becomes a gatekeeper that determines which brand is visible, repeatedly encountered, associated, and ultimately trusted by consumers.

Unlike traditional branding, where businesses consciously craft identity through packaging or mass advertising, algorithmic branding leverages machine learning systems that continuously adapt brand presentation based on behavioural data, conversion probability, competitor traffic interception, and ranking optimisation objectives. The commercial success of a mark is thus dependent on system-generated brand exposure metrics rather than consumer-driven discovery. This creates situations where origin perception is manipulated by ranking architecture, not by mark similarity, laying the foundation for trademark deception without formal infringement.

The most influential brand steering environments include:

- search result auctions run by Google Search
- advertising auctions orchestrated by Google Ads
- marketplace ranking and recommendations used by Amazon India
- social identity-driven product nudging on Instagram

These platforms structure visibility by prioritizing consumer-profile alignment, demand-prediction models, and paid prominence, rather than genuine origin neutrality.

4.1 How Algorithms Construct Brand Visibility

Algorithms execute brand steering through the following operational cycle:

1. **Behaviour Mapping**: A consumer's search queries, dwell time, clicks, purchases, and demographic patterns are logged to construct behavioural vectors.
2. **Intent Profiling**: The system predicts purchase likelihood and category preference, building a personalized demand index.
3. **Brand Auctioning**: Companies bid on consumer segments or competitor keywords to secure placement priority.
4. **Ranking Deployment**: Sponsored or profile-matching brands are ranked higher to maximise conversions.

5. **Recall Reinforcement**: The consumer is repeatedly exposed to the same steering pattern so that market memory aligns with algorithmic suggestion.

This turns a trademark into a cognitively positioned digital asset, not just a legal sign.

4.3 Legal Relevance

Indian law interprets deceptive "use in trade" broadly to prevent marks or branding mechanisms that manipulate association triggers. At the same time, competition law challenges arise when visibility steering is used by a dominant intermediary to distort final consumer choice or foreclose competitor brand recall.

Key statutory touchpoints that strengthen the legal framing include:

- misuse of algorithmic power to distort consumer choice may qualify as abuse of dominance, investigated by the Competition Commission of India under Competition Act, 2002 - Section 4
- consumer routing through misleading visibility layers may amount to unfair commercial impression, prohibited under Consumer Protection Act, 2019 - Section 2(47)
- when branding systems induce a false trade connection belief, even without mark copying, deception principles under the Trade Marks Act, 1999 are triggered

Additionally, global regulatory developments led by the European Commission increasingly expect algorithmic accountability where brand visibility impacts competition and consumer origin memory.

4.4. Practical Examples

Example 1: Sportswear Recall Hijack

A consumer searches for "Nike running shoes" on Google. The algorithm shows top sponsored placements for Puma Velocity Nitro, describing it as *"elite running performance used by global athletes"*, occupying the first scroll zone. The consumer may interpret Puma's product as the quality class they associated with Nike, even though the mark is not copied.

This is perception engineering, not trademark imitation.

Relevant brands involved:

- searched brand: Nike
- substituted brand: Puma

Example 2: Herbal Goods Association Mimicry

A consumer searches "Himalaya baby cream". The e-commerce platform repeatedly pushes Mamaearth Plant-Based Baby Cream in recommendations with caption *"same herbal softness trusted by parents, 100% toxin-free herbs."* There is no visual similarity or name copying, yet the algorithm mimics the consumer's association zone for herbal baby care, diverting recall.

Brands:

- recalled origin brand: Himalaya Wellness
- recommendation substitute: Mamaearth

Example 3: Invisible Keyword Traffic Interception

A seller uses Google Ads to bid on competitor traffic. When someone types "Adidas sports cap", the algorithm inventory stacks Decathlon sports caps at top placement to consumers who previously purchased athletic apparel. Even without copying the Adidas trademark, market association is influenced by data segment routing.

Marketplace used:

- visibility platform: Google Ads

Example 4: Private Label Placement Dominance

On Amazon India, more than 60% of users click only the first screen of results for electronic accessories. The platform ensures its most converting sellers or Amazon in-house brands like AmazonBasics 65W USB-C Laptop Charger appear before competitors. The mark becomes provider-associated through exposure frequency, not genuine discovery—showing how visibility = brand trust.

Modern trademark deception arises because:

- visibility: legitimacy in consumer perception
- repetition: recall dominance
- rankings: presumed origin authority
- data segments: competitor goodwill routing

4.5 Passing-Off & Deception in Algorithmic Markets: A Doctrinal Case for Extension

This creates origin confusion without mark similarity, goodwill diversion without mark copying, and competition impairment without explicit human intent—a category unanticipated by classical trademark infringement tests.

Unlike statutory infringement under Sections 29 and 30 of the Trade Marks Act, 1999, the doctrine of passing-off has never been confined to rigid notions of mark usage or formal similarity. Its doctrinal strength lies in its functional focus on consumer belief and trade origin, rather than on the mechanics of representation. This makes passing-off uniquely adaptable to algorithmic markets, where deception arises not from imitation of marks but from systemic distortion of consumer perception.

Indian courts have consistently treated passing-off as a dynamic, equitable doctrine, capable of evolving with market realities. The Supreme Court has repeatedly emphasised that the object of passing-off is not merely to protect proprietary rights in a mark, but to prevent commercial misrepresentation that misleads consumers and damages goodwill. This foundational orientation provides the doctrinal basis for extending passing-off to algorithmically engineered deception.

4.5.1 Misrepresentation Without Imitation: Indian Courts Have Already Accepted This Principle

A critical misconception is that passing-off requires imitation of a mark or trade dress. Indian jurisprudence clearly rejects this limitation.

In Kaviraj Pandit Durga Dutt Sharma v. Navratna Pharmaceutical Laboratories (1965), the Supreme Court drew a decisive conceptual distinction:

- Infringement protects the statutory right in the mark
- Passing-off protects the right to goodwill and correct trade origin perception

The Court expressly held that deception may exist even where infringement does not, because passing-off is concerned with whether the defendant's conduct is calculated to mislead consumers into believing a trade connection. Importantly, the Court clarified that misrepresentation need not be deliberate; it is sufficient if the market effect is misleading.

This principle directly supports algorithmic deception claims. Algorithmic substitution, ranking manipulation, and visibility steering may lack human intent or mark imitation, yet they can still produce predictable and scalable misrepresentation of trade origin.

4.5.2 Passing-Off Protects Consumer Belief, Not Formal Similarity

Indian courts have repeatedly emphasised that the mental impression of the consumer, not the technical similarity of marks, is the controlling factor.

In Laxmikant V. Patel v. Chetanbhai Shah (2002), the Supreme Court held that passing-off protects against any conduct that leads consumers to believe that the defendant's business is connected with or endorsed by the plaintiff. The Court stressed that:

- The inquiry is whether the defendant's conduct creates a likelihood of deception
- The protection extends to business reputation and market identity, not merely names or symbols

This reasoning is especially relevant in algorithmic markets, where platform-controlled context—ranking position, repeated exposure, interface design—creates an implied association or endorsement without any visual imitation. When a platform's architecture repeatedly positions substitute brands in the cognitive space of a searched trademark, it generates exactly the kind of false trade connection belief condemned in Laxmikant V. Patel.

4.5.3. Goodwill Exists Beyond Physical Markets and Requires Protection in Digital Form

Indian courts have long recognised that goodwill is not territorially or physically confined. This recognition is crucial for algorithmic markets.

In N.R. Dongre v. Whirlpool Corporation (1996), the Supreme Court protected the goodwill of a foreign brand despite minimal physical presence in India. The Court held that goodwill is rooted in consumer perception and reputation, not in the mechanics of market entry.

This principle is directly transferable to algorithmic branding. In digital ecosystems:

- Goodwill is often accessed before the product itself
- Consumer belief is shaped by search results, rankings, and recommendations
- Market presence is increasingly algorithmic rather than physical

If goodwill can exist without physical sales, it logically follows that goodwill can be misappropriated or distorted through algorithmic routing, even when no mark is copied. Passing-off doctrine, as articulated in Whirlpool, is therefore conceptually capable of addressing algorithmic misattribution.

4.5.4. Deception Is About Market Effect, Not Defendant's Intent

Indian passing-off jurisprudence consistently adopts an effect-based rather than intent-based analysis.

In Reckitt & Colman Ltd. v. Borden Inc. (1990) (the "Jif Lemon" case, adopted by Indian courts), the House of Lords formulation—accepted in India—requires proof of:

1. Goodwill
2. Misrepresentation likely to deceive
3. Damage or likelihood of damage

Notably, intent is irrelevant. What matters is whether the conduct is likely to mislead the public.

This doctrinal stance is critical for algorithmic markets, where deception is often autonomous and emergent, produced by machine-learning optimisation rather than conscious design. If Indian law required intent, passing-off would already be ineffective against many traditional cases. Since it does not, algorithmic deception fits squarely within existing doctrine.

4.5.5. Passing-Off Is Context-Sensitive and Market-Structure Aware

Indian courts have repeatedly emphasised that passing-off must be assessed in real market conditions, not in abstraction.

In Cadila Health Care Ltd. v. Cadila Pharmaceuticals Ltd. (2001), the Supreme Court held that courts must consider:

- Nature of goods
- Class of consumers
- Mode of purchase
- Surrounding circumstances affecting consumer perception

This flexible, contextual inquiry provides a doctrinal gateway for considering algorithmic architecture as a "surrounding circumstance." In digital markets:

- Consumers rely on rankings, not side-by-side comparison
- Trust is inferred from visibility and repetition

- Sponsored placement often substitutes for brand recognition

Ignoring these realities would contradict Cadila's insistence on realism in confusion analysis. Algorithmic interfaces are not neutral backdrops; they are active market participants shaping perception.

4.5.6. Why Passing-Off Must Be Extended—Not Reinvented

The extension of passing-off to algorithmic deception does not require doctrinal innovation; it requires doctrinal fidelity. The principles already recognised by Indian courts logically compel such an extension (Table 2).

Table 2.

Established Doctrine	Algorithmic Application
Protection of consumer belief	Protection against visibility-induced origin misattribution
Misrepresentation without intent	Deception arising from algorithmic optimisation
Goodwill independent of form	Digital goodwill shaped by rankings and recall
Contextual confusion analysis	Interface design and ranking architecture as context

Algorithmic markets merely change how misrepresentation occurs, not what misrepresentation means.

4.5.7. The Consequence of Non-Extension

If passing-off doctrine is not applied to algorithmic deception, a paradox emerges:

- Deception is legally recognised
- Goodwill diversion is economically real
- Consumer belief is demonstrably distorted

Yet no remedy exists, because the harm does not fit mark-centric infringement tests

Such an outcome would undermine the very purpose of passing-off as articulated by Indian courts: preserving honest market communication and consumer trust.

Indian passing-off jurisprudence, when read holistically, already contains the conceptual tools necessary to address algorithmic trademark deception. Courts have protected goodwill beyond physical markets, recognised deception without imitation, rejected intent as a prerequisite, and insisted on contextual analysis of consumer perception. Algorithmic branding does not rupture these principles—it activates them.

Extending passing-off to algorithmic markets is therefore not a radical doctrinal leap, but a principled continuation of Indian trademark law's consumer-centric foundations. In an era where trade origin is increasingly inferred from code rather than symbols, passing-off remains the most doctrinally coherent vehicle for preserving the integrity of trademarks and the autonomy of consumer choice.

5. TRADEMARK DECEPTION VS. TRADEMARK INFRINGEMENT: DOCTRINAL AND LEGAL DISTINCTION

In the contemporary digital economy, distinguishing trademark deception from trademark infringement is essential for both doctrinal clarity and enforcement strategy. While the two concepts are intertwined in protecting consumer trust and market integrity, they diverge fundamentally in legal focus, evidentiary requirements, and remedial scope.

5.1. Legal Foundation in India

Under the Trade Marks Act, 1999 - Sections 29 & 30, infringement occurs when a person uses a registered trademark or a deceptively similar mark in the course of trade for identical or related goods/services. Indian courts have clarified that intent to deceive is not required; the offense arises from actual use causing potential confusion, as established in:

- Kaviraj Pandit Durga Dutt Sharma v. Navaratna Pharmaceutical Laboratories (1965)

Deception falls within the common law doctrine of passing-off, protecting goodwill, consumer belief, and market perception, irrespective of registration. The elements are:

1. Existence of goodwill
2. Misrepresentation likely to deceive the public
3. Damage or potential damage to goodwill

The Supreme Court in India has held that deception can exist without infringement, and that goodwill and origin perception are protected even against unregistered marks, as seen in:

- Reckitt & Colman Ltd v. Borden Inc (1990)

- S. Syed Mohideen v. P. Sulochana Bai (2016)

5.1. Practical Illustration in the Digital Era

A user searches for "Nike running shoes", but the algorithm promotes Puma or Adidas listings in top positions. No logo is copied, but the consumer's trade-origin perception is diverted deceptive conduct without infringement.

If a competitor lists "Nike Air Zoom" shoes using Nike's logo without authorization, it constitutes infringement, regardless of whether consumers are deceived or not.

Overlap with Competition Law

Deception-based harms frequently intersect with competition concerns under the Competition Act, 2002, particularly when algorithmic systems redirect consumer demand, restrict visibility, or reinforce dominant-market brand

The Consumer Protection Act, 2019 - Section 2(47) also recognizes unfair trade practices where perception-based misrepresentation impacts purchasing decisions. Deceptive branding in Big Data environments often triggers simultaneous trademark, consumer protection, and competition law remedies. Infringement requires demonstrable mark use. Deception requires evidence of likelihood of confusion, which can include algorithm logs, click-through patterns, recommendation biases, and consumer surveys.

The L'Oréal v. eBay case of 2009 addressed algorithmic visibility of unauthorized products, highlighting that marketplace architecture can generate deception even without mark use.

In USA Courts have recognized "reverse confusion", where smaller brands mislead consumers about the origin of a larger, more established brand, often via search engine ad placement, reflecting algorithmic deception.

Doctrinal Takeaways

1. Trademark Infringement = mark-centric, statutory violation, strict liability.
2. Trademark Deception = consumer-perception-centric, protects goodwill and origin belief, may exist without mark copying, and increasingly incorporates algorithmic and data-driven influence.
3. Digital Markets Challenge Traditional Tests: Algorithms can amplify confusion without human intent, creating enforcement gaps if courts do not interpret "use in trade" and "likelihood of confusion" to include exposure engineering and memory diversion.
4. Enforcement frameworks must integrate trademark law, consumer protection law, and competition law to address modern algorithmic deception.

6.SECTION 29 AND THE VISUAL-TEXTUAL MODEL OF TRADEMARK USE

The Classical Meaning of "Use in the Course of Trade" Section 29 of the Trade Marks Act defines infringement in terms of unauthorized use of a registered mark or a deceptively similar mark in relation to goods or services. Judicial interpretation has consistently treated "use" as: visual or textual application of the mark, affixation to goods or packaging, use in advertising or commercial representation. In Kaviraj Pandit Durga Dutt Sharma v. Navaratna Pharmaceutical Laboratories (1965), the Supreme Court made clear that infringement analysis is mark-centric, focusing on whether the defendant has used the plaintiff's mark or a deceptively similar variant. Once such use is established, likelihood of confusion is presumed. This doctrinal approach assumes that the source of confusion is the mark itself, not the surrounding market architecture. The insufficiency of Sections 29 and 30 arises from a fundamental mismatch between: a mark-based infringement model, and a visibility-based market reality. Trademark law protects marks as indicators of origin, but algorithms treat trademarks as data points within demand-prediction systems. Confusion is no longer generated by similarity of signs, but by: ranking priority, repetition, interface dominance, and associative placement. Thus, even where consumer confusion and goodwill diversion are demonstrable, infringement analysis fails because the harm is architectural rather than representational. While statutory trademark infringement under Sections 29 and 30 of the Trade Marks Act, 1999 remains ill-suited to capture algorithmic market harms, the common law doctrine of passing off offers a more flexible and conceptually appropriate framework for addressing algorithmic trademark deception. Unlike infringement, passing off is not confined to the formal use of a mark; it is concerned with the protection of goodwill and consumer belief, making it doctrinally adaptable to evolving market structures.

6.1. "'Use in the Course of Trade' in Algorithmic Markets: Do Sections 29 and 30 Still Work?"

The concept of "use in the course of trade" under Sections 29 and 30 of the Trade Marks Act, 1999 occupies a central position in Indian trademark infringement jurisprudence. Traditionally, this requirement has served as a jurisdictional and doctrinal filter, ensuring that liability for infringement attaches only where a defendant makes a commercial use of the registered mark or a deceptively similar mark in relation to goods or services. The statutory language, judicial interpretation, and enforcement practice surrounding Sections 29 and 30 are, however, deeply rooted in a visual–

textual model of trademark use, which assumes that trademarks operate as visible signs consciously deployed by traders and consciously perceived by consumers.

In classical markets, "use in the course of trade" has been understood to mean the affixation of a mark on goods, packaging, labels, invoices, advertisements, or other commercial communications. Courts have consistently linked infringement to representational use—that is, the defendant's act of placing the plaintiff's mark (or a confusingly similar variant) before the public as an indicator of trade origin. Once such use is established, likelihood of confusion is either presumed or assessed through traditional similarity tests. This framework presupposes that deception flows from the mark itself and that market context is largely neutral.

Algorithmic markets fundamentally disrupt these assumptions.

In digital ecosystems governed by search engines, online marketplaces, and social media platforms, the most commercially significant uses of trademarks often occur without any visible reproduction of the mark by the alleged infringer. Instead, trademarks function as data triggers within algorithmic systems—inputs that activate auctions, rankings, recommendations, and personalised visibility outcomes. When a consumer types a brand name into a search bar or marketplace query field, the trademark is not merely "used" as a sign; it is processed as a signal of consumer intent. Algorithms then monetise this intent by reallocating attention toward competing products through sponsored placements, recommendation modules, or ranked results.

This raises a critical doctrinal question: can algorithmic exploitation of trademark intent amount to "use in the course of trade" even when the mark is not visually or textually displayed by the defendant?

Under Sections 29 and 30, the answer under current interpretation is largely negative. Indian infringement doctrine continues to require demonstrable use of the mark in advertising, labelling, or product identification. As a result, algorithmic practices such as competitor keyword bidding, sponsored substitution, and ranking-based diversion often fall outside the statutory definition of infringement, even where consumer confusion and goodwill diversion are empirically evident. The law, in effect, treats algorithmic steering as commercially invisible.

This doctrinal gap stems from the representational bias embedded in Sections 29 and 30. The provisions conceptualise trademark harm as arising from misrepresentation through sign usage, not from exposure engineering or visibility manipulation. Algorithms, however, do not "represent" marks in the traditional sense; they operationalise them. Trademarks are converted into behavioural vectors—signals that guide automated decisions about which products appear first, most prominently, or most frequently. The harm to trade origin arises not because the consumer sees the wrong mark, but because the consumer is led, through ranking and repetition, to attribute legitimacy, affiliation, or equivalence to a different source.

In this sense, algorithmic markets expose the limits of a mark-centric infringement model. Sections 29 and 30 presume a linear relationship between mark use and consumer confusion: mark → perception → confusion. In algorithmic environments, the relationship is circular and mediated: intent → algorithmic processing → visibility → perception → reinforced intent. Confusion emerges as a system outcome, not as the direct result of any single act of mark use. Consequently, even clear evidence of origin misattribution may fail to satisfy the statutory threshold of infringement.

The problem is compounded by the intent-neutral nature of infringement under Indian law. While intent is not a prerequisite for liability, use remains indispensable. Algorithmic systems, however, diffuse responsibility across advertisers, platforms, and automated processes. Advertisers may argue that they never used the trademark in their ads; platforms may claim neutrality by attributing outcomes to automated ranking logic; and algorithms themselves lack legal personhood. Sections 29 and 30, designed for bilateral disputes between trademark owners and infringers, struggle to accommodate this distributed architecture of decision-making.

Section 30, which provides defences for honest descriptive use and nominative reference, further illustrates the mismatch. These defences presuppose conscious human use of a mark for descriptive or referential purposes. Algorithmic substitution, by contrast, is neither descriptive nor referential in the traditional sense. It is predictive and probabilistic, driven by conversion optimisation rather than communicative intent. As a result, Section 30 neither clearly legitimises nor clearly restrains algorithmic brand steering, leaving courts without a coherent statutory basis to evaluate such practices.

Given these limitations, Sections 29 and 30 do not "fail" in an absolute sense, but they operate incompletely in algorithmic markets. They remain effective in cases of classic infringement—counterfeiting, deceptive similarity, and unauthorised advertising—but they are ill-equipped to address confusion generated through non-representational uses of trademarks. The statutory framework protects trademarks as symbols, while algorithmic systems exploit trademarks as signals of demand.

This doctrinal insufficiency explains why common law passing off has emerged as a more adaptable tool for addressing algorithmic deception. Passing off focuses on misrepresentation and likelihood of public confusion, not on formal mark use. It allows courts to examine market conduct holistically, including platform architecture, ranking design, and visibility bias. However, reliance on passing off alone is insufficient in markets dominated by powerful intermediaries, where deception is systemic rather than incidental.

Accordingly, the persistence of Sections 29 and 30 in their current interpretive form reveals a structural lag between trademark law and digital market realities. If "use in the course of trade" continues to be confined to visual or textual deployment of marks, large-scale algorithmic diversion of trademark goodwill will remain legally invisible. Addressing this gap does not necessarily require abandoning the concept of use, but it does require reconceptualising use to include algorithmic exploitation of trademark intent where such exploitation foreseeably distorts consumer origin perception.

In the absence of such reinterpretation or legislative clarification, Sections 29 and 30 will continue to protect trademarks against imitation, while leaving them vulnerable to a more pervasive threat: confusion engineered not by copying marks, but by code.

7. ALGORITHMIC INFLUENCE ON BRAND RECALL, COGNITIVE BIAS, AND ORIGIN MISATTRIBUTION

Algorithms have re-architected the informational conditions in which trademarks operate, transforming brand recall from a product of consumer-driven memory to a product of machine-steered reinforcement loops. In digital marketplaces and search ecosystems, consumer exposure is neither random nor neutral; it is governed by ranking hierarchies, behavioural predictions, and conversion-optimal routing. This creates origin misattribution, a new species of trademark deception, where the consumer's belief about source or affiliation is shaped not by mark similarity but by algorithmic visibility dominance and memory conditioning.

A. Understanding Brand Recall and Cognitive Bias in Legal Terms

Brand recall refers to a consumer's ability to associate a product or service with its trade source when prompted by a trademark. Traditionally, trademark law policed confusion arising from visual or phonetic similarity, presuming that memory is an autonomous cognitive result. However, algorithmic environments manufacture bias by inserting repeated associative cues and probability-based placement, creating what scholars call "visibility-induced legitimacy bias"—where consumers trust higher-ranked results even when unsolicited.

This introduces:

- **Exposure Bias**: Ranking priority creates perceived authenticity.
- **Association Bias**: Algorithms pair competitor goods in a trademark's memory neighborhood.
- **Recency & Repetition Bias**: Frequent nudges overwrite original trade-source memory.
- **Automation Shielding**: Platforms deny intent by attributing outcomes to AI.

B. Why Algorithmic Steering Creates Trademark Deception Without Infringement

Under Indian trademark jurisprudence, the essence of deception is a misrepresentation causing likely public confusion regarding trade connection, endorsement, or origin. In domains controlled by:

- Google Search
- Google Ads
- Amazon India
- Instagram

Confusion increasingly results from amplified brand substitution, mislabelled proximity, and interface ranking dominance, even when the competitor does not reproduce or imitate the trademark.

Indian courts recognise that deception may exist independently of infringement, especially where goodwill or trade-connection belief is diluted or diverted, as laid down in:

- Laxmikant V. Patel v. Chetanbhai Shah (2002)
- Cadila Health Care Ltd. v. Cadila Pharmaceuticals Ltd. (2001)

In algorithm-driven markets, *confusion arises cognitively*, even when trademarks are *formally dissimilar*.

C. Practical Mechanisms of Origin Misattribution

1. Competitor Traffic Hijack via Cognitive Neighborhood

A user searches "Nike jogging shoes"; the top half of the first screen displays *Puma* or *Adidas* in sponsored placements. The consumer associates the product class or quality cluster with Nike's goodwill, even though the trademark itself is not copied.

Entities involved:

- searched brand: Nike
- competing brand: Puma

This resembles goodwill routing, not infringement.

2. AI Recommendation Substitution

On Amazon India, a user who repeatedly purchases electronics sees a cheaper private-label charger appear before competitor listings when searching "Dell laptop charger," phrased as: *"Top choice for professionals, fast charging, premium reliability."* This creates associative source legitimacy, even without copying the mark of:

- Dell

The recommended brand becomes source-by-placement, not source-by-trademark.

3. Interface-Induced Legitimacy Bias

Search engines place the "Ad" label in lighter fonts or low contrast zones, knowing through Big Data that "72% of users do not scroll past the first 5 listings.""Empirical user-experience research consistently demonstrates that consumer attention is heavily concentrated on top-ranked search results, with a steep decline in engagement beyond the first screen or initial set of listings (Nielsen Norman Group; Pan et al.)." . UI visibility replaces trademark salience in determining origin belief.

4. Private Label Memory Capture

Marketplace owned brands like Amazfirst onBasics or Flipkart SmartBuy dominate first impressions because algorithms train on consumer click-through data showing that first-page results receive 8x higher trust. "Studies on ranking authority bias indicate that users tend to attribute greater legitimacy and relevance to higher-ranked results, often treating ranking position as a proxy for trustworthiness rather than independently evaluating source indicators (Pan et al.; Joachims et al.)."

This builds memory supremacy even when the mark is "distinct"—fulfilling deception tests under competition law rather than trademark law.

D. Intersection with Competition Law

Algorithmic steering turns trademark substitution into a competition law concern when conducted by a dominant intermediary. Under:

- Competition Act, 2002 - Section 4 (enforced by the Competition Commission of India) conduct may be anti-competitive when it:

1. Distorts consumer choice through predictive steering,

2. Prioritizes marketplace-owned brands to foreclose competitors,
3. Captures goodwill of searched trademarks via visibility dominance, and
4. Induces origin belief through placement architecture, not mark identity.

Thus:

- *Trademark infringement protects the mark itself.*
- *Trademark deception protects origin belief and goodwill.*
- *Competition law protects fairness when deception flows from platform dominance.*

E. Emerging Doctrinal Gap

Algorithms create three enforcement dilemmas:

1. No intent, yet deception exists → Who is liable? seller or platform?
2. No mark copying, yet origin belief is diverted → Does Section 29 TM Act apply?
3. Memory layers replace trademark distinctiveness as trade source cues → Classical confusion tests fall short.

Several international rulings acknowledge that market steering itself can create reverse confusion and competitive foreclosure, such as:

- L'Oréal SA v. eBay Inc (2009)
- FTC v. 1-800 Contacts (2021)

While jurisdictionally distinct, these illustrate how keyword auctions and ranking architectures influence digital origin and consumer belief zones without copying trademarks.

Deception occurs when algorithms manipulate *trade-source belief* even without similar marks.

Infringement occurs only when a registered mark or confusingly similar mark is *actually used in trade.*

Modern Confusion, unlike classical confusion, is *visibility-engineered, memory-conditioned, and platform-amplified.*

Enforcement must combine trademark cancellation, consumer remedies, and competition inquiry, not just infringement analysis.

8. BIG DATA AND AI AUTONOMOUS DECISION-MAKING: TRADEMARK DECEPTION WITHOUT HUMAN INTENT

The advent of Big Data coupled with autonomous decision-making has created markets where consumer confusion is not always the result of a deliberate human act, but rather the outcome of self-optimizing algorithms, predictive segmentation, and automated visibility engineering. This challenges a foundational premise of trademark enforcement: that deception presupposes an identifiable misrepresenting actor with intent or consciousness of wrongdoing. The digital economy reveals that trademark deception now frequently arises from structural algorithmic behaviour, shifting liability debates toward platforms, intermediaries, and automated systems.

Big Data platforms ingest vast datasets—search queries, click-through patterns, shopping histories, time-on-page, linguistic intent signals, device metadata, and competitor bidding behaviours—to train machine-learning systems that maximise engagement and conversions, rather than protect the trademark's source-integrity function.

Autonomous decision-making engines, such as:

- ranking decisions by Amazon India
- ad decision auctions by Google Ads
- personalised brand curation by Flipkart
- email-ecosystem nudging by Gmail

engineer visibility using probability models that often place substitutes next to (or ahead of) searched brands. This produces:

1. **Origin-by-Placement Bias** → higher-ranked products acquire perceived endorsement.
2. **Quality-Halo Borrowing** → competitors inherit cognitive product-class memories.
3. **Recirculation of Misleading Associations** → repeated suggestions overwrite authentic goodwill.
4. **Human-Intent Absence** → algorithm routes consumers based on predicted conformity, not intent.

Thus, deception exists in effect, but not necessarily in intent, a phenomenon trademark statutes did not envision explicitly.

- **Infringement** → requires actual use of the mark or confusing similarity.

- **Deception** → requires only a likelihood of public misperception, which may emerge from *contextual routing, visibility dominance, or cognitive adjacency engineering* even without any similarity between the marks.

This distinction was legally recognized in India long before algorithmic markets in:

- N.R. Dongre v. Whirlpool Corporation (1996), which protected consumer origin belief, not formal similarity.

Autonomous deception simply amplifies the same doctrine technologically.

The law protects marks as trade-origin indicators, but algorithms treat them as traffic-intent funnels.

A consumer searches for "iPhone charger" but sees first recommendation dominated by cheaper marketplace-owned chargers labelled as "Bestseller" because 83% of similar-segment buyers clicked them previously. Consumers infer Apple-grade reliability by ranking, not by trademark.

- Trademark searched: Apple
- Substitute ranking product family: marketplace private-label chargers (distinct marks)
- No copying → not infringement.
- **Inference manipulation** → deception.

A shoe retailer bids on "Adidas sneakers" in Google Ads. The ad is shown only to consumers predicted to like discounted athletic footwear, avoiding universal display. Platform shows the competitor above Adidas when relevant segment is detected.

- searched brand: Adidas

Seller mark is entirely distinct. Yet systems use consumer "propensity route" to legitimise competitor substitution. This is autonomous enforcement blind-spot exploitation.

On Flipkart, the platform positions its own brand products first for 9 out of 10 electronics searches after profile prediction of price sensitivity. Smaller brands lose recall not because their mark is similar, but because the algorithmic fidelity score promotes platform inventory first.

- Dominant platform: Flipkart
- Marketplace brand strategy zone: Flipkart SmartBuy (distinct mark family, no similarity)

This resembles competitive foreclosure through recall erasure, actionable under competition law, not infringement.

This introduces competing liability narratives:

1. **Seller Liability** → if bidding caused substitution.
2. **Platform Liability** → if UI, labels, or ranking foresaw deception but allowed it.
3. **Shared Liability** → if platform monetised competitor routing despite predictable confusion.

Courts globally have begun recognising that marketplace architecture which monetises intentional confusion at scale may amount to unfair competition or abuse of dominance, for example:

- Google LLC v. Australian Competition and Consumer Commission (2021)—held that ranking systems influencing consumer belief attract competition scrutiny.
- In the U.S., the FTC recognised that platforms enabling keyword-based perception capture and controlled rank-stacking can suppress genuine competition, moving deception harms into competition law.
- EU regulatory investigations increasingly expect intermediaries to adopt interface accountability where brand recall becomes the product.

Indian equivalent legal levers include:

- Bhartiya Nagrik Sanhita (BNS) for digital cognitive fraud effects at scale when public harm is foreseeable, and
- Bandwidth for inquiry under Section 4 of Competition Act

9. ALGORITHMIC BEHAVIOUR CREATING TRADEMARK HARM

Algorithmic systems within digital marketplaces generate a distinct set of trademark harms that diverge sharply from traditional infringement models. These harms occur not through imitation of marks but through distortions in visibility, ranking, recommendation architecture, and interface design. The consumer's perception of brand origin is shaped by what the algorithm chooses to display, prioritise, or suppress. As a result, confusion emerges from the structural behaviour of the platform, not from deliberate acts of copying by individual sellers.

One major source of harm arises from keyword advertising auctions. Platforms such as Google permit competitors to bid on the trademarks of well-known brands. When a consumer searches for a brand like "Bata shoes," the first result may be an advertisement for an unrelated competitor whose bid on the trademarked keyword was higher. The consumer, conditioned to trust top results, may assume an association or official endorsement. Confusion here arises even though the competing product may be visually and phonetically distinct. The distortion is created by algorithmic prioritisation rather than similarity of marks.

Another source of harm is the deliberate blending of sponsored and organic results. Many interfaces now obscure the distinction between paid advertisements and authentic listings. This creates a false impression of neutrality and can mislead consumers into believing that a sponsored product is the most relevant or official option. This "ad–organic blending" is increasingly recognised by scholars as a digital dark pattern capable of generating consumer deception at scale.

Algorithmic product substitution also plays a significant role. Recommendation systems that display "similar products" or "people also bought" suggestions can override consumer intention and redirect attention to competing brands. Such systems analyse behavioural data and frequently amplify products with higher probability of conversion, even if they bear no trademark similarity to the searched brand. The harm here lies not in the products themselves but in the automated redirection of consumer belief and attention.

Together, these practices reveal that trademark harm in digital markets is no longer limited to imitative conduct but emerges from behavioural engineering driven by large-scale data analytics and machine-learning systems.

10. COMPETITION LAW INTERSECTIONS AND THE ROLE OF THE CCI

The interplay between competition law and trademark law becomes increasingly relevant when algorithmic branding distorts consumer choice and market access. The Competition Act, 2002 provides the framework for examining whether platform-driven distortions amount to abuse of dominance, market foreclosure, or unfair trade practices. Algorithmic branding often raises competition concerns where platforms act as both marketplace operators and competitors within the same ecosystem.

A key concern involves self-preferencing, where platforms rank their own private labels or affiliated sellers above independent trademark owners. This can significantly reduce the visibility of the genuine trademark owner's goods and thereby erode brand equity. Such visibility distortions may not constitute infringement under the Trade Marks Act, yet they undermine the fundamental identity function of trademarks by preventing consumers from reaching the intended brand.

Another concern is predatory ranking, in which platforms artificially demote particular sellers or brands in favour of those who purchase advertising or share higher commissions. This may lead to competitive foreclosure, where smaller or non-advertising entities—despite having legitimate trademark rights—struggle to compete due to systematic ranking disadvantage. The Competition Commission of India (CCI) has shown willingness to address similar concerns in cases involving Google's search bias and MakeMyTrip's ranking practices, indicating a growing readiness to scrutinise digital marketplace conduct through a competition law lens.

Algorithmic behavioural exploitation represents a further dimension of harm. Platforms utilise consumer data not merely to present options but to shape preferences and subtly influence commercial decisions. The law traditionally focuses on consumer welfare from the perspective of price and output, but algorithmic manipulation introduces a more nuanced challenge: the exploitation of behavioural vulnerabilities to divert consumer attention away from genuine trademark owners. This raises questions regarding whether competition law should expand its behavioural standards to address manipulative interface design and perception steering.

The convergence of trademark and competition concerns suggests that algorithmic branding cannot be regulated in isolation. Both fields must work together to ensure that brand origin remains meaningful and that consumers retain the capacity to make informed decisions.

11. EVIDENTIARY CHALLENGES IN ESTABLISHING ALGORITHMIC CONFUSION

Proving confusion in algorithmic environments presents substantial evidentiary challenges. Traditional trademark litigation relies on comparison of marks, consumer surveys, and evidence of misrepresentation. However, algorithmic deception does not stem from visual or phonetic similarity but from opaque and dynamic processes embedded within digital platforms.

To establish confusion, litigants may require access to algorithmic decision logs, ranking data, impression statistics, click-through patterns, and internal design specifications of platform interfaces. These records are often proprietary and protected as trade secrets, creating an information imbalance between trademark owners and digital intermediaries. Without access to internal systems, it becomes extremely difficult to demonstrate how rankings were generated or how consumers were directed toward competitor products.

Courts may need to adopt new evidentiary presumptions to address this asymmetry. One approach is the presumption of confusion arising from opacity, where the burden shifts to platforms to demonstrate that their ranking or recommendation systems did not mislead consumers. Another approach involves mandating transparency measures, such as disclosure of factors influencing ranking or the introduction of independent algorithmic audits. Comparative developments in the European Union under the Digital Markets Act and Digital Services Act demonstrate increasing emphasis on transparency in automated decision systems, and these emerging norms may eventually influence Indian jurisprudence.

The lack of visibility into algorithmic processes raises foundational questions about the adequacy of existing legal standards. Courts must determine how to assess confusion in an environment where consumer impressions are shaped by personalized, non-transparent systems rather than uniform marketplace representations.

12. ALGORITHMIC TRANSPARENCY AND THE NEED FOR RANKING FAIRNESS

Regulatory developments in other jurisdictions highlight the need for algorithmic transparency and ranking fairness in platform governance. The European Union's legal framework now requires certain designated platforms to provide clear information on ranking parameters, to implement audit mechanisms, and to disclose the basis for personalised recommendations. These measures are designed to mitigate the risk of opaque algorithms distorting consumer choice and harming brand visibility.

India currently lacks explicit statutory obligations requiring platforms to disclose how their algorithms affect visibility or ranking. In the absence of such obligations, trademark owners face considerable difficulty in identifying whether harm stems from algorithmic behaviour or from legitimate competitive conduct. This deficiency creates a regulatory vacuum where deception can occur without any corresponding legal accountability.

Introducing transparency duties would enable courts and regulators to better evaluate whether algorithmic outputs create confusion. Such duties may include periodic algorithmic audits, disclosure of key ranking factors, labelling of sponsored or personalised results, and mechanisms enabling trademark owners to challenge discriminatory or misleading rankings. Without these measures, the marketplace becomes increasingly susceptible to invisible distortions that undermine both trademark protection and consumer trust.

13. TOWARDS A NEW LEGAL DOCTRINE OF ALGORITHMIC CONFUSION

The emerging challenges posed by digital marketplaces warrant recognition of a new legal category: algorithmic confusion. This doctrine would acknowledge that modern confusion often arises from the architecture of digital intermediaries rather than direct acts of infringement. It would incorporate concepts such as system-generated misrepresentation, automated origin distortion, and perception steering.

Under this doctrine, liability would not depend on the similarity of marks but on whether the platform's conduct materially affected the consumer's ability to correctly identify the commercial origin of goods or services. This approach aligns with the core purpose of trademark law, which is to protect the link between the mark and its source. It also responds to the evolving technological environment by shifting focus from the actions of individual sellers to the systemic behaviour of intermediaries.

A doctrine of algorithmic confusion would also harmonise trademark and competition law by recognizing that visibility manipulation can simultaneously mislead consumers and distort fair competition. Courts could then adopt more integrated approaches to analyzing cases involving algorithmic branding, recognizing that the harm spans both legal domains.

14. CONCLUSION

Algorithmic branding represents a structural transformation of the marketplace, where data-driven systems intermediate nearly every aspect of consumer decision-making. Traditional trademark principles, designed for tangible markets, are increasingly insufficient to address harms arising from algorithmic ranking, predictive recommendations, and behaviourally targeted advertising. These systems produce confusion not through imitation but through the re-engineering of visibility, relevance, and perceived authenticity.

To safeguard consumer autonomy, the integrity of brand origin, and the fairness of digital markets, legal reform must evolve in three directions: incorporating transparency obligations for platforms, expanding trademark doctrines to recognise system-generated confusion, and integrating competition law principles that address digital foreclosure and manipulation. Without these reforms, the law risks legitimizing a marketplace in which deception persists without infringement, and consumer choice becomes an artefact of algorithmic design rather than independent decision-making.

The engineering of confusion through algorithmic systems challenges the foundational assumptions of trademark law. Confusion arises: without mark similarity, without direct misrepresentation, and often without identifiable human intent.

Yet the effect on consumer perception and goodwill is real and measurable. This necessitates a doctrinal shift from evaluating trademark harm solely through similarity analysis toward recognizing system-generated deception as legally cognizable harm.

REFERENCES

.Advanced Web Ranking. (2023). *Organic CTR study.*

Cadila Health Care Ltd. v. Cadila Pharmaceuticals Ltd., (2001) 5 SCC 73 (India).

Competition Act. (2002).

Competition and Markets Authority (UK). (2022). *Online choice architecture and consumer harm*. CMA.

Competition Commission of India. (2022). *Market study on e-commerce in India*. CCI.

Consumer Protection Act, 2019 (India).

Dong, Y. (2021). Trademark confusion in digital marketplaces. *The Journal of World Intellectual Property*, *24*(4), 367–389.

European Commission. (2020). *Antitrust proceedings in the e-commerce and platform economy*. European Commission.

.Federal Trade Commission. (2013). *FTC staff letter on search engine advertising disclosures*. Consumer Reports. (2018). *Dark patterns and digital deception in online interfaces*.

.Federal Trade Commission v. 1-800 Contacts, Inc., 1:16-cv-02586 (D. Utah, 2021).

Google LLC v. Australian Competition and Consumer Commission, [2021] HCA 2 (High Court of Australia, 2021).

Hofmann, F., & Keates, J. (2013). Trade marks in cyberspace: The challenges of online enforcement. *European Intellectual Property Review*, *35*(3), 129–137.

Joachims, T., Granka, L., Pan, B., Hembrooke, H., & Gay, G. (2005). Accurately interpreting clickthrough data as implicit feedback. *Proceedings of the 28th Annual International ACM SIGIR Conference*, 154–161.

Katyal, S. K., & Grinvald, L. C. (2018). Trademark protection and consumer search costs on the internet. *Harvard Journal of Law & Technology*, *31*(2), 555–620.

Kaviraj Pandit Durga Dutt Sharma v. Navaratna Pharmaceutical Laboratories, AIR 1965 SC 980 (India).

Khachatryan, S. (2022). Online trademark infringement and platform liability. *Journal of Intellectual Property Law & Practice*, *17*(6), 463–472.

L'Oréal SA v. eBay International AG, Case C-324/09, EU:C:2011:474.

L'Oréal SA v. eBay International AG, Case C-324/09, EU:C:2011:474 (Court of Justice of the European Union, 2011).

Laxmikant V. Patel v. Chetanbhai Shah, (2002) 3 SCC 65 (India).

.Nielsen Norman Group. (2020). *Eyetracking research: How users read and interact with search results.*

N.R. Dongre v. Whirlpool Corporation, (1996) 5 SCC 714 (India).

Pan, B., Hembrooke, H., Joachims, T., Lorigo, L., Gay, G., & Granka, L. (2007). In Google we trust: Users' decisions on rank, position, and relevance. *Journal of Computer-Mediated Communication, 12*(3), 801–823.

Pasquale, F. (2015). *The black box society: The secret algorithms that control money and information.* Harvard University Press.

Reckitt & Colman Ltd. v. Borden Inc., [1990] 1 WLR 491 (HL).

Regulation (EU) 2022/1925 of the European Parliament and of the Council of 14 September 2022 on contestable and fair markets in the digital sector (Digital Markets Act). (2022).

Regulation (EU) 2022/2065 of the European Parliament and of the Council of 19 October 2022 on a Single Market for Digital Services (Digital Services Act). (2022).

Trademarks Act. (1999).

Yeung, K. (2018). Algorithmic regulation: A critical interrogation. *Regulation & Governance, 12*(4), 505–523.

Zuboff, S. (2019). *The age of surveillance capitalism: The fight for a human future at the new frontier of power.* PublicAffairs.

Chapter 7
Technological Change: Artificial Intelligence in Law and the Transformation of the Legal Profession From the Perspective of Progressive Legal Theory

Junaidi Junaidi
http://orcid.org/0000-0002-2948-696X
Sjakhyakirti University, Indonesia

ABSTRACT

The use of artificial intelligence is currently an important component of the advancement of information technology worldwide. Consequently, the intelligence of a system correlates directly with its ability to perform actions that could have legal consequences. AI has entered many industries, including healthcare and education. The ability of machines to perform tasks that typically require human intelligence is referred to as artificial intelligence. Technology plays a very important role in society today because it has the ability to influence the attitudes and actions of its members. Therefore, comprehensive legislation is needed to ensure that artificial intelligence is used fairly. According to progressive legal theory, AI can be used to meet human needs rather than maintain existing systems. Progressive legal theory is based on the "law for humans" paradigm. This theory links the values of Pancasila as the moral foundation of the Indonesian nation with the ethics of applying artificial intelligence and its consequences.

DOI: 10.4018/979-8-3373-7685-1.ch007

INTRODUCTION

Among the most significant aspects of contemporary human life is the transformation that is currently taking place in the technology industry. In order to keep up with the times, individuals need to be able to quickly adapt. Each and every facet of human existence must undergo change in order to ensure the survival of their culture, which includes the rules and ethical standards that govern it. According to Pabubung (2023), artificial intelligence (AI) provides assistance in a variety of other ways in addition to assisting humans in gaining access to information about the world as it exists today. The field of computer science known as artificial intelligence (AI) makes it possible for machines like computers to carry out tasks that are comparable to those that humans are capable of (Ririh et al., 2020; Jaya & Goh, 2021). The ambiguity surrounding the definition of artificial intelligence (AI) is a significant issue for academics, governments and the general public alike. There is still much debate surrounding the definition of artificial intelligence, and it is difficult to reach a consensus on this term across fields. Various devices described as 'smart', such as refrigerators, mobile phones and speakers, are often referred to as artificial intelligence, as are self-driving vehicles (Ghorayeb et al., 2021; Park et al., 2021). This lack of a standard definition hinders our understanding of whether society truly accepts artificial intelligence in practice, or just the concept of artificial intelligence (Kelly, et al, 2023).

An important step forward is represented by the implementation of artificial intelligence (AI). It is able to provide assistance with and automate a variety of aspects of the legal field (European Commission, 2021). AI is now being used for legal research, contract analysis, court decision analysis, and even case outcome projections. This marks the beginning of the legal technology era, also known as 'legal tech'. This new era increases the efficiency of legal processes while improving access to justice.

Artificial intelligence (AI) is defined by Russell and Norvig (2016) as the development of systems that can carry out operations that were previously limited to humans, such as data-driven decision-making. Legal systems have a lot of opportunity to react faster to such developments. According to Susskind (2019), the future of the legal system will be online and digital, with simple cases being handled automatically by artificial intelligence. This demonstrates how technology has had a significant impact on how the legal system has developed.

Artificial intelligence will soon be used for legal research, contract analysis, and the discovery phase to find crucial documents. Artificial intelligence is currently being used to assist with agreement droughting, forecast the results of legal proceedings, and offer advice on court decisions pertaining to penalties or incarceration.

Previous research has demonstrated that artificial intelligence and human solicitors are not equally accurate (Gellers, 2020).

For instance, in the United States, twenty solicitors collaborated with an AI system named Robot Ross to identify legal issues in about thirty cases in four hours. This test showed that Robot Ross identified legal issues with an accuracy rate of 94%, while human solicitors identified legal issues with an average accuracy rate of 85% (Dwiputro, 2020). Additionally, China is using artificial intelligence in legal experiments. An example of this is the AI Prosecutor, which is thought to have been created by the Shanghai Pudong People's Procuratorate (Chen, 2021).

This is evident from the artificial intelligence (AI) trials that have been carried out in a number of nations. China, for example, employed artificial intelligence in 2017 to decide digital cases involving online sales disputes, copyright, and e-commerce product liability. In a contract comprehension competition held in the United States, two seasoned solicitors faced off against an AI-based lawyer. The result shocked law professors at the University of Southern California, Duke University School of Law, and Stanford University. The AI lawyer had performed better than the other 20 lawyers, they said. Recently, artificial intelligence (AI) has been developed in the United Kingdom to help the public with legal matters. As of right now, it has helped about 160,000 people and rendered more than 1,100 legal services. Its success is demonstrated by numerous additional examples (Azis, 2023).

The legal industry will change as new, human-designed legal professions emerge. It is hoped that these new occupations will help legal professionals in their future endeavors. The use of artificial intelligence robots in a variety of legal domains is currently on the rise. Studies show that using this technology in the legal sector can significantly improve case resolution. For instance, chatbots designed to assist individuals with legal issues can provide more affordable and convenient solutions. The purpose of this study is to examine how Indonesian legal professionals use artificial intelligence (AI) in their daily work and personal lives. Artificial intelligence capabilities are required by law. This can reduce expensive mistakes and boost worker productivity. Artificial intelligence can also expedite law enforcement, investigations, and decision-making in exceptional circumstances.

The legal profession has changed as a result of the introduction of digital products like automation and artificial intelligence (AI) (Vlassis, 2007). Legal professionals can more quickly identify and analyses legal issues thanks to AI and automation, which improves client services. Automation and artificial intelligence are viewed as potential solutions for society, especially as access to qualified legal professionals becomes more challenging and expensive (Mahomed, 2019). The public's fear of the risks posed by automation and artificial intelligence has sparked a continuous search for answers to these problems. This includes technological adjustments, as well as potential changes to the legal field in future (Garingan & Pickard, 2023).

Artificial intelligence (AI) is currently being used extensively by lawyers worldwide. The Swedish law firm Freja Partner's Edward Stromstedt offered his opinions on the application of artificial intelligence in the legal field. This happened at the Swedish-Polish Chamber of Commerce's 'Innovation if You Want to Stay Competitive' seminar, which was conducted both online and offline on May 14, 2024. In his talk, “Innovating the Legal Profession with AI,” Edward talked about how he uses artificial intelligence in his legal practice, specifically to find information for ongoing projects (Surahmat et al., 2023).

Without clear regulations, the application of artificial intelligence (AI) in the legal field can cause problems such as loyalty to algorithms, confusion over who is responsible for system errors and potential human rights violations. It is therefore crucial for the Indonesian government and relevant parties to formulate appropriate policies immediately to ensure the safe and lawful use of artificial intelligence. Surden's (2014) study on machine learning and law is one of several previous studies that have examined the use of AI in law. This is in addition to Ashley's (2017) research, which demonstrates AI's ability to assist in the legal thought process. Across the country, a number of articles have begun to explore the relationship between law and technology. However, these articles are merely descriptive and do not provide an in-depth analysis of the ethical and regulatory issues that are the main concern. Consequently, more in-depth, critical analysis is required to determine how Indonesian law should respond to artificial intelligence technology developments in legal applications.

Artificial intelligence continues to evolve, creating better solutions for the future (Devianto & Dwiasnati, 2020). The increasing use and development of artificial intelligence technology brings many opportunities and consequences. In Indonesia, a country with diverse values, cultures, and local wisdom, it is important to consider the relationship between artificial intelligence technology and the principles upheld by the nation. By placing the nation's moral values at the heart of Indonesia's progress and civilization, the principle of Pancasila plays a key role in driving the country's advancement in artificial intelligence technology (Ramdhani & Dewi, 2022).

The legal profession is changing, with new AI-assisted roles set to enhance lawyers' careers in the future. Various legal fields are beginning to utilize artificial intelligence robots, and research shows that artificial intelligence is increasingly being incorporated into professional practice. In law, artificial intelligence has many potential benefits, such as increasing productivity and reducing errors. In certain situations, artificial intelligence can even accelerate decision-making, investigations and legal processes. However, if the legal profession is to implement artificial intelligence, it must consider progressive legal theory, which emphasizes that the law should prioritize human welfare and be in accordance with *Pancasila* values.

In this context, progressive law offers a relevant perspective. This legal approach prioritizes social justice, emphasizing that the law must be flexible and adaptable to technological and social developments. Progressive law encourages rules that consider humanity, fundamental rights, and the protection of the most vulnerable people. When it comes to utilizing artificial intelligence, progressive law can provide the basis for creating flexible regulations that govern not only how artificial intelligence is used, but also ensure that ethical principles underpin its implementation.

This article is divided into several sections. After an introduction and explanation of the research methodology, it will discuss the use of artificial intelligence and automation in the legal profession. Focusing on regulations related to the use of artificial intelligence in the legal field, the discussion will center on progressive legal theory. This theory emphasizes that those who think, innovate and develop information technology must prioritize humans, so that the technology they create improves human well-being. Next, the article will examine the use of artificial intelligence in law, emphasizing the ethical and legal aspects related to automation and artificial intelligence in the legal profession. Finally, the article will discuss professional legal competency standards and strategies for maintaining the sustainability of the legal profession amidst automation and artificial intelligence, as well as future projections for the legal profession.

RESEARCH METHOD

This research was conducted using a normative methodology and an in-depth literature review. Secondary data was obtained from scientific journals, internet sources discussing technology in the field of law ('legal tech'), case studies on the application of AI and other publications related to the research topic. Legal studies were conducted to resolve legal issues. The ultimate goal of this study was to make recommendations on the actions that should be taken. Three approaches were employed: the legal approach (statute approach), the conceptual approach and the comparative approach.

1. To ensure the research complies with applicable regulations, a legislative method is employed to investigate a legal issue by examining relevant legislation. This study will examine various concepts and theories relating to artificial intelligence, the noble values of *Pancasila* and progressive legal theory.
2. A conceptual approach is adopted to explain existing principles relating to the research topic, particularly where specific legislation is absent. This study uses the conceptual approach to examine, from the perspective of progressive legal theory, how artificial intelligence is applied in the legal realm and how it impacts

the legal profession. This conceptual approach aims to identify the relationship between ideas, theories and concepts related to law when assessing the legality of its utilisation.

3. This study compares Indonesian and other countries' legal regulations to identify similarities and differences. The study focuses on the influence of artificial intelligence (AI) on the future of law. A case study is conducted on countries in the European Union that have established regulations regarding the use of artificial intelligence in the legal field. Comparisons will be made to determine the advantages and disadvantages of the current regulations. The results can then be used to inform the development of improved legal models

REGULATIONS GOVERNING THE USE OF ARTIFICIAL INTELLIGENCE (AI) IN THE LEGAL FIELD FROM THE PERSPECTIVE OF PROGRESSIVE LEGAL THEORY

Advances in computer and communication technology have enabled the development of computer network systems spread across the globe. Computer network applications are used not only in laboratories and universities for scientific research, but also in many other areas. They are also used by businesses, banks, governments, the military and defense agencies, legal systems and the judiciary (Junaidi, 2020). Thanks to the internet, artificial intelligence can be applied more easily in various aspects of people's lives. However, this also creates challenges for the legal sector (Pirmansyah et al., 2021). The legal sector, like many other areas of life, has changed due to advances in information and communication technology (ICT), especially with the emergence of artificial intelligence (AI). AI can automate routine tasks and improve quality, speeding up processes that previously required human time and effort (Muhana, 2025). The main issue is not the technology itself, but how the law regulates artificial intelligence to ensure fairness (Judge, et al, 2025).

AI has great potential to improve the efficiency and effectiveness of decision-making in the legal sector, particularly in legal proceedings and courts (Putra, 2024). One important initiative impacting the provision of legal aid is the rollout of DoNotPay chat in the UK, which currently offers legal aid services in over 1,000 legal areas (Mannes, 2024). However, since AI is essentially a tool used by humans to accelerate their own work processes, AI operational systems cannot operate independently. Many people believe that big data generated by artificial intelligence (AI) can provide more comprehensive answers than human thought alone (Junaidi, 2023). Almost every aspect of human life is now influenced by the ever-evolving field of AI. Therefore, it is crucial to implement existing laws to control AI, especially in the legal field (Junaidi, 2025). This must be taken into consideration because

AI technology currently has the ability to interact and act like humans. Clear regulations regarding AI are essential for ensuring legal certainty. Current legal rules often cannot keep up with the rapid progress of society, particularly in today's era of rapid innovation. This can lead to a lack of legislation (Junaidi & Fadzil, 2024).

Advances in AI influence various aspects of the modern legal system, including legal research, contract drafting and predicting trial outcomes (Surden, 2019; Susskind, 2023). Advances in AI in the field of law have given rise to artificial intelligence lawyers and judges. To gain a better understanding of the current use of AI in law, it is helpful to conceptualize it in terms of three user groups. The first group consists of legal administrators, i.e. those who create and enforce legal regulations, such as judges, legislators, administrative officials and law enforcement officers. The second group consists of legal practitioners, i.e. those who utilize AI to create and enforce legal regulations. The third group consists of individuals or subjects of the law, i.e. people, companies and organizations that are under legal regulation and utilize the law to achieve their objectives (Surden, 2019).

AI is software that greatly assists human work. The author believes that AI is a machine with the ability to perform many tasks that humans carry out using their natural intelligence. AI is intended to describe aspects of human life such as task planning, problem solving, thought processes, idea and concept recognition, and improved analytical abilities, as well as various other actions that can increase work efficiency and speed (Quteishat et al., 2024). The legal sector has many opportunities to improve the administration of justice, including in the areas of the judiciary, legislation, and the economy. AI speeds up the decision-making process by using data as a basis due to its efficiency and effectiveness. However, as feelings, will and conscience are necessary for decision-making, AI cannot be used for this purpose (Putri, 2024).

AI technology enables legal professionals to provide better legal services to their clients and accelerate decision-making processes. Law has many AI applications, including:

1. **Legal Research and Jurisprudence Studies:** AI can help legal practitioners in this field become more efficient and accurate, and streamline processes. AI-powered platforms use natural language processing (NLP) and machine learning algorithms to analyze large volumes of legal documents, regulations and court decisions remarkably quickly and accurately. Lawyers can use these tools to conduct thorough legal research, identify relevant case law and analyze intricate legal issues. AI-supported analysis also enables the creation of predictive models for case outcomes, helping legal practitioners to make more data-driven decisions. AI technology can accelerate legal discovery and support

the provision of high-quality legal services by enhancing human capabilities and automating repetitive tasks (Ghani & Malik, 2020; Nadjia, 2024).

2. **Agreement Evaluation and Drafting:** Advanced AI capabilities can simplify and improve the efficiency of the process of evaluating and drafting agreements, transforming conventional methods. AI-powered contract evaluation systems use machine learning algorithms to examine and extract important clauses, terms and conditions from contract documents. This speeds up the assessment process while reducing the likelihood of errors. The platform can delve into and analyze legal language, enabling thorough reviews of contract terms to identify risks and inconsistencies. Additionally, artificial intelligence can assist in drafting agreements by offering formatting suggestions, improved language usage and recommendations based on industry standards and previous data. With AI, legal practitioners can reduce potential legal risks, improve agreement quality, and accelerate the negotiation process. Ultimately, this will generate greater value for clients and other relevant parties. Kira Systems and LawGeex are AI-based platforms designed to help legal teams review and analyze contracts more effectively by focusing on clauses, potential risks and significant inconsistencies. As well as ensuring compliance with applicable legal provisions, these platforms accelerate the due diligence stage in the merger and acquisition process (Goodall & Hodge, 2020; Biresaw & Saste, 2022).
3. **Predictive Analysis Related to Case Outcomes:** Artificial intelligence (AI) algorithms play a crucial role in the predictive analysis of case outcomes, enabling legal practitioners to predict potential litigation situations and plan strategies accordingly. AI can help legal practitioners predict and plan strategies by analyzing past case data, court decisions, and various contextual factors. These predictive models allow solicitors to evaluate the strengths and weaknesses of their legal arguments, anticipate potential issues and develop more informed litigation strategies. Furthermore, AI-powered predictive analytics assist in risk assessment and resource allocation, enabling law firms to optimize their litigation portfolios and focus on high-value cases. Ultimately, legal professionals can improve efficiency, enhance decision-making processes, and maximize resource utilization (Li & Zhang, 2019; Filipova, 2024).
4. **Legal Chatbot:** Legal services are using legal chatbots as AI applications. These tools are intended to provide basic legal assistance quickly and affordably to everyone. Various countries have used applications such as DoNotPay described as 'the world's first automated solicitor' to help users draft letters of objection or appeal, and even simple lawsuits relating to traffic fines and other administrative offences. These chatbots use an interactive dialogue interface based on natural language processing (NLP), allowing users to ask legal questions in everyday language and receive automatic answers quickly. The two main advantages of

legal chatbots are their accessibility and scalability. They can be accessed at any time and from anywhere, eliminating the need for expensive consultations or meetings with solicitors. Additionally, chatbots can be configured to comply with local regulations, provide relevant information and generate legal documents such as contracts, written statements or petitions. This is particularly helpful for marginalized communities or groups that previously had difficulty obtaining formal legal assistance due to cost, geographical barriers or a lack of information. However, legal chatbots have several shortcomings, as do all artificial intelligence technologies. They are still unable to handle complex legal issues or those requiring in-depth analysis, a task that only legal experts can perform. Furthermore, there is a risk that the information provided may be inaccurate or misleading if the training data or algorithms are not regularly updated to reflect changes in applicable laws. Legal chatbots should serve as the initial point of contact for legal matters, guiding users through legal processes. This includes advising users to consult a solicitor or legal aid agency if their issue exceeds the chatbot's capabilities. If used judiciously and tailored to existing legal systems, legal chatbots can be a strategic tool for improving access to technology-based legal services. These results support the idea that AI can play a significant part in enhancing the quality and effectiveness of legal practice. However, maximizing the benefits depends heavily on the preparedness of the regulations and the knowledge of users in the field of law (Chien & Lee, 2020).

The author argues that applying artificial intelligence (AI) to the legal field represents a paradigm shift and provides unprecedented opportunities to enhance productivity, accuracy and innovation. AI technology enables legal practitioners to automate daily tasks such as legal research and document analysis, providing more efficient and affordable legal services, as well as predictive analysis of case outcomes. However, responsible and ethical use of AI in law requires careful assessment of potential biases and transparency, as well as compliance with applicable ethical and legal standards. The legal profession can maximize the use of AI while upholding the principles of justice, accountability, and the protection of individual rights. AI can be leveraged to improve access to justice, drive innovation in the legal field, and uphold the rule of law in the digital age.

AI is also very helpful in the field of law and legal science in general. AI applications assist the legal reasoning process by providing tools and methods designed to solve specific legal problems, utilizing knowledge to find solutions. The legal community recognizes the role of AI in legal research and reasoning processes. Legal reasoning is the process of creating and delivering accountable responses to specific legal issues. For instance, legal text databases can be used to find cases related to current court proceedings (Alzbeta, 2017). Additionally, artificial intelligence technology assists in filtering out irrelevant data during the legal research process in court. Furthermore, many AI systems can analyze and resolve legal issues independently (Tu et al., 2024). Similarly, various types of artificial intelligence are employed in different areas of legal studies. For instance, legal logic can be employed to describe legal precedents, correct errors in legal documents, validate regulations or identify ambiguities within them (Sergot, 2010). Conversely, many technologies help advocates conduct legal research. For instance, they can identify problematic contract clauses or develop winning strategies in intellectual property cases. Online dispute resolution, which aims to resolve disputes between parties who have reached an agreement via a digital platform, is another example of AI's application in the legal field (Niebla, 2018).

Therefore, most people agree that combining human oversight with technical AI intelligence can produce excellent legal outcomes (Brynjolfsson & McAfee, 2014). For instance, while solicitors may not screen documents directly, they play a vital role in the e-discovery process (Susskind, 2023). It appears that AI will continue to evolve and change in the future, making it a popular tool in legal research and practice. In 2017, the British House of Lords established a select committee to examine the economic, legal and social implications of the development of artificial intelligence, recognizing its inevitable influence (Najafli, 2025). Similarly, 25 European countries signed the EU Declaration on Cooperation on Artificial Intelligence in 2017 (The EU Declaration on Cooperation on Artificial Intelligence, 2018). There are variations in how countries implement regulations, and these variations can be seen in the way in which the regulations are applied (Blind & Munch, 2024).

Table 1. Comparison of Artificial Intelligence Regulations in Various Countries

Aspect	Indonesia	China	European Union
AI Regulations	There are no specific regulations yet	However, there are smart court regulations	There are strict rules regarding transparency and accountability
AI usage	Still in the research phase	It is used for case analysis and mediation	The focus is on protecting human rights
Accountability	This depends on law enforcement	AI can make light legal decisions	Judges have full control

This table provides a comparative analysis of the rule of law regarding artificial intelligence (AI) in various countries, classified by the strictness of its enforcement. It is crucial that the legal system has AI regulations to determine how this technology can be used to support legal processes. Some countries have enacted broad legislation to ensure transparency and accountability, while others are still developing their policy frameworks. These differences in legislation reflect how each country assesses the benefits and risks of AI in the legal field. The table illustrates global trends in AI regulation and its impact on the performance of legal systems. Consequently, this comparative research can assist policymakers in creating appropriate AI regulations that balance legal rights and encourage innovation. However, this progress also presents challenges for legal practitioners. Regulations are needed to protect human rights, prevent the emergence of unfair practices within algorithmic systems, and establish the responsibilities of the relevant parties (Borgesius, 2020; EU Artificial Intelligence Act (2021/2024).

Legal regulations should not be reduced to a fixed system that cannot be changed (Rahardjo, 2006a). Progressive legal theory argues that using AI in the legal system could undermine its primary objectives. Law enforcement that relies solely on practical reasoning tends to make rigid and unreasonable decisions. If the legal decision-making process does not consider conscience, punishment can be reduced to a mechanical tool. According to Rahardjo (2009a), progressive law holds that the purpose of law is to achieve justice, welfare and happiness for humanity. It is not an absolute and final institution, but rather a means of helping people. Therefore, according to Rahardjo (2006), the doctrine of progressive law emphasizes adopting a critical attitude towards existing legislation rather than simply complying with it. Conscience plays an important role in realizing moral justice in a legal state based on the principles of the philosophy of Pancasila (Rahardjo, 2003). Progressive law is an attempt to change the legal paradigm, which is often trapped in narrow formal justice.

The main principle of this theory is that laws are made for the benefit of society. When a legal problem arises, it is not the legal system itself that needs to be solved, but rather the parties that are forced to become involved in it. The purpose of legislation is to create a just, prosperous and happy society. Therefore, the law is always changing, or it can be described as a process: the process of law being created (Junaidi et al., 2024).

When discussing progressive law, it is important to consider the underlying philosophy that law is created for the benefit of humanity (Rahardjo, 2007a). This philosophy is considered the foundation of progressive law. Punishment exists to fulfil human needs, not the other way around. Therefore, human interests cannot be separated from the law. The extent to which the law improves societal well-being determines its quality. Consequently, legal progressives believe that law should promote justice and society (Rahardjo, 2007).

According to the principle of progressive law, the legal system should serve to meet the needs of society, rather than merely maintaining the status quo. The two main components that form the basis of progressive law are: (1) the desire to continuously improve the legal system's services to society through ongoing efforts to enhance their quality; and (2) the desire to continuously encourage society to apply the law, alongside the belief that law can change the world (Junaidi, 2025).

Satjipto Rahardjo (2007) also discussed the philosophy of the nation, stating that the legitimate legal basis should be Pancasila, emphasizing essence over legal procedures. In short, the law should demonstrate deep justice, not just procedural justice. Furthermore, according to Rahardjo (2003), efforts to achieve moral justice or the rule of law priorities consideration of conscience within the context of the state of law based on the principles of the philosophy of the nation, or 'Pancasila'. One could describe the movement to implement progressive law as an effort to change the course of law, which has historically tended towards formal justice.

Progressive law is a process that liberates itself from conventional concepts that are no longer relevant in order to meet modern needs. According to Satjipto Rahardjo, this interpretation is not necessarily based on logic alone, but can also stem from the habit of logical thinking. This is because the interpretive process involves leaps, with no logical connection between existing and newly emerging ideas. Therefore, progressive interpretation is not limited to a literal reading of the text (Rahardjo, 2006).

The presence of AI in the legal system can undermine the goals of progressive law. If the law is only applied for operational purposes, overly simplistic and polarized conclusions will be reached in cases. Law will only function as a mechanical tool if conscience is not involved in legal decision-making. The theory of progressive law is based on the fundamental belief that law is a tool created to help people lead just, prosperous and happy lives. This theory does not portray law as an absolute and definitive institution, but is instead influenced by law's ability to serve human interests (Rahardjo, 2009). Progressive law's core teaching is to be critical rather than compliant or accepting of rules (Rahardjo, 2006).

The author believes that Satjipto Rahardjo's focus on progressive law is rooted in humanity. Innovators, developers and thinkers in the IT field must follow these principles to ensure that their innovations bring happiness to humanity. The process of drafting laws and regulations cannot be viewed from a sociological perspective as an entirely independent action. According to this perspective, the law-making process is based on social elements, aims to achieve social goals, is influenced by social intervention and has social consequences. In order to reduce the tension caused by differing interests, it is crucial to use methods that encourage community participation. This ensures that the needs and interests of the community are reflected in the resulting legislation. These methods align with Nonet and Selznick's theory of responsive law and Rahardjo and Dimyati's (2002) theory of progressive law.

The progressive law does not only consider how the law should be implemented literally; it also considers the deeper meaning and motivation behind the law. Additionally, its implementation incorporates spiritual intelligence, suggesting that it is not solely focused on cognitive aspects. In other words, law enforcement based on belief, empathy, contribution and dedication to alleviating societal suffering must be combined with the courage to find more efficient solutions (Rahardjo, 2009).

According to Satjipto Rahardjo, progressive law is not a fixed system, but an entity that evolves alongside human life. Sanctions should not be considered in isolation from their context. The norms that regulate social interaction are a source of law. Therefore, to ensure justice, legal analysis and investigation must be conducted in various ways. In conclusion, progressive legal theory has three main characteristics: (1) law aims to promote human welfare rather than personal gain; (2) law is constantly changing and evolving; and (3) law functions as an institution based on human values (Rahardjo, 2004).

The author believes that the values of Pancasila are the ideal foundation on which to build progressive law and achieve social justice. Progressive law must absolutely be based on the values of Pancasila, particularly social justice, because without these values, progressive law will not be relevant to the Indonesian legal system. Progressive law ensures that the law continues to adapt to the dynamics of community life. Progressive law emphasizes the independence of law enforcement by abandoning a dogmatic approach to achieve justice. However, this freedom must still be in harmony with the basic principles of Indonesian law and of the ideology of the state, Pancasila.

The author argues that creating rules based on values is becoming increasingly important. Justice, transparency and accountability must form the basis of AI ethics. Procedures and operational standards must be in place to evaluate artificial intelligence systems in the legal field. In cases of errors or misuse of technology, clear oversight and accountability systems must be in place. Legal and human resource capabilities must be improved to ensure proper understanding and control of AI systems. The use of AI in the legal field can increase the efficiency and legitimacy of the legal system, improving public trust in justice. Overall, technological advancements, especially in information technology, impact human life and the environment. Placing humanitarian issues at the heart of AI development puts people first, in accordance with the principles of Pancasila. According to progressive law, researchers, innovators and developers of information technology must prioritise people. It is therefore hoped that the technology created will bring happiness to humanity.

Interpreting the law in a new or neo-textual way is the same as giving law enforcement responsibilities to an indifferent application system. Progressive law enforcement means applying the law based not just on literal rules, but also on the law's true purpose and meaning. However, artificial intelligence (AI) that relies on big data only follows the letter of the law, not its true meaning, because understanding deeper meaning requires deep introspection and contemplation. Based on the fundamental concepts of progressive law explained above, discussions about progressive law should be considered an important component in the development of rules for artificial intelligence technology. It is hoped that this will facilitate technological progress while also benefiting humanity. Conversely, there is a risk that artificial intelligence technology could turn into a system that enslaves humans, rather than freeing them.

THE USE OF ARTIFICIAL INTELLIGENCE IN TRANSFORMING THE LEGAL PROFESSION IN THE FUTURE

Rapid technological advances are having a significant impact on the legal world. The public's demand for easier access to legal services is being met by technology companies that offer artificial intelligence (AI) systems and tools for creating legal documents. However, these changes are expected to alter the perception and application of laws significantly in the Society 5.0 era, which encompasses digitalisation, AI, and big data. As these changes could disrupt the legal profession, particularly affecting law firms, notaries, and judicial institutions, this issue must be addressed. The impact of AI on the legal field is often not given sufficient attention (Agustini et al., 2022).

Artificial intelligence (AI) has the remarkable ability to transform the world through the use of the latest technology. It is crucial to implement AI ethically and with the full participation of all stakeholders. AI can be used to prepare for future problems (Junaidi, 2025). In the future, technology-focused companies will be the market leaders, and the legal profession will encounter a wide variety of highly diverse clients. According to Silva and Kenney (2019), legal professionals must adapt to the unique culture of digital companies. Firstly, they must be flexible and agile. This technology company is designed in such a way as to allow it to adapt quickly to market changes and technological developments. They emphasized the importance of flexibility when it comes to implementing layouts and procedures. Secondly, network-based operations: Technology companies operate by leveraging networks and platforms that enable more people to collaborate and connect with each other beyond physical and conventional limitations. Thirdly, innovation is a key focus for technology companies, who develop innovations in terms of products, services, and business models. They continue to strive to find new ways to generate value and leverage current technological opportunities. Fourthly, decision-making is decentralized. Company technology typically uses a more decentralized management structure. This enables decisions to be made more quickly and in closer proximity to the action itself. Fifthly, it creates an environment that supports cooperation. Technology companies create a collaborative ecosystem in which different groups of people, such as advocates, work together to achieve shared objectives. Sixthly, digital and data-driven: Technology companies rely heavily on digitalization and information to streamline their operations and make data-driven decisions. In such situations, legal experts must acquire new skills and expand their understanding of technology and how they can leverage these advancements to provide more efficient and effective legal services. They must also prepare to collaborate with people from various scientific disciplines and demonstrate strong project management skills in the ever-changing digital world (Busemeyer, 2022).

The legal profession should contribute significantly to the creation of solutions related to the application of the latest technologies. In the future, rather than simply providing legal solutions, the legal profession should function as Transaction Engineering (Crawford, 2021). For instance, as well as having legal responsibilities such as making innovative provisions to protect high-risk investors, lawyers can also be involved in unlawful actions in commercial transactions. According to Brian (2019), legal experts can act as mediators in such situations, including during the drafting of agreements and conciliation, and can serve as an important 'filtering tool' in legal transactions. Ultimately, the legal and contractual systems managed by lawyers can reduce the information imbalance that occurs in commercial transactions.

However, the problem is that the legal profession is often unable to carry out this transaction engineering task. Sometimes, the legal profession can hinder the transaction process. According to Thylstrup (2019), this situation can arise for a variety of reasons. One of these is the work involved in the legal field, which can slow down business transactions for procedural reasons. For instance, legal professionals often spend a long time evaluating the elements present in contracts and agreements rather than completing business transactions quickly. Additionally, they tend to focus on less important transactions. Consequently, lawyers are considered one of the least reliable professions. The following issues often arise in business transactions involving legal professionals: lengthy processes, lack of attention to clients, unresponsiveness, excessive costs, lack of empathy towards clients, wasting time on unimportant matters, lack of information provided to clients, excessive emphasis on legal aspects and unclear, non-concise communication (Agrawal et al., 2019).

In a highly competitive and volatile environment, the legal profession must strive to redefine its position as effective transaction engineers. These engineers can assist various parties in facilitating business interactions and activities. In the modern world, expenses such as regulation, supervision, transactions, agents and compliance must be reduced (Nijman, 2016). In this context, there is a significant opportunity for the legal profession to 'add value'. For the legal profession to function effectively as transaction engineers and contribute positively to the future use of digital technology, the legal sector must undergo various changes. Those working in law must be prepared to act as 'project managers' or, at the very least, be active members of cross-disciplinary teams working together to find innovative solutions to upcoming challenges.

A comparative analysis shows that some countries have taken creative steps to address the use of AI in law (Kristianti & Rolando, 2025):

1. The European Union's Artificial Intelligence Act (AI Act) categories artificial intelligence systems used in judicial administration as high-risk technology, requiring them to meet transparency, accountability and auditability standards.
2. The National Institute of Standards and Technology (NIST) has issued guidelines on the ethical use of AI and is funding research to reduce bias in legal algorithms.
3. Singapore has created an AI Governance Framework setting out the rules for using AI in various fields, including the justice system and the public service sector.

Comparisons can provide countries with policy references that they can use or modify when creating appropriate national regulatory frameworks. Additionally, the guidelines on the regulation of artificial intelligence robot use state that future legislative instruments relating to the liability of artificial intelligence robots should apply strict liability. Therefore, in order to claim compensation, it is sufficient to demonstrate that damage occurred and that there is a causal link between the robot's harmful actions and the losses suffered by the affected party (Ravizki & Yudhantaka, 2022).

Based on the explanation of the challenges faced in formulating the concept of AI in regulations in several countries, it is possible that AI will have a significant impact in various places and around the world. Countries must acknowledge that special provisions for AI are necessary to ensure safety, mitigate associated risks, and establish regulations that foster innovation while safeguarding public interest.

The ability to collaborate and communicate effectively with a variety of partners will become increasingly important. In the modern era, legal professionals need to work with more than just traditional professional 'partners', such as accountants or financial consultants. They will also need to work alongside designers, engineers, architects and other technology experts on projects and business transactions. Under this new legal service model, legal professional bodies will transform into a kind of legal 'platform'. Their focus will be on building relationships and collaborating with legal experts and other professionals.

The author believes that AI could help to make the process of analyzing and drafting legal documents more efficient. From a legal perspective, however, AI can only explore the field of legal thought, as it is capable of swiftly searching databases and analyzing legal elements. Law is subjective and often requires individual consideration, which makes it difficult to apply artificial intelligence in this context. In terms of legal drafting, however, AI can help overcome problems caused by unclear language. Thus, recognizing the language to be used in lawmaking will become easier. Additionally, AI can assist in devising winning strategies in the judicial process. Lawyers can use AI to assess relevant laws and regulations, which makes it easier for them to plan legal processes. Therefore, fundamentally, AI can be very helpful in resolving legal issues in reasoning competitions. However, there are legal considerations where AI cannot develop too far. This is because legal considerations are a broad concept encompassing an accountable process for providing answers (Jumantoro, 2024).

There are many algorithms that can be used in law, such as the following:

1. **Machine Learning:** As the name suggests, machine learning or *pembelajaran mesin* in Indonesian is a branch of artificial intelligence (AI) algorithms. This field enables computers to acquire knowledge through instructions and data. Machine learning (ML) can function independently of human assistance. By combining various scientific fields, such as data mining, mathematics and statistics, this technology enables machines to recognize patterns in data without the need for reprogramming or specific instructions (Kubat, 2021).
2. **Deep Learning:** Deep learning is a method of artificial intelligence (AI) that teaches machines to analyze data in a way that is similar to the way the human brain works. Deep learning models enable machines to identify intricate patterns within diverse data types, including sound, text, images, and other information. This enables them to provide accurate insights and forecasts. Deep learning techniques can be leveraged to automate tasks that typically require human intelligence, such as explaining images or converting audio files to text (Janiesch et al., 2021).

Technology based on artificial intelligence uses machine learning and deep learning algorithms to analyze data. In machine learning, an algorithm is the first thing to receive data, or input, for the device to learn from. Machines then generate output based on this information, which individuals receive as additional input. Machines can use this iterative process to predict problems with general artificial intelligence models. Therefore, the amount of available data greatly affects the accuracy of AI prediction models. Consequently, machine learning and big data are crucially interconnected for the success of artificial intelligence (Ramadhan & Putri, 2018). Deep learning is a method of data learning that aims to generate hierarchical data representations using multiple processing layers. It is a branch of machine learning that focuses more on the ability of learning algorithms to automatically generate data representations (Heryadi, 2021).

Additionally, deep learning is crucial in new technologies such as self-driving vehicles and virtual reality. A deep learning model is a computer program that has been trained by data scientists to perform specific tasks using predefined algorithms or sets of procedures. There are ongoing efforts to use this model to analyze data and make predictions in various application areas. Neural networks are a key component of deep learning, which distinguishes it from machine learning (Mishra & Gupta, 2016).

In addition to the artificial intelligence technology mentioned earlier, there are eight further artificial intelligence tools designed to handle various types of unstructured data. These tools include Autonomous Learning Machine (ALM), Clarabridge CX Analytics, Facebook Ad Planner, Google Cloud Platform Natural Language API, IQ Bot, Quid, The R Project for Statistical Computing and Word nerds. State-owned companies in Indonesia have used chatbots to interact with their consumers. Examples include Sabrina (BRI's New Intelligence Assistant) from BRI, Cinta (Chat with Your Intelligence Advisor) from BNI and Mita (Mandiri Intelligence Assistant) from *Bank Mandiri* (Abdullah, 2020). Professionals in the legal field can demonstrate this particularly when dealing with their clients.

It must be remembered that the application of law by machines or devices will differ from the application of law by people. When handling cases, judges have three types of justice at their disposal: legal, moral and social. Abdurrahman Rahim also stated that artificial intelligence (AI) cannot benefit law enforcement because it cannot make judgements, deliver justice or consider the benefits of a case, even though it relies on algorithms. Furthermore, AI cannot take over the role of judges because it cannot think like humans (Doly, 2023).

AI justice is rigid and does not consider conscience or humanitarian principles. Therefore, matters cannot be represented by devices or tools in the decision-making process. However, systems like AI can assist law enforcement by performing case administration techniques, such as making consistent, effective and easily understandable decisions. AI has the potential to transform law enforcement processes by selecting suitable judges to handle cases and taking their workloads into account. Additionally, AI can help law enforcement to identify criminals by tracking individuals involved in criminal activity. However, human instinct and conscience are still required for decision-making in matters of criminal offence.

The author believes that artificial intelligence (AI) cannot replace judges or other individuals responsible for making legal decisions within the judiciary. Law enforcement requires not only accuracy and logic, but also elements of feeling, intention and conscience that cannot be replicated by common sense alone. Therefore, in order to maintain integrity and human values within the legal system, AI should only ever be used as an aid, not as a replacement. To welcome the digital law era, firm and fair regulations that support human values are needed. Several steps can be taken to implement AI in the legal field, including:

1. **Manifesting Clear Guidelines:** The government and relevant authorities should immediately create specific regulations governing the use of artificial intelligence (AI) in the legal field. These rules should cover important aspects such as defining who is legally responsible if AI makes a mistake, protecting personal and confidential information, setting quality and reliability standards for AI, and establishing a monitoring system to ensure AI usage aligns with the principles of fairness and transparency (Disemadi, 2021). Clear guidelines like these will make legal practitioners and the public more comfortable and confident in using AI.
2. **Escalating Technological Understanding:** Legal practitioners need a better understanding of technology, particularly in relation to artificial intelligence (AI) and legal technology. Law schools and professional training programs should educate students on how AI works, its advantages and its limitations. Armed with this knowledge, legal professionals can use artificial intelligence wisely and effectively. They can also offer additional value that AI cannot provide, such as critical thinking and empathy when dealing with legal cases (Wahyuni, 2023).
3. **Strengthening the Data Fortress:** Given the importance of legal information, legal institutions must implement strict cybersecurity standards to protect digitally managed data. These standards include using strong encryption to keep data confidential, implementing layered authentication systems to prevent unauthorized access and conducting regular security audits to identify and prevent data breaches and cyberattacks (Mahameru et al., 2023).

We hope that, as a result, AI will serve as both a sophisticated tool and a reliable partner in building a more efficient, effective, just and transparent legal system.

To bring the law closer to justice, we need human policies that make decisions based on emotion and legal logic. This hypothesis suggests that legal decisions based on conscience are superior to those that rely solely on conventional legal reasoning. Under this legal framework, artificial intelligence machines can only offer 'legal certainty', meaning the status of the legal profession is considered to be higher than that of AI. Legal professionals contribute to subsequent tasks in their efforts to find and deliver justice in society. The goal is to bring the law closer to justice. Consequently, the legal profession of the future will be filled with extraordinary individuals, namely those with unquestionable integrity and moral intelligence. Currently, the field of legal education focuses on legal skills, but it should also teach important lessons about the philosophy of justice and professional ethics in order to foster moral intelligence. Despite the challenges posed by disruption and the rise of AI, legal professionals continue to play a leadership role in legal civilization in the millennial era thanks to these legal developments.

The author believes that AI can be a very effective tool for supporting law enforcement. AI can provide accurate information about legal aspects, documents and cases, including the regulations required by Indonesian law enforcement officers. AI can achieve a faster law enforcement process because it can complete tasks quickly. For instance, a Colombian judge used ChatGPT to assist in drafting legal opinions during court hearings. However, given the significant impact of existing legal issues, any AI technology used to support law enforcement processes must be safe and trustworthy.

The government plays a crucial role in promoting the development and use of AI in the legal system. It can do the following:

1. **Create a regulatory authority:** The government should establish a regulatory authority specifically responsible for overseeing the development and use of AI within the legal system.
2. **Set national standards:** Set national standards for the development and use of AI within the legal system.
3. **Enhance digital literacy:** Educate the public, especially law enforcement officials, about digital technology and its impact on the legal system.
4. **Promote research and innovation:** The government should provide assistance for research and innovation in the field of artificial intelligence related to the legal system.

In order to ensure that artificial intelligence (AI) is used positively and in accordance with the moral values of Indonesian society, it is crucial to apply the principles of Pancasila and ethics when using AI, without compromising the ethical and moral values that form part of this nation's culture and identity (Akbar & Najicha, 2022). In order to develop and utilise AI, the principles contained within the five pillars of Pancasila must be applied: social justice, cooperation, ethical and dignified humanity, unity, and democracy:

1. **Mutual Cooperation:** This involves facilitating cooperation and collaboration between government agencies, businesses and academic institutions to achieve common goals, such as accelerating innovation and enhancing technological understanding. For instance, a research project utilizing artificial intelligence could address social issues such as poverty or climate change through collaboration.
2. **Just and Civilized Humanity:** Ensuring that this technology is not used in decision-making processes that could harm specific groups or individuals. 3. Unity: Ensuring that this technology is not used to disrupt the harmony and unity of the country. For example, algorithms are used to prevent the spread of content that could be provocative or disrupt unity on social media platforms.

3. **Democracy:** Encouraging public and stakeholder participation in decision-making processes related to AI. Public consultations and open discussions should, for example, be held during the decision-making process regarding AI regulations.
4. **Social Justice:** Ensuring that this technology benefits everyone, not just a select few or large corporations.

The author believes that the principles of progressive legal theory are the main foundation of the state and the source of all laws. The values of social justice, humanity, unity and morality align with the principles of progressive legal theory. Therefore, not only is Pancasil a philosophical foundation, it is also a moral and normative guideline for creating laws that serve the interests of the people and achieve the ideals of social justice. By strengthening the values of Pancasila in the legal system, it is hoped that citizens will develop a better understanding of these values through their practical application in law. This will create a synergy between law and Pancasila, driving the realization of social justice.

It is hoped that this issue will be minimized through the use of artificial intelligence. This is because the use of artificial intelligence technology provides insights and recommendations that can be applied to specific situations based on the data entered into the AI system. Therefore, evaluating artificial intelligence in a legal context is expected to provide a more objective assessment of the parties involved and the case. Under these conditions, the law can achieve its goal of fair and non-discriminatory law enforcement.

CONCLUSION

The regulations to be developed here relate not only to progressive legal theory governing humans, but also to laws governing the relationship between humans and technology. Legal regulations should accommodate both human and technological interests to advance science and human well-being. Technological advancements are increasingly based on humanitarian issues, particularly in the development of artificial intelligence. The true goal is to ensure that humans remain in the most important position, as outlined in the Pancasila. According to the principle of progressive law, intellectuals, innovators and information technology developers should priorities human welfare so that the technology they create can benefit humanity. Advances in AI and automation will have a significant impact on the future of the legal field. To prevent human interaction in the legal world from being entirely replaced by technology, ethical considerations are crucial. Those working in the legal field must devise strategies to survive and transition from legal engineers to transactional engineers, who will play an active role in innovation and business. Thus, the legal profession has the ability to reduce information inequality and enhance its role in the use of digital technology.

The government must immediately create laws regarding artificial intelligence (AI) technology, as AI requires strict regulation and sanctions for violations. It is hoped that the government will soon establish an AI Committee to monitor and penalize unethical use of AI. This will enable the benefits and drawbacks of using AI technology to be monitored.

REFERENCE

Abdullah, A. (2020). Public relation in the era of artificial intelligence: Peluang atau ancaman? *Jurnal Aristo: Social, Politic. Humaniora, 8*(2), 406–417. DOI: 10.24269/ars.v8i2.2629

Agustini, A., Nurlaily, N., & Seroja, T. D. (2022). Technological Advancement in The Society 5.0 Era for Notary in Indonesia: Glory or Obsolete? *Legal Brief, 11*(3), 1589–1597. DOI: 10.35335/legal.Technological

Agrawal, A., Gans, J., & Goldfarb, A. (2019). *The economics of artificial intelligence: An agenda*. University of Chicago Press., DOI: 10.7208/chicago/9780226613475.001.0001

Akbar, H. M., & Najicha, F. U. (2022). Upaya memperkuat jati diri bangsa melalui pemahaman wawasan nusantara di era gempuran kebudayaan asing. *Jurnal Kewarganegaraan, 6*(1), 2122–2127. DOI: 10.31316/jk.v6i1.2939

Alzbeta, K. (2017). Intersections between law and artificial intelligence. *International Journal of Computer, 27*(1), 55–68. DOI: 10.53896/ijc.v27i1.1071

Ashley, K. D. (2017). *Artificial Intelligence and Legal Analytics New Tools for Law Practice in the Digital Age*. Cambridge University Press., DOI: 10.1017/9781316761380

Azis, R. A., Susetio, W., Nurhayani, N., & Hikmawati, E. (2023). Pengaturan dan Pertanggung Jawaban Pemanfaatan Artificial Intelligence (AI) di Indonesia dalam Perspektif Hukum. *Forum Ilmiah Indonusa, 20*(4), 243–254.

Biresaw, S. M., & Saste, A. U. (2022). The impacts of artificial intelligence on research in the legal profession. *International Journal of Law and Society, 5*(1), 53–65. DOI: 10.11648/j.ijls.20220501.17

Blind, K., & Münch, F. (2024). The interplay between innovation, standards and regulation in a globalising economy. *Journal of Cleaner Production, 445*(15), 1–11. DOI: 10.1016/j.jclepro.2024.141202

Borgesius, F. J. Z. (2020). Strengthening legal protection against discrimination by algorithms and artificial intelligence. *International Journal of Human Rights, 24*(10), 1572–1593. DOI: 10.1080/13642987.2020.1743976

Brynjolfsson, E., & McAfee, A. (2014). *The second machine age: Work, progress, and prosperity in a time of brilliant technologies*. W. W. Norton & Company.

Brian, C. S. (2019). *The Promise of Artificial Intelligence: Reckoning and Judgment.* MIT Press., DOI: 10.7551/mitpress/12385.001.0001

Busemeyer, M., Kemmerling, A., van Kersbergen, K., Marx, P., Wren, A., Eichhorst, W., Glassmann, U., Iversen, T., Rehm, P., Kurer, T., Hausermann, S., Gingrich, J., Kua, A., Chrisp, J., Martinelli, L., Guarascio, D., Sacchi, S., Zepeda, S., & Picot, G. (2022). *Digitalization and The Welfare State.* Oxford University Press., DOI: 10.1093/oso/9780192848369.001.0001

Chen, S. (2021). *Chinese scientists develop AI 'prosecutor' that can press its own charges.* https://www.scmp.com/news/china/science/article/3160997/chinese-scientists-develop-ai-prosecutor-can-press-its-own

Chien, S., & Lee, M. (2020). Legal technology and artificial intelligence: Implications for the legal profession. *The Journal of Legal Studies, 45*(3), 227–245. DOI: 10.2139/ssrn.3353292

Crawford, K. (2021). *The Atlas of AI: Power, politics, and the planetary costs of artificial intelligence.* Yale University Press., DOI: 10.2307/j.ctv1ghv45t

Devianto, Y., & Dwiasnati, S. (2020). Kerangka kerja sistem kecerdasan buatan dalam meningkatkan kompetensi sumber daya manusia Indonesia. *Jurnal Telekomunikasi dan Komputer*, 10(1), 19-24. https://doi.org/DOI: 10.22441/incomtech.v10i1.7460

Disemadi, H. S. (2021). Urgensi regulasi khusus dan pemanfaatan artificial intelligence dalam mewujudkan perlindungan data pribadi di Indonesia. *Jurnal Wawasan Yuridika, 5*(2), 177–199. DOI: 10.25072/jwy.v5i2.460

Doly, D. (2023). Pemanfaatan *artificial intelligence* dalam penegakan hukum di Indonesia. Info Singkat: Kajian Singkat terhadap Isu Aktual dan Strategis, 15(19), 1-5. https://berkas.dpr.go.id/pusaka/files/info_singkat/Info%20Singkat-XV-19-I-P3DI-Oktober-2023-208.pdf

Dwiputro, W. (2020). Disrupsi dan Masa Depan Profesi Hukum. *Jurnal Mimbar Hukum, 32*(1), 192–29. DOI: 10.22146/jmh.42928

European Commission. (2021). Proposal for a regulation of the European Parliament and of the Council laying down harmonized rules on artificial intelligence (Artificial Intelligence Act). https://ec.europa.eu/info/sites/info/files/commission-proposal-regulation-artificial-intelligence-2021_en.pdf

Artificial Intelligence Act, EU (2021/2024)

Filipova, I. A. (2024). Legal regulation of artificial intelligence: Experience of China. *Journal of Digital Technologies and Law, 2*(1), 46–73. DOI: 10.21202/jdtl.2024.4

Garingan, D., & Pickard, A. J. (2021). Artificial Intelligence in Legal Practice: Exploring Theoretical Frameworks for Algorithmic Literacy in the Legal Information Profession. *Legal Information Management*, *21*(2), 97–117. DOI: 10.1017/S1472669621000190

Gellers, J. C. (2020). *Rights for robots: Artificial intelligence, animal, and environmental law* (1st ed.). Routledge., DOI: 10.4324/9780429288159

Ghani, I., & Malik, M. I. (2020). The impact of artificial intelligence on the legal profession: A review. *International Journal of Legal Information*, *48*(2), 121–138. DOI: 10.1017/jli.2020.19

Ghorayeb, A., Comber, R., & Gooberman-Hill, R. (2021). Older adults' perspectives of smart home technology: Are we developing the technology that older people want? *International Journal of Human-Computer Studies*, *147*, 102571. DOI: 10.1016/j.ijhcs.2020.102571

Goodall, J. R., & Hodge, G. (2020). Artificial intelligence in the legal profession: Opportunities and challenges. *Legal Technology Review*, *23*(4), 34–48. DOI: 10.2139/ssrn.3504165

Heryadi, Y. (2021). *Dasar-dasar deep learning dan implementasinya*. Gava Media.

Janiesch, C., Zschech, P., & Heinrich, K. (2021). Machine learning and deep learning. *Electronic Markets*, *31*, 685–695. DOI: 10.1007/s12525-021-00475-2

Jaya, F., & Goh, W. (2021). Analisis Yuridis terhadap Kedudukan Kecerdasan Buatan atau *Artificial Intelligence* sebagai Subjek Hukum pada Hukum Positif Indonesia. *Jurnal Supremasi Hukum*, *17*(2), 1–11. DOI: 10.33592/jsh.v17i2.1287

Judge, B., Nitzberg, M., & Russell, S. (2025). When code isn't law: Rethinking regulation for artificial intelligence. *Policy and Society*, *44*(1), 85–97. DOI: 10.1093/polsoc/puae020

Jumantoro, T. R. P. (2024). Menilik pro dan kontra pemanfaatan dan penetapan status hukum artificial intelligence dalam hukum Positif Indonesia. *Journal of Analytical Research. Statistics and Computing*, *3*(1), 51–70. DOI: 10.4590/jarsic.v3i1.28

Junaidi, J. (2020). Kajian yuridis pasal 362 Kitab Undang-Undang Hukum Pidana dan pasal 30 Undang-Undang Nomor 11 Tahun 2008 tentang Informasi dan Transaksi Elektronik terhadap pencurian internet Wi-Fi. *Jurnal Wajah Hukum*, *4*(2), 325–330. DOI: 10.33087/wjh.v4i2.190

Junaidi, J. (2023). Artificial Intelligence in The Implementation of Criminal Case Settlement Law Using Restorative Justice Based on Progressive Law. In *Proceedings of the First International Cyber Law Conference (ICL-C 2023)*, 198-204. EAI. http://dx.doi.org/DOI: 10.4108/eai.11-11-2023.2351325

Junaidi, J., Pujiyono, P., & Fadzil, R. M. (2024). Legal Reform of Artificial Intelligence's Liability to Personal Data Perspectives of Progressive Legal Theory. *Journal of Law and Legal Reform*, *5*(2), 587–612. DOI: 10.15294/jllr.vol5i2.3437

Junaidi, J., & Fadzil, R. M. (2024). Urgency of legal personal data protection in e-commerce transactions involving artificial intelligence. *Walisongo Law Review (Walrev)*, *6*(2), 96–108. DOI: 10.21580/walrev.2024.6.2.25548

Junaidi, J. (2025a). Transformation of Literary Culture in the Digital Era Through the Use of Artificial Intelligence as a Form of Copyright Protection. *in Role of AI in Producing, Evaluating, and Interpreting Literary Materials. IGI Global Scientific Publishing*, 177-204, http://dx.doi.org/DOI: 10.4018/979-8-3373-1057-2

Junaidi, J. (2025). Education Reform in the Application of Artificial Intelligence in Supporting Learning Media: AI and Education for Sustainable Development Goals (SDGs), *in AI, Policy, and the Future of Human-Centered Education, IGI Global Scientific Publishing,* 57-84. https://doi.org/DOI: 10.4018/979-8-3373-5781-2.ch003

Kelly, S., Kaye, S. A., & Trespalacios, O. O. (2023). What factors contribute to the acceptance of artificial intelligence? A systematic review. *Telematics and Informatics*, *77*, 101925. DOI: 10.1016/j.tele.2022.101925

Kubat, M. (2021). *An introduction to machine learning* (3rd ed.). Springer Nature Switzerland., DOI: 10.1007/978-3-030-81935-4

Kristianti, N., & Rolando, B. (2025). Pemanfaatan artificial intelligence dalam praktik hukum: Peluang dan tantangan regulasi di Indonesia. *Belom Bahadat: Jurnal Hukum Agama Hindu*, *15*(1), 82–95. DOI: 10.33363/bb.v15i1.1483

Li, S., & Zhang, R. (2019). Legal implications of artificial intelligence in China: A regulatory approach. *Journal of Chinese Law*, *35*(4), 75–92. DOI: 10.2139/ssrn.3384760

Mahameru, D. E., Nurhalizah, A., Badjeber, H., Wildan, A., & Rahmadia, H. (2023). Implementasi UU Perlindungan Data Pribadi terhadap Keamanan Informasi Identitas di Indonesia. *Jurnal Esensi Hukum*, *5*(2), 115–131. DOI: 10.35586/jsh.v5i2.240

Mahomed, S. (2019). Healthcare, artificial intelligence and the Fourth Industrial Revolution: Ethical, social and legal considerations. *South African Journal of Bioethics and Law*, *11*(2), 93–95. DOI: 10.7196/SAJBL.2018.v11i2.00664

Mannes, J. (2024). *Legal Aid at the Click of a Button: The Power of DoNotPay's 1,000 Bots*. https://fxis.ai/edu/legal-aid-at-the-click-of-a-button-the-power-of-donotpays-1000-bots/

Mishra, C., & Gupta, D. L. (2016). Deep machine learning and neural networks: An overview. *International Journal of Hybrid Information Technology*, *6*(2), 66–73. DOI: 10.11591/ijai.v6.i2.pp66-73

Muhana, A. F. (2025). Legal drafting: Optimalisasi hukum melalui artificial intelligence (AI) di Indonesia. *Jurnal Hukum Ekualitas*, *1*(1), 84–94. DOI: 10.56607/9hdrcw80

Nadjia, M. (2024). The impact of artificial intelligence on legal systems: Challenges and opportunities. *Problem of Legality*, *1*(164), 285–303. DOI: 10.21564/2414-990X.164.289266

Najafli, A. (2025). The impact of artificial intelligence on the legal system: Benefits, risks, legal, and ethical challenges. *Acta Globalis Humanitatis et Linguarum*, *2*(4), 247–263. DOI: 10.69760/aghel.0250040012

Niebla, Z. J. M. (2018). Artificial Intelligence and Legal Analytics: New Tools for Law Practice in the Digital Age. *Script-ed*. Advance online publication. DOI: 10.2966/SCRIP.150118.156

Nijman, J. E. (2016). Non-state actors and the international rule of law: Revisiting the 'realist theory' of international legal personality. In *Non-state actor dynamics in international law*. Routledge.

Pabubung, M. R. (2023). Era Kecerdasan Buatan dan Dampak terhadap Martabat Manusia dalam Kajian Etis. *Jurnal Filsafat Indonesia*, *6*(1), 66–74. DOI: 10.23887/jfi.v6i1.49293

Park, J., Hong, E., & Le, H. T. (2021). Adopting autonomous vehicles: The moderating effects of demographic variables. *Journal of Retailing and Consumer Services*, *63*, 102687. DOI: 10.1016/j.jretconser.2021.102687

Pirmansyah, R., Junaidi, J., & Merta, M. M. (2021). *Law transformation: The law of personal data protection in the pandemic time COVID-19 on electronic system*. In *Proceedings of OSC 2021, Faculty of Law, Social and Political Sciences, Universitas Terbuka* (Theme 1). https://www.cips-indonesia.org/post/siaran-pers-kebocoran-data-ingatkan-pentingnya-legislasi-ruu-perlindungan-data-pribadi

Putra, I. N. G. A., & Silaban, J. K. P. (2024). Penerapan Kecerdasan Artifisial dalam Pengawasan Kekuasaan Kehakiman sebagai Upaya Mereduksi Disparitas Putusan Pidana di Indonesia. *Ma'mal. Jurnal Laboratorium Syariah Dan Hukum*, *5*(4), 297–320. DOI: 10.15642/mal.v5i4.382

Putri, M. C., Febyanti, A., Azzahra, S., & Putri, N. A. (2024). Pengaruh penggunaan artificial intelligence dalam pembentukan peraturan perundang-undangan. *TERANG: Jurnal Kajian Ilmu Sosial, Politik dan Hukum,* 1(2), 266-284. https://doi.org/DOI: 10.62383/terang.v1i2.235

Rahardjo, S., & Dimyati, K. (2002). *Sosiologi Hukum, Perkembangan, Metode dan Pilihan Masalahnya.* Muhammadiyah University Press.

Rahardjo, S. (2003). *Suatu Versi Indonesia tentang Rule of Law, Sisi-sisi Lain dari Hukum Indonesia.* Kompas.

Rahardjo, S. (2004). *Hukum Progresif (Penjelajahan Suatu Gagasan).* Majalah Hukum Newsletter, 59 Jakarta: Yayasan Pusat Pengkajian Hukum.

Rahardjo, S. (2006a). *Hukum dalam Jagat Ketertiban.* UKI Press.

Rahardjo, S. (2006). *Hukum Progresif sebagai Dasar Pembangunan Ilmu Hukum, dalam buku Menggagas Hukum Progresif Indonesia.* Semarang: Kerjasama Pustaka Pelajar, IAIN Walisongo dan Program Doktor Ilmu Hukum UNDIP

Rahardjo, S. (2007a). *Biarkan Hukum Mengalir: Catatan Kritis tentang Pergulatan Manusia dan Hukum.* Kompas.

Rahardjo, S. (2007). Arsenal Hukum Progresif. *Jurnal Hukum Progresif, 3*(1), 1. DOI: 10.14710/hp.3.1.1

Rahardjo, S. (2009a). *Hukum Progresif Sebuah Sintesa Hukum Indonesia.* Genta Publishing.

Rahardjo, S. (2009). *Penegakan Hukum Suatu Tinjauan Sosiologis.* Genta Publishing.

Ramdhani, D. N., & Dewi, D. A. (2022). Menerapkan nilai-nilai Pancasila dalam menghadapi perkembangan ilmu pengetahuan dan teknologi. *Jurnal Kewarganegaraan, 6*(1), 1081–1088. DOI: 10.31316/jk.v6i1.2676

Ramadhan, A., & Putri, A. (2018). *Big data, kecerdasan buatan, blockchain, dan teknologi finansial di Indonesia.* Direktorat Jenderal Aplikasi Informatika, Kementerian Komunikasi dan Informatika

Ravizki, E. N., & Yudhantaka, L. (2022). *Artificial intelligence* sebagai subjek hukum: Tinjauan konseptual dan tantangan pengaturan di Indonesia. *Jurnal Notaire, 5*(3), 351–376. DOI: 10.20473/ntr.v5i3.39063

Ririh, K. R., Laili, N., Wicaksono, A., & Tsurayya, S. (2020). Studi Komparasi dan Analisis Swot pada Implementasi Kecerdasan Buatan (Artificial Intelligence) di Indonesia. *J@ti Undip. Jurnal Teknik Industri, 15*(2), 122–133. DOI: 10.14710/jati.15.2.122-133

Russell, S., & Norvig, P. (2016). *Artificial intelligence: A modern approach* (3rd ed.). Pearson Education Limited.

Sergot, M., Cory, T., Hammond, P., Kowalski, R., Kriwaczek, F., & Sadri, F. (2010). Formalisation of the British nationality act. *International Review of Law Computers & Technology, 2*(1), 40–52. DOI: 10.1080/13600869.1986.9966229

Silva, S., & Kenney, M. (2019). Algorithms, Platforms, And Ethnic Bias. *Communications of the ACM, 62*(11), 37–39. DOI: 10.1145/3318157

Surden, H. (2014). Machine Learning and Law. *Washington Law Review (Seattle, Wash.), 89*(2), 87–126. DOI: 10.2139/ssrn.2410530

Surden, H. (2019). Artificial Intelligence and Law: An Overview. *Georgia State University Law Review, 35*(4), 1306–1339. https://readingroom.law.gsu.edu/gsulr/vol35/iss4/8

Surahmat, A., Ahmad, N., Fitri, H., Widarma, A., Ardilla, Y., Hasan. N.F., Satria, S., Army, W.L., & Wati, V. (2023). *Kecerdasan buatan dalam data mining*. Widina Bhakti Persada.

Susskind, R. (2019). *Online courts and the future of justice*. Oxford University Press., DOI: 10.1093/oso/9780198838364.001.0001

Susskind, R. (2023). *Tomorrow's lawyers: An introduction to your future* (3rd ed.). Oxford University Press., DOI: 10.1093/9780192864727.001.0001

The EU Declaration on Cooperation on Artificial Intelligence. (2018). *The European Parliament Resolution on Civil Law Rules on Robotics* (2015/2103 (INL)) (2018/C 252/25) 2017. https://eur-lex.europa.eu/legal-content/EN/TXT/?uri=CELEX:52018DC0237

Thylstrup, N. B. (2019). *The Politics of Mass Digitization*. MIT Press., DOI: 10.7551/mitpress/11404.001.0001

Tu, S. S., Cyphert, A., & Perl, S. J. (2024). Artificial intelligence: Legal reasoning, legal research and legal writing. *Minnesota Journal of Law, Science & Technology*, *25*(2), 105–125. https://ssrn.com/abstract=4817765

Vlassis, N. (2007). *A concise introduction to multiagent systems and distributed artificial intelligence*. Springer Nature., DOI: 10.2200/S00091ED1V01Y200705AIM002

Quteishat, E. M. A., Qtaishat, A., & Quteishat, A. M. A. (2024). Exploring the role of AI in modern legal practice: Opportunities, challenges, and ethical implications. *Journal Electrical Systems*, *20*(6s), 3040–3050. DOI: 10.52783/jes.3320

Wahyuni, W. (2023). Praktisi hukum perlu bersiap hadapi isu hukum di era artificial intelligence. *Hukumonline.* https://www.hukumonline.com/berita/a/praktisi-hukum-perlu-bersiap-hadapi-isu-hukum-di-era-artificial-intelligence-lt652951251562f

Chapter 8
Taming the Digital Tempest:
Consumer Sovereignty, State Power, and the Challenge of Global Governance

Shovonita Acharjee
http://orcid.org/0000-0002-3208-4750
Amity Law School, Amity University, Mumbai, India

Rohan Rajeev Ghosh
http://orcid.org/0009-0004-5954-5686
Thakur Ramnarayan College of Law, Mumbai, India

ABSTRACT

This study critically examines consumer protection in India's digital marketplace, exposing vulnerabilities in data-driven commerce and introducing the concept of a "Cyber Sherpa" to guide and safeguard consumers. Using a doctrinal legal approach, it analyses global frameworks, landmark cases, and governance models related to cybersecurity, corporate accountability, and data privacy. The findings reveal major gaps in consumer protection and highlight the need for empowerment and legal reform to ensure a secure, trustworthy digital economy. The innovative "Cyber Sherpa" framework redefines policy reform, accountability, and consumer education, positioning India to lead in digital consumer rights.

DOI: 10.4018/979-8-3373-7685-1.ch008

INTRODUCTION

Consumerism in India has emerged due to factors such as shortages in essential goods and services, inflation, low levels of technology, poor quality of goods, unethical business practices, and misleading advertisements (Adam Smith,1776). The main objectives of the consumer movement in India include protecting consumers' interests, promoting consumer awareness, establishing and improving healthy buyer-seller relationships, preventing exploitation, promoting consumer education, providing quality testing facilities, and supplying relevant consumer information (Selvi D et al., 2021). However, the progress of the movement in India has been slow compared to Western counterparts due to poverty, illiteracy, ignorance, lack of market information, and lack of consumer involvement and interest in market-related issues.(Gupta SC, 1999) The Indian government has implemented various legal protective measures to safeguard consumers' interests, although their implementation could be improved (Latha, KL, 2022). According to Adam Smith, the consumer is the sole end purpose of all production, and marketers must analyze, organize, plan, and control resources to satisfy the needs and wants of chosen customer groups at a profit (Muhammad, A et.al 2012). Peter F. Drucker defines marketing as a process that converts distinct knowledge into a contribution of economic value in the marketplace (UNCTAD, 2016). At the same time, Theodore Levitt emphasizes that management must think of itself as buying customers and doing things that will make people want to do business with it (Blasio, GD,2008). Consumers have certain basic expectations from traders, such as fair pricing, good quality, accurate weights, product safety, assured supply, redress of complaints against fraudulent businessmen, service after-sales, and protection against unfair trade practices. The traditional doctrine of "Caveat Emptor," which placed the burden of ensuring the quality of goods on the buyer, has evolved to recognize the importance of protecting consumers' interests. The noble aspirations of the consumer movement in India echo a call to safeguard consumer interests, foster awareness, cultivate healthy buyer-seller relations, curb exploitation, and promote consumer education (Helberger et al., 2017). Yet, the journey of this movement has been marked by sluggish progress, hindered by poverty, illiteracy, dearth of market information, and consumer apathy, in stark contrast to the vigour witnessed in Western societies. In this era of data-driven commerce, consumer empowerment hinges on the protection of personal information. Recent breaches and regulatory responses illuminate the delicate balance between consumer trust, data security, and corporate responsibility (Svantesson, D. J. B. (2017). The convergence of data and consumer protection policies signals a paradigm shift, fraught with challenges and opportunities (Rott, P. (2017). The interplay between legislative frameworks such as the GDPR and consumer rights frameworks exemplifies the complexities inherent in aligning policy agendas. Against this backdrop, the ethos of consumerism emerges as a beacon of empowerment, rallying citizens and governments to fortify consumer rights and counter unfair trade practices . The historic Consumer Protection Act of 1986 stands as a milestone in India's journey towards socio-economic justice, yet its efficacy hinges on consumer awareness and active participation. In this high-stakes arena, where rights and responsibilities intertwine, the quest for equitable commerce continues. This paper delves into the labyrinthine realm of consumer protection, traversing recent trends and challenges, offering insights, and charting a course towards a fairer marketplace.

NEED FOR CONSUMER PROTECTION AND CONSUMER AWARENESS IN THE PRESENT SCENARIO

Consumer protection stands as a cornerstone of trust and confidence within a nation's economic framework. Laws governing consumer rights not only ensure the safety and quality of products and services but also foster a conducive environment for economic growth by bolstering consumer trust in producers (EDPS, 2014). In a landscape where inexperienced consumers are susceptible to substandard products and fraudulent sales tactics, consumer protection laws serve as a shield against deceptive practices, misleading advertisements, and unsafe goods. Herein lies the pressing need for robust consumer protection policies in the present scenario. Consumer protection plays a crucial role in building trust and encouraging economic activities in a country. With numerous brands and products available in the market today, consumers need protection from poor-quality products, unethical practices, and misleading advertisements. (Singh, J., & Sharma, D.,2014) Consumer protection laws aim to ensure that consumers are not taken advantage of by unscrupulous business owners and are informed about their rights.

Reasons for the Need for Consumer Protection

1. Poor Quality Products: Companies sometimes use low-quality materials to save costs, leading to defective products. Only consumer protection complaints can discourage this behaviour and force manufacturers to maintain high-quality standards.
2. Unethical Business Practices: In the highly competitive modern economy, some business owners resort to unethical practices that compromise the safety and health of consumers. Group legal plans can inform and educate consumers about their rights and guide them through legal proceedings. (Latha, K. L. (2022)

3. Illiteracy and Ignorance: Consumers in India are often illiterate and unaware of their rights. An efficient system is needed to protect them from unscrupulous businessmen (Chawla, Y. 2018).
4. Dispersed and Unorganized Consumers: Unlike producers and traders, consumers are widely dispersed and lack unity. Organizing consumers and fighting against unfair trade practices is crucial (Prakash, S., & Raju, K. S.,2018).
5. Duplicate Products: Distinguishing between genuine and fake products can be challenging for consumers. Ensuring compliance with prescribed quality and safety norms is vital to protect consumers from exploitation.
6. Deceptive Advertising: Misleading information about products and services can lead to confusion and disappointment for consumers. Mechanisms need to be put in place to prevent misleading advertisements.
7. Adulteration: Consumers often receive impure or substandard goods despite paying high prices. Reporting incidents of adulteration can result in action against offenders.
8. Irregular Supply: Artificial scarcity created by organizations leads to high prices and inconvenience for consumers. Strict measures need to be taken to regulate supply chains and ensure regular availability of goods.
9. Other Issues: Malpractices, deceptive techniques, false warranties or guarantees, black marketing, and other forms of exploitation require strict regulation and monitoring (Goel, A., 2019).

Recent Challenges and Trends in Consumer Protection in India

1. New Digital Products and Services: The emerging trend of digital products and services requires regulatory oversight to ensure transparency and reliability.
2. Internet Use for Information Purposes: The widespread use of the Internet for purchasing decisions necessitates mechanisms to verify authenticity and quality.
3. Electronic Payments: Secure payment systems need to be established to protect consumers from cybercrime and scams.
4. Redefined Exchanges: Technology and peer communities are changing traditional modes of exchange. Appropriate checks and balances are necessary to ensure fair practices.
5. M-commerce: Mobile commerce is gaining popularity, requiring appropriate regulations and guidelines.

Existing Laws for Consumer Protection in India

Various acts aimed at protecting consumers from different forms of exploitation exist in India, including the Indian Penal Code, 1860; Indian Contract Act, 1872;

Drugs Control Act, 1950; Industries (Development and Regulation) Act, 1951; and Consumer Protection Act, 1986, among others. These laws aim to address various aspects of consumer protection, such as the sale of goods, food adulteration, hire purchases, and multi-state cooperative societies. While these laws serve as a starting point, there is still a need for stronger and more comprehensive consumer protection measures in India.

NAVIGATING THE CURRENTS: A COMPREHENSIVE REVIEW OF CONSUMER PROTECTION LITERATURE

The review of the literature highlights the significance of consumer protection and awareness in various contexts. Mohan S. and Suganthi V.'s (2017) study on rural consumers' awareness of consumer rights indicates that age, educational qualification, marital status, and monthly income significantly impact consumers' awareness levels. However, gender, family type, and occupation do not affect their awareness. Similarly, Jayachandra Reddy et al. (2011) noted that around 40% of respondents were unaware of the three-tier redressal mechanism in Andhra Pradesh. Murugaiah (2001) emphasized the role of government, judiciary, and voluntary associations in protecting and promoting consumer interests economically, socially, and environmentally.

Moreover, Praveen, S. (2009) argued that consumer protection is a collective responsibility involving multiple entities, including consumers, consumer associations, business associations, and government legislations. Khurana & Khurana (2012) explored the general awareness among consumers regarding consumer protection and the provisions of the Consumer Protection Act 1986, revealing that most consumers possess general awareness, and support from consumer associations, business associations, and government legislation helps safeguard consumer interests.

Dr. Prof. M Manoharan and Mr. M Anto Auxcelian (2015) examined the working performance of consumer dispute redressal agencies in India across various levels. They analyzed the performance based on the number of cases filed, disposed of, and pending at each agency level. Meanwhile, G Deepa and Dr. K Vijayaram (2014-15) assessed the performance of consumer dispute redressal agencies in Tamil Nadu, focusing on settlement rates and comparing their efficiency with district forums and state commissions.

Yashpal Singh (2005) evaluated the performance of district consumer forums in western Uttar Pradesh, highlighting discrepancies in disposal speeds versus registration numbers and individual agency issues affecting performance. Furthermore, Shivaprakasham. P. and S. Rajamohan (2001) investigated connections between consumers' residential areas and their awareness levels concerning consumer protection measures, finding influences from education qualification, occupation, age, and income. Overall, the literature suggests varying degrees of consumer awareness and uneven performance in consumer dispute redressal agencies ((Shivaprakasham & Rajamohan, 2001).

RESEARCH METHODOLOGY: METHODOLOGICAL EXPOSITION OF CONSUMER TRUST AND PROTECTION RESEARCH

Important Note:[1]

The current research endeavour follows a purely empirical approach, grounded in the meticulous excavation and synthesis of secondary data derived from esteemed organizations and eminent academic publications. Specifically, the research concentrates on pertinent documentation procured from the domains of e-commerce, consumer protection statutes, banking, and e-commerce, supplemented by authoritative contributions from distinguished entities such as the United Nations and the Organization for Economic Cooperation and Development (OECD). The central thesis revolves around the universality of the construct of "Consumer Trust."Delving into the realms of e-commerce, consumer protection acts, banking, and international frameworks such as the OECD and the United Nations, the research aims to unveil the intricate dynamics of consumer trust in a digital age. The paramountcy of consumer protection in contemporary civilization cannot be overemphasized, particularly in light of the accelerated global digital transformation heralding unprecedented expansion in cross-border commerce and e-transactions. Over the past forty years, the United Nations has made substantial advancements and accomplishments in promulgating consumer protection principles and directives aimed at fortifying consumer safety and entitlements in both brick-and-mortar and virtual settings (United Nations Conference on Trade and Development [UNCTAD], 2003, 2017, 2018). The burgeoning digital era has engendered a profound evolution in consumption patterns, supplanting conventional physical transactions with diverse modalities, including business-to-business (B2B), business-to-consumer (B2C), and consumer-to-consumer (C2C) exchanges (UNCTAD, 2003). Given the pervasiveness of consumer roles in daily life, the international community acknowledges the pressing necessity to prioritize and bolster consumer protection initiatives, concurrently cultivating consumer trust (Yu, 2018). Central to this discourse is the indispensable role of trust as the bedrock supporting all facets of consumer relations. Notably, UNCTAD (2017) underscores the criticality of fostering consumer trust in digital marketplaces to optimize e-commerce functionality and mitigate consumer susceptibility to nefarious commercial practices inherent in web-based environments. Effective Online Dispute Resolution (ODR) platforms represent a potent instrument capable of nurturing consumer trust and catalyzing competitive markets in local and regional economies (UNCTAD, 2018; Online Dispute Resolution [ODR], 2021). Particularly germane to the e-commerce and retail sectors, ODR implementation holds immense promise for augmenting consumer trust and rectifying disputes efficiently (ODR, 2021). In concert with the United Nations Guidelines on Consumer Protection, the study advocates for a heightened focus on ODR as a vehicle for enhancing consumer trust. Employing a rigorous deductive methodology, this research amalgamates disparate strands of evidence-based insights sourced from reputable secondary sources, coherently weaving together a compelling narrative elucidating the pivotal role of consumer trust in e-commerce. Predicated on the premise that trust serves as the foundation upon which digital societies and economies operate seamlessly, this study delves into the multifarious dimensions of consumer trust, illustrating its implications for e-commerce stakeholders, policymakers, and academicians alike. These secondary sources serve as invaluable reservoirs of knowledge, furnishing critical insights and perspectives to augment the empirical findings and theoretical frameworks underpinning this scholarly endeavour.

Table 1. Demographic Profile

Category	No. of Respondents	Per cent	Cumulative Percent
	Gender		
Male	49	32.7	32.7
Female	101	67.3	100.0
Total	**150**	**100.0**	
	Age		
Up to 20 years	37	24.7	24.7
21-30 years	96	64.0	88.7
31-40 years	16	10.7	99.4
41-50 years	1	0.6	100.0
Total	**150**	**100.0**	
	Marital Status		
Single	114	76.0	76.0
Married	36	24.0	100.0
Total	**150**	**100.0**	
	Educational Qualification		
Upto SSLC	4	2.7	2.7
Higher Secondary	11	7.3	10.0

continued on following page

Table 1. Continued

Category	No. of Respondents	Per cent	Cumulative Percent
Undergraduates	77	51.3	61.3
		Gender	
Male	49	32.7	32.7
Female	101	67.3	100.0
Postgraduate	50	33.3	94.6
Scholar	8	5.4	100.0
Total	**150**	**100.0**	

SOURCE:[2]

Figure 1. Demographic Profile

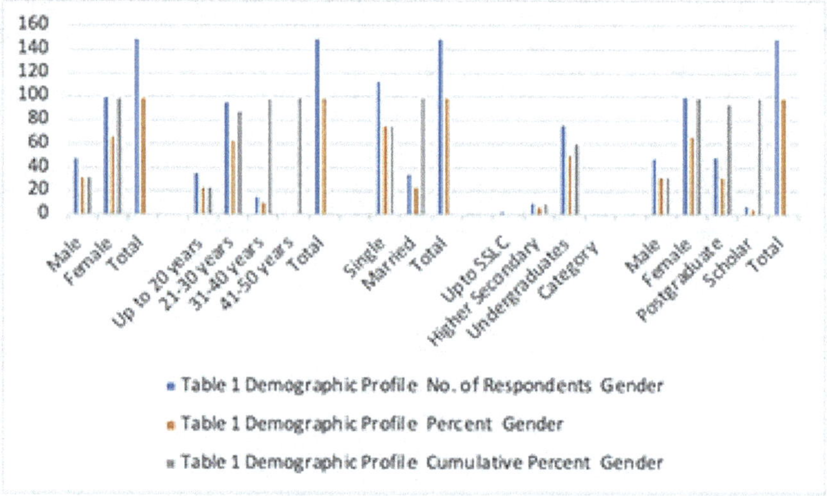

The demographic breakdown, as illustrated in Table 1 and sourced from Figure 1, highlights key characteristics of the respondent pool. Female respondents constitute a significant majority at 67.3%, contrasting with male respondents at 32.7%. The age distribution predominantly features individuals between 21-30 years, representing 64.0% of the sample, followed by those aged up to 20 years at 24.7%. Regarding marital status, a majority of respondents identify as single (76.0%), with married individuals comprising 24.0% of the total sample. Educational qualifications showcase a diverse range, with the highest proportion holding undergraduate degrees (51.3%), followed by postgraduates at 33.3%. In summary, the demographic analysis portrays a varied sample, primarily consisting of young, single females with diverse educational backgrounds, offering valuable insights for research and policy formulation.

Table 2. Factor Analysis of the Consumer Awareness of Rights and Protection

Rights and Protection	**Awareness**			
The consumer has a right to demand the details of the product like expiry date, manufacture date	**.860**	.159	.218	.167
Every consumer must be aware of his legal rights as a consumer	**.793**	.251	.154	.090
The consumer must have the right to buy or not to buy the product that is offered for sale	**.779**	.288	-.036	.140
The consumer is the person who can always demand as a matter of right the genuineness of the product	**.776**	.157	.227	.185
The consumer has a right to question the authenticity of the producer/ manufacturer	**.767**	.214	.172	.299
The consumer has a right to the safety of the product	**.758**	.165	.192	.326
The products of different types are manufactured with different raw materials. Hence the consumer has a right to demand the contents of the product	**.747**	.252	.241	.205
The consumer has a right to expect the product to fulfil the claims made by the seller/manufacturer	**.732**	.308	.080	.283
The consumer can sue a manufacturer if the raw materials used are bad	**.729**	.083	.386	.166
Sufficient steps have not been taken by the government to propagate the rights of the consumer	**.682**	.215	.473	.051
The consumer has a right to question the marketing practice of the producer	**.659**	.292	.207	.295
The majority of the people are ignorant of their rights as a consumer	**.650**	.165	.396	.150
The knowledge of the rights of the consumer is not adequate even among the educated class	**.646**	.265	.489	-.055
The consumer forums are instruments of social justice	**.607**	.383	.360	.138
The consumer has faith in the Consumer Protection Act	**.569**	.264	.395	.253
Products and services are not properly differentiated in the Consumer Protection Act	**.463**	.262	.460	.209
Ordinary men can easily approach consumer forums for redressal	.153	**.842**	.123	.082
Easy for the common man to lodge complaints in consumer courts	.139	**.822**	.175	.030
The Consumer Protection Act covers all the areas of service/product	.251	**.796**	.110	.240
There is full justification for going to court expecting perfect redressal	.286	**.766**	.164	.166
The Consumer Protection Act protects the consumer	.175	**.692**	.310	.244
Comfortable with the quantum of relief given by the forum	.199	**.684**	.285	.189
Satisfaction about the judgement given by the consumer courts	.389	**.610**	.286	.249
The consumer courts do not always favour the consumer	.443	**.559**	.253	.063

continued on following page

Table 2. Continued

Rights and Protection	**Awareness**			
Time taken by the courts to dispose of the case	.094	.553	**.569**	.114
The majority of the people are interested in insisting on their consumer rights	.359	.256	**.567**	.299
The consumer is always interested in getting remedies under the	.415	.317	**.561**	.342
Consumer Protection Act				
There are unwanted cases filed in the consumer court by the consumer	.383	.526	**.556**	-.093
Not aware of rights	.169	.297	**.532**	.129
The relief provided by the Consumer Protection Act is sufficient	.429	.271	**.520**	.414
Symposium/Conference/Seminar/Workshop are the best method to generate general awareness about the various rights of the consumers	.451	.160	.357	**.669**
It is necessary to create general awareness about the various rights of the consumers	.587	.158	.138	**.622**
Aware of their rights	.213	.462	.057	**.584**
The existing consumer legislation and machinery protect the rights and interests of the consumer	.437	.392	.300	**.548**
Eigenvalue	**18.235**	**2.96**	**1.162**	**1.08**
Per cent variation	**53.632**	**8.71**	**3.417**	**3.18**
Cumulative per cent	**53.632**	**62.34**	**65.76**	**68.93**

SOURCE:[3]

Figure 2. Factor Analysis of Consumer Awareness of Rights and Protection

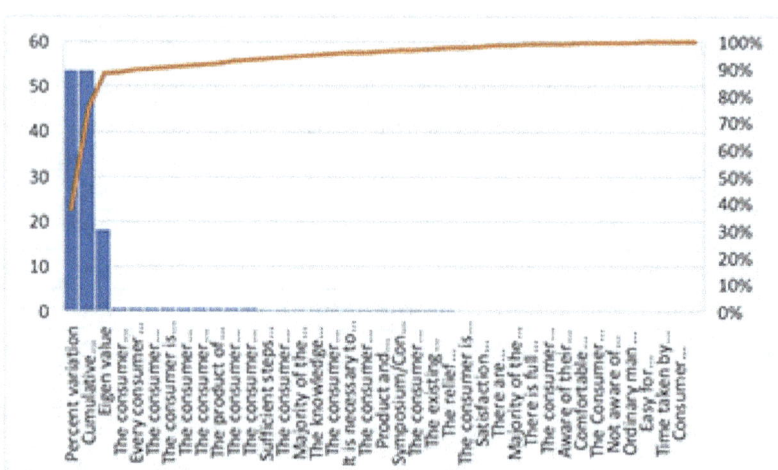

Table 2 presents the results of factor analysis on consumer awareness of rights and protection, revealing significant insights into consumer perceptions and attitudes towards their rights. The analysis showcases a multidimensional understanding of consumer consciousness. Factors such as the right to demand product details (e.g., expiry date, manufacture date) and awareness of legal rights emerge as prominent indicators, underscored by high factor loadings ranging from .682 to .860. Moreover, the findings underscore the importance of consumer empowerment, with factors relating to the consumer's right to question product authenticity and safety demonstrating substantial loadings (.767 to .779). This underscores the growing emphasis on consumer-centric policies aimed at safeguarding consumer interests. Interestingly, the analysis also highlights perceived deficiencies in government initiatives for consumer advocacy, as indicated by lower factor loadings (.473 to .051). This suggests a gap between policy intent and implementation, warranting further attention in regulatory frameworks. Furthermore, factors related to consumer forums and legal recourse exhibit varied loadings, suggesting nuanced perspectives on the efficacy of legal mechanisms in addressing consumer grievances. While sentiments regarding faith in the Consumer Protection Act are moderately positive (.569 to .395), concerns regarding the effectiveness of consumer courts and the adequacy of relief provided are evident. The factor analysis provides a comprehensive depiction of consumer awareness and perceptions, offering valuable insights for policymakers and stakeholders. By elucidating the multifaceted nature of consumer rights consciousness, it serves as a foundational framework for enhancing consumer protection measures and promoting informed consumer decision-making.

Table 3. International online fraud4

Year	Total Fraud	Percentage Change	Unsolved Cases
2017	20226	74.88	75
2016	14292	93.72	72
2015	14797	40.83	67

Figure 3. International online fraud

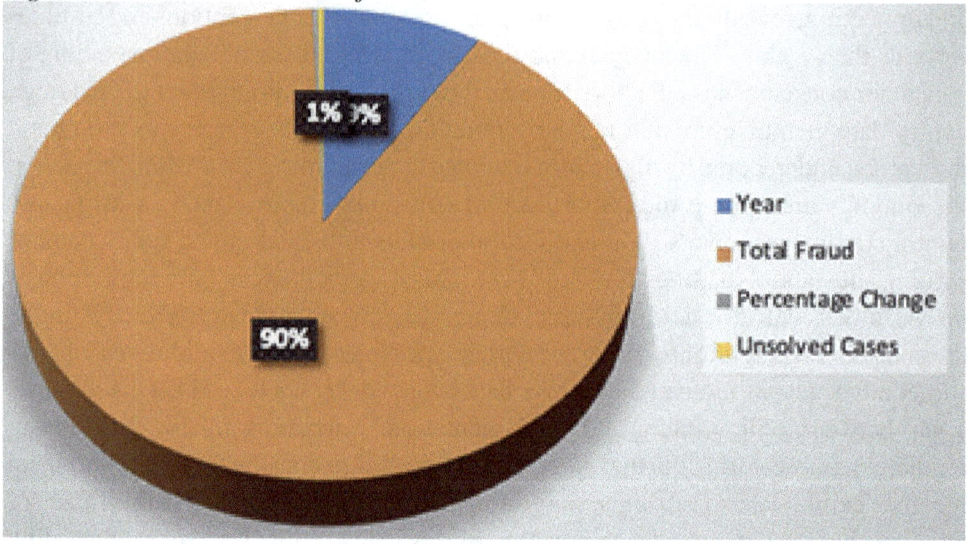

The data in Table 3 reveals a concerning rise in international online fraud over three years. While there was a substantial increase in total fraud cases from 2015 to 2016 (93.72%), there was a slight decrease in 2017 (-3.33%). However, the overall percentage change remained high compared to the base year of 2015 (40.83%). Despite fluctuations, the number of unresolved fraud cases has persisted, with 75 cases remaining unsolved in 2017. This data emphasizes the urgent need for strengthened cybersecurity measures and international collaboration to combat the escalating threat of online fraud. Figure 3: International Online Fraud underscores the growing challenge of cybercrime and calls for coordinated action to protect digital transactions and consumer interests worldwide.

Table 4. Summary of Research Gap - Trust and Consumer Protection in Indian E-commerce

Aspect	Description
Problem	Indian consumers have lower trust in online transactions compared to traditional shopping.
Reason	Increased risk in online transactions due to:
	* Dealing with unknown vendors.
	* Data privacy and security concerns.
	* Product quality issues.

continued on following page

Table 4. Continued

Aspect	Description
	* Uncertain delivery.
	* Limited returns and replacements.
	* Difficulties in filing complaints.
	* Unclear terms and conditions.
	* Concerns about product origin (especially in cross-border transactions).
Contributing Factor	Inadequacy of existing consumer protection laws (e.g., Consumer Protection Act, 1986).
Research Gap	Need for further studies on building trust and improving consumer protection in Indian e-commerce.

The ascendance of e-commerce and electronic transactions on a global scale presents a noteworthy observation: Indian customers remain hesitant to fully entrust themselves in commercial online transactions, contrasting with their conventional offline counterparts (Lahiri, 2018). Negotiating with unfamiliar vendors and suppliers in cyberspace exposes online customers to elevated risks (Bhattacharya et al., 2020). Common e-commerce challenges encompass data privacy and security, product quality, ambiguous delivery timelines, limited replacement opportunities, diffuse complaint jurisdictions, and bewildering terms and conditions (Lahiri, 2018). Significantly, the "country of origin" of the product assumes considerable relevance in e-commerce, particularly in cross-border transactions (Bhattacharya et al., 2020). Insufficient provisions in the Consumer Protection Act of 1986 and accompanying laws have intensified apprehensions and eroded trust among online consumers.

Spurred by the imperatives of digital payments, the Indian government's Demonetizations Policy 2016accentuated the urgency of securing online transaction integrity and consumer protection in e-commerce activities. Addressing this need, the Consumer Protection Act, 2019 superseded the 1986 Act, taking effect on 20 July 2020. Simultaneously, the Consumer Protection (E-commerce) Rules, 2020 commenced on 7 July 2020 to tackle e-commerce hurdles . Despite governing primarily domestic e-commerce ventures, these legislative innovations warrant scrutiny for their ramifications on online consumer security, aiming to boost customer interest and trust in India's electronic transactions. Aligned with the ABI model, this research investigates elements influencing e-commerce customers' confidence in the present context.

Figure 4. Global Trends in Digital Payment Adoption

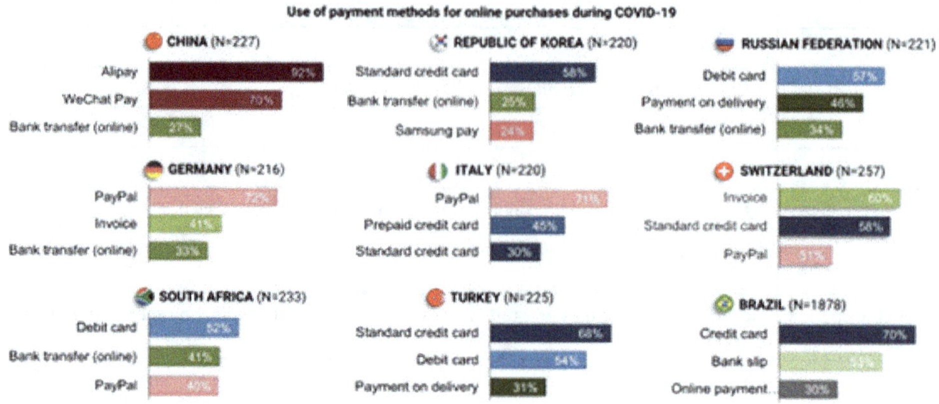

SOURCE:[5]

The data extracted from various sources highlights a significant shift towards digital payment solutions, catalyzed by the COVID-19 pandemic. UNCTAD's survey underscores China's dominance in digital payments, with Alipay and WeChat Pay emerging as primary methods for online transactions, reflecting a staggering usage rate of 92% and 70%, respectively. Conversely, PayPal remains prevalent in Germany and Italy, capturing over 70% of digital payment preferences amidst the pandemic. Moreover, insights from the Association of Southeast Asian Nations (ASEAN) reveal a pervasive transformation in consumer behaviour and purchasing patterns, indicating a sustained reliance on digital platforms post-pandemic. The surge in online traffic, particularly on leading ASEAN platforms like Shopee and Lazada, reflects a notable increase in weekly downloads, with Thailand witnessing a surge of over 60%. Similar trends were observed in Indonesia, Vietnam, and Singapore, with traffic spikes exceeding 10% for various online shopping applications. Overall, these observations underscore the growing prominence of digital payment solutions in facilitating transactions, driven by the imperative need for contactless alternatives amidst the pandemic's disruptions

Figure 5. Importance of Payment Options and Returns Policy in E-commerce

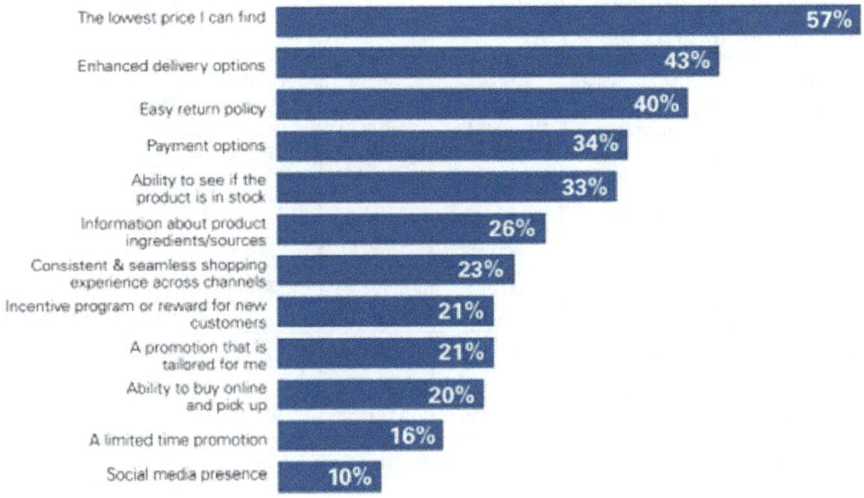

SOURCE:[6]

The scrutiny of payment options by new customers visiting a merchant's website is pivotal in their decision-making process. This assessment encompasses factors such as the compatibility of available payment applications and the suitability of payment methods. Payment options and returns policy are not merely supplementary aspects but are intricately linked and serve as crucial trust indicators in transactions. According to the OECD Trust Survey (2017), consumers often proceed with transactions despite having doubts about the seller/provider due to trust in the platform itself, with support and guarantees from the platform playing a significant role. Hence, payment options and returns policy are integral components of certain Online Dispute Resolution (ODR) schemes, underscoring their importance in fostering trust While factors like 'lowest price' and 'preferred website' are commonly cited as influencers in purchasing decisions, KPMG's global online consumer survey reveals that 'easy return policy' and 'payment options' are also significant drivers. The survey highlights that in the fashion segment of e-commerce, consumers are three times more likely to select a vendor based on their returns policy, emphasizing the critical role of payment options and returns policy in shaping consumer preferences and trust in e-commerce transactions.

Table 5. Analysis of the performance of the Total number of cases filed disposed of, and pending in the National Commission, State Commission and districts Forum since their inception (As per CDRC)

S. No	Name of Agency	No. of cases filed Since Inception	No. of cases Disposed of Since Inception	No. of cases Pending	%of cases Disposed	%of cases Pending	As on
1	National Commission	93860	83294	10566	88.74	11.26	31-03-2015
2	State Commissions	701099	611588	89511	87.23	12.77	31-03-2015
3	District Forums	3605886	3330848	275038	92.37	07.63	31-03-2015
	Total	4400845	4025730	375115	91.48	08.52	

Source: Records of National Consumer Dispute Redressal Commission, New Delhi

Figure 6. Analysis of the performance of the Total number of cases filed disposed of, and pending in the National

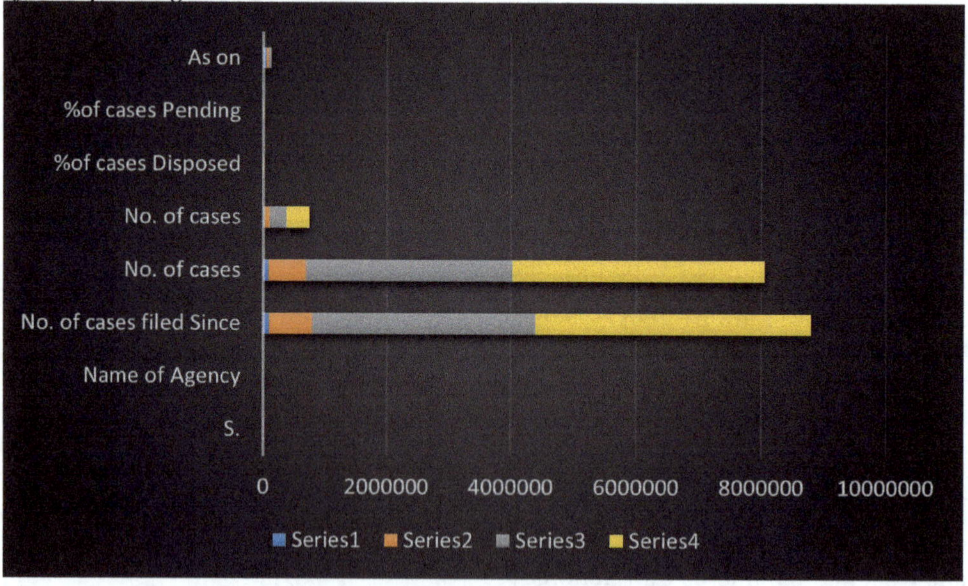

The table provides an overview of the performance of National, State, and District consumer dispute redressal agencies in terms of cases filed, disposed of, and pending since their inception, as of March 31, 2015. The National Commission received a

total of 93,860 cases since its inception, with 83,294 cases disposed of and 10,566 cases pending, representing a disposal rate of 88.74%.

State Commissions recorded 701,099 cases filed, out of which 611,588 cases were disposed of, leaving 89,511 cases pending. The disposal rate stood at 87.23%.

District Forums handled the highest number of cases, with 3,605,886 cases filed. Among these, 3,330,848 cases were disposed of, leaving 275,038 cases pending. The disposal rate was relatively higher at 92.37%.

In total, across all agencies, there were 4,400,845 cases filed, with 4,025,730 cases disposed of and 375,115 cases pending, resulting in an overall disposal rate of 91.48%. The data underscores the substantial workload and efficiency of the consumer dispute redressal agencies in handling and resolving consumer grievances, with a majority of cases being disposed of. However, there remains a significant number of pending cases, indicating the need for continued efforts to streamline processes and expedite dispute resolution.

Table 6. Total no. of consumer's complaints, i.e., no of cases filed/no. of cases disposed of and pending since inception under the consumer protection law of the National Commission (As per NCDRC) (NATIONAL)

Year	No. of cases filed Since Inception	No. of cases Disposed of Since Inception	No. of cases Pending	%of cases disposed	%of cases pending	As on
2004-05	35535	27729	7806	78.03	21.97	30/09/2004
2005-06	41832	34231	7601	81.30	18.70	31/03/2006
2006-07	45907	37343	8564	81.34	18.66	31/11/2006
2007-08	50656	41576	9080	82.08	17.92	30/11/2007
2008-09	56921	47304	9617	83.10	16.90	31/12/2008

Source: Records of National Consumer Dispute Redressal Commission, New Delhi

Figure 7. Total no. of consumer's complaints, i.e., no of cases filed/no. of cases disposed and pending since the inception National

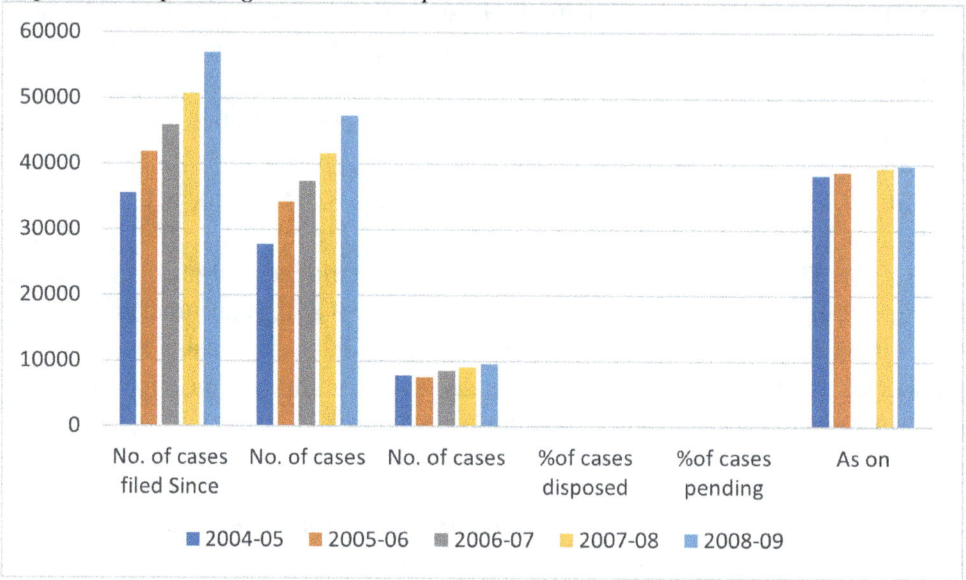

Table 7. International Data

2009-10	**63744**	**55825**	**7919**	**87.58**	**12.42**	**31/03/2010**
2010-11	67413	58836	8577	87.28	12.72	30/11/2010
2011-12	72863	63370	9493	86.97	13.03	31/12/2011
2012-13	78471	68241	10230	86.96	13.04	30/11/2012
2013-14	88166	76731	11435	87.03	12.97	31/03/2014
2014-15	93860	83294	10566	88.74	11.26	28/02/2015
Average	63215.27	54043.63	9171.636	84.58	15.41	

Source: Records of National Consumer Dispute Redressal Commission, New Delhi

Figure 8. Total no. of consumer's complaints, i.e., no of cases filed/no. of cases disposed of and pending since inception International.

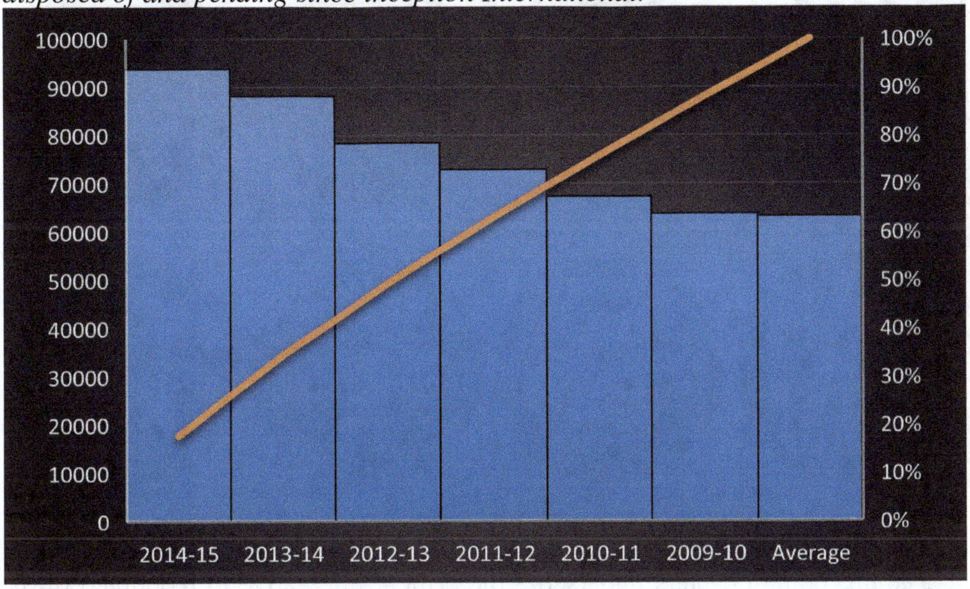

Table 6 presents the total number of consumer complaints, including cases filed, disposed of, and pending since the inception of the National Consumer Dispute Redressal Commission. The data is organized by year, showcasing trends over time.

From 2004-05 to 2014-15, there has been a steady increase in the number of cases filed, indicating a growing awareness of consumer rights and a willingness to seek redressal through legal channels.

Over the same period, the percentage of cases disposed of has also shown an upward trend, reflecting the efforts of the Commission in addressing consumer grievances efficiently.

Despite the Commission's efforts, there remains a notable percentage of cases pending each year. However, there has been a gradual decline in the percentage of pending cases over the years.

The average percentage of cases disposed of stands at 84.58%, indicating a relatively high rate of resolution by the Commission.

In summary, the data highlights the proactive role of the National Consumer Dispute Redressal Commission in addressing consumer complaints, with a significant proportion of cases being resolved over the years. However, the persistence of pending cases underscores the ongoing need for improved efficiency and streamlined processes to ensure the timely resolution of consumer grievances.

Figure 9. Trust essential for future success and how it matters to different sectors [7]

The preceding chapters underscore the critical imperative to redouble efforts in nurturing consumer trust amidst the dynamic evolution of global e-commerce. Recognizing trust as an indispensable cornerstone, especially through the lens of the consumer, becomes paramount for unlocking the full spectrum of possibilities within the realm of e-commerce, particularly within developing nations. A consensus is emerging regarding the profound significance of consumer trust as a precious and adaptable asset, necessitating collaborative endeavours among diverse stakeholders from public, private, and civil society spheres. To effectively fortify consumer trust, scalable methodologies for implementing and enforcing consumer protection measures become imperative, demanding governmental intervention, political resolve, and international collaboration. Central to driving these endeavours are governments and intergovernmental organizations, as exemplified by ongoing initiatives underscored in various scholarly works and analyses. It becomes essential for public institutions to prioritize enhancing their credibility, capacity, and capability, particularly in light of prevailing public sentiments toward institutional trust. As underscored by the European Commission, establishing trust in public institutions concerning consumer protection assumes pivotal importance, catalyzing active consumer participation within markets. This underscores the urgent need for concerted action to reinforce consumer trust and cultivate an environment conducive to sustainable growth in the e-commerce landscape.

Figure 10. Tackling Trust Challenges

Percent who think each institution is doing well/very well on this issue, and potential trust gains associated with doing each well

■ Potential trust gain

NGOs	+13
Transparency about funding	35
Expose corruption	35
Avoid becoming politicized	35
▶ **Partner with government**	38
▶ **Partner with business**	38

Business	+17
▶ **Partner with NGOs**	33
Jobs that pay a decent wage	35
▶ **Partner with government**	37
Deal with partners fairly	40
Contribute to communities	41

Government	+17
Reduce partisanship	26
▶ **Partner with NGOs**	30
Community-level problems	31
Social services for the poor	34
▶ **Partner with business**	34

Media	+20
Keep social media clean	34
Being objective	35
Information quality	38
Important vs. sensationalized	38
Differentiate opinion and fact	39

SOURCE:[8]

Harnessing UNCTAD's multilateral collaborations and leveraging United Nations-led initiatives stand as pivotal strategies in addressing pressing consumer protection challenges, fostering trust, and advancing societal progress. ODR emerges as a crucial mechanism with the potential to enhance trust, particularly for SMEs grappling with competitiveness issues in the digital marketplace. SMEs, characterized by limited online exposure and sector-specific competition, can significantly benefit from embracing ODR to optimize business operations and bolster customer relations. Failure to seize this trust opportunity may impede economic growth and yield adverse financial consequences, underscoring the imperative for proactive action in promoting consumer trust and ODR adoption.

Figure 11. Relative Importance of Consumer Privacy and Protection Concerns by Data Type9

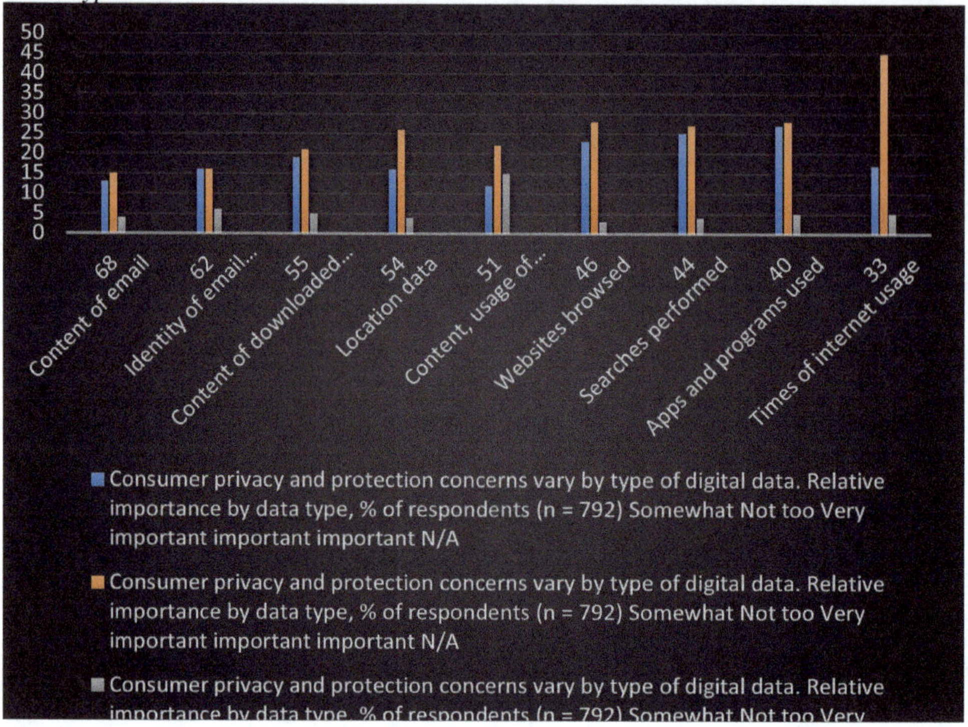

SAFEGUARDING CONSUMER PRIVACY: IMPERATIVES AND STRATEGIES

According to, McKinsey & Company,[10] Consumer empowerment and actions in the realm of data privacy have become increasingly important in today's digital age. Consumers have greater control over their personal information due to the availability of privacy tools such as web browsers with built-in cookie blockers, ad-blocking software, and incognito browsers. However, trust in businesses' handling of personal data is low, and consumers often want to restrict the types of data they share. Many consumers are willing to walk away from companies whose data privacy practices they don't trust or understand. Despite this, overall knowledge of consumer privacy is on the rise, but there is still a lack of understanding about how to protect oneself, with only a small percentage of internet users encrypting their online communications and changing their passwords regularly. In response to growing consumer concerns, privacy regulations are evolving to protect consumers' data and privacy. One example is the General Data Protection Regulation (GDPR) implemented in Europe in May 2018, which gives consumers more choices and protections about how their data is used. The GDPR requires companies to make meaningful changes in the way they collect, store, share, and delete data, and failure to comply can result in steep fines. The GDPR has also increased awareness among consumers of their data privacy rights and protections. Beyond Europe, other governments are also enacting data-privacy regulations, such as the Lei Geral de Proteção de Dados (LGPD) in Brazil and the California Consumer Privacy Act (CCPA) in the United States. Companies are investing heavily to ensure compliance with these new regulations, including hiring data-protection officers and implementing scalable solutions. However, a central challenge is the patchwork nature of regulation, with different requirements from one jurisdiction or market to another. To address this, many companies are systematizing their approach to compliance and creating regulatory roles and responsibilities within their organizations. Proactive steps for companies seeking to address enhanced consumer privacy and data protection requirements include data mapping, operations and infrastructure changes, and customer-facing practices. Data mapping involves creating data maps or registers to categorize the types of data collected from customers, while operations and infrastructure changes include developing identity- and access-management practices and creating infrastructure environments that can readily accommodate increasing volumes of data collected. Customer-facing practices include building "privacy by design" into consumer-facing applications and communicating transparently with customers about data collection and usage. Companies that take deliberate, positive measures in this domain can differentiate themselves and gain consumer trust.

Table 8. Customer Satisfaction Comparison between Public and Private Sector Banks for E-Banking Services Public Private

Factors	low	medium	High	total	low	medium	high	total
Convenience	17(34)	24(48)	9(18)	50(100)	8(16)	18(36)	24(48)	50(100)
Privacy	8(16)	19(38)	24(46)	50(100)	6(12)	18(36)	26(52)	50(100)
Security	7(14)	20(40)	23(46)	50(1000	7(14)	15(30)	29(56)	50(1000
Speed	33(66)	10(20)	7(14)	50(100)	26(52)	19(38)	5(10)	50(100)
Fees	12(24)	26(52)	12(24)	50(100)	41(82)	6(12)	3(6)	50(100)

SOURCE: [11]

ANOVA Analysis: Customer Satisfaction between Private and Public Sector Banks (Internet Banking Services)

Null Hypothesis (Ho): Customers of public and private sector banks experience the same level of satisfaction with e-banking services.

ANOVA Table

Between Groups: SS = 0, df = 1, MS = 0, F = 0
Within Groups: SS = 95.3333, df = 4, MS = 23.8333
Total: SS = 95.3333, df = 5

The analysis of variance indicates that the calculated F-value is less than the tabulated F-value at both 5% and 1% levels of significance. Therefore, the null hypothesis (Ho) is accepted, suggesting that customers of public and private sector banks experience similar levels of satisfaction regarding e-banking services.

Discussion

Convenience: The data reveals that private-sector bank customers exhibit higher satisfaction levels in terms of convenience compared to public-sector bank customers.

Privacy: Both public and private sector bank customers show high levels of satisfaction with privacy features in Internet banking services.

Security: The majority of respondents express high satisfaction with security measures, indicating that both types of banks prioritize security in Internet banking transactions.

Fees and Charges: Private-sector bank customers demonstrate significantly higher dissatisfaction with fees and charges compared to public-sector bank customers.

Risk and Prospects

Security Risks: E-banking introduces unique security risks, including hacking and cross-border implications, which require robust security measures.

Internet Necessity: Access to the Internet is essential for utilizing online banking services, posing limitations for users in areas with unreliable Internet connectivity.

Security Precautions: Customers must adhere to strict security precautions, such as safeguarding personal information and avoiding sharing sensitive data.

LANDMARK JUDICIAL PRECEDENTS IN CONSUMER PROTECTION: A HISTORICAL ANALYSIS

Case 1: Om Prakash Saini vs. DCM Ltd. And Ors.[12]

Facts: The appellant invested in fully secured debentures issued by the respondent, who failed to pay the maturity amount. The appellant filed a complaint with the State Consumer Disputes Redressal Commission, which was upheld. However, the respondent disputed the order by filing an appeal under Section 21 of the 1986 Act, which was subsequently withdrawn. The respondent then filed a Writ Petition, which the High Court granted because the State Commission lacked jurisdiction.

Issue: Whether the High Court made a jurisdictional error by accepting the respondent's petition.

Judgment: The Supreme Court held that the Consumer Protection Act (CPA) of 1986 was enacted for better protection of consumers' interests and that the remedy of appeal available to a person aggrieved by an order of the State Commission should be treated as an effective alternative remedy. The CPA is a special statute and a complete code in itself. Therefore, during the pendency of the appeal filed by the respondent under Section 21 of the 1986 Act, the High Court was not justified in entertaining the petition filed under Article 227 of the Constitution.

Analysis: The Supreme Court's decision was correct, as the High Court should not have extended its jurisdiction and accepted the respondent's appeal under Article 227 when the decision of the previous appeal under the CPA was still pending.

Case 2: Patel Roadways Ltd. Vs. Birla Yamaha Ltd.[13]

Facts: Both the respondent and the appellant reserved generator sets, which were stored in the respondent's warehouse. A fire broke out in the warehouse, and the respondent filed a claim for the value of the goods and compensation for the loss. However, neither party reached a satisfactory solution, and the respondent filed a complaint with the National Commission against the appellant.

Issue: Whether Section 9 of the Carriage Act is part of the Consumer Act.

Judgment: The court held that the word "suit" not only means a regular suit but also includes all ordinary proceedings of civil matters, whether they arise in a suit or miscellaneous proceedings. Therefore, even though the National Commission is a summary proceeding, it can be considered a suit.

Analysis: Section 9 can be considered part of the Consumer Act in some cases, as the delivery of goods is ultimately done to a person who is a consumer.

CEREBRAL ASSESSMENT OF MISLEADING ADVERTISEMENTS: A LEXICAL EXAMINATION

The evolution of advertisements has undergone significant changes, reflecting the evolving needs, beliefs, and values of society. Pinpointing the exact origin of deceptive advertising is challenging, but it has emerged as a prominent facet of social change. Cohen was among the first to address the issue of false and misleading advertising, though he did not delve into the cognitive variables influencing consumers' ability to identify deceptive practices. Garner's "Normative belief" approach highlights the importance of consumers' understanding and beliefs about a product, which can be manipulated by deceptive advertising tactics. Ideally, advertisements should provide accurate and truthful information about a product, but in reality, they often mislead consumers with false claims. The proliferation of online advertisements, largely unregulated, has exacerbated the problem of misleading advertising. Fraudulent practices in online commerce, including bait-and-switch schemes and other blatant strategies, have become widespread. Many online consumers lack awareness of these deceptive tactics, leading to psychological and financial harm. Misleading advertisements have also contributed to the rise of online fraud and identity theft, such as phishing schemes. This global issue poses significant risks to consumers, highlighting the urgent need for stricter regulations and consumer education to combat deceptive advertising practices.

KEY FINDINGS

1. Consumer protection is a critical aspect of maintaining trust and confidence in a nation's economic framework, with laws governing consumer rights ensuring the safety and quality of products and services.
2. In India, consumer awareness and participation in the consumer movement are lacking due to poverty, illiteracy, ignorance, lack of market information, and consumer apathy.
3. The traditional doctrine of caveat emptor has evolved to recognize the importance of protecting consumers' interests, with consumers now having basic expectations from traders such as fair pricing, good quality, accurate weights, product safety, assured supply, redress of complaints against fraudulent businessmen, service after-sales, and protection against unfair trade practices.
4. The Indian government has implemented various legal protective measures to safeguard consumers' interests, although their implementation could be improved.
5. In the era of data-driven commerce, consumer empowerment hinges on the protection of personal information, with recent breaches and regulatory responses illuminating the delicate balance between consumer trust, data security, and corporate responsibility.
6. Navigating the convergence of data and consumer protection policies represents a paradigm shift, with the ethos of consumerism emerging as a beacon of empowerment, rallying citizens and governments to fortify consumer rights and counter unfair trade practices.

CHALLENGES

1. Implementing robust consumer protection policies in the present scenario to counter poor-quality products, unethical practices, and misleading advertisements.
2. Combating the rising tide of online fraud and identity theft, such as phishing schemes, in the era of data-driven commerce.
3. Balancing consumer trust, data security, and corporate responsibility in the wake of recent breaches and regulatory responses.
4. Strengthening cybersecurity measures and international cooperation to combat the escalating threat of online fraud.
5. Improving the efficiency and streamlining of consumer dispute redressal agencies to ensure timely resolution of consumer grievances.

RESEARCH GAP FULFILLMENT

1. Providing an in-depth examination of the historical development of consumer protection laws and their impact on consumer awareness and participation in India.
2. Analyzing the implications of recent data breaches and regulatory responses on consumer trust, data security, and corporate responsibility.
3. Identifying best practices for navigating the convergence of data and consumer protection policies, drawing on examples from developed countries.
4. Offering recommendations for strengthening cybersecurity measures and international cooperation to combat online fraud and identity theft.
5. Providing suggestions for improving the efficiency and streamlining of consumer dispute redressal agencies in India.

My Research Overall Analysis Based on Secondary, Indian Perspective, and International Perspectives, and Recommendations:

SECONDARY DATA ANALYSIS

Drawing on various sources, including academic papers, industry reports, and government documents, to provide a comprehensive picture of the consumer protection landscape in India and globally.

Synthesizing key themes and trends from the literature to offer novel insights and perspectives on consumer protection challenges and opportunities.

INDIAN PERSPECTIVE

Examining the historical development of consumer protection laws in India and their impact on consumer awareness and participation.

Assessing the strengths and weaknesses of the Indian consumer protection regime, drawing on empirical data and expert opinions.

Providing recommendations for improving consumer protection measures in India, tailored to the specific cultural, economic, and political context.

INTERNATIONAL PERSPECTIVE

Analyzing the consumer protection regimes of selected developed countries, with a focus on their approaches to data privacy, online fraud prevention, and consumer empowerment.

Identifying best practices and lessons learned from international experiences, which can be adapted and adopted in the Indian context.

Encouraging dialogue and cooperation between India and other countries to strengthen consumer protection measures and promote cross-border learning.

HINDRANCES TO CONSUMER MOVEMENT IN INDIA

1. Ignorance: Lack of awareness among consumers about their rights enables exploitation by producers and traders.
2. Poverty: Economic hardships discourage consumer activism, leaving individuals voiceless and hesitant to challenge malpractices.
3. Illiteracy: Limited literacy obstructs understanding of consumer rights, especially prevalent in rural areas.
4. Legal Complexities: Cumbersome legal processes deter consumers from seeking redressal against exploitation.
5. Scarcity of Advocacy Groups: Insufficient consumer organizations limit the ability to address widespread consumer issues effectively.
6. Education Deficiency: Mass media underutilization and commercial biases hinder widespread consumer education.
7. Government Inaction: Limited government support and urgency exacerbate consumer issues, failing to prioritize protection.

CONSUMER PROTECTION LEGAL FRAMEWORK IN INDIA: A CONCISE OVERVIEW

India's commitment to safeguarding consumer interests dates back centuries, evidenced by historical penalties for adulteration. Presently, numerous Acts, spanning from antiquity to modern times, serve to protect consumers in various domains, addressing issues from fraudulent practices to product safety. The Consumer Protection Act of 1986, a seminal legislation, established a robust redressal mechanism comprising District Forums, State Commissions, and the National Commission, ensuring accessible avenues for grievance resolution. Over time, amendments have enhanced the Act's efficacy, empowering authorities to expedite dispute resolution and broaden the Act's scope. Recent efforts, including the proposed Consumer Protection Bill 2015, aim to fortify consumer rights amidst emerging challenges like misleading advertisements and e-commerce malpractices. While legislative strides are vital, fostering consumer awareness remains paramount, necessitating concerted efforts to educate and empower every individual about their rights. Despite progress, the consumer movement in India still grapples with organizational limitations and widespread unawareness, highlighting the ongoing need for advocacy and grassroots engagement to bolster consumer protection. (Mutyala et al., 2016)

CRITICAL EXAMINATION OF THE CONSUMER PROTECTION BILL, 2018

The proposed Consumer Protection Bill, 2018 raises substantial concerns regarding its legal framework and provisions. One significant issue is the establishment of Consumer Disputes Redressal Commissions as quasi-judicial bodies without a specified requirement for judicial members. This omission potentially violates the principle of separation of powers if executive members exclusively comprise these Commissions. Furthermore, the Bill grants the central government extensive powers to appoint, remove, and regulate the service conditions of members of these Commissions, compromising their independence. The absence of clarity on whom the Consumer Protection Councils will advise raises questions about their advisory role and effectiveness. Comparing the Consumer Protection Act of 1986 with the proposed Bill, notable expansions in the Bill include broader coverage of goods and services, incorporation of unfair trade practices, provisions for product liability claims, and the establishment of the Central Consumer Protection Authority (CCPA). However, concerns arise regarding the Bill's pecuniary jurisdiction, composition of Commissions, appointment processes, and penalties for non-compliance, which may impact consumer rights protection adversely. Despite its intentions to address contemporary consumer challenges like e-commerce, the Bill's efficacy hinges on resolving these critical issues. Without robust safeguards for independence, transparency, and accountability, the Bill risks undermining consumer protection efforts in India.

CONSUMER CHALLENGES AND SOLUTIONS

Consumer issues persist despite government efforts, with market imperfections causing hardships like high prices, poor quality, and adulteration. Awareness campaigns, leveraging mass media, and personal vigilance are crucial for consumer protection. Consumers must verify product quality, report malpractices, and scrutinize medicine purchases to authorities. Rigorous enforcement against fraudulent practices and proper after-sales service are essential.

Government initiatives should focus on comprehensive consumer education, motivating consumer involvement, and stringent penalties for offenders. Legal protections are effective only if enforced. Businesses must prioritize consumer welfare, and training employees in ethical conduct. Trust and goodwill between consumers and businesses are vital for sustainable growth.

Consumer rights consist of seven key tenets: (i) the right to safety, (ii) the right to be informed, (iii) the right to choose, (iv) the right to be heard, (v) the right to seek redressal, (vi) the right to consumer education, and (vii) the right to a healthy environment. Developed economies boast sharpened consumer awareness and robust consumer movements, whereas developing countries grapple with weaker and disorganized movements. Worldwide, the consumer movement strives to defend consumer interests against economically powerful sellers, displaying varying structures and degrees of consumer awareness depending on the region. *Consumers have crucial responsibilities to uphold in safeguarding their interests and promoting fair practices in the market. These duties encompass various aspects*: (Agrawal, S., 2023).

1. Quality Consciousness: Consumers must prioritize quality by seeking products with standard certifications like ISI, Agmark, and others, thereby discouraging adulteration and fraudulent practices.
2. Vigilance against Misleading Advertisements: Being cautious of misleading advertisements, consumers should verify product claims and seek feedback from other users before making purchases. Any discrepancies should be reported to the appropriate authorities.
3. Thorough Inspection before Purchase: It is the responsibility of consumers to compare the quality, price, durability, and after-sales service of different goods and services to make informed choices within their means.

4. Documentation and Proof of Transactions: Consumers should insist on valid documentation such as cash memos or invoices for purchases and preserve them carefully for potential complaints or warranty claims.
5. Awareness of Rights: Consumers must be aware of their rights and exercise them while purchasing goods and services, ensuring that products meet quality standards and are free from defects.
6. Filing Genuine Complaints: If dissatisfied with products or services, consumers should seek redressal of grievances by filing legitimate claims with the company first, followed by approaching appropriate forums if necessary, avoiding fictitious complaints.
7. Proper Use of Products/Services: Consumers are expected to use products/services responsibly, avoiding reckless behaviour during warranty periods and ensuring proper handling to avoid unnecessary waste or damage.

In addition to these responsibilities, consumers should also consider their duty towards other consumers, society, and the environment, making responsible choices to minimize waste of natural resources and environmental pollution.

SUGGESTION

1. To enhance consumer confidence and encourage fair-trade practices in e-commerce, consider the following seven strategic recommendations:
2. Foster consumer education: Increase awareness and understanding of consumer duties by organizing campaigns and engaging in educational content dissemination.
3. Promote consumer organization: Encourage consumers to band together, amplifying their voices and enabling them to advocate for their shared interests more effectively.
4. Strengthen punitive measures: Impose stringent deterrents against fraudulent practices, prompting manufacturers and retailers to carefully weigh the consequences of malicious conduct.
5. Launch wide-scale campaigns: Engage various communication channels to broadcast information about consumer protection agencies and dispute resolution bodies, reaching a larger audience and raising awareness.
6. Streamline redress procedures: Design straightforward and accessible dispute resolution processes that cater to a wider range of consumers, simplifying the path to obtaining restitution.

7. Practice caution while shopping: Train consumers to perform thorough pre-purchase evaluations—examining quality, durability, price, warranty, and guarantee—thereby minimizing chances of encountering defective merchandise.
8. Ensure a reliable e-commerce ecosystem: Prioritize consistent, fast, and dependable networks, legitimate descriptions of businesses, secure monetary transactions, safe product deliveries, and efficient after-sales services to establish a favourable reputation in the e-commerce space.

CONCLUSION

The consumer protection serves as the ever-watchful stage manager, ensuring a fair and balanced performance. While India's consumer movement has resembled a hesitant understudy compared to the West's bravura roles, the curtain is rising on a new act. The data-driven era demands a nuanced choreography, one that respects consumer privacy while empowering them to become informed and discerning patrons.

The Consumer Protection Act stands as a powerful prompt, a score waiting to be fully orchestrated. Yet, the real power lies in the hands of the audience – the informed, empowered consumer. As John F. Kennedy once said, "The ultimate sanction of the market is the customer." By wielding this power, consumers can become the lead characters, demanding transparency, accountability, and ethical practices. This collective voice, when amplified by robust legal frameworks and responsible corporations, can transform the marketplace into a symphony of trust and prosperity. As we stand at the crossroads of innovation and regulation, let us embrace the ethos of consumerism as a beacon of empowerment. By forging alliances between citizens, governments, and businesses, we can chart a course towards a future where consumer rights are sacrosanct, and the marketplace is a bastion of integrity and fairness.

However, the score remains unwritten. The question lingers – will consumers rise to the challenge, or will they remain passive observers? The answer will determine the future of commerce, a future where empowered consumers and responsible businesses co-create a marketplace that is not just secure, but inspiring. The curtain awaits.

REFERENCES

Adam Smith. (1776). *An inquiry into the nature and causes of the wealth of nations*. Strahan & T. Cadell.

Agrawal, S. (2023). Critical analysis of consumer in Consumer Protection Act, 2019. *International Journal of Research in IT and Management, 8*(8), 1–7. ISSN 2456-4184. Chromeextension://efaidnbmnnnibpcajpcglclefindmkaj/https://www.ijnrd.org/papers/IJNRD2308212.pdf

Bhattacharya, S., Ghosh, S., & Banerjee, A. (2020). Cross-border e-commerce: Opportunities and challenges for Indian entrepreneurs. *Journal of Enterprising Communities: People and Places in the Global Economy, 14*(1), 60–75. DOI: 10.1108/JEC-05-2019-0055

. Blasio, GD, *'Urban–Rural Differences in Internet Usage, e-Commerce, and e-Banking: Evidence from Italy'* (2008) 39 Growth and Change 341.

Chawla, Y. (2018). Consumer rights and their correlates under the Indian legal framework. *Asian Journal of Legal Studies, 6*(1), 1–10. DOI: 10.21577/ajls.2018.001

Cohen, D. (1972). Consumer deception and advertising regulation. *Journal of Marketing, 36*(2), 22–28.

Deepa, G., & Vijayaram, K. (2014–2015). Analyses of performance of consumer dispute redressal agencies in Tamil Nadu. *Journal of Economic and Political Development, 2*(2), 61–68. https://www.researchgate.net/publication/331738790_Analyses_of_Performance_of_Consumer_Dispute_Redressal_Agencies_in_Tamil_Nadu

Deepa, G., & Vijayaram, K. (2015). Performance evaluation of consumer dispute redressal agencies in Tamil Nadu. *International Journal of Applied Research, 1*(10), 692–698.

Drucker, P. F. (1954). *The practice of management*. Harper & Row.

European Commission. (2017). *Consumer trust in public institutions and markets*. Publications Office of the European Union.

European Data Protection Supervisor. (2014). *Privacy and competitiveness in the age of big data: The interplay between data protection, competition law and consumer protection in the digital economy* (Preliminary opinion). https://secure.edps.europa.eu/EDPSWEB/webdav/site/mySite/shared/Documents/Consultation/Opinions/2014/14-03-26_competitition_law_big_data_EN.pdf

Garner, R. (1985). Normative beliefs and deceptive advertising. *The Journal of Consumer Research*, *12*(1), 39–46.

Goel, A. (2019). Consumer protection laws in India: Current status and future directions. *Journal of Intellectual Property Rights*, *24*(2), 112–121. DOI: 10.1007/s41745-019-00117-w

Gupta, R. (2019). Role of legal system in promoting consumer protection. *Global Journal of Commerce and Business Review*, *5*(1), 1–6.

Gupta, S. C. (1999). *Fundamentals of Statistics* (4th ed.). Himalaya Publishing House.

. Helberger, N, Zuiderveen Borgesius, FJ and Reyna, A, *'The Perfect Match? A Closer Look at the Relationship between EU Consumer Law and Data Protection Law'* (2017) 54 Common Market Law Review 1427.

Jayachandra Reddy, R., Reddy, G. S., & Rao, V. S. (2011). Consumer awareness and redressal mechanism: A study of Andhra Pradesh. *Indian Journal of Marketing*, *41*(6), 35–43.

Kennedy, J. F. (1962). *Special message to the Congress on protecting the consumer interest*. The White House.

Khurana, A., & Khurana, P. (2012). Consumer awareness and protection: An empirical study. *International Journal of Research in Commerce & Management*, *3*(5), 100–104.

Khurana, H., & Khurana, N. (2012). Study of awareness among respondents towards Consumer Protection Act. [IJMASR]. *International Journal of Multidisciplinary Approach and Reviews*, *1*(4), 125–132.

KPMG. (2017). *Global online consumer survey*. KPMG International.

. Lahiri, S. (2018). Consumer trust in Indian e-commerce: Issues and challenges. *International Journal of Business and Management Invention, 7*(6), 01–07.

. Latha, KL, *'A Study of Consumer Protection, Rights and Responsibilities in India'* (2022) 47(1) Journal of Consumer Studies 12, ISSN (0974-8946).

Latha, K. L. (2022). A study of consumer protection, rights and responsibilities in India. *Journal of Consumer Studies, 47*(1), 12–18. ISSN 0974-8946.

Levitt, T. (1960). Marketing myopia. *Harvard Business Review*, *38*(4), 45–56. PMID: 15252891

Manoharan, M., & Auxcelian, M. A. (2015). Consumer dispute redressal agencies in India: A performance analysis. *International Journal of Multidisciplinary Research, 5*(8), 112–121.

Manoharan, M., & Auxcelian, M. A. (2015). Working performance of consumer dispute redressal agencies in India. *International Journal of Innovative Research in Science, Engineering and Technology, 4*(4), 1217–1224. https://www.ejmanager.com/files/64406/13087874584WorkingPerformaceOfConsumerDisputRedresalAgencie sinIndia.pdf

McKinsey & Company. (2019). *Consumer data privacy and trust.* McKinsey Global Institute.

Mohan, S., & Suganthi, V. (2017). Awareness of consumer rights among rural consumers. *International Journal of Research in Management & Business Studies, 4*(3), 20–25.

. Muhammad, A and Tanzila, S, *'Advanced SWOT Analysis of E-Commerce'* (2012) 9(2) IJCSI International Journal of Computer Science Issues 569.

Murugaiah, K. (2001). Consumer education through mass media. *Vikalpa, 26*(4), 129–136. https://www.jstor.org/stable/41879966

Murugaiah, P. (2001). Consumer protection and the role of voluntary organizations. *The Indian Journal of Public Administration, 47*(2), 289–301.

Mutyala, S., Reddy, M. L., & Reddy, K. (2016). Consumer protection law in India: Some challenges and measures in the global market milieu. *International Journal of Research in IT and Management, x*(x), 19–27. https://www.researchgate.net/publication/386253859_CONSUMER_PROTECTION_LAW_IN_INDIA_SOME_CHALLENGES_AND_MEASURES_IN_GLOBAL_MARKET_MILIEU

OECD. (2017). *Trust and public policy: How better governance can help rebuild public trust.* OECD Publishing., DOI: 10.1787/9789264268920-

Online Dispute Resolution. (2021). *ODR and consumer trust in digital markets.* ODR Institute.

Patel Roadways Ltd. v. Birla Yamaha Ltd., (2000) 4 SCC 91 (India).

Prakash, S., & Raju, K. S. (2018). Consumer protection in India: Contemporary issues and challenges. *International Journal of Law, Crime and Justice, 54*, 1–11. DOI: 10.1016/j.ijlcj.2018.05.001

Praveen, S. (2009). Consumer protection as a collective responsibility. *Indian Journal of Law and Society, 2*(1), 55–62.

Praveen, S. (2009). Consumer protection in India (with special reference to Andhra Pradesh). *International Journal of Social Science and Interdisciplinary Research, 1*(1), 1–10. https://www.researchgate.net/publication/277900279_Consumer_Protection_in_India_With_Special_Reference_to_Andhra_Pradesh

Rott, P. (2017). Data protection law as consumer law: How consumer organisations can contribute to the enforcement of data protection law. *Journal of European Consumer and Market Law, 6*, 113–116.

Schulte-Nölke, H. (2017). The brave new world of EU consumer law: Without consumers, or even without law? *Journal of European Consumer and Market Law, 6*, 117–120.

Selvi, D., & Goele, S. *'Critical Evaluation of Awareness of Consumer Rights and Protection'* (2021) https://www.researchgate.net/publication/352704563 accessed 3rd Feb, 2026.

Singh, J., & Sharma, D. (2014). Consumer Protection Act, 1986: Analysis and critique. *International Journal of Scientific Research in Management, 5*(1), 1–5.

Singh, Y. (2005). Performance evaluation of district consumer forum in western Uttar Pradesh. *International Journal of Home Science, 19*(1), 1–9. https://www.semanticscholar.org/paper/Performance-Evaluation-of-District-Consumer-Forum-Singh-Upadhyaya/09820bc0ea2c82c8a578829820a3e002c82cdaa5

Svantesson, D. J. B. (2017). Enter the quagmire: The complicated relationship between data protection law and consumer protection law. *Computer Law & Security Review, 33*(5), 646–656. DOI: 10.1016/j.clsr.2017.07.004

UNCTAD. (2003). *E-commerce and development report*. United Nations.

UNCTAD. *'Consumer Protection in E-Commerce'* (2016) chrome-extension://efaidnbmnnnibpcajpcglclefindmkaj/https://unctad.org/system/files/official-document/cicplpd7_en.pdf accessed 3rd Feb, 2026.

UNCTAD. (2017). *Consumer protection in electronic commerce*. United Nations.

UNCTAD. (2018). *Manual on consumer protection and dispute resolution*. United Nations.

ENDNOTES

1 This scholarly endeavour to proffer a distinctive approach to societal and global quandaries. The data herein harnessed is exclusively designated for academic inquiry and not for pecuniary or commercial ends. The author herein acknowledges their position as not the progenitor of said data, which pertains to the respective entities, publications, authors, and esteemed journals. All attributions and entitlements are duly vested in the original entities. Any data utilized within this treatise shall be suitably credited and acknowledged through scholarly conventions and footnotes. It is paramount to underscore that this research manuscript is intended solely for academic contemplation, with all references provided for scholarly and academic inquiry exclusively.

2 Selvi, DV and Anusuya, A, *'Critical Evaluation of Awareness of Consumer Rights and Protection'* (2021) 8(2) *Primax International Journal of Commerce and Management Research* 1 https://doi.org/10.17605/OSF.IO/Q83SB accessed 4 March 2024.

3 Selvi, DV and Anusuya, A, *'Critical Evaluation of Awareness of Consumer Rights and Protection'* (2021) 8(2) *Primax International Journal of Commerce and Management Research* 1 https://doi.org/10.17605/OSF.IO/Q83SB accessed 4 March 2024.

4 Data compiled from https://public.tableau.com/proile/federal.trade.commission #!/viz home/consumer/Infographic and https://www.statista.com/outlook/243/ 100/ecommerce/worldwide, Accessed 10 March 2024,

5 UNCTAD, *COVID-19 and E-commerce: A Global Review* (2020, October) https://unctad.org/system/files/official-document/dtlstictinf2020d1_en.pdf accessed 8 March 2024.

6 KPMG, The KPMG Survey of Corporate Responsibility Reporting 2017 (2017) https://kpmg.com/xx/en/home/insights/2017/10/the-kpmg-survey-of-corporate -responsibility-reporting-2017.html accessed 12 March 2024.

7 Edelman, *2020 Edelman Trust Barometer* (2020, Edelman) https://www.edelman .com/trust/2020-trust-barometer accessed 11 March 2024.

8 UNCTAD, *Consumer Trust in the Digital Economy: The Case for Online Dispute Resolution* (2021, UNCTAD) https://unctad.org/system/files/official -document/ser-rp-2021d15_en.pdf accessed 12 March 2024.

9 Anant, V and others, *'The Consumer-Data Opportunity and the Privacy Imperative'* (2020, McKinsey & Company) https://www.mckinsey.com/business

-functions/risk/our-insights/the-consumer-data-opportunity-and-the-privacy-imperative accessed 8 March 2024.

10 *Ibid.*

11 Siddiq, A and Janefer, C, *'E-banking and consumer protection'* (2016) 5(1) *International Journal of Commerce and Management Research* 1 https://www.researchgate.net/publication/321973136_E-banking_and_consumer_protection accessed 10 March 2024.

12 *Om Prakash Saini v DCM Ltd and Ors*, (2002) 8 SCC 196.

13 *Patel Roadways Ltd v Birla Yamaha Ltd*, (2000) 4 SCC 91, [2000] 2 SCR 594.

Chapter 9
Utilizing Artificial Intelligence to Advance Legal Procedures in India: A Global Perspective

Leny Ramadhani Setiawan
http://orcid.org/0009-0008-2518-6450
Universitas Esa Unggul, Indonesia

Binastya Anggara Sekti
http://orcid.org/0000-0001-5489-4888
Universitas Esa Unggul, Indonesia

ABSTRACT

The integration of Artificial Intelligence (AI) into legal systems marks a paradigm shift in how justice is delivered and legal processes are managed. In India, AI offers unprecedented opportunities to enhance legal research, case management, contract analysis, and judicial decision-making. By leveraging machine learning and natural language processing, legal professionals can reduce human error, improve efficiency, and increase access to justice. This chapter examines how AI technologies are transforming India's legal landscape through digital infrastructure, predictive analytics, and intelligent automation. It also compares India's legal transformation with global trends, highlighting implications for regulation, privacy, intellectual property, and ethical governance. By exploring both opportunities and challenges, the chapter aims to provide a practical framework for the responsible adoption of AI in legal systems.

DOI: 10.4018/979-8-3373-7685-1.ch009

1. INTRODUCTION

The rapid advancement of Artificial Intelligence (AI) has increasingly reshaped public institutions worldwide, including the administration of justice and systems of judicial governance. This transformation has prompted governments and international institutions to develop regulatory frameworks aimed at balancing technological innovation with ethical safeguards, accountability, and the protection of fundamental rights, most notably reflected in the European Union's Artificial Intelligence Act as the first comprehensive, rights-based approach to AI governance (Tanujaya & Sekti, 2025). Traditionally, legal systems have relied extensively on human expertise, voluminous documentation, and time-intensive procedural mechanisms. In large and complex jurisdictions such as India, these conventional approaches have struggled to adequately address long-standing challenges, including judicial backlogs, prolonged case resolution, limited access to legal resources, and inconsistencies in legal research and decision-support processes.

India currently faces one of the largest judicial backlogs globally, with more than 49 million cases pending across various levels of the judiciary. While digital initiatives such as the e-Courts Project have improved case management, transparency, and accessibility, digitalization alone has proven insufficient to address structural inefficiencies within the judicial system. Consequently, AI technologies particularly machine learning, natural language processing, and data analytics are increasingly viewed as complementary tools that move judicial reform beyond basic digitalization toward data-driven decision support and enhanced procedural efficiency (Sekti, 2025b).

At the global level, several jurisdictions have begun integrating AI-based systems into judicial workflows with varying degrees of success. Singapore has introduced Smart Courts supported by legal analytics and decision-support technologies, while the United States has experimented with AI-assisted legal research and risk assessment tools. China, meanwhile, has implemented large-scale "Smart Court" initiatives incorporating AI-driven case filing, transcription, and document analysis. Collectively, these developments illustrate the growing role of AI as a judicial support mechanism rather than an autonomous decision-maker. Recent regulatory and interdisciplinary scholarship further emphasizes that the effectiveness and legitimacy of such AI integration depend on clear, legally sound definitions of AI systems and their functional scope. Comparative experiences, however, also reveal significant governance challenges, particularly with respect to transparency, accountability, algorithmic bias, and judicial independence arising from ambiguities in how AI systems, general-purpose AI, and generative AI are conceptualized within legal frameworks (Fernández et al., 2025).

Despite its potential benefits, the deployment of AI within judicial systems raises critical legal and ethical concerns. Predictive and generative AI systems may reinforce historical biases embedded within training data, undermine due process when deployed without adequate explainability, and create accountability gaps when algorithmic recommendations influence judicial outcomes. As highlighted in recent interdisciplinary scholarship on explainable artificial intelligence (XAI), the opacity of certain AI models particularly deep learning systems poses significant challenges for legal accountability, where transparency and reason-giving are fundamental requirements (Richmond et al., 2024). Furthermore, issues related to data protection, intellectual property rights, and the increasing reliance on private legal technology vendors pose additional risks to judicial legitimacy and public trust.

From an institutional perspective, effective AI adoption requires not only technological capability but also strategic management frameworks that align AI deployment with organizational objectives, human oversight, and ethical accountability (Sekti, 2025a). Against this backdrop, this chapter critically examines the role of AI in advancing judicial procedures in India by situating national developments within a broader global context. Rather than advocating the full automation of judicial decision-making, the chapter conceptualizes AI as a decision-support tool that must operate within clearly defined governance frameworks, under sustained human oversight, and in accordance with ethical and legal safeguards. By integrating comparative insights and policy analysis, this chapter seeks to contribute to the evolving discourse on responsible, transparent, and sustainable AI adoption in judicial systems.

Objectives of the Chapter

By the end of this chapter, readers will be able to:

- Understand the institutional drivers behind AI adoption within India's judicial system.
- Examine key AI-enabled applications supporting judicial administration and legal research.
- Compare India's approach to judicial AI with global best practices and cautionary examples.
- Identify ethical, regulatory, and governance challenges associated with AI-assisted justice.
- Recognize future pathways for responsible AI deployment that enhance access to justice while preserving judicial legitimacy.

1.1 Background

The adoption of Artificial Intelligence in judicial systems reflects a broader shift toward data-driven governance and digital public infrastructure. In India, judicial reforms such as the e-Courts Project, National Judicial Data Grid, and digital filing systems represent important steps toward transparency and administrative efficiency. AI extends these reforms by enabling automated document analysis, multilingual translation support, real-time transcription, and advanced case analytics. When deployed responsibly, these tools can improve access to justice, particularly in a linguistically diverse and resource-constrained legal environment such as India.

1.2 Research Problem and Gap

Despite increasing interest in judicial AI, several unresolved challenges limit its effective adoption in India:

- Fragmented judicial data systems and uneven digital capacity across courts
- Limited regulatory guidance on explainable and accountable AI in judicial contexts
- Insufficient institutional readiness and technical literacy among legal professionals
- Ethical risks related to bias, fairness, due process, and data protection

Existing literature largely focuses on technological capabilities or isolated pilot projects, with limited critical evaluation of governance structures and long-term implications for judicial legitimacy in India. This chapter addresses this gap by offering a comparative and governance-oriented analysis of judicial AI adoption, emphasizing accountability, institutional safeguards, and policy coherence.

1.3 Methodology and Approach

This chapter adopts a qualitative research approach grounded in:

- A structured review of academic literature on AI in judicial systems
- Comparative analysis of AI deployment in selected global jurisdictions
- Examination of documented AI initiatives within Indian courts
- Review of relevant legal, ethical, and policy frameworks governing AI and data protection

Both peer-reviewed academic sources and verified governmental and institutional reports are used to ensure analytical rigor.

1.4 Contribution and Significance

This chapter contributes to the existing body of knowledge by:

- Providing a judicial-focused analysis of AI adoption in India
- Highlighting governance, ethical, and institutional challenges often overlooked in technical discussions
- Proposing policy-oriented recommendations for responsible judicial AI implementation
- Offering comparative insights that support policymakers, researchers, and legal practitioners

1.5 Chapter Organization

This chapter is organized as follows:

- Section 2 discusses the digital transformation of India's judicial system.
- Section 3 examines AI-supported applications within judicial procedures.
- Section 4 analyzes regulatory, privacy, and intellectual property considerations.
- Section 5 presents comparative global perspectives on judicial AI.
- Section 6 explores ethical risks, public trust, and accountability concerns.
- Section 7 proposes a framework for responsible AI governance in courts.
- Section 8 concludes with key reflections and implications.
- Section 9 outlines future research directions and policy recommendations.
- Section 10 discusses the limitations of the study.

2. DIGITAL TRANSFORMATION IN INDIA'S JUDICIAL SYSTEM

The digital transformation of India's judicial system has progressed steadily over the past two decades in response to chronic institutional challenges, including excessive case pendency, procedural delays, limited accessibility, and heavy reliance on manual documentation. According to the National Judicial Data Grid (NJDG), more than 50 million cases remain pending across Indian courts, with district courts accounting for the largest share. These structural pressures have highlighted the limitations of traditional court administration and underscored the need for systemic technological intervention.

Initial digital reforms focused on Information and Communication Technology (ICT) enabled court administration, aiming to improve record management, transparency, and procedural efficiency. More recently, Artificial Intelligence (AI) has been introduced as an extension of this digital foundation, shifting the system from basic digitization toward data-assisted judicial support. Importantly, AI adoption in India's courts remains largely assistive in nature, designed to support judges and court officials rather than to automate judicial decision-making. This section examines the evolution of India's judicial digital infrastructure, the institutional role of AI, and India's position within the broader global smart courts landscape.

2.1 Evolution of Digital Judicial Infrastructure in India

India's judicial digitalization formally began with the National Policy and Action Plan for ICT Enablement of the Judiciary, which sought to modernize court operations through electronic records and case management systems. Over time, this initiative evolved into a multi-tiered national infrastructure supporting:

- Electronic filing and case tracking
- Digitized court records and judgments
- Automated scheduling and cause lists
- Online access to court orders for litigants and lawyers
- Remote participation through virtual hearings

This transformation represents a gradual institutional shift from paper-based administration toward digitally coordinated judicial workflows. Recent developments have explored the use of Natural Language Processing (NLP) tools to assist in judgment search, legal research, and document summarization. However, these tools function primarily as internal aids for judges and clerks rather than as independent analytical systems, reflecting continued judicial caution regarding algorithmic intervention in legal reasoning.

Parallel investments under the Digital India initiative have improved nationwide connectivity, enabling more equitable digital access to courts across urban and rural regions. Nevertheless, disparities in digital maturity across states and court levels persist, limiting uniform implementation.

2.2 e-Courts Mission Mode Project

The e-Courts Mission Mode Project, launched in and currently operating under Phase III constitutes the backbone of India's digital judiciary. Its primary objectives include:

- End-to-end online case filing and tracking
- Secure video-conferencing for judicial proceedings
- Electronic issuance and service of summons and notices
- Digital payment systems for court-related fees
- Mobile access for citizens and legal practitioners

During the COVID-19 pandemic, Indian courts conducted millions of virtual hearings, demonstrating the system's capacity to sustain judicial continuity under extraordinary conditions. While these developments significantly improved procedural resilience, they also revealed limitations related to digital literacy, infrastructure reliability, and unequal access.

AI-based tools introduced within the e-Courts ecosystem such as SUVAS (Supreme Court Vidhik Anuvaad Software) focus on language translation and document accessibility rather than adjudicatory decision-making. These applications highlight India's emphasis on inclusivity and efficiency while preserving judicial discretion and authority.

2.3 National Judicial Data Grid (NJDG)

The National Judicial Data Grid represents one of the most extensive judicial data repositories globally, aggregating structured information on millions of cases across court levels. Its institutional functions include:

- Transparency in case pendency and disposal rates
- Administrative analytics for judicial workload allocation
- Identification of regional and subject-matter bottlenecks
- Empirical support for judicial reform planning

While NJDG provides a critical data foundation for future AI-assisted analytics, its current role remains primarily descriptive rather than predictive. The potential use of AI for case duration forecasting or workload optimization is still largely experimental, constrained by data standardization issues, interoperability challenges, and concerns over algorithmic bias. As such, NJDG functions as an enabling infrastructure rather than an autonomous intelligence system.

2.4 Online Dispute Resolution (ODR) and Digital Lok Adalat

Online Dispute Resolution (ODR) platforms represent a complementary component of India's justice delivery ecosystem, primarily addressing low-stakes civil, commercial, and consumer disputes. These platforms offer:

- Reduced litigation costs
- Faster dispute resolution outside formal courts
- Hybrid online–offline mediation mechanisms
- Improved accessibility for underserved populations

The Digital Lok Adalat initiative, supported by NITI Aayog, has demonstrated scalability in resolving high-volume, low-complexity cases, such as traffic violations and financial disputes. AI tools in this context are used selectively to screen cases suitable for settlement and to assist mediators with contextual information. Importantly, ODR operates outside formal adjudication and does not replace judicial authority, reinforcing the principle that AI-supported mechanisms should complement rather than substitute judicial processes.

2.5 Comparative Perspective: India and Global Smart Courts

Several jurisdictions have adopted AI-enabled judicial technologies at varying institutional depths. Table 1 provides a comparative overview of selected global approaches. This regional constitutional perspective is reinforced by recent Southeast Asian scholarship, which examines the compatibility of e-Court systems with constitutional principles and judicial independence (Ruzayana et al., 2025).

Table 1. Comparative Use of AI in Judicial Systems

Country	AI Applications in Courts	Institutional Emphasis
Singapore	Smart courtrooms, legal analytics, digital case management	Efficiency and procedural optimization
China	AI-assisted filing, document review, virtual court services	Large-scale automation with centralized governance
U.S./EU	Risk assessment tools, e-discovery, legal analytics	Strong emphasis on regulatory oversight
India	AI-assisted translation, research support, digital courts	Human-centered, assistive AI model

While India benefits from strong national infrastructure and large-scale data availability, its judicial system has deliberately avoided autonomous AI decision-making tools. This cautious approach reflects concerns regarding constitutional safeguards, judicial independence, and accountability. India's trajectory aligns most closely with a hybrid judicial AI model, where technology augments human judgment without displacing it.

Summary of Section 2

India's judicial digital transformation has evolved from basic computerization to institutionally embedded digital systems capable of supporting AI-assisted judicial functions. While the foundational infrastructure is robust, AI adoption remains deliberately restrained, emphasizing administrative efficiency, access to justice, and human oversight. This cautious yet scalable approach positions India to develop a context-sensitive model of judicial AI that balances innovation with constitutional and ethical safeguards.

3. AI-ASSISTED INNOVATION IN INDIA'S JUDICIAL SYSTEM AND LEGAL PRACTICE

Artificial Intelligence (AI) has begun to reshape selected components of India's judicial system and legal profession, primarily as a decision-support and administrative enhancement tool rather than as an autonomous adjudicatory mechanism. Given the constitutional centrality of judicial independence and due process, AI adoption in India remains cautious and largely assistive in scope. Current implementations focus on legal research augmentation, document management, case analytics, and courtroom accessibility, all designed to complement rather than substitute human legal reasoning.

This section examines AI-assisted innovation within courts and legal practice, deliberately excluding operational law enforcement functions except where explicitly distinguished. By maintaining this institutional boundary, the analysis aligns ethical, governance, and accountability considerations with the judiciary's unique constitutional role.

3.1 AI for Legal Research and Judicial Knowledge Management

Legal research in India traditionally requires manual examination of voluminous judgments, statutes, and precedents across multiple court hierarchies and jurisdictions. AI-based Natural Language Processing (NLP) tools now assist lawyers and judges by enabling:

- Semantic (intent-based) search rather than keyword matching

- Automated summarization of lengthy judgments
- Identification of legally similar cases based on fact patterns
- Multilingual translation of judicial texts

Indian Judicial and Legal Practice Use Cases

- SUVAS (Supreme Court Vidhik Anuvaad Software): Facilitates translation of judgments and legal documents into 22 constitutionally recognized Indian languages, enhancing accessibility rather than influencing legal interpretation.
- Manupatra AI: Provides citation linkage and contextual case relevance indicators to support legal research.
- Indian Kanoon: Uses AI-assisted indexing to improve public access to judicial decisions.

While studies suggest significant reductions in research time, such findings are typically based on practitioner surveys and workflow observations rather than controlled experimental designs As such, efficiency gains should be interpreted as indicative rather than definitive, particularly given variations in case complexity and user proficiency.

Comparative Perspective

Table 2. Selected AI Tools in Legal Research

Jurisdiction	Tool	Functional Emphasis
United States	Westlaw Edge AI	Litigation analytics and citation networks
United Kingdom	CaseIQ	Risk assessment and litigation strategy support
Singapore	LawNet AI	Integrated judicial knowledge management

Rather than replicating foreign models, India's approach emphasizes linguistic inclusivity and access to justice, reflecting its constitutional and demographic context.

3.2 Document Automation and Contract Analysis in Legal Practice

A substantial portion of legal practice involves repetitive drafting and review tasks, including notices, agreements, compliance filings, and standardized pleadings. AI-assisted document automation tools support legal professionals by:

- Generating draft documents based on structured templates
- Flagging clause anomalies and compliance risks
- Standardizing documentation for routine legal transactions
- Reducing clerical workload in high-volume practices

Indian Context

Platforms such as VakilSearch and SpotDraft offer AI-assisted contract review and drafting support primarily for commercial and corporate legal services. Reported efficiency improvements often cited in the range of 40–50% are derived from internal productivity assessments rather than peer-reviewed empirical studies. These tools therefore function best as productivity aids, not substitutes for professional legal judgment.

Crucially, final responsibility for accuracy, interpretation, and legal consequence remains with the human practitioner, consistent with professional ethical obligations.

3.3 AI-Assisted Judicial Analytics and Decision Support

Within courts, AI adoption is most carefully constrained. Existing systems focus on information extraction and pattern recognition, not on generating binding legal outcomes. Common applications include:

- Case summarization and relevance extraction
- Analytics dashboards for administrative oversight
- Pattern identification to support consistency in reasoning

Table 3. AI Tools Supporting Judicial Functions in India

Tool	Function	Institutional Scope
SUPACE	Case summarization and precedent relevance	Supreme Court
SCALES	Judicial analytics dashboards	High Courts
Sentencing Analytics (Pilot)	Risk indicators for bail/parole	Limited trial settings

AI outputs in these systems are advisory. Judges retain full discretion to accept, modify, or reject AI-generated insights, consistent with a human-in-the-loop model. When studies report reductions in administrative workload such as paperwork processing time these results reflect operational efficiency, not changes in judicial outcomes or fairness.

Notably, evidence regarding AI's impact on substantive justice such as consistency, bias reduction, or appeal rates remains limited and under-researched.

3.4 Institutional Boundary: Law Enforcement vs. Judicial Systems

AI applications in law enforcement such as predictive policing, biometric identification, and crime analytics operate under fundamentally different institutional mandates and oversight frameworks than courts. While such systems may influence the criminal justice pipeline, they do not constitute judicial decision-making.

However, the legal implications of AI adoption vary significantly depending on which elements of the judicial decision-making process are automated (Barysė & Sarel, 2024). emphasise that automating discrete components of judicial reasoning carries different normative, ethical, and institutional consequences, particularly in relation to judicial discretion, accountability, and the preservation of judicial independence.

Accordingly, law enforcement AI is not analyzed as part of judicial innovation in this chapter. Experiences from jurisdictions such as the United States, including controversies surrounding algorithmic risk assessment tools, illustrate the risks of conflating policing intelligence with adjudicatory fairness. Algorithmic discrimination in AI judicial tools underscores the necessity of explainable models that allow legal practitioners and litigants to critically evaluate AI outputs and mitigate bias (Herrera-Tapias et al., 2025). This distinction is essential to preserving constitutional due process and judicial independence.

3.5 Structural and Ethical Constraints on AI Adoption

Despite technical progress, several constraints limit the expansion of AI within India's judicial system:

Table 4. Key Challenges in Judicial AI Adoption

Challenge	Judicial Implication
Data bias and incompleteness	Risk of distorted analytical outputs
Limited explainability	Difficulty in contesting AI-assisted recommendations
Uneven digital literacy	Inconsistent adoption across courts
Governance gaps	Ambiguity in accountability structures
Privacy risks	Exposure of sensitive judicial data

Any AI deployment must comply with constitutional guarantees under Article, particularly regarding personal liberty, dignity, and procedural fairness. Ethical AI in courts therefore requires not only technical safeguards but also institutional accountability mechanisms.

3.6 AI Integration in Supreme Court and High Courts

India's highest courts have adopted AI primarily to enhance accessibility and procedural efficiency, rather than adjudication. Key initiatives include:

- AI-assisted translation and live transcription
- Automated cause list generation
- Court information chatbots for litigants

Table 5. Selected AI Deployments in Indian High Courts

High Court	Application	Purpose
Delhi HC	Petition categorization	Reduce filing errors
Kerala HC	Digital case bundling	Trial preparation efficiency
Karnataka HC	Digital evidence validation	Procedural accuracy

These implementations signal a transition from pilot experimentation to limited institutional integration, while maintaining judicial control over substantive legal reasoning.

Section 3 Summary

AI-assisted innovation in India's judicial system is characterized by incremental, human-centered adoption focused on research support, administrative efficiency, and accessibility. While early results suggest operational benefits, robust empirical evidence regarding long-term impacts on fairness, consistency, and justice quality remains limited. India's restrained approach reflects constitutional priorities and positions the judiciary to adopt AI cautiously while preserving legitimacy and public trust.

4. POLICY, PRIVACY, AND INTELLECTUAL PROPERTY IMPLICATIONS OF AI IN INDIA'S JUDICIAL SYSTEM

While Artificial Intelligence (AI) offers efficiency and accessibility gains for India's judicial system, its integration raises complex policy questions related to data protection, intellectual property, competition, and ethical accountability. Unlike commercial AI deployment, judicial AI systems operate within a constitutional framework that prioritizes due process, transparency, and fundamental rights. As such, regulatory clarity is not optional but foundational to legitimate adoption.

This section critically examines India's evolving legal and policy environment governing AI in courts, with particular attention to data protection under the Digital Personal Data Protection Act (DPDP), intellectual property ownership of AI-generated legal content, competition risks in legal technology markets, and ethical governance requirements.

4.1 Data Privacy and Judicial AI under the DPDP Act

Judicial AI systems rely extensively on large volumes of sensitive data, including litigant identities, case histories, criminal records, and judicial reasoning. The Digital Personal Data Protection Act (DPDP) establishes India's first comprehensive statutory framework for regulating such data use.

Key DPDP Principles Relevant to Judicial AI

- **Purpose Limitation and Data Minimization** Judicial data may only be processed for clearly defined legal functions. AI models trained on court data must therefore demonstrate necessity and proportionality, particularly for decision-support tools.
- **Transparency and Notice Obligations** Litigants should be informed when their data contributes to AI-assisted processes such as analytics dashboards or predictive models, even if the final decision remains human-made.
- **Grievance Redressal and Accountability** Courts and judicial administrations must provide mechanisms allowing individuals to challenge improper data use, erroneous outputs, or security breaches.
- **Data Localization and Security** Sensitive judicial datasets are expected to remain within India's jurisdiction, raising practical constraints on cross-border AI collaboration and cloud-based model training.

Implementation Challenges

Despite statutory safeguards, several unresolved issues remain:

- Courts vary significantly in technical capacity and awareness of DPDP compliance obligations.
- Anonymization of judicial data for AI training is technically complex and inconsistently implemented.
- The DPDP Act does not yet provide judiciary-specific rules governing AI-assisted decision-support systems.

Unlike the EU's GDPR Article, which explicitly regulates automated decision-making, India lacks equivalent judicial guidance. Without supplementary rules, AI deployment risks uneven compliance and legal uncertainty. In the European context, legal analysis shows that generative AI systems pose complex regulatory challenges across liability, privacy, and intellectual property domains, underscoring the need for integrated legal frameworks to safeguard fundamental rights and accountability before deployment (Novelli et al., 2024).

4.2 Intellectual Property and Liability in AI-Generated Legal Content

AI systems increasingly assist in drafting legal documents, summarizing judgments, and organizing precedents. While such outputs may appear derivative, they raise non-trivial questions of authorship, ownership, and liability.

Authorship and Ownership

Across most jurisdictions, AI is not recognized as a legal author or rights-holder. As summarized in Table 6, India follows the prevailing global position that intellectual property rights vest in the human or organization deploying the AI system.

Table 6. Legal Recognition of AI Authorship

Jurisdiction	AI as Author?	Rights Holder
India	No	Human operator or institution
United States	No	Human or organization
United Kingdom	Limited (statutory fiction)	Person making arrangements

However, judicial reliance on AI-generated summaries introduces institutional liability risks. If AI-assisted outputs contain inaccuracies or omissions, responsibility ultimately lies with the human decision-maker or institution that relied upon them. In the European context, legal analysis shows that generative AI systems pose complex regulatory challenges across liability, privacy, and intellectual property domains, underscoring the need for integrated legal frameworks to safeguard fundamental rights and accountability before deployment (Novelli et al., 2024).

Emerging Legal Risks

- Unclear ownership of AI-generated annotations or summaries used in judgments
- Potential copyright conflicts if training data includes proprietary legal databases
- Absence of clear liability rules when AI errors influence judicial reasoning

India therefore requires a judicial AI–IP framework that clarifies:

- Permissible training data sources
- Attribution of responsibility for erroneous outputs
- Distinction between assistive drafting and authoritative legal text

4.3 Competition Law and Market Concentration in Legal AI

The rapid expansion of legal technology platforms introduces competition risks that extend beyond traditional software markets. AI systems derive competitive advantage from exclusive datasets, proprietary algorithms, and network effects.

Competition Concerns

- Dominant vendors may control access to high-quality judicial data
- Algorithmic pricing and bundling may disadvantage smaller law firms
- Vendor lock-in may limit institutional autonomy of courts

The Competition Commission of India (CCI) will need to address emerging risks such as algorithmic collusion, discriminatory licensing practices, and data monopolization. Internationally, the EU Data Act emphasizes equitable data access a principle that could inform Indian regulatory adaptation for legal AI markets.

4.4 Ethical Governance and Explainability in Judicial AI

This understanding aligns with contemporary legal scholarship emphasizing that explainable AI in judicial contexts is not merely a technical requirement, but a normative condition for accountability, legitimacy, and the right to contest algorithmic influence (Fernåndez et al., 2025).

Ethical governance is central to AI legitimacy in justice systems. Key risks include algorithmic bias, opacity, unequal access, and excessive institutional reliance on automated outputs.

Operational Meaning of Ethical Principles

Terms such as *explainable AI* and *human-in-the-loop* require concrete interpretation in judicial contexts:

- **Explainability** does not require judges to understand mathematical models, but it does require:
- clarity on data sources
- reasoning pathways (why a recommendation was produced)
- known limitations and confidence levels
- **Human-in-the-loop** implies that:
- judges may override AI outputs without justification to the system
- AI recommendations are non-binding
- responsibility remains exclusively human

Ethical Checklist for Judicial AI

Table 7. Ethical Governance Requirements

Principle	Judicial Function
Explainability	Enables meaningful challenge and review
Non-discrimination	Protects vulnerable groups
Auditability	Supports accountability and oversight
Human oversight	Preserves judicial independence

India may draw on the European Commission's Ethics Guidelines for Trustworthy AI, but judicial adaptation must reflect constitutional due process and institutional realities.

Section 4 Summary

AI adoption in India's judicial system cannot be governed solely through general technology regulation. It requires context-specific legal frameworks addressing privacy, intellectual property, competition, and ethics. While the DPDP Act establishes a foundational privacy regime, further judicial guidance is necessary to operationalize AI accountability, explainability, and liability. Without such safeguards, efficiency gains risk undermining trust, legitimacy, and constitutional guarantees.

5. COMPARATIVE GLOBAL PERSPECTIVES ON AI IN LEGAL SYSTEMS

The global deployment of Artificial Intelligence (AI) within judicial systems demonstrates varied approaches shaped by differing legal traditions, governance models, and socio-political priorities. Comparative analysis of international practices provides valuable insights into how India can refine its AI-enabled judicial transformation while preserving constitutional values. This section examines AI adoption in Singapore, China, the United States, and Europe, with emphasis on efficiency, accountability, human rights protection, and governance frameworks.

In addition to large-scale institutional deployments, recent empirical studies have begun to examine the implications of generative AI tools within judicial settings. A pilot case study conducted in Colombia explores the use of ChatGPT as a decision-support instrument in judicial reasoning, highlighting both its potential to enhance analytical efficiency and the risks it poses to judicial autonomy, consistency, and accountability (Perona et al., 2025). This experience illustrates how emerging generative AI systems introduce new comparative dimensions beyond traditional rule-based or analytics-driven judicial technologies.

5.1 Smart Courts in Singapore: Precision and Digital Maturity

Singapore is widely recognized as a global benchmark for judicial digitalization. Its Smart Courts initiative integrates AI-powered case triaging, electronic filing systems, online dispute resolution mechanisms for low-value claims, real-time language translation, automated speech recognition, and AI-assisted sentencing recommendations. These technologies are embedded within a highly standardized and centralized judicial infrastructure, supported by strong institutional coordination and advanced digital literacy among legal professionals.

Singapore's experience highlights the importance of treating AI as an enabler of judicial efficiency rather than a substitute for judicial discretion. Clear regulatory guidance governs the use of AI tools, ensuring that judges retain full authority over final decisions while benefiting from analytical support.

For India, Singapore's model underscores several areas for improvement, including the development of a unified national judicial infrastructure, systematic digital capacity-building among legal professionals, and centralized governance mechanisms for AI deployment. These measures would allow AI to enhance consistency and efficiency while safeguarding judicial independence.

Table 8. Lessons from Singapore's AI-Driven Judiciary

Singapore's Strength	**India's Current Gap**	**Adaptation Strategy for India**
Strong digital foundation	Uneven infrastructure across states	Unified national judiciary cloud
High digital literacy	Resistance to technological adoption	Mandatory AI competency training
Clear legal policies on AI use	Fragmented regulatory readiness	Centralized AI governance framework

5.2 China's AI Judicial Automation: Efficiency Versus Accountability

China has adopted an aggressive approach to judicial automation, deploying AI-enabled virtual courtrooms where litigation can be conducted via mobile platforms. Advanced technologies such as facial recognition are used for identity verification, AI systems assist in preliminary rulings for simple disputes, and blockchain is employed to authenticate digital evidence.

While these innovations have significantly improved efficiency and accessibility, they have also attracted substantial criticism. Concerns include limited transparency in algorithmic decision-making, extensive state surveillance enabled by centralized data control, and reduced institutional independence for legal professionals.

For India, China's experience serves as a cautionary case. Although technological modernization is necessary to address systemic inefficiencies, it must be carefully balanced against constitutional ethics, judicial autonomy, and the protection of privacy and human rights. Rapid automation without robust accountability mechanisms risks eroding public trust in the justice system.

5.3 The United States and Europe: Accountability-Oriented AI Governance

In contrast to China's efficiency-driven model, the United States and the European Union prioritize accountability, transparency, and rights-based governance in the use of AI within legal systems. In the United States, AI adoption is largely driven by private legal analytics platforms that support litigation strategy and risk assessment. However, systems such as COMPAS have faced legal challenges due to demonstrated racial and socioeconomic bias, leading to increased calls for algorithmic audits and judicial scrutiny.

The European Union has adopted a more comprehensive regulatory approach through the proposed AI Act, which emphasizes transparency, explainability, and risk-based classification of AI systems. Central to this framework is the recognition of individuals' rights to understand and challenge automated decisions that significantly affect them.

Table 9. Rights-Based AI Governance in the United States and Europe

Region	Governance Focus	Key Risk Controls
United States	Market-driven legal analytics	Audits and litigation addressing biased models
European Union	Regulatory oversight under the AI Act	Explainability and "right to explanation"

India can benefit from these approaches by institutionalizing explainable AI standards, embedding audit mechanisms within judicial AI tools, and ensuring enforceable accountability for automated recommendations.

5.4 India's Strategic Opportunity: A Hybrid Model of Legal Innovation

India occupies a distinctive position in the global AI landscape. The country possesses strong digital public infrastructure initiatives such as Aadhaar, the National Judicial Data Grid, and the e-Courts program, alongside a rapidly expanding LegalTech startup ecosystem. Additionally, India's extensive multilingual judicial datasets provide a valuable foundation for AI development, while its democratic legal framework emphasizes fairness, inclusion, and procedural justice.

To capitalize on these strengths, India should adopt a hybrid strategy that combines Singapore's operational efficiency, the accountability and transparency frameworks of the United States and Europe, and a clear avoidance of excessive automation that compromises judicial independence. Such an approach would allow India to position itself as a global model for human-centric, ethically governed AI-enabled justice, balancing innovation with constitutional legitimacy.

The comparative perspectives discussed in Section 5 illustrate that while AI integration in judicial systems can deliver substantial gains in efficiency, accessibility, and administrative coordination, these benefits are highly contingent upon the ethical and governance conditions under which AI operates. Experiences from Singapore, China, the United States, and Europe collectively demonstrate that technological sophistication alone is insufficient to ensure legitimacy, fairness, or public confidence in AI-assisted justice.

Across jurisdictions, recurring concerns emerge regarding algorithmic bias, opacity in decision-support systems, unclear attribution of responsibility, and the potential dilution of judicial independence when AI tools are insufficiently regulated. These challenges are particularly salient for India, where constitutional values, socio-legal diversity, and public trust in judicial institutions form the foundation of the justice system. As India seeks to adopt a hybrid model of judicial AI innovation, the ethical implications of AI deployment cannot be treated as secondary considerations.

Accordingly, the analysis now moves beyond comparative institutional models to examine the ethical risks, public trust implications, and accountability challenges associated with AI-assisted judicial processes. Section 6 addresses these concerns in detail, providing a normative basis for the responsible AI governance framework proposed in Section 7.

6. ETHICAL RISKS, PUBLIC TRUST, AND ACCOUNTABILITY CONCERNS

The integration of Artificial Intelligence (AI) into judicial systems introduces ethical risks that are qualitatively different from those encountered in commercial, administrative, or purely technical environments. Courts function as constitutional institutions whose legitimacy derives not only from procedural efficiency, but from adherence to fairness, transparency, reasoned decision-making, and public accountability. Consequently, ethical evaluation of judicial AI must extend beyond performance metrics and address its structural implications for justice delivery and institutional trust. Critical theoretical perspectives highlight that AI systems in judicial settings can reproduce structural inequalities embedded in existing legal processes, raising questions about neutrality, fairness, and social justice in AI-supported justice delivery(Dias & Sátiro, 2024)

Unlike administrative automation, judicial AI operates within decision-making processes that directly affect fundamental rights, including personal liberty, property, and access to justice. Even when AI systems are formally classified as decision-support tools, their outputs may exert indirect normative influence on judges through framing effects, perceived objectivity, or cognitive anchoring. Ethical risks therefore arise not only from autonomous decision-making, but also from subtle shifts in human judgment influenced by algorithmic recommendations.

6.1 Algorithmic Bias and Fairness Risks

Recent legal scholarship analysing generative AI in judicial domains highlights the persistent accountability gaps that emerge when algorithmic systems are deployed without robust oversight frameworks, where automation bias and over-reliance on AI can undermine human agency and the rule of law if not mitigated by comprehensive accountability mechanisms (Carnat, 2024).

Algorithmic bias represents one of the most significant ethical challenges in AI-assisted judicial systems. AI models trained on historical judicial data may reproduce and amplify pre-existing structural inequalities embedded in past legal outcomes. In India, such risks are particularly salient given long-standing disparities linked to caste, gender, socio-economic status, geographic location, and differential access to legal representation.

Bias may emerge at multiple stages of the AI lifecycle, including data selection, feature engineering, model training, and output interpretation. For example, case prioritization tools trained on historical disposal rates may implicitly deprioritize cases involving marginalized litigants if such cases historically experienced longer delays. Similarly, analytics used in bail or sentencing contexts may reflect patterns shaped by unequal policing practices rather than neutral assessments of risk.

Even when judges retain formal decision-making authority, reliance on algorithmic indicators may introduce *automation bias*, where AI-generated outputs are afforded undue credibility. This risk underscores the need for continuous bias evaluation, disaggregated data analysis, and institutional mechanisms capable of detecting discriminatory patterns before they affect judicial outcomes.

6.2 Transparency and Explainability Challenges

Transparency and explainability are central to judicial legitimacy. Judicial reasoning must be intelligible, reviewable, and contestable by affected parties. AI systems that generate recommendations without clear explanatory pathways pose a direct challenge to these principles. In order to strengthen perceptions of fairness and public trust, procedural justice principles such as participatory elements and due process by design should be embedded within AI decision-making systems, especially in high-stakes judicial contexts (Fischman-Afori, 2025).

In judicial contexts, explainability should not be interpreted narrowly as technical interpretability of algorithms. Rather, it requires that AI-assisted outputs be accompanied by legally meaningful explanations, including the data sources relied upon, the relevance criteria applied, and known limitations or confidence levels. Without such contextual clarity, AI systems risk becoming opaque authority structures incompatible with principles of natural justice.

The absence of explainability also complicates appellate review and procedural safeguards. If parties cannot ascertain whether, how, or to what extent AI influenced judicial reasoning, meaningful legal challenge becomes difficult. Transparency is therefore not merely an ethical aspiration but a procedural necessity.

Comparative studies illustrate that when AI tools are used in civil proceedings without transparency safeguards, such automation may compromise core procedural rights such as the right to be heard and judicial impartiality, demanding robust explainability standards (Selçuk et al., 2025).

6.3 Accountability and Attribution of Responsibility

AI integration disrupts traditional accountability frameworks within judicial institutions. While judges remain formally responsible for decisions, the increasing use of AI-generated analytics introduces ambiguity regarding responsibility for errors, bias, or unjust outcomes.

Accountability gaps may arise when AI tools are perceived as neutral or technically authoritative, thereby diffusing responsibility across technological systems, vendors, and institutional actors. In such cases, adverse outcomes may be attributed to "systemic error" rather than being subject to clear legal or administrative review.

To preserve accountability, judicial institutions must establish explicit responsibility attribution rules. AI outputs must be clearly documented, their advisory status formally acknowledged, and their influence on judicial reasoning transparently recorded where relevant. Responsibility for outcomes must remain unequivocally human, ensuring that technological mediation does not weaken institutional accountability.

6.4 Public Trust and Judicial Legitimacy

Public trust constitutes the normative foundation of judicial authority. The introduction of AI into courts risks undermining this trust if perceived as opaque, externally imposed, or insufficiently regulated. Concerns may intensify where AI systems are developed by private vendors operating under proprietary constraints, limiting public scrutiny.

Trust erosion is particularly likely if AI adoption is framed primarily as an efficiency-enhancing measure rather than as a rights-preserving institutional reform. Citizens may perceive algorithmic assistance as prioritizing speed over fairness or cost reduction over due process.

Sustaining public trust therefore requires that AI adoption be explicitly aligned with constitutional values, judicial independence, and procedural fairness. Ethical governance must be institutionally embedded, publicly communicated, and continuously reinforced through oversight and accountability mechanisms.

6.5 Automation Bias and Cognitive Dependence on AI Systems

Beyond technical bias embedded in datasets, AI-assisted judicial tools introduce a subtler yet equally significant ethical risk: automation bias. Automation bias refers to the human tendency to over-rely on algorithmic outputs, particularly when such systems are perceived as objective, data-driven, or technologically authoritative. In judicial contexts, this risk manifests when judges, clerks, or court administrators unconsciously defer to AI-generated recommendations in areas such as case prioritization, bail analytics, or precedent relevance assessment.

Even when AI systems are formally designated as non-binding, their influence on judicial cognition can be substantial. Research in decision science suggests that repeated exposure to algorithmic recommendations can shape human judgment through anchoring effects, framing biases, and confirmation reinforcement. In courts operating under conditions of heavy caseloads and time pressure such as India's district and high courts these cognitive effects may be amplified.

The ethical concern here is not that AI replaces judicial discretion, but that it subtly restructures how discretion is exercised. Without explicit safeguards, training, and reflective awareness, AI-assisted tools risk transforming judicial reasoning from independent evaluation to algorithmically guided validation. This phenomenon directly implicates due process and judicial independence, even in the absence of formal automation.

6.6 Ethical Asymmetry Between Efficiency and Justice Values

A recurring tension in judicial AI deployment lies in the ethical asymmetry between efficiency-oriented objectives and justice-centered constitutional values. While AI systems are frequently justified on the basis of backlog reduction, speed, and administrative optimization, judicial legitimacy is grounded not in efficiency alone but in fairness, transparency, and reasoned decision-making.

Comparative experience demonstrates that efficiency gains achieved through AI may coexist with declining perceptions of procedural justice if litigants are unable to understand how decisions are shaped. In India, where courts serve as critical sites of constitutional accountability and social redress, prioritizing efficiency without parallel ethical safeguards risks instrumentalizing justice delivery.

This asymmetry underscores the need to treat ethical governance not as a constraint on innovation, but as a condition of sustainable legitimacy. AI systems that accelerate processes while obscuring reasoning may undermine the very trust they seek to restore. Ethical risk assessment must therefore evaluate not only technical accuracy but also the normative compatibility of AI tools with judicial values.

Table 10. Ethical Risk Dimensions in Judicial AI Systems

Ethical Risk	Judicial Impact	Governance Implication
Algorithmic bias	Unequal treatment	Continuous bias audits
Lack of explainability	Due process erosion	XAI standards
Automation bias	Cognitive dependence	Judicial AI literacy
Accountability gaps	Responsibility dilution	Clear attribution rules
Public trust deficit	Legitimacy loss	Transparency & disclosure

7. FRAMEWORK FOR RESPONSIBLE AI GOVERNANCE IN COURTS

In light of the ethical risks and legitimacy concerns identified in Section 6, a structured governance framework is essential to ensure that AI adoption in judicial systems remains constitutionally grounded, ethically defensible, and institutionally sustainable. Rather than treating AI governance as a technical compliance exercise, this framework conceptualizes governance as an extension of judicial responsibility and public accountability.

AI governance highlights the importance of structured frameworks that integrate ethical principles with operational practices, enabling coherent oversight, accountability, and monitoring mechanisms across the AI lifecycle (Papagiannidis et al., 2025).

7.1 Human-in-the-Loop and Judicial Control

Judicial AI systems must operate strictly under a human-in-the-loop model. Judges must retain exclusive authority over legal reasoning and final determinations, with AI outputs explicitly designated as advisory and non-binding. This distinction is critical to preventing the de facto delegation of judicial power to algorithmic systems.

Human-in-the-loop governance also requires capacity-building initiatives. Judges and court administrators must possess sufficient technical literacy to critically assess AI outputs, understand their limitations, and recognize potential sources of error or bias. Without such institutional competence, formal human oversight risks becoming nominal rather than substantive.

7.2 Explainable and Contestable AI Systems

Responsible judicial AI governance requires minimum explainability standards tailored to legal contexts. AI systems should provide interpretable justifications that enable judges to assess relevance and allow litigants to meaningfully contest algorithmic influence.

Contestability extends beyond technical transparency to procedural rights. Litigants should be informed when AI-assisted tools are used in case management or decision-support processes and should have access to mechanisms for challenging their use. This approach aligns AI deployment with due process guarantees and appellate review norms.

7.3 Institutional Oversight and Audit Mechanisms

Continuous oversight is essential to prevent ethical drift and unintended consequences. Judicial AI systems should be subject to periodic audits assessing bias, accuracy, data integrity, and compliance with ethical standards. Oversight structures may include judicial committees, independent technical experts, and data protection authorities operating under clearly defined mandates.

Audits serve both preventive and corrective functions, enabling early identification of risks while reinforcing institutional accountability. Importantly, audit findings should inform policy refinement and system recalibration rather than remaining purely technical assessments.

7.4 Data Governance and Privacy Safeguards

Data governance constitutes a core pillar of responsible judicial AI. Given the sensitivity of judicial data, strict compliance with data protection obligations under the Digital Personal Data Protection Act, is essential. Anonymization, access controls, and secure data storage must be institutionally enforced rather than left to vendor discretion.

Robust data governance also mitigates risks of vendor lock-in and data monopolization. Judicial institutions should retain control over core datasets and ensure that AI deployment does not compromise institutional autonomy or public accountability.

7.5 Institutional Coordination and Policy Coherence

Finally, effective AI governance requires coordination across judicial, executive, and regulatory institutions. Fragmented implementation risks inconsistent standards, uneven rights protection, and regulatory ambiguity. A centralized policy framework while respecting judicial independence can promote coherence, interoperability, and long-term sustainability.

Table 11. Ethical Risks and Governance Responses in Judicial AI

Ethical Risk	Judicial Implication	Governance Response
Algorithmic bias	Unequal treatment and discrimination	Bias audits and disaggregated data analysis
Lack of explainability	Weak due process and contestability	Minimum explainability standards
Accountability gaps	Diffusion of responsibility	Explicit attribution rules
Public trust erosion	Legitimacy deficit	Transparency and public communication

7.6 Phased and Context-Sensitive Implementation Strategy

Responsible AI governance in courts requires not only normative principles but also a realistic implementation pathway. Given the heterogeneity of India's judicial system across court levels, regions, and institutional capacities a phased and context-sensitive approach is essential.

Rather than pursuing uniform nationwide deployment, AI systems should be introduced incrementally, beginning with low-risk, high-utility applications such as document translation, legal research assistance, and administrative analytics. Higher-risk applications involving predictive insights or behavioral assessments should be subject to enhanced scrutiny, pilot evaluation, and sunset clauses.

Phased implementation enables institutional learning, iterative governance refinement, and evidence-based calibration of AI tools. It also reduces the risk of systemic harm arising from premature scaling. Importantly, such an approach aligns technological adoption with judicial autonomy, allowing courts to retain control over the pace and scope of AI integration.

8. KEY IMPLICATIONS

This chapter has examined the integration of Artificial Intelligence (AI) into India's judicial system through institutional, technological, ethical, and governance perspectives. The analysis demonstrates that AI adoption in Indian courts is neither a purely technological reform nor an efficiency-driven modernization agenda. Instead, it represents a structural transformation that directly affects judicial discretion, procedural fairness, and public trust in the justice system. A unified regulatory framework that integrates ethical, legal, and accountability dimensions is critical to reconcile innovation with societal safeguards in judicial and other high-risk AI deployments(Mansouri et al., 2025).

Rather than advocating automated adjudication, this chapter consistently positions AI as a judicial decision-support mechanism that must remain subordinate to human authority. Across Sections 1–5, it has been shown that while India possesses strong digital judicial infrastructure such as the e-Courts Project and the National Judicial Data Grid AI deployment remains fragmented, uneven, and weakly governed. This creates a critical gap between technological capability and institutional readiness.

8.1 Synthesis of Core Findings

The key analytical conclusions emerging from this study can be summarized across four dimensions.

First, India's judicial system has successfully transitioned from basic digitization to data-enabled administration. However, AI adoption remains largely experimental and assistive, focusing on translation, research support, and administrative analytics rather than adjudicatory decision-making. This cautious approach reflects constitutional priorities but also limits the transformative potential of AI.

Second, comparative analysis shows that India occupies a hybrid position globally. Unlike China's automation-heavy model, India has avoided delegating judicial authority to algorithms. At the same time, unlike the U.S. and EU, India lacks formalized explainability, audit, and accountability standards specific to judicial AI.

Third, ethical risks particularly algorithmic bias, opacity, and data misuse—remain under-addressed at the institutional level. While judges retain final authority, the absence of standardized governance frameworks increases the risk of indirect automation bias and inconsistent application across courts.

Finally, public trust emerges as a central determinant of AI legitimacy in the judiciary. Without transparency regarding how AI tools are used, litigants may perceive judicial decision-making as opaque or technocratic, even when human oversight is preserved.

Table 12. Consolidated Implications of Judicial AI Adoption in India

Dimension	Key Insight	Implication
Technology	AI is assistive, not autonomous	Judicial authority preserved
Governance	Lack of unified standards	Risk of inconsistency
Ethics	Bias and opacity insufficiently regulated	Threat to fairness
Legitimacy	Trust depends on transparency	Need for disclosure

8.2 Implications for Judicial Independence and Due Process

Although AI systems do not formally decide cases, they shape how information is presented, prioritized, and interpreted. This indirect influence has significant implications for due process. If judges are not trained to critically assess AI-generated outputs, there is a risk of cognitive deference to algorithmic recommendations.

To safeguard judicial independence, AI outputs must remain explicitly non-binding, contestable, and explainable. Responsibility for legal outcomes must remain exclusively human. AI, therefore, should be treated as an informational aid rather than an epistemic authority.

8.3 Implications for Institutional Reform

The findings indicate that judicial AI reform cannot be addressed solely through technology procurement. It requires coordinated institutional reform involving judicial leadership, regulatory clarity, capacity building, and public communication. Without such alignment, AI risks reinforcing existing inequalities rather than enhancing access to justice.

A systematic review of AI in justice systems finds that while innovation offers efficiency gains, significant ethical challenges including bias, transparency constraints, and weak human oversight persist, affirming the need for robust governance structures to uphold justice and legitimacy(Borgesano et al., 2025)

9. FUTURE RESEARCH DIRECTIONS AND POLICY RECOMMENDATIONS

Emerging research proposes procedural justice frameworks to resolve value conflicts inherent in AI governance, allowing democratic deliberation, inclusion, and transparency to inform ethical AI deployment a direction that aligns with future research needs for judicial AI governance (de Fine Licht, 2025).

Building on the conclusions above, this section outlines future research priorities and policy interventions necessary to ensure responsible and sustainable AI integration within India's judicial system.

9.1 Future Research Directions

Current judicial AI discourse in India is predominantly conceptual and descriptive. There is a clear need for empirical, interdisciplinary research that evaluates AI's real-world impact on judicial outcomes and institutional behavior.

Priority research areas include:

- Measuring whether AI-assisted tools improve consistency and efficiency in judicial reasoning
- Examining how bias enters judicial AI systems through historical datasets
- Defining minimum standards of explainability required to satisfy due process
- Studying how AI alters judicial cognition and decision-making behavior

Such research is essential to move from speculative optimism to evidence-based judicial reform.

9.2 Policy Recommendations

To address the governance gaps identified in this chapter, the following policy measures are recommended.

Table 13. Policy Priorities for Responsible Judicial AI in India

Policy Area	Recommendation	Purpose
Governance	Judiciary-issued AI usage guidelines	Uniform standards
Accountability	Mandatory bias and impact audits	Prevent systemic harm
Transparency	Disclosure of AI-assisted processes	Maintain public trust
Capacity	AI literacy training for judges	Informed oversight
Data protection	Court-specific DPDP compliance rules	Privacy assurance

These measures should be led by judicial institutions rather than external technology vendors to preserve institutional autonomy.

9.3 Long-Term Strategic Outlook

India's long-term opportunity lies in developing a human-centric judicial AI model that combines operational efficiency with constitutional safeguards. By learning selectively from global practices adopting efficiency from Singapore, accountability from the EU, and avoiding excessive automation India can establish a globally relevant framework for ethical judicial AI.

Ultimately, the success of AI in India's legal system will not be measured by speed alone, but by its ability to strengthen fairness, transparency, and trust. AI should enhance justice delivery without diminishing the human judgment that lies at the core of judicial legitimacy.

10. LIMITATIONS OF THE STUDY

Despite offering a comprehensive analysis of artificial intelligence integration within India's judicial system, this chapter is subject to several conceptual, methodological, and contextual limitations. Acknowledging these limitations is essential to ensure academic rigor and to prevent overgeneralization of the findings.

10.1 Conceptual and Scope Limitations

First, this study adopts a policy-oriented and governance-focused perspective, rather than a technical evaluation of AI systems. As a result, the chapter does not assess algorithmic performance metrics such as accuracy rates, model validation techniques, or system-level optimization. While this approach aligns with legal scholarship, it limits the ability to quantitatively evaluate AI effectiveness in judicial outcomes. Comprehensive reviews of AI regulation highlight that ethical principles such as transparency, accountability, and privacy must be integrally considered in judicial AI policies to balance innovation with societal protection (Cajueiro & Celestino, 2026).

Second, the comparative global analysis emphasizes institutional models rather than jurisdiction-specific case law. Although examples from Singapore, China, the United States, and Europe are used to extract governance lessons, the chapter does not conduct a doctrinal comparison of judicial decisions influenced by AI tools. Consequently, legal nuances at the micro-level may not be fully captured.

Third, the scope of AI examined is largely confined to court-facing judicial functions, such as case management, legal research assistance, and procedural automation. AI applications used by law enforcement agencies, prosecutors, or private legal platforms are not analyzed in depth, even though they indirectly influence judicial processes.

10.2 Empirical and Data Limitations

This chapter relies primarily on secondary sources, including policy documents, institutional reports, academic literature, and publicly available information on judicial digitization initiatives. Due to limited access to internal court data and proprietary AI systems, the study does not include primary empirical data such as judicial interviews, system usage logs, or outcome-based statistical analyses.

Additionally, India's judicial AI initiatives are still at an early and evolving stage, which restricts the availability of longitudinal data. As a result, the chapter cannot conclusively assess long-term impacts on judicial consistency, backlog reduction, or litigant satisfaction. Any observations regarding future implications should therefore be interpreted as analytical projections rather than definitive outcomes.

10.3 Regulatory and Temporal Constraints

The regulatory environment governing AI in India is currently under development, particularly following the introduction of the Digital Personal Data Protection Act. Since judicial-specific AI regulations have not yet been formally enacted, the analysis necessarily operates within a dynamic legal landscape. Future statutory or judicial interventions may alter the relevance of certain governance recommendations presented in this chapter. Legal analyses of fairness in AI underline that while frameworks such as Europe's AI Act aim to ensure non-discrimination and accountability, divergent legal standards and incomplete regulatory clarity continue to challenge comprehensive trustworthiness assessments reflecting a key limitation in current judicial AI governance research (Kattnig et al., 2024).

Moreover, rapid advancements in AI technologies especially in generative AI and large language models mean that some technological assumptions may evolve faster than institutional adoption. This temporal limitation underscores the need for continuous reassessment of AI governance frameworks within the judiciary.

CONCLUSION

The integration of Artificial Intelligence (AI) into India's judicial system presents both significant opportunities and complex ethical challenges. AI is currently employed as an assistive tool for case management, legal research, and administrative analytics rather than autonomous decision-making. Its implementation has the potential to improve efficiency and consistency, but judicial authority and discretion remain exclusively human, ensuring that AI serves as a support mechanism rather than a replacement for judicial reasoning.

Ethical risks including algorithmic bias, automation bias, and lack of explainability are critical concerns that can affect fairness, due process, and public trust. AI systems trained on historical judicial data may unintentionally reinforce structural inequalities, while human reliance on algorithmic recommendations may subtly influence decision-making. Maintaining transparency, contestability, and accountability is essential to prevent unintended consequences and safeguard the legitimacy of the judiciary.

Responsible AI governance requires clear institutional oversight, phased implementation, and capacity building to ensure that AI adoption aligns with constitutional values and judicial independence. Regular audits, explainable outputs, robust data protection, and public disclosure are necessary to preserve trust and ethical compliance. Ultimately, the success of AI in the judicial context depends not on speed or efficiency alone, but on its ability to enhance fairness, transparency, and trust while keeping human judgment at the center of legal decision-making.

REFERENCES

Barysė, D., & Sarel, R. (2024). Algorithms in the court : Does it matter which part of the judicial decision - making is automated? *Artificial Intelligence and Law*, *32*(1), 117–146. DOI: 10.1007/s10506-022-09343-6 PMID: 36643574

Borgesano, F., De Maio, A., Laghi, P., & Musmanno, R. (2025). Artificial intelligence and justice: A systematic literature review and future research perspectives on Justice 5.0. *European Journal of Innovation Management*, *28*(11), 349–385. https://doi.org/https://doi.org/10.1108/EJIM-01-2025-0117

Cajueiro, D. O., & Celestino, V. R. R. (2026). A comprehensive review of Artificial Intelligence regulation: Weighing ethical principles and innovation. *Journal of Economy and Technology*, *4*, 77–91. https://doi.org/https://doi.org/10.1016/j.ject.2025.07.001

Carnat, I. (2024). Addressing the risks of generative AI for the judiciary: The accountability framework(s) under the EU AI Act. *Computer Law & Security Review*, *55*, 106067. https://doi.org/https://doi.org/10.1016/j.clsr.2024.106067

de Fine Licht, K. (2025). Resolving value conflicts in public AI governance: A procedural justice framework. *Government Information Quarterly*, *42*(2), 102033. https://doi.org/https://doi.org/10.1016/j.giq.2025.102033

Dias, S. A. de J., & Sátiro, R. M. (2024). Artificial intelligence in the judiciary: A critical view. *Futures*, *164*, 103493. https://doi.org/https://doi.org/10.1016/j.futures.2024.103493

Fernández, D., Emilia, L., Ignacio, G., & Mazzini, G. (2025). An interdisciplinary account of the terminological choices by EU policymakers ahead of the final agreement on the AI Act : AI system, general purpose AI system, foundation model, and generative AI. *Artificial Intelligence and Law*, *33*(4), 875–888. DOI: 10.1007/s10506-024-09412-y

Fischman-Afori, O. (2025). Due process by design: Enhancing fairness and trust in AI decision-making. *Social Sciences & Humanities Open*, *12*, 102178. https://doi.org/https://doi.org/10.1016/j.ssaho.2025.102178

Herrera-Tapias, B. A., Guzmán, D. H., Zambam, N. J., Turatti, L., Rodríguez, F. A., Fröhlich, S., Staffen, M. R., Muñoz, P. C., Reyes, A. G., de la Torre, G. S., Duarte, N. R., & Ramos, E. P. (2025). Algorithmic discrimination and explainable artificial intelligence in the judiciary: A case study of the Constitutional Court of Colombia. *Procedia Computer Science*, *257*, 1227–1232. https://doi.org/https://doi.org/10.1016/j.procs.2025.03.164

Kattnig, M., Angerschmid, A., Reichel, T., & Kern, R. (2024). Assessing trustworthy AI: Technical and legal perspectives of fairness in AI. *Computer Law & Security Review, 55*, 106053. https://doi.org/https://doi.org/10.1016/j.clsr.2024.106053

Mansouri, O., Yusuf, N., & Kooli, C. (2025). Ethical frontiers and legal boundaries: Proposing a unified framework for AI regulation and accountability. *Next Research, 2*(4), 101087. https://doi.org/https://doi.org/10.1016/j.nexres.2025.101087

Novelli, C., Casolari, F., Hacker, P., Spedicato, G., & Floridi, L. (2024). Computer Law & Security Review : The International Journal of Technology Law and Practice Generative AI in EU law : Liability, privacy, intellectual property, and cybersecurity. *Computer Law & Security Review, 55*(October), 106066. DOI: 10.1016/j.clsr.2024.106066

Papagiannidis, E., Mikalef, P., & Conboy, K. (2025). Responsible artificial intelligence governance: A review and research framework. *The Journal of Strategic Information Systems, 34*(2), 101885. https://doi.org/https://doi.org/10.1016/j.jsis.2024.101885

Perona, R., Carrillo, Y., & Rosa, D. (2025). Unveiling AI in the courtroom : Exploring ChatGPT ' s impact on judicial decision - making through a pilot Colombian case study. *AI & Society, 40*(4), 2533–2540. DOI: 10.1007/s00146-024-01943-x

Richmond, K. M., Muddamsetty, S. M., Gammeltoft-hansen, T., Olsen, H. P., & Moeslund, T. B. (2024). Explainable AI and Law: An Evidential Survey. In *Digital Society* (Vol. 3, Issue 1). Springer International Publishing. https://doi.org/DOI: 10.1007/s44206-023-00081-z

Ruzayana, Z., Hidayah, R. N., & Firsha, M. (2025). Judicial System Digitalization. *The Constitutionality of the E-Court System in Southeast Asia., 4*(1), 127–138. DOI: 10.57255/hakamain.v4i1.1343

Sekti, B. A. (2025a). AI Technology Management Concepts and Strategies. In *AI Technology Management and Value Creation* (pp. 1–32). https://doi.org/DOI: 10.4018/979-8-3373-2497-5.ch001

Sekti, B. A. (2025b). Machine Learning vs. AI: Key Concepts. In *Implementing Enterprise Cybersecurity With AI* (pp. 1–27). https://doi.org/DOI: 10.4018/979-8-3373-2252-0.ch001

Selçuk, S., Kurt Konca, N., & Kaya, S. (2025). AI-driven civil litigation: Navigating the right to a fair trial. *Computer Law & Security Review, 57*, 106136. https://doi.org/https://doi.org/10.1016/j.clsr.2025.106136

Tanujaya, C. N., & Sekti, B. A. (2025). Global Regulatory Landscape: The European Union Al Act Comparative International Perspectives. In *Navigating Social Trust in the AI Era* (pp. 95–121). https://doi.org/DOI: 10.4018/979-8-3373-7011-8.ch005

Chapter 10

Fuzzy Logic-Driven Governance Models for Responsible AI Adoption in India's Legal and Cybersecurity Ecosystem

Ajoy Kanti Das
http://orcid.org/0000-0002-9326-1677
Tripura University, India

Nandini Gupta
http://orcid.org/0009-0000-5450-9783
Bir Bikram Memorial College, India

Ebenezer Aquisman Asare
http://orcid.org/0000-0003-1185-1479
Northeastern University, USA

Takaaki Fujita
http://orcid.org/0009-0007-1509-2728
Independent Researcher, Japan

Suman Patra
Tripura University, India

Ruhit Bardhan
Indian Institute of Teacher Education, India

ABSTRACT

India is rapidly implementing AI in the courts, police, government services, banking, and cybersecurity. These technologies can benefit the country, but they also introduce additional hazards like bias, privacy concerns, and ambiguous conclusions. Traditional yes/no criteria are insufficient to control these risks. This chapter discusses how fuzzy logic might aid in responsible AI governance in India. Fuzzy logic allows for degree-based decisions rather than precise answers. It can provide more accurate measurements of fairness, openness, privacy, and cybersecurity risk. The chapter discusses fuzzy risk models, fuzzy rule-based systems, and fuzzy MCDM

DOI: 10.4018/979-8-3373-7685-1.ch010

methods for assessing AI technologies. A step-by-step governance framework is presented to assist policymakers in monitoring AI systems, evaluating risks, and making balanced judgments. The chapter demonstrates that fuzzy logic is a versatile, straightforward, and successful strategy to establishing safe, equitable, and trustworthy AI governance in India.

1. INTRODUCTION

India is experiencing a rapid digital transition. AI systems help make choices in courts, police, banking, hospitals, and national security. These systems bring both new opportunities and new threats. India requires responsible AI governance to address these risks. Governance entails developing rules, policies, and processes for responsible AI use. AI works with unclear and incomplete data. It processes patterns that aren't necessarily clear or precise. Legal and cybersecurity judgments both involve ambiguity. The law addresses imperfect evidence. Cybersecurity deals with evolving dangers. In these unpredictable situations, fuzzy logic (Zadeh, 1965) is useful. Values between 0 and 1 are handled by it. Instead of providing predetermined solutions, this provides graded decisions. When we are unable to respond with a simple "yes" or "no," fuzzy logic (Zadeh, 1965) can be helpful. It encourages India to adopt AI responsibly. Flexible regulations are frequently needed for AI governance. A choice might not be entirely dangerous or complying. It might lie in the middle of these two extremes. This intermediate zone is modeled by fuzzy logic. Cybersecurity teams, courts, and governments all benefit from it. AI rulings must be fairly judged by India's judicial system. Teams in charge of cybersecurity must anticipate unknown dangers. AI systems must be ranked by policymakers using a variety of factors. A straightforward and useful method for doing this is fuzzy logic (Zadeh, 1965). It uses membership functions and equations. These equations guide balanced and clear decisions.

Fuzzy logic improves decision-making in the face of ambiguity and supports responsible AI governance in India's legal and cyber systems. Hu et al. (2023) used fuzzy decision models to regulate artificial intelligence audits. Their model makes it easier for businesses to securely validate AI technologies. Singh and Sodhi (2025) discussed the cybersecurity and legal requirements for AI. They highlighted how important it is that Indian laws get updated. Venkatesh et al. (2025) applied AI incentives to improve legal services. Their strategy improves digital marketplace efficiency. R and Salman (2023) investigated the current legal oversight of artificial intelligence in India. Their work displays the oversight and verification of artificial intelligence tools. N and Rajagopal (2024) proved the significance of AI in preventing cybercrime. According to their research, AI can identify threats early. Ravishankar

(2025) looked into the use of AI in arbitration. He explained how AI could expedite the resolution of disputes. Chen (2025) used fuzzy logic to retrieve legal content. When it comes to recognizing lawful information, his model performs better. Wirtz et al. (2022) introduced a framework for risk-based AI governance. Their framework guides the safe and moral use of AI. Mcintosh et al. evaluated cybersecurity recommendations for large language models (2024). Their study exposes flaws in AI safety laws. Sane and Thombre (2025) presented a plan for AI in legal services. Their approach facilitates the ethical application of AI. Toapanta et al. (2025) developed a cybersecurity governance model using blockchain and artificial intelligence. Their model helps companies protect digital systems more effectively. Malik et al. (2020) used fuzzy models to predict drought in India. Their method shows how fuzzy logic handles unclear climate data. Dixit et al. (2025) investigated the use of AI in courts and law enforcement. They highlighted these domains' promise and hazards. Aljohani (2025) developed AI-based ESG decision frameworks. His philosophy promotes ethical and environmentally friendly decisions. Taeihagh (2021) described global AI governance concepts. The importance of responsible policy is emphasized in his work. Devarajan et al. (2025) assessed cybersecurity risks using fuzzy networks. Their approach makes it easier for businesses to comprehend digital risks. Misra et al. (2023) looked at the use of AI in Indian government. They brought attention to issues with trust and infrastructure. Sharma et al. (2020) looked at IoT governance issues in smart cities. Their research highlights the need for secure online platforms. Shah (2024) discussed ethical AI and trust in the digital economy. He emphasized how strong governance promotes user trust.

Recent studies highlight that responsible AI adoption in legal and cybersecurity domains demands structured governance frameworks supported by fuzzy logic–based decision models. Research on sustainable and AI-enabled systems (Das et al., 2023; Singh et al., 2023) shows that complex, uncertain environments benefit from fuzzy approaches for prioritising risks and improving accountability. In the legal domain, scholars have identified major challenges in AI adoption and emphasised systematic evaluation mechanisms (Kim et al., 2025; Kumar, 2025). Emerging governance gaps in cybersecurity and e-commerce ecosystems further reinforce the need for transparent and bias-resistant AI systems (Kolo, 2025). Global initiatives on responsible AI engineering and pattern-based governance (Lu et al., 2022; Madanchian & Taherdoost, 2025) also provide guiding principles applicable to India's evolving digital governance landscape. In the Indian context, AI-driven public decision-making continues to expand (Manoj & Jeevanandhan, 2025), while regulatory debates stress the urgency of robust oversight for frontier AI technologies (Radanliev, 2025). Together, these works justify the development of fuzzy logic–driven governance models tailored to India's legal and cybersecurity ecosystem, where ambiguity, multi-criteria risk factors, and ethical considerations must be addressed simultaneously.

For MCDM, Das and Granados (2022a) created a fuzzy parameterized intuitionistic fuzzy soft multiset theory. Their research on FP-intuitionistic multi-fuzzy N-soft sets enhanced MCDM models' adaptability (Das and Granados, 2022b). To further this study, they later presented IFP-intuitionistic multi-fuzzy N-soft sets (Das and Granados, 2023a). Weighted fuzzy soft multisets were suggested by Das (2018) as a novel MCDM tool. Previously, preference fuzzy rough relations and intuitionistic fuzzy rough relations were studied by Das (2016) and Das & Granados (2023b). Their collaborative study presented a fuzzy soft group MCDM technique in 2021. It employed weighted average ratings to enhance MCDM theory and practical analysis (Das and Granados, 2021). New operations on F Ss were proposed by Das et al. (2022). They demonstrated how these operations aid in the efficient resolution of MCDM issues. Weighted hesitant bipolar-valued FS s were later introduced by Das et al. (2023). These sets provide a more thorough method of contrasting and assessing several choices. A fuzzy MCDM model was also created by Das et al. (2025b) to investigate how human activity affects the water quality of urban rivers. An important addition to environmental MCDM research is this work. It assessed the Gomati and Haora Rivers' contamination levels. Water contamination was also graded using FSS models and weighted hesitant FS (Das et al., 2024a; 2024b; 2025a). Mukherjee and Das's work are also used in the development of fuzzy soft multiset theories in MCDM (2016a). In their 2015 work, interval-valued intuitionistic fuzzy soft multi-sets were applied to practical MCDM situations (Mukherjee and Das, 2015b). Additionally, they investigated the application of intuitionistic FSSs with interval values in investment decision-making (Mukherjee and Das, 2015a).

In 2022, they also developed Einstein operations on fuzzy soft multisets and MCDM (Mukherjee & Das, 2022). In their 2023 book, they go into greater detail about the theoretical underpinnings and practical applications (Mukherjee & Das, 2023). Mukherjee & Das focus even further on the topological and relational paradigm of fuzzy and rough sets (2015c; 2016b). Granados et al. (2022) introduced the continuous neutrosophic distributions with neutrosophic parameters that give a possibility to represent the uncertainty probabilistically. Granados et al. (2023) proposed the weighted neutrosophic soft multiset approach, which Das et al. (2025c) have recently thoroughly examined. Das et al. (2025d) recently introduced the fuzzy logic decision-support system to streamline the concept of an adaptive inventory management system within the retailing context. Das et al. (2025e) have developed a new weighted hypersoft expert system MCDM paradigm. They provide helpful strategies on how to deal with uncertainty, make decisions more precisely, and address difficult real-life problems (Das et al., 2025f). Das et al. (2025g; 2025h; 2025i) investigated how urban river water is impacted by human activity. Das et al. (2025j) investigated the groundwater quality in Agartala, Northeast India using an effective fuzzy MCDM model. Das et al. (2025k) studied the impact of management of interactive learning environments on mathematical proficiency. Fuzzy logic applications in multicultural marketing were investigated by Das et al. (2026a). Das et al. (2026b) examined smart luxury goods co-branding in a different study. They made decisions using a neutrosophic multi-criteria method. Neutrosophic sets were also used in environmental recovery by Das et al. (2026c). A generalized interval-valued neutrosophic rough soft set structure was presented by Mukherjee et al. (2026). Recently, Gupta et al. (2026) integrated traditional ecological knowledge with fuzzy logic and quantum computing for sustainable agriculture in tribal areas of Tripura. Their work offers useful approaches for managing uncertainty, enhancing the precision of decisions, and tackling challenging real-world issues. This chapter explains how fuzzy logic supports AI governance. It expands concepts with examples, formulas, and Indian cases. It builds a complete model for India's legal and cybersecurity ecosystem.

2. BASICS OF FUZZY LOGIC AND CONCEPTUAL FRAMEWORK

2.1 Fuzzy Logic

Partial truth values are the subject of fuzzy logic (Zadeh, 1965). It simulates uncertainty in the range of 0 to 1. This aids in more accurate description of real-world circumstances. Strict bounds are used in crisp logic. For instance, a person may or may not be young. Threats might be either high or low. A system is either secure or risky. This dichotomous perspective is frequently impractical. Middle values are permitted by fuzzy logic. A system may be "partially safe." A circumstance may be "moderately risky." This is a reflection of actual cybersecurity and legal behavior. On universe U, a fuzzy set A is:

$$A = \{(x, \mu_A(x)) : x \in U\}$$

Here, $\mu_A(x)$ **is the membership value. It lies between 0 and 1:**

$$0 \leq \mu_A(x) \leq 1$$

It shows how strongly x **belongs to A. Real Governance Context Example**
Let,
U be AI tools used in courts.
Define fuzzy set Responsible AI. Membership indicates responsibility level.

Examples:

$\mu(ExplainableAI) = 0.9$

$\mu(ModeratelyTransparentAI) = 0.6$

$\mu(BlackboxAI) = 0.2$

This helps judges assess risk levels.

Membership Functions

A membership function assigns value between 0 and 1. It shows how much an input belongs to a fuzzy set.

A common function is triangular:

$$\mu(x) = \begin{cases} 0, x < a \\ \frac{x-a}{b-a}, a \le x \le b \\ \frac{c-x}{c-b}, b \le x \le c \\ 0, x > c \end{cases}$$

This function is simple and clear. It models gradual change. Use in Cybersecurity Let,

x **be threat score.**

Low threat decreases gradually as score rises. High threat increases gradually. This avoids sudden category change.

Example:

A threat score of 0.45 may have:

$\mu_{Low} = 0.2$

$\mu_{Medium} = 0.6$

$\mu_{High} = 0.1$

This helps teams respond before threats become severe.

Fuzzy Operations

Fuzzy sets use standard operations.
Union:

$$\mu_{A \cup B}(x) = max\left(\mu_A(x), \mu_B(x)\right)$$

Intersection:

$$\mu_{A \cap B}(x) = min\left(\mu_A(x), \mu_B(x)\right)$$

Complement:

$$\mu_{A^c}(x) = 1 - \mu_A(x)$$

These operations help combine rules in governance models.

Example in AI Regulation

Suppose:

$$AITransparencymembership = 0.7$$

$$AISafetymembership = 0.5$$

To combine as "Overall Trustworthiness" using intersection:

$$\mu = min(0.7, 0.5) = 0.5$$

This gives a fair trust score.

Real Example: Cyber Threat Level

Define fuzzy sets for threat levels.
Let,

$$\mu_{Low} = 0.2$$

$$\mu_{High} = 0.7$$

Union gives:

$$\mu_{Union} = 0.7$$

Intersection gives:

$$\mu_{Intersection} = 0.2$$

This shows both low and high elements exist. This mixed value helps analysts judge situations better.

The Applicability of Fuzzy Logic to Indian Governance

Indian systems handle unpredictability and variety. States and regions have very different cases. Cyberthreats are constantly evolving. Incomplete evidence is a factor in legal conflicts. AI choices must be carefully considered. These conflicting circumstances are supported by fuzzy logic. It produces results that are fair and understandable.

2.2 CONCEPTUAL FRAMEWORK: FUZZY LOGIC–DRIVEN RESPONSIBLE AI GOVERNANCE FRAMEWORK (FL-RAIGF)

2.2.1 Introduction to the Conceptual Framework

To provide a coherent theoretical foundation for the chapter, a comprehensive conceptual model titled the Fuzzy Logic–Driven Responsible AI Governance Framework (FL-RAIGF) is introduced. This framework establishes the analytical structure through which Responsible AI practices, governance maturity, and regulatory compliance within India's legal and cybersecurity ecosystem are systematically evaluated. By adopting fuzzy logic principles, the framework integrates qualitative judgement, ambiguity, and linguistic variables into a consistent decision-making system.

2.2.2 Core Components of the FL-RAIGF

The proposed FL-RAIGF consists of five interconnected components that collectively operationalise Responsible AI governance assessment:

(a) Input Determinants

These serve as the primary governance indicators:

- Risk Exposure (technological, operational, ethical)
- Organisational Readiness (infrastructure, human capability, digital maturity)
- Regulatory & Ethical Compliance (alignment with AI policies, cybersecurity acts, and ethical guidelines)

(b) Fuzzy Membership Functions

Each input variable is mapped to linguistic variables such as *Low, Medium,* and *High* using fuzzy membership functions.

This step captures:

- uncertainty present in governance indicators
- ambiguity in legal–ethical assessment
- gradual variation rather than binary classifications

(c) Rule Base and Inference Engine

A structured set of fuzzy IF–THEN rules encodes governance expectations, legal norms, and ethical principles.

The inference engine processes:

- stakeholder-defined governance rules
- domain-specific Responsible AI criteria
- multi-criteria interactions among inputs

(d) Fuzzy Inference Mechanism

The inference mechanism aggregates all activated rules to generate a fuzzy output representing the institution's Responsible AI governance maturity.

(e) Defuzzification Process

The final fuzzy output is converted into a crisp numerical value known as the Governance Readiness Score (GRS)

This score quantifies an institution's overall preparedness to deploy Responsible AI.

2.2.3 Functional Flow of the Framework

The FL-RAIGF operates through a structured step-wise process:

1. Input indicators (risk, readiness, compliance) are collected from organisational and regulatory sources.
2. These indicators undergo fuzzification to convert raw values into fuzzy sets.

3. The fuzzy rule base evaluates the interactions of all input variables.
4. The inference engine applies fuzzy reasoning to produce a governance assessment.
5. The fuzzy output is finally defuzzified into the Governance Readiness Score for interpretation and decision-making.

This flow translates complex legal, ethical, and organisational uncertainties into a transparent and computable governance model.

2.2.4 Technical Illustration of the FL-RAIGF

Illustration of the Fuzzy Logic–Driven Responsible AI Governance Framework (FL-RAIGF). This schematic presents the structure of the proposed fuzzy governance model, including the Input Layer, Membership Function Blocks, Rule Base and Inference Engine, Defuzzification Stage, and Final Governance Readiness Score.

2.2.5 Theoretical Foundation

The FL-RAIGF is grounded in classical fuzzy set theory (Zadeh, 1965) and contemporary fuzzy decision-making approaches. Fuzzy logic is particularly suitable for Responsible AI governance because it accommodates:

- interpretive ambiguity in legal compliance,
- vagueness in ethical norms, and
- qualitative expert judgements in regulatory environments.

By integrating these principles, the framework offers a mathematically robust, uncertainty-aware method for evaluating governance readiness in complex AI ecosystems.

2.2.6 Integration with Chapter Structure

The conceptual framework introduced above forms the foundational structure for the remainder of the chapter. All subsequent sections—including the literature review, model development, analysis, and policy recommendations—are aligned with the FL-RAIGF. This ensures conceptual coherence, methodological alignment, and a clear narrative progression throughout the chapter.

3. GOVERNANCE CHALLENGES IN AI ADOPTION

When implementing AI, India confronts significant obstacles. These issues arise in the fields of cybersecurity, ethics, and law. Many of these problems are addressed by fuzzy logic.

3.1 LEGAL GAPS IN AI ACCOUNTABILITY

AI systems are employed in surveillance, welfare, courts, and law enforcement. However, liability regulations are still ambiguous. It is challenging to assign blame when AI commits a mistake. Legal ambiguity results from this. AI judgments are frequently partially accountable. This can be captured using a fuzzy model.

Let, responsibility R depend on:

$AlgorithmError(E)$

$DataBias(B)$

$HumanOversightLevel(H)$

The fuzzy equation is:

$$R = 0.5E + 0.3B + 0.2(1 - H)$$

If:

$E = 0.6$

$B = 0.4$

$H = 0.8$

Then:

$$R = 0.5(0.6) + 0.3(0.4) + 0.2(0.2) = 0.46$$

R = 0.46 means moderate responsibility.
Courts can interpret this clearly.

Legal Example: Bias in Bail Decisions

Suppose an AI bail tool shows bias.

$Biasvalue = 0.7.$

$Transparency = 0.3.$

Court can compute fuzzy fairness score:

$Fairness = 1 - (0.6B + 0.4(1 - T))$

This avoids extreme "fair/unfair" judgments.

3.2 CYBERSECURITY THREAT GROWTH

In India, AI raises cyber dangers. AI is used by attackers to produce deepfake videos. They produce phishing scams. They crack cryptography. Threats do not appear out of nowhere. This gradual shift is modeled by fuzzy logic. Threat level TS is based on:

$NetworkAnomalyScoreA$

$SuspiciousLoginScoreL$

$MalwareDetectionScoreM$

$TS = 0.4A + 0.3L + 0.3M$

If $TS = 0.55$, **membership might be:**

- Medium = 0.7
- High = 0.3

This shows rising danger.
Teams can respond early.

3.3 RISING DATA PRIVACY REQUIREMENTS

Clear compliance is required with India's Digital Personal Data Protection (DPDP) Act. AI systems make advantage of private information. Levels of compliance might not be zero or full. They are in the middle. This partial compliance is measured by fuzzy logic. Let privacy level P be determined by:

$DataEncryptionLevel(DE)$

$UserConsentStrength(UC)$

$DataMinimizationScore(DM)$

$\boldsymbol{P=0.3DE+0.4UC+0.3DM}$

This gives graded output. Governance teams can compare systems.

3.4 LACK OF TRANSPARENCY IN AI DECISIONS:

A lot of AI models are mysterious. They display findings without justification. India's judicial system demands responsibility. Transparency scores are provided by fuzzy logic.

Example:

$Hightransparency = 0.8$

$Medium = 0.4$

$Low = 0.1$

These values guide governance.

3.5 NEED FOR FLEXIBLE RISK EVALUATION

The risks associated with AI differ by industry. Police, finance, and healthcare all require different regulations. This variation cannot be captured by crisp rules. Fuzzy models are easily adjustable. The AI Governance Risk Index (GRI) as a whole is:

$GRI = 0.4B + 0.3T + 0.3PR$

A score between 0 and 1 gives flexible decisions.

4. FUZZY RISK ASSESSMENT FOR AI SYSTEMS

Different hazards are introduced by AI systems. There are no rigid yes/no patterns for these dangers. They undergo gradual transformation. They rely on a number of unknown variables. These slow changes are captured by fuzzy logic. AI tools are used in Indian courts, law enforcement, banking, welfare, and cybersecurity. The degree of risk varies by industry. These dangers need to be quantified precisely. This risk assessment is supported by fuzzy models. We are now developing fuzzy risk assessment formulae. These formulas demonstrate how governance is supported by fuzzy logic.

4.1 TYPES OF AI RISKS

AI systems have several major risks:

$Biasrisk$

$Privacyrisk$

$Securityrisk$

$Reliabilityrisk$

$Ethicalrisk$

$Explainabilityrisk$

Each risk lies between 0 and 1.
A higher value means higher risk.
Let:

$B = BiasRisk$

$P = PrivacyRisk$

$S = SecurityRisk$

$R = ReliabilityRisk$

$E = EthicalRisk$

$X = ExplainabilityRisk$

4.2 FUZZY RISK SCORE FORMULA

The overall fuzzy risk score is:

$$FR = w_1 B + w_2 P + w_3 S + w_4 R + w_5 E + w_6 X$$

Where:

$$0 \leq w_i \leq 1$$

$$\sum_{i=1}^{6} w_i = 1$$

This formula captures the combined risk.

Real Example: Indian Government Example

Consider a realistic Indian Government scenario involving an AI-based CCTV surveillance tool deployed in a smart city project. The government evaluates this system using six key governance indicators:

Now assume values:

$B = \text{Bias Risk} = 0.6$

$P = \text{Privacy Vulnerability} = 0.8$

$S = \text{System Accuracy} = 0.5$

$R = \text{Regulatory Compliance} = 0.4$

$E = \text{Ethical Transparency} = 0.7$

$\text{X} = \text{Explainability Level} = 0.3$

The government assigns the following weights to reflect national priorities:

$w_1 = 0.25$

$w_2 = 0.20$

$w_3 = 0.20$

$w_4 = 0.15$

$w_5 = 0.10$

$w_6 = 0.10$

Using the fuzzy readiness computation:

$$FR = 0.25(0.6) + 0.20(0.8) + 0.20(0.5) + 0.15(0.4) + 0.10(0.7) + 0.10(0.3)$$

$$FR = 0.15 + 0.16 + 0.10 + 0.06 + 0.07 + 0.03 = 0.57$$

Thus $FR = 0.57$

The tool has moderate risk. The government must monitor it carefully.

4.3. MEMBERSHIP FUNCTIONS FOR RISK CATEGORIES

Define three fuzzy sets:

$LowRisk(LR)$

$MediumRisk(MR)$

$HighRisk(HR)$

Membership values depend on FR:

Triangular Membership

Low Risk:

$$\mu_{LR}(FR) = \begin{cases} 1, FR \leq 0.2 \\ \frac{0.4 - FR}{0.2}, 0.2 < FR < 0.4 \\ 0, FR \geq 0.4 \end{cases}$$

Medium Risk:

$$\mu_{MR}(FR) = \begin{cases} 0, FR < 0.3 \\ \frac{FR - 0.3}{0.2}, 0.3 \leq FR < 0.5 \\ \frac{0.7 - FR}{0.2}, 0.5 \leq FR < 0.7 \\ 0, FR \geq 0.7 \end{cases}$$

High Risk:

$$\mu_{HR}(FR) = \begin{cases} 0, FR < 0.5 \\ \frac{FR - 0.5}{0.2}, 0.5 \leq FR < 0.7 \\ 1, FR \geq 0.7 \end{cases}$$

Interpretation Example

For $FR = 0.57$:

$$\mu_{LR} = 0$$

$$\mu_{MR} = 0.65$$

$$\mu_{HR} = 0.35$$

For the most part, the system is medium-risk. However, there are high-risk components. This enables governance teams to operate in a balanced manner.

4.4 EXAMPLE: AI TOOL IN INDIAN COURTS

Let, an AI tool recommend sentencing.
Risks:

$$Bias = 0.65$$

$$Transparency = 0.30$$

$$Privacy = 0.80$$

Overall risk using weights 0.4, 0.3, 0.3:

$$FR = 0.4(0.65) + 0.3(0.30) + 0.3(0.80)$$

$FR = 0.26 + 0.09 + 0.24 = 0.59$

Thus, risk is moderate-high. Court must supervise the tool heavily.

4.5 WHY FUZZY RISK FITS GOVERNANCE

Crisp rules fail when risk is uncertain. Fuzzy models show smooth transitions. Benefits include:

- More realistic risk modeling
- Clear formulas
- Easy interpretation
- Better public accountability
- Support for Indian laws

Fuzzy logic provides mathematical clarity.
This helps law and cybersecurity teams.

5. FUZZY RULES FOR LEGAL COMPLIANCE

AI in India requires well-defined legal frameworks. Transparency, equity, and privacy regulations must be adhered to by AI tools. However, adherence to the law is rarely perfect. It is in the range of 0 to 1. Compliance levels can be measured with the aid of fuzzy if-then rules. They integrate several criteria. This promotes cybersecurity and responsible adoption in courts.

5.1 FUZZY RULE STRUCTURE

The format of a fuzzy rule is IF condition THEN output. For instance, compliance is strong if both transparency and fairness are high. Fuzzy sets are used in each section. Every value fall between 0 and 1.

5.2 MAIN COMPLIANCE CRITERIA

Let the criteria be:

$Transparency(T)$

$PrivacyProtection(PP)$

Explainability(EX)

BiasReduction(BR)

DataQuality(DQ)

Each value lies in [0,1].
Compliance score C **is:**

$$C = w_1 T + w_2 PP + w_3 EX + w_4 BR + w_5 DQ$$

Weights sum to 1.

5.3 EXAMPLE RULE BASE

Rule 1:

IF Transparency is High AND Explainability is High
Then Compliance is Strong.

Rule 2:

IF Privacy is Low AND Bias is High
THEN Compliance is Weak.

Rule 3:

IF Data Quality is Medium AND Transparency is Medium
THEN Compliance is Moderate.

Rule 4:

IF Bias is Low AND Privacy is High
THEN Compliance is Strong.
Rule bases can grow large. They adapt to different sectors.

5.4 EXAMPLE

Assume:

$T = 0.6$

$PP = 0.8$

$EX = 0.4$

$BR = 0.3$

$DQ = 0.7$

Weights:

$w_1 = 0.25$

$w_2 = 0.25$

$w_3 = 0.20$

$w_4 = 0.15$

$w_5 = 0.15$

Compute:

$$C = 0.25(0.6) + 0.25(0.8) + 0.20(0.4) + 0.15(0.3) + 0.15(0.7)$$

$$C = 0.15 + 0.20 + 0.08 + 0.045 + 0.105 = 0.58$$

Thus, compliance is moderate. Governance teams should monitor the AI system.

5.5 LEGAL EXAMPLE: DPDP ACT COMPLIANCE

DPDP Act requires:

Userconsent

Dataminimization

Purposelimitation

Secureprocessing

Let:

$$ConsentStrength = 0.7$$

$$DataMinimization = 0.5$$

$$SecurityScore = 0.8$$

Then privacy compliance:

$$PC = 0.3(0.7) + 0.3(0.5) + 0.4(0.8)$$

$$PC = 0.21 + 0.15 + 0.32 = 0.68$$

Thus, privacy compliance is fairly strong.

5.6 EXAMPLE: AI POLICING TOOL

AI may track suspects. Compliance requires fairness and privacy.
Assume values:

$$T = 0.4$$

$$PP = 0.3$$

$$EX = 0.2$$

$$BR = 0.5$$

$$DQ = 0.4$$

Compute:

$$C = 0.25(0.4) + 0.25(0.3) + 0.20(0.2) + 0.15(0.5) + 0.15(0.4)$$

$$C = 0.10 + 0.075 + 0.04 + 0.075 + 0.06 = 0.35$$

Compliance is weak.
The tool should not be deployed widely.

5.7 WHY FUZZY RULES FIT INDIA'S LEGAL SYSTEM

There is confusion in Indian legal procedures. Gradual conclusions are supported by fuzzy rules. Intermediate compliance can be interpreted by judges. It gives clear rules for making decisions. This boosts confidence in AI technologies.

5.8 TECHNICAL ILLUSTRATION OF THE FUZZY GOVERNANCE MODEL

To enhance the clarity and operational understanding of the proposed framework, a technical illustration of the fuzzy logic–based governance model is provided in this section. The model is constructed using standard fuzzy inference components, including input variables, membership functions, rule bases, and defuzzification mechanisms. The illustration demonstrates how governance indicators are transformed into fuzzy linguistic values, processed through fuzzy decision rules, and converted into final governance readiness scores.

1. Input Variables and Membership Functions

Three primary governance criteria—AI Risk Severity, Regulatory Readiness, and Ethical Compliance—are modeled as fuzzy input variables.

For each variable, triangular or trapezoidal membership functions are assigned under linguistic terms such as Low, Medium, and High.

These functions allow smooth handling of uncertainty inherent in legal and cybersecurity assessments.

2. Fuzzy Rule Base Construction

A rule base is created using the format:

IF (Risk Severity is High) AND (Regulatory Readiness is Low) THEN Governance Readiness is Poor.

More than 20 rule combinations are formed to capture real-world governance scenarios in the Indian AI ecosystem.

3. Inference Mechanism

The Mamdani-type fuzzy inference system (FIS) is used to compute aggregated decision outputs.

Each rule's firing strength is calculated using fuzzy AND operations, and the output membership values are aggregated using maximum composition.

4. Defuzzification Process

The final governance score is obtained using the centroid (CoA) defuzzification method.

This converts the fuzzy output into a crisp value between 0 and 1, representing the system's responsible AI governance readiness level.

5. Example Calculation

For instance, when:
Risk Severity = High,
Regulatory Readiness = Medium,
Ethical Compliance = High,
the FIS processes the related rules and produces a governance readiness score of approximately 0.62, indicating moderate readiness.

6. Technical Illustration Diagram

Figure 1. Internal computation and decision-making workflow of the proposed fuzzy governance model

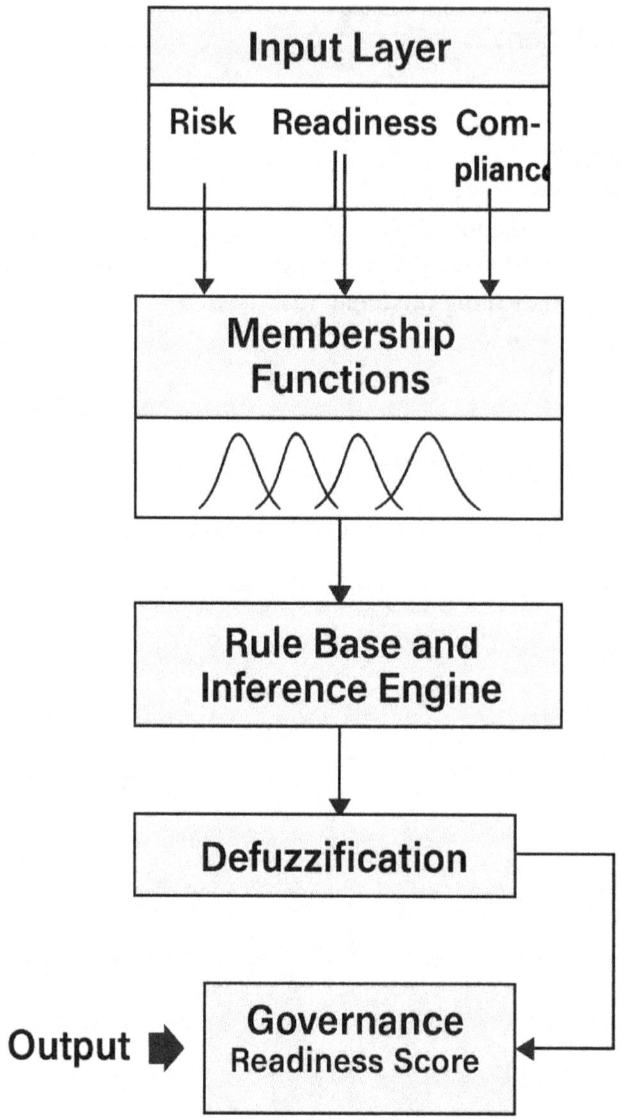

Fig. 1 visually explains the internal computation and decision-making workflow of the proposed fuzzy governance model.

6. FUZZY MULTI-CRITERIA DECISION-MAKING (FMCDM) IN GOVERNANCE

AI governance necessitates comparing various systems. Many judgments require more than one factor. FMCDM helps to aggregate all criteria into a single score. It can rank AI tools for deployment. India makes extensive use of artificial intelligence technologies. Different ministries employ various instruments. FMCDM makes it easier to select the best one.

6.1 FMCDM FORMULA

Let, AI systems be:

$$A_1, A_2, A_3$$

Criteria:

$$C_1: Transparency$$

$$C_2: Reliability$$

$$C_3: PrivacySafety$$

$$C_4: EthicalCompliance$$

Let membership value be μ_{ij}
where $i = system, j = criterion.$
Combined score:

$$S(A_i) = \sum_{j=1}^{4} w_j \mu_{ij}$$

Where w_j are weights.
Highest S **gives best system.**

6.2 EXAMPLE WITH THREE SYSTEMS

Let weights:

$w_1 = 0.3$

$w_2 = 0.3$

$w_3 = 0.2$

$w_4 = 0.2$

Now fuzzy ratings:

Table 1.

Criterion	A_1	A_2	A_3
$C_1(T)$	0.7	0.4	0.6
$C_2(R)$	0.6	0.8	0.5
$C_3(P)$	0.5	0.6	0.4
$C_4(E)$	0.8	0.5	0.6

Compute $S(A_1)$:

$$S(A_1) = 0.3(0.7) + 0.3(0.6) + 0.2(0.5) + 0.2(0.8)$$

$$S(A_1) = 0.21 + 0.18 + 0.10 + 0.16 = 0.65$$

Compute $S(A_2)$:

$$S(A_2) = 0.3(0.4) + 0.3(0.8) + 0.2(0.6) + 0.2(0.5)$$

$$S(A_2) = 0.12 + 0.24 + 0.12 + 0.10 = 0.58$$

Compute $S(A_3)$:

$$S(A_3) = 0.3(0.6) + 0.3(0.5) + 0.2(0.4) + 0.2(0.6)$$

$$S(A_3) = 0.18 + 0.15 + 0.08 + 0.12 = 0.53$$

Ranking:

$A_1 = 0.65$

$A_2 = 0.58$

$A_3 = 0.53$

Thus A_1 is the best choice for deployment.

6.3. APPLICATION IN INDIAN GOVERNANCE

Use Case 1: Selecting Court AI Tool

- Ministry must pick best AI system for courts.
- Criteria include transparency and reliability.
- FMCDM gives clear ranking.

Use Case 2: Choosing Cybersecurity AI

- Systems must detect attacks.
- Criteria include accuracy and speed.
- FMCDM supports selection.

Use Case 3: Choosing AI for Public Services

- AI may manage rations, pensions, or welfare.
- FMCDM ensures fairness and trust.

6.4. ADDING MORE GOVERNANCE CRITERIA

Additional criteria may include:

- Human oversight level
- Explainability
- Data security
- Environmental impact
- Cost effectiveness
- Compliance with DPDP Act

FMCDM can handle any number of criteria. It adapts to government needs.

6.5 WHY FMCDM FITS GOVERNANCE

- Combines multiple indicators
- Produces clear and simple ranking
- Uses numerical and fuzzy values
- Helps policy makers with balanced decisions

FMCDM is simple but powerful.
It fits India's governance requirements.

7. FUZZY GOVERNANCE ARCHITECTURE FOR RESPONSIBLE AI IN INDIA

Fuzzy governance generates flexible, adaptive decision systems that are appropriate for India's complicated legal and cybersecurity settings. Traditional binary rules (approve/reject) cannot handle ambiguous, changing, or uncertain AI behavior. Fuzzy logic enables graded and explainable governance decisions.

7.1 CORE RISK DIMENSIONS

AI risk varies across domains. Four major risk types are considered: - Legal Risk - Privacy Risk - Cybersecurity Risk - Fairness and Bias Risk

Each risk is mapped to fuzzy membership levels: Low (L) - Medium (M) - High (H)

Example membership functions: -

$$\mu_L(x) = max\left(0, \frac{(0.4 - x)}{0.4}\right)$$

$$\mu_M(x) = max\left(0, 1 - \frac{|x - 0.5|}{0.3}\right)$$

$$\mu_H(x) = max\left(0, \frac{(x - 0.6)}{0.4}\right)$$

These functions allow nuanced comparison of AI systems.

7.2 COMPONENTS OF THE FUZZY GOVERNANCE ARCHITECTURE

The architecture includes four layers:

- Fuzzy Evaluation Layer – Computes fuzzy scores for transparency, privacy, bias, and threats.
- Decision Layer – Applies fuzzy rules to determine approve/modify/reject outcomes.
- Monitoring Layer – Tracks AI behaviour over time and updates scores.
- Review Layer – Experts revise rules, weights, and membership functions.

7.3 FUZZY EVALUATION LAYER

Each criterion is converted to fuzzy membership values.
Example:

$$Transparencyscore = 0.6 \rightarrow \mu_M(0.6) = 0.8.$$

This allows partial classification.

7.4 DECISION LAYER (RULE-BASED)

This layer interprets fuzzy scores using rules such as: -
IF Privacy is High AND Bias is Low → Approve
IF Transparency is Low → Require explanation

$$Mathematicalevaluation: \alpha = min\left(\mu_{privacy}, \mu_{bias}\right)$$

$$If \alpha \geq 0.7 \rightarrow Accept$$

$$If 0.4 \leq \alpha < 0.7 \rightarrow Modify$$

$$If \alpha < 0.4 \rightarrow Reject$$

7.5 MONITORING LAYER

AI performance changes with new data. To track updates: $S_{t+1} = 0.8 S_t + 0.2 S_{new}$. This ensures stable but responsive oversight.

7.6 REVIEW LAYER

Human experts refine: - Membership functions - Weights - Governance rules This keeps the system aligned with new laws and emerging AI risks.

8. FUZZY INFERENCE SYSTEM FOR INDIA'S AI GOVERNANCE

A fuzzy inference system (FIS) can support India.
It uses three steps: Fuzzification Inference Rules Defuzzification
Example output: Governance Risk Index (GRI).
Inputs: Bias Level (BL) Data Sensitivity (DS) Cyber Threat Level (CTL)
Rule example: IF BL is High AND DS is High THEN GRI is Very High.
Defuzzification uses:

$$GRI = \frac{\sum_i x_i \mu(x_i)}{\sum_i \mu(x_i)}$$

This gives crisp governance outputs.

9. FUZZY MODEL FOR RESPONSIBLE AI

This section provides a realistic example. It illustrates how fuzzy logic might benefit Indian courts. It demonstrates how fuzzy guidelines can govern responsible AI use.

Assume an AI tool T is employed in court. It predicts case outcomes. It offers advice to judges. It must be fair and safe. India need clear evaluation rules. Fuzzy logic facilitates this.

9.1 CRITERIA FOR COURT AI EVALUATION

We evaluate the AI tool using three criteria: Fairness (F) Data Quality (DQ) Privacy Protection (PP)

Each criterion is fuzzy. Each value lies between 0 and 1. Higher value means better performance.

Examples: $F = 0.7 means moderately fair.$

DQ = 0.5 means medium-quality data.

PP = 0.9 means very strong privacy.

9.2 FUZZY WEIGHTED SCORE

We use a weighted score. Weights show importance. Courts may choose: 0.4 for Fairness 0.3 for Data Quality 0.3 for Privacy Protection

The fuzzy weighted score W **is:**

$$W = 0.4F + 0.3DQ + 0.3PP$$

This score supports decisions. If W is high, the tool is acceptable. If W is low, the system needs review.

9.3 EXAMPLE CALCULATION

Take: F = 0.7, DQ = 0.5, PP = 0.9

Now compute W:

$$W = 0.4(0.7) + 0.3(0.5) + 0.3(0.9)$$

$$W = 0.28 + 0.15 + 0.27 = 0.70$$

Thus $W = 0.70$. **This shows the AI system is acceptable. It performs well in privacy and fairness. Its data quality needs improvement.**

9.4 INTERPRETATION IN INDIAN GOVERNANCE

Courts can use W to decide adoption. If $W > 0.75$, **AI is highly reliable. If** $0.60 \leq W \leq 0.75$, **AI is acceptable with monitoring. If** $W < 0.60$, **AI must be improved.**

These thresholds are fuzzy. They allow flexible judgments. They help reflect real-world uncertainty. They support responsible AI adoption.

9.5 EXTENDED EXAMPLE: ADDING TRANSPARENCY

India focuses on transparency. Let a new factor TPR (Transparency) be added.

Let, weight be 0.2.

Then update weights:

$$Fairness = 0.35$$

$DataQuality = 0.25$

$PrivacyProtection = 0.20$

$Transparency = 0.20$

New formula:

$$W' = 0.35F + 0.25DQ + 0.20PP + 0.20TPR$$

Suppose TPR = 0.6. Calculate:

$$W' = 0.35(0.7) + 0.25(0.5) + 0.20(0.9) + 0.20(0.6)$$

$$W' = 0.245 + 0.125 + 0.18 + 0.12 = 0.67$$

Thus transparency reduces the score. This shows the AI tool lacks clarity. Courts can demand more openness.

9.6 WHY FUZZY MODELS HELP INDIA

The AI systems deployed in these scenarios are questionable. Fuzzy values capture incomplete truths. They avoid making rigid yes/no decisions. They demonstrate varying degrees of tolerance. They support legal and cybersecurity bodies. They promote safe AI deployment. They protect citizens' rights.

10. IMPLEMENTATION FRAMEWORK FOR INDIA

A flexible governance framework for responsible AI must be practical. It must be appropriate for India's legal, administrative, and cybersecurity environments. This section describes each stage in depth. It also includes formulas, models, and examples appropriate for Indian institutions.

10.1 STEP-WISE IMPLEMENTATION MODEL

The full implementation process includes eight core steps:

1. Define governance goals.
2. Identify AI risk domains.

3. Select evaluation criteria.
4. Assign fuzzy membership functions.
5. Construct decision rules.
6. Compute fuzzy scores.
7. Generate recommendations.
8. Review and update scores.

Each step is explained in detail below.

Step 1: Define Governance Goals

India must define clear objectives before deploying AI systems. Common goals include:

- responsible AI usage,
- promoting justice and fairness,
- supporting transparency,
- strengthening cyber defence,
- protecting data under the DPDP Act.

Goal design uses fuzzy priority values.
Let, goals be:

$$G = Fairness$$

$$G = Privacy$$

$$G = Cybersecurity$$

$$G = Transparency$$

$$G_5 = Accountability$$

Assign fuzzy importance weights:

$$W = \{w_1, w_2, w_3, w_4, w_5\}$$

Example values:

$$w_1 = 0.9(veryhighpriority)$$

$w_2 = 0.8$

$w_3 = 0.85$

$w_4 = 0.7$

$w_5 = 0.75$

These values may be defined by:

- Ministry of Electronics and IT (MeitY),
- law officers,
- cybersecurity experts,
- judicial bodies.

Step 2: Identify AI Risk Domains

AI systems in India operate in multiple domains:

$D : LegalAI$

Examples:

- judgment prediction,
- legal document summarization,
- evidence classification,
- bail-risk scoring.

$D : CybersecurityAI$

Examples:

- intrusion-detection systems,
- phishing detection,
- fraud analysis,
- ransomware behaviour analysis.

$D : AdministrativeAI$

Examples:

- e-governance platforms,
- Aadhaar-enabled services,
- document verification.

$D : Law - EnforcementAI$

Examples:

- facial recognition for missing persons,
- crime pattern analysis,
- hotspot prediction.

Fuzzy Risk-Level Assignment

Each domain gets a fuzzy risk score:

$R_d \in [0,1]$

Example:

$LegalAI : R_1 = 0.9$

$CyberAI : R_2 = 0.85$

$AdministrativeAI : R_3 = 0.6$

$Law - enforcementAI : R_4 = 0.95R$

These scores help prioritize regulation.

Step 3: Select Evaluation Criteria

Criteria should reflect the needs of Indian stakeholders.

$Letcriteria =$

$C = Transparency$

$C = Reliability$

$C = PrivacyCompliance$

$C = Bias \ \& \ Fairness$

$C_5 = CybersecurityStrength$

$C_6 = LegalAccountability$

For each AI system A_i values μ_{ij} must be assigned. Example for AI Tool Used in Courts System: AI Sentencing Support Tool

Criteria values:

- Transparency: 0.5
- Reliability: 0.7
- Privacy compliance: 0.9
- Fairness: 0.65
- Cybersecurity strength: 0.8
- Accountability: 0.6

Step 4: Assign Fuzzy Membership Functions

Membership functions convert real values into fuzzy meaning.

Linguistic Terms

Typical terms:

$Low(L)$

$Medium(M)$

$High(H)$

$VeryHigh(VH)$

Triangular Membership Example

For Privacy Compliance (PC):

$$\mu_L(x) = \frac{0.4 - x}{0.4 - 0.2}, 0.2 \leq x \leq 0.4$$

$$\mu_M(x) = \frac{x - 0.3}{0.6 - 0.3}, 0.3 \leq x \leq 0.6$$

$$\mu_H(x) = \frac{x - 0.5}{0.9 - 0.5}, 0.5 \leq x \leq 0.9$$

Interpretation

$$x = 0.9, gives\, \mu_H(x) = 1.0$$

$$x = 0.5 is a boundary case$$

$$x = 0.3 is mostly low or medium$$

This helps convert subjective judgment into mathematical form.

Step 5: Construct Fuzzy Rules

Rules guide decision making.

Example Rule Set

Rule 1:
IF Privacy is High AND Fairness is High
THEN Accept System
Rule 2:
IF Transparency is Low
THEN Require Audit
Rule 3:
IF Cybersecurity is Medium AND Risk is High
THEN Strengthen Defence
Rule 4:
IF Accountability is Low
THEN Increase Oversight

Mathematical Form

For Rule 1:

$$\alpha_1 = min(\mu_{PC}, \mu_F)$$

If:

- $\mu_{PC} = 0.9,$

$\mathbf{v}\ \mu_F = 0.65,$

Then:

$$\alpha_1 = min(0.9, 0.65) = 0.65$$

Thus Rule 1 fires with strength 0.65.

Step 6: Compute Fuzzy Scores

You already established the formula:

$$S(A_i) = \sum_{j=1}^{n} w_j \mu_{ij}$$

Extended Example (6 Criteria)

Criteria weights:

$$w = 0.15$$

$$w = 0.20$$

$$w = 0.20$$

$$w = 0.15$$

$$w_5 = 0.15$$

$$w_6 = 0.15$$

Values:

$$\mu = 0.5$$

$$\mu = 0.7$$

$$\mu = 0.9$$

$$\mu = 0.65$$

$$\mu_5 = 0.8$$

$\mu_6 = 0.6$

$$S(A)=0.15(0.5)+0.20(0.7)+0.20(0.9)+0.15(0.65)+0.15(0.8)+0.15(0.6)$$

$$S(A) = 0.075 + 0.14 + 0.18 + 0.0975 + 0.12 + 0.09$$

$$S(A) = 0.7025$$

Thus, the AI system receives a score of 0.70.
India may use thresholds for decision making.

Step 7: Provide Final Recommendations

Based on fuzzy scores:

$$If S > 0.80 \rightarrow Fully Approve$$

$$If 0.65 \leq S \leq 0.80 \rightarrow Approve with Monitoring$$

$$If 0.50 \leq S < 0.65 \rightarrow Improve and Re-evaluate$$

$$If S < 0.50 \rightarrow Reject System$$

In our example, $S = 0.70$
Thus:
Approve with Monitoring
This ensures accountability.

Step 8: Review and Update

AI governance must be dynamic.
Fuzzy scores change when:

- new risks appear,
- laws are updated,
- datasets evolve,
- system behaviour changes.

Let, S_t be the score at time t.

Let, λ be the update factor.
The updated score:

$$S_{t+1} = \lambda S_t + (1 - \lambda)S_{new}$$

Example:

$$\lambda = 0.8$$

$$old = 0.70$$

$$new = 0.75$$

$$S_{t+1} = 0.8(0.70) + 0.2(0.75) = 0.71$$

This shows stability and controlled change.

Figure 2.

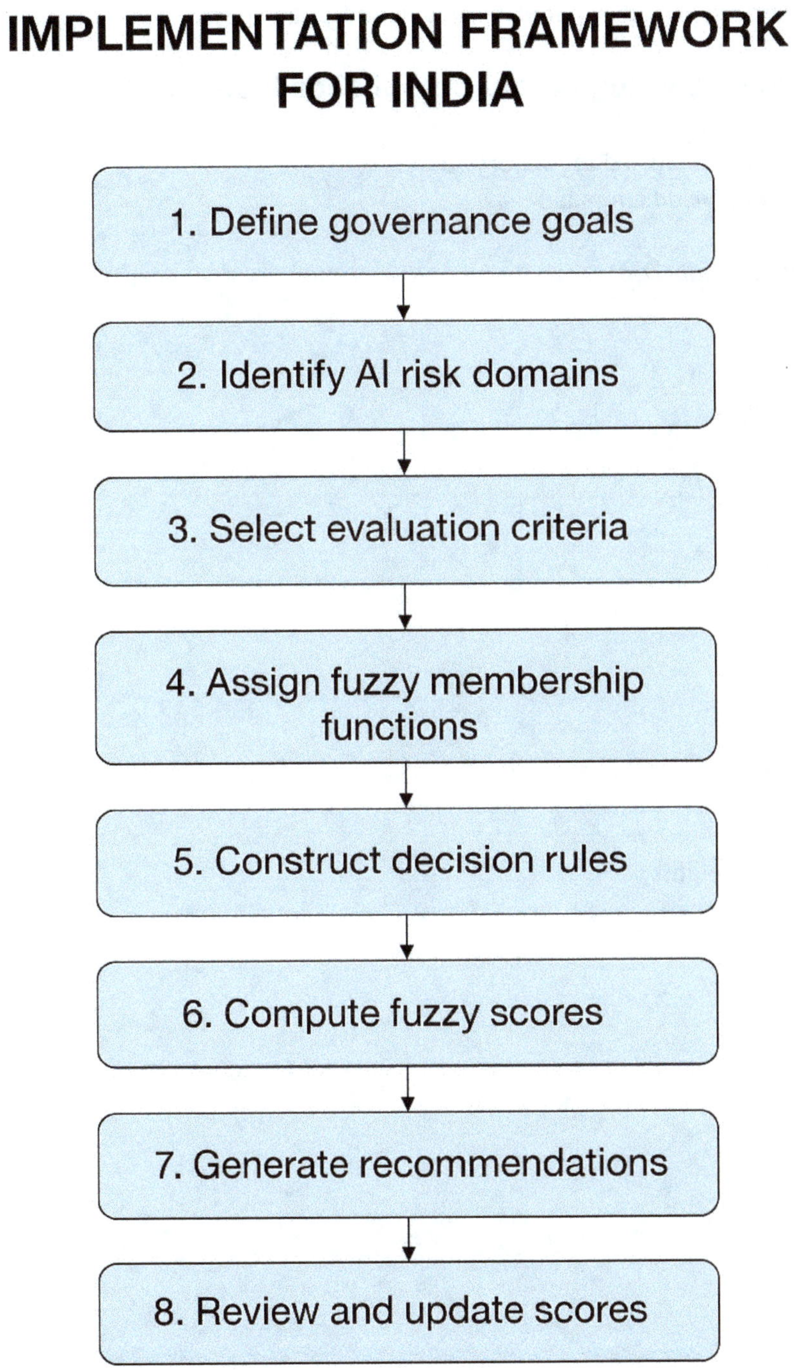
IMPLEMENTATION FRAMEWORK FOR INDIA
1. Define governance goals
2. Identify AI risk domains
3. Select evaluation criteria
4. Assign fuzzy membership functions
5. Construct decision rules
6. Compute fuzzy scores
7. Generate recommendations
8. Review and update scores

11. FUZZY GOVERNANCE MODELS FOR INDIA

This section provides complete models India can adopt.

Model 1: Fuzzy Regulatory Compliance Index (FRCI)

India needs a unified regulatory score.
Let compliance factors be:

$DataMinimization(DM)$

$Privacy(PP)$

$Accountability(AC)$

$Transparency(TR)$

$BiasControl(BC)$

$Safety(SF)$

Define:

$$FRCI = \sum_i w_i \mu_i$$

Example weights:

DM:0.10

PP:0.20

AC:0.20

TR:0.15

BC:0.20

SF:0.15

If all values are assigned, agencies can compute a compliance score.

Model 2: National Fuzzy Risk Index (NFRI)

This model estimates national-level AI risk.
Let risk dimensions be:

$R:DataMisuse$

$R:SurveillanceAbuse$

$R:AlgorithmicBias$

$R:CyberThreat$

$R_5:LegalGaps$

NFRI:

$$NFRI = max(R_1, R_2, R_3, R_4, R_5)$$

Interpretation:

- If any risk is high, overall risk is high.
- This follows fuzzy union logic.

Model 3: Fuzzy Court AI Acceptance Model (FCAAM)

Yes/No decisions for courts cannot be crisp.
Fuzzy acceptance is more appropriate.
Let factors:

$FairnessF$

$ExplainabilityE$

$ErrorConsistencyC$

$Human - in - the - loopIntegrationH$

Acceptance score:

$$A = min(F, E, H)$$

All must meet basic thresholds.
If:

F = 0.7

E = 0.6

H = 0.9

Then:

$$A = min(0.7, 0.6, 0.9) = 0.6$$

Thus, system requires improvement.

Model 4: Fuzzy Cybersecurity Readiness Model

Let readiness factors:

$$IntrusionDetectionStrength(ID)$$

$$EncryptionLevel(EN)$$

$$ResponseSpeed(RS)$$

$$CSR = min(ID, EN, RS)$$

This highlights weakest links.

Advantages of Fuzzy Logic for Indian AI Governance

India's AI governance environment is uncertain and evolving.
Fuzzy logic matches this complexity.

Advantages

1. handles vague laws,
2. supports interdisciplinary evaluations,

3. combines expert judgment,
4. improves transparency of decisions,
5. reduced risk of rigid rules,
6. assists dynamic policy updating.
7. aligns with the DPDP Act and global guidelines

Limitations and Considerations

Even fuzzy models have constraints.

- membership assignment requires expertise,
- subjective bias may enter rating scales,
- needs continuous calibration,
- requires staff training,
- cannot solve political disputes alone,
- must integrate with classical regulation.

Limitations and Challenges

While the proposed fuzzy logic–driven governance framework offers multiple advantages for responsible AI adoption in India, several limitations and challenges must be acknowledged to maintain academic transparency and balance.

1. Data Availability Constraints: Many legal and cybersecurity institutions in India still lack high-quality, structured, and interoperable datasets. Since fuzzy-based evaluation relies on expert input and contextual data, limited data availability may affect the accuracy of the fuzzy scores and risk assessments.
2. Institutional Readiness Gaps: The implementation of fuzzy governance models requires trained personnel, technical capacity, and institutional readiness. Variations in preparedness across Indian courts, regulatory bodies, and cybersecurity institutions may restrict uniform adoption.
3. Interpretability and Complexity Issues: Although fuzzy logic enhances decision-making under uncertainty, the underlying membership functions, rule bases, and inference systems may appear complex to non-technical stakeholders. This may hinder widespread acceptance among legal practitioners and policymakers.
4. Challenges in Standardizing Governance Criteria: India's AI ecosystem is highly diverse, spanning sectors such as law enforcement, healthcare, e-commerce, judiciary, and cybersecurity. Creating a single standardized set of fuzzy evaluation criteria for all these domains is difficult and may require continuous customization.

5. Dependence on Expert Judgments: Fuzzy systems depend heavily on expert-assigned weights, risk ratings, and membership functions. Variation in expert perspectives may introduce subjectivity, affecting consistency across different evaluations.
6. Evolving Nature of AI Risks: AI risks and governance threats evolve rapidly, especially in cybersecurity, data privacy, and algorithmic bias. Fuzzy rules and criteria must therefore be updated frequently. Static or outdated rule-bases can weaken the reliability of the governance framework.
7. Limited Real-World Validation: Although the model is theoretically robust, large-scale empirical validation in Indian legal and cybersecurity institutions is still limited. Pilot testing across courts, CERT bodies, and digital governance platforms is necessary to confirm practical effectiveness.
8. Policy and Regulatory Uncertainty: India's responsible AI ecosystem is still evolving, with multiple guidelines but limited binding regulation. Changes in digital public policy may require modifications in the governance model, leading to implementation uncertainty.

Policy Recommendations for India

To strengthen fuzzy-governance adoption:

Recommendation 1: Create a National Fuzzy AI Evaluation Framework (NFAIEF).
Recommendation 2: Train judiciary and officials in fuzzy methods.
Recommendation 3: Include fuzzy risk ratings in licensing AI systems.
Recommendation 4: Integrate fuzzy models in cybersecurity audits.
Recommendation 5: Mandate fuzzy transparency scoring for high-risk AI.

12. CONCLUSION

India is aggressively adopting AI in courts, policing, government services, and cybersecurity. These technologies have numerous benefits, but they also pose significant hazards such as bias, privacy violations, lack of transparency, and new types of cyber threats. Traditional rule-based techniques cannot adequately address these issues since AI choices are frequently unclear and unpredictable.

This chapter demonstrated that fuzzy logic is a powerful and useful tool for responsible AI governance in India. Fuzzy logic allows us to express judgment in degrees rather than just "yes" or "no" answers. It allows policymakers to more precisely assess fairness, risk, openness, privacy, and security. It also helps in decision-making when information is incomplete or imprecise.

We introduced fuzzy risk models, fuzzy rule-based systems, and fuzzy multi-criteria decision-making methods for evaluating and monitoring artificial intelligence systems. These models can assist courts, government departments, and cybersecurity teams in making more secure and balanced decisions. The step-by-step architecture presented in this chapter demonstrates how India may create a flexible and adaptable governance structure that updates itself as AI technologies advance.

Overall, fuzzy logic provides India with a straightforward, clear, and dependable approach to responsible AI management. It can assist to defend citizens' rights, build trust, and ensure that AI technology are employed safely and fairly. As AI advances, fuzzy logic will remain a crucial instrument for India's digital future, ensuring its security and ethics.

Future Works

There is still much to discover in the subject of AI governance with fuzzy logic. Future research can concentrate on developing stronger and more accurate fuzzy models that meet India's actual demands. More research is needed to evaluate these models in actual courts, police departments, government offices, and cybersecurity centers. This will allow us to better understand how fuzzy logic works in real-world situations.

Future work could entail creating larger datasets to train and evaluate AI systems. Improved data will make fuzzy decisions more reliable. Another major path is to combine fuzzy logic with other modern technologies like machine learning, blockchain, and quantum computing to improve security and transparency.

India also requires systems that can automatically track AI behaviour over time. Creating real-time fuzzy dashboards for judges, politicians, and cybersecurity professionals may be a beneficial move. Future research can also look into how fuzzy logic can help support new laws and policies under the DPDP Act, as well as impending national AI regulations.

Finally, more training programs should be developed for government officials, legal experts, and cybersecurity specialists to help them comprehend and apply fuzzy models successfully. With more study and actual testing, fuzzy logic has the potential to provide an even stronger basis for secure, fair, and trustworthy AI governance in India.

REFERENCES

Aljohani, A. (2025). A decision-support framework for evaluating AI-enabled ESG strategies in the context of sustainable manufacturing systems. *Scientific Reports, 15*. Advance online publication. DOI: 10.1038/s41598-025-09569-9 PMID: 40615575

Chen, J. (2025). BiLSTM-enhanced legal text extraction model using fuzzy logic and metaphor recognition. *PeerJ. Computer Science, 11*. Advance online publication. DOI: 10.7717/peerj-cs.2697 PMID: 40062303

Das, A. K. (2016). On partially included intuitionistic fuzzy rough relations. *Afrika Matematika, 27*, 993–1001. DOI: 10.1007/s13370-016-0395-2

Das, A. K. (2018). Weighted fuzzy soft multiset and decision-making. *International Journal of Machine Learning and Cybernetics, 9*, 787–794. DOI: 10.1007/s13042-016-0607-y

Das, A. K., Das, R., Das, S., Debnath, B. K., Granados, C., Shil, B., & Das, R. (2025c). A comprehensive study of neutrosophic SuperHyper BCI-semigroups and their algebraic significance. *Transactions on Fuzzy Sets and Systems, 4*(2), 80–101. DOI: 10.71602/tfss.2025.1198050

Das, A. K., Das, R., Datta, R., & Granados, C. (2025e). An Innovative Approach to Group Decision-Making Based on Weighted Hypersoft Expert System. In Smarandache, F., Jdid, M., & Leyva-Vazquez, M. (Eds.), *Neutrosophic and Plithogenic Inventory Models for Applied Mathematics* (pp. 483–518). IGI Global Scientific Publishing., DOI: 10.4018/979-8-3693-3204-7.ch019

Das, A. K., & Granados, C. (2021). An advanced approach to fuzzy soft group decision-making using weighted average ratings. *SN Computer Science, 2*, 471. DOI: 10.1007/s42979-021-00873-5

Das, A. K., & Granados, C. (2022a). A new fuzzy parameterized intuitionistic fuzzy soft multiset theory and group decision-making. *Journal of Current Science and Technology, 12*(3), 547–567. DOI: 10.14456/jcst.2022.42

Das, A. K., & Granados, C. (2022b). FP-intuitionistic multi fuzzy N-soft set and its induced FP-Hesitant N soft set in decision-making. *Decision Making: Applications in Management and Engineering, 5*(1), 67–89. DOI: 10.31181/dmame181221045d

Das, A. K., & Granados, C. (2023a). IFP-intuitionistic multi fuzzy N-soft set and its induced IFP-hesitant N-soft set in decision-making. *Journal of Ambient Intelligence and Humanized Computing, 14*, 10143–10152. DOI: 10.1007/s12652-021-03677-w

Das, A. K., & Granados, C. (2023b). Preference intuitionistic fuzzy rough relation and its theoretical approach. *Journal of the Indian Mathematical Society*, *90*(3-4), 199–212.

Das, A. K., Granados, C., & Bhattacharya, J. (2022). Some new operations on fuzzy soft sets and their applications in decision-making. *Songklanakarin Journal of Science and Technology*, *44*(2), 440–449. DOI: 10.14456/sjst-psu.2022.61

Das, A. K., Gupta, N., Das, R., Das, S., Das, R., Granados, C., & Debnath, B. K. (2026a). Fuzzy Logic-Driven Strategies for Diversity and Inclusion in Multicultural Marketing. In Tarnanidis, T., Sousa, B., Vlachopoulou, M., Papachristou, E., & Kittu Manda, V. (Eds.), *Diversity and Inclusion-Driven Marketing for Multicultural Marketplaces* (pp. 189–236). IGI Global Scientific Publishing., DOI: 10.4018/979-8-3373-2111-0.ch009

Das, A. K., Gupta, N., Das, R., Granados, C., & Das, S. (2026c). Neutrosophic Sets for Decision-Making in Natural Disasters and Environmental Recovery. In Ezaier, Y., Gaamouche, R., & Lahby, M. (Eds.), *Computational Intelligence and Optimization Methods for Sustainable Water Management* (pp. 119–162). IGI Global Scientific Publishing., DOI: 10.4018/979-8-3373-2700-6.ch004

. Das, A. K., Gupta, N., Das, R., Mallik, R., & Das, S. (2025i). Interval-valued neutrosophic rough soft set based intelligent multi-criteria decision-making framework. Boletim da Sociedade Paranaense de Matemática (3rd Series), 43, 1–26. https://doi .org/DOI: 10.5269/bspm.76016

Das, A. K., Gupta, N., Fujita, T., Das, S., Granados, C., Debnath, B. K., & Das, R. (2026b). Advanced Co-Branding Strategies for Smart Luxury Products: A Multi-Criteria Decision-Making Approach Using Neutrosophic Sets. In Tarnanidis, T., Sousa, B., Vlachopoulou, M., Papachristou, E., & Kittu Manda, V. (Eds.), *Co-Branding Strategies for Smart Luxury Products* (pp. 203–258). IGI Global Scientific Publishing., DOI: 10.4018/979-8-3373-3010-5.ch006

Das, A. K., Gupta, N., & Granados, C. (2023). Weighted hesitant bipolar-valued fuzzy soft set in decision-making. *Songklanakarin Journal of Science and Technology*, *45*(6), 681–690. https://sjst.psu.ac.th/journal/45-6/10.pdf

Das, A. K., Gupta, N., Granados, C., Das, R., & Das, S. (2024b). Neutrosophic Approach to Water Quality Assessment: A Case Study of Gomati River, the Largest River in Tripura, India. *Neutrosophic Systems with Applications*, *22*, 1–12. DOI: 10.61356/j.nswa.2024.22386

Das, A. K., Gupta, N., Mahmood, T., Das, R., Das, S., & Granados, C. (2025j). *Assessment of groundwater quality in Agartala, Tripura, Northeast India using an effective fuzzy multicriteria decision-making model.* In J. Das, B. Pradhan, R. Mitra, P. Chouhan, C. Lee, & U. Chatterjee (Eds.), *Developments in Environmental Science* (Vol. 19, pp. 311–333). Elsevier. https://doi.org/DOI: 10.1016/B978-0-443-33787-1.00023-X

Das, A. K., Gupta, N., Mahmood, T., Tripathy, B. C., Das, R., & Das, S. (2024a). Assessing anthropogenic influences on the water quality of Gomati River using an innovative weighted fuzzy soft set based water pollution rating system. *Discover Water*, *4*, 73. DOI: 10.1007/s43832-024-00136-3

Das, A. K., Gupta, N., Mahmood, T., Tripathy, B. C., Das, R., & Das, S. (2025a). An efficient water quality evaluation model using weighted hesitant fuzzy soft sets for water pollution rating. In Kumar, A., Kumar, P., Rathee, S., & Kumar, B. (Eds.), *Mechatronics: Concepts, Tools, Applications, and New Trends* (1st ed., p. 17). CRC Press., DOI: 10.1201/9781003494478-10

Das, A. K., Gupta, N., Mahmood, T., Tripathy, B. C., Das, R., & Das, S. (2025b). An innovative fuzzy multi-criteria decision making model for analyzing anthropogenic influences on urban river water quality. *Iran Journal of Computer Science*, *8*, 103–124. DOI: 10.1007/s42044-024-00211-x

Das, A. K., Gupta, N., Mahmood, T., Tripathy, B. C., Das, R., & Das, S. (2025g). Anthropogenic Impacts on Urban River Water Quality for Rating Water Pollution Using an Effective Fuzzy Soft Multi Criteria Group Decision Making Model. *Iraqi Journal of Science*, *66*(9), 3921–3937. DOI: 10.24996/ijs.2025.66.9.32

Das, A. K., Gupta, N., Mahmood, T., Tripathy, B. C., Das, R., & Das, S. (2025h). Analyzing seasonal changes and anthropogenic impacts on urban river water quality using a weighted fuzzy soft set-based multi-criteria decision-making model: A case study of the Manu River, India. *Arabian Journal of Geosciences*, *18*, 228. DOI: 10.1007/s12517-025-12323-0

Das, A. K., Mahmood, T., Das, R., & Das, S. (2025d). Optimizing Inventory Levels in Retail: Fuzzy Logic-Based Decision Support Systems for Adaptive Inventory Management. In Jana, S., Basu Mallik, B., Sarkar, A., & Jana, C. (Eds.), *Applications of Fuzzy Logic in Decision Making and Management Science. Information Systems Engineering and Management* (Vol. 29). Springer., DOI: 10.1007/978-3-031-77719-6_8

Das, A. K., Patra, S., & Granados, C. (2025f). An innovative approach to hesitant bipolar fuzzy soft sets in multi-criteria group decision-making. Adv. in Comp. *Int.*, *5*, 4. DOI: 10.1007/s43674-025-00082-0

Das, S., Barve, A., Sahu, N., & Muduli, K. (2023). Enabling artificial intelligence for sustainable food grain supply chains: An agri 5.0 and circular economy perspective. *Operations Management Research*, *16*, 2104–2124. DOI: 10.1007/s12063-023-00390-z

. Das, S., Mallik, R., Shil, B., Bardhan, R., Das, A.K. (2025k) The Impact of Management of Interactive Learning Environments on Mathematical Proficiency: A Neutrosophic Overview, Boletim da Sociedade Paranaense de Matemática (3rd Series), 43, 1–6. https://doi.org/DOI: 10.5269/bspm.76458

Devarajan, M., Khan, M., Sandeep, K., Hamza, L., Soujanya, K., & Munirathinam, S. (2025). Smart Manufacturing Assessment on Cybersecurity Risks using Bayesian and Hybrid Fuzzy Logic Networks. *2025 International Conference on Computational Innovations and Engineering Sustainability (ICCIES)*, 1-6. https://doi.org/DOI: 10.1109/iccies63851.2025.11032583

Dixit, S., Tripathi, T., & Singh, R. (2025). *Incorporating Artificial Intelligence into India's Judicial and Law Enforcement Systems*. International Journal For Multidisciplinary Research., DOI: 10.36948/ijfmr.2025.v07i02.41822

. Granados, C., Das, A.K., Das, B. (2022). Some continuous neutrosophic distributions with neutrosophic parameters based on neutrosophic random variables. Advances in the Theory of Nonlinear Analysis and its Applications, 33(2): 293-308. https://doi.org/DOI: 10.31197/atnaa.1056480

. Granados, C., Das, A.K., Osu, B. (2023). Weighted neutrosophic soft multiset and its application to decision making. Yugoslav journal of operations research, 33(2): 293-308. https://doi.org/DOI: 10.2298/YJOR220915034G

Gupta, N., Das, A. K., & Granados, C. (2026). Integrating Traditional Ecological Knowledge with Fuzzy Logic and Quantum Computing for Sustainable Agriculture in Tribal Areas of Tripura. In Horng, M., Khalaf, O., Shieh, C., & Jain, V. (Eds.), *Revolutionizing Sustainable Food Production With Quantum Computing* (pp. 177–214). IGI Global Scientific Publishing., DOI: 10.4018/979-8-3373-3957-3.ch006

Hu, K., Chen, F., Hsu, M., & Tzeng, G. (2023). Governance of artificial intelligence applications in a business audit via a fusion fuzzy multiple rule-based decision-making model. *Financial Innovation*, *9*, 1–31. DOI: 10.1186/s40854-022-00436-4

Kim, S., Yi, S., & Park, S. (2025). Prioritizing challenges in AI adoption for the legal domain: A systematic review and expert-driven AHP analysis. *PLoS One*, *20*. Advance online publication. DOI: 10.1371/journal.pone.0326028 PMID: 40554557

. Kolo, F. (2025). Responsible AI for Cybersecurity: Assessing the Barriers, Biases and Governance Gaps in Implementation with E-commerce Systems. *Journal of Engineering Research and Reports*. https://doi.org/.DOI: 10.9734/jerr/2025/v27i51520

Kumar, N. (2025). From Surveillance to Sentencing: Evaluating AI's Role in Indian Criminal Justice. *Science Bulletin*, *30*, 68–78. DOI: 10.2478/bsaft-2025-0008

Lu, Q., Zhu, L., Xu, X., Whittle, J., Zowghi, D., & Jacquet, A. (2022). Responsible AI Pattern Catalogue: A Collection of Best Practices for AI Governance and Engineering. *ACM Computing Surveys*, *56*, 1–35. DOI: 10.1145/3626234

Madanchian, M., & Taherdoost, H. (2025). Ethical theories, governance models, and strategic frameworks for responsible AI adoption and organizational success. *Frontiers in Artificial Intelligence*, *8*. Advance online publication. DOI: 10.3389/frai.2025.1619029 PMID: 40741285

Malik, A., Kumar, A., Salih, S., Kim, S., Kim, N., Yaseen, Z., & Singh, V. (2020). Drought index prediction using advanced fuzzy logic model: Regional case study over Kumaon in India. *PLoS One*, *15*. Advance online publication. DOI: 10.1371/journal.pone.0233280 PMID: 32437386

Manoj, C., & Jeevanandhan, L. (2025). *AI in Indian Governance*. Electronic Journal of Social and Strategic Studies., DOI: 10.47362/ejsss.2025.6607

. Mcintosh, T., Sušnjak, T., Liu, T., Watters, P., Nowrozy, R., & Halgamuge, M. (2024). From COBIT to ISO 42001: Evaluating Cybersecurity Frameworks for Opportunities, Risks, and Regulatory Compliance in Commercializing Large Language Models. ArXiv, abs/2402.15770. https://doi.org/.DOI: 10.1016/j.cose.2024.103964

Misra, S., Sharma, S., Gupta, S., & Das, S. (2023). A framework to overcome challenges to the adoption of artificial intelligence in Indian Government Organizations. *Technological Forecasting and Social Change*. Advance online publication. DOI: 10.1016/j.techfore.2023.122721

Mukherjee, A., & Das, A. K. (2015a). Application of interval valued intuitionistic fuzzy soft set in investment decision making, *2015 Fifth International Conference on Advances in Computing and Communications (ICACC)*, Kochi, India, 2015, pp. 61-64, https://doi.org/DOI: 10.1109/ICACC.2015.37

Mukherjee, A., & Das, A. K. (2015b). Interval valued intuitionistic fuzzy soft multi set theoretic approach to decision making problems, 2015 International Conference on Computer, Communication and Control (IC4), Indore, India, 2015, pp. 1-5, https://doi.org/DOI: 10.1109/IC4.2015.7375640

Mukherjee, A., & Das, A. K. (2022). Einstein operations on fuzzy soft multisets and decision making. *Boletim da Sociedade Paranaense de Matematica*, *40*, 1–10. DOI: 10.5269/bspm.32546

Mukherjee, A., & Das, A. K. (2023). Essentials of fuzzy soft multisets: Theory and applications, Springer Nature Singapore Pte Ltd., 1-151. ISBN: 978-981-19-2759-1, https://doi.org/DOI: 10.1007/978-981-19-2760-7

Mukherjee, A., Das, A. K., Gupta, N., Patra, S., Mahmood, T., Das, S., & Das, R. (2026). A novel generalized interval-valued neutrosophic rough soft set framework for enhanced decision-making: Application in water quality assessment. *Transactions on Fuzzy Sets and Systems*, *5*(1), 1–25. DOI: 10.71602/tfss.2026.1194037

. N, S., & Rajagopal, A. (2024). A study on role of artificial intelligence in detecting and preventing cyber crimes in India. International Journal of Advanced Research in Science. *Tongxin Jishu*. Advance online publication. DOI: 10.48175/ijarsct-22635

. R, C., & Salman, S. (2023). The Present State of Artificial Intelligence in the Indian Legal System and its Monitoring. June-July 2023. https://doi.org/.DOI: 10.55529/jls.34.12.21

Radanliev, P. (2025). Frontier AI regulation: What form should it take? *Frontiers in Political Science*. Advance online publication. DOI: 10.3389/fpos.2025.1561776

Ravishankar, S. (2025). *The role of artificial intelligence in arbitration: Prospects for India*. International Journal for Multidisciplinary Research., DOI: 10.36948/ijfmr.2025.v07i02.41005

Sane, G., & Thombre, S. (2025). Artificial Intelligence in Indian Legal Services: Challenges and a Strategic Framework. 2025 1st International Conference on AIML-Applications for Engineering & Technology (ICAET), 1-6. https://doi.org/DOI: 10.1109/icaet63349.2025.10932285

Shah, S. (2024). *Trust Dynamics in the Digital Economy: Ethical AI and Data Governance Frameworks*. Premier Journal of Artificial Intelligence., DOI: 10.70389/pjai.100005

Sharma, M., Joshi, S., Kannan, D., Govindan, K., Singh, R., & Purohit, H. (2020). Internet of Things (IoT) adoption barriers of smart cities' waste management: An Indian context. *Journal of Cleaner Production*, *270*, 122047. DOI: 10.1016/j.jclepro.2020.122047

. Singh, A., Dwivedi, A., Agrawal, D., & Singh, D. (2023). Identifying issues in adoption of AI practices in construction supply chains: towards managing sustainability. *Operations Management Research*, 1 - 17. https://doi.org/.DOI: 10.1007/s12063-022-00344-x

Singh, M., & Sodhi, P. (2025). *The role of law in the growing realm of Artificial Intelligence vis-a-vis the concern of Cyber Security*. International Journal for Multidisciplinary Research., DOI: 10.36948/ijfmr.2025.v07i02.39608

Taeihagh, A. (2021). Governance of artificial intelligence. *Policy and Society*, *40*, 137–157. DOI: 10.1080/14494035.2021.1928377

Toapanta, T. M., Buenaño, J. J., Vayas, C. S., Nogales, P. R., Del Pozo, D. R., Orizaga, T. A., & Andrade, A. D. (2025). Perspectives on a Cybersecurity Governance Framework Integrating Blockchain, Artificial Intelligence, and Legal Base for one Organization. *Journal of Posthumanism*, *5*(5), 2701–2718. DOI: 10.63332/joph.v5i5.1664

Venkatesh, P., Mukesh, V., Kumar, S., & Gowtham, G. (2025). Optimizing Legal Service Delivery Using AI-Based Incentives for E-Marketplaces in India. *2025 International Conference on Knowledge Engineering and Communication Systems (ICKECS)*, 1-10. https://doi.org/DOI: 10.1109/ickecs65700.2025.11035228

Wirtz, B., Weyerer, J., & Kehl, I. (2022). Governance of artificial intelligence: A risk and guideline-based integrative framework. *Government Information Quarterly*, *39*, 101685. DOI: 10.1016/j.giq.2022.101685

Zadeh, L. A. (1965). Fuzzy sets. *Information and Control*, *8*(3), 338–353.

Chapter 11
"Click, Trap, Repeat": Dark Patterns and the Illusion of Choice in the Digital Market

Akanksha
http://orcid.org/0009-0002-8975-3967
Christ University, India

ABSTRACT

This chapter will look into how AI has transformed the traditional methods of dark patterns, which are deceptive, manipulative designs used to trick users into decisions that wouldn't have been made if such patterns were not introduced. It will analyse how such patterns use predictive reasonings across e-commerce, social media, and fintech platforms, influencing consumer behavior and their decision-making. The chapter highlights the wide regulatory gap in addressing the manipulations and ethical implications by drawing on global developments from the European Union, the United States, and Asia. The study aims to provide a multidisciplinary understanding of how AI boosts digital deception and to propose a legal framework that safeguards user autonomy, promotes transparency, and ensures accountability in an AI-mediated consumer environment

A. INTRODUCTION TO DARK PATTERNS: DEFINITION, ORIGIN, AND EVOLUTION

1. Background and Context

The digital revolution has enormously transformed how consumers engage with technology. From online shopping to social networking and mobile applications, the global digital economy is now a part of everyday life. However, the ease and

DOI: 10.4018/979-8-3373-7685-1.ch011

innovation often conceal a troubling development - the manipulation of user behavior through deceptive interface designs called dark patterns. Dark patterns are designed to take advantage of psychological biases and cognitive limits, leading consumers toward choices that benefit businesses at the expense of consumer welfare (Mathur et al., 2021).

While unintentional design flaws can lead to dark patterns, deliberately designed dark patterns produce influence over user behavior. Through dark patterns, the distinction between persuasive and deceptive design has been blurred, eroding trust, autonomy, and fairness in digital markets. Dark patterns are becoming more nuanced as e-commerce, fintech, and social media platform markets increasingly depend on algorithmic recommendation systems and artificial intelligence systems (Gray et al., 2023).

2. Definition and Conceptual Understanding

The term dark pattern was coined by Harry Brignull in 2010. He defined it as " *tricks used in websites and apps that make you do things that you didn't mean to"(*Brignull 2010). Since then, these patterns have evolved from simple interfaces like pre-checked boxes and disguised ads into complex systems driven by AI. These designs use consumer data, behaviour profiling, and algorithm predictions to affect decision-making in real time. What was once a static design trick has now become a dynamic system of persuasion powered by artificial intelligence, enabling platforms to personalize manipulation based on users' emotions, preferences, and vulnerabilities. Brignull's work sparked a lot of research on how interface design can influence cognitive biases, such as scarcity, urgency, and loss aversion. This can lead users to take actions they didn't intend (Leiser, 2020). Originally seen in e-commerce and app design, dark patterns now exist in many areas, including financial technology, healthcare apps, social media, and AI-driven personalization systems (Mathur, Mayer, & Kshirsagar, 2021).

Globally, these patterns have become a growing concern as they undermine user autonomy. By masking manipulative tactics as convenience or personalization, companies hide how much control they really have over online decision-making. Studies show that both younger and older adults respond differently to these patterns, highlighting an age-related vulnerability to online deception (Ghaiumy Anaraky et al., 2023). This manipulation often happens without the user's clear awareness, damaging trust and causing digital fatigue. Beyond individual harm, these practices disrupt fair competition and market transparency by favouring manipulative design over ethical innovation (Day et al., 2019).

3. Historical Evolution

Initially, dark patterns originated with rapid increases in online buying in the late 1990s and early 2000s. For instance, misleading advertising, fake scarcity ("Only two seats left!"), and the cancellation process was obscured. These were static designs, applying the same manipulation for all users.

However, this shifted dramatically in the decade of data analytics, algorithmic personalization, and AI in the 2010s. Modern dark patterns are no longer static, instead being adaptive in nature—they adapt to user data, behaviour, and emotional signals. AI algorithms analyse users' browsing history, time spent on pages, and even facial or vocal signals to optimize what would be most likely to compel them to click or buy (Deligoz, 2025). It could be, for example, that the platform sends their "deal of the day" late at night, i.e., while they are tired, or produces a reordered list of search results to show higher profit items first.

The transition from the use of vague interface deception to the use of data to drive deception behaviour has distinctively changed how users' psychological weaknesses can be manipulated at scale. These behavioural manipulations augmented by AI are also referred to as "adaptive dark patterns," a far more powerful, personalized, and difficult to track type of manipulation (Gray et al., 2023).

4.Psychological Mechanisms Behind Dark Patterns

The power of dark patterns is indebted to humans' cognitive biases that are mental shortcuts allowing us to make quick decisions, but that often lead to predictable errors. The following cultural biases are among the most common:

- Scarcity bias- Users perceive items to have more value when it appears they are less available (e.g., "Only 1 left in stock!").
- Social proof -Products seem more trustworthy with fake or exaggerated product reviews (e.g., "5,000 people bought this today").
- Loss aversion -Humans are more afraid of losing something than a missed gain (e.g., "Your discount expires in 5 minutes!").
- Anchoring effect - Initial price information creates a psychological anchor (e.g., "Was 999, now 499"), even with a false discount.
- Default bias -Users stay with the pre-selected option; therefore, companies can pre-check boxes for data sharing or subscriptions. These manipulations create an illusion of user control, whereas their options are pre-structured to benefit the corporation despite apparent user agency (Binns, 2022). The blurring of persuasive design and AI personalization allows companies to target

each user's unique weaknesses and treat decision-making as a data-driven psychological experiment.

5. Worldwide Significance and Consequences

Dark patterns have emerged as a global issue, extending beyond geography, language, and legal frameworks. In developed economies like the U.S. and the European Union, authorities have begun to consider them unfair or deceptive trade practices. The EU Digital Services Act (2024) expressly prohibits designs that "deceive or materially distort" user behaviour, while in the U.S. the Federal Trade Commission has begun enforcement actions against companies that use manipulative subscription traps and false urgency tactics (FTC, 2023).

Conversely, in developing economies - particularly in Asia, Africa, and Latin America - digital literacy tends to be lower, and there is limited awareness or understanding of manipulative design practices. Millions of new internet users are entering online markets without a basic understanding of how their data and choices are being manipulated. This creates a global asymmetry in power where technology companies can take advantage of the regulatory gaps and cultural vulnerabilities. In this sense, dark patterns increasingly impact not only individual users but also the overall picture of systemic digital inequality.

6. The Role of Artificial Intelligence

Artificial intelligence has radically shifted the nature and extent of dark patterns. While dark patterns of the past were designed manually, contemporary AI systems automate the optimization of designs to pursue business aims, such as maximizing engagement or sales. For example, machine learning models automatically test interface layouts and alter them depending on how users respond, in effect learning how to manipulate a user.

So, AI, for example, could identify when users linger or demonstrate hesitation at the checkout page before payment is completed, and immediately generate an emotional cue, such as flashing messages that say "limited time offer," to put them into the impulse purchase category. AI can also profile a user and manipulate the defaults, notifications, content visibility, and other manipulative design elements to influence action (Deligoz, 2025). So, while AI comprises an intelligent analysis of the user's behaviour, it also equivocates between personalization and coercion. Emerging research on algorithms highlights fundamental ethical questions about algorithms, accountability, and informed consent.

7. Need for Regulation and Ethical Design

The worldwide expansion of dark patterns has created an increasing demand for ethical design principles and improved legal frameworks. Ethical design centres on transparency, autonomy, and fairness, allowing users to truly understand their choices. Scholars such as Mathur et al. (2021) and Narayanan et al. (2020) contend that deceptive design risks adversely affect digital democracy, and this manipulation must be addressed through regulation and awareness.

Regulators across the world are beginning to take action, but with varying urgency. The European Union, the United States, and India are beginning to add anti-dark-pattern factors into consumer protection and data privacy laws. The challenge is that manipulative design is difficult to prove, evolves quickly, and can be hidden by technology.

Ultimately, combating dark patterns needs the cooperation of technologists, lawmakers, psychologists, and designers alike. The ambition is not just to punish deception but to reimagine digital design as a force for good, a context where technology will enhance human agency rather than degrade it.

B.TYPES AND MECHANISM OF DARK PATTERNS

Dark patterns appear in various forms throughout online platforms, and each type specifically seeks to exploit certain cognitive biases and impact consumer behaviour. Dark patterns are common in e-commerce, social media, fintech, and apps. Each platform uses an intentionally constructed design in its user interface (UI) and user experience (UX) to intentionally lead consumers' behaviour. Dark patterns can be very basic, such as deceptive design, to more complex operations that incorporate algorithmic behaviour and artificial intelligence. It is important to understand dark patterns to identify, regulate, and eliminate them.

1. Traditional Dark Patterns

Standard dark patterns are static and generic manipulations that do not rely on user-specific data. They exploit psychological tricks in interface design and were among the earliest types noted by Harry Brignull (2010). There are many repeating categories:

- Roach Motel: A pattern involving design that allows users to sign up easily, but it is extremely difficult to unsubscribe or delete an account. For example, streaming services where it takes five clicks to cancel a subscription.

- Confirm shaming: Any language that may induce guilt or shame in users for opting teaching users out. An example would be a pop-up message that said "No thanks. I don't want to save money," when declining an offer.
- Basket Sneaking: Adding products or services, such as insurance or accessories, to the consumer's shopping cart without user consent, such as pre-ticked boxes at checkout.
- Forced continuity: Users are charged after a free trial or charged after 30 days without any clear way to cancel. This is often seen in many online entertainment subscriptions, and app trials, etc.
- Trick questions: Using ambiguous wording or double negatives to confuse users. For example, one might say "Uncheck this box if you don't want to receive promotional emails".
- Hidden Costs: Indicating additional costs (like taxes or delivery fees) during the last stage of checkout to take advantage of the user's sunk-cost bias.
- False Urgency: Provide a bogus perception that either there is a shortage of items ("Only 1 item left!) or that time is short ("Offer valid for 5 minutes") and encourage impulsive purchasing.

Traditional dark patterns assume that users act reasonably quick and with little attention online. This is effective, because dark patterns exploit bounded rationality, the tendency of people to rely on shortcuts when there is too much information, or too little time (Narayanan et al., 2020).

2. AI-Based and Algorithmic Dark Patterns

The emergence of AI and data analytics has led to the invention of adaptive dark patterns, which change in real-time based on user behaviour and emotional data (Gray et al., 2023). In contrast to static manipulation, AI-driven patterns use predictive algorithms, personalized approaches, and reinforcement learning to customize trickery/user behaviour for each user.

Examples of some new agreements are:

- Customized Nudging: Algorithms will observe a user's unit of activity, for example, how long they have browsed, or are hesitating at checkout, and personalize nudging pop-ups or offers ("Don't leave without something in the cart- here is 10%!").
- Behaviour Targeting: An AI model may observe demographics, preferences, and emotional state to manipulate pricing or promotion. For example, a user with increased purchase power may see higher "recommended" pricing models.

- Infinite Scroll and Autoplay: Continuous scroll, also known as infinite scroll or autoplay, reveals that platforms as social media and streaming services, developed a trap for users to deem their endless viewing or usage as their "idea" to engage. The system learns the type of content that triggers a longer engagement session and manipulates users accordingly.
- Dark Personalization: Changing the manipulation of visibility to a possibility option, for example, maybe a high value user will not be seen the "cancel" or "delete" buttons more prominently, but rather the "continue" or "upgrade" visibility as a form of manipulation.
- Algorithmic Payment: AI dynamically manipulates pricing for products, based on a user's previous browsing history or urgency indicators.

AI-driven dark patterns represent a new stage in manipulation like contextual deception, where algorithms continuously learn and evolve. They exploit behavioural feedback loops, creating an ecosystem where manipulation is optimized over time (Deligoz, 2025).

3. Psychological Mechanisms Behind Dark Patterns

Dark patterns work because they exploit deep-rooted psychological and cognitive mechanisms. Research in behavioural economics identifies several biases that dark patterns weaponize:

Table 1.

Bias	Description	Example of Dark Pattern
Scarcity Effect	People value things more when they appear limited.	"Only 2 left at this price!"
Anchoring Bias	People rely heavily on the first piece of information they see.	"Was $999, now $499."
Loss Aversion	People fear losses more than they value equivalent gains.	"Your cart will expire soon!"
Social Proof	People follow others' actions to validate their choices.	"5,000 users bought this today."
Default Effect	Users stick with pre-selected choices.	Pre-checked subscription boxes.

These manipulations succeed because they reduce decision effort while stimulating emotional urgency. As a result, users feel in control but are unknowingly guided toward pre-engineered outcomes (Mathur et al., 2021). This erosion of free will is subtle yet profound—it replaces informed consent with coerced behaviour disguised as choice.

4. Global Examples of Dark Patterns

Dark patterns are a global phenomenon, appearing across regions, industries, and platforms. Major case studies include:

- Amazon (USA): The U.S. Federal Trade Commission sued Amazon in 2023 for "trapping" consumers in Amazon Prime subscriptions through a labyrinthine cancellation process, a classic "roach motel" pattern (FTC, 2023).
- LinkedIn (Global): Accused of sending automatic invitations to contacts without explicit user consent, exploiting social proof bias.
- Booking.com (EU): Displayed fake scarcity messages such as "Only 1 room left at this price," misleading users into quick purchases.
- Zomato and Swiggy (India): The Central Consumer Protection Authority (CCPA) warned these food delivery platforms for false urgency and hidden pricing tactics (CCPA, 2023).
- Facebook (Norway): The Norwegian Data Protection Authority fined Facebook for "privacy dark patterns" that pushed users to enable data tracking under misleading prompts.

5. Mechanism of AI-Based Manipulation

Dark patterns enabled by AI work by feeding off a cycle of data collection, prediction, and reinforcement. Each action performed by the user clicks, scrolling, dwell time represents behavioural data. Algorithms process these signals to determine the user's psychological state (e.g., boredom, excitement, hesitation). Depending on the prediction, the algorithm then intelligently prompts the user with designated stimuli such as notifications, colours, or prices. This fosters a self-learning feedback mechanism, akin to reinforcement learning, where the algorithm refines its manipulation strategies based on what it learns over time.

As noted by Gray et al. (2023), "the machine is a behavioural scientist," and a machine is not merely using the data to signal to the user, but more so, the machine is constantly running experiments on the user to discover the best method of persuasion. Such personalized manipulation renders AI dark patterns invisible and eludes simple ethical categorization. Unlike other ways of deceiving there is the assumption that the user can read and anticipate, while algorithmic levels of manipulation can operate below conscious awareness while establishing covert behavioural governance.

C. LEGAL AND REGULATORY FRAMEWORK ON DARK PATTERNS (GLOBAL COMPARATIVE PERSPECTIVE)

Over time the legal response to dark patterns has been different in each jurisdiction. The European Union and the United States are among the few regions that have taken the lead with specific regulations, while others, mainly in the Global South, are still at the initial stage of addressing dark patterns as a legal matter. The difficulty comes from the fact that dark patterns are not easy to define, as they span consumer protection, data privacy, and digital design ethics—areas that are treated differently in each country. This part includes a comparison of the major legal systems with respect to creating the concept, prohibiting it, and enforcing regulations against manipulative interface design, with the focus on the main jurisdictions and developing international norms.

1. European Union:

The Most Comprehensive Framework. The European Union (EU) has set itself as the world's foremost regulator of dark patterns through a comprehensive framework that simultaneously integrates consumer rights, data protection, and digital service regulation.

1.1. The General Data Protection Regulation (GDPR)

The GDPR of the EU (2018), though mainly a data protection law, indirectly deals with dark patterns through its provisions of transparency, informed consent, and limitation of purpose. Consent, according to Article 7, must be provided through "clear affirmative action", thus making the use of misleading or auto-ticked consent boxes illegal. On the same lines, Recital 32 prohibits designs that "silence, hide or obscure" the information necessary for valid consent. One can see the case examples of CNIL v. Google (2022) and Meta Platforms Ireland Ltd. (2023) showing the EU´s actions against privacy dark patterns that pushed users to consent to data tracking. The consent interfaces were found to be unclear, and thus, the regulators ruled that such practices were against the principle of free consent as per GDPR.

1.2. The Digital Services Act (DSA) 2024

The Digital Services Act (DSA) of the EU is the most obvious legislative recognition of dark patterns. It is said to be so because Article 25 of the DSA prohibits "deceptive or misleading interfaces" that effectively impact or limit user choice. This law is applicable to all online middlemen, which include social media, marketplaces, and app stores. The law further provides for transparency in recommending systems, calling for the disclosure of the algorithmic criteria that are used to personalize content. Moreover, the Digital Markets Act (DMA) works alongside the DSA by imposing limitations on "gatekeepers", preventing them from applying manipulative design strategies that disadvantage rival services. The DSA and DMA together create a holistic EU platform that integrates the Ethics of design into platform regulations.

Table 2.

Regulation	Key Provision	Target Behaviour	Enforcement Authority
GDPR	Article 7 – Valid consent	Misleading consent boxes	Data Protection Authorities
DSA	Article 25 – Prohibition of deceptive design	Manipulative interfaces	European Commission
DMA	Article 6 – Fair competition	Self-preferencing, biased defaults	DG Competition

2. United States: Fragmented but Evolving Approach

The United States does not have a comprehensive omnibus privacy or consumer protection law similar to the EU. Rather, enforcement against a dark pattern occurs through agency processes and state-level action.

2.1. Federal Trade Commission (FTC)

Central to this process is the Federal Trade Commission (FTC), an agency with authority under Section 5 of the FTC Act prohibiting "unfair or deceptive acts or practices." In 2022, the FTC published a report called Bringing Dark Patterns to Light that identifies categories of manipulative designs, which they grouped into misleading interfaces, covert data collection, obstructing cancellation, and forced action (FTC, 2022).

2.2. State-Level Laws and Emerging Trends

California's Consumer Privacy Act (CCPA, 2020) and the updated California Privacy Rights Act (CPRA, 2023) explicitly prohibit the use of dark patterns that subvert user consent. Similarly, the Colorado Privacy Act (CPA, 2023) defines dark patterns as any design that "substantially subverts or impairs" user choice.

3. India: The Emerging Digital Regime

India, a rapidly growing digital economy, has recently considered dark patterns in its consumer protection and digital governance framework.

3.1. Consumer Protection Act, 2019 and CCPA Guidelines, 2023

The Consumer Protection Act, 2019, defines "unfair trading practices" broadly as manipulative online designs under Section 2(47). Following this, the Central Consumer Protection Authority (CCPA) published the Guidelines for Prevention and Regulation of Dark Patterns, 2023, formally recognizing dark patterns as unlawful. The Guidelines detail 13 categories of prohibited dark patterns, such as: Basket sneaking, forced action, False urgency, Subscription traps, Drip pricing, nagging, and confirm shaming

These rules apply to online platforms, e-commerce entities, and any advertiser. Accordingly, India joins the EU and the U.S. as some of the few jurisdictions to issue dedicated regulatory guidance. However, challenges remain, especially weak enforcement mechanisms and the absence of explicit provisions for AI-driven manipulations.

3.2. The Digital Personal Data Protection Act, 2023 (DPDP Act)

The DPDP Act emphasizes notice and consent, aiming to align with GDPR principles. As an example, if consent is obtained through a dark pattern, such as by providing mandatory consent for unrelated data processing, that consent cannot be regarded as valid consent.

India's approach is especially notable in combining consumer protection and data privacy regulation.

4. Gaps and Challenges in Global Regulation

While significant progress has taken place, various challenges will develop from the effective regulation of dark patterns worldwide:

- Lack of Consistent Definitions: Terms such as "deceptive design," "choice architecture," and "dark patterns" are sometimes used synonymously with one another, causing interpretative inconsistencies.
- Intersection of Jurisdictions: A single form of manipulation may overlap with both consumer protection and privacy regulations, establishing confusion over enforcing order.

- AI and Creepy Complexity: Existing regulations tend to focus on visible instances of such deceptive interfaces, as opposed to adaptive manipulations in algorithmic systems. Enforcement: Authorities may not regulate dark patterns because they do not have the technical skills or bandwidth to verify the intention of the manipulative design. Global Platforms, Local Laws. Multinational digital corporations operate in various jurisdictions, making global enforcement very difficult.
- These gaps highlight the need for a mixed international structure, possibly through multilateral governance over digital design like OECD Guidelines for Consumer Protection in E-Commerce and UNCTAD Digital Economy Reports.

5. Other Jurisdictions: A Growing Global Trend

Many countries are now taking action by identifying and restricting manipulative design practices:

- United Kingdom: The Competition and Markets Authority (CMA) published its report on "Online Choice Architecture" in 2022, which discussed dark patterns in retail, travel, and subscription platforms.
- Australia: The Australian Competition and Consumer Commission (ACCC) began its Digital Platform Services Inquiry and indicated that manipulative consent interfaces would be under scrutiny.
- Canada: Privacy regulators have initiated investigations of dark patterns in consent forms under the Personal Information Protection and Electronic Documents Act (PIPEDA).
- Norway: The Norwegian Data Protection Authority fined Meta for deceptive privacy settings in 2023, which is among the strongest EU-aligned enforcement actions to date.
- Japan: The Ministry of Economy, Trade and Industry (METI) suggested amendments to consumer laws curbing online misleading designs.

Table 3.

Country	Key Regulation/Action	Year	Focus Area	Enforcement Body
EU	Digital Services Act	2024	Manipulative interface	European Commission
USA	FTC Enforcement	2022–23	Deceptive subscriptions, data consent	Federal Trade Commission
India	CCPA Guidelines	2023	Unfair trade practices	CCPA
UK	CMA Report	2022	Choice architecture	Competition & Markets Authority
Australia	ACCC Inquiry	2022	Online consent	ACCC
Norway	Meta Privacy Case	2023	Data manipulation	Datatilsynet

6. Towards a Global Regulatory Framework

A unified response to dark patterns requires integrating principles from both consumer protection and data governance. Experts suggest three pillars for a global model:

- Transparency-by-Design: Platforms must disclose how their interfaces influence user decisions, with mandatory "consent dashboards."
- Algorithmic Accountability: Companies should conduct regular audits of AI-driven designs to prevent exploitative personalization.
- User Empowerment: Legislation must prioritize consumer education, ensuring users can recognize and resist manipulative tactics.

Recent academic proposals advocate the establishment of an international code of conduct for ethical interface design, enforced through transnational cooperation among data protection authorities and consumer regulators (Leiser, 2020).

D. IMPACT OF DARK PATTERNS ON CONSUMER AUTONOMY AND BEHAVIOUR

The emergence of dark patterns signifies a new paradigm of the influence of digital environments on human behavioural outcomes. In contrast to traditional marketing techniques dependent on persuasion and transparency, dark patterns engage users through deceit, often preying on cognitive bias. Their design cultivates user confusion regarding choice, often resulting in actions that are detrimental to the user, e.g., disclosing excessive personal information, unintended purchase, or providing consent for unwanted tracking. The impacts of these deceptive patterns represent a threat to more than just economic outcomes, eroding user autonomy, user trust, and users' psychological well-being, while creating complexities at both ethical and regulatory levels around the globe.

1. Psychological and Behavioural Impact

Fundamentally, dark patterns exist because they exploit human cognition. Behavioural economics identifies the fact that people are rarely "fully rational" in their choice, relying instead on the use of heuristics (i.e., mental shortcuts) to minimize effort and time (Kahneman, 2011). Dark patterns use tendencies to nudge users toward predetermined outcomes.

1.1. Decision Fatigue and Cognitive Overload

Repeatedly being exposed to the design of an interface that nudges behaviour leads to decision fatigue, a state in which the choice-making, within an intentional frame, mental effort has been depleted. This states that users are more likely to accept defaults, such as opting in for data tracking or auto-renewal of subscriptions. Platforms such as social media and e-commerce are engaged in this already through endless scrolling.

For instance, studies show that users are up to 60% more likely to accept data collection when presented with multiple confusing consent screens rather than a clear choice (Ghaiumy Anaraky et al., 2023). Over time, such patterns lead to psychological exhaustion and a loss of perceived control.

1.2. Emotional Manipulation and Guilt Induction

Many dark patterns intentionally use emotional triggers to compel action. Confirm shaming—expressions like "No, I'd rather pay full price" traffic in guilt to ensure compliance. Similarly, "fear of missing out" (FOMO) fairness-based (time-based) tactics, such as countdown timers or counterfeit scarcity messages, exploit anxiety and urgency.

Research by Chun and Rha (2025) showed that dark patterns elicit emotional responses such as regret, frustration, and stress, which strongly impact trust and consumer satisfaction. The emotional leveraging associated with dark patterns not only promotes impulsive decision-making, rather it also undermines users' ability to rationally evaluate situations.

1.3. Habit Formation and Addictive Design.

AI-driven platforms further encourage manipulative behaviour through the use of reinforcement learning algorithms designed to retain users. Infinite scroll, autoplay, and push notifications take advantage of the dopamine reward system in the brain, the same effects that contribute to gambling addiction in the context of continuous reward anticipation, creating conditioning for users to increase their time and attention on the platforms through compulsion.

In reality, the intersection of dark patterns makes the platforms transition from instruments of convenience to systems of behavioural dependence, creating an illusion of voluntary engagement while users are intentionally being nudged algorithmically.

2. Economic and Data-Related Harms

Beyond psychological manipulation, dark patterns create real-world economic costs and violate user privacy. Dark patterns compromise pricing transparency, coerce users into unwanted purchases, and obtain data based on false premises.

2.1. Financial Violation

E-commerce sites often rely on drip pricing, where only part of the total cost is displayed first, and additional costs are revealed just prior to checkout. Airline and hotel booking sites, as an example, routinely show users a "base fare" before taxes and/or mandatory fees are disclosed at checkout. This technique exploits the user's anchoring bias toward the initial price and makes the pricing appear favourable when it is not (Ro ca, 2024).

Subscription traps impose a financial obligation without consent. The Federal Trade Commission (2022) formally sanctioned Epic Games for knowingly developing a confusing refund process and pre-selecting several in-app purchases, resulting in millions of dollars in unwanted charges without consent. All forms of predatory behaviour can cause public distrust in digital commerce and undermine the fair market process.

2.2. Data Extraction and Pertinent Privacy Violations

Dark patterns also extort data, relying on a variety of data extraction methods. Platforms that use manipulative consent interfaces rely on implicit consent to collect personal data. Data extraction that relies on misleading consent under the guise of privacy defaults relies on pre-selected data sharing boxes that violate the tenet of informed consent under privacy laws such as the EU GDPR and California Consumer Privacy Act (CCPA).

3. Impact on Consumer Autonomy and Consent

Dark patterns' deepest damage is to users' autonomy, the ability to make informed and, more importantly, voluntary decisions. Once users are nudged towards decisions based on deceit, the foundation for digital consent has eroded.

3.1. The Facade of Choice

Dark patterns provide users with an illusion of control while reducing options. For example, an interface design for a user to click "accept all" in order to proceed, while not offering a clearly visible "reject" option, creates consent instead of seeking it. The European Data Protection Board (EDPB, 2022) has determined this type of design renders consent "invalid" under GDPR.

Compounding this illusion is the erosion of the moral legitimacy of a digital transaction. Even if a user could be said to agree to the terms, because these decisions take place against asymmetrical information and design coercion, the moral principle of autonomy has been violated.

3.2. Impacts Disproportionately Affect Those Most Vulnerable

Dark patterns disproportionately impact users with low digital literacy, children, and older adults; those who could be assumed to be equally unable to spot deceptive design signals. For example, older adults are 40% more likely to stay "false urgency" messages, while younger users exhibit impulsivity to gamified incentives (Ghaiumy Anarakay et al., 2023).

This leaves open a wider ethical divide in the digital economy, because the most vulnerable consumer segments bear the greatest risk. As Chauhan (2024) explains, the impacts of AI

4. Ethical Implications: Persuasion vs. Coercion

The ethical quandary of dark patterns is the line between persuasion (an ethical influence strategy) and coercion (an unethical manipulation strategy). In relation to this, persuasion is a means of informing and empowering users, while coercion typically rests on exploiting cognitive or emotional vulnerabilities and is not transparent.

According to Schafer et al. (2023), dark patterns blur this line between persuasion and coercion. Dark patterns have made it exceptionally difficult in some circumstances to ascertain manipulation concealed as user-centred design. For example, "nudge" techniques initially posited in behavioural economics relay that nudging is simply promoting specific decisions that are deemed to be advantageous (like saving money or exercising). In particular, when a corporation takes nudging that is ethically aligned and applies it for the sole purpose of profit, nudging becomes essentially sludge: a coercive form of choice architecture.

This presents the ethical issue that even if manipulative techniques "work" and increase engagement, does it make it ethical? If systems are designed to obfuscate intent, how likely is user consent to be conscientious? Without ethical "guardrails" in place, using AI-based dark patterns has the potential to transform human choice into a predictable variable for algorithmic decision-making.

5. Case Studies Illustrating Global Impact

The following real-world examples highlight that dark patterns can cause demonstrable harm across industries and countries:

- Meta (Norway, 2023): The Norwegian Data Protection Authority found that the way Meta had designed privacy settings misled users into making data-sharing choices and ruled that their violation of the GDPR.
- Amazon (USA, 2023): The Federal Trade Commission revealed that it had prepared to sue Amazon for "a labyrinthine cancellation process" that appeared to induce customers to pay for Amazon Prime and cancel only upon sharing their credit information.
- Zomato and Swiggy (India, 2023): The Consumer Choice Protection Agency warned against Zomato and Swiggy for their use of deception and manipulation tactics to elicit false urgency, hidden pricing, and unwanted subscriptions.
- Booking.com (EU, 2022): Booking.com received a monetary penalty from an EU consumer protection authority for notifying customers of fake scarcity, e.g., "Only 1 room left!" that was allegedly generated by algorithms.

These examples show that the reach and importance of dark patterns can be worldwide and cross-design sectors.

Table 4.

Platform	Country	Type of Dark Pattern	Legal Action/Outcome
Amazon	USA	Subscription trap	FTC lawsuit (2023)
Booking.com	EU	False urgency	Fined by the EU Commission
Meta	Norway	Privacy manipulation	GDPR violation
Zomato/Swiggy	India	Drip pricing, forced action	CCPA warning

6. The Need for Digital Trust and Consumer Empowerment

To lessen the impact of these threats, digital systems must be reoriented toward trust and empowering users. To do this, we must have transparency-by-design; for example, consent interfaces should be simple, honest, and reversible. User education to enhance digital literacy should also help users recognize deceptive behavioural influences.

In addition, companies need to be held accountable in a way that includes audits, ethical design standards, and transparency of the AI/machine learning systems they use, which must be a larger part of platform governance. As Ro ca (2024) argues, the aim is not just compliance but also to create what she calls "digital dignity," which is a digital marketplace redesigned so that autonomy, fairness, and honesty have been embedded into the design.

E. ETHICAL AND TECHNICAL COUNTERMEASURES AGAINST DARK PATTERNS

Dark patterns expose a widening gap between technological progress and ethical responsibility. As artificial intelligence, persuasive design, and behavioural analytics converge, the line between influence and manipulation blurs. Addressing this challenge requires a dual approach: embedding ethical design principles into digital architectures and deploying technical countermeasures capable of detecting, auditing, and deterring deceptive interfaces. This section explores both dimensions of ethical norms shaping responsible design and emerging technologies for real-time accountability.

1. Ethics-by-Design: Re-centring Human Autonomy

Ethics-by-design denotes the belief that moral values such as autonomy, fairness, and transparency should be encoded into technology from the very outset, not tacked on after harm has occurred (Cowls et al., 2019). Applied to interface design, ethics-by-design means that systems must prioritize user understanding over conversion.

Statements of a shared framework for ethics (e.g., "Ethics Guidelines for Trustworthy AI," which has been created by the EU High-Level Expert Group, 2019; or "Ethically Aligned Design" from the IEEE, 2021) support more specific ethical principles, such as explainability, informed consent, and human oversight. When considering ethical measures for designing digital commerce, these principles can translate into three actionable ethical principles:

- Informed Interaction: interfaces must provide truthful, understandable information about the consequences of user action (e.g., a clear cancellation button, an easy-to-understand breakdown of pricing, and an explicit consent form).

- Freedom of Reversal: ethical systems should allow the user to easily withdraw consent or reverse decisions without consequence or penalty.
- Proportional Persuasion: designers may encourage productive behaviour (e.g., security updates), but should not coerce or induce persuasive disagreement.

This trend is already apparent, as companies like Mozilla and DuckDuckGo implement "user-first" guidelines for these ethical design principles, showing potential for ethical design to coexist with profit.

2. Corporate Accountability and Governance Mechanisms

Corporate governance has a vital function in preventing manipulative practices. Some multinational corporations have established an internal AI ethics board and algorithmic audit committee to guarantee legal compliance with new legislation such as the EU Digital Services Act and California Privacy Rights Act. Accountability functions are increasingly incorporating:

- Algorithmic Impact Assessments (AIAs): The structure of AIAs, which aim to evaluate the potential for manipulative design or biased targeting, is modelled after environmental assessments (Kaminski & Malgieri, 2021).
- Transparency Reports: Large platforms such as Meta and Google have started doing annual transparency disclosures that detail interface experiments, although they concede to self-regulation (meaning there is no independent outside entity to keep them responsible for anything other than what they have to comply with to be legal).
- Independent Auditing: Independent third-party UX audits can identify whether these designs are exploiting behavioural biases; this is also supported by the OECD's 2022 Consumer Policy Guidance on Online Disclosure (pp. 32-33).

These types of tools are moving away from reacting to enforcement and toward proactive representation of responsibility, or measurable ethical compliance, rather than aspirational ethical compliance.

3. Technical Countermeasures: Detection and Monitoring Tools

Technological interventions work to complement ethical frameworks by automatically identifying designs that rely on manipulative practices. In recent studies in computer science, researchers have explored detection using machine learning and a user-side/browser-level shield.

3.1. Automated Detection Frameworks

Ramteke et al. (2024) provide an example of an AI model they built that classifies e-commerce interfaces relative to 13 different dark design types, relying on convolutional neural networks to analyse thousands of web page screenshots. In their use cases of spotting drip-pricing and confirm-shaming cues, the accuracy of the model was over 90%. This shows that using an algorithmic tool/approach demonstrates the ability to expose algorithmic designers who will engage in deception.

Mathur et al. (2021) built on this work by developing the "Dark Patterns Detection Project", a browser-based tool that analyzes web pages and interacts with users in detecting manipulative phrase placements and misleading button placement practices. This represents movement and the juxtaposition between manual audits and pulling data on a large scale.

3.2. Browser Extensions and User-Side Shields

There are open-source tools developed to alert users when a webpage employs the practice of coercing users to act. The "Deceptive Design Detector" (University of Trento, 2023) and Mozilla's experimental Privacy Badger fork flag anomalous behaviour in font size, colour contrast, or button hierarchy that may play a role in influencing an authentication decision. The existence of detection plugins is are example of consumer-empowering technologies that give users immediate feedback and reestablish some transparency lost by opaque algorithms.

3.3. Data Forensics and Blockchain Logging

In the efforts to preserve evidence that the user was manipulated, researchers have Immutable ledger record interface, ensuring tamper-proof documentation for regulators (Deshmukh et al., 2022). This approach allows cross-jurisdictional verification of deceptive practices, strengthening digital-evidence chains.

4. AI Transparency and Explainability

AI-powered personalization is a prevalent form of modern dark patterns. Addressing these dark patterns requires mitigating the lack of transparency within the algorithmic decision-making process. The EU Artificial Intelligence Act (2024) specifically identifies manipulative or subliminal AI systems as "high-risk" and demands that these AI systems maintain transparency, including addressing human oversight, documenting risk mitigation strategies, and addressing explainability, that is, demonstrating how algorithmic outputs can be made comprehensible or interpretable to regulators and consumers, as expected as part of the mandate.

To enable auditors to visualize how particular input data affects algorithm output, technical frameworks like SHAP (Shapley Additive Explanations) and LIME (Local Interpretable Model-Agnostic Explanations) have emerged. For instance, one could use SHAP and/or LIME when auditing recommender systems, to determine if an online marketplace user's product suggestions Favor corporate profit rather than consumer welfare.

Notably, researchers have suggested "algorithm-focused nutrition labels" or simplified dashboards clarifying what data is collected, how recommendations are made, and how users can opt out (Kugler et al., 2025). Pilot tests, with one in the Netherlands and another in Canada, found slightly more than 20% participants embraced the use of algorithm nutrition labels favourably, and as a result of using algorithmic nutrition labels, 27% of participants reduced their accidental purchases when shopping online.

Table 5.

Transparency Tool	Function	Outcome	Example Platform
SHAP/LIME	Model interpretability	Exposes hidden biases	Research labs (Google AI)
Algorithmic Nutrition Labels	Consumer disclosure	Builds trust, informed consent	Dutch E-Commerce Test 2024
AI Impact Assessment	Regulatory audit	Pre-deployment accountability	EU AI Act compliance

5. Regulatory and Multilateral Strategies

International coordination remains essential because manipulative platforms operate globally while laws remain national. Recent initiatives indicate growing convergence:

- **OECD (2023):** Issued *Global Principles for Responsible Digital Design*, urging member states to prohibit deception-based "choice architectures."
- **UNCTAD Digital Economy Report (2024):** Recommended algorithmic audits as a standard element of consumer-protection regimes in developing economies.
- **Council of Europe Recommendation CM/Rec(2024)1:** Called for cross-border cooperation among data-protection authorities to address manipulative UX in AI systems.

At the regional level, Asia-Pacific Economic Cooperation (APEC) economies are drafting an *AI Ethics and Fair-Design Charter* to harmonize best practices across digital markets in Singapore, Japan, and Australia.

Global coordination is critical for two reasons: (1) to avoid regulatory arbitrage by multinational platforms; and (2) to standardize definitions of deceptive design, ensuring consistent enforcement.

6. Design-Ethics Education and Consumer Empowerment

Technical and regulatory solutions will only continue to be partial solutions without fundamentally changing the culture in which we train our digital professionals. Adding ethics to UX/UI and computer science curricula can begin to change the culture of designer responsibility.

Universities like Stanford, MIT, and the University of Amsterdam have begun stating that "Persuasive Technology and Ethics" modules will soon be required. These courses require training students to identify design triggers that manipulate users and implement those triggers responsibly using behavioural science.

Consumer leaves parallel initiatives that build awareness-teaching users to recognize visual deception, for example, hidden unsubscribe buttons, or fake urgency with marketing tactics. For example, on March 27, 2023, the European Consumer Organisation launched a "Clean Choice Campaign" that builds awareness to recognize this visual deception. There is a similar project, the CCPA Digital Nudge Awareness Drive, happening in India, where they expertly appraise existing outreach in vernacular languages.

These educational strategies support the development of digital resiliency--a social capacity to doubt the prompts that are presented on digital formats and resist blindly accepting their demands.

7. Future of Countermeasures: Toward Symbiotic Regulation

The upcoming evolution entails the concept of symbiotic regulation, which takes place when ethical design, automated detection, and legal compliance coalesce into mutually reinforcing layers. The advancing possibilities include:

- Real-time interface auditors - Embedded APIs to score each webpage for manipulative risk before it goes live.
- Dynamic consent dashboards - Centralized tools to allow users to view and modify all platform permissions across devices.
- Collaborative AI watchdogs - International databases to which regulators can contribute dark-pattern configurations they have observed.

By harnessing the combined power of human ethics and machine intelligence, a self-correcting ecosystem can be developed, one in which manipulative design is both discoverable and financially unsustainable.

F. GLOBAL CHALLENGES AND FUTURE DIRECTIONS IN REGULATING AI-DRIVEN DARK PATTERNS

Despite growing international awareness and regulatory efforts, the problem of dark patterns, particularly those enhanced by artificial intelligence, continues to evolve faster than legal systems can respond. These manipulative designs have become deeply embedded in digital ecosystems, hidden within algorithmic personalization, behavioural analytics, and predictive modelling. As a result, even well-structured laws such as the EU Digital Services Act (2024) or the California Privacy Rights Act (2023) face practical and conceptual limits. This section explores the multifaceted global challenges in regulating AI-driven dark patterns and the future directions necessary to ensure that digital markets remain transparent, fair, and accountable.

1. The Technological Challenge: Adaptive and Invisible Manipulations

Dark patterns powered by AI differ from traditional deceptive design because they are dynamic, contextually aware, and invisible. Machine learning models continuously improve interface displays and content to specifically exploit an individual's behavioural vulnerabilities. These adaptive dark patterns are personalized to each user rather than relying on static forms of "confirm shaming" or "false urgency."

For example, recommender systems utilize reinforcement learning algorithms, on behalf of the tech company, indiscriminately trying to determine which design features (colour, position, timing) reliably push specific users towards desired outcomes. This means that every user interface is a different version of manipulation that is exponentially more challenging for users to detect or regulators to assess (Brennecke, 2023).

The potential for real-time optimization of deception also accelerates with AI. Algorithms can be used to track immediate reactions (cursor movements, eye-tracking features, dwell time, etc.) to reinforce or "turn up" coercive prompting. This kind of hyper-personalization can quickly turn dark patterns into behavioural feedback loops where the system is always learning how to manipulate a user more effectively. Regulation is impossible because there is no consistent "design evidence" of manipulation, only code functioning in ever-changing learned patterns within neural networks.

2. The Legal Challenge: Fragmented and Reactive Frameworks

Legal systems across the world remain divided, unresponsive, and jurisdictionally limited in scope. While different laws can prohibit unfair or deceptive acts and practices, laws often do not provide sufficient clarity on algorithmic manipulation.

2.1. Definition Uncertainty

There is no consistent definition for dark patterns in any global legal context. Terms including "deceptive design", "choice architecture", and "misleading interface" are used interchangeably in laws, which contributes to an unclear interpretive landscape. For example, the FTC Act (United States) prohibits "deceptive practices", while the Digital Services Act (EU) names dark patterns explicitly, and India's CCPA Guidelines (2023) define 13. This disunity in definitions inhibits international frameworks from developing and cross-border enforcement more widely.

2.2. Jurisdictional & Enforcement Gaps

While digital platforms operate across national borders, consumer protection and privacy laws are still territorial. For example, while one jurisdiction fines a company, other jurisdictions may not do the same, creating regulatory arbitrage, where companies relocate to jurisdictions with less enforcement (Ro ca, 2024). For example, while the EU imposed fines against Meta due to privacy violations, the similar design patterns persisted in jurisdictions without such laws.

Further, regulators usually do not have the technical knowledge or capacity to indicate that a manipulative design exists, and enforcement relies on whistleblowers or entities that perform academic audits. Additionally, due to limited resources, many violations go unnoticed or unheeded.

2.3. Enforcement After the Fact

Most laws that exist today address dark patterns after harm has occurred. Conversely, investigations take significant time, evidence fades, and manipulative designs evolve. This reactive model contrasts sharply with the speed of AI development, allowing unethical practices to proliferate before legal consequences arise.

3. The Ethical Challenge: Manipulation vs. Personalization

One of the most significant challenges is in differentiating ethical persuasion from manipulative coercion. AI invariably persuades; it tailors an experience to increase relevance and user engagement. The troubling part comes when that persuasion becomes deceitful, diminishing user agency without direct coercive pressure.

Since Kugler et al. (2025) contend, people often agree to be persuaded for their convenience, like suggested recommendations. Nevertheless, they hardly recognize how much their user experience influences their feelings and decision-making. This raises ethical concerns: should the designer, the data scientist, or the corporation be ethically responsible when manipulation occurs without malicious intent but is systematic?

The challenge is compounded by the subsequent wave of affective computing when AI predicts emotional dispositions with only facial expressions or idea-level typing patterns. The platform alters the tone, hue, or urgency of different interface features based on presumed emotional states—entering psychological manipulation (Deligoz, 2025). This may be harmless without ethical peril, but it offers a pathway toward normalizing emotional exploitation under a framework of "improving a user experience."

4. The Economic and Political Challenge: Incentives for Manipulation

Dark patterns endure because they are not so much a technology failure as they are a market design feature. The economics of platforms reward engagement and attentiveness, not ethical behaviour. Models of digital business, particularly in e-commerce, fintech, and social media, are optimized for whatever maximizes attention and conversion rates; metrics that can be enhanced through manipulative design.

Indeed, as Day et al. (2019) point out, dark patterns can also emerge as anti-competitive behaviour. If larger platforms use some of the aforementioned design strategies to lock users into an ecosystem (like a service where subscriptions are hidden and deceptively easy to purchase) or where aesthetic defaults are used to manipulate attention, they not only create market dominance, but also limit potential competitors—an issue for both consumers as well as smaller, evolving platforms. Thus, dark patterns not only harm consumers, but they also distort entire markets by generating asymmetry of information while simultaneously providing large platforms with a monopolistic advantage.

Politically, the economic power of these larger platforms tends to discourage regulators from limiting dark patterns. The lobbying power of technology companies stalls reforms, while developing countries prioritize growing the digital economy over protecting their citizens. The salient risks for a global digital economy are developing into a "persuasion marketplace", a marketplace where our attention is manipulated into a monetized asset.

5. The Cultural Challenge: Low Digital Literacy and Consent Fatigue

Low levels of digital literacy and consent fatigue allow dark patterns to flourish. On average, users face dozens of consent requests every day for cookies or app permissions, leading to a situation in which they fall into a pattern of consent, rather than informed consent (Li, 2024).

In the case of emerging economies like India and Indonesia, and some parts of Africa, users are often even unaware that they are facing manipulative designs, and are thereby ripe for exploitation on economic grounds. Asymmetries that exist between a technologically sophisticated corporation and users who may be digitally naïve create a new kind of inequality around the digital space, whereby users are targeted for manipulation and are least capable of resisting it.

Even educated users will additionally experience "learned helplessness," a psychological state of getting accustomed to manipulation interfaces through repeated experiences. Before long, users would exhibit a failure to distinguish between ethical and unethical design, and ultimately consider deception a normal part of living in a digital world.

Table 6.

Socio-Cultural Factor	Effect on Regulation	Examples
Low digital literacy	Users fail to identify manipulative cues	Emerging economies
Consent fatigue	Users click "agree" without reading	Cookie banners
Trust erosion	Users disengage from platforms	Data scandals
Learned helplessness	Acceptance of deception	Persistent pop-ups, defaults

6. The Institutional Challenge: Lack of Interdisciplinary Collaboration

Coordinating responses to AI-triggered dark patterns necessitates experts working together to combine laws, behavioural science, data ethics, and computer engineering. Unfortunately, in practice, these institutions are typically siloed—consumer protection authorities rarely share information with AI auditors, and UX designers are rarely working with some type of legal oversight.

Kowalczyk et al. (2023) detail how Internet of Things (IoT) ecosystems deepen this fragmentation. Smart-home devices utilize dark patterns that rely on voice interfaces—a subtle nudge in the tone of the assistant or a slight delay in responses—

creating difficulty in responding to manipulation rationally with established legal categories; legal definitions will not likely fit easily here. These multi-modal dimensions of manipulation add further complexity to developing pooled or cross-disciplinary governance—drawing together technologists, ethicists, and regulators toward certain frameworks to build shared systems.

Modern initiatives like the Global Partnership on AI (GPAI) or the OECD AI Policy Observatory attempt to implement pooled value frameworks and promote norms that include cooperation across traditional boundaries, but operational co-operation remains low. The lack of convergence across institutions risks regulation remaining abstract, while at the same time, manipulation becomes more complex.

7. Future Directions: Constructing a Transparent and Accountable Digital Tomorrow

Addressing these challenges requires global governance to shift from a reactive model of enforcement to a preventive one founded on transparency, interoperability, and shared accountability. The following strategies represent the beginning stages of a roadmap towards future success:

7.1. Mandates on Algorithmic Transparency

Governments should mandate that platforms provide transparency on key features of their recommendation and personalization systems. "Explainability reports" would help make technological influence auditable by regulators and available to consumers, similar to environmental or nutrition labels.

7.2. International Harmonization of "Dark Patterns" Vocabulary

Multilateral organizations such as the OECD, UNCTAD, and G20 Digital Economy Task Force could work together to define dark patterns and develop model clauses for national consumer law. This would reduce jurisdictional discrepancies and provide a coordinated vehicle for enforcement.

7.3. Certification for Ethical Design

An "Ethical UX Seal" (similar to energy efficiency ratings) could be developed to motivate platforms to engage in transparency in how they design their services. This mark could be provided by international organizations that were awarded based on periodic audits of the algorithms.

7.4. Human-Centric AI

Any frameworks created with ethical measures around AI should explicitly centre human autonomy as a core constraint on design. The EU AI Act (2024), for example, will address particularly dangerous systems, namely, many forms of systems that "materially distort human behaviour." Regardless, this will ultimately depend on enforcement through ongoing oversight of AI, including algorithm testing and public reporting.

7.5. Enhance Digital Literacy and Consumer Empowerment

Long-term solutions require strengthening digital literacy through education, public campaigns, and interface transparency tools. Empowered consumers are the strongest deterrent against manipulative design.

7.6. Global Regulatory Cooperation

Cross-border enforcement networks, like the International Consumer Protection and Enforcement Network (ICPEN), could facilitate coordinated action against multinational offenders. This approach mirrors global collaboration in antitrust and environmental regulation.

G. CASE STUDIES

Around the world, the recognition of dark patterns as a form of digital manipulation has prompted significant legal and regulatory action. Enforcement agencies are increasingly treating deceptive interface design as an unfair trade practice, a privacy violation, or even an anticompetitive strategy. This section highlights key enforcement cases across jurisdictions and analyses emerging global trends in tackling dark patterns.

1. Case Study 1: Norwegian Consumer Council v. Meta (Facebook) (2022)

The Norwegian Consumer Council (Forbrukerradet) lodged a complaint against Meta (Facebook) for using forced consent and default bias to collect user data for targeted advertising. The EU Data Protection Board found that users had been coerced into consenting due to interface pressure and a lack of a true choice. Meta was subsequently fined €390 million for violating the GDPR principles of transparency and free consent (European Data Protection Board, 2023). This case established a precedent that coercive consent flows are equivalent to non-consensual data processing under the law.

2. Case Study 2: Amazon EU Srl – "Prime Cancellation Flow" (2022)

In 2022, after an inquiry by the European Commission and national consumer authorities, it was determined that Amazon had made it unnecessarily difficult for consumers to cancel subscriptions through an obstructive cancellation flow (misleading buttons and lengthy repeated confirmations). Under EU pressure, Amazon redesigned its interface across all of its European domains in 2022. The case reinforced that "subscription traps" are violations of both the Unfair Commercial Practices Directive (UCPD) and the DSA, and highlight Europe's proactive approach to combating manipulative UX.

3. Case Study 3: Epic Games (Fortnite) Settlement (2023)

In December 2022, the FTC imposed a $520 million fine against Epic Games for utilizing a misleading interface design for its popular game Fortnite. The commission found that Epic's "counterintuitive, inconsistent, and confusing button configuration" caused players to make unintended transactions in the game. The settlement contained $245 million in consumer reimbursement, the largest penalty for utilizing dark patterns in the FTC's history (FTC, 2023). This case established a forcible precedent that misleading interface design is a deceptive trade practice and not just poor interface design.

4. Case Study 4: Age of Learning Inc.'s ABC Mouse (2020)

ABC Mouse was accused by the FTC of using subscription traps, which make it simple for users to sign up but nearly impossible to cancel. The business consented to update its cancellation procedure and pay $10 million in settlements (FTC, 2020). The FTC's 2022 "Bringing Dark Patterns to Light" Report, which currently directs enforcement and policymaking throughout the digital sectors, was impacted by this case.

5. Case Study 5: CMA's 2019–2020 Study of Online Hotel Reservations

The CMA discovered that websites such as Booking.com and Expedia employed deceptive ranking algorithms and fake urgency (e.g., "Only one room left!"). Significant interface reforms, such as transparent pricing and more lucid sponsored listing labelling, were agreed upon by the platforms (CMA, 2020). Similar actions have been taken by the Australian Competition and Consumer Commission (ACCC), which has brought charges against Google and Trivago for making false statements based on dark patterns. These cases affirm a global convergence toward defining dark patterns as unfair trade practices.

6. Case Study 6: Zomato and Swiggy Consumer Complaints (2024)

Following widespread consumer backlash, the **Consumer Affairs Ministry** investigated "Buy One Get One" and "Pro" memberships on food delivery apps for *drip pricing* and *false urgency*. The companies were instructed to modify their promotional design, marking India's first official enforcement instance (Consumer Affairs Report, 2024).

7. Case Study 7: MakeMyTrip and Golbibo (2022)

The Competition Commission of India (CCI) found that MakeMyTrip used algorithmic ranking manipulation to Favor partnered hotels, misleading consumers. The CCI fined the company 223 crores, citing abuse of dominant position.

This case bridged competition law and consumer protection, showing that dark patterns can be anticompetitive.

H. GLOBAL ENFORCEMENT TRENDS

Across jurisdictions, a **pattern of convergence** emerges:

- **Shift from privacy to consumer protection:** Early enforcement under data laws (GDPR) has expanded into broader trade and competition regulation.
- **Algorithmic accountability:** Regulators are increasingly demanding algorithmic transparency to detect dark patterns hidden in code.
- **Joint investigations:** Cross-border cooperation is growing, e.g., between EU consumer bodies, US FTC, and APEC economies.

- **AI regulation overlap:** The EU AI Act (2024) and OECD AI Principles explicitly prohibit AI systems that "materially distort human behaviour."

Table 7.

Jurisdiction	Regulatory Body	Key Law	Notable Case	Outcome
EU	European Commission	DSA, GDPR	Meta (2022)	€390M fine
US	FTC	FTC Act S5	Epic Games (2023)	$520M settlement
UK	CMA	Consumer Protection Regs	Expedia/Booking (2020)	Reforms mandated
India	CCPA	CPA 2019 + Guidelines (2023)	Zomato/Swiggy (2024)	Policy revision
Australia	ACCC	ACL	Google (2022)	Fined for deception

BENEFITS, LIMITATIONS AND RECOMMENDATIONS

1. Advantages of the Existing Regulation

Three significant accomplishments have been made by the current dark-pattern regulation:

- Awareness and Recognition: Lawmakers now openly recognize that dark patterns are destructive manipulations.
- Legal Categorization: They fall under the category of unfair trade practices in jurisdictions like the EU and India, which grant regulators direct control.
- Corporate Accountability: In response to pressure from around the world, major platforms, including Amazon, Meta, and Google, have updated their user experience flows.

These advancements signal a shift in digital governance from voluntary ethics to legally binding regulations.

2. Limitations

Despite advances in technology, plenty of limitations still exist:

- Reactive Enforcement: Additionally, there is no preventive system in place; investigations are conducted after harm has been done.

- Fragmented Global Approach: Every single country has its own definitions, sanctions, and parameters.
- AI Complexity: Adaptive, customized manipulations are not covered by current legal language.
- Underdeveloped Technical Capacity: Regulators frequently lack the resources or know-how necessary to identify patterns of manipulative design.
- Low Public Awareness: Due to a lack of digital literacy, consumers in developing nations continue to be at risk.

3. Policy Recommendation

• This chapter recommends a few modifications to get over the following challenges:

Algorithmic Transparency Mandates: Must all of the major digital platforms reveal their patterns of data usage and UX testing procedures?

- Pre-Deployment Auditing: For platforms with more users or revenue than a certain threshold, implement Ethical Design Certification, which is related to ISO compliance.
- Cross-Jurisdictional Cooperation: For sharing enforcement data, create a Global Digital Fairness Network under UNCTAD or OECD.
- AI-Specific Provisions: Make AI-driven dark patterns a clear violation of current consumer and data laws.
- Behavioural Data Ethics Boards: Use independent algorithmic audit committees to promote corporate self-regulation.
- Public Awareness Programs: Start government-sponsored initiatives, similar to internet security campaigns, to inform users about manipulative design.
- Legal Standing for Consumer Associations: Give NGOs the ability to file lawsuits against dishonest interfaces in the form of public interest litigation (PIL).

CONCLUSION

One of the most challenging moral and legal issues of the digital age can be seen in dark patterns. Subtle design clues have provided a way to AI-powered persuasion architectures that sell off human attention and consent. From the EU's DSA to India's CCPA Guidelines, the growing global regulatory momentum represents a significant step in the direction of restoring user autonomy and transparency.

However, enforcement is still dispersed, reactive, and behind the times in terms of innovations in technology.

Adaptive, international governance based on human rights and moral AI is necessary for the future. Algorithmic transparency, collaboration across borders, and digital literacy can help societies move away from a "deceptive design economy" and toward one that prioritizes trust and informed decision-making. In the end, restricting dark patterns is important to ensuring human autonomy in the era of algorithms, not just for protecting consumers.

REFERENCES

Binns, R. (2022). Human Judgment in algorithmic loops: Individual justice and automated decision-making. *Regulation & Governance, 16*(1), 197–211.

Chauhan, K. D. S. (2024). *Darker patterns? AI-generated persuasion and the regulatory void in Indian law.* Journal of Development Policy and Practice.

Chun, Y., & Rha, J. (2025). *Influence of dark patterns on consumer responses: A use of a qualitative approach.* Social Science Research Network.

Cowls, J., King, T., Taddeo, M., & Floridi, L. (2019). Designing AI for social good: Seven essential factors. *Available at SSRN* 3388669.

Day, G., Stemler, A., & Stemler, A. (2019). *Are dark patterns anticompetitive?* Social Science Research Network. DOI: 10.2139/ssrn.3468321

Deligoz, K. (2025). *Consumer manipulation with artificial intelligence: Dark patterns and hidden techniques.* DOI: 10.58830/ozgur.pub710.c3029

European Data Protection Board. (2023). *Decision on Meta Platforms Ireland Limited (No. 01/2023).* Brussels.

Federal Trade Commission. (2022, September). Bringing dark patterns to light [Staff report]. https://www.ftc.gov/reports/bringing-dark-patterns-light

Federal Trade Commission (FTC). (2020). *FTC charges ABC Mouse with illegal subscription practices.* https://www.ftc.gov

Federal Trade Commission (FTC). (2023). *FTC takes action against Epic Games for dark patterns and privacy violations.* https://www.ftc.gov

Ghaiumy Anaraky, R., Lowens, B., Li, Y., Byrne, K. A., Risius, M., Page, X., Wisniewski, P., Soleimani, M., Soltani, M., & Knijnenburg, B. P. (2023). *Older and younger adults are influenced differently by dark pattern designs.* arXiv.Org, abs/2310.03830. /arxiv.2310.03830DOI: 10.48550

Gray, K., Yam, K. C., Zhen'An, A. E., Wilbanks, D., & Waytz, A. (2023). The psychology of robots and artificial intelligence. *The handbook of social psychology*, 1-91.

Kahneman, D. (2011). *Fast and slow thinking*. Allen Lane and Penguin Books.

Kowalczyk, M. E., Choffnes, D., Dubois, D. J., & Hartzog, W. (2023). Understanding dark patterns in home IoT devices. *International Conference on Human Factors in Computing Systems.* DOI: 10.1145/3544548.3581432

Kugler, M. B., Strahilevitz, L., Chetty, M., & Mahapatra, C. (2025). *Can consumers protect themselves against privacy dark patterns?* Social Science Research Network. DOI: 10.2139/ssrn.5084827

Leiser, M. R. (2020). *"Dark patterns": The case for regulatory pluralism.* Social Science Research Network. DOI: 10.2139/ssrn.3625637

Li, Z. (2024). *Digital advertising and EU digital regulation.*, DOI: 10.4324/9781003168485-25

Mathur, A., Mayer, J., & Kshirsagar, M. (2021). *What makes a dark pattern... dark? Design attributes, normative considerations, and measurement methods.* DOI: 10.1145/3411764.3445610

Narayanan, A., Mathur, A., Chetty, M., & Kshirsagar, M. (2020). Dark Patterns: Past, Present, and Future: The evolution of tricky user interfaces. *Queue, 18*(2), 67–92.

Ramteke, A., Tembhurne, S., Sonawane, G., & Bhimanpallewar, R. N. (2024). *Detecting deceptive dark patterns in e-commerce platforms.* arXiv.Org. /arxiv.2406. 01608DOI: 10.48550

Riaz, R., Vasconcelos, A., & Pinto, P. (2024). *An overview of user psychological manipulation techniques in UI/UX web design* (pp. 1–6). DOI: 10.1109/ cars61786.2024.10778887

Ro ca, C. (2024). *Digital arms for digital consumer harms – Mapping legal and technical solutions for dark patterns in EU consumer law.* DOI: 10.26481/mup.2403

Schäfer, R., Preuschoff, P. M., & Borchers, J. (2023). *Investigating visual countermeasures against dark patterns in user interfaces.* DOI: 10.1145/3603555.3603563

Chapter 12

Artificial Intelligence and Human Rights: Safeguarding Data Privacy and Ethical Values in the Digital Age

Vijeta Verma
http://orcid.org/0000-0001-9255-9132
Christ University, India

Priyanshu Kumar
http://orcid.org/0009-0000-2712-6242
Christ University, India

ABSTRACT

In the 21st century, the rapid advancement of Artificial Intelligence (AI) presents governments with the dual challenge of fostering technological innovation while safeguarding the rights and freedoms of their citizens. This comparative analysis examines how India addresses data privacy, human rights and ethical concerns arising from AI deployment. The study begins by tracing the evolution of India's legal and policy framework, from the Information Technology Act, 2000 to the Digital Personal Data Protection Act, 2023, assessing how these measures respond to emerging AI-related threats and their implications for individual privacy and civil liberties. Further, the paper evaluates India's engagement with international standards and best practices. Lastly, the study examines ethical and human rights challenges posed by AI applications, including algorithmic bias, automated decision-making, surveillance and deepfakes with a focus on high-stakes sectors like law enforcement, and welfare delivery.

DOI: 10.4018/979-8-3373-7685-1.ch012

1. INTRODUCTION

Artificial Intelligence (AI) is reshaping human life at an unprecedented pace, offering transformative opportunities alongside profound risks. AI offers both great opportunities and serious risks. On one hand, it can transform industries, increase efficiency, and help solve major social issues. On the other hand, it raises important ethical concerns, especially about human rights. Many experts and policymakers are worried that AI could violate basic rights like privacy and equal treatment (Temperman and Quintavalla 2023). This is mainly because AI systems are often complex and unclear working like "*black boxes*" where it's hard to see how decisions are made or who is responsible (Pasquale 2015). One major concern is the use of AI for mass surveillance, which can harm people's right to privacy. For example, China has used facial recognition and social credit systems in ways that many see as government overreach and a threat to civil freedoms (Mozur 2018). Another issue is algorithmic bias when AI systems unfairly treat people based on race, gender, or other factors. This can happen in job hiring, policing, or loan approvals, and often makes existing inequalities worse (O'Neil 2016). Because AI decision-making is not always clear or explainable, it also raises tough questions about who is accountable when things go wrong (Zuboff 2019). Although there are many views on how AI might harm people, most experts agree that strong laws and systems are needed to protect citizens and deal with these challenges.

India's primary data protection legislation, the Digital Personal Data Protection (DPDP) Act, 2023 aims to regulate the collection, storage and processing of personal data. The Act mandates explicit consent especially in the context of sensitive and children's data and imposes obligations on data fiduciaries to ensure transparency and accountability. However, it faces limitations in addressing AI-specific threats such as algorithmic opacity, profiling and automated decision-making. The absence of clear provisions on explainability, fairness and discrimination leave room for human rights risks especially in high-stakes sectors like law enforcement, financial services and welfare delivery.

The Information Technology Act, 2000 along with its rules such as the Intermediary Guidelines and Digital Media Ethics Code, 2021 indirectly address concerns relating to data misuse and harmful content generated by AI. Yet, these laws were not designed with keeping AI in mind and thus struggle to deal with emerging challenges like deepfakes, AI-enabled surveillance and non-consensual data harvesting. While the Supreme Court of India has affirmed the right to privacy as a fundamental right in the case of Justice K.S. Puttaswamy v. Union of India, 2017 which translated that right into practical safeguards in AI governance remains a work in progress.

Furthermore, at the International level, countries like the European Union have taken pioneering steps through the General Data Protection Regulation (GDPR) and the newly adopted AI Act which establish robust standards for data protection, algorithmic transparency and accountability. Similarly, the OECD Principles on AI and UNESCO's Recommendation on the Ethics of AI offer guiding frameworks for balancing innovation with human dignity. India, as a major digital economy can draw from these global models to craft a future-ready AI regulatory ecosystem.

Recent developments in India (2021–2025) reveal multiple real-life instances of AI misuse and rights violations that strengthen the background of this chapter. For example, errors in Aadhaar-based authentication have led to wrongful exclusion from ration and welfare schemes in Jharkhand, Rajasthan and Odisha, demonstrating the risks of automated identity verification for vulnerable groups. Similarly, AI-enabled facial recognition used by Delhi Police was reported to have extremely low accuracy rates during protest surveillance, raising concerns about arbitrary targeting and disproportionate privacy intrusions.

Although India enacted the Digital Personal Data Protection (DPDP) Act in 2023, the regulatory framework remains insufficient for governing AI systems involving profiling, automated decision-making, and high-risk data processing. Existing laws including the DPDP Act and the Information Technology Act, 2000 do not impose explicit duties regarding explainability, auditability or algorithmic transparency, creating a widening gap between technological deployment and rights protection.

A deeper understanding of India's AI governance must also recognise the political economy driving digitalisation. State-led platforms such as Aadhaar, India Stack and large-scale data infrastructures incentivise rapid datafication and automated public service delivery. This institutional ecosystem creates strong political and techno-economic incentives for automation and surveillance often at the expense of due process and transparency.

This paper study titled '*Data Privacy, Human Rights and Ethical Values in the Age of Artificial Intelligence*' will provide the issue with the challenges posed by Artificial Intelligence on individual privacy, human rights and ethical standards. Despite India's recent step of enacting the Digital Personal Data Protection Act, 2023, there remain gaps in addressing AI-specific risks such as algorithmic bias, profiling, opacity and automated decision-making. The study will also examine how the absence of strong safeguards impacts fairness, accountability and civil liberties especially in high-stakes areas like law enforcement, finance and welfare. A comparative analysis with global models such as the GDPR, EU AI Act, OECD Principles and UNESCO AI Ethics will be undertaken to identify best practices. *This research is segmented into 5 Chapters.*

2. RESEARCH PROBLEM

Artificial Intelligence (AI) is growing rapidly in India and across the world While it improves efficiency in areas like healthcare, education, business and governance, it also creates serious risks for data privacy, human rights and ethical values. Although AI enhances productivity and service delivery, its integration into governance and industry often comes at the expense of privacy and equality. Indian laws such as the DPDP Act, 2023 and IT Act, 2000 offer basic protections but lack provisions for algorithmic accountability or transparency (ICLG, 2025). For instance, studies highlight algorithmic discrimination in recruitment and credit scoring systems globally which remain unaddressed in Indian regulation (Floridi et al., 2018). Without reform, marginalized communities are disproportionately exposed to these harms. Current scholarship extensively documents global AI risks but provides limited India-specific analysis on how institutional weaknesses, socio-technical conditions, and constitutional constraints shape these harms. Moreover, little attention has been paid to the deeper causes of India's regulatory gaps, including weak oversight mechanisms, broad state surveillance powers, limited transparency obligations, and lack of procedural safeguards. The absence of strong accountability mechanisms and ethical standards may lead to violations of fundamental rights especially for vulnerable and marginalized communities. Therefore, the central problem this study examines is the misalignment between India's rapid AI adoption and its insufficient legal, ethical and accountability frameworks necessary to safeguard privacy, fairness and human dignity.

3. OBJECTIVE OF THE PAPER

1. To critically examine the challenges AI poses to data privacy, human rights, and ethical standards in India.
2. To analyse the adequacy of Indian legal frameworks such as the DPDP Act, 2023 and the IT Act, 2000 in addressing AI-related risks.
3. To study comparative global practices (like GDPR, EU AI Act, UNESCO and OECD guidelines) and identify lessons for India.
4. To propose policy and regulatory measures that balance technological innovation with protection of individual rights.

4. RESEARCH METHODOLOGY

This research has been conducted by employing a research methodology which is doctrinal research also known as library-based research and the researcher in this paper has also used a qualitative approach. Data has been collected from both primary sources such as Statutes like the *Digital Personal Data Protection Act, 2023 and the Information Technology Act, 2000, Reports, Orders and Judgments* delivered by the Supreme Court of India as well as relevant foreign courts, and international instruments such as the *EU GDPR, EU AI Act, OECD Principles on AI and UNESCO's Recommendation on the Ethics of AI.* Moreover, the secondary sources used include books, journals, research articles, policy papers and newspapers which provide scholarly analysis and critical perspectives on Artificial Intelligence, data privacy, human rights and ethics. Data sources include Google Scholar, Hein Online, and JSTOR. *Keywords used were AI governance, algorithmic bias, human rights and data privacy India.* Only works published between 2018 and 2025 were included. The data were analysed using comparative synthesis and thematic categorization. Limitations include reliance on secondary sources and the evolving nature of AI regulation. Keeping in mind the statement of problem and objectives of research, the researcher has adopted the doctrinal method to critically examine the adequacy of the Indian legal framework, compare it with global practices and propose measures for developing a rights-based and ethical AI ecosystem.

5. LITERATURE REVIEW

The academic discourse on Artificial Intelligence and human rights has grown significantly in recent years, reflecting widespread concern that AI systems may entrench bias, undermine privacy and exacerbate structural inequalities. While existing scholarship offers valuable insights into AI's ethical, legal and societal implications, much of the literature remains either heavily descriptive or predominantly centred on Western regulatory frameworks. There is limited attention to India's unique socio-technical landscape, constitutional principles and institutional constraints.

Of course, there are some studies that in one way or another discuss the tension between technological/state objectives and individual rights. For the present study, the researcher has reviewed an extensive body of literature but only a review of selected, representative works is attempted here. To achieve the objective of the study, the following literature has been extensively reviewed by the researcher.

Maria Devi Angerhofer et al. (2024), "*Privacy in the Age of Artificial Intelligence: Addressing the Ethical and Legal Implications*". In this article, the authors discussed how AI-driven data collection and automated decision-making are eroding traditional notions of individual privacy in multiple sectors (healthcare, fintech, social media) and examine regulatory gaps using GDPR and Indian laws. The paper highlights practical risks (bias in hiring/credit scoring, covert data collection) and stresses the need for transparency, robust regulatory measures and public awareness. However, it does not deeply analyse India's new DPDP Act along with rules or practical enforcement challenges.

Tripti Bhushan (2025), "*AI, Surveillance and Privacy in India: Human Rights in the Age of Technology*", OHRH, This article shows how systems like the Automated Facial Recognition System (AFRS) and Delhi Police's use of facial recognition during the anti-CAA protests can discourage people from protesting or speaking freely which violates Articles 19 and 21 of the Constitution of India. The article also says that predictive policing in states like Uttar Pradesh and Telangana can be unfair because the databases used by police already contain caste, class and community biases, meaning marginalised groups may be targeted more. It also points out that India's new Digital Personal Data Protection Act, 2023 is weak because it allows the government to bypass many rules has almost no checks on surveillance and does not protect citizens as strongly as global laws like the GDPR. The main warning of the article is that India may slowly become a surveillance-heavy society if AI tools are used without transparency or proper legal limits. But the gap is that this article talks only about surveillance and does not cover other important AI problems like bias in welfare benefits, banking or government decision-making, or the lack of India-specific rules for high-risk AI. It also does not compare India's legal system with major global AI laws such as the EU AI Act or UNESCO guidelines.

(Gyandeep Chaudhary & Aditi Nidhi, 2022), "*Human rights and legal issues in the age of artificial intelligence: Challenges, gaps and vulnerabilities*", ILI Law Review. This article explains different types of bias like when the data represents only one group, when surveys are uneven, or when hidden human opinions influence algorithms and shows that these mistakes mostly harm poor people, women, migrants and racial minorities. The paper also discusses how governments use technologies like facial recognition, predictive policing, drones and mass surveillance, which can reduce people's privacy, limit free movement and even silence their freedom of speech. It also talks about global rules such as the EU's AI laws, which try to make AI safe, transparent and accountable. But the main gap in this paper is that it does not focus on India. It does not study India's new Digital Personal Data Protection Act, 2023 or how AI is affecting Indian sectors like policing, welfare schemes, banking or governance. It also does not compare India's laws with global models like the GDPR, EU AI Act or UNESCO guidelines. Your paper fills this gap by studying India's situation, identifying AI risks specific to India (like bias, profiling and lack of transparency) and suggesting how India can make stronger laws to protect privacy, fairness and human dignity.

Rowena Rodrigues (2020), *'Legal and Human Rights Issues of AI: Gaps, Challenges and Vulnerabilities'*, Rodrigues offers a panoramic and rights-based taxonomy of AI legal problems like algorithmic opacity, cybersecurity vulnerabilities, unfairness/bias, lack of contestability, liability and accountability and frames these through a "vulnerability" lens to show which social groups are most exposed. The paper also surveys proposed technical and regulatory remedies (impact assessments, human-in-the-loop, auditing standards) and maps each legal issue to affected human-rights principles. However, the study is more descriptive and does not provide case-based or Indian-specific analysis.

Fatima Roumate (2021), *'Artificial Intelligence, Ethics and International Human Rights Law'*. Roumate reviewed AI concerns within international human rights and humanitarian law, discussing threats from autonomous weapons, large-scale surveillance and algorithmic manipulation of public opinion (deepfakes, microtargeting). The paper argues for international ethical instruments, stronger multilateral cooperation, and adaptation of existing UN human-rights mechanisms to AI risks. However, the suggestions are broad and lack focus on India's institutional capacity or enforcement.

Rahul Kailas Bharati (2024), *'The Right to Privacy in the Age of Artificial Intelligence: Challenges and Legal Frameworks'*. Bharati reviews privacy challenges from AI, traces legal antecedents (e.g., UDHR) and compares regulatory regimes (GDPR) as models. The paper stresses the invisibility of data collection and the need for strong oversight (especially for biometric/emotion-recognition systems). However, It gives more of a technical view and less focus on legal or rights-based aspects.

Existing literature highlights that AI's rapid growth outpaces governance. Angerhofer et al. (2024) examine privacy erosion from AI's automated decision-making but overlook India's enforcement challenges. Rodrigues (2020) frames AI's legal risks via a vulnerability lens. Roumate (2021) links AI with international human-rights law, calling for global cooperation. Bharati (2024) focuses on privacy but misses ethical and accountability dimensions. These studies reveal descriptive gaps but lack integrated theoretical frameworks. To address this, the present This chapter addresses these gaps by Integrating rights-based, vulnerability-based, and accountability-based theoretical frameworks into the analysis of AI's human-rights implications, Providing India-specific insights grounded in real-world examples such as Aadhaar-related exclusions, biased welfare algorithms, and error-prone facial recognition systems, Critically evaluating India's DPDP Act, IT Act, and constitutional jurisprudence for their ability to address AI-specific harms. Lastly, actionable lessons from global frameworks such as GDPR, EU AI Act, OECD Principles and UNESCO Ethics while evaluating their adaptability to Indian realities.

6. HUMAN RIGHTS AND SOCIAL JUSTICE CONCERNS IN AI APPLICATIONS

Artificial Intelligence holds transformative potential across diverse sectors, including healthcare, financial services, governance, and social welfare. However, as AI systems increasingly influence critical human decisions, profound concerns emerge regarding their impact on human rights and social justice.

A central challenge is algorithmic bias, wherein AI systems perpetuate or even amplify historical and societal inequities embedded in their training data. This bias manifests in discriminatory outcomes across hiring practices, credit approvals, policing, and judicial decision-making, disproportionately affecting marginalized groups based on race, gender, socioeconomic status, or ethnicity (O'Neil, 2016; Floridi et al., 2018). For example, facial recognition technologies have been documented to exhibit higher error rates for individuals with darker skin tones, potentially leading to unfair treatment or wrongful surveillance (Pasquale, 2015). In India, this materialised during the Delhi Police's use of facial recognition to identify protestors, where the system reportedly achieved accuracy rates as low as 2% raising concerns of arbitrariness and disproportionate state power.

AI-driven governance also threatens the right to privacy, which the Supreme Court recognised as a fundamental right in Justice K.S. Puttaswamy v. Union of India (2017). Unlike traditional surveillance, AI-enabled monitoring is continuous, silent and capable of inferring sensitive information such as caste, religion, political preferences, behavioural tendencies, or emotional states. With the rapid expansion of CCTV networks linked to facial recognition systems, India risks normalising mass surveillance without adequate oversight or legal constraints. Such pervasive monitoring can produce a chilling effect, discouraging individuals from exercising free speech, participating in protests or engaging in political dissent.

AI's reliance on extensive personal data raises significant privacy and surveillance issues. Mass surveillance systems empowered by AI, particularly facial recognition and behaviour prediction, threaten the fundamental right to privacy and may facilitate intrusive monitoring without due process or consent (Mozur, 2018; Zuboff, 2019). This pervasive surveillance fosters chilling effects on freedom of expression and assembly, undermining democratic participation and civil liberties.

Moreover, the opacity of AI decision-making processes often characterized as "*black boxes*" complicates accountability and transparency. When individuals receive adverse decisions from AI, such as loan denials or employment rejection, they frequently lack sufficient explanation or recourse to challenge those decisions, significantly undermining principles of fairness and due process (Pasquale, 2015; Raso et al., 2018). For example, in several states, automated Aadhaar-based authentication errors have led to wrongful exclusion from ration systems, pensions, and welfare schemes. These exclusions disproportionately harm the elderly, rural populations, and low-income communities who lack the resources or digital literacy to challenge automated decisions.

AI deployment in surveillance, welfare, and policing raises serious concerns under the proportionality framework articulated in Puttaswamy (2017). The test requires that any rights-infringing measure must: (a) pursue a legitimate state aim, (b) be necessary in the sense of adopting the least intrusive method and (c) include robust procedural safeguards to prevent abuse. AI-enabled facial recognition, predictive policing and biometric-based welfare exclusion mechanisms often fail to meet these requirements. Less intrusive alternatives frequently exist, and the absence of transparent oversight, notice, or meaningful appellate mechanisms reveals deep constitutional vulnerabilities in India's current AI governance model.

Social justice concerns also arise from the uneven distribution of AI benefits and harms. Marginalized communities often face greater exposure to harmful AI practices while having limited access to its benefits, thereby exacerbating existing inequalities (Kriebitz & Lütge, 2020). Additionally, AI-facilitated online abuse, disinformation, and suppression of dissent disproportionately affect vulnerable populations, threatening the pluralism and inclusiveness essential for social justice (Nicolau, 2021). AI contributes to informational harms including online manipulation, targeted misinformation and algorithmically amplified hate speech. Deepfakes and microtargeted political messaging can distort democratic processes and exacerbate communal tensions, particularly when deployed without accountability or transparency.

7. RIGHT BASED AND ETHICAL AI ECOSYSTEM IN INDIA

Building a rights-based and ethically grounded Artificial Intelligence ecosystem in India requires more than scattered policy initiatives or generic ethical guidelines. It demands a coherent governance architecture that aligns technological development with constitutional values particularly dignity, equality, privacy and due process. As AI becomes embedded in welfare delivery, policing, education, finance and digital governance, the need for a comprehensive ethical and legal framework becomes urgent.

A genuinely ethical AI ecosystem must begin with clear, enforceable regulatory standards. Although the Digital Personal Data Protection (DPDP) Act, 2023 establishes a baseline framework for personal data processing, it does not address AI-specific obligations such as algorithmic explainability, impact assessments, bias audits, human oversight or transparency requirements. These omissions are significant because AI systems frequently operate through high-risk decision-making that directly affects rights, entitlements, and access to essential services. (Chambers Global Practice Guides, 2025). Therefore, India requires dedicated AI legislation that defines high-risk AI systems and mandates greater scrutiny for domains such as welfare eligibility, credit scoring, predictive policing, biometric surveillance and healthcare diagnostics.

Secondly, The creation of an independent AI regulatory authority empowered to oversee, audit and enforce compliance. Such a body must possess investigative powers, the ability to mandate algorithmic audits, the authority to review high-risk AI systems before deployment, and mechanisms to impose penalties for non-compliance. (Legal500, 2025; IJLLR, 2025) Without an independent regulator, AI governance in India will remain fragmented, reactive, and vulnerable to political and corporate influence particularly given the extensive discretion enjoyed by government agencies. (Drishti IAS, 2025).

An ethical AI ecosystem must also adopt a multi-stakeholder governance model, ensuring participation from technologists, civil society groups, industry actors, human-rights organisations, academic experts and the communities most affected by AI deployment. Participatory governance helps reduce information asymmetry, enhances the legitimacy of policy formulation, and ensures that AI systems are designed with a holistic understanding of social realities.

Further, AI systems in India must embrace ethics-by-design, embedding principles such as fairness, proportionality, contestability, and human oversight at every stage of development and deployment. Mandatory mechanisms such as algorithmic impact assessments, bias testing, explainability standards, and post-deployment monitoring should be integrated to ensure continuous accountability. In all high-stakes decisions, human-in-the-loop mechanisms must be preserved to prevent complete reliance on opaque automated systems. (Floridi et al., 2018).

At the societal level, an ethical ecosystem requires strengthening public awareness and digital literacy. India's deep digital divide means that millions of citizens do not understand how their data is collected, profiled, or used by AI systems. Awareness initiatives integrated into school curricula, community programmes, and public campaigns are essential to ensure that individuals can meaningfully exercise their rights, challenge adverse automated decisions, and hold institutions accountable.

However, no ethical AI framework is complete without addressing innovation-related counterarguments. Policymakers and industry actors frequently argue that stringent regulations such as mandatory audits, explainability requirements and prior authorisation for high-risk systems may slow innovation and impose compliance burdens on start-ups. (Huridocs, 2025). Given India's aspiration to become a global AI hub and its reliance on rapid digital public infrastructure development, there are concerns that rigid regulatory frameworks might hinder experimentation and competitiveness. India also faces institutional constraints, including limited technical expertise within regulatory bodies and fragmented oversight structures. Therefore, AI governance in India must strike a careful balance, protecting fundamental rights without stifling innovation or technological growth.

To sum up, an ethical AI ecosystem for India must be grounded in the country's constitutional ethos. AI governance should operationalise the principles of dignity, equality, fairness, and justice by embedding them into enforceable legal and institutional mechanisms. Only through a rights-based and accountability-driven approach can India ensure that AI serves as a tool for social empowerment rather than a driver of exclusion, discrimination or unchecked surveillance.

8. RESULTS

8.1. Ethical Concerns

AI is no longer a futuristic concept, it is a powerful tool that has already begun reshaping industries, societies, and daily life. From healthcare diagnostics and financial decision-making to facial recognition and smart assistants, AI's capabilities are rapidly expanding. The most persistent ethical concern in India's AI ecosystem is the opacity of algorithmic decision-making. Unlike jurisdictions governed by the GDPR or EU AI Act where risk classification, transparency obligations, and human oversight are mandated that India lacks requirements for explainability, algorithmic disclosures or automated decision-making safeguards. Individuals adversely affected by AI-driven decisions therefore lack meaningful ability to seek clarity, contest decisions or access effective remedies.

One of the most widely discussed ethical issues is algorithmic bias. Since AI systems learn from data, they can reflect and reinforce existing societal biases present in that data. For instance, if a hiring algorithm is trained on data from a company that has historically favoured male applicants, it may replicate and perpetuate gender discrimination. Studies have shown that AI used in facial recognition tends to be less accurate for people with darker skin tones, potentially leading to false arrests or surveillance abuses. Such biases not only reproduce historical injustices but also violate the principles of equality and non-discrimination, enshrined in human rights law.

When AI systems make wrong or harmful decisions, it can be unclear who is responsible: the programmer, the company or the machine itself. This lack of accountability complicates the assignment of legal or moral responsibility. In traditional systems, decision-makers are identifiable and their actions can be challenged. With AI, especially with autonomous systems, the chain of accountability may be fragmented, leading to a gap in justice and redress mechanisms.

AI technologies like facial recognition, predictive policing, and behaviour analysis rely heavily on the collection and processing of personal data. Without proper safeguards, such tools can be misused by governments and corporations to monitor citizens, often without consent. For example, mass surveillance systems implemented in some countries using AI have raised alarms about the erosion of privacy rights and civil liberties. The right to privacy, upheld by courts in many jurisdictions (such as Justice K.S. Puttaswamy v. Union of India in India), is directly threatened by unchecked AI surveillance. AI's increasing influence over personal and professional decisions raises concerns about human autonomy. When AI makes decisions about medical treatment, employment, or access to public benefits, human beings may lose the ability to make informed choices or challenge automated outcomes. This can undermine human dignity, a core ethical value, especially if people are reduced to mere data points in decision-making systems.

8.2. Data Privacy

The results show that the Digital Personal Data Protection (DPDP) Act, 2023 provides only partial protection against AI-related privacy harms. While it establishes a consent-based data processing framework, it does not regulate profiling, automated decision-making, behavioural inference or algorithmic prediction all of which are central to AI. Because biometric, demographic and transactional data are routinely used to train AI systems, the lack of transparency obligations leaves individuals vulnerable to intrusive monitoring and discrimination. The misuse of personal data is another serious concern linked to AI models and the risks they pose to human rights. These models can sometimes generate content that includes personal information from the data they were trained on, violating individuals' privacy. For example, a study by Carlini et al. (2021) found that text produced by models like GPT-2 occasionally contained publicly available personal details such as names, email addresses, and phone numbers. Damani and Engler (2024) raise an important question: What happens if a lawyer uploads a full contract, including sensitive client data and asks the AI model to revise it? In such cases, the model may learn from that personal information, which could then influence future responses. This raises serious concerns about how such actions affect a person's right to privacy.

Due to these concerns, companies like OpenAI warn users not to share personal data while interacting with their platforms. They clearly mention that any content users provide may be used to further train their models. For example, OpenAI states: "When you use our services for individuals such as ChatGPT, we may use your content to train our models." Additionally, they admit that they monitor user conversations to ensure they follow safety and policy standards. This highlights the need for users to be careful when using AI tools and to avoid sharing sensitive or private information. Lastly, Protecting personal data is essential to safeguarding one's right to privacy in the age of AI.

Data privacy has changed a lot in a short time as technology has advanced. In the past, privacy mainly meant keeping papers, records, and face-to-face meetings confidential. But with the digital age came massive data collection, storage, and processing, which required stronger rules and clearer privacy rights (Warren & Brandeis, 1890). The famous article "The Right to Privacy" by Warren and Brandeis (1890) is often seen as the starting point of modern privacy laws.

Over the years, privacy challenges became more complex, leading to the creation of strict standards like the General Data Protection Regulation (GDPR) in the European Union in 2018. GDPR not only set high standards for protecting personal data in Europe but also influenced global privacy regulations, pushing the world toward a more unified approach (Solove, 2006). These rules give individuals more control over their personal information and require organizations to follow strict data protection measures.

8.3. AI in Welfare Delivery System

The findings reveal that India's use of AI in welfare governance produces disproportionate harm for vulnerable populations. Aadhaar-based biometric authentication failures have led to wrongful exclusion from essential programmes such as the Public Distribution System (PDS), pensions and social security schemes. These errors often stem from biometric mismatches, low-quality datasets, connectivity issues, or rigid automated verification systems. Artificial Intelligence is increasingly shaping governance and everyday life in India but several context-specific challenges require closer examination. In the social welfare sector, algorithmic tools now determine eligibility for schemes such as the Public Distribution System (PDS), Direct Benefit Transfers (DBT), and pension programmes and automated error-detection systems have led to wrongful deletion of beneficiary names, an exclusion that disproportionately harms marginalised communities. Similar concerns arise in policing, where states such as Telangana and Uttar Pradesh have piloted predictive policing and crime-mapping systems that rely on biased historical data, creating a heightened risk of over-surveillance of specific socio-economic groups. In the private sector, major Indian technology companies (including Infosys, TCS, Wipro and Jio Platforms) have established internal AI ethics boards, yet these mechanisms remain largely voluntary, opaque, and without regulatory oversight. Compounding these issues is India's significant gap in digital literacy and AI awareness; many citizens lack the capacity to understand consent, data rights or the implications of automated decision-making.

8.4. Gaps in Legal and Regulatory Framework in India and Global Lessons

India's legal framework addressing data privacy and artificial intelligence is currently anchored primarily by the Digital Personal Data Protection (DPDP) Act, 2023, alongside related legislation such as the Information Technology Act, 2000. The DPDP Act represents a crucial legislative step toward regulating the collection, processing, and storage of personal data with a mandate for explicit consent, transparency, purpose limitation, and accountability (Drishti IAS, 2025; Legal500, 2025). However, the Act, while comprehensive on data privacy fundamentals, falls short in explicitly addressing AI-specific challenges such as algorithmic transparency, explainability, automated decision-making, and profiling dimensions are essential for safeguarding human rights within AI ecosystems. For instance, the DPDP Act does not provide particular mandates regarding the explainability of AI decisions, the mitigation of algorithmic bias, or mechanisms ensuring fairness within automated systems, leaving significant regulatory gaps (IJLLR, 2025).

Similarly, the Information Technology Act, 2000, along with its subsidiary rules including the Intermediary Guidelines and Digital Media Ethics Code, 2021, provides ancillary safeguards concerning data misuse, digital content, and intermediary liabilities but was initially designed for earlier digital threats, lacking provisions tailored for AI phenomena like deepfakes, AI-driven surveillance, or automated profiling (Chambers Global Practice Guides, 2025). The Indian judiciary has recognized the right to privacy as fundamental in landmark judgments such as Justice K.S. Puttaswamy v. Union of India (2017), affirming privacy's constitutional protection. However, operationalizing these rights effectively within AI governance frameworks remains an ongoing challenge (ICLG, 2025).

The government is taking preliminary steps to bridge these gaps by creating committees focused on responsible AI development and issuing governance guidelines recommending institutional frameworks, risk assessment protocols, and redressal mechanisms specifically targeted at AI use cases. Yet, the absence of a dedicated AI regulatory authority, unlike data protection authorities in other jurisdictions, tempers enforcement effectiveness (Legal500, 2025; Chambers Global Practice Guides, 2025).

Consequently, while the Indian legal system provides a solid foundation for data privacy, a more nuanced, AI-centric legal framework integrating transparency, fairness, accountability, and non-discrimination is essential to adequately protect human rights in the AI era.

Globally, various international legal and ethical frameworks offer robust models for AI governance aligned with human rights and ethical values. The European Union's General Data Protection Regulation (GDPR) is a landmark regulation that sets stringent standards for personal data protection, embedding principles of informed consent, data minimization, and individual rights such as access, correction, and deletion of data (Solove, 2006). Building upon GDPR, the new EU AI Act introduces regulatory requirements targeting high-risk AI systems, emphasizing transparency, risk management, human oversight, and mitigation of bias. This pioneering legislation demands pre-use conformity assessments and continuous post-market monitoring, establishing a comprehensive accountability mechanism to prevent harm to individuals (Global Legal Insights, 2025).

Beyond the EU, multilateral efforts such as the OECD AI Principles provide foundational international standards advocating for inclusive growth, innovation, human-centred values, transparency, security, accountability, and respect for democratic principles. These principles underscore the necessity for governments and private sector actors to ensure AI systems do not erode human rights and to promote trustworthy AI development (OECD, 2024).

UNESCO's Recommendation on the Ethics of Artificial Intelligence (2021) further addresses AI's societal implications by recommending policies that emphasize human dignity, non-discrimination, accessibility, environmental sustainability, and participatory governance. This framework advocates for embedding these ethical principles from design through deployment, guiding states to nurture AI ecosystems that serve humanity equitably (Huridocs, 2025).\

9. SUGGESTIONS

Based on the findings of this study, it is clear that India must adopt a multi-layered, rights-based approach to Artificial Intelligence regulation in order to safeguard constitutional values while supporting responsible technological innovation. The following suggestions outline legal, institutional, and ethical reforms necessary for establishing a transparent, accountable and socially just AI governance framework in India. Artificial Intelligence (AI) has already begun reshaping governance, business, and social life in India. But the existing regulatory framework mainly the IT Act, 2000 and the Digital Personal Data Protection (DPDP) Act, 2023 does not adequately cover AI-specific risks like algorithmic bias, profiling, or mass surveillance. To make AI development both safe and rights-respecting, India needs a multi-pronged strategy. Firstly, India needs a dedicated AI law that clearly defines high-risk AI systems, establishes mandatory transparency requirements and introduces rights against adverse automated decision-making. Such legislation should require algorithmic explainability, fairness standards, human oversight and clear liability frameworks. This is essential because existing laws like the DPDP Act and IT Act do not address AI-specific harms. For example, if an AI system denies a person access to a loan or job, that person should have the right to question and challenge the decision (Floridi et al., 2018). Such legal safeguards would ensure accountability and prevent unfair discrimination. Secondly, A strong regulatory authority dedicated solely to AI is essential. Similar to data protection regulators in the European Union, such a body would be responsible for enforcing standards, carrying out audits, and investigating complaints. Without an independent oversight mechanism, the risk of unchecked AI misuse especially by powerful corporations or state authorities remains high (Global Legal Insights, 2025). This authority should also act as a mediator between citizens and AI developers, ensuring that grievances are addressed effectively. Thirdly, Merely having laws is not enough; AI systems must also be designed with ethics at their core. The concept of "*ethics by design*" suggests that fairness, transparency, and accountability should be built into AI systems from the very beginning. For example, bias testing and fairness audits should be mandatory before an AI tool is rolled out. Moreover, explainable AI (XAI) should be encouraged so that users can understand how decisions are made (Pasquale, 2015). These measures would reduce the "*black box*" nature of AI, where even developers sometimes cannot explain outcomes. Lastly, Not all AI applications carry the same level of risk. For instance, AI used in medical diagnosis has higher stakes than AI used in a music recommendation app. Therefore, India should introduce a system of "AI impact assessments" where applications are classified as low-risk, medium-risk, or high-risk. High-risk AI should undergo stricter testing, approval, and monitoring before deployment. This approach is already part of the EU's AI Act and could be adapted to India's socio-legal environment (OECD, 2024).

India should draw lessons from the GDPR, EU AI Act, OECD Principles, and UNESCO Ethics but adapt them to local constraints such as institutional capacity, digital inequality, and socio-economic diversity. A hybrid regulatory model combining global standards with Indian constitutional principles is the most viable approach.

10. CONCLUSION

Artificial Intelligence is a double-edged sword for India. On one hand, it promises to transform industries like healthcare, education, agriculture, and governance, bringing efficiency and growth. On the other, it raises serious concerns regarding privacy, equality, and human dignity. Without proper checks, AI can reinforce existing social inequalities and create new forms of injustice (O'Neil, 2016; Zuboff, 2019).

Currently, India relies mainly on the DPDP Act, 2023 and the IT Act, 2000. While these are important, they are not sufficient for AI's unique risks. For instance, they do not fully address problems like algorithmic opacity, automated profiling or large-scale surveillance. This creates a legal vacuum where citizens may lack protection against harmful AI practices (IJLLR, 2025).

Internationally, frameworks such as the GDPR, the EU AI Act, the OECD AI Principles, and the UNESCO Ethics Recommendations show that it is possible to regulate AI without stifling innovation (OECD, 2024; UNESCO, 2021). These models prove that human rights and technological development can go hand-in-hand. India can draw lessons from these while tailoring them to its socio-economic conditions. Going forward, India needs to draft AI-specific legislation, establish a strong and independent regulatory body, mandate transparency and accountability in AI systems, and focus on empowering citizens through education and awareness. Implementing these measures will not only make AI safer but also ensure that technology serves the people rather than working against their interests. Ultimately, the true success of AI will not be judged by how advanced the technology becomes, but by how effectively it respects and safeguards human rights.

REFERENCES

Angerhofer, M. D.. (2024). Privacy in the age of artificial intelligence: Addressing the ethical and legal implications. *Journal of AI & Society*, *42*(3), 215–234.

Bharati, R. K. (2024). The right to privacy in the age of artificial intelligence: Challenges and legal frameworks. *Indian Journal of Law and Technology*, *16*(1), 45–67.

Carlini, N., Tramer, F., Wallace, E., Jagielski, M., Herbert-Voss, A., Lee, K., & Song, D. (2021). Extracting training data from large language models. *Proceedings of the 30th USENIX Security Symposium*, 2633–2650.

Chambers Global Practice Guides. (2025). Technology, media, and telecommunications in India. Retrieved from https://chambers.com

Damani, S., & Engler, A. (2024). Data privacy and AI in legal practice: Emerging concerns. *International Journal of Legal Technology*, *8*(2), 101–120.

Drishti, I. A. S. (2025). *Artificial intelligence governance and ethics: Policy overview*. Drishti Publications.

Floridi, L., Cowls, J., Beltrametti, M., Chatila, R., Chazerand, P., Dignum, V., & Vayena, E. (2018). AI4People-An ethical framework for a good AI society: Opportunities, risks, principles, and recommendations. *Minds and Machines*, *28*, 689–707. DOI: 10.1007/s11023-018-9482-5

Global Legal Insights. (2025). Artificial intelligence regulations 2025: India. Retrieved from https://www.globallegalinsights.com/practice-areas/artificial-intelligence-laws-and-regulations/india

. Huridocs. (2025). AI ethics and human rights: Global perspectives. New Delhi: Huridocs Publications.

ICLG. (2025). Data protection and privacy laws in India. Retrieved from https://iclg.com

IJLLR. (2025). Emerging issues in AI governance and human rights in India. International Journal of Law. *Language & Regulation*, *12*(1), 55–79.

Kriebitz, R., & Lütge, C. (2020). Ethics of AI: Societal impacts and justice perspectives. *AI and Ethics*, *1*, 123–135. DOI: 10.1007/s43681-020-00004-x

Mozur, P. (2018, April 10). Inside China's dystopian dreams: AI, shame, and control. The New York Times. Retrieved from https://www.nytimes.com

Nicolau, L. (2021). Social justice and AI: Addressing inequities in algorithmic systems. *Journal of Human Rights and Technology*, *3*(2), 34–52.

O'Neil, C. (2016). *Weapons of math destruction: How big data increases inequality and threatens democracy.* Crown Publishing.

OECD. (2024). OECD principles on artificial intelligence. Paris: Organisation for Economic Co-operation and Development. Retrieved from https://www.oecd.org/ai

Pasquale, F. (2015). *The black box society: The secret algorithms that control money and information.* Harvard University Press.

Raso, F. A.. (2018). Artificial intelligence & human rights: Opportunities and challenges. *European Journal of Risk Regulation*, *9*(2), 177–194.

Solove, D. J. (2006). A taxonomy of privacy. *University of Pennsylvania Law Review*, *154*(3), 477–564.

Temperman, J., & Quintavalla, L. (2023). AI, law, and human rights: Ethical implications and safeguards. *International Journal of Law and Information Technology*, *31*(1), 1–25.

UNESCO. (2021). Recommendation on the ethics of artificial intelligence. Paris: UNESCO. Retrieved from https://unesdoc.unesco.org

Warren, S. D., & Brandeis, L. D. (1890). The right to privacy. *Harvard Law Review*, *4*(5), 193–220.

Zuboff, S. (2019). *The age of surveillance capitalism: The fight for a human future at the new frontier of power.* PublicAffairs.

Chapter 13
Technical and Ethical Perspectives on Building Intelligent Legal Assistants With LLM and RAG Pipelines:
Building a Legal Chatbot With LLMs and RAG

Jessica Mbounkap
Aivancity, La Grande Ecole De L'intelligence Artificielle Et De La Data, France

Habiba Djigo
Aivancity, La Grande Ecole De L'intelligence Artificielle Et De La Data, France

Tasnim Masheh
Aivancity, La Grande Ecole De L'intelligence Artificielle Et De La Data, France

Aymrick Nzooh
http://orcid.org/0009-0004-9695-0840
Aivancity, La Grande Ecole De L'intelligence Artificielle Et De La Data, France

Anuradha Kar
http://orcid.org/0000-0002-2543-1697
Aivancity, La Grande Ecole De L'intelligence Artificielle Et De La Data, France

DOI: 10.4018/979-8-3373-7685-1.ch013

ABSTRACT

The rapid advancement of Large Language Models (LLMs) has opened new possibilities for intelligent legal assistants that support research, drafting, case analysis, and decision preparation. This article presents how LLMs combined with Retrieval-Augmented Generation (RAG) can power context aware and reliable legal AI systems. The article outlines technical foundations of such assistants, describing how RAG pipelines integrate legal documents to produce outputs based on reliable sources and reduce hallucinations. Key technical challenges such as constructing legal knowledge bases and managing computational demands are also discussed. Beyond technical design, the article explores the ethical implications of deploying legal chatbots, including bias, unequal access, accountability, and overreliance on automated interpretations. We highlight the requirements for responsible AI in these chatbots, covering explainability, human oversight, and compliance. The article defines a roadmap for developing legal assistants that are accurate, transparent, and aligned with legal and societal norms.

1. INTRODUCTION

Access to accurate, comprehensible, and reliable legal information remains a persistent challenge in present day societies, despite the widespread availability of digitized legal documents and statutes. While much of this information is publicly accessible, it is often presented in formal legal language and complex structures that require specialized training to interpret. Individuals without a legal background frequently face significant barriers in understanding their rights, obligations, or available legal remedies. Even experienced legal professionals can spend substantial time locating relevant statutes, jurisprudence, procedural requirements, or regulatory guidelines.

This gap between the availability of legal information and its accessibility underscores a growing need for technological solutions that can reliably support legal research, public legal education, and professional practice. Despite digitization and open-access platforms, legal information remains difficult to navigate. Several factors contribute to this problem, such as 1)Complexity of legal language: Legal documents are often densely structured and filled with terms of art, cross-references, and layered interpretations. 2)Fragmentation of information: Relevant materials may be spread across statutes, case law, administrative rules, and commentary. 3) High expertise threshold: Effective legal research requires training in legal reasoning and a deep understanding of domain-specific frameworks. 4)Limited access to professional counsel: Cost, geography, and systemic barriers often hinder timely access to legal advice. AI systems offer the potential to bridge these barriers by providing efficient, context-aware, and user-friendly access to legal knowledge (Bench-Capon et al., 2012; Dzienkowski, 2013; McKeown et al., 2020; Nikolskaia & Naumov, 2020). However, unlike open-domain chatbots (like ChatGPT), legal chatbots must be grounded in verifiable legal sources and adhere to high standards of accuracy, fairness, and transparency. LLMs such as GPT, LLaMA, or Mistral have demonstrated remarkable capabilities in natural language understanding and generation (Alarie et al., 2018; Brooks et al., 2020; McGinnis & Pearce, 2014; Muthuraju et al., 2025). Their ability to synthesize complex information, interpret user queries, and produce fluent text makes them strong candidates for legal conversational systems (Bhagwat et al., 2025; Khatri et al., 2021; Patil et al., 2025). However, LLMs alone are insufficient for legal contexts because: 1)They can hallucinate information, creating plausible-sounding but incorrect statements. 2) Their training data is broad but not necessarily tailored to specific jurisdictions. 3) Legal knowledge must be grounded in authoritative and updated sources. Therefore, LLMs must be paired with robust retrieval mechanisms to ensure factual grounding.(Y Arcas, 2022; Chernyavskiy et al., 2021; Radford et al., 2019; Surana et al., 2021) Retrieval-Augmented Generation (RAG) addresses LLM limitations by combining two components: 1) A retrieval system that identifies relevant documents (statutes, regulations, case law) 2) An LLM generator that synthesizes responses based on retrieved content. This architecture improves accuracy, traceability, and domain specificity.

This chapter demonstrates how RAG-enabled LLM systems (Brown et al., 2020; Chung et al., 2024; Devlin et al., 2018; Lewis et al., 2019; Zhang et al., 2021) offer a promising software architecture for achieving this balance that is suitable for both legal professionals and generic users. We first present how using advanced artificial intelligence(AI), especially Large Language Models (LLMs) and Retrieval Augmented Generation (RAG), a legal chatbot can be built which is capable of generating contextually relevant answers to legal questions from diverse fields like civil, criminal and intellectual property law. This chapter then explores the potential applications and ethical challenges associated with building such legal chatbots. It guides readers through the principles, design choices, implementation workflows, and evaluation considerations involved in creating a responsible legal chatbot. Then it explores the practical challenges of using such chatbots in real life judiciary systems and state-of-the-art legal applications. The chapter provides practical insights on how RAG pipelines integrate several components to generate accurate, grounded responses. It begins with document ingestion, where legal texts are cleaned, segmented, and embedded for efficient retrieval. These embeddings are stored in a vector database to enable semantic search of relevant information. The LLM reasoning layer synthesizes this retrieved information into coherent, legally grounded answers. Finally, memory and conversation handling tools, such as those in LangChain, manage interactions, maintain context, and ensure smooth, consistent dialog flow in a legal chatbot. The chapter will provide information on software frameworks and tools that can be used to build the end to end legal chatbot framework.

A substantial part of the chapter walks readers through the complete process of building a functional legal chatbot using a RAG-based architecture(Touvron, Martin, Stone, Albert, Almahairi, Babaei, & Scialom, 2023; Wang et al., 2022; Wei et al., 2022). It begins with designing the system workflow, integrating document ingestion and embedding components, configuring retrievers, linking LLMs to the retrieval layer (Boiko et al., 2023; Webb et al., 2023), and crafting prompt templates suited to legal queries. The chapter then moves into hands-on pipeline construction, demonstrating how to connect different chatbot components with the vector databases for semantic retrieval (Salemi & Zamani, 2024; Gao et al., 2023; Lewis et al., 2020; Rackauckas, 2024; Shao et al., 2023). Readers learn to implement core functionalities such as query analysis, retrieval operations, and, where appropriate, multimodal reasoning, enabling them to assemble a fully operational legal chatbot (Salemi & Zamani, 2024; Gao et al., 2023; Lewis et al., 2020; Rackauckas, 2024; Shao et al., 2023).

In order to build chatbots we also created a robust and comprehensive document library that spans constitutional law, civil and criminal codes, family and financial law, international and environmental laws. Building such a knowledge base involves acquiring authoritative legal sources, preprocessing and segmenting the texts, enriching them with metadata such as jurisdiction, enactment dates, and case identifiers, and embedding them into vector formats for semantic search. In the chapter, we demonstrate this process step by step, showing how to collect documents from official repositories, clean and structure them using python programming-based preprocessing pipelines, generate embeddings, and store them efficiently in a vector database. This hands-on walkthrough illustrates how each component of the data pipeline contributes to a well-organized and traceable document library, which is essential not only for accurate information retrieval and effective chatbot performance but also for maintaining transparency and legal reliability in real-world applications.

User interface development for the chatbot is carried out using web development technologies, which provides a straightforward yet effective platform for capturing user questions and managing conversation history. This design approach enhances usability and transparency for both legal professionals and general users. Evaluation and testing then focus on key criteria such as accuracy, faithfulness to retrieved documents, completeness of responses, and safety to ensure the system avoids misleading or harmful guidance. By integrating automated evaluation with expert review, developers can verify that the chatbot meets essential quality and reliability standards.

After describing the construction process of the legal chatbot, we discuss its potential application areas. Legal chatbots can provide meaningful value across a wide range of domains. They can support legal aid and public information by helping individuals understand their rights and navigate basic legal procedures (Dzienkowski, 2013; McGinnis & Pearce, 2014; McKeown et al., 2020; Nikolskaia & Naumov, 2020), while also assisting organizations with compliance and risk management by interpreting regulatory requirements. For legal professionals, these systems offer rapid access to summaries, statute lookups, and cross-referencing tools that enhance research efficiency (Bhagwat et al., 2025; Brooks et al., 2020; Muthuraju et al., 2025; Patil et al., 2025). In government and public administration, chatbots streamline citizen access to administrative processes and legal obligations. They also contribute to legal education by offering structured explanations and case-based reasoning guidance. The chapter illustrates these applications through practical workflows and context-specific examples.

The deployment of legal chatbots introduces significant ethical challenges, including risks of inaccuracy and hallucination that can have serious legal consequences, making factual grounding and oversight essential. In this chapter we discuss the aspect of bias and fairness concerns that arise from systemic inequities embedded in legal datasets, requiring audits, test cases, and mitigation frameworks. Ensuring interpretability and transparency is equally crucial, with users needing clarity on retrieved sources, reasoning processes, and model uncertainty. Legal chatbots must also comply with evolving AI safety standards, professional ethics, and data protection regulations. A key issue is avoiding unauthorized legal practice, addressed through disclaimers, scope limits, and escalation to human experts. The chapter follows a hands-on structure covering foundations, implementation, evaluation, and future directions, concluding that RAG-enabled legal chatbots can expand access to legal knowledge when developed responsibly.

2. FOUNDATIONS OF BUILDING A LEGAL CHATBOT

In this section we present the conceptual and technological building blocks that underpin such systems. It introduces core ideas from types of law, information retrieval, and legal AI that are essential for understanding subsequent design choices. By grounding the discussion in these foundational principles, the section provides the basis for analyzing more advanced architectures, such as retrieval-augmented and graph-based approaches, developed in the later sections of this chapter.

2.1.1 The Legal Domain and Types of Law

Law is a vast field made up of multiple branches, each addressing different kinds of rights, responsibilities, and disputes. Criminal law deals with offenses against the state, such as theft, assault, or fraud, where the goal is to punish wrongdoing. Civil law governs disputes between individuals or organizations, including contracts, property issues, family matters, and personal injuries. Corporate and commercial law regulates business entities, commercial transactions, and corporate governance. Constitutional law defines the structure of the government and protects fundamental rights, while administrative law oversees how government agencies create and enforce regulations. Employment and labour law governs the relationship between employers and employees, covering contracts, workplace safety, and discrimination. Intellectual property law protects creations like inventions, art, and trademarks. Environmental law regulates how individuals and companies interact with the environment, while banking and finance law manages financial transactions, lending, and regulatory compliance. Tax law, family law, immigration law, and consumer protection law are additional areas that touch everyday life but are often confusing for the general public. Below we describe further some of the main branches of law, based on which we will be presenting our legal chatbot results later in the chapter.

Figure 1. The different branches of legal system

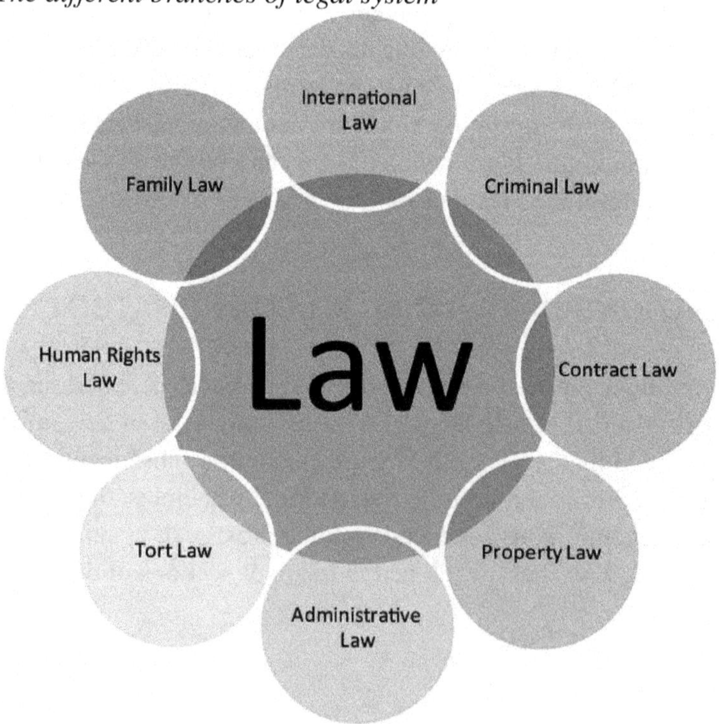

a) Banking and Finance Law

It is a broad and diverse practice area covering the legal regulation of financial institutions and the wide variety of financial transactions they engage in. At its core, practitioners in banking and finance law help structure and document the relationships between lenders and borrowers. This involves complex loan agreements, security arrangements, debt financing, and other credit facilities for corporations, public-sector borrowers, SMEs, or institutional investors.

Within this field, there are several sub-specializations:

- **Acquisition and leveraged finance**: Laws concerning financing leveraged buy-outs, takeovers, recapitalizations or major acquisitions. These deals often require sophisticated intercreditor agreements and collaboration between M&A, tax, and regulatory specialists.
- **Asset and leasing finance**: covering finance for high-value assets or equipment, for example, aircraft, ships, telecom equipment, rail or energy infrastructure, where the lawyer drafts and advises on leasing, security over assets, regulatory implications and financing structure.
- **General loans and lending**: advising banks, financial institutions or corporate/industrial borrowers on standard or bespoke credit facilities, whether for property development, business expansion, asset purchase, or working capital.
- **Structured finance and securitisation**: pooling different debt obligations (e.g. mortgages, loans, credit-card debt) and repackaging them into securities or bonds, a complex area involving detailed transaction structuring and regulatory compliance.
- **Project finance and real-estate finance**: financing large-scale infrastructure, energy or real estate development projects, often requiring coordination across banking, real estate, tax, regulatory, and construction-law experts.
- **Debt capital markets**: supporting the issuance of public debt (bonds, notes) by companies or governments, including drafting prospectuses, listing documents, regulatory compliance, and due diligence.
- **Regulatory banking law and compliance**: advising institutions on bank licensing, capital adequacy rules, securities distribution, marketing rules, and ensuring compliance with banking and financial regulations, a dynamic area given regulatory reforms and market shifts.

b) Civil Law

Civil law is the branch of private law that governs legal relations and disputes between individuals, organizations, or entities rather than crimes punishable by the state. It provides a systematic framework, often codified in statutes or civil codes (in countries with a civil-law tradition), which enables clarity, predictability, and fairness in resolving non-criminal disputes. Unlike criminal law, where the objective is punishment, civil law seeks remedies, typically compensation or specific performance, when one party's rights are harmed by another's breach or wrongful act. Civil law deals with the rights and duties of individuals or entities in their private interactions, for example, contracts, property ownership, family relations, or personal damages and allows aggrieved parties to bring lawsuits seeking restitution or injunctions. Civil law is subdivided into many specialized domains.

Figure 2. Core principles of civil law

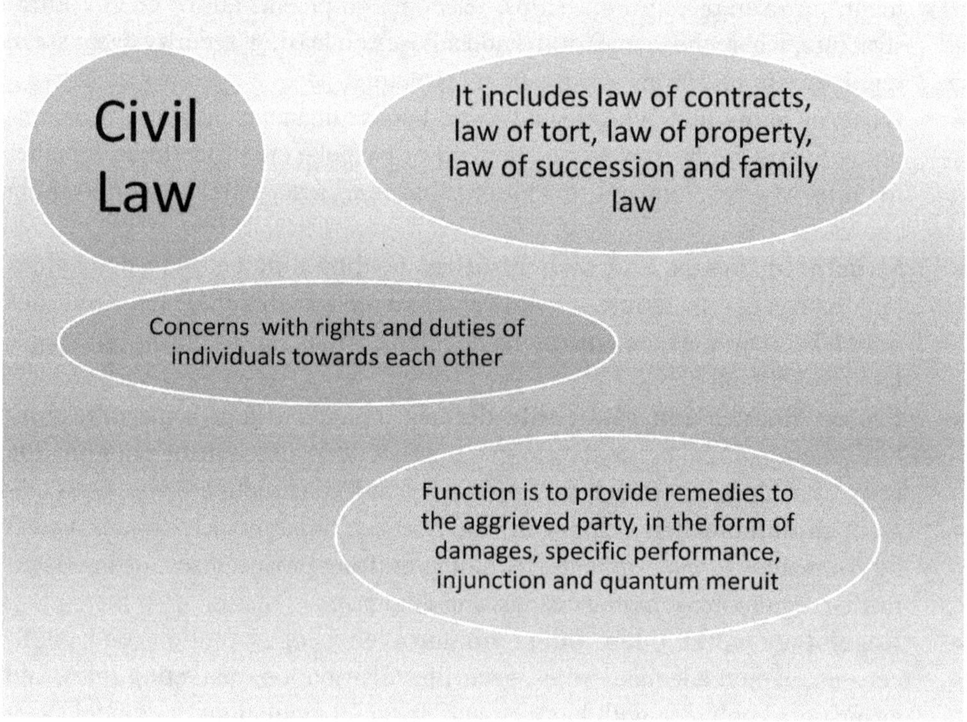

Some of the principal categories are:

- **Contract Law**: Governing legally enforceable agreements between parties for goods, services, employment, leases, or other arrangements. It defines when a contract is valid, how obligations are enforced, and what remedies are available in case of breach.
- **Property Law**: Regulating ownership, use, transfer, and rights over property both real property (land, buildings) and personal property (movables, intangible assets). It defines how property can be bought, sold, inherited, or secured, and resolves disputes over possession, boundaries, or rights.
- **Family Law**: Dealing with legal matters within families: marriage, divorce, child custody, adoption, maintenance, succession and related rights. It governs the personal and patrimonial relations among family members under civil law.
- **Tort Law / Civil Wrong / Liability Law**: Addressing non-contractual civil wrongs when one party's negligence, breach of duty, or intentional wrongdoing causes harm to another. This includes personal injury, defamation, negligence, property damage, and allows injured parties to claim compensation for losses.
- **Corporate / Commercial Law**: Governing the legal status, rights, and duties of business entities and contractual relationships between companies, including business transactions, trade, company formation, investments, sale of goods, and obligations between commercial parties.

Other less centralized but still significant domains include inheritance and succession law, consumer protection, employment law, or specialized private-law areas such as intellectual property. In civil cases, the plaintiff (the harmed party) brings the action against the defendant; the burden of proof typically falls on the plaintiff to demonstrate harm or contract breach. Civil law underpins many aspects of everyday life — from buying a house, signing a contract, inheriting property, to protecting personal rights, resolving family disputes or seeking damages, civil law aims to ensure fairness, clarity, and predictability in private relations.

c) Criminal Law

Criminal law is the body of law that defines criminal offenses, regulates the apprehension, charging, and trial of suspected offenders, and fixes penalties and modes of treatment applicable to convicted persons. At its core, criminal law serves as one of society's main mechanisms for protecting public safety, deterring wrongful conduct, and ensuring social order. Criminal law includes two main components:

- **Substantive criminal law**, which defines the behaviors that constitute crimes, such as theft, assault, fraud, homicide, and sets the corresponding punishments.
- **Procedural criminal law**, which establishes the rules and procedures for investigating, prosecuting, and adjudicating criminal cases, ensuring due process, fair trial, and protections for defendants.

Over time, many criminal-law systems have been codified into penal codes, replacing older common-law traditions, offering greater clarity, consistency, and modern definitions of crimes and procedures. Modern criminal law has also been shaped by evolving social principles — combining punishment with prevention, rehabilitation, and protection of societal values such as public safety and human rights.

d) International Law

International law refers to the set of legal rules, norms, and standards that govern the interactions between sovereign states and other recognized international actors—such as international organizations and, increasingly, individuals. It serves as a common framework enabling cooperation, conflict resolution, and collaboration on global issues that transcend national boundaries. Unlike domestic law which is enforced internally by governments, international law relies heavily on state consent, conventions, treaties, and customary practices. Its legal authority is derived from agreements states voluntarily enter into, or consistent practices that states adopt and treat as binding.

Figure 3. The two main branches of international law

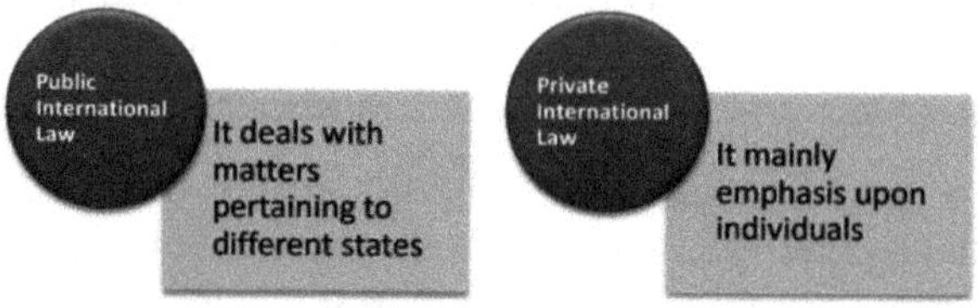

Over time, the scope of international law has expanded considerably. Originally focused on inter-state relations, it now covers a wide array of domains including human rights, environmental protection, international trade, maritime law, international criminal justice, international organizations, and global security. Key features and principles of international law include the equality and sovereignty of states, respect for treaties, recognition of customary norms, freedom of navigation and commerce, and self-defense rights under certain conditions. Disputes between states or other international actors are often resolved through negotiation, arbitration, or adjudication via bodies such as the International Court of Justice (ICJ). Compliance depends largely on mutual interest, reciprocity, diplomatic pressure, and reputation within the international community. As globalization deepens and global challenges, such as climate change, migration, pandemics, transnational crime continue to grow and international law continues to adapt. It provides a shared legal language, structured processes for cooperation, and a framework for collective action across borders.

e) Environmental & Natural Resources Law

Environmental law is the branch of law that regulates how humans interact with the natural world. It comprises a body of statutes, regulations, treaties, conventions and common-law principles whose goal is to protect ecosystems, natural resources, and public health from the harmful effects of pollution, habitat destruction, over-exploitation, and environmental degradation. At its core, environmental law seeks to balance ecological protection with sustainable development allowing economic and social activity while ensuring natural resources (air, water, forests, wildlife, soil) remain viable for future generations. Under environmental law the following issues are addressed.

- **Pollution control:** regulating emissions to air, water, and soil; managing chemical and hazardous waste; limiting industrial discharge and ensuring safe environmental quality.
- **Natural-resources law:** governing the use, extraction, and conservation of resources such as forests, minerals, water, fisheries — ensuring sustainable exploitation and protecting biodiversity.
- **Biodiversity and wildlife protection:** establishing rules to conserve endangered species, protect habitats, regulate land use and prevent ecological destruction.
- **Environmental impact assessment and land-use regulation:** requiring assessment of proposed projects (construction, industrial, mining, infrastructure) to evaluate and mitigate environmental harm.
- **Climate and global environmental law:** rising importance of laws and treaties addressing global challenges like climate change, ozone depletion, transboundary pollution, and sustainable development frameworks.

Figure 4. Main features of environmental law and its directions

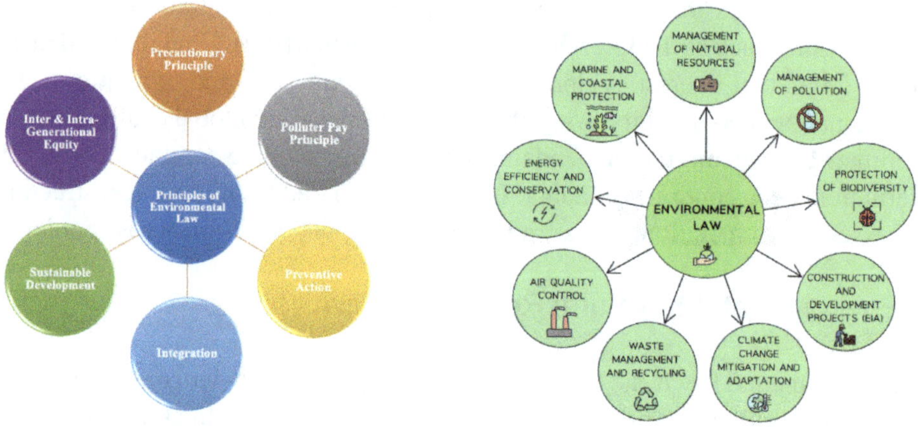

Environmental law rests on several guiding principles:

- **Precautionary principle:** When an activity risks serious or irreversible harm to the environment, legal action should be taken even if scientific certainty is not yet complete.
- **Prevention principle:** It is better to prevent environmental damage than to remediate it, as laws often regulate waste generation, emissions, harmful substances, and industrial processes accordingly.
- **Polluter-pays principle:** Those who cause environmental damage are responsible for bearing mitigation and cleanup costs, internalizing what would otherwise be external social or ecological costs.
- **Sustainable development principle:** Development must satisfy present needs without compromising the ability of future generations to meet theirs, integrating environmental protection with economic and social goals.
- **Public participation and transparency:** Environmental decision-making often requires public consultations, access to information, and participation, allowing communities and stakeholders to influence environmental governance.

Environmental law thus forms a complex, multidisciplinary legal framework, combining domestic statutes, regulations, international treaties, and common law to regulate pollution, resource use, land development, and ecological protection. Its purpose is not only to prevent and remedy environmental damage, but to ensure long-term sustainability, ecological balance, and protection of both nature and human health. As environmental pressures grow globally, climate change, biodiversity loss, pollution, resource depletion, the importance and complexity of environmental law continues to rise, making it a key pillar for sustainable modern societies.

2.1.2 Motivation for a Legal Chatbot

From the above description it can be easily understood that for an ordinary user, the difficulty lies in the complexity and fragmentation of the legal system. Each branch of law brings its own rules, procedures, terminology, and documentation. Legal language is often technical and filled with nuances that are hard for non-experts to interpret. Laws also vary between jurisdictions and are frequently updated, making it nearly impossible for a typical user to stay informed. Additionally, people may struggle to identify which area of law their problem falls under—for instance, whether a workplace conflict is an employment issue, a contractual dispute, or a matter of harassment law.

Because of these challenges, an AI-powered legal chatbot can be extremely helpful. It can guide users by explaining legal concepts in plain language, identifying which legal category their issue belongs to, summarizing relevant regulations, and directing them toward appropriate resources or professionals. This lowers the barrier to understanding law, empowers individuals to make informed decisions, and offers support without requiring deep legal expertise.

2.2 CHATBOTS: FUNCTIONALITY AND TYPES

A chatbot is a conversational system designed to streamline user requests and provide automated responses by imitating written or spoken human dialogue (Aleedy et al., 2019; Giovis & Rozsa, 2024; Kulkarni et al., 2024; Rajamalli Keerthana et al., 2021). While some chatbots are fairly simple, offering predefined menus or scripted choices—more sophisticated versions rely on artificial intelligence (AI) and natural language processing (NLP) to interpret user input and conduct fluid, human-like exchanges. A chatbot can be used to simulate real-time human interactions through text or voice. It can be integrated with websites, mobile apps, and instant messaging applications to interact with website visitors, app users, or customers 24/7 to provide real-time assistance through live chat.

Figure 5. A schematic workflow diagram of how AI chatbots function

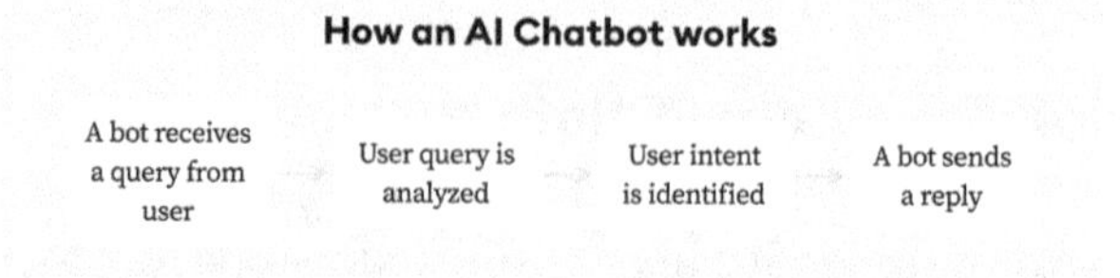

In essence, chatbots are software tools that answer user questions by replicating natural conversations through text or voice. Ranging from rule-based systems to intelligent virtual assistants, these technologies have become central to modern web interactions. Organizations deploy them to engage customers, strengthen support services, and deliver smoother, more efficient user experiences.

Chatbots come in several forms, but they can broadly be grouped into rule-based and AI-driven systems. Rule-based chatbots guide users through predefined options or decision trees. They rely on if-then logic and linguistic patterns, such as keywords, synonyms, and word order to trigger specific responses. These bots are ideal for predictable, repetitive tasks like answering FAQs, where organizations clearly understand the typical queries they receive.

In contrast, AI and NLP chatbots use artificial intelligence, natural language processing (NLP), and machine learning to interpret user intent rather than just specific keywords. They learn over time, adapt to new inputs, and can sustain more natural, context-aware conversations. Compared with rule-based bots that react only to predefined patterns, AI chatbots analyze full sentences or dialogue context, enabling more flexible and human-like interaction.

AI chatbots fall into several categories. Knowledge-base (FAQ) chatbots retrieve answers from an existing information repository and understand differently phrased questions using natural language understanding. Generative AI chatbots, by contrast, produce new responses with natural language generation, adapting tone and style to match the user. Hybrid chatbots combine rule-based logic with AI reasoning, using structured flows for simple queries and intelligent interpretation for complex ones. Finally, voice chatbots rely on speech recognition and NLP to engage users through spoken dialogue, powering many modern virtual assistants.

Figure 6. Applications of AI chatbots and key characteristics

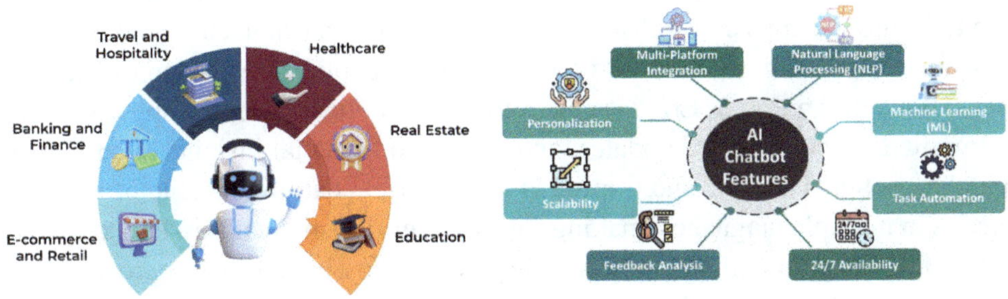

Chatbots have become essential tools across industries, transforming how organizations deliver services, engage users, and streamline operations. In healthcare, conversational agents support both clinicians and patients by facilitating symptom tracking, preliminary diagnosis guidance, and treatment recommendations. For instance, Babylon Health uses AI-powered chatbots to help users describe their symptoms and receive triage recommendations based on medical databases and clinical models. Similarly, Ada Health provides personalized health assessments, asking patients a series of adaptive questions and generating a detailed summary they can share with physicians. Healthcare providers also deploy chatbots for administrative support; the Mayo Clinic's chatbot, integrated into its patient portal, assists users with appointment scheduling, follow-up reminders, and medication management. For chronic disease monitoring, conversational tools such as Sensely's virtual nurse "Molly" help patients log daily symptoms, receive encouragement, and adhere to care pathways, demonstrating how chatbots can scale continuous patient engagement across large populations.

In insurance, chatbots streamline policy discovery, automate routine transactions, and improve customer service efficiency. Many insurers now use conversational interfaces to help users find policies that meet their needs by simulating the questioning style of a human agent. For example, Lemonade Insurance employs its chatbot "Maya" for onboarding, helping customers secure renters or homeowners insurance in minutes through a conversational flow. Claims processing has also become increasingly automated: Lemonade's AI chatbot can approve simple claims almost instantly, reducing operational costs and improving customer satisfaction. Traditional insurers have adopted similar tools; GEICO's virtual assistant answers policy-related questions, provides billing details, and guides users through quote generation without requiring human intervention. These systems help insurance companies deliver round-the-clock support while reducing wait times and operational bottlenecks.

In the banking sector, chatbots are widely used for customer service, multilingual assistance, and secure digital transactions. Banks integrate conversational agents into their mobile apps and websites to help customers check account balances, review recent transactions, transfer funds, and begin applications for credit cards or loans. Bank of America's Erica is one of the most sophisticated examples, offering bill reminders, credit score updates, and proactive financial insights by analyzing spending patterns. HSBC and Capital One also offer chatbots capable of handling queries in multiple languages, making financial services more accessible to diverse user groups. By automating routine banking interactions, institutions improve service availability and minimize the need for call center support.

In financial services, chatbots extend beyond basic account management to provide financial advice, budgeting assistance, and travel planning. For personal finance management, apps like Cleo and Plum use conversational AI to give users spending breakdowns, encourage saving habits, and set budgetary limits. These chatbots often communicate in a friendly, engaging tone, making financial literacy more approachable. In corporate contexts, American Express's virtual assistant helps cardholders plan business trips by recommending hotels and flights based on loyalty programs and past bookings. Travel platforms such as Expedia and Kayak also employ conversational agents that search itineraries, compare prices, and propose optimized travel schedules. By combining financial insights with real-time travel data, these chatbots simplify complex planning tasks and enhance customer convenience.

Across these diverse domains, chatbots demonstrate their versatility—supporting clinical decision-making, automating insurance processes, facilitating multilingual banking assistance, and guiding both personal and business financial planning. Through real-world deployments, they illustrate how conversational AI is reshaping service delivery and improving user experience across sectors.

2.3 BENEFITS OF AI CHATBOTS

AI-powered chatbots offer a range of advantages that make them valuable across industries, regardless of an organization's specific needs (Bauer et al., 2019; Divya et al., 2018; Itelman et al., 2024). One of the most significant benefits is their ability to respond to user questions instantly, delivering information or guidance within seconds. This not only enhances the overall customer experience but also helps users resolve issues or complete tasks far more quickly than traditional support channels (Banerjee et al., 2023; Bauer et al., 2019; Touvron, Martin, Stone, Albert, Almahairi, Babaei, & Scialom, 2023).

AI chatbots can also boost conversion rates, particularly in sales and marketing contexts. By automatically identifying and routing qualified leads to the appropriate representatives, they ensure that follow-ups happen sooner—an approach consistently shown to increase the likelihood of successful conversions.

From an internal operations perspective, AI chatbots contribute to greater employee engagement and productivity. By automating repetitive, low-value tasks, they allow staff to dedicate more time to meaningful, strategic, and creative work. This reduction in manual workload often translates into improved job satisfaction.

A further benefit is cost efficiency. Because chatbots can reliably handle a wide range of tasks, they reduce the need for large support teams and minimize operational costs over time. Their scalability also means they can manage high volumes of requests without a proportional increase in staffing.

Finally, implementing AI chatbots can provide competitive differentiation. Many organizations have yet to fully adopt advanced conversational AI, so being an early mover can create a distinct market advantage. Offering smarter, faster, and more personalized interactions can help a company stand out and retain customers in a crowded landscape. Overall, AI chatbots enhance user satisfaction, streamline business processes, and strengthen a company's strategic position—all while reducing costs and enabling more agile operations.

In the following section we describe in detail the artificial intelligence and computational techniques involved in building a chatbot, followed by details about our implementation of our legal chatbot following these principles.

2.4 STATE OF THE ART DEVELOPMENTS IN LEGAL CHATBOTS

Recent advances in legal chatbots increasingly leverage large language models (LLMs) combined with structured retrieval mechanisms to improve factual accuracy, interpretability, and task effectiveness. Applied systems such as AttorneyGPT (Adheshvar et al., 2025) and L.E.G.A.L. (Chia et al., 2024)utilize Retrieval-Augmented Generation (RAG) to ground responses in legal text, mitigating hallucinations and enabling users to navigate complex legal documents with more precision. Efforts like LexRAG (LexRAG Consortium, 2025) contribute benchmarking frameworks and evaluation protocols specific to multi-turn legal consultation, highlighting the importance of rigorous assessment in this domain. To address trust and auditability, frameworks such as HalluGraph (Noël et al., 2025) explore hallucination detection through alignment with knowledge graphs, enhancing reliability in legal reasoning.

Additionally, work on LLM-augmented knowledge graph construction (Kane et al., 2025), exemplified by the Senegalese legal texts structuration project, demonstrates the potential of graph-centric representations for capturing rich legal semantics at scale. Together, these developments reflect a shift toward hybrid architectures that integrate symbolic structures with generative models to meet the demanding accuracy, explainability, and contextual reasoning requirements of legal applications. Other notable recent works on legal chatbots may be found in (Ioannidou et al., 2025; Keerthana et al., 2025; Rivas-Echeverría et al., 2025).

2.5 KEY CONTRIBUTIONS OF THIS WORK

This chapter advances the state of the art in legal chatbots by moving beyond document-level retrieval and generic RAG-based question answering toward a graph-centric, agentic, and legally grounded conversational system. In contrast to recent legal RAG systems that primarily focus on grounding responses in retrieved text or benchmarking retrieval performance, our work makes the following key contributions:

1. End-to-End GraphRAG Pipeline Tailored to Legal Documents

While prior work explores RAG-based legal assistants and isolated knowledge graph extraction, we present a fully integrated GraphRAG pipeline that transforms raw legal documents into structured knowledge graphs capturing entities, clauses, obligations, and cross-references. This enables preservation of legal structure and relationships that are typically lost in chunk-based retrieval systems.

2. Agentic ReAct-Style Legal Reasoning Over Knowledge Graphs

Unlike existing legal chatbots that rely on a single retrieve-and-generate step, our system employs an agentic architecture that performs iterative reasoning, targeted graph searches, and query refinement. This allows the system to support multi-hop legal reasoning, handle ambiguous queries, and synthesize relationships across clauses.

3. Support for Both Local and Global Legal Queries

By combining entity-level graph traversal with community detection and summarization, the system explicitly supports both fine-grained factual questions and global document-level queries (e.g., risk allocation, party obligations), which remain a limitation of many current legal RAG systems.

4. Conflict Handling and Source-Grounded Legal Answers

We introduce mechanisms for detecting conflicting legal information, applying legal precedence rules, and maintaining hierarchical source attribution. Each response is traceable to specific document sections, addressing trust, auditability, and explainability concerns highlighted in recent literature.

5. Deployment-Aware Design for Real Legal Workflows

Unlike benchmark-focused studies, this work emphasizes practical deployment considerations, including conversation-specific knowledge bases, context isolation across legal matters, ambiguity handling via clarification actions, and safeguards for agent termination.

Together, these contributions position our work as a practical, explainable, and structurally aware legal chatbot architecture, complementing recent advances in legal RAG systems while addressing their limitations in multi-hop reasoning, document-level understanding, and real-world legal usability.

3. BUILDING AN INTELLIGENT LEGAL ASSISTANT- A STEP BY STEP METHODOLOGY

In this section we present how the technical foundations underlying legal chatbots described in Section 2 can be translated into a concrete, step-by-step methodology for designing and implementing an intelligent legal assistant in practice.

The most effective way to build a reliable LLM-powered chatbot is through Retrieval-Augmented Generation (RAG). RAG combines the generative abilities of a large language model with a retrieval system capable of extracting factual, context-specific information from an enterprise knowledge base(Asai et al., 2023; Behnia et al., 2022; Lv et al., 2024; Peters et al., 2019; Ram et al., 2023). This approach ensures responses are accurate, grounded in organizational data, and less prone to hallucination.

Figure 7. A schematic operational workflow of an LLM-RAG architecture for a chatbot

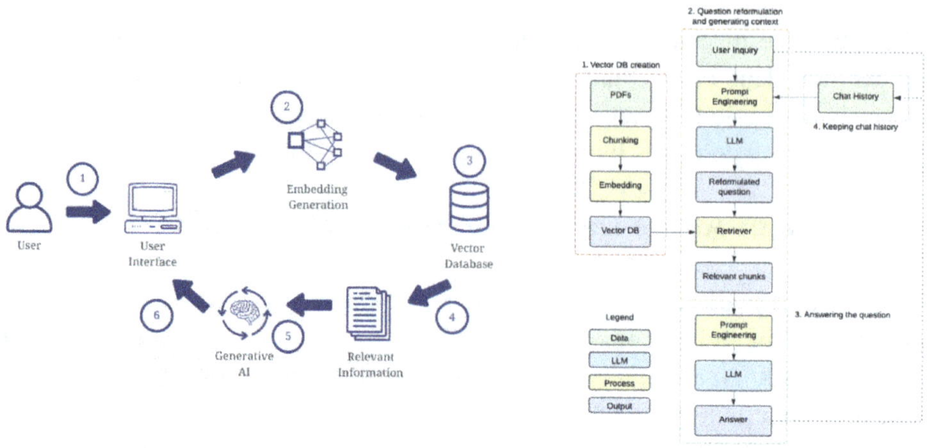

3.1 An Overview of Architecture of RAG Based Chatbots

A RAG architecture consists of several interconnected components that work together to deliver context-aware responses which are described below:

3.1.1 Data Ingestion and Vector Database Creation

The foundation of any RAG system is its vector database, which stores domain-specific knowledge in a form that LLMs can retrieve efficiently (Chan et al., 2022; Es et al., 2024; Hu et al., 2023; Izacard et al., 2021; Shi et al., 2024). The data can come from PDFs, text reports, webpages, patient records, internal manuals, or any structured/unstructured documents. The ingestion pipeline typically includes:

- Chunking: Large documents are split into smaller, meaningful text segments—usually a few hundred tokens—so retrieval can be precise.
- Embeddings Generation: Each chunk is converted into a numerical vector using an embedding model. These vectors represent semantic meaning.
- Storage in a Vector Database: Tools like ChromaDB, Neo4j, Pinecone, or FAISS store the vectors and allow similarity search.

For example, in a hospital scenario, patient experiences, medical procedures, physician data, and insurance information are embedded and stored so the chatbot can access hospital-specific knowledge.

3.1.2 User Query Reformulation and Context Handling

User questions in real conversations often depend on earlier context. To answer properly, the system must turn these conversational prompts into stand-alone questions. An LLM is used to: Examine the chat history, Reformulate the query into a self-contained question (e.g., "What insurance do I need?" → "What insurance is relevant?") This step ensures the retrieval system can search the database effectively. The chat history is stored and updated with each interaction, enabling multi-turn conversations and coherent follow-up answers.

3.1.3 Retrieval of Relevant Information

Once the question is reformulated, a retriever searches the vector database to find the text chunks most semantically similar to the user query. These chunks form the context that the LLM will use to answer. If no relevant data exists, the chatbot is instructed to say it cannot answer—reducing hallucination and increasing trust (Aleedy et al., 2019; Hsueh & Chou, 2022; Kuang et al., 2024; Lakatos et al., 2025). For example In a hospital RAG system, retrieval might pull records about patient demographics, hospital locations, physician specialties, past visits, insurance rules.

3.1.4 LLM Response Generation

Next, the system passes both the reformulated question and the retrieved context to the LLM with a carefully designed prompt. The LLM (e.g., GPT-4, Gemini 1.5) generates a grounded, factual response(Banerjee et al., 2023; Bauer et al., 2019; Giovis & Rozsa, 2024; Kulkarni et al., 2024; Rajamalli Keerthana et al., 2021; Touvron, Martin, Stone, Albert, Almahairi, Babaei, & Scialom, 2023). Because it is restricted to the retrieved context, the output is far more accurate than free-form generation.

3.1.5 Conversation Logging and Updating State

Each new user input and system response is appended to the conversation history. This log enables coherent multi-turn interactions, correct interpretation of follow-up questions, and future auditability.

3.1.6 User Interface Layer

Finally, frameworks like Streamlit, Flask, or enterprise dashboards provide the front-end interface. Streamlit's chat components make it easy to deploy a conversational UI where users can interact with the RAG chatbot in real time.

3.2 Implementation Steps of Our Legal Chatbot

The architecture and implementation of an autonomous legal document chatbot leverages GraphRAG (Graph Retrieval Augmented Generation) for intelligent document analysis. Unlike traditional RAG systems that rely on simple vector similarity, GraphRAG constructs knowledge graphs from legal documents, enabling the system to understand complex relationships between entities such as parties, clauses, obligations, and legal concepts. The system employs an agentic architecture where a Large Language model autonomously decides when to search the knowledge base, how to refine queries, and when sufficient information has been gathered to provide a response.

Legal professionals spend a significant portion of their time reviewing documents, extracting relevant information, and understanding the relationships between different elements. This section describes a system designed to address these challenges through three key innovations:

- GraphRAG-based knowledge representation that preserves document structure and entity relationships
- An agentic architecture that enables autonomous decision making about information retrieval
- Conversation specific knowledge base that maintains context isolation between different legal matters.

3.2.1 System Architecture Overview

The system follows a three-tier architecture consisting of a frontend interface, a robust backend where all the AI processes executes and a relational database to store conversation history per conversations. In these sections we mainly describe the data layer including document ingestion, creation of knowledge graphs, evaluation and optimization of the pipeline and creation of knowledge bases for the chatbot.

3.2.1.1 Components Overview

- Front end Layer: A minimalist chat interface that allows users to create conversation, upload legal documents, trigger knowledge graph indexing, and interact with the AI assistant.
- Backend Layer: A RestfulAPI application that orchestrates all system operations. It handles document processing, manages the agentic chat loop, interfaces with the LLM provider, and coordinates GraphRAG operations

- Data Layer: PostgresSQL stores conversation metadata, message history,and document references. Each conversation's GraphRAG artifacts (knowledge graphs, embeddings, entity tables) are stored in isolated directories on the file system.
- External Services: Ollama provides local LLM inferences for the agentic chat loop while OpenAI's API powers the GraphRAG index process (entity extraction and embeddings). It can also be done with a local LLM.

Figure 8. GraphRag chatbot system architecture

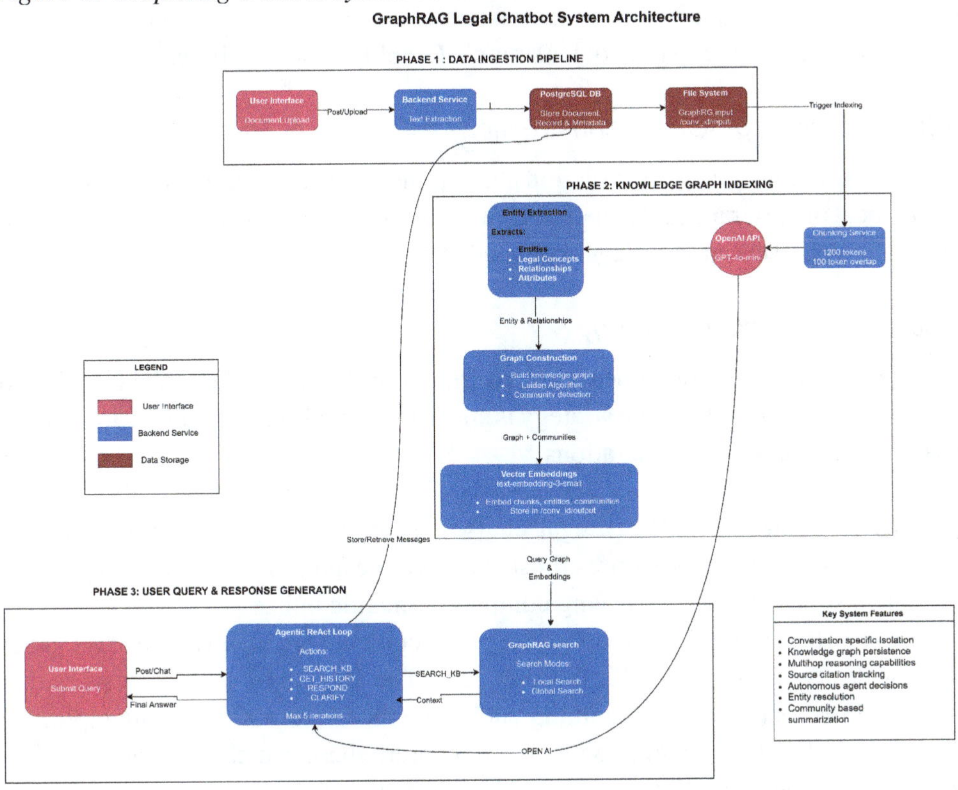

3.2.2 Ingestion and Preprocessing of Legal Documents

The data ingestion pipeline transforms raw legal documents into queryable knowledge graph. This process involves several stages, each critical to the system's ability to answer complex legal questions.

3.2.2.1 Document Upload and Text Extraction

When a user uploads a document, the system first extracts its contextual content. For pdf files, which are common in legal practice, the system extracts text while preserving paragraph structure. The extracted text undergoes cleaning to remove excessive whitespaces while maintaining semantic boundaries between sections.

The document service performs the following operations:

- Receive the uploaded file(s) and validates its format (PDF, TXT, or Markdown)
- Extract text content using format-appropriate parsers
- Clean and normalize the extracted text
- Save the text file to the conversation's GraphRAG input directory

3.2.2.2 Knowledge Graph construction

The knowledge graph construction phase is the most computationally demanding component of the GraphRAG pipeline, transforming raw documents into a structured, queryable representation of legal knowledge.

Document Chunking Strategy

The system divides documents into overlapping chunks of 1200 tokens with 100 tokens overlap. This chunking strategy is specifically optimized for legal documents based on several key considerations:

- Legal context Window: Legal clauses typically span 300-800 tokens. The 1200 token window ensures most clauses are captured in their entirety within atleast one chunk; preserving complete semantic unit.
- Cross-Reference Preservation: Legal documents frequently reference other sections (e.g as defined in Section 3.2). The 100 token overlap ensures that ensures that clauses containing such references are not artificially split, allowing the entity extraction model to capture these critical relationships.
- Entity Boundary Handling: The overlap region serves as a buffer zone that captures entities and relationships that might chunk boundaries. Testing showed that 100 tokens provides sufficient context while minimizing redundant processing.

This overlap is particularly important for legal documents where clauses references often span multiple paragraphs. For example, a liability limitation clause may reference definitions from earlier sections and be subject to exceptions in later sections, all of which need to be co-locates in at least one chunk for proper graph construction.

Entity and Relationship Extraction

Next, each chunk undergoes entity and relationship extraction using a large language model (GPT-4o). The model identifies named entities such as organizations, individuals, dates, monetary values, and locations, along with legal concepts including clause categories, obligations, rights, definitions, and contract types. Additionally, it extracts explicit relationships such as payment obligations, dependencies between clauses, or references across sections and attributes like roles, addresses, or amounts. This stage transforms unstructured text into a detailed map of the actors, concepts, and interactions embedded in the document.

Graph Construction and Community Detection

These extracted elements serve as inputs for graph construction, where entities become nodes and relationships become edges. The system then applies the Leiden community detection algorithm to identify clusters of closely related entities. In legal documents, such communities naturally correspond to thematic groupings, such as termination clauses, financial obligations, or sets of parties and their associated duties. To enhance global understanding, GraphRAG generates community-level summaries, producing clear natural-language descriptions of each cluster and its internal relationships. This enables global search capabilities that reflect the document's broader structure rather than isolated facts.

Embedding Generation

Finally, the system computes vector embeddings for all chunks, entities, and community summaries. These semantic representations allow the chatbot to perform similarity search and retrieve relevant legal information efficiently during the query phase.

Why GraphRAG over naive RAG for legal documents

Traditional Retrieval Augmented Generation (RAG) systems chunks documents, embed the chunks, and retrieve the most semantically similar chunk to a query. While effective for simple factual retrieval, this approach has significant limitations when applied to legal documents.

Limitation of Naive RAG in Legal Context

Loss of Structural Relationships: Legal documents are highly structured. A limitation of liability clause may reference definitions from an earlier section and be subject to conditions in later sections. Naive RAG treats each chunk independently, losing these critical cross-references.

Difficulty with Multi-Hop Questions: Question like "What happens if Party A fails to meet the delivery deadline specified in Clause 4?" require understanding multiple connected concepts: who Party A is, what the delivery obligations are, what the deadline is, and what the consequences of breach are. These concepts may be scattered across different chunks.

Inability to answer Global Questions: Questions such as "What are the main obligations of each party?" or "Summarize the risk allocation in this contract" requires understanding the document as a whole, not just retrieving similar chunks.

Entity Resolution Challenges: The same entity may be referred differently throughout a document ('the company', 'ABC corporation', 'Seller'). Naive RAG does not perform entity resolution, potentially missing relevant information.

How GraphRAG addresses these limitations

Preserved Relationships: By extracting entities and their relationships explicitly, GraphRAG maintains the web of connections that gives legal documents their meaning. When a user asks about termination rights, the system can traverse the graph to find not just the termination clause, but also the notice requirements, the events that trigger termination, and the consequences thereof.

Multi-Hop Reasoning: The graph structure enables multi-hop queries. To answer 'What are Party A's obligations if the force majeure clause is triggered?', the system can follow edges from Party A to its obligations, filter for those related to force majeure, and return a comprehensive answer.

Global Understanding via Communities: The community detection and summarization process creates high-level representations of document themes. This enables answering broad questions about the document's overall structure and purpose.

Entity Resolution: During extraction, the LLM performs implicit entity resolution, recognizing that 'the Company' and 'ABC Corporation' refer to the same entity and consolidating information accordingly.

Knowledge Graph Visualization:

Figure9. A sample knowledge graph

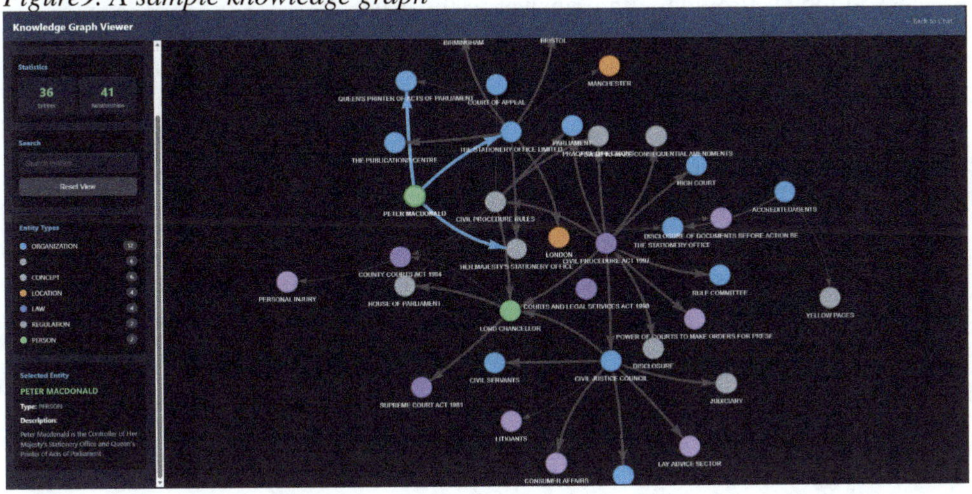

This figure 9 illustrates a knowledge graph constructed for uk_cilvil_war. The graph captures entities and their relationships. This structure enables the system to answer complex queries by traversing relationships between nodes.

The Agentic Question-Answering Architecture

Rather than using a simple retrieve then generate pipeline, this system employs an agentic architecture where the LLM autonomously decides how to handle each query. This approach is particular valuable for legal questions, which often require multiple searches, reasoning about search results, and iterative refinement.

The ReAct Loop

The agent follows a Reasoning and Acting (ReAct) pattern. For each user query, the agent enters a loop where it:

1. Reasons about what information it needs
2. Select an action to take
3. Observe the results, and
4. Decides whether to continue or respond.

The agent has access to four actions:

- SEARCH_KNOWLEDGE_BASE: query the GraphRAG index with a specific search string

- GET_CONVERSATION_HISTORY: retrieve previous messages for context on follow up questions
- RESPOND: Provide a final answer to the user
- CLARIFY: ask for clarification when the query is ambiguous

The Agent Decision Process

At each iteration, the agent receives the initial query, whether documents are available, whether the knowledge base has been indexed, a log of all previous actions and observations in this turn, and the conversation history. The agent then outputs its reasoning ("thought"), selected action, and action input in a structured JSON format.

Consider a user asking: 'What are the indemnification obligations and how do they relate to the liability cap?' The agent might proceed as follows:

- Iteration 1: Thought: 'I need to find information about indemnification first.' Action: SEARCH_KNOWLEDGE_BASE with query 'indemnification obligations'
- Iteration 2: After receiving search results, Thought: 'I found the indemnification clause. Now I need to find the liability cap.' Action: SEARCH_KNOWLEDGE_BASE with query 'liability cap limitation'
- Iteration 3: After receiving both sets of results, Thought: 'I have information about both topics and can now explain their relationship.' Action: RESPOND with a comprehensive answer

Handling Conflicting Information and Source Citation

The agentic system incorporates several mechanisms to handle conflicting information and ensure accurate source citation:

- Conflict Detection: When the agent retrieves information from multiple graph communities or document sections, it evaluates consistency across sources. If conflicting information is detected (e.g., different notice periods mentioned in different clauses), the agent flags this in its reasoning step.
- Hierarchical Source Attribution: Each piece of information retrieved from the knowledge graph includes metadata about its source document, section, and specific text span. The system maintains a citation chain from the final answer back to the original document locations.
- Precedence Rules: For legal documents, the system applies precedence rules when conflicts arise. Amendment clauses typically take precedence over original provisions, specific terms override general terms, and later-dated modifications supersede earlier versions.

- Explicit Uncertainty Communication: When the agent cannot resolve conflicts or lacks sufficient information, it explicitly communicates uncertainty to the user and may use the CLARIFY action to request additional context.

The citation mechanism works as follows: each entity and relationship in the knowledge graph stores references to the original text chunks from which they were extracted. When the agent constructs a response, it includes inline references (e.g., '[Section 4.2, p. 12]') that link back to specific document locations, enabling users to verify the information source.

Safeguards and Termination

To prevent infinite loops, the system enforces a maximum iteration count (default: 5). If the agent hasn't reached a RESPOND or CLARIFY action by the final iteration, the system forces a response using all information gathered so far. This ensures users always receive a response, even if the agent's reasoning was suboptimal.

Query Processing: From Question to Answer

When the agent decides to search the knowledge base, the query is processed through GraphRAG's retrieval system. GraphRAG supports two search modes, each suited to different types of questions.

Local Search

Local search is optimized for specific, factual questions. It operates by:

1. Embedding the query
2. Finding the most similar entity description and text chunks
3. Transversing the graph to find related entities and relationships
4. Assembling a context window with the most relevant information

This mode excels at questions like 'What is the notice period for termination?' or Who are the parties to this agreement?'

Global Search

Global search leverages community summaries to answer broad questions. It retrieves the most relevant community summaries, shuffles them to avoid position bias, and generates an answer that synthesizes information across the entire document. This mode is ideal for questions like 'What are the main risks allocated to the buyer?' or 'Summarize the intellectual property provisions.'

4. RESULTS

4.1 Chatbot interface and responses

Our legal chatbot interface looks as shown in the figure 10 below. It accepts user queries and responds with relevant solutions. For testing the chatbot we used our knowledge base containing legal documents from five law categories: civil, criminal, finance, environmental and international law from countries like India, USA and UK. For each law category approximately 30 megabytes of documents were used (total nearly 200 MB of data (were used for ingestion into the chatbot pipeline). A set of queries for each law category was asked and the corresponding chatbot answers recorded. These are presented in Tables 1-5. It is observable that our chatbot provides useful and relevant answers with a typical delay of 2-5 seconds.

Figure 10. Snapshot of our chatbot interface with legal query

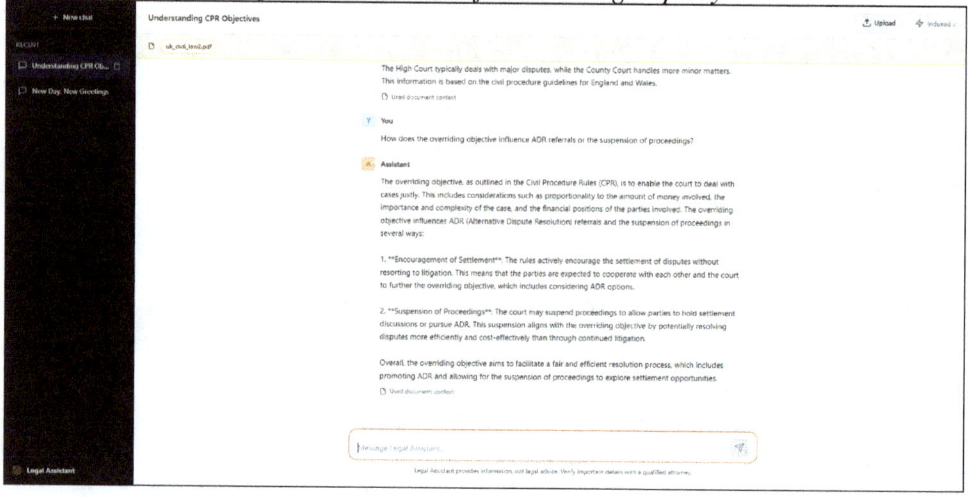

Table 1. Questions and answers on finance law provided by our legal chatbot

No.	Questions	Answers by our legal chatbot
1.	What are some tax laws in India?	The provided context discusses specific provisions of the Income Tax Act, 1961, in India. Here are some tax laws mentioned: 1. Interim Dividend: "any interim dividend shall be deemed to be the income of the previous year in which the amount of such dividend is unconditionally made available by the company to the member who is entitled to it." 2. Income Deemed to Accrue or Arise in India: "all income accruing or arising, whether directly or indirectly, through or from any business connection in India, or through or from any property in India, or through or from any asset or source of income in India." 3. Business Operations: "the income of the business deemed under this clause to accrue or arise in India shall be only such part of the income as is reasonably attributable to the operations carried out in India." 4. Non-Resident Income: "in the case of a non-resident, no income shall be deemed to accrue or arise in India to him through or from operations which are confined to the purchase of goods in India for the purpose of export."
2.	What are some banking laws in India?	The context mentions the following banking laws in India: 1. Banking Regulation Act, 1949 - This act applies to banking companies and is referenced in relation to time deposits: "time deposits with a banking company to which the Banking Regulation Act, 1949 (10 of 1949) applies." 2. Reserve Bank of India Act, 1934 - This act is mentioned concerning guidelines issued for business correspondents of banking companies: "in accordance with the guidelines issued in this regard by the Reserve Bank of India under the Reserve Bank of India Act, 1934 (2 of 1934)." 3. Payment and Settlement Systems Act, 2007 - This act is referenced in relation to the authorization of white label automated teller machine operators: "in accordance with the authorisation issued by the Reserve Bank of India under the Payment and Settlement Systems Act, 2007 (51 of 2007)."
3.	What are some of the financial regulations by RBI in India?	The financial regulations by the Reserve Bank of India (RBI) in India include: 1. Banking Arrangements: "The Reserve Bank of India (RBI) shall be the banker to the Government. It shall maintain cash balance of the Government and provide banking facilities to the Ministries and subordinate or attached offices." 2. Accredited Bank Nomination: "RBI shall, in consultation with the Controller General of Accounts, nominate a bank to function as Accredited Bank of a Ministry or Department." 3. Payment Procedures: "All payments shall be made through these identified bank branches. These branches shall also collect departmental and other receipts." 4. Tax Revenue Collection: "Tax revenues of the Government shall be collected by the RBI through its own offices or through the nominated branches of its agent banks." 5. Remittance Procedures: "Detailed procedure to be followed for remittance of Government receipts into Government cash balance and reimbursement of payments made on behalf of Government by the banks are laid down in the Memoranda of Instructions issued by the Reserve Bank of India."
4.	What are some of the general insurance regulations in India?	Some of the insurance regulations in India mentioned in the context include: 1. Definition of Life Insurance Business: "life insurance business" is defined as per clause (11) of section 2 of the Insurance Act, 1938. 2. World Income Computation: For a person not resident in India carrying on life insurance business, "the world income... shall be computed in the manner laid down in this Act for the computation of the profits and gains of life insurance business carried on in India." 3. Unit Linked Insurance Policy: Defined as "a life insurance policy which has components of both investment and insurance and is linked to a unit as defined in clause (ee) of regulation 3 of the Insurance Regulatory and Development Authority of India (Unit Linked Insurance Products) Regulations, 2019."

Table 2. Questions and answers on civil law provided by our legal chatbot

No.	Questions	Answers by our legal chatbot
1.	What are some rights related to private and family life in the UK?	Some rights related to private and family life in the UK, as protected under the ECHR, include: ○ Right to respect for family and private life (Article 8): "right to respect for family and private life." ○ Freedom of thought, conscience and religion (Article 9): "freedom of thought, conscience and religion." ○ Freedom of expression: "freedom of expression." These rights are part of the broader framework of human rights legislation that influences the English legal system
2.	What are some laws related to healthcare safety?	Some laws related to healthcare safety mentioned in the context include: 1. Draft Health Service Safety Investigations Bill: This bill aims to establish a duty of candour on providers of NHS services, requiring them to follow a prescribed process whenever someone suffers an adverse outcome that could result in more than minimal harm. 2. Healthcare Safety Investigation Branch: The role of this body is to conduct investigations into patient safety incidents, ensuring compatibility with human rights obligations. 3. Requirement for NHS trusts: There is a call for NHS trusts to ensure that data on deaths caused by failures of care is disaggregated by protected characteristic, analyzed, and published.
3.	What are some key elements in the European Convention on Human Rights?	The key elements in the European Convention on Human Rights (ECHR) include: 1. International Treaty: The ECHR is described as "an international treaty which was drafted in 1950 and came into effect in 1953." 2. Council of Europe: It was established by countries that are members of the "Council of Europe," which is separate from the European Union. 3. Signatory Countries: The UK was one of the first countries to sign the Convention in 1953, and currently, "some 47 countries have now signed up to the Convention." 4. Response to Historical Events: The ECHR was created as a reaction to the "horrors of the Second World War," reflecting a collective hope to protect human rights. These elements highlight the foundational purpose and structure of the ECHR as a significant legal instrument for human rights in Europe.
4.	What are some liabilities related to road safety?	Some liabilities related to road safety mentioned in the context include: 1. Gross Negligence or Intentional Misconduct: A motorized off-road vehicle entity can be liable for injuries caused by their "gross negligence or intentional misconduct with regard to the safety of the motorized off-road vehicle area or the motorized off-road vehicle activity participant." 2. Negligence with Equipment: Liability can arise from "negligence with regard to a motorized off-road vehicle or related equipment provided by the entity to the participant." 3. Dangerous Conditions: The entity may be liable for injuries caused by "a potentially dangerous condition at the motorized off-road vehicle area," which they knew or reasonably should have known about, excluding conditions inherent to driving. 4. Failure to Train Employees: Liability can also stem from "the motorized off-road vehicle entity's failure to train or improper training of an employee" involved in the activities. These points highlight the responsibilities of motorized off-road vehicle entities in ensuring safety and the potential liabilities they face if they fail to meet those responsibilities.

Table 3. Questions and answers on criminal law provided by our legal chatbot

No.	Questions	Answers by our legal chatbot
1.	What are the key differences between felonies and misdemeanors, and how do courts usually determine the severity of an offence?	The key differences between felonies and misdemeanors are primarily based on the severity of the punishment. A felony is defined as "a crime punishable by death or by imprisonment for more than one year," while a misdemeanor is "a crime punishable by less than a year in prison." Courts usually determine the severity of an offense based on "the punishment provided in the statute under which an individual is convicted rather than by the actual punishment imposed." Additionally, jurisdictions may further classify felonies and misdemeanors into classes or degrees to distinguish between the seriousness of criminal acts.
2.	What laws in the USA are against theft in connection with a bank?	The laws in the USA against theft in connection with a bank include: 1. Theft by bank examiner - This is specifically mentioned as a type of theft statute. 2. Theft, embezzlement, or misapplication by bank officer or employee - This addresses misconduct by individuals in positions of trust within banks. 3. Theft or embezzlement in connection with health care - While not exclusively about banks, it can involve financial institutions that deal with health care funds.
3.	What legal protections exist for victims of crime, and how can victims access support services?	Victims of crime have several legal protections and rights as outlined in the provided context. These include: 1. Protection from the Accused: Victims have the right to be "reasonably protected from the accused" (§ 3771(a)(1)). 2. Notification of Proceedings: They are entitled to "reasonable, accurate, and timely notice of any public court proceeding" involving the crime or the accused's release (§ 3771(a)(2)). 3. Right to Attend Proceedings: Victims have the right not to be excluded from public court proceedings unless specific conditions are met (§ 3771(a)(3)). 4. Opportunity to be Heard: They have the right to be "reasonably heard at any public proceeding" related to the case (§ 3771(a)(4)). 5. Access to Support Services: Law enforcement personnel are required to ensure that victims receive emergency social and medical services and are informed about various support options, including: ○ Availability of crime victim compensation. ○ Community-based victim treatment programs. ○ The role of the victim in the criminal justice process (Title II, § 1408(b)(1)(A)-(D)).
4.	How does the criminal justice process work from arrest to trial, and what are the main steps involved in each jurisdiction? Please provide a concise reply in 50 words and 5 bullet points	The criminal justice process involves several key steps from arrest to trial: ○ Application by Prosecutor: Includes identifying information and alleged crimes (e.g., "The application of the Prosecutor shall contain..."). ○ Warrant of Arrest: Issued with specific details about the person and crimes (e.g., "The warrant of arrest shall contain..."). ○ Provisional Arrest: Court may request arrest based on the warrant (e.g., "On the basis of the warrant of arrest..."). ○ Summons Issuance: Alternative to arrest, ensuring appearance (e.g., "the Prosecutor may submit an application requesting..."). ○ Arrest Proceedings: State Party must act on arrest requests (e.g., "A State Party which has received a request...").

Table 4. Questions and answers on international law provided by our legal chatbot

SL no.	Questions	Answers by our legal chatbot
1.	What are the main international laws on trade-related environmental measures?	The main international laws on trade-related environmental measures (TREMs) mentioned in the context include: 1. Basel Convention - This treaty spells out the principle of prior informed consent (PIC). 2. PIC Convention - Another treaty that also involves the principle of prior informed consent. 3. Cartagena Protocol on Biosafety - Focuses on the safe handling of living modified organisms. 4. CITES (Convention on International Trade in Endangered Species) - Aims to protect endangered species through trade control. 5. Montreal Protocol - Addresses substances that deplete the ozone layer, including trade measures. 6. POP Convention (Stockholm Convention on Persistent Organic Pollutants) - Involves trade measures typically banning transfers of certain substances. These treaties illustrate the potential conflicts between trade and environmental regulations, with some primarily imposing trade restrictions and others using trade measures as one of several implementation tools.
2.	What is UNFCCC?	The UNFCCC, or the United Nations Framework Convention on Climate Change, is a treaty that enshrines the principle of Common But Differentiated Responsibilities (CBDR). It states that "The Parties should protect the climate system for the benefit of present and future generations of humankind, on the basis of equity and in accordance with their common but differentiated responsibilities and respective capabilities." The UNFCCC establishes that developed country Parties should take the lead in combating climate change.
3.	What is the role of international organizations, such as the United Nations, in enforcing international law?	The role of international organizations, such as the United Nations, in enforcing international law includes being recognized as legal entities that possess the competence necessary to discharge their functions. The context states, "the United Nations is a legal entity separate and distinct from the member States" and is described as "an international person, clothed by its Members with the competence necessary to discharge its functions." Additionally, Article 104 of the UN Charter provides that the organization "shall enjoy in the territory of each of its Members such legal capacity as may be necessary for the exercise of its functions and the fulfillment of its purposes." This indicates that international organizations have a recognized legal status that supports their role in the enforcement of international law.
4.	What is International law on humanitarian assistance?	International law on humanitarian assistance suggests that "States have a duty under International Law either to provide humanitarian assistance to their own populations or to accept external humanitarian assistance." Additionally, it is indicated that "in appropriate circumstances, other States could provide such help, presumably without the consent of the State whose populace is in need of such 'intervention.'" Furthermore, access by private humanitarian organizations to victims without government consent "must be considered lawful."

Table 5. Questions and answers on environmental law provided by our legal chatbot

No.	Questions	Answers by our legal chatbot
1.	What are the main multilateral environmental agreements that govern global environmental protection?	1. Ramsar Convention on Wetlands 2. FAO instruments concerning agriculture and fisheries 3. Basel Convention on the Control of Transboundary Movements of Hazardous Wastes and Their Disposal 4. Rotterdam Convention on the Prior Informed Consent Procedure for Certain Hazardous Chemicals and Pesticides in International Trade 5. Stockholm Convention on Persistent Organic Pollutants 6. UN Convention on the Law of the Sea 7. Vienna Convention for the Protection of the Ozone Layer
2.	What environmental laws are there on environmental pollution ? Can you specify the law name?	The context provides several environmental laws related to pollution, but it does not specify law numbers or IDs. Here are the mentioned laws: 1. Clean Air Act 2. Clean Water Act 3. Superfund 4. CERCLA (Comprehensive Environmental Response, Compensation, and Liability Act) 5. RCRA (Resource Conservation and Recovery Act) 6. NEPA (National Environmental Policy Act) 7. Toxic Substances Control Act These laws are referenced as examples of environmental law terms that can be used in searches for articles and materials related to environmental pollution.
3.	What are three most important regulations on green energy?	1. Energy Policy and Conservation Act of 1975: This act requires certain appliances and equipment to carry labels with information on energy efficiency and estimated energy costs, which helps consumers make informed choices (U.S. Congress, Office of Technology Assessment 1992). 2. Energy Star Program: Developed by the EPA and the U.S. Department of Energy, this program allows energy-efficient products to display an Energy Star label, promoting awareness and encouraging the purchase of energy-efficient products. 3. Top Runner Programme in Japan: Introduced in 1999, this program sets energy efficiency standards for over 20 product categories, encouraging competition among manufacturers to meet these standards and achieve the 'Top Runner' label at point of sale.
4.	What laws exist on sustainable development?	The context mentions several laws related to sustainable development: 1. China: The 13th Five-Year Plan for Economic and Social Development (2016–2020) includes commitments to building a "Beautiful China" through measures focused on resource efficiency and environmental protection. 2. European Union: The EU has established a wide range of laws, policies, and programmes relevant to sustainable development, with the European Commission reviewing them for their ability to deliver the Sustainable Development Goals. 3. Republic of Korea: The 2015 Sustainable Development Act and the 2010 Framework Act on Low Carbon, Green Growth create a national system for low-carbon sustainable development. 4. Mexico: The 2003 General Law for Sustainable Forest Development provides a framework for the development and management of forest goods and services, including safeguards for indigenous peoples' rights to natural resources.

4.2 Evaluation of Legal Chatbot Responses

To assess the quality of above answers generated by our legal chatbot built, we implemented a set of quantitative and qualitative metrics. These metrics help measure not only the accuracy of the answers but also their legal reliability and trustworthiness.

4.2.1. Dataset

We evaluated the system on the 20 question-answer pairs, where each pair consists of:

- Question: A legal query from a user.
- Reference Answer: The expected answer based on legal sources.
- Generated Answer: The chatbot's response.

4.2.2. Evaluation Metrics

4.2.2.1 Quantitative Metrics

To evaluate the performance of the legal chatbot, we employed several quantitative metrics. Exact Match (EM) measures whether the generated answer exactly matches the reference answer, making it particularly useful for short, factual responses. F1 Score computes the token-level overlap between the generated and reference answers, providing a more forgiving measure than exact match by accounting for paraphrasing or minor variations in wording. Citation Presence evaluates whether the generated answer includes references to legal sources, such as "section," "article," "law," or "act," ensuring that the chatbot's responses are grounded in relevant legal material. Finally, Hallucination Rate measures the fraction of words in the generated answer that do not appear in the reference answer, with higher rates indicating unsupported or potentially incorrect information.

4.2.2.2 Qualitative Considerations

While quantitative metrics provide an automated assessment of answer quality, human evaluation remains essential in the legal domain. Key qualitative factors include correctness, ensuring that answers are legally accurate; completeness, verifying that all relevant aspects of the question are addressed; clarity, ensuring the language is understandable to the intended audience; relevance, confirming that answers remain focused and free of unnecessary information; and supportability, assessing whether responses can be traced to specific graph nodes or legal sources.

4.2.3 Evaluation Procedure

To systematically compute these metrics, we implemented an algorithmic evaluation pipeline. For each question-answer pair, the generated and reference answers are first tokenized. Exact Match and F1 Score are then calculated to measure lexical accuracy, while legal citations are detected using keyword matching. The hallucination fraction is computed to identify unsupported content. Finally, results are aggregated across all 20 QA pairs to provide an overall assessment of chatbot performance.

4.2.4 Sample Results

The legal chatbot was evaluated on a dataset of above 20 question-answer pairs using both quantitative and qualitative metrics. The key results are as follows: Exact Match (EM): 0.00, F1 Score: 0.66, Citation Presence: 0.52, and Average Hallucination Rate: 0.30.

The Exact Match score of 0.00 indicates that none of the generated answers perfectly matched the reference answers. This is expected given the complex, paraphrased nature of legal responses produced by a RAG-based system. The F1 score of 0.66 demonstrates substantial lexical overlap with the reference answers, indicating that the chatbot generally captures the relevant legal information even when phrasing differs. A Citation Presence of 0.52 shows that just over half of the answers contain explicit references to legal sources (e.g., "act," "law," "section," or "article"), highlighting moderate traceability and adherence to legal referencing. The Average Hallucination Rate of 0.30 suggests that about 30% of the words in the generated answers do not appear in the reference answers, indicating some degree of unsupported or extraneous content.

Overall, these results suggest that our chatbot is capable of retrieving and presenting relevant legal information with reasonable accuracy and relevance. However, improvements are needed in exact referencing and minimizing hallucinations to ensure higher reliability and trustworthiness in legal applications.

4.2.5. Discussion

The evaluation demonstrates that the chatbot provides mostly accurate and relevant answers, though exact matches are lower due to paraphrasing. Ensuring legal citations and traceability to graph nodes is critical to maintain trustworthiness.

This combined approach of automated quantitative metrics and human qualitative review provides a comprehensive framework for evaluating legal chatbots and can be extended as the dataset grows.

4.3 The importance of GraphRAG in legal Applications

Legal practice has several characteristics that make it particularly well-suited to GraphRAG-based systems:

a. Complex Document Structures

Legal documents are not flat text. They contain hierarchical structures (articles, sections, clauses), cross-references ('as defined in Section 1.2'), and conditional logic ('if X occurs, then Y applies unless Z'). GraphRAG's entity-relationship model captures this complexity in a way that simple embeddings cannot.

b. Precision Requirements

In legal work, nuance matters. The difference between 'shall' and 'may,' or between 'material breach' and 'breach,' can have significant consequences. By extracting and preserving these distinctions as entity attributes and relationship types, GraphRAG enables more precise retrieval than systems that treat all text as undifferentiated content.

c. Multi-Document Analysis

Legal matters often involve multiple related documents: a master agreement and its amendments, a contract and its exhibits, or a set of related agreements in a transaction. GraphRAG's ability to maintain entity identity across documents makes it possible to ask questions that span multiple files.

d. Auditability

Legal professionals need to verify the sources of information. The graph structure provides natural traceability: every answer can be traced back to specific entities and relationships, which in turn link to specific passages in the source documents. This is superior to naive RAG, where the connection between retrieved chunks and the final answer may be opaque.

4.4 Deployment Considerations for Production Systems

While this chapter focuses primarily on systems design, successful deployment of such systems in production environments requires careful attention to scalability and reliability concerns.

High Traffic Handling and Load Balancing

For organizations deploying this system to handle multiple concurrent users or high query volumes, load balancing becomes essential. Load balancers are network devices or software services that distribute incoming requests across multiple server instances to prevent any single server from becoming overwhelmed.

In our architecture, load balancing would be implemented at two levels:

- Application Load Balancing: Multiple instances of the FastAPI backend can be deployed behind an application load balancer (e.g., NGINX, HAProxy, or cloud-native solutions like AWS ALB). The load balancer distributes incoming API requests across healthy backend instances using algorithms such as round-robin, least connections, or IP hash.
- Database Connection Pooling: PostgreSQL connection pools (e.g., PgBouncer) manage database connections efficiently, preventing connection exhaustion under high load. Each backend instance maintains a connection pool, and the pooler aggregates connections across all instances.

For the LLM inference components, rate limiting and request queuing ensure graceful handling of burst traffic. Auto-scaling policies can dynamically adjust the number of backend instances based on CPU utilization, memory usage, or request queue depth.

Scalability Patterns

Large-scale deployments benefit from several architectural patterns:

- Stateless Backend Design: The FastAPI backend is stateless, storing all persistent data in PostgreSQL. This enables horizontal scaling adding more servers to handle increased load without complex state synchronization.
- Caching Strategies: Frequently accessed knowledge graph queries can be cached using Redis or Memcached, reducing database load and improving response times for common questions.
- Asynchronous Processing: Document indexing (the most computationally intensive operation) is handled asynchronously, allowing users to continue interacting with the system while indexing proceeds in the background.

4.5 Practical Challenges and Opportunities for Improvement

The proposed GraphRAG-based legal chatbot performance depends on several factors. In this section we describe some limitations and possible challenges. First, the quality of the knowledge graph is highly dependent on the accuracy of LLM-based entity and relationship extraction. Errors in extraction—such as missed obligations, incorrect role assignments, or incomplete cross-references—can propagate through the graph and lead to incomplete or misleading responses, even if downstream reasoning is correct.

Second, while the chunking strategy is optimized for typical legal clause lengths, very long or highly nested clauses may still span multiple chunks in ways that challenge complete semantic capture. In such cases, relationships between definitions, exceptions, and conditions may be only partially represented, affecting multi-hop reasoning accuracy.

Third, the system assumes that legal documents are internally consistent or that conflicts can be resolved using standard precedence rules. In practice, poorly drafted contracts, jurisdictional overlaps, or contradictory amendments may lead to unresolved conflicts. Although the agent is designed to flag uncertainty and request clarification, users may still misinterpret such responses as definitive legal guidance.

Fourth, the agentic ReAct loop relies on a bounded number of reasoning iterations. Complex legal questions that require extensive exploration across multiple communities or documents may exceed this limit, forcing the system to produce a response based on partial information.

From a deployment perspective, performance and scalability remain open challenges. Knowledge graph construction and community detection are computationally expensive, and large document collections or concurrent users may introduce latency beyond acceptable thresholds in production settings.

Finally, real-world failure cases may arise from ambiguous or underspecified user queries, such as vague references to "liability" or "termination," which can lead the agent to retrieve overly broad or irrelevant graph segments. While the system includes clarification mechanisms, user non-cooperation or misunderstanding may still result in suboptimal answers.

These limitations highlight the need for careful deployment, user education, and continued evaluation when applying such systems in high-stakes legal environments.

5. ETHICAL PERSPECTIVES OF LEGAL CHATBOTS

A growing range of AI tools now support legal work, helping lawyers research cases, summarize documents, and draft memos or contracts. Among professional tools, Lexis+ AI integrates directly into the LexisNexis research platform to generate case summaries, legal memos, and answers to doctrinal questions. Westlaw CoCounsel, part of Thomson Reuters, assists with research, document review, and contract analysis and is widely used in major law firms. Harvey AI, built on GPT technology, is adopted by firms like Allen & Overy for advanced drafting and analysis. Casetext CoCounsel, now owned by Thomson Reuters, also focuses on legal research and document review.

In the consumer space, several chatbots provide basic legal guidance without offering full legal advice. DoNotPay assists with simple tasks such as contesting parking tickets or generating letters, though it remains controversial. LegalZoom's AI Assistant helps users prepare wills, create business entities, and file trademarks. Ailira, used in Australia, generates documents and answers straightforward legal questions. Some courts and public agencies also deploy legal chatbots. India's Nadia, California's Lina, and Wisconsin's Ask Madison help users navigate procedures or complete forms.

However, legal chatbots cannot replace licensed attorneys, must avoid offering full legal advice, and must comply with regulations governing unauthorized practice of law. In the legal domain AI chatbots offer particular advantages. For example, they enhance efficiency, reduce costs, and expand access to justice. Yet, as shown in recent research on chatbots in public administration, their deployment raises a wide range of ethical, legal, and governance challenges. These challenges become even more critical in the legal domain, where chatbot errors may directly affect citizens' rights, obligations, and livelihoods. The following sections outline the core ethical concerns.

Figure 11. Main application areas of chatbots in the legal domain

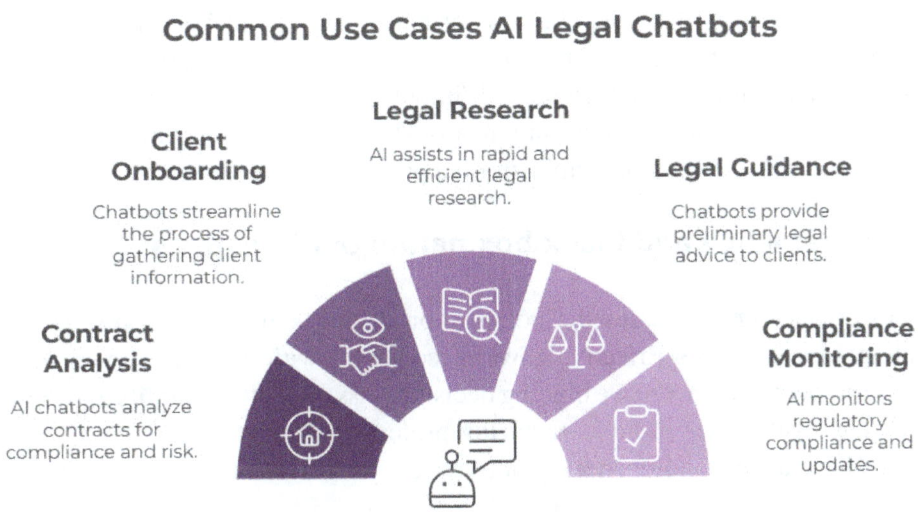

We describe the major risks, ethical challenges and corresponding guidelines which are to be followed by AI chatbots for their successful adaptation in the legal domain.

Figure 12. Major ethical constraints and challenges legal chatbots

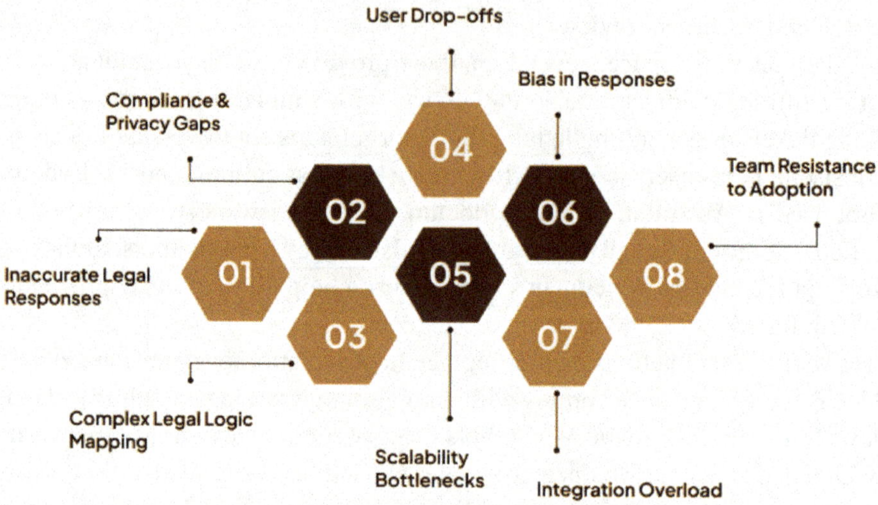

5.1. Principle of Legality and Good Administration

Legal chatbots must operate consistently with principles of legality and fair treatment. Because administrative and legal decisions require strict procedural safeguards, chatbots risk violating these principles if they misinterpret legal rules or apply concepts incorrectly. Their outputs may appear authoritative, yet lack the nuance required for lawful reasoning. Without clear legal frameworks governing their deployment, chatbots may unintentionally undermine citizens' procedural rights and compromise good administrative practice.

5.2. Governance and black box nature of AI Systems

Governance encompasses the policies, processes, and oversight mechanisms guiding AI system use. Effective governance begins with defining system scope: legal chatbots should not make binding decisions, assess guilt or liability, or provide definitive legal advice in areas requiring professional judgment. Their role is to support legal understanding, not replace lawyers, judges, or administrative officers.

Organizations should establish governance committees including legal experts, AI specialists, and ethics officers to review system documentation, risk assessments, performance metrics, user feedback mechanisms, and incident reports. The EU AI Act (2024) establishes a risk-based regulatory framework with specific implications for legal chatbots. While general-purpose chatbots fall under "limited-risk" provisions requiring transparency disclosures, AI systems used in the "administration of justice and democratic processes" are classified as high-risk (Article 6 and Annex III). Legal chatbots deployed in court systems, administrative proceedings, or legal aid contexts may therefore be subject to mandatory conformity assessments, risk management systems, data governance standards, technical documentation requirements, and human oversight obligations.

5.3. Accountability and Responsibility

The autonomous nature of AI creates a "responsibility gap." When a chatbot provides incorrect legal guidance with harmful consequences, it is unclear who should be held accountable—the developer, the deploying institution, or the end user. This ambiguity is ethically problematic in legal settings where clear liability is essential. Human oversight must remain central: even when AI systems provide preliminary interpretations, legal professionals remain responsible for validating outputs before relying on them in practice. The system must clearly state that it does not replace human legal judgment and that users should consult qualified professionals for complex or high-stakes issues.

Accountability applies across the value chain: developers must document model limitations, known risks, and appropriate use scenarios; deploying institutions must define liability structures ensuring users understand which outputs can be relied upon; legal professionals using AI tools remain professionally responsible for verifying outputs; and end users must be informed of system limitations and their responsibility to seek professional advice. Traceability—keeping records of prompts, retrieved documents, and system versions—is essential for attributing responsibility in case of errors or disputes.

5.4. Privacy and Data Protection

Legal queries frequently involve highly sensitive personal information about work conflicts, family issues, financial disputes, immigration circumstances, or criminal allegations. Such information belongs to the most sensitive categories of personal data. Under the General Data Protection Regulation (GDPR), legal chatbots must uphold data minimization (collecting only information strictly necessary to answer the question), purpose limitation (no repurposing without explicit consent), transparency about data processing, and privacy by design principles. Technical safeguards include encryption, strict access control, isolation of private content, and local deployment approaches that ensure sensitive queries are not transmitted to third-party servers. Institutions must implement clear retention and deletion policies, specifying how long conversation logs are stored and how users can request removal. Legal confidentiality is not just a technical matter but an ethical and sometimes statutory obligation—breaches may cause financial, reputational, or personal harm.

5.5. Data Quality and Algorithmic Bias

The accuracy and fairness of chatbots depend on the quality of their training data. Biased or low-quality data can lead to discriminatory recommendations, especially in areas such as eligibility assessments, complaint filing, or legal risk scoring. Examples from European public-sector AI demonstrate how predictive systems can disproportionately target vulnerable populations, highlighting the danger of embedding structural inequalities into automated legal tools.

5.6 Transparency and Explainability

Transparency is essential for trust and legitimacy in legal contexts. Users must understand how the system generates its responses, which sources it relies on, and what assumptions guide its reasoning. The opacity of "black-box" algorithms makes it difficult to understand how conclusions are generated, limiting the ability of regulators, courts, or users to evaluate fairness, accuracy, or compliance with legal standards. The EU AI Act (European Commission, 2024) places chatbots in the "limited-risk" category by default, yet they may become "high-risk" when used in contexts impacting legal rights—triggering stricter requirements for transparency, accuracy, cybersecurity, and data governance. RAG architectures offer inherent transparency advantages that should be leveraged. The system should explicitly display the statutes, regulations, or case-law excerpts retrieved during the query, helping users verify the factual basis of responses. Legal chatbots should articulate their reasoning in a structured form, explaining how retrieved sources apply to the user's question. The system should also communicate uncertainty explicitly, as legal texts are often ambiguous. Contestability is equally crucial: users must be able to challenge outputs by requesting alternative interpretations, clarifications, or access to additional sources. Follow-up prompts such as "Would you like to see relevant case law?" encourage critical engagement rather than passive acceptance and support due process principles.

5.7 Specialization, Expertise, and Workforce Impact

Developing and supervising legal chatbots requires advanced expertise, which may widen skill gaps and create dependence on a small group of specialists. This raises concerns about inequality within the legal profession. Additionally, automation may reshape legal work, shifting roles from advisory tasks to supervision of AI outputs, requiring retraining and new competencies.

5.8 Human–Machine Interaction and Social Acceptance

The success of legal chatbots ultimately depends on how users perceive and interact with them. Chatbots often lack contextual sensitivity and emotional awareness, leading to misunderstandings in delicate legal situations such as family disputes, criminal allegations, or employment conflicts. Trust depends on transparency (users knowing they interact with AI), fairness (equitable treatment regardless of background), data security, and the perception that AI enhances rather than replaces human judgment. Interfaces should display clear disclaimers about the system's advisory nature, provide verifiable source citations, offer pathways to human assistance, use accessible language, and acknowledge uncertainty when confidence is low.

The integration of AI tools will likely reshape legal work: professionals may shift from routine research to supervising AI outputs, requiring new competencies in AI literacy and critical evaluation of AI-generated content. While AI can democratize access to legal knowledge, concerns about professional inequality arise, well-resourced firms gaining advantages over smaller practices. Ensuring equitable access to legal AI technologies and the expertise required to use them effectively is an important policy consideration for the future of legal practice.

6. HUMAN FACTORS AND GOVERNANCE PERSPECTIVES ON LEGAL CHATBOTS

In this section we study how ethical principles governing legal chatbots manifest in human–AI interaction, user trust, governance mechanisms, and interface-level design decisions in real-world legal contexts.

In high-stakes domains such as law, the effectiveness of AI-driven legal chatbots cannot be evaluated solely on technical performance or accuracy. Equally critical is how users understand, interpret, and trust AI-generated legal explanations (Bardhan & Kandarp, 2025; Pustry & Bardhan, 2025) . Legal advice interfaces operate under conditions of uncertainty, power asymmetry, and potentially severe consequences, making human-centered considerations central rather than peripheral.

Empirical studies across human–AI interaction suggest that users often struggle to interpret probabilistic or conditional explanations provided by AI systems, especially when these explanations mimic authoritative legal language. This can lead to misplaced confidence, over-reliance, or conversely heightened anxiety, depending on the user's legal literacy, prior experiences, and perceived system authority. In legal contexts, such effects are amplified: users may incorrectly assume legal validity, conflate explanation with advice, or fail to recognize jurisdictional limitations embedded in AI outputs.

Table 6 synthesizes the relationship between key technical components of legal chatbots, corresponding ethical principles, and their implications for human-centered interaction design. Rather than treating ethics as an external compliance layer, the table illustrates how ethical considerations are operationalized through concrete design and implementation choices. For example, transparency is realized not only through explainable language models but through explanations that explicitly communicate uncertainty in a form users can meaningfully interpret. Similarly, fairness extends beyond dataset composition to encompass retrieval mechanisms that influence how legal information is contextualized across jurisdictions and user populations. By linking confidence framing and human-in-the-loop escalation to non-maleficence and accountability, the table highlights how interface-level decisions directly affect risks of over-reliance and misplaced trust. Overall, this mapping underscores that ethical, trustworthy legal chatbots emerge from the integration of technical architecture, human-centered design, and governance-aware interaction practices.

Table 6. Linking Technical Components with Ethical and Human-Centered Design Considerations in Legal Chatbots

Technical Component	Ethical Principle	Human-Centered Implication
Language models and reasoning engines	Transparency	Comprehensible, uncertainty-aware explanations that support user understanding
Training data and retrieval mechanisms	Fairness	Reduced bias across legal contexts, jurisdictions, and user groups
Confidence scoring and response framing	Non-maleficence	Mitigation of over-reliance, false certainty, and inappropriate legal trust
Human-in-the-loop escalation mechanisms	Accountability	Support for responsible legal decision-making and access to qualified professionals
Interface design and interaction flow	Autonomy	User empowerment through informed choice rather than automation bias

6.1 User Confidence, and Over-Reliance in High-Stakes AI Systems

Interaction with legal chatbots can trigger forms of legal anxiety, analogous to well-documented phenomena such as mathematical or technological anxiety. Users facing legal uncertainty such as disputes, immigration issues, or contractual obligations, often approach AI systems in emotionally charged states. In such contexts, AI explanations may either:

- Increase user confidence by providing structured guidance and perceived clarity, or
- Increase anxiety through ambiguity, inconsistent responses, or over-complex legal phrasing.

Importantly, a parallel can be drawn with prior research on user psychological modeling (Pustry & Bardhan, 2025), where user confidence is strongly shaped by how information is framed and explained. Extending these insights to legal chatbots suggests that uncertainty-aware and cognitively sensitive explanation design is essential. Rather than presenting deterministic outputs, legal chatbots should communicate uncertainty explicitly, contextualize confidence levels, and support gradual sense-making thereby mitigating both anxiety and over-reliance.

6.2 Governance, accountability & responsibility in AI-mediated legal assistance

Governance frameworks such as the EU AI Act play a pivotal role in structuring the responsible deployment of legal chatbots by explicitly classifying AI systems used in legal decision support as high-risk applications, thereby subjecting them to heightened obligations around transparency, human oversight, risk management, and documentation. In the context of AI-mediated legal assistance, these regulatory requirements directly intersect with user experience: mandated disclosures regarding system limitations, confidence levels, and intended use are essential to preventing user misunderstanding, over-reliance, and false perceptions of legal authority. Beyond statutory regulation, legal tech governance must also align with professional responsibility frameworks, including duties of competence, non-deception, and client protection traditionally imposed on legal practitioners. When legal chatbots are deployed by law firms, courts, or public institutions, governance mechanisms must ensure that AI outputs do not constitute unauthorized legal advice and that clear pathways to qualified human professionals are preserved. In this sense, governance operates not merely as external compliance but as a socio-technical design constraint that shapes how trust, accountability, and human agency are negotiated at the interface level, reinforcing ethical human-centered design in legally consequential human–AI interactions.

In Table 7 below shows how legal chatbots are placed within emerging regulatory frameworks that emphasize transparency, human oversight, accountability, and user trust.

Table 7. Mapping international governance frameworks with AI based legal chatbot capabilities

Framework / Report	Jurisdiction	Scope	Key Provisions Relevant to Legal Chatbots
EU AI Act (2024)	European Union	Binding regulation	Risk-based classification; high-risk obligations for legal and justice-related AI; transparency, human oversight, logging, and accountability
OECD Governing with AI (2025)	International	Policy guidance	Institutional AI governance, risk management, lifecycle oversight, public-sector AI deployment
Council of Europe AI Convention (2024)	International	Binding treaty	Alignment of AI with human rights, due process, access to remedies, rule of law
IAPP AI Governance in Practice (2024)	Global	Practitioner report	Organizational governance models, accountability structures, AI risk controls
IAPP AI Governance Profession (2025)	Global	Workforce & governance	Emerging roles, skills, and compliance practices for AI governance

6.3 Glossary of Legal and AI terms

To enhance accessibility for readers from diverse backgrounds, we provide definitions of key technical and legal terminology used throughout this chapter:

AI and Machine Learning Terms:

- Embedding: A numerical vector representation of text that captures semantic meaning, enabling mathematical comparison of textual similarity.
- Hallucination: When a language model generates information that is not supported by its input context or training data, potentially producing plausible-sounding but incorrect statements.
- Knowledge Graph: A structured representation of information as entities (nodes) and their relationships (edges), enabling reasoning about connections between concepts.

- Large Language Model (LLM): An AI system trained on vast amounts of text data to understand and generate human-like text, capable of tasks like question answering and summarization.
- RAG (Retrieval-Augmented Generation): An approach where a language model retrieves relevant information from a knowledge base before generating a response, improving factual accuracy.
- Semantic Search: Information retrieval based on meaning rather than exact keyword matching, using techniques like embeddings to find conceptually related content.

Technical Architecture Terms:

- API (Application Programming Interface): A set of protocols and tools that allow different software applications to communicate and exchange data.
- FastAPI: A modern Python web framework for building APIs quickly and efficiently.
- Load Balancer: A system that distributes network traffic across multiple servers to ensure no single server becomes overwhelmed.
- PostgreSQL: An open-source relational database management system known for its reliability and feature richness.

7. CONCLUSION

Legal chatbots represent a powerful innovation with the potential to reshape how individuals, institutions, and legal professionals interact with the law. By offering rapid access to legal information, procedural guidance, and structured explanations, these systems can expand access to justice, enhance research efficiency, and streamline administrative processes. As discussed throughout this article, legal chatbots can support legal aid services, assist public administration, strengthen compliance workflows, and contribute to legal education. Their value lies not only in accelerating information retrieval but also in democratizing legal knowledge for users who may otherwise struggle to obtain timely legal support.

However, the promise of legal chatbots must be balanced with a careful assessment of the ethical and regulatory challenges they introduce. Issues such as legality, governance, accountability, privacy, data quality, bias, transparency, and public trust require deliberate attention. Inaccuracies, hallucinations, or misinterpretations can carry severe legal consequences, underscoring the importance of robust oversight, factual grounding, and continuous monitoring. Bias embedded in training data can reinforce systemic inequities, making fairness audits and mitigation strategies essential. Transparency and interpretability remain central: users must understand how chatbot conclusions are reached, what sources they rely on, and where uncertainties remain. Furthermore, compliance with evolving regulatory frameworks such as data protection laws, AI safety standards, and restrictions on unauthorized legal practice—is indispensable for responsible deployment.

Importantly, this article not only analyzes the ethical landscape of legal chatbots but also provides a practical guide on how to build such systems and rigorously test their capabilities. By combining technical instruction with critical ethical reflection, the article aims to equip practitioners, researchers, and students with the tools to design RAG-enabled legal chatbots that are both effective and trustworthy. Ultimately, legal chatbots can meaningfully enhance access to legal knowledge—provided they are developed with care, transparency, and respect for the fundamental rights of the individuals they serve.

Future research will extend this work through longitudinal user studies of legal chatbots, systematic evaluation of chatbot accuracy, explainability, robustness, and uncertainty handling, and deeper analysis of legal anxiety and over-reliance. From a systems perspective, we plan to conduct stress and load testing under concurrent user scenarios to analyze latency, throughput, and overall system stability, as well as evaluate scalability by progressively increasing document corpus size and graph complexity while measuring ingestion time and retrieval latency. Closer alignment with evolving AI governance frameworks and human-centered evaluation methodologies remains essential. Finally, due to the diversity of legal systems and document structures, systematic cross-system and jurisdiction-specific benchmarking remains an important direction for future work as standardized legal QA benchmarks mature.

REFERENCES

Salemi, A., & Zamani, H. (2024, July). Evaluating retrieval quality in retrieval-augmented generation. In *Proceedings of the 47th International ACM SIGIR Conference on Research and Development in Information Retrieval* (pp. 2395-2400).

Adheshvar, A., Jessiah Inbaraj, P., Patturajan, T., & Rajesh, K. (2025). AttorneyGPT – Multilingual Generative Artificial Intelligence Law Chatbot using Retrieval Augmented Generation. In Proceedings of the 4th International Conference on Information Technology, Civil Innovation, Science, and Management (ICITSM 2025). EAI.

Alarie, B., Niblett, A., & Yoon, A. H. (2018). How artificial intelligence will affect the practice of law. *University of Toronto Law Journal, 68*, 106–124.

Aleedy, M., Shaiba, H., & Bezbradica, M. (2019). Generating and analyzing chatbot responses using Natural Language Processing. *International Journal of Advanced Computer Science and Applications, 10*(9). Advance online publication. DOI: 10.14569/ijacsa.2019.0100910

Alqaidi, S. H., Albugami, S. M., Alzahrani, W. S., Badri, S., & Wali, A. (2024). Network-integrated medical chatbot for enhanced healthcare services. *Telematics and Informatics Reports, 15*, 100153.

Y Arcas, , B. A. (2022). Do large language models understand us? *Daedalus, 151*(2), 183–197.

Asai, A., Schick, T., Lewis, P., Chen, X., Izacard, G., Riedel, S., & Yih, W. T. (2023, July). Task-aware retrieval with instructions. In *Findings of the Association for Computational Linguistics* (pp. 3650–3675). ACL.

Babu, A., & Boddu, S. B. (2024). BERT-based medical chatbot: Enhancing healthcare communication through natural language understanding. *Exploratory Research in Clinical and Social Pharmacy, 13*(Mar), 100419. PMID: 38495953

Banerjee, D., Singh, P., Avadhanam, A., & Srivastava, S. (2023). Benchmarking LLM powered chatbots: methods and metrics. arXiv preprint arXiv:2308.04624.

Bardhan, R., & Kandarp, A. (Eds.). (2025). REIMAGINING HIGHER EDUCATION WITH AI. Krishna Publication House.

Bauer, T., Devrim, E., Glazunov, M., Jaramillo, W. L., Mohan, B., & Spanakis, G. (2019, September). #MeTooMaastricht: Building a chatbot to assist survivors of sexual harassment. In *Joint European Conference on Machine Learning and Knowledge Discovery in Databases* (pp. 503-521). Cham: Springer International Publishing.

Behnia, R., Ebrahimi, M. R., Pacheco, J., & Padmanabhan, B. (2022, November). Ew-tune: A framework for privately fine-tuning large language models with differential privacy. In *2022 IEEE International Conference on Data Mining Workshops (ICDMW)* (pp. 560-566). IEEE.

Bench-Capon, T., Araszkiewicz, M., Ashley, K., Atkinson, K., Bex, F., Borges, F., Bourcier, D., Bourgine, P., Conrad, J. G., Francesconi, E., Gordon, T. F., Governator, G., Leidner, J. L., Lewis, D. D., Loui, R. P., McCarty, L. T., Prakken, H., Schilder, F., Schweighofer, E., & Walton, D. N. (2012). A history of ai and law in 50 papers: 25 Years of the international conference on ai and law. *Artificial Intelligence and Law*, *203*, 215–319.

Bhagwat, S., Panchangam, S., Sawant, A., Sharma, P., & Nayak, U. (2025, June). NyAI Saathi-Legal Research Tool leveraging GenAI (RAG). In 2025 5th International Conference on Intelligent Technologies (CONIT) (pp. 1-10). IEEE.

Boiko, D. A., Mac Knight, R., & Gomes, G. (2023). *Emergent autonomous scientific research capabilities of large language models*. arXiv preprint arXiv: 2304.05332.

Brooks, C., Gherhes, C., & Vorley, T. (2020). Artificial intelligence in the legal sector: Pressures and challenges of transformation. *Cambridge Journal of Regions, Economy and Society*, *13*(1), 135–152.

Brown, T., Mann, B., Ryder, N., Subbiah, M., Kaplan, J. D., Dhariwal, P., & Amodei, D. (2020). Language models are few-shot learners. *Advances in Neural Information Processing Systems*, *33*, 1877–1901.

Chan, C. S., Kong, H., & Guanqing, L. (2022, May). A comparative study of faithfulness metrics for model interpretability methods. In *Proceedings of the 60th annual meeting of the association for computational linguistics* (volume 1: Long papers) (pp. 5029-5038).

Chernyavskiy, A., Ilvovsky, D., & Nakov, P. (2021). Transformers: "the end of history" for natural language processing? In Machine Learning and Knowledge Discovery in Databases. *Research Track: European Conference, ECML PKDD 2021*, Bilbao, Spain, September 13–17, 2021 [Springer International Publishing.]. *Proceedings*, *21*(Part III), 677–693.

Chia, H., Zhang, G. Z., Russo-Batterham, D., Manandhar, K., Quang, U. T., Wang, Z., & Paterson, J. M. (2024). L.E.G.A.L.: A RAG-Based System for Legal Document Navigation. *Proceedings of the ALTA Conference*.

Chung, H. W., Hou, L., Longpre, S., Zoph, B., Tay, Y., Fedus, W., & Wei, J. (2024). Scaling instruction-finetuned language models. *Journal of Machine Learning Research, 25*(70), 1–53.

Council of Europe. (2024). *Framework convention on artificial intelligence, human rights, democracy and the rule of law*. Council of Europe Publishing.

Devlin, J., Chang, M. W., Lee, K., & Toutanova, K. (2018). *Bert: Pre-training of deep bidirectional transformers for language understanding*. arXiv preprint arXiv: 1810.04805.

Divya, S., Indumathi, V., Ishwarya, S., Priyasankari, M., & Devi, S. K. (2018). A self-diagnosis medical chatbot using artificial intelligence. *J. Web Develop. Web Designing, 3*(1), 1–7.

Dzienkowski, J. S. (2013). The future of big law: Alternative legal service providers to corporate clients. *Fordham Law Review, 82*, 2995–3040.

Es, S., James, J., Anke, L. E., & Schockaert, S. (2024, March). Ragas: Automated evaluation of retrieval augmented generation. In Proceedings of the 18th conference of the european chapter of the association for computational linguistics: system demonstrations (pp. 150-158).

European Commission. (2024). *Regulation (EU) 2024/1689 laying down harmonised rules on artificial intelligence (Artificial Intelligence Act)*. Official Journal of the European Union.

Gao, Y., Xiong, Y., Gao, X., Jia, K., Pan, J., Bi, Y., . . . Wang, H. (2023). Retrieval-augmented generation for large language models: A survey. arXiv preprint arXiv:2312.10997, 2(1), 32.

Giovis, R., & Rozsa, E. (2024). *Transforming customer service: How generative AI is changing the game*. IBM Artificial Intelligence.

Hsueh, Y.-L., & Chou, T.-L. (2022). A Task-Oriented Chatbot Based on LSTM and Reinforcement Learning. *ACM Transactions on Asian and Low-Resource Language Information Processing, 22*(1), 127. DOI: 10.1145/3529649

Hu, Z., Wang, L., Lan, Y., Xu, W., Lim, E.-P., Bing, L., Xu, X., Poria, S., & Lee, R. K.-W. (2023). "LLM-adapters: An adapter family for parameter-efficient fine-tuning of large language models, arXiv:2304.01933.

International Association of Privacy Professionals (IAPP). (2024). *AI governance in practice: Organizational approaches to responsible AI*. IAPP.

Ioannidou, E., Promikyridis, R., & Tambouris, E. (2025). Legal and Ethical Issues Arising from the Use of Chatbots in Public Administration. *Proceedings of the 28th Pan-Hellenic Conference on Progress in Computing and Informatics*, 211–215. doi:DOI: 10.1145/3716554.3716586

Itelman, E., Golovchiner, G., Barsheshet, A., Kornowski, R., & Erez, A. (2024, October). Balancing innovation and professionalism: The emerging role of AI-powered chatbots in medical consultation. *Heart Rhythm*, *21*(10), 2037–2039. PMID: 38588991

Izacard, G., Caron, M., Hosseini, L., Riedel, S., Bojanowski, P., Joulin, A., & Grave, E. (2021). "Unsupervised dense information retrieval with contrastive learning," arXiv:2112.09118.

Kane, O., Allaya, M. M., Samb, D., & Bousso, M. (2025). An Senegalese Legal Texts Structuration Using LLM-Augmented Knowledge Graph. arXiv preprint 2510.02353.

Keerthana, D., N.S., Gowda, V., & Vali, S. (2025, May 28). Ethical and legal implications of AI chatbots in legal sector. *2025 International Conference on Computational Robotics, Testing and Engineering Evaluation (ICCRTEE)*, 1–5. Presented at the 2025 International Conference on Computational Robotics, Testing and Engineering Evaluation (ICCRTEE), Virudhunagar, India. doi:DOI: 10.1109/iccrtee64519.2025.11053085

Khatri, M., Agrawal, A., & Garg, A. (2021). PoliceBOT-An Informative RASA Powered Chatbot based Crime Registration and Crime Awareness System. International Research Journal of Engineering and Technology, 8(06).

Kuang, W., Qian, B., Li, Z., Chen, D., Gao, D., Pan, X., & Zhou, J. (2024, August). Federatedscope-llm: A comprehensive package for fine-tuning large language models in federated learning. In *Proceedings of the 30th ACM SIGKDD Conference on Knowledge Discovery and Data Mining* (pp. 5260-5271).

Kulkarni, M., Tangarajan, P., Kim, K., & Trivedi, A. (2024). Reinforcement learning for optimizing rag for domain chatbots. arXiv preprint arXiv:2401.06800.

Kumar, S. S., Ahmed, S. T., Fathima, A. S., Nishabai, M., & Sophia, S. (2024, January). Medical ChatBot assistance for primary clinical guidance using machine learning techniques. *Procedia Computer Science*, *233*, 279–287.

Lakatos, R., Pollner, P., Hajdu, A., & Joó, T. (2025, February). Investigating the performance of retrieval-augmented generation and domain-specific fine-tuning for the development of AI-driven knowledge-based systems. *Mach. Learn. Knowl. Extraction*, *7*(1), 15.

Lewis, M., Liu, Y., Goyal, N., Ghazvininejad, M., Mohamed, A., Levy, O., . . . Zettlemoyer, L. (2019). *Bart: Denoising sequence-to-sequence pre-training for natural language generation, translation, and comprehension*. arXiv preprint arXiv: 1910.13461.

Lewis, P., Perez, E., Piktus, A., Petroni, F., Karpukhin, V., Goyal, N., Küttler, H., Lewis, M., Yih, W.-T., Rocktäschel, T., Riedel, S., & Kiela, D. (2020). "Retrieval-augmented generation for knowledge-intensive NLP tasks," in Proc. *Advances in Neural Information Processing Systems*, •••, 9459–9474.

LexRAG Consortium. (2025). LexRAG: Benchmarking Retrieval-Augmented Generation in Multi-Turn Legal Consultation. arXiv preprint 2502.20640.

Lv, K., Yang, Y., Liu, T., Guo, Q., & Qiu, X. (2024, August). Full parameter fine-tuning for large language models with limited resources. In *Proceedings of the 62nd Annual Meeting of the Association for Computational Linguistics* (Volume 1: Long Papers) (pp. 8187-8198).

McGinnis, J. O., & Pearce, R. G. (2014). The great disruption: How machine intelligence will transform the role of lawyers in the delivery of legal services. *Fordham Law Review*, *82*, 3041–3306.

McKeown, T., Mustafina, J., Magizov, R., & Gataullina, C. (2020, December). AI in law practices. In 2020 13th International Conference on Developments in eSystems Engineering (DeSE) (pp. 27-32). IEEE.

Muthuraju, V., Patnaik, S. L., Paul, G. S., & Sadhu, H. (2025, July). LexBot: AI-Powered Legal Help. In 2025 2nd International Conference on New Frontiers in Communication, Automation, Management and Security (ICCAMS) (pp. 1-4). IEEE.

Nikolskaia, K., & Naumov, V. (2020, October). Artificial intelligence in law. In 2020 International Multi-Conference on Industrial Engineering and Modern Technologies (FarEastCon) (pp. 1-4). IEEE.

. Noël, V., Seidou, E. Y., Capo-Chichi, C. K., & Amari, G. (2025).HalluGraph: Auditable Hallucination Detection for Legal RAG Systems via Knowledge Graph Alignment. arXiv preprint 2512.01659.

Organisation for Economic Co-operation and Development (OECD). (2025). *Governing with artificial intelligence: Policy frameworks and institutional practices*. OECD Publishing.

Patil, B., Alam, R., Kalal, T. V., Porwal, P., Kushwaha, N. S., & Sharma, N. (2025, April). BNS Mitra: RAG-Optimized LLM Based AI-Powered Legal Virtual Assistant. In 2025 3rd International Conference on Communication, Security, and Artificial Intelligence (ICCSAI) (Vol. 3, pp. 1501-1506). IEEE.

Peters, M. E., Ruder, S., & Smith, N. A. (2019, August). To tune or not to tune? adapting pretrained representations to diverse tasks. In Proceedings of the 4th Workshop on Representation Learning for NLP (RepL4NLP-2019) (pp. 7-14).

Pustry, R. N., & Bardhan, R. (2025). Improving accessibility to abstract mathematical concepts us- ing generative multimodal explanations. In *Mathematics Education in the Era of Education 4.0* (Vol. 1, pp. 187–199). KBD Publication.

Rackauckas, Z. (2024). Rag-fusion: a new take on retrieval-augmented generation. arXiv preprint arXiv:2402.03367.

. Radford, A., Wu, J., Child, R., Luan, D., Amodei, D., & Sutskever, I. (2019). Language models are unsupervised multitask learners. *OpenAI blog*, 1 (8),

Rajamalli Keerthana, R., Fathima, G., & Florence, L. (2021). Evaluating the performance of various deep reinforcement learning algorithms for a conversational chatbot. 2021 2nd International Conference for Emerging Technology (INCET). DOI: 10.1109/incet51464.2021.9456321

Ram, O., Levine, Y., Dalmedigos, I., Muhlgay, D., Shashua, A., Leyton-Brown, K., & Shoham, Y. (2023, November). In-context retrieval-augmented language models. *Transactions of the Association for Computational Linguistics*, *11*, 1316–1331.

Rivas-Echeverría, F., Ramos, L. T., Ibarra, J. L., Zerpa-Bonillo, S., Arciniegas, S., & Asprino-Salas, M. (2025). LegalBot-EC: An LLM-Based Chatbot for Legal Assistance in Ecuadorian Law. *IEEE Access : Practical Innovations, Open Solutions*, *13*, 106817–106833. DOI: 10.1109/ACCESS.2025.3580488

Shao, Z., Gong, Y., Shen, Y., Huang, M., Duan, N., & Chen, W. (2023, December). Enhancing retrieval-augmented large language models with iterative retrieval-generation synergy. In *Findings of the Association for Computational Linguistics* (pp. 9248–9274). EMNLP.

Shi, Y., Zi, X., Shi, Z., Zhang, H., Wu, Q., & Xu, M. (2024). Eragent: Enhancing retrieval-augmented language models with improved accuracy, efficiency, and personalization. arXiv preprint arXiv:2405.06683.

Surana, S., Chekkala, J., & Bihani, P. (2021). Chatbot based crime registration and crime awareness system using a custom named entity recognition model for extracting information from complaints. International research journal of engineering and technology, 8(04).

Touvron, H., Martin, L., Stone, K., Albert, P., Almahairi, A., Babaei, Y., . . . Scialom, T. (2023). Llama 2: Open foundation and fine-tuned chat models. arXiv preprint arXiv:2307.09288.

Wang, Y., Kordi, Y., Mishra, S., Liu, A., Smith, N. A., Khashabi, D., & Hajishirzi, H. (2022). *Self-instruct: Aligning language models with self-generated instructions*. arXiv preprint arXiv: 2212.10560.

Webb, T., Holyoak, K. J., & Lu, H. (2023). Emergent analogical reasoning in large language models. *Nature Human Behaviour*, *7*(9), 1526–1541. PMID: 37524930

Wei, J., Tay, Y., Bommasani, R., Raffel, C., Zoph, B., Borgeaud, S., . . . Fedus, W. (2022). *Emergent abilities of large language models*. arXiv preprint arXiv: 2206.07682.

Zhang, Z., Gu, Y., Han, X., Chen, S., Xiao, C., Sun, Z., & Sun, M. (2021). CPM-2: Large-scale cost-effective pre-trained language models. *AI Open*, *2*, 216–224.

Chapter 14

Theories of Fraud, the Metaverse, and the Role of Forensic Accounting in Ensuring Security

Dibya Jyoti Acharya
http://orcid.org/0009-0004-7614-928X
Alliance University, India

Nandini G.
http://orcid.org/0000-0003-4643-0199
Alliance Ascent College, Alliance University, India

Senthil Kumar A. V.
http://orcid.org/0000-0002-8587-7017
Nehru Institute of Information Technology and Management, India

ABSTRACT

This chapter delves into foundational and contemporary theories related to fraud- such as the Fraud Triangle, Diamond, Pentagon, Scale, and Circle- illustrated with cases that made history like the Ponzi fraud, Enron, Satyam, WorldCom, the Harshad Mehta scam and many more in order to make clear the reasons behind fact. The chapter presents the behavioural, psychological, and situational elements behind the fact and discusses the significance of forensic accounting in the effort to detect, safeguard, and investigate fraud in the corporate, banking, insurance, securities sectors, and even in the Metaverse's virtual economies by mitigating novel digital risks like NFT scams and blockchain laundering. The chapter also addresses the work with regulators and the integration of emerging technological advances like

DOI: 10.4018/979-8-3373-7685-1.ch014

Artificial Intelligence (AI) in the pursuit of fraud deterrence, which establishes a modern role for forensic accounting as being part of the global effort to prevent the integrity of finances across traditional and virtual domains.

1. INTRODUCTION

Today's economy is flooded with the threat of Financial Fraud for corporations, financial institutions, and public entities and increasingly those operating in the digital and virtual world (Association of Certified Fraud Examiners [ACFE], 2022; PricewaterhouseCoopers [PwC], 2022). Financial Fraud can be thought of as any act of deliberately misrepresenting or deceiving someone for financial gain, whether that be because someone wants to make money, hold a position of power, maintain a high level of status, or fulfil an ideological objective (Wells, 2017; Kranacher, Riley, & Wells, 2019). In a corporate environment, those who commit financial fraud can be any of the following: employees, managers, executives, board members, and/or owners (ACFE, 2022). It is the overlap of pressures, opportunities, and rationalizations that allows someone to commit fraud, regardless of their title at an organization. From these circumstances, The Forensic Approaches emerged to systematically identify all the different types of misconduct that occur in organizations. This application is based on the integration of Accounting, Auditing, Investigations, and Law to determine the factors involved in concealing financial manipulations and provide how to hold entities accountable for their actions.

Forensic Analysis is the application of scientific methodologies and analytical methodologies to perform investigations of crimes/disputes (Crumbley, Heitger, & Smith, 2015). In the financial and corporate settings, Forensic accounting has developed into a specialized area of study. The focus of this area is on the examination of Financial Records and Financial Controls, as well as the processes and evidence needed to determine the causes and effects of all forms of fraud. Forensic accounting can be distinguished from Traditional Auditing by its emphasis on Investigation, Evidentiary Requirements, and Event Reconstruction suitable for Presentation in a Court of Law (Golden, Skalak, Clayton, & Pill, 2011; Rezaee, 2009). Forensic accounting has become critical to the detection, deterrence, and explanation of fraud and has increasingly taken a role in helping to develop a foundation upon which fraud prevention efforts can be based (Rezaee, 2009; Bhasin, 2013).

To understand how fraud is committed, it is essential to utilize a theoretical model that examines the individual behaviors of perpetrators and the shortcomings of the systems wherein fraud occurred. Here, an integrated fraud-forensics-Metaverse framework is proposed as a new way to combine traditional fraud theory with digital forensics evidence for guiding both professional practice and policy response in virtual economies. In contrast to existing narrative reviews, this chapter presents a framework that links existing fraud drivers directly with specific investigative tools, control mechanisms and regulatory considerations for fraud in the Metaverse. Numerous theories have been implemented to assist in defining how seemingly "honest" individuals can engage in behaviours that are contrary to both their ethical and legal obligations. The Fraud Triangle developed by Dr. Edwin Cressey defines three distinct elements that together are likely to cause a person to commit fraud (Pressure, Opportunity, and Rationalization). Pressure comes from a variety of sources, including personal financial needs and performance expectations. Opportunity arises from either ineffective internal control systems or ineffective management. Rationalization gives rise to the belief that the behaviour of an individual is acceptable or justifiable based on the circumstances surrounding them (Cressey, 1953). The Fraud Diamond added a fourth element to this model, the dimension is Capability, which encompasses the skills, authority, and confidence of the perpetrator who utilises the weaknesses or ineffectiveness of the internal controls to commit fraud or to design and implement complex fraudulent schemes (Wolfe & Hermanson, 2004). Other models such as Palmer's Fraud Scale and the MICE (Money, Ideology, Coercion, Ego) model further enrich the understanding of both motivational and situational causes of fraudulent behaviour (Albrecht, Howe, & Romney, 1984; Kranacher et al., 2011).

Forensic accounting is considered a practice in the application of accounting to solve problems through the interpretation of financial evidence with investigative methods and legal knowledge. Forensic accountants use standard audit techniques with advanced tools, including data mining, ratio and trend analysis and continuous monitoring systems, to identify the movement of irregularly transacted assets, to identify the historical movement of those assets, and finally to determine the events that occurred in the historical record (Wells, 2017; Bologna & Lindquist, 1995). In addition to those applications, forensic accountants assist in prevention and deterrence by assessing fraud risk, strengthening internal controls, providing guidance on corporate governance, and fostering a business ethics culture that supports regulators, investors, and other stakeholders. Because the forensic work of forensic accountants is becoming increasingly intermingled with global laws, such as Sarbanes-Oxley, the UK Bribery Act, and the Indian Prevention of Corruption (Amendment), the laws are emphasizing the need for transparency, accountability, and strong anti-fraud controls.

By connecting theories of fraud to the practices of forensic accounting, forensic investigators will be better able to recognize and address red flags, or warning signs, of fraud and risk, before they escalate into significant events. Examples of significant historical failures, such as Enron, Wirecard, Satyam and various Ponzi schemes, exemplify the ongoing cycle wherein there are many instances in which there is an opportunity to commit fraud (pressure), there is an opportunity/ability to commit fraud (capability), and there are multiple rationalizations to commit fraud (rationalization) where there has been a breakdown of internal controls (governance) (Healy & Palepu, 2003; Staff, 2009; *McCrum, D. (2020, June 25). Wirecard the Timeline. Financial Times. - References - Scientific Research Publishing*, n.d.; Lewis, 2010). Forensic Accounting is now becoming more proactive in the assessment of risks and prediction of future risks through the use of analytical models and technology-based tools for the analysis of fraud-related issues, and therefore, we are witnessing a move toward predictive analytics as a result (Huber, 2017; Dzuranin & Malaescu, 2015). The move toward Proactive Fraud Risk Assessment and Predictive Analytic Models (PAM) for Fraud will become increasingly more relevant especially as business activities continue to shift to Virtual/decentralized environments.

The growth of the Metaverse and other Virtual Ecosystems has created many other areas of fraud and security risk that have developed (Dionisio, Burns, & Gilbert, 2013; David, 2023), such as Identity Manipulation, Avatar Impersonation, Theft of Virtual Property, NFT and Crypto-Based Schemes, and Money Laundering in Complex Typologies using Decentralized Platforms (Smaili & De Rancourt-Raymond, 2022; Forbes Council, n.d.; Mazer, 2024). These Virtual Environments not only blur the jurisdictions we have today but rely on digital identities, smart contracts, and Blockchain technology to record transactions (Qin et al., 2025; "The Rising Concern of Financial Crimes in the Metaverse – AML Screening as a Solution," 2022), thereby providing both new ways to produce evidence and create additional vulnerabilities in terms of security. As a result, the role of Forensic Accountants in this new environment will require that they continue to utilize the skills and tools of Cyber Security; Digital Forensics; and Blockchain Programs (James, 2023; (Admin & Admin, 2025), to investigate and detect fraud in both Virtual and Traditional Environments.

To conduct this research, a combined approach will be taken using both academic literature as well as concepts and themes developed by using case studies on old- and new-generation corporate frauds. The objective of this Chapter is to present key theories regarding potential fraud schemes and their application to Real-World Corporate Scandals; outline the changing roles of Forensic Accountants based upon developments in the Fraud/Corruption Prevention/Risk Assessment arena; and examine how Forensic Accountants assist in maintaining the integrity of the financial reporting system in both Virtual and Traditional Marketplace Operations.

Problem Statement

The central problem addressed in this chapter is that, despite advancements made in fraud theory and forensic accounting, there still remains a gap between the theoretical development of these tools and the development of an Integrated Framework, which would create a methodology for organizations and regulators to use to prevent, detect, and respond to fraud, both within traditional financial institutions as well as emerging environments found within the Metaverse – environments that include virtual asset transactions and the use of electronic currencies.

2. BACKGROUND

As the metaverse & virtual worlds continue to expand, how fraud happens, and how it is controlled have changed (Smaili & De Rancourt-Raymond, 2022). Traditional fraud theory still can describe offender behaviour; however, it needs to be adapted to consider the new digital pressures, opportunities and rationalisation (Chimonaki, Papadakis & Lemonakis, 2023; Lokanan & Sharma, 2023). Forensic accounting and digital forensics have also become a central component of tracing the flow of virtual assets and maintaining financial integrity in the online environment (Lokanan, 2022). A literature review is conducted to examine previous research regarding fraud theory; risks associated with the metaverse; and the role of forensic accounting to provide security.

Chimonaki, C. et al. (2023) gave Systematic Literature Review on the major fraud models used in the modern world, highlighting an over-reliance on the Fraud Triangle and insufficient use of extended models. Noting the need for theoretical frameworks that reflect Culture, Behaviour and Technology and call for greater empirical testing.

Christian, N. et al. served Quantitative Study using surveys with reliability and regression analysis shows that Pressure, Opportunity, Rationalisation together with Capability and Arrogance increase the perceived fraud risk. The study suggests that Diamond/Pentagon Models are better suited for Assessment of Fraud Risks.

Taheri, M. (2020) performed Conceptual/Content Analysis of three models. Identifies the similarities and unique features of the models; introduces the concept of 'competence' and 'collusion'; proposes a Combined, Contextualised Fraud model.

Lokanan, M. (2015) outlined Qualitative Case Study on Financial Statement fraud. Identifies that Capability is Critical in addition to the Classic Triangle. The study calls upon Regulators and Auditors to consider the Power and Skill of Perpetrators.

Smaili & De Rancourt-Raymond, N. (2022) accomplished qualitative mapping of fraud risk to the Metaverse platforms using examples. The study finds that Anonymity and Speculation coupled with Weak Regulations create an enabling environment for scams and manipulation. The study advocates for adapting existing Fraud Risk Models/Controls for use with Virtual Assets.

Karapatakis, A. (2024) carried out a Legal Analysis of English Law concerning crimes in the Metaverse identifies significant legal gaps related to Jurisdiction, Property and Evidence. The study also advocates for targeted Legislative Reform and Guidance.

In "An Overview of the Challenges Facing Accounting in the Metaverse" we found the conceptual analysis of issues relating to Accounting and Assurance for Virtual Assets highlights issues of Valuation, Ownership and Control. The study advocates for a new set of standards and forensic expertise to evaluate Virtual Assets.

The "Navigating Virtual Economies: Transformative Impacts and Challenges for Forensic Accounting in the Metaverse" journal examined how virtual economies create an environment where economic and fraud risks are amplified through increased levels of information asymmetry, speculative bubbles, and transnational crime. Emphasizes the importance of employing an interdisciplinary approach to prevention by combining existing controls with investigative research and forensic oversight.

"Blockchain and the Metaverse: A Dual-Tech Approach to transforming medical data and patient care" executed a framework indicating the interaction between blockchain technology and the Metaverse has the potential to enhance the future of auditing through better forms of transparency but also create new risks associated with smart contracts and off-chain data management. It develops integrated solutions to both the blockchain and the application/platform that enables logging activities.

Tziakouris (2024) provided practitioners with technical advice on how to collect and analyze digital evidence, identifying various potential sources such as logs, traffic data, and blockchain activity, while reinforcing the need to engage in efficient, systematic forensic workflows for the purpose of enabling accountability and attribution.

Admin & Admin (2025) summarized the lessons learned from past real-world Metaverse incidents, indicating that one key issue experienced in almost all of these cases was the difficulty associated with working with an excessive amount of evidence and the increased complexity of interpreting evidence from multiple geographic/jurisdictional locations.

"Decentralized Identity Verification in Metaverse Auditing using Blockchain Technology" presented the explanation of blockchain-based identity structure for performing audits in the Metaverse. States how decentralised identification methods reduce impersonation and support Know Your Customer (KYC) processes and audit trails. Suggests integration across platforms.

"The Metaverse and Accounting: A Paradigm Shift in Emerging Technologies and their Implications on Accounting Research" discussed about how the Metaverse will evolve how audit and assurance are performed. Describes how the evolution of the Metaverse includes real-time data collection as well as programmable assets, both of which will require new methods of audit and forensic investigation. Recommends accountants take on an investigative, technology-supported role.

"The impact of cyber forensic accounting on quality of metaverse integrated reporting quality in metaverse local government" highlighted empirical review to demonstrate how digital forensics and analytical technology assist in the detection of fraudulent activities. Evidence provided that utilizing digital forensic and analytical technology, along with established control measures, has significantly improved the likelihood of detecting fraud. Recommends that forensic analytical methods should be included in standard audit procedures.

Taken together, the fraud theory studies have progressed from evaluating fraud using fundamental, individual-level variables to using more complex models, which include the ideas of capability, arrogance, and colluding groups of people. However, in the realm of the digital or metaverse, there has been precious little empirical research to date (Chimonaki et al., 2023; Christian, et al., n.d.; Taheri, 2020; Lokanan, 2015). While there have been substantial statistical analyses done by Christian et al. (n.d.) of the extended model, the majority of the other contributions in this field are merely theoretical or conceptual. It tells us that there is a gap in the evidence base of the theories of fraud as they pertain to digital/cybersecurity environments, under conditions of an abundance of technology.

Across the spectrum of literature on Metaverse and virtual economy, there is a large consensus that anonymity, speculation, and a fragmented system of regulation tend to raise the likelihood of traditional drivers of fraud. Yet the overwhelming majority of these discussions are descriptive in nature rather than being framework-driven (Smaili & De Rancourt-Raymond, 2022; Karapatakis, 2024; Rehman & Muhammad, 2024). The papers on issues related to accounting stress the issues surrounding valuation, ownership and control in the Metaverse space, but they do not seem to work together to connect these issues back to the conceptual constructs of traditional models of fraud (An Overview of the Challenges Facing Accounting in the Metaverse; The Metaverse and Accounting). This illustrates a second gap: the lack of an integrated framework to connect the features of the Metaverse to the existing concepts of fraud.

Studies in digital forensics, as well as forensic accounting show that, to effectively investigate digital transactions in the Metaverse, investigators will need - to safeguard both on-chain and off-chain transaction logs, methods for establishing digital identity, to utilise cross-jurisdictional cooperation between law enforcement agencies (Tziakouris, 2024; Admin & Admin, 2025; Decentralized Identity Verification; Impact of Cyber Forensic Accounting). Currently, the majority of relevant literature is either very technical or aimed primarily at practitioners, with little basis in established theories of fraud. This makes it unclear as to how certain forensic tools can be used to implement constructs such as pressure, rationalisation, and systemic risk. Thus, the final identified gap is the absence of a standardised model connecting theoretical drivers of fraud with concrete evidence sources and analytical techniques within the context of the Metaverse.

2.1 Critical issues in the literature

Current research reflects divergence in opinions on whether or not the Fraud Triangle continues to be applicable to online environments, and if the use of extended models provides meaningful improvements in predicting fraud. However, very few works have compared the various frameworks directly with one another. The majority of studies conducted within the Metaverse have relied on descriptive analyses and/or a legal perspective with little or no empirical analysis of fraud mechanisms or controls. Digital Forensics literature has produced a significant amount of technical guidance; however, most digital forensic publications do not explicitly reference any particular fraud theory, which tends to leave the relationship between constructs, as well as the relationship between constructs and forensic evidence, under-specified.

As graphical and written materials in metaverse-related research vary significantly and are at such an early stage, we consider this chapter a narrative review as opposed to a systematic review. This chapter synthesizes fraud theory, case evidence, and forensic methodologies that clearly demonstrate how these methods fit into the overall conceptual model of fraud development in the metaverse.

While core drivers like pressure, opportunity, and rationalization remain, Metaverse environments reshape how these factors manifest, particularly around identity, technology, and evidence.

Table 1. Comparison of Traditional Fraud Factors vs. Metaverse Fraud Factors

Dimension	Traditional fraud factors	Metaverse fraud factors
Actors & identity	Identifiable employees, managers, executives; real-world KYC and HR files.	Pseudonymous avatars, wallet addresses, anonymous teams and influencers.
Pressure / incentives	Earnings targets, bonuses, debt, job insecurity, market competition.	Speculative FOMO, token/NFT price swings, hype-driven communities, "degen" culture.
Opportunity (controls)	Weak internal controls, poor segregation of duties, management override.	Weak platform governance, smart-contract bugs, poor wallet security, cross-platform gaps.
Rationalization / culture	"Everyone does it," short-termism, tolerant or toxic corporate culture.	Normalized flipping, wash trading, "it's just a game," anonymous group norms.
Capability / competence	Financial engineering, accounting manipulation, access to core systems.	Coding/smart-contract skills, protocol knowledge, bot networks, cross-chain expertise.

continued on following page

Table 1. Continued

Dimension	Traditional fraud factors	Metaverse fraud factors
Collusion & environment	Intra-firm collusion, sector norms, local regulatory weaknesses.	Discord/Telegram coordination, global regulatory arbitrage, pseudonymous laundering paths.
Evidence & forensics	Ledgers, emails, physical documents, ERP logs.	Blockchain records, smart-contract logs, platform/server logs, on-chain analytics.

3. OBJECTIVES

a) To examine the major fraud theories and models as presented in various frameworks that identify the motivation and mechanism for dishonest behaviour.
b) To analyse the behavioural and psychological aspects of fraud that encourage both individuals and businesses to commit immoral and illegal acts.
c) To examine the role of forensic accounting and legal structures in detecting, preventing, and investigating fraud.
d) To understand emerging fraud risks in Metaverse environments and the need for security-focused forensic methods.

4. METHODOLOGY

Using a qualitative research design based on secondary data sources, this chapter provides an analysis of the role of forensic accounting in detecting, preventing and investigating financial fraud involving both traditional and evolving digital environments (Creswell, 2014; Flick, 2018). The Narrative Literature Review methodology will create a structured format in which the current scholarly and professional literature and regulations developed for the analysis of fraud theories and forensic accounting practices can be organized, integrated, and examined (Tranfield, Denyer, & Smart, 2003; Snyder, 2019). The structured approach will provide the necessary level of transparency for conducting the review, from identifying research sources through the conduct of the study, thereby allowing for enhanced reliability and replicability of or the results of the study for both academic and professional audiences.

The most important type of source for data gathering are Secondary sources. In general, secondary sources include academic journals with peer review (Cressey, 1953; Wolfe & Hermanson, 2004; Albrecht et al., 1984; Kranacher et al., 2019; Rezaee, 2009), authoritative publications from professional organizations such as

ACFE and ICAI as well as fraud-related global surveys and thematic reports published by global firms such as PwC (ACFE, 2022;Institute of Chartered Accountants of India [ICAI], 2017; PwC, 2022). These sources were selected based on their methodological integrity, relevance to fraud/forensic accounting and ability to provide empirical information that informs observable patterns of deception, forensic methods used to examine fraud & breakdowns in controls across industries. Further, International organisation and law enforcement/regulatory body reports (Sarbanes-Oxley Act of 2002; UK Bribery Act 2010; Prevention of Corruption (Amendment) Act 2018) and position papers regarding financial crime risk relating to digital and the Metaverse (such as the development of assets and NFTs, cyber enabled money laundering etc.) were also reviewed to provide context for how the evolving nature of fraud relates to activity within Virtual ecosystems (Financial Action Task Force [FATF], 2022; Smaili & De Rancourt-Raymond, 2022; "The Rising Concern of Financial Crimes in the Metaverse – AML Screening as a Solution," 2022; Dionisio et al., 2013; Qin et al., 2025).

Complementary to the themes from the literature; the analysis within the framework of the study will use comparative case analysis for illustrative examples of physical fraud that has occurred in large multinational companies (e.g. Enron, Satyam, Wirecard etc.) as well as representative case studies on Ponzi schemes (Healy & Palepu, 2003; Staff, 2009; Houben & Snyers, 2020; Lewis, 2010). Each case will include typology; methods of perpetration & concealment; governance breakdowns and the role of both forensic accounting & auditing in discovering conduct contrary to law. Documented instances of digital and virtual asset frauds e.g. - Cryptocurrency Exchange Failures and NFT Manipulations, provide examples of various fraud techniques re-applied to technology-mediated environments and how forensic disciplines adapt to new types of digital forensics, blockchain analytics etc. (Forbes Council, n.d.; Mazer, 2024; David, 2023).

This chapter establishes a relationship between various theoretical models of fraud i.e. The Fraud Triangle, The Fraud Diamond, the Fraud Pentagon, The Fraud Scale, The Fraud Circle, etc., along with the empirical literature from selected cases/ reports (Cressey, 1953; Wolfe & Hermanson, 2004; Albrecht et al., 1984; Kranacher et al., 2011; Rezaee, 2009). The synthesis of these materials allows for the analysis of recurring patterns associated with manipulation strategies, behavioural indicators associated with fraud and control failures, as well as differences regarding the context between Traditional Corporate environments and Metaverse related or Cryptocurrency (cryptocurrency) intensive ecosystems. Thus, the conclusions drawn can be used by practitioners to assess risk, design controls, and perform forensic investigations (Beasley, Carcello, & Hermanson, 2010; Bhasin, 2013; Dionisio et al., 2013; Qin et al., 2025).

The methodology employed in this research is intended to be rigorous, integrative and sensitive to context. It combines a systematic review of the literature with a structured analysis of the selected cases to provide both academic contribution and practice-oriented guidance. As such, it highlights how forensic accounting can contribute to increasing the transparency and ethical governance of corporations while enhancing the security of both traditional (existing) financial systems and emerging Virtual Economies (cryptocurrencies) (Snyder, 2019; Rezaee, 2009; FATF, 2022).

5. MAIN DISCUSSION

5.1 Integrated fraud–forensics–Metaverse framework

When considered separately, the Fraud Triangle, Diamond, Pentagon, Scale and Circle illustrate a number of key motivating factors for fraud. However, by grouping them into three broad categories, they can provide insight into individuals' motivational factors (the individual incentive & belief). Structural conditions & capabilities (opportunity, ability & competence) create an environment that allows fraud to occur & therefore provide a platform for individuals to commit fraud. Lastly, the systemic context considers the culture in which the fraud is occurring, as well as its implications for society as a whole. Examples of traditional frauds (Enron, Satyam, Wirecard & Harshad Mehta) illustrate how the interaction of high pressure & rationalization on the individual level combine with a concentrated level of capability & an organizational culture encouraging fraud results in a situation where fraud at scale is practiced, rather than the result of a singular factor or set of factors.

The same three dimensions of motivation, ability & environment can still be identified in Metaverse platforms, although the interaction of these three factors is modified by the digital platform design, the economy created around NFTs & the virtual assets created within the environment. In the virtual world, the effect of pressure is amplified by speculative unconventional wealth narratives, as opportunity is facilitated by the anonymity associated with participating in an already established environment and weak regulations regarding policing of the environment. The environment also provides a greater opportunity for individuals to use their programming & blockchain skills, as well as exploit their position in the community through social media & transitioned into a different jurisdiction with differing regulations. Forensic accounting & digital forensics assist prosecutors, investigators & courts by defining the scope of each dimension and aligning those with factual evidence that can be used at trial, to detect evidence of other dimensions.

This chapter expands on an integrated fraud-forensics-metaverse framework. It suggests that classical fraud models should not compete against each other but rather serve as additional methods for analyzing and understanding(all forms of fraud) while using new forms of forensics. This is to provide clear, objective analysis of fraud from both a traditional and virtual world perspective. The five models when used together will support the design of multiple layers of control and regulation across all environments.

5.2 Detailed explanation of each theory

5.2.1 Fraud Triangle

To support fraud examiners' understanding of, investigation of and mitigation against fraud, the Fraud Triangle creates a structure to assist fraud examiners with acquiring the three fundamental components of fraud; pressure, opportunity and rationalization (Cressey, 1953). The pressure component includes the reason(s) a person may commit fraud because of the possibility that they experience pressure or stressful conditions that cause them to commit fraud, including but not limited to financial difficulties, job insecurity, wanting a higher social status, or the ability to meet aggressive performance goals set by their employer. To analyse and evaluate the pressure component, a fraud examiner evaluates both personal stressors (debts, addictions and family obligations, etc.) and employer-based stressors (deadlines, competitive strain and fear of termination) by way of interview, background check and through the evaluation of both internal and external records (ACFE, 2022; Kranacher et al., 2019).

Opportunity refers to the conditions that create the ability for fraud to be perpetrated; and these conditions usually arise due to weak internal controls, poor segregation of duties, dishonesty or the ability of an employee or manager to override regulation. In order to assess opportunity as the second component of fraud, a fraud examiner reviews and evaluates process maps, internal audit reports, and the control environment using forensic data analysis and analysis of individual transaction ledgers/purchase orders (i.e. transaction mappings) to identify weaknesses, gaps and uncharacteristic patterns of accessing required enterprise systems. Rationalisation (the third component of fraudulent activity) is the process whereby the perpetrator rationalizes the act of fraud to themselves (i.e. "I deserve this"; "everybody else does it"; "this is in the best interest of my company"). Rationalizations can be investigated through behavioral interviews and analysis of communications that a perpetrator uses to justify their illegal or unethical behavior (Wells, 2017). Scandals with major impact like those connected to Satyam, Enron and WorldCom illustrate how the Fraud Triangle demonstrates these three components of the Fraud Triangle (Healy & Palepu, 2003; Staff, 2009). It is the Fraud Triangle that provides the framework within which the Fraud Examiner evaluates fraud risk and how they approach interviewing and providing organizational remedies and determines methods of control evaluation and Ethics Intervention.

5.2.2 Fraud Diamond

The Fraud Diamond extends the Fraud Triangle to incorporate a fourth element called 'Capability'; this helps explain the ability of individuals to perpetrate and conceal prominent fraud schemes (Wolfe & Hermanson, 2004). Capability refers to all those characteristics that allow the fraud perpetrator to manipulate and conceal their fraud: technical skills, authority, intelligence, confidence and the ability to cope under pressure are all necessary to exploit control weaknesses and sustain a fraud scheme for many years to come. Capability is also determined by reviewing a fraud examiner's professional background and profile, the degree of unusual success attained by that fraud examiner, access to systems and controls, and involvement in roles that were both technically advanced and risky.

In the majority of instances of large-scale fraud, such as Enron and WorldCom, capability was concentrated at the executive level of organizations; at this level, individuals possessed vast amounts of knowledge with respect to financial engineering, had extensive access to expansive systems and resources, and possessed the courage to override or manipulate controls for extended periods of time (Healy & Palepu, 2003; Lewis, 2010). Examinators can distinguish between people who have motive and opportunity (in terms of potential) and people who can make and follow through with advanced fraud schemes (in practical situations). They can do so by analyzing each defendant's skill and authority level, and how that affects the potential to cause fraud. The Fraud Diamond supports this by giving guidance on developing controls, and monitoring systems, allowing organizations to provide greater oversight for positions of higher authority, specialist knowledge, or privileged system access, rather than treating every employee as having an equal level of risk.

5.2.3 Fraud Pentagon

Through two additional constructs, competence and arrogance, the Fraud Pentagon builds on previous models to add dimensions for examining behavior and profiling associated with fraudulent activity (Marks, 2012; Yesiariani & Rahayu, 2017). Competence means having sufficient technical proficiency, experience, and ability to solve problems to understand and manipulate intricate systems. Examiners look to education, work history, and the complexity of past projects to evaluate a person's ability to circumvent intricate controls. Arrogance is associated with having a belief in one's own superiority; entitlement; or a lack of respect for rules and processes, which is usually demonstrated by rule breaking; having an excess of confidence; and not being willing to cooperate with audits or show any respect for audit mechanisms.

Examples from history like Harshad Mehta's manipulation of the stock market, and the actions of top executives at Enron and Satyam show how much arrogance combined with capability can increase the likelihood of fraudulent behavior occurring (Staff, 2009; *Satyam Scandal: Inside India's Enron*, n.d.). Furthermore, since leadership affects both the overall culture and the systems of an entire organization, the chances of fraud occurring are even greater when someone in a leadership role exhibits these two traits. The Fraud Pentagon allows Fraud Examiners to create detailed prefabricated profiles of individuals who possess technical skill sets related to their job, while also looking for additional correlations with behaviors that indicate an inclination to take risks and/or not respect limits and boundaries. Then based on this analysis, appropriate controls can then be implemented that identify and consider behavior-related indicators as well as technical access rights.

5.2.4 Fraud Scale

The Fraud Scale approach enables Fraud Examiners to assess all three traditional elements of fraud (pressure/gain, opportunity, rationalization) not just for presence (yes/no) but also for each element's impact (Albrecht et al., 1984). This way, Fraud Examiners could perform more precise evaluations of risk levels associated with all three elements over time rather than only performing binary evaluations. By rating risks along a continuum from low to high, Fraud Examiners were then able to gather additional information, such as incentive programs, debt levels, the ability to override controls, exception rates and frequent rationalization habits, to create a more precise risk profile.

The Fraud Scale provides a means of prioritizing audit and investigative resources by enabling the differentiation of minor policy violations committed to benefit minor gain and large organized schemes motivated by significant incentives, as well as the whole range of systemic weaknesses exposed through collective efforts -- where organizations can embed the Fraud Scale into various scoring models and matrices that capture the survey data, findings from internal audits, and key financial indicators in order to better understand where the highest level of fraud prevalence might occur, such as in cases of Executive Bonus Driven Misreporting (EBDM) in banking and insurance venues (Beasley et al., 2010). Therefore, as a result, fraud examiners can monitor layers of fraud based on its level of severity and likelihood of being committed.

5.2.5 Fraud Circle

The Fraud Circle represents a combination of multiple factors that create an environment in which fraud can flourish. While fraud may be facilitated by the individual perpetrator's personal characteristics, it is more likely to be the product of creating an environment where the factors are connected (organizational culture, leadership, group dynamics, external environment) (Tommasetti et al., 2021). The Fraud Circle is especially relevant in cases of heightened levels of systemic, or widespread fraud, where the organizational culture, use of incentives, and organizational structure(s) allowing for and/or hiding fraudulent behavior are working together to reinforce each other, and thus, provide additional opportunities for fraud. In creating a model of fraud based on the elements derived from the fraud circle, criminal fraud examination professionals may examine and identify the culture of the organization and the overall governance of the organization by reviewing and examining its policies and procedures, conducting ethics audits, conducting an analysis of whistleblower reports, and reviewing the communications made by leadership and any type of incentive that those leadership members may receive for good performance.

To combat collusion between teams, they conduct workflow analysis and approved chain analysis and compare it to systematic approaches, industry standards, and macroeconomic conditions. The situations presented by Enron and Satyam illustrate that a culture of aggressive performance regardless of cost, permissive supervision, and collusion with each team member may allow fraudulent behavior to be accepted by all levels in an organization, thus making previously isolated acts of misconduct systemic fraud (Staff, 2009; Houben & Snyers, 2020). The overall framework promotes investigative and remedial efforts to identify and address root cause issues, rather than simply focusing on the actions of individual fraudsters.

5.3 Linking theories to real-world and Metaverse frauds

5.3.1 Traditional frauds

Various tools and models exist within the academic and business literature to assist in analyzing and deriving insight into significant corporate frauds and organized patterns of technological fraud - Fraud Triangle, Fraud Diamond, Fraud Pentagon, Fraud Scale and Fraud Circle (Cressey, 1953; Albrecht et al., 1984; Wolfe & Hermanson, 2004; Kranacher et al., 2019; Tommasetti et al., 2021). These models and connections assist in analyzing corporate fraud in either traditional environments (such as Enron, Satyam, WorldCom, the Harshad Mehta scam, and numerous Ponzi schemes) or new forms of fraud enabled by technological advancement (Healy & Palepu, 2003; Staff, 2009; Bhasin, 2013; Lewis, 2010; Forbes Council, n.d.). Most traditional corporate fraud cases fit within one or more of the primary components of pressure, opportunity, rationalization, capability, competence, and arrogance, along with organizational issues related to culture, control, and regulatory oversight (Wolfe & Hermanson, 2004; Yesiariani & Rahayu, 2017; Beasley et al., 2010; Kranacher et al., 2019). For example, the characteristics of high-performance and reputation-driven pressure experienced by Satyam executives combined with the opportunities provided by the creation of ineffective internal control systems and a rationale that retained the status of jobs or shareholder value resulted in systemic, significant corporate fraud (Staff, 2009; Post et al., 2009; *Satyam Scandal: Inside India's Enron*, n.d.). Enron and WorldCom illustrate how highly competent and confident executives effectively exploited complex institutional relationships and weaknesses in the oversight structure over extended periods to perpetuate extensive corporate fraud (Healy & Palepu, 2003; Benston and Hartgraves, 2002; Lewis, 2010).

Similarly, sector-specific weaknesses can be analyzed through the same lens as developed in reference to banking and securities models (Bhasin, 2013; Beasley et al., 2010). In the banking and securities industry, the Harshad Mehta case highlighted how a failure of regulation, combined with collusion across institutional boundaries, created a situation where risk-laden behaviors were normalized (Bhasin, 2013). The characteristics of the Harshad Mehta case were consistent with both the Fraud Scale (i.e. there was a high level of pressure and opportunity) and the Fraud Circle (the toxic culture involved, the group dynamic) (Albrecht et al., 1984; Tommasetti et al., 2021; Bhasin, 2013). The classic Ponzi schemes provide another excellent example of how the combination of personal charisma, social proof and the fear of missing out can encourage the rationalization of behavior by the investor: and, how regulatory arbitrage and a lack of due diligence on the part of investors create opportunities for individuals to perpetrate fraud (Lewis, 2010; ACFE, 2022; PwC, 2022). Forensic accountants and regulators can identify and better understand the reason for a certain Ponzi scheme to escalate, where controls broke down, and what sequences of behavior (including behavior's that exhibited traits such as executive arrogance or group collusion) should have warranted earlier intervention and action (Rezaee, 2009; Kranacher et al., 2019; Beasley et al., 2010).

5.3.1.1 Theory-Linked Case Write-Ups

(a) Enron Scandal – Pressure, Opportunity, Capability

The Enron scandal serves as a most evident indication of the combined influences of extreme pressure, unlimited opportunities, and extraordinary abilities create an environment conducive to substantial fraudulent activities in connection to financial statements. The motivation of senior executives from an uninterrupted stream of capital market pressure to achieve ever increasing earnings and to maintain a high price per share led to creating an environment wherein there was a strong temptation to avoid reporting earnings volatility or losses and report only consistently increasing earnings relative to prior periods or forecasts (Healy & Palepu, 2003). When the actual operating performance of the company's underlying businesses did not equate to the company's original expectation of operating performance, the performance-related pressures on the executives in the form of aggressive bonus programs that rewarded accomplishments based on short term results contributed heavily towards facilitating Executive Attention towards engaging in fraudulent behavior consistent with the pressure side of the Fraud Triangle and Fraud Diamond (Healy & Palepu, 2003).

The web of special purpose entities (SPEs), opaque derivative contracts, and accounting for marks, created a complex environment for hiding debt, hiding losses from view, and manipulating reported profits, where the lack of corporate internal controls, top management acceptance of aggressive structures and low auditor skepticism, all provided Enron's management with more opportunities to circumvent internal controls with virtually no challenge (Healy & Palepu, 2003; Benston and Hartgraves, 2002). The characteristics of opportunity, capability, and pressure in the Fraud Diamond were very concentrated in a few senior executives and structuring specialists who all had the highest level of expertise in accounting rules, financial engineering, off-balance sheet structures and were empowered to take advantage of this capacity for years (Wolfe & Hermanson, 2004; Healy & Palepu, 2003). A detailed examination of the Enron fraud case illustrates how this alignment of opportunity, capability and pressure created the conditions necessary for sophisticated fraud to occur and go unreported until a major external disruption, or an investigation, forced the company to make it public (Healy & Palepu, 2003; Benston and Hartgraves, 2002).

(b) Satyam Scandal – Rationalization and Arrogance

Systematic and long-term financial manipulation as shown by the Satyam Computer Services scandal exemplifies, through rationalization, through executive arrogance and the confluence of external performance pressure and weak governance systems, the perpetuation of artificial financial results. For many years, the founder/chairman of Satyam admitted to intentionally overstating cash balances, revenue, and profit, thereby creating a false narrative of the company's performance (Staff, 2009). Publicly, Satyam management described it as a rapidly growing comparable peer of Indian IT companies thereby creating expectations that were greater than what could be satisfied as market conditions evolved (Staff, 2009). Internally, rationalization arguments emerged around protecting the company's image (retroactively), protecting jobs, and aligning with shareholder expectations. These rationalization arguments allowed those in the decision-making roles to consider fictitious numbers to be either temporary or justifiable, consistent with the rationalization element of the Fraud Triangle, as well as associated behavioral models (Staff, 2009; Post et al., 2009).

The arrogance evident in the fraud pentagon analysis of Satyam reflects the excessive concentration of power in the chairman of Satyam and the fact that the board deferred to him. It also reflects the willingness of the chairman to pursue controversial related-party transactions, as highlighted by the planned purchase of Maytas, to camouflage bogus assets with real assets (Post et al., 2009; *Satyam Scandal: Inside India's Enron*, n.d.). This arrogance of being above the normal boundaries, combined with the confidence the chairman had in his ability to work with regulators, auditors and investors, shows the nature of the behaviors of many executive leaders that exacerbate the likelihood of frauds (Yesiariani & Rahayu, 2017). The continued failure of external auditors to challenge the inaccurate reporting of implausible cash positions and governance issues perpetuated this culture (Staff, 2009). Forensic accountants analyzing the history of Satyam demonstrate how the entrenched belief system (or rationalized culture) combined with the arrogance of an executive leader allows fraud to grow to a size that becomes "too big to unwind" without a major crisis. Thus, forensic accountants analyze not only the numeric anomalies of a financial report, but also the leadership behaviors, related-party structures and cultural signals (Staff, 2009; Post et al., 2009).

(c) Wirecard – Weak Controls and Organizational Collusion

The Wirecard Scandal illustrates excessive opportunities to commit substantial cross-border accounting fraud as the result of weak internal controls and organizational collusion between several defense lines. Following several investigations and parliamentary inquiries, serious structural weaknesses in Wirecard's control environment were identified, including a lack of segregation of duties, an over-concentration of pooled authority among a small cadre of leadership, unclear Third Party Acquirer (TPA) relationships, and a governance structure that did not support an independent challenge (Houben & Snyers, 2020). Senior management personnel, including the CEO and COO, possessed an inordinate amount of authority over the oversight of all offshore operations and escrow accounts, while there were severe deficiencies in the authority and independence of the management of internal risk and compliance functions to question any discrepancies. Thus, these issues demonstrate that there is a systemic failure of control and not isolated deficiencies (Houben & Snyers, 2020; *McCrum, D. (2020, June 25). Wirecard the Timeline. Financial Times. - References - Scientific Research Publishing*, n.d.).

Senior management of the organization coordinated through their misrepresentation of the company's financial statements to its shareholders, (i) kept information from reaching their employees and (ii) imposed their individual wills on to other shareholders to a greater extent than their standing as the CEO or majority shareholder entitled them to do (Houben & Snyers, 2020). External auditors increasingly relied on confirmations from auditors instead of independently verifying accounts held at banks by the corporation, (i) regulators were slow to respond to whistleblower revelations, and (ii) the investigative work done by journalists was never taken seriously by regulators (Houben & Snyers, 2020; *McCrum, D. (2020, June 25). Wirecard the Timeline. Financial Times. - References - Scientific Research Publishing*, n.d.). Wirecard fraud serves as a vivid example of the significant increased opportunity created when both internal controls and external oversight of an organization fail (Houben & Snyers, 2020).

The Fraud Circle focuses on organizational culture, leadership and systemic environment to explain fraud that results from the joint and integrated efforts of those at all levels of the organization rather than from a single rogue actor; thus, it is essential in determining how and why a company committed fraud and engaged in collusive schemes.

5.3.2 Metaverse frauds

In the metaverse and the virtual asset space, the same theories from above continue to exist but appear in a different form. Similar to traditional speculative markets, the metaverse has created a volatile and speculative marketplace for tokens; in the metaverse there is some speculation around the value of non-fungible tokens (NFTs) as a function of growing demand for NFTs in particular communities; and there may be significant pressure created by community expectations to generate rapid returns and gains ("get-rich-quick" narratives) (Forbes Council, n.d.; Mazer, 2024).

The behavior encouraged by the metaverse will continue to exhibit the same cognitive processes as currently exist in traditional financial markets. This is demonstrated by the fact that very little due diligence exists on the part of individuals, as to the nature of what constitutes fair market practices and ethical behavior in the metaverse (e.g. wash trading, market manipulation, or "rug pulls"), as such behaviors continue to be endorsed as legit forms of trading rather than as fraud (David, 2023). The capability, competence, and arrogance of those who create, develop, and use sophisticated virtual realities can be seen both technically, in how they use the coding expertise (the "whales") and protocols as well as having access to privileged knowledge (administrative keys), to create virtual land scams, manipulate token launches, or launder NFTs in ways that the average user can't (ACM, 2024).

Case 1: NFT "Rug Pull" In A Metaverse Gaming Project – Pressure, Opportunity, Capability

A growing trend in the Metaverse is to commit fraud through NFTs by "rug pulling". In an NFT rug pull, a developer creates a highly marketed virtual project (like an avatar or collection) and promotes it heavily to get funds through the NFT sale or in-game tokens, only to terminate the project without any notice to the investors, taking their money with them. There are examples of teams who created hype for Metaverse games and virtual worlds, created unrealistic expectations of future utility of the assets, exclusive features in the metaverse, and future values that could be realized in the secondary market, and then relied on social media and endorsements from other people to create a fear of missing out (Forbes Council, n.d.; Mazer, 2024; White, 2025). Through the lens of fraud theory, the increase in pressure on investors comes from the speculative nature of the culture surrounding cryptocurrencies, the unpredictability of the market, and the many community-based narratives around the need to "get in early"; similarly, the pressure on founders of projects to meet unrealistic expectations or generate revenue quickly (Forbes Council, n.d.).

The creation of opportunities for crypto projects is enabled by pseudonymous teams, low disclosure requirements, and the lack of detailed due diligence and listing requirements on many NFT and token marketplaces. Typically, funds raised through smart contracts are routed to wallets that are held by a small number of insiders, with few on-chain protections and no escrow mechanisms, allowing these insiders to exit quickly after the initial sale goals are met (Mazer, 2024; David, 2023). Using the terminology of Fraud Diamond, the developers or technically skilled insiders have the capability to create the appearance of legitimacy through their knowledge of the contract code, tokenomics, and marketing dynamics that allow them to create the mechanism by which they can maintain control over the project's treasury and the metadata while creating the illusion of legitimacy (Wolfe & Hermanson, 2004). Forensic investigation of these cases often includes tracing the transaction flow from the minting wallet to the personal wallets of the scammers, identifying instances of wash trading that were used to artificially increase the perceived demand for the project, and compiling the on-chain evidence with the off-chain marketing activities to create a case to demonstrate that there was intentional misrepresentation and coordinated actions to withdraw liquidity (Forbes Council, n.d.; White, 2025).

Case 2: Avatar Impersonation And Wallet Compromise On A Metaverse Platform – Identity, Security Breach, Collusion

Security breaches involving taking over users' accounts in the Metaverse are on the rise, with attackers gaining access to an individual's avatar, using that identity to commit fraud, theft or activation of virtual assets. Industry research has identified that when hackers obtain compromised authentication credentials through a security breach or exploitable vulnerabilities in VR devices or connected applications, they are able to see other people's profiles and interact impersonally (Identity Management Institute, 2022). Once they have gained control of an avatar, criminals may solicit their friends to request crypto transfers, approve malicious smart contract activity or sell/transfer valuable NFTs or virtual property held in a linked wallet. Identity theft and asset fraud are often combined (Bajpai & Ciso, 2025).

Opportunity is increased through the design choices made by the platforms, which include single-factor logins; device security weaknesses; lack of awareness of transaction signing; and lack of verification of the in-world high-valued transactions (Identity Management Institute, 2022). Fraud Circle is also relevant here because of how the culture and rules of platforms (trust, speed of transactions and informal verification) contribute to user vulnerability to social engineering scams that target hijacked avatars (Qin et al., 2025; David, 2023). In many cases of fraud, collusion and/or negligence by organizations occur because of the lack of appropriate monitoring systems to detect compromises, the failure to immediately investigate reports of compromises, or the lack of adequate records for forensics (Admin & Admin, 2025). Digital forensics and forensic accounting teams investigate these types of compromises by correlating platform logs with IP/device information and blockchain records to create the timeline of the compromise, identify unauthorized approval and transfer, and determine if additional users or insiders helped facilitate and/or hide the breach (Admin & Admin, 2025; Smaili & De Rancourt-Raymond, 2022).

Understanding systemic frauds in the Metaverse through a Fraud Circle framework provides insight into the interaction of the culture, leadership, and dynamics within groups that operate in this environment. Highly speculative groups, influencer driven narratives, anonymous groups on social networks and gaming platforms, and lightly regulated exchanges operating overseas can create norms that are consistent with high-risk behavior while providing ways to disguise colluding, as rapid technological advancements outpace legal and supervisory responses (Identity Management Institute, 2022; David, 2023). Forensic proficiency can be obtained through the analysis of the different methods of a forensic analysis through use of the Fraud Circle Model (FCM). For example, identifying, tracking and auditing both on-chain flows, smart contract contracts, plus platform rules, incentives, plus communications channels will provide insights into how cultural norms and group behaviors combined can lead to recurring patterns of fraud (White, 2025; "Metaverse and Money Laundering – How Shufti's AML Screening Helps," 2022; Bajpai & Ciso, 2025; Qin et al., 2025). By creating an integrated theory for traditional and Metaverse types of fraud it will allow for cross-contextual analyses and create a foundation for designing effective control measures, governance of reform and regulatory approaches that can work across both types of economies.

5.3.3 Cross Case Synthesis

In analyzing the cases of Enron, Satyam, Wirecard and the Metaverse, there are four consistent elements that were present: (1) Speculation or performance pressure; (2) Internationally built systems that create opportunity and control gaps; (3) Concentration of both technical and positional competence; and (4) Cultures that foster normalisation of breaking established rules and collusion.

The evidence suggests that fraud theory should focus more on how these factors interact in different environments, rather than focusing solely on industry type.

5.4 Role of forensic accountants in traditional and Metaverse environments

To avoid conceptual overlap and clarify professional boundaries, it is important to distinguish the assurance-oriented role of auditing from the investigative role of forensic accounting before discussing the forensic accountants' tools and responsibilities.

The term 'Audit' refers to recurring type assurance-oriented engagements to provide some reasonable assurance on financial statements / controls which use the materiality approach and sampling-based approach in conducting an audit. Forensic Accounting, on the other hand, takes a more narrow and investigative aspect by focusing on the examination of suspicious activity, tracing through the transactions in great detail and preserving sufficient evidence for presentation in court during legal proceedings. While both types of services require similar accounting skills, forensic engagements are typically not recurring in nature and adversarial in nature and therefore would be held to a standard of evidential quality consistent with that of the court system (i.e., criminal investigations).

The focus of external and internal auditing is primarily on recurrent assurance engagements (financial statement audits and reviews of internal controls), which utilize sampling and materiality thresholds as the basis for performing their duties. Routine compliance testing and continuous audits are primarily the audit functions of the auditor. It also aims to provide reasonable assurance by performing audit procedures that are free from material misstatement.

Forensic accountants build upon theories of fraud and behavioral information and create tangible products and methods for identifying and preventing fraud across all sectors and types of technology. In the general corporate, banking, insurance, and securities industries, forensic accountants utilize data analytics, continuous auditing, transaction mapping, and anomaly detection techniques to identify unusual behaviors, trace and map financial transactions, and uncover concealment schemes through fictitious revenue, off-balance sheet transactions, circular debt, and improper classifications of expense transactions. Notable examples of corporate fraud examples include the Enron, Satyam, WorldCom, and Harshad Mehta scandals, the forensic procedures, in conjunction with internal and regulatory auditing methods, resulted in investigations that identified the complexity of the fraud schemes through the potential for management override, collusion, and a systemic failure in internal controls (Healy & Palepu, 2003; Staff, 2009; Bhasin, 2013; Houben & Snyers, 2020). Evidence obtained through forensic accounting procedures provided the basis for many enforcement actions, governance reforms, and improved internal controls.

In addition to performing ex post investigations, forensic accountants also provide a preventive governance function. Forensic accountants utilize well-established models, such as the Fraud Triangle, Fraud Diamond, and the Fraud Circle, to assist organizations with assessing fraud risk, developing, implementing, and testing effective internal controls, monitoring activities based on capabilities and access, and establishing ethics and whistleblower systems that align with the culture of the organization (Rezaee, 2009; Kranacher et al., 2019). Through ongoing partnerships with regulatory and enforcement organizations like the SEC and SEBI (Securities and Exchange Board of India), forensic accountants help provide an understanding of forensic accounting investigations through forensic audits, and also assisting in litigation through writing litigation-ready forensic audit reports, as well as providing expert witness opinions in cases relating to the Sarbanes-Oxley Act, the Bribery Act (United Kingdom), the Prevention of Corruption (Amendment) Act of 1988 (India) and similar statutes in other nations (Rezaee, 2009). These efforts ensure the admissibility of forensic evidence as well as compliance with the International Standards of Practice adopted by the profession worldwide.

The expansion of digital and Metaverse environments has also resulted in an increasing overlap between the functional roles of forensic accountants, cyber security professionals, and digital forensics specialists. The development of new virtual economies that rely on blockchain-based assets and smart contracts, as well as the use of avatars to create an interface for transaction-related interactions, has resulted in new types of forensic evidence that are complex and challenging to trace, but that are still capable of providing forensic accountants information about the activity of individuals involved in such virtual environments (Dionisio et al., 2013; Qin et al., 2025). For example, forensic accountants can utilize blockchain analytics for purposes such as clustering wallets, tracing token flows, detecting NFT wash trading, identifying the use of mixers and tumblers as indicators of money laundering, and linking transactions across multiple exchanges or marketplaces that appear to be suspicious (Smaili & De Rancourt-Raymond, 2022; James, 2023). In addition to working with platform operators and law enforcement agencies, the forensic accountant analyzes past user activity, such as server logs and device fingerprints, and looks through all avenues of private communications (chats, social media, etc.) To find possible links between pseudonymous avatars to real-life identities in furtherance of investigations for virtual land scams, phishing-based account takeovers, and impersonation of legitimate projects, they also have a forensic theory based upon existing Fraud Theories, such as the Fraud Scale and Fraud Circle, to help define what virtual assets should be monitored more closely (Admin & Admin, 2025; Identity Management Institute, 2022; David, 2023; Qin et al., 2025; White, 2025).

In addition, advances in artificial intelligence and machine learning will continue to be incorporated into current forensic workflows, both in traditional and Metaverse settings, to automate the detection of anomalies, create behavioral and transactional risk scoring mechanisms, and provide alerts from very large data streams with high velocity (Dzuranin & Malaescu, 2015; Dalwai et al., 2022). In summary, forensic accountants are now right in the middle of the intersection of Accounting, Law, Technology, and Cybersecurity, and will continue to play an important role in protecting the integrity of financial transactions throughout all financial ecosystems—physical, digital, and the Metaverse (Rezaee, 2009; FATF, 2022).

5.5 Metaverse-based fraud models

Virtual worlds and the Metaverse have led to both a shift in the context of fraud statutes and how they are interpreted (as previously discussed) (Smaili & De Rancourt-Raymond, 2022; David, 2023). In these environments, users may engage with each other via their avatars, sell and purchase virtual land and items, transact using cryptocurrencies and NFTs (which frequently operate under pseudonymous conditions and in jurisdictions with fragmented regulations), all of which create greater volume of certain opportunity for fraud, but also present forensic accountants with a greater variety of new evidence types (and therefore New Generations of Evidence) and challenges in taking control of this evidence and regulating it (London, n.d.; "The Rising Concern of Financial Crimes in the Metaverse – AML Screening as a Solution," 2022; FATF, 2022).

An analysis of the Fraud Triangle perspective on Metaverse fraud may include certain pressures arising from speculative cultures that develop with your ability to speculate on the pricing changes of virtual land (they may also arise from "fear of missing out" on a potential NFT boom), as well as opportunities in these environments (Smaili & De Rancourt-Raymond, 2022; London, n.d.; Smaili & De Rancourt-Raymond, 2022). It is not unusual for users to charge high fees to facilitate these transactions and transfer these fees to both the seller and purchaser or offer their own personal services for large sums of money or multiple accounts (London, n.d.; "The Rising Concern of Financial Crimes in the Metaverse – AML Screening as a Solution," 2022). Community narratives (the expectations and belief systems of the individuals who interact within a community) may further develop the rationalization of participants engaged in such speculative behavior by normalizing "flipping," "insider" advantage, and aggressive speculation as being appropriate arbitrage as opposed to fraud (Smaili & De Rancourt-Raymond, 2022; David, 2023).

The capability dimension of the Fraud Diamond is particularly relevant in Metaverse fraud schemes, as these schemes typically involve at least three capabilities: a solid understanding of blockchain protocols and technology; specific coding abilities to execute a series of transactions across various platforms; and the technical capability to run coordinated Bot activity or impersonate avatars across many platforms (Liang et al., 2023; Tziakouris, 2024; Qin et al., 2025).

The leadership aspects as well as systemic aspects of Metaverse fraud are illuminated additionally by using the Fraud Pentagon and Fraud Circle (Marks, 2012; Lokanan, 2015). The competence and arrogance of project founders/influencers who exploit informational asymmetries to generate hype around tokens, inflate NFT floor prices, or misappropriate pooled funds is one instance of the implications of the Fraud Pentagon and Fraud Circle with respect to individual actors (London, n.d.; "Metaverse and Money Laundering – How Shufti's AML Screening Helps," 2022; Smaili & De Rancourt-Raymond, 2022). At the adapt level of fraud within the Metaverse ecosystem level, culture, interpersonal and group dynamics, and other environmental factors/contexts all contribute to factors that normalize high risk behavior and collusion (David, 2023; Smaili & De Rancourt-Raymond, 2022). For example, highly speculative communities (e.g., virtual property investing), anonymous Discord and social media groups, laxer regulatory/oversight controls of offshore exchanges, etc., contribute to normalizing high risk behaviour and collusion; rapid innovations in technology combined with deficient, confused, or non-existent regulatory frameworks further exacerbate these issues (London, n.d.; FATF, 2022; Smaili & De Rancourt-Raymond, 2022). Because of these issues, forensic accountants and fraud investigators must adapt the Fraud Pentagon and Fraud Circle models to also include cues associated with a particular individual's avatar identity, "social" cues, wallet clustering and other supporting evidences (cross-platform social signals), along with other indicators associated with behaviour and systemic risk in the context of frauds perpetrated within the Metaverse (Tziakouris, 2024; Qin et al., 2025; Liang et al., 2023).

In the context of Metaverse, digital forensics and blockchain analytics are essential tools for forensic practitioners (Tziakouris, 2024; Liang et al., 2023; Qin et al., 2025). Practitioners can follow the track of an NFT throughout the chain of transactions to determine whether NFT wash trading has occurred, and through tracing patterns of how an individual tokenised asset has been mixed (i.e., determining whether that token was acquired through money laundering), coordinate price manipulation through the action on multiple exchanges, etc. (London, n.d.; FATF, 2022; Smaili & De Rancourt-Raymond, 2022). The use of platform logs, IP addresses (to the extent they are available) and communications that occur outside of the blockchain to connect the actions of avatars (represented by pseudonyms) with their real-life counterparts and reconstruct frauds that are committed on the blockchain, for example; virtual land frauds, phishing-based account Takeovers, impersonation of authentic projects etc. (Tziakouris, 2024; "Metaverse and Money Laundering – How Shufti's AML Screening Helps," 2022; Qin et al., 2025). This integration of fraud theory with these tools will provide forensic accountants with the ability to advance from analyzing frauds that occur in isolation, to mapping the risks of the entire Metaverse through model-based inference (Smaili & De Rancourt-Raymond, 2022; Qin et al., 2025).

5.6 Ethical, privacy and technological constraints

The extensive use of blockchain and monitoring has led to numerous issues regarding privacy, compliance with Data Protection Laws, and the proportionality of surveillance in that not all pseudo-anonymous blockchain activity that has been flagged as suspected should be presumed to be in breach of the law (e.g., GREATER concern for compliance with AML and KYC than with GDPR). Furthermore, when financial institutions maintain large volumes of historical transaction data, device fingerprints, and behavioural profiles of users beyond what is necessary to prevent the commission of fraud or other financial crimes, this practice is associated with risk of excessive profiling, misuse of the data by third parties, and data breaches. Additionally, Anomaly Detection systems (artificial intelligence) generate alerts that are sometimes biased based on the data used to train the systems, which can result in a high number of false positives based on characteristics associated with specific user categories or types of transactions. Such false-positive alerts may be difficult or impossible to explain or defend in litigation. Thus, the use of human expertise, well-documented models, evidence chains, and governance controls (validation, bias testing, and legal review) is essential to ensure that forensic technologies are both effective and respect users' rights.

The comparative matrix below summarises how key fraud models differ in focus, strengths, and best-fit use cases, providing a practical guide for applying theory in both traditional and Metaverse fraud contexts.

Table 2. Comparative matrix of fraud theories

Basis	Triangle	Diamond	Pentagon	Scale	Circle
Core elements	Pressure, Opportunity, Rationalization	Triangle + Capability	Triangle + Competence, Arrogance	Pressure, Opportunity, Personal Integrity (graded)	Culture, Leadership, Group Dynamics, Environment
Unique additions	Foundational "three-condition" model	Focus on skills, authority, access	Behavioural profiling of high-risk actors	Risk "intensity" measurement	Systemic and environmental focus
Strengths	Simple, intuitive; applicable across sectors	Distinguishes who can actually execute large schemes	Targets leadership-driven, ego-driven misconduct	Supports prioritised, risk-based audits and monitoring	Reveals root-cause patterns and collusive networks
Limitations	Too coarse for complex, tech-enabled or collusive schemes	Underplays culture, group collusion, and ecosystem factors	Requires behavioural data; more complex to operationalize	Subjective scoring; needs good data on incentives and control	Less useful for isolated, small-scale individual frauds
Best-fit scenarios (traditional)	Everyday fraud awareness, baseline audits, staff training	Executive/insider fraud, high-skill or privileged-access roles	Leadership and governance failures, tone-at-the-top issues	Enterprise-wide risk assessment, audit planning	Post-crisis reviews, systemic fraud in sectors or conglomerates
Metaverse / digital relevance	Explains FOMO-driven speculation, weak platform controls, and rationalization in NFT/crypto hype cycles.	Captures developers, admins, or "whales" with technical and financial capacity to run rug-pulls or exploit smart contracts.	Illuminates charismatic founders/influencers who hype tokens, overrule controls, and dismiss regulatory/safety concerns.	Helps rank Metaverse fraud risks (e.g., petty avatar scams vs. large NFT laundering) to allocate analytic and compliance resources.	Frames Metaverse as an ecosystem: community norms, anonymous groups, platform design, and regulatory gaps that jointly enable new fraud "marketplaces.

Taking all of these models together, forensic accountants will have a multi-layered toolkit that covers the psychological profile of individual fraudsters in addition to their technical and quantitative capabilities, their ability to take advantage of their operational environment and the cultural norms of the communities in which they operate (Cressey, 1953; Wolfe & Hermanson, 2004; Marks, 2012; Lokanan, 2015). In traditional finance, these models will assist auditors in planning their audits, designing their controls, and creating their investigative strategies (Kranacher et al., 2019; Rezaee, 2009). In the Metaverse, they will assist forensic accountants in understanding the unique factors that shape the way fraudsters behave and take advantage of the environment and how to convert classical fraud theory into a format that will continue to apply in the digital borderless environment of the Metaverse (Smaili & De Rancourt-Raymond, 2022; Qin et al., 2025).

6. IMPLICATIONS

By integrating fraud theory with forensic accounting practice, it opens up new avenues for collaboration among business organizations, policymakers and academics as the emergence of the Metaverse and other new ways to commit financial crimes grows rapidly (Rezaee, 2009; FATF, 2022). By consciously thinking through the implications of combining these two concepts, businesses, government and academics can develop more efficient fraud prevention, detection and response systems, both traditional and virtual (Kranacher et al., 2019; David, 2023).

6.1.1 For companies: governance, ethical culture, fraud risk, Metaverse readiness

It is necessary for organizations to develop strong board governance and an ethical culture based on information gained from the Fraud Triangle, Diamond, Pentagon, Scale, and Circle (Cressey, 1953; Wolfe & Hermanson, 2004; Albrecht et al., 1984; Kranacher et al., 2019; Tommasetti et al., 2021). According to findings in empirical literature, organizations with strong and independent boards and active audit committees who provide robust whistleblower protection mechanisms and have clearly defined accountabilities at all levels of the organization will observe fewer instances of fraud (Beasley et al., 2010; ACFE, 2022). This underscores how these forms of oversight provide an effective deterrent to fraud (Beasley et al., 2010; PwC, 2022). As part of enterprise risk management, boards must manage fraud risk (Rezaee, 2009). They should conduct ongoing assessments of their organizations' internal controls and fraud risk assessment processes, including regular reviews of the organization's culture and behaviors indicative of the tone at the top, group think, and the degree to which rules are tolerated to be broken (Kranacher et al., 2019; Treviño, Weaver, & Reynolds, 2006).

Organizations that have included forensic thinking such as continuous monitoring, developing analytical techniques to analyze data, and assessment of culture and behaviors are positioned to better prevent and detect fraud as part of a risk management process (Dzuranin & Malaescu, 2015; Rezaee, 2009). Other departments within the organization, such as finance, internal audit, IT, cyber security, and compliance, will work together to collaboratively identify fraud risk anomalies and respond quickly to incidents (Kranacher et al., 2019; IFAC, 2018). As organizations continue to conduct business involving virtual assets such as NFTs, gaming tokens, virtual land, and developing metaverse customer experiences, the organization's fraud risk frameworks must cover virtual (avatar) identity management, security of wallets, governance of smart contracts, and on-chain/off-chain reconciling of transactions, all reinforced by utilizing blockchain forensics and responses to incidents (FATF, 2022; Smaili & De Rancourt-Raymond, 2022; James, 2023; Identity Management Institute, 2022).

6.1.2 For policymakers: reporting standards, compliance mandates, and virtual-asset regulation

The regulatory environment determines how risks, for instance fraud should be dealt with, as well as the position of forensic accounting in assisting with that risk reduction, is determined by their policies (Rezaee, 2009; IOSCO, 2020; IFAC, 2018). New laws like the Sarbanes Oxley Act; the UK Bribery Act; and the Prevention of Corruption Amendment acts in India are examples of reforms that increase the responsibility of managers, boards of directors, and other members of the firm to protect themselves from potential fraud resulting from their own actions through stronger certifications, attestation of internal controls or oversight duties, etc. (IBM, 2025). The ongoing improvement of Disclosure Standards related to fraud or potential weaknesses of internal controls, and the remediation of those weaknesses will assist companies to move towards a more active fraud prevention approach (IOSCO, 2020; IFAC, 2018).

Regulators must also address the new fraud schemes that are associated with digital assets like virtual land and NFTs, as well as platforms that operate on the blockchain (decentralized finance platforms), by making clear to users of these new digital assets and platforms the legal status of their digital assets and any obligations to comply with anti-money laundering (AML) and know your customer (KYC) regulations (FATF, 2019; FATF, 2021; Raza, 2025; Smaili & De Rancourt-Raymond, 2022). Additionally, regulators need to provide guidance on protecting your digital identity and safeguarding the custody of customer assets when on-line or through a platform (FATF, 2021; Raza, 2025). As a result, in order for regulators, financial intelligence units (FIUs), and law enforcement agencies to effectively respond to fraudulent activity occurring across different national borders and jurisdictions in relation to the virtuous economy, secure data sharing, mutual legal assistance, and cooperation between FIUs, securities regulators, and Law Enforcement, including providing support for blockchain forensic investigations into money laundering, market manipulation, and other fraudulent activity occurring on multiple platforms, must happen (FATF, 2019; FATF, 2021; IOSCO, 2020). By embedding the principles of forensic accounting into regulatory guidelines - such as audit trails, log files, and virtual asset platform evidence retention - Digital Evidence will be of higher quality & of greater admissibility (IFAC, 2018; FATF, 2021).

6.1.3 For academia: forensic education, certification, and Metaverse-focused training

In the continuous growth of fraud, the maturing of Physical and Digital/Virtual Economic Markets has brought about increased demands on academia (Rezaee, 2009; IFAC, 2018). Colleges & universities need to reconsider their curriculums, Research priorities, the incorporation of behavioral sciences into Forensic Accounting Curriculum - Integrating Models of Fraud (Triangle, Diamond, Pentagon, Scale, Circle) - (Behavioral Models) (Kranacher et al., 2019; Rezaee, 2009). Integrating Review of /via Case Studies of Fraudulent Schemes (Enron, Satyam, Wirecard, Harshad Mehta), Ponzi Schemes, WorldCom. Teaching these Models through the way of Case Study Method emphasizes this Integration into Education (Healy & Palepu, 2003; Bhasin, 2013; *International Journal Publication | Research Paper Publication and Submission - IJARIIT*, 2021). Programmes must focus on developing practical skills in data analytics, anomaly detection (AI), Digital Forensics, and Blockchain Analysis for use in technology-enabled environments (Dzuranin & Malaescu, 2015; Dalwai et al., 2022).

Professional certifications - Certified Fraud Examiner (CFE) and other certifications for forensic accounting - provide employers with examples of competence and ethical standards and their importance to employers is growing (ACFE, 2022; Rezaee, 2009). Universities can provide pathways for professional certifications through the development of certification aligned modules, practicum/internships, and collaborations between universities and professional/regulatory bodies as part of degree curricula (IFAC, 2018; ICAI, 2023). Various aspects of metaverse fraud are emerging as new areas of interest for researchers from different fields, including digital evidence, digital asset regulation, and cross-border enforcement (FATF, 2021). These new topics provide an opportunity for collaboration among accounting, law, computer science, and criminology to develop new publications (Qin et al., 2025).

Building on this new body of knowledge through inclusion of topics related to Metaverse fraud readiness (identity risk, virtual asset security, platform governance, digital evidence collection) will prepare the next generation of forensic accountants and auditors to protect the financial integrity of organizations both in traditional markets and through online transactions (Smaili & De Rancourt-Raymond, 2022; Liang et al., 2023; Qin et al., 2025).

The expanding digital and Metaverse landscape require forensic accountants to build on traditional investigative competencies with advanced technological, analytical, and virtual-asset skills, creating distinct but overlapping profiles for traditional and digital-forensic practice.

Table 3. Skills required for traditional vs. digital-forensic accountants

Skill area	Traditional forensic accountant	Digital / Metaverse-focused forensic accountant
Core accounting & audit	Advanced financial accounting, auditing standards, IFRS/GAAP, controls.	Same core accounting/audit plus understanding of crypto, tokens, and virtual-asset flows.
Investigation & evidence	Interviewing, document review, transaction tracing, litigation support.	Same, plus handling digital evidence, logs, and chain-of-custody for electronic records.
Data analytics	Excel, sampling, basic CAATs, ratio/trend analysis.	Big-data tools, scripting, AI/ML-based anomaly detection, real-time monitoring.
Legal & regulatory	Fraud/AML laws, SOX, PCA, company law, court procedures.	Above + virtual-asset/crypto/Metaverse regulation, AML/KYC for platforms, data-privacy.
Technology & security	ERP systems, basic IT controls, email/log analysis.	Blockchain and wallet forensics, smart-contract basics, cyber-security and incident response.
Behavioural / communication	Behavioural fraud understanding, interviewing, reporting to management and regulators.	Same, plus ability to explain complex digital-forensic findings and Metaverse risks to non-technical stakeholders.

6.2 Future Research Directions

6.2.1 Fraud theories through the virtual world

- Devise quantitative models that allow the testing of different ways to study fraud using existing datasets.
- Create a virtual environment (e.g., VR) to study whether the Fear of Missing Out (FOMO), Anonymity, and Community Narrative have an impact on how people are pressured into committing fraud, rationalising their actions, and creating a joint effort to commit the fraud.
- Create studies that will allow for direct comparison of different legal definitions of fraud and virtual property, especially in regards to how laws (such as the Fraud Acts) are enforced, and how those enforcement practices impact/facilitate fraud on the Metaverse.

6.2.2 Forensic Accounting, Evidence and Technology

- Empirical investigation of the combinations of on-chain indicators, platform-log signals and off-chain communications that best predict the following fraud types:
    - Rug Pulls
    - Impersonation
    - Wash Trading
    - Phishing
- Review of the evidentiary standards for blockchain forensic evidence, including:
    - Chain-of-Custody
    - Authentication of Wallet Linkages
    - Treatment of Algorithmically-Generated Risk Scores in Court
- Review of the performance, bias and explainability of ai-based forensic tools for financial-crime detection, including:
    - The impact of model design on false-positives and legal defensibility

6.2.3 Governance, Privacy and Ethics

- Review of the impact of data-protection/privacy regimes (e.g., GDPR) and models of data protection/privacy by design, on the nature of forensic monitoring in the context of the metaverse, including proposals for models that strike a balance between surveillance and rights protection.
- Review of ethical frameworks establishing guidelines for the forensic use of immersive data (e.g., biometrics, motion capture, voice) for investigative purposes, including the necessity for consent, the establishment of proportionality and the secondary use of high-sensitivity data.

7. CONCLUSION

This chapter's exploration of the development of fraud theories and forensic accounting has shown that there are models (e.g., Fraud Triangle; Fraud Diamond; Fraud Pentagon; Fraud Scale; Fraud Circle) that help to explain both why people commit fraud and how fraud is supported through the structures created by organizations (Kranacher et al., 2019). While all the models provide some context, strengths, and limitations, they also provide researchers, practitioners, and regulators with a comprehensive toolkit for understanding and combating financial crime across multiple sectors.

Case history demonstrates that fraud is not usually an isolated technical issue, but rather belongs in the context of interacting psychological, behavioral, structural and environmental elements which often combine within weak governance and ethically vulnerable cultures (Albrecht et al., 1984). The Satyam, Enron, and WorldCom cases, as well as the Harshad Mehta fraud and various Ponzi schemes, illustrate how the co-existence of pressure or opportunity, rationalization, competence, arrogance, and collusion can exist in an environment of weak governance and ethical culture (Coffee, 2006; Khanna & Palepu, 2010). The scams provide compelling evidence supporting the identification of strong boards, credible oversight, and embedded fraud risk management roles in corporate governance systems (Beasley, et al., 2010; "G20/OECD PRINCIPLES OF CORPORATE GOVERNANCE 2015," 2015).

In addition, forensic accounting has evolved from a primarily reactive, post-event investigator role to a more proactive, risk management-driven discipline integrated with integrity systems (Singleton et al., 2010; Kranacher et al., 2019). Data analytics, continuous auditing techniques, transaction mapping and digital forensics facilitate the detection of fraud and the investigation and analysis of complex transactions (Kogan et al., 2014). Forensic accountants convert theoretical concepts into operational fraud control and red flag frameworks that limit potential for fraud and provide for prompt intervention. Close cooperation with regulators and following of legal and regulatory standards such as Sarbanes-Oxley and the UK Bribery Act and India's Prevention of Corruption (Amendment) Act helps to ensure that evidence gathered is robust and admissible as well as compliant with the highest level of accountability globally.

Technological advancements will dramatically change the types of fraud risk we face and how we react to them from a forensic accounting perspective. Using artificial intelligence (AI) and machine learning (ML), organizations can now perform real-time analysis of vast, heterogeneous datasets, advanced anomaly detection, and predictive scoring for risk purposes (Beneish M-score, 2015; Kokina & Davenport, 2017). Blockchain and distributed ledger technology creates a transparent, tamper-resistant record. With these technologies comes new avenues for committing fraud, but they also provide a strong evidentiary trail to follow in the investigation of fraud (Tapscott & Tapscott, 2016; Schmitz & Leoni, 2019).

The emergence of the Metaverse and the related ecosystem of virtual assets has introduced new types of fraud that need to be addressed in different ways; how are we going to deal with a virtual land scam, NFT wash trading, avatar impersonation, or laundering with cryptocurrency? This new area of digital fraud will require forensic accountants to combine the skills of blockchain analysis, cyber security, and digital identity forensics to perform a complete fraud examination (Houben & Snyers, 2018).

The importance of the behavioral and educational facets of fraud continues to be just as critical as technological developments. There is ongoing research into the motive and rationalization for committing fraud, the factors that create an ethical climate, and the culture in which we live (Cressey, 1953; Kranacher et al., 2019). All of this plays an important role in developing a more effective profile for assessing fraud risk and informing our strategies for improving organizational governance and directing ethics training and developing leaders (Albrecht et al., 1984). As forensic accounting and fraud examination practitioners, we need to develop academic and professional certification programs that encompass both classical fraud theory and new skills necessary for digital forensics, including virtual asset related risks, to educate our practitioners to be prepared for the merging of the physical and virtual financial systems (Golden et al., 2011). The growing recognition of the need for greater harmonization of international fraud and corruption legislation has led to increased collaboration between international organizations including IOSCO (International Organization of Securities Commissions) and IFAC (International Federation of Accountants) (International Organization of Securities Commissions [IOSCO], 2020; International Federation of Accountants [IFAC], 2018). Increasing cross-border cooperation and information sharing are critical to combatting fraud and corruption that span multiple countries and digital environments.

Collectively, the future of fraud control requires a multifaceted approach built upon behavioral insights, technology innovations, sound governance, and regulatory coordination (Albrecht et al., 1984; Kranacher et al., 2019). By building upon evolving theories of fraud and the development of forensic accounting capabilities, and extending that readiness into digital and Metaverse contexts, organisations and communities will have an opportunity to close the gap between understanding fraud and preventing fraud, ultimately enhancing trust and transparency in the world's financial systems (Golden et al., 2011; Houben & Snyers, 2018).

REFERENCES

Admin, & Admin. (2025, March 21). Digital Forensics specialists master metaverse challenges. *ecsInfotech* -. https://www.ecsinfotech.com/how-digital-forensics-specialists-cracks-metaverse-crimes/

Albrecht, W. S., Romney, M. B., Howe, K. R., & Albrecht, C. (1984). *Deterring fraud: The internal auditor's perspective*. The Institute of Internal Auditors Research Foundation.

Association of Certified Fraud Examiners. (2022). *Occupational fraud 2022: A report to the nations*. Association of Certified Fraud Examiners. https://www.acfe.com/about-the-acfe/newsroom-for-media/press-releases/press-release-detail?s=2022-RTTN-launch

Bajpai, P., & Ciso, E. (2025, November 13). The unsafe metaverse: VR harassment, avatar theft and new cyber threats. *ETCISO.in*. https://ciso.economictimes.indiatimes.com/news/cybercrime-fraud/the-unsafe-metaverse-vr-harassment-avatar-theft-and-new-cyber-threats/125289677

Beasley, M. S., Hermanson, D. R., Carcello, J. V., & Neal, T. L. (2010). *Fraudulent financial reporting: 1998-2007 : an analysis of U.S. public companies*. Committee of Sponsoring Organizations of the Treadway Commission (COSO). https://egrove.olemiss.edu/cgi/viewcontent.cgi?article=1534&context=aicpa_assoc

Benston, G. J., & Hartgraves, A. L. (2002). *Enron What happened and what we can learn from it. Journal of Accounting and Public Policy, 21, 105-127. - References - Scientific Research Publishing*. https://www.scirp.org/reference/referencespapers?referenceid=1922733

Bhasin, M. L. (2013). Corporate Accounting Fraud: A Case study of Satyam Computers Limited. *Open Journal of Accounting*, *02*(02), 26–38. DOI: 10.4236/ojacct.2013.22006

Bologna, G. J., & Lindquist, R. J. (1995). *Fraud auditing and forensic accounting: New tools and techniques* (2nd ed.). John Wiley & Sons.

Bribery Act. 2010, c. 23. *United Kingdom* (2010). http://legislation.gov.uk/ukpga/2010/23/contents

Chimonaki, C., Papadakis, S., & Lemonakis, C. (2023). Perspectives in fraud theories – A systematic review approach. *F1000 Research*, *12*, 933. DOI: 10.12688/f1000research.131896.1

Christian, N., Basri, Y. Z., & Arafah, W. (n.d.). Analysis of Fraud Triangle, Fraud Diamond and Fraud Pentagon Theory to detecting Corporate Fraud in Indonesia. In *The International Journal of Business Management and Technology* (pp. 73–74). The International Journal of Business Management and Technology. [Journal-article], https://www.theijbmt.com/archive/0928/608343945.pdf

Coffee, J. C. (2006). *Gatekeepers: The professions and corporate governance.* Oxford University Press., DOI: 10.1093/oso/9780199288090.001.0001

Cressey, D. R. (1953). *Other people's money: A study in the social psychology of embezzlement.* Free Press.

Creswell, J. W. (2014). *Research design: Qualitative, Quantitative, and Mixed Methods Approaches* (4th ed.). SAGE.

Crumbley, D. L., Heitger, L. E., & Smith, G. S. (2015). *Forensic and investigative accounting* (7th ed.). CCH., https://www.scribd.com/document/484261659/Forensic-and-Investigative-Accounting-pdf

Dalwai, T. A. R., Madbouly, A., & Mohammadi, S. S. (2022). An investigation of artificial intelligence application in auditing. In *Artificial Intelligence and COVID Effect on Accounting* (pp. 101–114). Springer Nature., DOI: 10.1007/978-981-19-1234-5_6

David, R. C. (2023, February 15). *What are worldwide AML regulations for cryptocurrency?* Pideeco. https://pideeco.be/articles/worldwide-aml-regulations-virtual-assets/#:~:text=However%2C%20the%20rules%20for%20stablecoins,asset%20services%20and%20related%20activities

Dionisio, J. D. N., Burns, W. G., III, Gilbert, R., & Loyola Marymount University. (2013). 3D Virtual Worlds and the Metaverse: current status and future possibilities. *Computer Science Faculty Works.* https://digitalcommons.lmu.edu/cs_fac/8

Dzuranin, A. C., & Malaescu, I. (2015). The current state and future direction of data analytics in accounting and auditing. *Journal of Information Systems, 30*(3), 131–148. https://papers.ssrn.com/sol3/papers.cfm?abstract_id=2663167

FATF. (2019). *Guidance for a risk-based approach to virtual assets and virtual asset service providers.* Financial Action Task Force. https://www.fatf-gafi.org/en/publications/Fatfrecommendations/Guidance-rba-virtual-assets.html

FATF. (2021). *Updated guidance for a risk-based approach to virtual assets and virtual asset service providers.* Financial Action Task Force. https://www.fatf-gafi.org/en/publications/Fatfrecommendations/Guidance-rba-virtual-assets-2021.html

FATF. (2022). *Targeted update on implementation of the FATF standards on virtual assets and virtual asset service providers*. Financial Action Task Force. https://www.fatf-gafi.org/en/publications/Fatfrecommendations/Targeted-update-virtual-assets-vasps.html

Flick, U. (2018). Doing Qualitative Data Collection – Charting the Routes. In *The SAGE Handbook of Qualitative Data Collection.* (pp. 3–16). https://doi.org/DOI: 10.4135/9781526416070.n1

Forbes Councils. (n.d.). *Forbes councils*. https://councils.forbes.com/

G20/OECD Principles of Corporate Governance. 2015. (2015). In *OECD Publishing eBooks*. https://doi.org/DOI: 10.1787/9789264236882-en

Golden, T. W., Skalak, S. L., Clayton, M. M., & Pill, J. S. (2011). *A guide to forensic accounting investigation* (2nd ed.). John Wiley & Sons., https://download.e-bookshelf.de/download/0000/5848/25/L-G-0000584825-0002384529.pdf

Healy, P. M., & Palepu, K. G. (2003). The fall of Enron. *The Journal of Economic Perspectives*, *17*(2), 3–26. DOI: 10.1257/089533003765888403

Houben, R., & Snyers, A. (2018). Cryptocurrencies and blockchain: Legal context and implications for financial crime, money laundering and tax evasion. In European Parliament's Special Committee on Financial Crimes, Tax Evasion and Tax Avoidance, *European Parliament's Special Committee on Financial Crimes, Tax Evasion and Tax Avoidance* (Report PE 619.024). https://repository.uantwerpen.be/docman/irua/80a4a6/152140.pdf

Houben, R., & Snyers, A. (2020). Crypto-assets - Key developments, regulatory concerns and responses. In European Parliament, *European Parliament* (Study PE 648.779). https://www.europarl.europa.eu/RegData/etudes/STUD/2020/648779/IPOL_STU(2020)648779_EN.pdf https://www.sciencedirect.com/

Huber, W. D. (2017). Forensic accounting, fraud theory, and the end of the fraud triangle. *Journal of Theoretical Accounting Research*, *12*(2), 28–48. https://papers.ssrn.com/sol3/papers.cfm?abstract_id=2423809

IBM X-Force 2025 Threat Intelligence Index. (n.d.). IBM. https://www.ibm.com/thought-leadership/institute-business-value/en-us/report/2025-threat-intelligence-index

ICAI. (2017). *Study on forensic accounting and fraud detection*. Institute of Chartered Accountants of India. https://pqc.icai.org/assets/announcement_files/1550140046.pdf

ICAI. (2023). *Forensic accounting and investigation standards (FAIS)*. Institute of Chartered Accountants of India. https://resource.cdn.icai.org/75009daab030723.pdf

International Journal Publication | Research paper publication and Submission - IJARIIT. (2021, February 20). IJARIIT. https://www.ijariit.com/

IOSCO. (2020). *Issues, risks and regulatory considerations relating to crypto-asset trading platforms*. International Organization of Securities Commissions. https://www.iosco.org/library/pubdocs/pdf/IOSCOPD649.pdf

James, M. (2023). Blockchain and forensic accounting enhancing transparency and accountability. SSRN *Electronic Journal*. https://doi.org/DOI: 10.2139/ssrn.4642347

Karapatakis, A. (2024). Metaverse crimes in virtual (Un)reality: Fraud and sexual offences under English law. *Journal of Economic Criminology*, *7*, 100118. DOI: 10.1016/j.jeconc.2024.100118

Khanna, T., & Palepu, K. G. (2010). Winning in Emerging Markets: A Road map for Strategy and Execution. *NHRD Network Journal*, *3*(3), 75. DOI: 10.1177/0974173920100316

Kogan, A., Alles, M. G., Vasarhelyi, M. A., & Wu, J. (2014). Design and evaluation of a continuous data level auditing system. *Auditing*, *33*(4), 221–245. DOI: 10.2308/ajpt-50844

Kokina, J., & Davenport, T. H. (2017). The Emergence of Artificial Intelligence: How Automation is Changing Auditing. *Journal of Emerging Technologies in Accounting*, *14*(1), 115–122. DOI: 10.2308/jeta-51730

Kranacher, M.-J., Riley, R. A., & Wells, J. T. (2011). *Forensic accounting and fraud examination*. John Wiley & Sons.

Kranacher, M.-J., Riley, R. A., & Wells, J. T. (2019). *Forensic accounting and fraud examination* (2nd ed.). John Wiley & Sons.

Liang, G., Xin, J., Wang, Q., Ni, X., Guo, X., & Chen, P. (2023). Research on metaverse security and forensics. *Computers, Materials & Continua/Computers. Materials & Continua (Print)*, *77*(1), 799–825. DOI: 10.32604/cmc.2023.038403

Lokanan, M. (2022). Predicting Money Laundering using Machine Learning and Artificial Neural Networks Algorithms in Banks. *Research Square*. https://doi.org/DOI: 10.21203/rs.3.rs-2161095/v1

Lokanan, M. E. (2015). Challenges to the fraud triangle: Questions on its usefulness. *Accounting Forum*, *39*(3), 201–224. DOI: 10.1016/j.accfor.2015.05.002

Lokanan, M. E., & Sharma, P. (2023). Two Decades of Accounting Fraud Research: The Missing Meso-Level Analysis. *SAGE Open, 13*(3). Advance online publication. DOI: 10.1177/21582440231197305

London. (n.d.). *Blockchain Analytics & Crypto Compliance Solutions | Elliptic*. https://www.elliptic.co/

Marks, J. T. (2012). Fraud Pentagon: An enhancement to the fraud triangle and other models. *Crowe Horwath* white paper.

Mazer Trainer. (2024, January 9). *Metaverse scams and how to avoid them*. https://mazerspace.com/metaverse-scams-and-how-to-avoid-them/

McCrum, D. (2020). *Wirecard The Timeline. Financial Times. - References - Scientific Research Publishing*. https://www.scirp.org/reference/referencespapers?referenceid=3100404

Metaverse and Money Laundering – How Shufti's AML Screening Helps. (2022, March 17). *Shufti Pro*. https://shuftipro.com/blog/metaverse-and-money-laundering-how-shufti-pros-aml-screening-helps/

Post, J. E., Varma, J. R., Menon, K., Desai, A., Raghavan, A., Srinivasan, V., Parekh, S. P., & Vohra, N. (2009). The Satyam Story: Many questions and a few answers. *Vikalpa, 34*(1), 69–88. DOI: 10.1177/0256090920090106

PricewaterhouseCoopers. (2022). *PwC's global economic crime and fraud survey 2022*. PricewaterhouseCoopers. https://www.pwc.com/gx/en/services/forensics/economic-crime-survey/2022.html

Qin, H. X., Wang, Y., & Hui, P. (2025). Identity, crimes, and law enforcement in the Metaverse. *Humanities and Social Sciences Communications, 12*(1). *Nature*. Advance online publication. DOI: 10.1057/s41599-024-04266-w

Raza, A. (2025, October 20). *Top 4 Game-Changing AML Solutions in 2025*. AML Watcher. https://amlwatcher.com/blog/4-game-changing-aml-solutions-in-2025/

Rehman, A. & Muhammad Ali Siddiqui. (2024). Navigating Virtual Economies: Transformative Impacts and Challenges for Forensic Accounting in the Metaverse. A Conceptual overview. In *Grenze International Journal of Engineering and Technology* (Vol. 10, Issue 2, p. 916). https://thegrenze.com/pages/servej.php?fn=916.pdf&name=Navigating%20Virtual%20Economies:%20Transformative%20Impactsand%20Challenges%20for%20Forensic%20Accounting%20in%20theMetaverse.%20A%20Conceptual%20Overview&id=2932&association=GRENZE&journal=GIJET&year=2024&volume=10&issue=2

Rezaee, Z. (2009). *Financial statement fraud: Prevention and detection* (2nd ed.). John Wiley & Sons.

Sarbanes–Oxley Act of. 2002, Pub. L. No. 107–204, 116 Stat. 745 (2002). https://www.dol.gov/sites/dolgov/files/oalj/PUBLIC/WHISTLEBLOWER/REFERENCES/STATUTES/SARBANES_OXLEY_ACT_OF_2002.PDF

Schmitz, J., & Leoni, G. (2019). Accounting and Auditing at the time of Blockchain Technology: A research agenda. *Australian Accounting Review, 29*(2), 331–342. DOI: 10.1111/auar.12286

Singleton, T. W., Singleton, A. J., Bologna, G. J., & Lindquist, R. J. (2010). *Fraud auditing and forensic accounting* (4th ed.). John Wiley & Sons., https://content.e-bookshelf.de/media/reading/L-580553-2336f26274.pdf

Smaili, N., & De Rancourt-Raymond, A. (2022). Metaverse: Welcome to the new fraud marketplace. *Journal of Financial Crime, 31*(1), 188–200. DOI: 10.1108/jfc-06-2022-0124

Smaili, N., & Rancourt-Raymond, A. (2022). *We need to anticipate and address potential fraud in the metaverse*. The Conversation., DOI: 10.64628/aam.559prpde6

Snyder, H. (2019). Literature review as a research methodology: An overview and guidelines. *Journal of Business Research, 104*, 333–339. DOI: 10.1016/j.jbusres.2019.07.039

Staff, K. W. (2009, January 9). Scandal at Satyam: Truth, lies and corporate governance. *Knowledge at Wharton*. https://knowledge.wharton.upenn.edu/article/scandal-at-satyam-truth-lies-and-corporate-governance/

Taheri, M. (2020). A comparison of Triangle, Diamond and Pentagon fraud models in fraud risk assessment. *Iranian Journal of Value and Behavioral Accounting, 4*(8), 339–369. DOI: 10.29252/aapc.4.8.339

Tapscott, D., & Tapscott, A. (2016). *Blockchain revolution: How the technology behind bitcoin is changing money, business, and the world*. Portfolio/Penguin. https://itig-iraq.iq/wp-content/uploads/2019/05/Blockchain_Revolution.pdf

The impact of cyber forensic accounting on quality of metaverse integrated reporting quality in metaverse local government. (2024). *Journal of Science and Technology - HaUI, 60*(11E). https://doi.org/DOI: 10.57001/huih5804.2024.341

The Rising Concern of Financial Crimes in the Metaverse – AML Screening as a Solution. (2022, November 10). *Shufti Pro*. https://shuftipro.com/blog/the-rising-concern-of-financial-crimes-in-the-metaverse-aml-screening-as-a-solution/

Tommasetti, R., De Oliveira Leite, R., Maia, V. M., & Da Silva Macedo, M. A. (2021). Revisiting the Accounting Fraud Components: A Bottom-Up approach using the Twitter platform. *SAGE Open*, *11*(4). Advance online publication. DOI: 10.1177/21582440211058190

Tranfield, D. R., Denyer, D., & Smart, P. (2003). Towards a methodology for developing Evidence-Informed management knowledge by means of systematic review. *British Journal of Management*, *14*(3), 207–222. DOI: 10.1111/1467-8551.00375

Treviño, L. K., Weaver, G. R., & Reynolds, S. J. (2006). Behavioral Ethics in Organizations: A review. *Journal of Management*, *32*(6), 951–990. DOI: 10.1177/0149206306294258

Tziakouris, G. (2024, July 9). *Digital forensics for investigating the metaverse*. Cisco Blogs. Retrieved December 19, 2025, from https://blogs.cisco.com/security/digital-forensics-for-investigating-the-metaverse

Wells, J. T. (2017). *Principles of fraud examination* (4th ed.). John Wiley & Sons.

White, M. (2025, December 16). *Web3 is Going Just Great*. https://www.web3isgoinggreat.com/

Wolfe, D. T., & Hermanson, D. R. (2004). The fraud diamond: Considering the four elements of fraud. *The CPA Journal*, *74*(12), 38–42. https://digitalcommons.kennesaw.edu/cgi/viewcontent.cgi?article=2546&context=facpubs

Yesiariani, M., & Rahayu, I. (2017). Deteksi financial statement fraud: Pengujian dengan fraud diamond. *Jurnal Akuntansi & Auditing Indonesia*, *21*(1), 49–60. DOI: 10.20885/jaai.vol21.iss1.art5

Yip, E. (2024). The metaverse future: legal gaps in data privacy, regulation, and democracy. SSRN *Electronic Journal*. https://doi.org/DOI: 10.2139/ssrn.4908442

Compilation of References

A., A. (2025, March 21). Artificial intelligence and intellectual property: How AI is changing the landscape of intellectual property rights. World Intellectual Property Organization. https://www.wipo.int/edocs/pubdocs/en/wipo-pub-econstat-wp-77-en-artificial-intelligence-and-intellectual-property-an-economic-perspective.pdf

A., S. (2025, March 21). Artificial intelligence and intellectual property: "Intellectual property rights and AI: A greener future". World Intellectual Property Organization. https://www.wipo.int/edocs/pubdocs/en/wipo-pub-econstat-wp-77-en-artificial-intelligence-and-intellectual-property-an-economic-perspective.pdf

Aayog, N. I. T. I. (2021). *Responsible AI for all: Operationalizing principles for responsible AI*. Government of India. https://www.niti.gov.in/sites/default/files/2021-08/Part2-Responsible-AI-12082021.pdf

Aayog, N. I. T. I. (2022). *Responsible AI for All: Strategy for India*. Government of India. https://www.niti.gov.in/sites/default/files/2022-11/Ai_for_All_2022_02112022_0.pdf

Abbott, R. (2020). *The reasonable robot: Artificial intelligence and the law*. Cambridge University Press.

Abdullah, A. (2020). Public relation in the era of artificial intelligence: Peluang atau ancaman? *Jurnal Aristo: Social, Politic. Humaniora*, *8*(2), 406–417. DOI: 10.24269/ars.v8i2.2629

Adam Smith. (1776). *An inquiry into the nature and causes of the wealth of nations*. Strahan & T. Cadell.

Adheshvar, A., Jessiah Inbaraj, P., Patturajan, T., & Rajesh, K. (2025). AttorneyGPT – Multilingual Generative Artificial Intelligence Law Chatbot using Retrieval Augmented Generation. In Proceedings of the 4th International Conference on Information Technology, Civil Innovation, Science, and Management (ICITSM 2025). EAI.

Admin, & Admin. (2025, March 21). Digital Forensics specialists master metaverse challenges. *ecsInfotech -*. https://www.ecsinfotech.com/how-digital-forensics-specialists-cracks-metaverse-crimes/

Agrawal, S. (2023). Critical analysis of consumer in Consumer Protection Act, 2019. *International Journal of Research in IT and Management, 8*(8), 1–7. ISSN 2456-4184. Chromeextension://efaidnbmnnnibpcajpcglclefindmkaj/https://www.ijnrd.org/papers/IJNRD2308212.pdf

Agrawal, A., Gans, J., & Goldfarb, A. (2019). *The economics of artificial intelligence: An agenda*. University of Chicago Press., DOI: 10.7208/chicago/9780226613475.001.0001

Agustini, A., Nurlaily, N., & Seroja, T. D. (2022). Technological Advancement in The Society 5.0 Era for Notary in Indonesia: Glory or Obsolete? *Legal Brief, 11*(3), 1589–1597. DOI: 10.35335/legal.Technological

Akbar, H. M., & Najicha, F. U. (2022). Upaya memperkuat jati diri bangsa melalui pemahaman wawasan nusantara di era gempuran kebudayaan asing. *Jurnal Kewarganegaraan, 6*(1), 2122–2127. DOI: 10.31316/jk.v6i1.2939

Akter, S., McCarthy, G., Sajib, S., Michael, K., Dwivedi, Y. K., D'Ambra, J., & Shen, K. N. (2021). Algorithmic bias in data-driven innovation in the age of AI. *International Journal of Information Management, 60*, 102387. DOI: 10.1016/j.ijinfomgt.2021.102387

Alarie, B., Niblett, A., & Yoon, A. H. (2018). How Artificial Intelligence Will Affect the Practice of Law. *University of Toronto Law Journal, 68*(Supplement 1), 106–124. DOI: 10.3138/utlj.2017-0052

Alarie, B., Niblett, A., & Yoon, A. H. (2018). How artificial intelligence will affect the practice of law. *University of Toronto Law Journal, 68*, 106–124.

Albrecht, W. S., Romney, M. B., Howe, K. R., & Albrecht, C. (1984). *Deterring fraud: The internal auditor's perspective*. The Institute of Internal Auditors Research Foundation.

Aldoseri, A., Al-Khalifa, K. N., & Hamouda, A. M. (2023). Re-thinking data strategy and integration for artificial intelligence: Concepts, opportunities, and challenges. *Applied Sciences (Basel, Switzerland), 13*(12), 7082. DOI: 10.3390/app13127082

Aleedy, M., Shaiba, H., & Bezbradica, M. (2019). Generating and analyzing chatbot responses using Natural Language Processing. *International Journal of Advanced Computer Science and Applications, 10*(9). Advance online publication. DOI: 10.14569/ijacsa.2019.0100910

Aletras, N., Tsarapatsanis, D., Preoţiuc-Pietro, D., & Lampos, V. (2016). Predicting Judicial Decisions of the European Court of Human Rights: A Natural Language Processing Perspective. *PeerJ. Computer Science*, *2*, e93. DOI: 10.7717/peerj-cs.93

Ali, M. A., & Kamraju, M. (2023, December). Impact of artificial intelligence on intellectual property rights: Challenges and opportunities. ResearchGate. https://www.researchgate.net/publication/376751087_Impact_of_Artificial_Intelligence_on_Intellectual_Property_Rights_Challenges_and_Opportunities

Aljohani, A. (2025). A decision-support framework for evaluating AI-enabled ESG strategies in the context of sustainable manufacturing systems. *Scientific Reports*, *15*. Advance online publication. DOI: 10.1038/s41598-025-09569-9 PMID: 40615575

Al-kfairy, M., Mustafa, D., Kshetri, N., Insiew, M., & Alfandi, O. (2024). Ethical challenges and solutions of generative AI: An interdisciplinary perspective. *Informatics (MDPI)*, *11*(3), 58. DOI: 10.3390/informatics11030058

Alqaidi, S. H., Albugami, S. M., Alzahrani, W. S., Badri, S., & Wali, A. (2024). Network-integrated medical chatbot for enhanced healthcare services. *Telematics and Informatics Reports*, *15*, 100153.

Alvarez, J. M., Colmenarejo, A. B., & Elobaid, A.. (2024). Policy advice and best practices on bias and fairness in AI. *Ethics and Information Technology*, *26*, 31. DOI: 10.1007/s10676-024-09746-w

Alzbeta, K. (2017). Intersections between law and artificial intelligence. *International Journal of Computer*, *27*(1), 55–68. DOI: 10.53896/ijc.v27i1.1071

Amazon.com NV Investment Holdings LLC v. Future Retail Ltd., 2021 SCC OnLine Del 1279 (Delhi High Court).

Amodei, D., Olah, C., Steinhardt, J., Christiano, P., Schulman, J., & Mané, D. (2016). Concrete problems in AI safety. arXiv preprint arXiv:1606.06565.

Angerhofer, M. D.. (2024). Privacy in the age of artificial intelligence: Addressing the ethical and legal implications. *Journal of AI & Society*, *42*(3), 215–234.

An, Q., Rahman, S., Zhou, J., & Kang, J. J. (2023). A comprehensive review on machine learning in healthcare industry: Classification, restrictions, opportunities, and challenges. *Sensors (Basel)*, *23*(9), 4178. DOI: 10.3390/s23094178 PMID: 37177382

Artificial Intelligence Act, EU (2021/2024)

Asai, A., Schick, T., Lewis, P., Chen, X., Izacard, G., Riedel, S., & Yih, W. T. (2023, July). Task-aware retrieval with instructions. In *Findings of the Association for Computational Linguistics* (pp. 3650–3675). ACL.

Ashley, K. D. (2017). *Artificial Intelligence and Legal Analytics: New Tools for Law Practice in the Digital Age*. Cambridge University Press., DOI: 10.1017/9781316761380

Association of Certified Fraud Examiners. (2022). *Occupational fraud 2022: A report to the nations*. Association of Certified Fraud Examiners. https://www.acfe.com/about-the-acfe/newsroom-for-media/press-releases/press-release-detail?s=2022-RTTN-launch

Azis, R. A., Susetio, W., Nurhayani, N., & Hikmawati, E. (2023). Pengaturan dan Pertanggung Jawaban Pemanfaatan Artificial Intelligence (AI) di Indonesia dalam Perspektif Hukum. *Forum Ilmiah Indonusa*, *20*(4), 243–254.

Babu, A., & Boddu, S. B. (2024). BERT-based medical chatbot: Enhancing healthcare communication through natural language understanding. *Exploratory Research in Clinical and Social Pharmacy*, *13*(Mar), 100419. PMID: 38495953

Bajpai, P., & Ciso, E. (2025, November 13). The unsafe metaverse: VR harassment, avatar theft and new cyber threats. *ETCISO.in*. https://ciso.economictimes.indiatimes.com/news/cybercrime-fraud/the-unsafe-metaverse-vr-harassment-avatar-theft-and-new-cyber-threats/125289677

Balayn, A., Lofi, C., & Houben, G. J. (2021). Managing bias and unfairness in data for decision support: A survey of machine learning and data engineering approaches to identify and mitigate bias and unfairness within data management and analytics systems. *The VLDB Journal*, *30*, 739–768. DOI: 10.1007/s00778-021-00671-8

Banerjee, D., Singh, P., Avadhanam, A., & Srivastava, S. (2023). Benchmarking LLM powered chatbots: methods and metrics. arXiv preprint arXiv:2308.04624.

Bardhan, R., & Kandarp, A. (Eds.). (2025). REIMAGINING HIGHER EDUCATION WITH AI. Krishna Publication House.

Barysė, D., & Sarel, R. (2024). Algorithms in the court : Does it matter which part of the judicial decision - making is automated? *Artificial Intelligence and Law*, *32*(1), 117–146. DOI: 10.1007/s10506-022-09343-6 PMID: 36643574

Bauer, T., Devrim, E., Glazunov, M., Jaramillo, W. L., Mohan, B., & Spanakis, G. (2019, September). #MeTooMaastricht: Building a chatbot to assist survivors of sexual harassment. In *Joint European Conference on Machine Learning and Knowledge Discovery in Databases* (pp. 503-521). Cham: Springer International Publishing.

Beasley, M. S., Hermanson, D. R., Carcello, J. V., & Neal, T. L. (2010). *Fraudulent financial reporting: 1998-2007 : an analysis of U.S. public companies*. Committee of Sponsoring Organizations of the Treadway Commission (COSO). https://egrove.olemiss.edu/cgi/viewcontent.cgi?article=1534&context=aicpa_assoc

Behnia, R., Ebrahimi, M. R., Pacheco, J., & Padmanabhan, B. (2022, November). Ew-tune: A framework for privately fine-tuning large language models with differential privacy. In *2022 IEEE International Conference on Data Mining Workshops (ICDMW)* (pp. 560-566). IEEE.

Belenguer, L. (2022). AI bias: Exploring discriminatory algorithmic decision-making models and the application of possible machine-centric solutions adapted from the pharmaceutical industry. *AI and Ethics, 2*, 771–787. DOI: 10.1007/s43681-022-00138-8 PMID: 35194591

Bench-Capon, T., Araszkiewicz, M., Ashley, K., Atkinson, K., Bex, F., Borges, F., Bourcier, D., Bourgine, P., Conrad, J. G., Francesconi, E., Gordon, T. F., Governator, G., Leidner, J. L., Lewis, D. D., Loui, R. P., McCarty, L. T., Prakken, H., Schilder, F., Schweighofer, E., & Walton, D. N. (2012). A history of ai and law in 50 papers: 25 Years of the international conference on ai and law. *Artificial Intelligence and Law, 203*, 215–319.

Bennett Moses, L., & Chan, J. (2016). Algorithmic prediction in policing: Assumptions, evaluation, and accountability. *Policing and Society, 28*(7), 806–822. DOI: 10.1080/10439463.2016.1253695

Benston, G. J., & Hartgraves, A. L. (2002). *Enron What happened and what we can learn from it. Journal of Accounting and Public Policy, 21, 105-127. - References - Scientific Research Publishing*. https://www.scirp.org/reference/referencespapers?referenceid=1922733

Bhagwat, S., Panchangam, S., Sawant, A., Sharma, P., & Nayak, U. (2025, June). NyAI Saathi-Legal Research Tool leveraging GenAI (RAG). In 2025 5th International Conference on Intelligent Technologies (CONIT) (pp. 1-10). IEEE.

Bharati, R. K. (2024). The right to privacy in the age of artificial intelligence: Challenges and legal frameworks. *Indian Journal of Law and Technology, 16*(1), 45–67.

Bhasin, M. L. (2013). Corporate Accounting Fraud: A Case study of Satyam Computers Limited. *Open Journal of Accounting, 02*(02), 26–38. DOI: 10.4236/ojacct.2013.22006

Bhattacharya, S., Ghosh, S., & Banerjee, A. (2020). Cross-border e-commerce: Opportunities and challenges for Indian entrepreneurs. *Journal of Enterprising Communities: People and Places in the Global Economy*, *14*(1), 60–75. DOI: 10.1108/JEC-05-2019-0055

Bin Rashid, A., & Karim Kausik, M. A. (2024). AI revolutionizing industries worldwide: A comprehensive overview of its diverse applications. *Hybrid Advances*, *7*, 100277. DOI: 10.1016/j.hybadv.2024.100277

Binns, R. (2022). Human Judgment in algorithmic loops: Individual justice and automated decision-making. *Regulation & Governance*, *16*(1), 197–211.

Biresaw, S. M., & Saste, A. U. (2022). The impacts of artificial intelligence on research in the legal profession. *International Journal of Law and Society*, *5*(1), 53–65. DOI: 10.11648/j.ijls.20220501.17

Blind, K., & Münch, F. (2024). The interplay between innovation, standards and regulation in a globalising economy. *Journal of Cleaner Production*, *445*(15), 1–11. DOI: 10.1016/j.jclepro.2024.141202

Boiko, D. A., Mac Knight, R., & Gomes, G. (2023). *Emergent autonomous scientific research capabilities of large language models*. arXiv preprint arXiv: 2304.05332.

Bologna, G. J., & Lindquist, R. J. (1995). *Fraud auditing and forensic accounting: New tools and techniques* (2nd ed.). John Wiley & Sons.

Bommarito, M. J., Katz, D. M., & Casey, A. (2022). Evaluating the Performance of Legal AI Systems. *Artificial Intelligence and Law*, *30*(3), 343–372.

Bommasani, R., Hudson, D. A., Adeli, E., Altman, R., Arora, S., von Arx, S., ... (2021). On the opportunities and risks of foundation models. arXiv preprint arXiv:2108.07258.

Borgesano, F., De Maio, A., Laghi, P., & Musmanno, R. (2025). Artificial intelligence and justice: A systematic literature review and future research perspectives on Justice 5.0. *European Journal of Innovation Management*, *28*(11), 349–385. https://doi.org/https://doi.org/10.1108/EJIM-01-2025-0117

Bourreau, M., & de Streel, A. (2020). *Digital conglomerates and EU competition policy*. Centre on Regulation in Europe (CERRE). https://cerre.eu/news/digital-conglomerates-and-eu-competition-policy/

Brian, C. S. (2019). *The Promise of Artificial Intelligence: Reckoning and Judgment*. MIT Press., DOI: 10.7551/mitpress/12385.001.0001

Bribery Act. 2010, c. 23. *United Kingdom* (2010). http://legislation.gov.uk/ukpga/2010/23/contents

Brink, D. O. (2021). *Fair Opportunity and Responsibility*. Oxford University Press., DOI: 10.1093/oso/9780198859468.001.0001

Brooks, C., Gherhes, C., & Vorley, T. (2020). Artificial intelligence in the legal sector: Pressures and challenges of transformation. *Cambridge Journal of Regions, Economy and Society*, *13*(1), 135–152.

Brown, T., Mann, B., Ryder, N., Subbiah, M., Kaplan, J. D., Dhariwal, P., & Amodei, D. (2020). Language models are few-shot learners. *Advances in Neural Information Processing Systems*, *33*, 1877–1901.

Brożek, B., Furman, M., & Jakubiec, M.. (2024). The black box problem revisited: Real and imaginary challenges for automated legal decision making. *Artificial Intelligence and Law*, *32*, 427–440. DOI: 10.1007/s10506-023-09356-9

Brynjolfsson, E., & McAfee, A. (2014). *The second machine age: Work, progress, and prosperity in a time of brilliant technologies*. W. W. Norton & Company.

Burton, J. (2023). Algorithmic extremism? The securitization of artificial intelligence (AI) and its impact on radicalism, polarization, and political violence. *Technology in Society*, *75*, 102262. DOI: 10.1016/j.techsoc.2023.102262

Busemeyer, M., Kemmerling, A., van Kersbergen, K., Marx, P., Wren, A., Eichhorst, W., Glassmann, U., Iversen, T., Rehm, P., Kurer, T., Hausermann, S., Gingrich, J., Kua, A., Chrisp, J., Martinelli, L., Guarascio, D., Sacchi, S., Zepeda, S., & Picot, G. (2022). *Digitalization and The Welfare State*. Oxford University Press., DOI: 10.1093/oso/9780192848369.001.0001

C., A. (2025, March 21). Artificial intelligence and intellectual properties: Legal and ethical considerations. ResearchGate. https://www.researchgate.net/publication/376885311_Artificial_Intelligence_and_Intellectual_Properties_Legal_and_Ethical_Considerations

Cadila Health Care Ltd. v. Cadila Pharmaceuticals Ltd., (2001) 5 SCC 73 (India).

Cajueiro, D. O., & Celestino, V. R. R. (2026). A comprehensive review of Artificial Intelligence regulation: Weighing ethical principles and innovation. *Journal of Economy and Technology*, *4*, 77–91. https://doi.org/https://doi.org/10.1016/j.ject.2025.07.001

Calvano, E., Calzolari, G., Denicolò, V., & Pastorello, S. (2020). Artificial intelligence, algorithmic pricing, and collusion. *The American Economic Review, 110*(10), 3267–3297. DOI: 10.1257/aer.20190623

Cardellino, C., Teruel, M., Alemany, L. A., & Villata, S. (2017). A Low-Cost, High-Coverage Legal Named Entity Recognizer, Classifier and Linker. In *Proceedings of the 16th International Conference on Artificial Intelligence and Law* (pp. 9–18). https://doi.org/DOI: 10.1145/3086512.3086514

Carlini, N., Tramer, F., Wallace, E., Jagielski, M., Herbert-Voss, A., Lee, K., & Song, D. (2021). Extracting training data from large language models. *Proceedings of the 30th USENIX Security Symposium*, 2633–2650.

Carnat, I. (2024). Addressing the risks of generative AI for the judiciary: The accountability framework(s) under the EU AI Act. *Computer Law & Security Review, 55*, 106067. https://doi.org/https://doi.org/10.1016/j.clsr.2024.106067

Castell, S. (2018). The Future Decisions of RoboJudge HHJ Arthur Ian Blockchain: Dread, Delight or Derision? *Computer Law \& Security Review, 34*(4), 739–753. https://doi.org/DOI: 10.1016/j.clsr.2018.05.011

Chalkidis, I., Fergadiotis, M., Malakasiotis, P., Aletras, N., & Androutsopoulos, I. (2020). LEGAL-BERT: The muppets straight out of law school. In Findings of the Association for Computational Linguistics: EMNLP 2020 (pp. 2898-2904).

Chalkidis, I., Fergadiotis, M., Malakasiotis, P., Aletras, N., & Androutsopoulos, I. (2020). LEGAL-BERT: The Muppets Straight Out of Law School. In *Findings of the Association for Computational Linguistics: EMNLP 2020* (pp. 2898–2904). Association for Computational Linguistics. https://doi.org/DOI: 10.18653/v1/2020.findings-emnlp.261

Chambers Global Practice Guides. (2025). Technology, media, and telecommunications in India. Retrieved from https://chambers.com

Chan, C. S., Kong, H., & Guanqing, L. (2022, May). A comparative study of faithfulness metrics for model interpretability methods. In *Proceedings of the 60th annual meeting of the association for computational linguistics* (volume 1: Long papers) (pp. 5029-5038).

Chatterjee, S., & S., N. S. (2022). Artificial intelligence and human rights: A comprehensive study from Indian legal and policy perspective. *International Journal of Law and Management, 64*(1), 110–134. DOI: 10.1108/IJLMA-02-2021-0049

Chauhan, K. D. S. (2024). *Darker patterns? AI-generated persuasion and the regulatory void in Indian law.* Journal of Development Policy and Practice.

Chawla, Y. (2018). Consumer rights and their correlates under the Indian legal framework. *Asian Journal of Legal Studies*, *6*(1), 1–10. DOI: 10.21577/ajls.2018.001

Chen, B., Zeng, W., & Lin, Y. (2014). Applications of artificial intelligence technologies in credit scoring: A survey of literature. In *2014 10th International Conference on Natural Computation (ICNC)* (pp. 658-664). IEEE. https://doi.org/DOI: 10.1109/ICNC.2014.6975914

Chen, S. (2021). *Chinese scientists develop AI 'prosecutor' that can press its own charges*. https://www.scmp.com/news/china/science/article/3160997/chinese-scientists-develop-ai-prosecutor-can-press-its-own

Chen, J. (2025). BiLSTM-enhanced legal text extraction model using fuzzy logic and metaphor recognition. *PeerJ. Computer Science*, *11*. Advance online publication. DOI: 10.7717/peerj-cs.2697 PMID: 40062303

Chen, Z. (2023). Ethics and discrimination in artificial intelligence-enabled recruitment practices. *Humanities & Social Sciences Communications*, *10*, 567. DOI: 10.1057/s41599-023-02079-x

Chernyavskiy, A., Ilvovsky, D., & Nakov, P. (2021). Transformers: "the end of history" for natural language processing? In Machine Learning and Knowledge Discovery in Databases. *Research Track: European Conference, ECML PKDD 2021*, Bilbao, Spain, September 13–17, 2021 [Springer International Publishing.]. *Proceedings*, *21*(Part III), 677–693.

Chia, H., Zhang, G. Z., Russo-Batterham, D., Manandhar, K., Quang, U. T., Wang, Z., & Paterson, J. M. (2024). L.E.G.A.L.: A RAG-Based System for Legal Document Navigation. *Proceedings of the ALTA Conference*.

Chien, S., & Lee, M. (2020). Legal technology and artificial intelligence: Implications for the legal profession. *The Journal of Legal Studies*, *45*(3), 227–245. DOI: 10.2139/ssrn.3353292

Chimonaki, C., Papadakis, S., & Lemonakis, C. (2023). Perspectives in fraud theories – A systematic review approach. *F1000 Research*, *12*, 933. DOI: 10.12688/f1000research.131896.1

Chiriatti, M., Ganapini, M., & Panai, E.. (2024). The case for human–AI interaction as system 0 thinking. *Nature Human Behaviour*, *8*, 1829–1830. DOI: 10.1038/s41562-024-01995-5 PMID: 39438682

Christian, N., Basri, Y. Z., & Arafah, W. (n.d.). Analysis of Fraud Triangle, Fraud Diamond and Fraud Pentagon Theory to detecting Corporate Fraud in Indonesia. In *The International Journal of Business Management and Technology* (pp. 73–74). The International Journal of Business Management and Technology. [Journal-article], https://www.theijbmt.com/archive/0928/608343945.pdf

Chung, H. W., Hou, L., Longpre, S., Zoph, B., Tay, Y., Fedus, W., & Wei, J. (2024). Scaling instruction-finetuned language models. *Journal of Machine Learning Research, 25*(70), 1–53.

Chun, Y., & Rha, J. (2025). *Influence of dark patterns on consumer responses: A use of a qualitative approach.* Social Science Research Network.

Coffee, J. C. (2006). *Gatekeepers: The professions and corporate governance.* Oxford University Press., DOI: 10.1093/oso/9780199288090.001.0001

Cohen, D. (1972). Consumer deception and advertising regulation. *Journal of Marketing, 36*(2), 22–28.

Company, M. (2025, March 21). The state of AI in 2022—and a half decade in review. McKinsey & Company. https://www.mckinsey.com/~/media/mckinsey/business%20functions/quantumblack/our%20insights/the%20state%20of%20ai%20in%202022%20and%20a%20half%20decade%20in%20review/the-state-of-ai-in-2022-and-a-half-decade-in-review.pdf

Competition Act. (2002).

Competition and Markets Authority (CMA). (2021). *Algorithms: How they can reduce competition and harm consumers.* UK Government. https://www.gov.uk/government/publications/algorithms-how-they-can-reduce-competition-and-harm-consumers

Competition and Markets Authority (UK). (2022). *Online choice architecture and consumer harm.* CMA.

Competition Commission of India. (2022). *Market study on e-commerce in India.* CCI.

Competition Commission of India. (2025). *Market study on artificial intelligence and competition.* Competition Commission of India. https://www.cci.gov.in/images/marketstudie/en/market-study-on-artificial-intelligence-and-competition1759752172.pdf

Consumer Protection Act, 2019 (India).

Council of Europe. (2024). *Framework convention on artificial intelligence, human rights, democracy and the rule of law.* Council of Europe Publishing.

Cowls, J., King, T., Taddeo, M., & Floridi, L. (2019). Designing AI for social good: Seven essential factors. *Available at SSRN* 3388669.

Crawford, K. (2021). *The Atlas of AI: Power, politics, and the planetary costs of artificial intelligence.* Yale University Press., DOI: 10.2307/j.ctv1ghv45t

Cressey, D. R. (1953). *Other people's money: A study in the social psychology of embezzlement.* Free Press.

Creswell, J. W. (2014). *Research design: Qualitative, Quantitative, and Mixed Methods Approaches* (4th ed.). SAGE.

Crumbley, D. L., Heitger, L. E., & Smith, G. S. (2015). *Forensic and investigative accounting* (7th ed.). CCH., https://www.scribd.com/document/484261659/Forensic-and-Investigative-Accounting-pdf

Dakalbab, F., Abu Talib, M., Abu Waraga, O., Bou Nassif, A., Abbas, S., & Nasir, Q. (2022). Artificial intelligence & crime prediction: A systematic literature review. *Social Sciences & Humanities Open*, *6*(1), 100342. DOI: 10.1016/j.ssaho.2022.100342

Dalwai, T. A. R., Madbouly, A., & Mohammadi, S. S. (2022). An investigation of artificial intelligence application in auditing. In *Artificial Intelligence and COVID Effect on Accounting* (pp. 101–114). Springer Nature., DOI: 10.1007/978-981-19-1234-5_6

Damani, S., & Engler, A. (2024). Data privacy and AI in legal practice: Emerging concerns. *International Journal of Legal Technology*, *8*(2), 101–120.

Das, A. K., Gupta, N., Mahmood, T., Das, R., Das, S., & Granados, C. (2025j). *Assessment of groundwater quality in Agartala, Tripura, Northeast India using an effective fuzzy multicriteria decision-making model.* In J. Das, B. Pradhan, R. Mitra, P. Chouhan, C. Lee, & U. Chatterjee (Eds.), *Developments in Environmental Science* (Vol. 19, pp. 311–333). Elsevier. https://doi.org/DOI: 10.1016/B978-0-443-33787-1.00023-X

Das, A. K. (2016). On partially included intuitionistic fuzzy rough relations. *Afrika Matematika*, *27*, 993–1001. DOI: 10.1007/s13370-016-0395-2

Das, A. K. (2018). Weighted fuzzy soft multiset and decision-making. *International Journal of Machine Learning and Cybernetics*, *9*, 787–794. DOI: 10.1007/s13042-016-0607-y

Das, A. K., Das, R., Das, S., Debnath, B. K., Granados, C., Shil, B., & Das, R. (2025c). A comprehensive study of neutrosophic SuperHyper BCI-semigroups and their algebraic significance. *Transactions on Fuzzy Sets and Systems*, *4*(2), 80–101. DOI: 10.71602/tfss.2025.1198050

Das, A. K., Das, R., Datta, R., & Granados, C. (2025e). An Innovative Approach to Group Decision-Making Based on Weighted Hypersoft Expert System. In Smarandache, F., Jdid, M., & Leyva-Vazquez, M. (Eds.), *Neutrosophic and Plithogenic Inventory Models for Applied Mathematics* (pp. 483–518). IGI Global Scientific Publishing., DOI: 10.4018/979-8-3693-3204-7.ch019

Das, A. K., & Granados, C. (2021). An advanced approach to fuzzy soft group decision-making using weighted average ratings. *SN Computer Science*, *2*, 471. DOI: 10.1007/s42979-021-00873-5

Das, A. K., & Granados, C. (2022a). A new fuzzy parameterized intuitionistic fuzzy soft multiset theory and group decision-making. *Journal of Current Science and Technology*, *12*(3), 547–567. DOI: 10.14456/jcst.2022.42

Das, A. K., & Granados, C. (2022b). FP-intuitionistic multi fuzzy N-soft set and its induced FP-Hesitant N soft set in decision-making. *Decision Making: Applications in Management and Engineering*, *5*(1), 67–89. DOI: 10.31181/dmame181221045d

Das, A. K., & Granados, C. (2023a). IFP-intuitionistic multi fuzzy N-soft set and its induced IFP-hesitant N-soft set in decision-making. *Journal of Ambient Intelligence and Humanized Computing*, *14*, 10143–10152. DOI: 10.1007/s12652-021-03677-w

Das, A. K., & Granados, C. (2023b). Preference intuitionistic fuzzy rough relation and its theoretical approach. *Journal of the Indian Mathematical Society*, *90*(3-4), 199–212.

Das, A. K., Granados, C., & Bhattacharya, J. (2022). Some new operations on fuzzy soft sets and their applications in decision-making. *Songklanakarin Journal of Science and Technology*, *44*(2), 440–449. DOI: 10.14456/sjst-psu.2022.61

Das, A. K., Gupta, N., Das, R., Das, S., Das, R., Granados, C., & Debnath, B. K. (2026a). Fuzzy Logic-Driven Strategies for Diversity and Inclusion in Multicultural Marketing. In Tarnanidis, T., Sousa, B., Vlachopoulou, M., Papachristou, E., & Kittu Manda, V. (Eds.), *Diversity and Inclusion-Driven Marketing for Multicultural Marketplaces* (pp. 189–236). IGI Global Scientific Publishing., DOI: 10.4018/979-8-3373-2111-0.ch009

Das, A. K., Gupta, N., Das, R., Granados, C., & Das, S. (2026c). Neutrosophic Sets for Decision-Making in Natural Disasters and Environmental Recovery. In Ezaier, Y., Gaamouche, R., & Lahby, M. (Eds.), *Computational Intelligence and Optimization Methods for Sustainable Water Management* (pp. 119–162). IGI Global Scientific Publishing., DOI: 10.4018/979-8-3373-2700-6.ch004

Das, A. K., Gupta, N., Fujita, T., Das, S., Granados, C., Debnath, B. K., & Das, R. (2026b). Advanced Co-Branding Strategies for Smart Luxury Products: A Multi-Criteria Decision-Making Approach Using Neutrosophic Sets. In Tarnanidis, T., Sousa, B., Vlachopoulou, M., Papachristou, E., & Kittu Manda, V. (Eds.), *Co-Branding Strategies for Smart Luxury Products* (pp. 203–258). IGI Global Scientific Publishing., DOI: 10.4018/979-8-3373-3010-5.ch006

Das, A. K., Gupta, N., & Granados, C. (2023). Weighted hesitant bipolar-valued fuzzy soft set in decision-making. *Songklanakarin Journal of Science and Technology*, *45*(6), 681–690. https://sjst.psu.ac.th/journal/45-6/10.pdf

Das, A. K., Gupta, N., Granados, C., Das, R., & Das, S. (2024b). Neutrosophic Approach to Water Quality Assessment: A Case Study of Gomati River, the Largest River in Tripura, India. *Neutrosophic Systems with Applications*, *22*, 1–12. DOI: 10.61356/j.nswa.2024.22386

Das, A. K., Gupta, N., Mahmood, T., Tripathy, B. C., Das, R., & Das, S. (2024a). Assessing anthropogenic influences on the water quality of Gomati River using an innovative weighted fuzzy soft set based water pollution rating system. *Discover Water*, *4*, 73. DOI: 10.1007/s43832-024-00136-3

Das, A. K., Gupta, N., Mahmood, T., Tripathy, B. C., Das, R., & Das, S. (2025a). An efficient water quality evaluation model using weighted hesitant fuzzy soft sets for water pollution rating. In Kumar, A., Kumar, P., Rathee, S., & Kumar, B. (Eds.), *Mechatronics: Concepts, Tools, Applications, and New Trends* (1st ed., p. 17). CRC Press., DOI: 10.1201/9781003494478-10

Das, A. K., Gupta, N., Mahmood, T., Tripathy, B. C., Das, R., & Das, S. (2025b). An innovative fuzzy multi-criteria decision making model for analyzing anthropogenic influences on urban river water quality. *Iran Journal of Computer Science*, *8*, 103–124. DOI: 10.1007/s42044-024-00211-x

Das, A. K., Gupta, N., Mahmood, T., Tripathy, B. C., Das, R., & Das, S. (2025g). Anthropogenic Impacts on Urban River Water Quality for Rating Water Pollution Using an Effective Fuzzy Soft Multi Criteria Group Decision Making Model. *Iraqi Journal of Science*, *66*(9), 3921–3937. DOI: 10.24996/ijs.2025.66.9.32

Das, A. K., Gupta, N., Mahmood, T., Tripathy, B. C., Das, R., & Das, S. (2025h). Analyzing seasonal changes and anthropogenic impacts on urban river water quality using a weighted fuzzy soft set-based multi-criteria decision-making model: A case study of the Manu River, India. *Arabian Journal of Geosciences*, *18*, 228. DOI: 10.1007/s12517-025-12323-0

Das, A. K., Mahmood, T., Das, R., & Das, S. (2025d). Optimizing Inventory Levels in Retail: Fuzzy Logic-Based Decision Support Systems for Adaptive Inventory Management. In Jana, S., Basu Mallik, B., Sarkar, A., & Jana, C. (Eds.), *Applications of Fuzzy Logic in Decision Making and Management Science. Information Systems Engineering and Management* (Vol. 29). Springer., DOI: 10.1007/978-3-031-77719-6_8

Das, A. K., Patra, S., & Granados, C. (2025f). An innovative approach to hesitant bipolar fuzzy soft sets in multi-criteria group decision-making. Adv. in Comp. *Int.*, *5*, 4. DOI: 10.1007/s43674-025-00082-0

Das, S., Barve, A., Sahu, N., & Muduli, K. (2023). Enabling artificial intelligence for sustainable food grain supply chains: An agri 5.0 and circular economy perspective. *Operations Management Research*, *16*, 2104–2124. DOI: 10.1007/s12063-023-00390-z

David, R. C. (2023, February 15). *What are worldwide AML regulations for cryptocurrency?* Pideeco. https://pideeco.be/articles/worldwide-aml-regulations-virtual-assets/#:~:text=However%2C%20the%20rules%20for%20stablecoins,asset%20services%20and%20related%20activities

Day, G., Stemler, A., & Stemler, A. (2019). *Are dark patterns anticompetitive?* Social Science Research Network. DOI: 10.2139/ssrn.3468321

de Fine Licht, K. (2025). Resolving value conflicts in public AI governance: A procedural justice framework. *Government Information Quarterly*, *42*(2), 102033. https://doi.org/https://doi.org/10.1016/j.giq.2025.102033

Deepa, G., & Vijayaram, K. (2014–2015). Analyses of performance of consumer dispute redressal agencies in Tamil Nadu. *Journal of Economic and Political Development*, *2*(2), 61–68. https://www.researchgate.net/publication/331738790_Analyses_of_Performance_of_Consumer_Dispute_Redressal_Agencies_in_Tamil_Nadu

Deepa, G., & Vijayaram, K. (2015). Performance evaluation of consumer dispute redressal agencies in Tamil Nadu. *International Journal of Applied Research*, *1*(10), 692–698.

Deligoz, K. (2025). *Consumer manipulation with artificial intelligence: Dark patterns and hidden techniques.* DOI: 10.58830/ozgur.pub710.c3029

Devarajan, M., Khan, M., Sandeep, K., Hamza, L., Soujanya, K., & Munirathinam, S. (2025). Smart Manufacturing Assessment on Cybersecurity Risks using Bayesian and Hybrid Fuzzy Logic Networks. *2025 International Conference on Computational Innovations and Engineering Sustainability (ICCIES)*, 1-6. https://doi.org/ DOI: 10.1109/iccies63851.2025.11032583

Devianto, Y., & Dwiasnati, S. (2020). Kerangka kerja sistem kecerdasan buatan dalam meningkatkan kompetensi sumber daya manusia Indonesia. *Jurnal Telekomunikasi dan Komputer*, 10(1), 19-24. https://doi.org/DOI: 10.22441/incomtech.v10i1.7460

Devlin, J., Chang, M. W., Lee, K., & Toutanova, K. (2018). *Bert: Pre-training of deep bidirectional transformers for language understanding*. arXiv preprint arXiv: 1810.04805.

Devlin, J., Chang, M. W., Lee, K., & Toutanova, K. (2019). BERT: Pre-training of deep bidirectional transformers for language understanding. In *Proceedings of NAACL-HLT 2019* (pp. 4171-4186).

Dias, S. A. de J., & Sátiro, R. M. (2024). Artificial intelligence in the judiciary: A critical view. *Futures, 164*, 103493. https://doi.org/https://doi.org/10.1016/j.futures .2024.103493

Dionisio, J. D. N., Burns, W. G., III, Gilbert, R., & Loyola Marymount University. (2013). 3D Virtual Worlds and the Metaverse: current status and future possibilities. *Computer Science Faculty Works*. https://digitalcommons.lmu.edu/cs_fac/8

Disemadi, H. S. (2021). Urgensi regulasi khusus dan pemanfaatan artificial intelligence dalam mewujudkan perlindungan data pribadi di Indonesia. *Jurnal Wawasan Yuridika*, *5*(2), 177–199. DOI: 10.25072/jwy.v5i2.460

Divya, S., Indumathi, V., Ishwarya, S., Priyasankari, M., & Devi, S. K. (2018). A self-diagnosis medical chatbot using artificial intelligence. *J. Web Develop. Web Designing*, *3*(1), 1–7.

Dixit, S., Tripathi, T., & Singh, R. (2025). *Incorporating Artificial Intelligence into India's Judicial and Law Enforcement Systems*. International Journal For Multidisciplinary Research., DOI: 10.36948/ijfmr.2025.v07i02.41822

Doly, D. (2023). Pemanfaatan *artificial intelligence* dalam penegakan hukum di Indonesia. Info Singkat: Kajian Singkat terhadap Isu Aktual dan Strategis, 15(19), 1-5. https://berkas.dpr.go.id/pusaka/files/info_singkat/Info%20Singkat-XV-19-I -P3DI-Oktober-2023-208.pdf

Dong, M., & Bocian, K. (2024). Responsibility gaps and self-interest bias: People attribute moral responsibility to AI for their own but not others' transgressions. *Journal of Experimental Social Psychology, 111*, 104584. DOI: 10.1016/j.jesp.2023.104584

Dong, Y. (2021). Trademark confusion in digital marketplaces. *The Journal of World Intellectual Property*, *24*(4), 367–389.

Drishti, I. A. S. (2025). *Artificial intelligence governance and ethics: Policy overview*. Drishti Publications.

Drucker, P. F. (1954). *The practice of management*. Harper & Row.

Duan, Y., Edwards, J. S., & Dwivedi, Y. K. (2019). Artificial intelligence for decision making in the era of Big Data – Evolution, challenges, and research agenda. *International Journal of Information Management*, *48*, 63–71. DOI: 10.1016/j.ijinfomgt.2019.01.021

Durand, T., & Hattingh, M. (2020). *Data mining and artificial intelligence techniques used to extract big data patterns*. In *Proceedings of the 2020 2nd International Multidisciplinary Information Technology and Engineering Conference (IMITEC)* (pp. 1-8). IEEE. https://doi.org/DOI: 10.1109/IMITEC50163.2020.9334069

Dwiputro, W. (2020). Disrupsi dan Masa Depan Profesi Hukum. *Jurnal Mimbar Hukum*, *32*(1), 192–29. DOI: 10.22146/jmh.42928

Dzienkowski, J. S. (2013). The future of big law: Alternative legal service providers to corporate clients. *Fordham Law Review*, *82*, 2995–3040.

Dzuranin, A. C., & Malaescu, I. (2015). The current state and future direction of data analytics in accounting and auditing. *Journal of Information Systems*, *30*(3), 131–148. https://papers.ssrn.com/sol3/papers.cfm?abstract_id=2663167

Egede, L. E., Walker, R. J., & Williams, J. S. (2024). Addressing structural inequalities, structural racism, and social determinants of health: A vision for the future. *Journal of General Internal Medicine*, *39*, 487–491. DOI: 10.1007/s11606-023-08426-7 PMID: 37740168

Es, S., James, J., Anke, L. E., & Schockaert, S. (2024, March). Ragas: Automated evaluation of retrieval augmented generation. In Proceedings of the 18th conference of the european chapter of the association for computational linguistics: system demonstrations (pp. 150-158).

European Commission. (2017). *Consumer trust in public institutions and markets*. Publications Office of the European Union.

European Commission. (2020). *Antitrust proceedings in the e-commerce and platform economy*. European Commission.

European Commission. (2021). Proposal for a regulation of the European Parliament and of the Council laying down harmonized rules on artificial intelligence (Artificial Intelligence Act). https://ec.europa.eu/info/sites/info/files/commission-proposal-regulation-artificial-intelligence-2021_en.pdf

European Commission. (2022). *The Digital Markets Act (DMA)*. Publications Office of the European Union. https://digital-markets-act.ec.europa.eu/about-dma_en#:~:text=Following%20the%20initial%20proposal%20of,applicable%20on%202%20May%202023

European Commission. (2023). *Digital Markets Act and Artificial Intelligence Act: Ensuring fair and transparent digital markets*. https://digital-strategy.ec.europa.eu

European Commission. (2024). *Regulation (EU) 2024/1689 laying down harmonised rules on artificial intelligence (Artificial Intelligence Act)*. Official Journal of the European Union.

European Commission. (2024). *Regulation (EU) 2024/1689 Laying Down Harmonised Rules on Artificial Intelligence*. Artificial Intelligence Act.

European Data Protection Board. (2023). *Decision on Meta Platforms Ireland Limited (No. 01/2023)*. Brussels.

European Data Protection Supervisor. (2014). *Privacy and competitiveness in the age of big data: The interplay between data protection, competition law and consumer protection in the digital economy* (Preliminary opinion). https://secure.edps.europa.eu/EDPSWEB/webdav/site/mySite/shared/Documents/Consultation/Opinions/2014/14-03-26_competitition_law_big_data_EN.pdf

European Union. (2022). *Digital Markets Act (Regulation (EU) 2022/1925). Official Journal of the European Union*. https://eur-lex.europa.eu/eli/reg/2022/1925/oj

Ezrachi, A., & Stucke, M. E. (2016). *Virtual competition: The promise and perils of the algorithm-driven economy*. Harvard University Press.

Faiyazuddin, M., Rahman, S. J. Q., Anand, G., Siddiqui, R. K., Mehta, R., Khatib, M. N., Gaidhane, S., Zahiruddin, Q. S., Hussain, A., & Sah, R. (2025). The impact of artificial intelligence on healthcare: A comprehensive review of advancements in diagnostics, treatment, and operational efficiency. *Health Science Reports*, *8*(1), e70312. DOI: 10.1002/hsr2.70312 PMID: 39763580

FATF. (2019). *Guidance for a risk-based approach to virtual assets and virtual asset service providers*. Financial Action Task Force. https://www.fatf-gafi.org/en/publications/Fatfrecommendations/Guidance-rba-virtual-assets.html

FATF. (2021). *Updated guidance for a risk-based approach to virtual assets and virtual asset service providers*. Financial Action Task Force. https://www.fatf-gafi.org/en/publications/Fatfrecommendations/Guidance-rba-virtual-assets-2021.html

FATF. (2022). *Targeted update on implementation of the FATF standards on virtual assets and virtual asset service providers*. Financial Action Task Force. https://www.fatf-gafi.org/en/publications/Fatfrecommendations/Targeted-update-virtual-assets-vasps.html

Federal Trade Commission (FTC). (2020). *FTC charges ABC Mouse with illegal subscription practices*. https://www.ftc.gov

Federal Trade Commission (FTC). (2023). *FTC takes action against Epic Games for dark patterns and privacy violations*. https://www.ftc.gov

Federal Trade Commission. (2021). *Aiming for truth, fairness, and equity in your company's use of AI*. U.S. Federal Trade Commission. https://www.ftc.gov/system/files/ftc_gov/pdf/p241200_ftc_comment_to_copyright_office.pdf

Federal Trade Commission. (2022, September). Bringing dark patterns to light [Staff report]. https://www.ftc.gov/reports/bringing-dark-patterns-light

Fernández, D., Emilia, L., Ignacio, G., & Mazzini, G. (2025). An interdisciplinary account of the terminological choices by EU policymakers ahead of the final agreement on the AI Act : AI system, general purpose AI system, foundation model, and generative AI. *Artificial Intelligence and Law*, *33*(4), 875–888. DOI: 10.1007/s10506-024-09412-y

Filipova, I. A. (2024). Legal regulation of artificial intelligence: Experience of China. *Journal of Digital Technologies and Law*, *2*(1), 46–73. DOI: 10.21202/jdtl.2024.4

Fischman-Afori, O. (2025). Due process by design: Enhancing fairness and trust in AI decision-making. *Social Sciences & Humanities Open*, *12*, 102178. https://doi.org/https://doi.org/10.1016/j.ssaho.2025.102178

Flick, U. (2018). Doing Qualitative Data Collection – Charting the Routes. In *The SAGE Handbook of Qualitative Data Collection*. (pp. 3–16). https://doi.org/DOI: 10.4135/9781526416070.n1

Floridi, L., Cowls, J., Beltrametti, M., Chatila, R., Chazerand, P., Dignum, V., & Vayena, E. (2018). AI4People-An ethical framework for a good AI society: Opportunities, risks, principles, and recommendations. *Minds and Machines*, *28*, 689–707. DOI: 10.1007/s11023-018-9482-5

Forbes Councils. (n.d.). *Forbes councils*. https://councils.forbes.com/

Fourati, H., Maaloul, R., & Chaari, L. (2021). A survey of 5G network systems: Challenges and machine learning approaches. *International Journal of Machine Learning and Cybernetics*, *12*(2), 385–431. DOI: 10.1007/s13042-020-01178-4

Fournier-Tombs, E. (2021). Towards a United Nations internal regulation for artificial intelligence. *Big Data & Society*, *8*(2). Advance online publication. DOI: 10.1177/20539517211039493

G20/OECD Principles of Corporate Governance. 2015. (2015). In *OECD Publishing eBooks*. https://doi.org/DOI: 10.1787/9789264236882-en

Gal, M., & Aviv, O. (2020). The competitive effects of the GDPR. *Journal of Competition Law and Economics*. https://ssrn.com/abstract=3548444

Gal, M. S., & Elkin-Koren, N. (2017). Algorithmic consumers. *Harvard Journal of Law & Technology*, *30*(2), 309–352.

Gao, Y., Xiong, Y., Gao, X., Jia, K., Pan, J., Bi, Y., . . . Wang, H. (2023). Retrieval-augmented generation for large language models: A survey. arXiv preprint arXiv:2312.10997, 2(1), 32.

Garcia, A. C. B., Garcia, M. G. P., & Rigobon, R. (2024). Algorithmic discrimination in the credit domain: What do we know about it? *AI & Society*, *39*, 2059–2098. DOI: 10.1007/s00146-023-01676-3

Garingan, D., & Pickard, A. J. (2021). Artificial Intelligence in Legal Practice: Exploring Theoretical Frameworks for Algorithmic Literacy in the Legal Information Profession. *Legal Information Management*, *21*(2), 97–117. DOI: 10.1017/S1472669621000190

Garner, R. (1985). Normative beliefs and deceptive advertising. *The Journal of Consumer Research*, *12*(1), 39–46.

Gellers, J. C. (2020). *Rights for robots: Artificial intelligence, animal, and environmental law* (1st ed.). Routledge., DOI: 10.4324/9780429288159

Gengler, E. J. (2024). Sexism, racism, and classism: Social biases in text-to-image generative AI in the context of power, success, and beauty. *Wirtschaftsinformatik 2024 Proceedings*, (48). Retrieved from https://aisel.aisnet.org/wi2024/48

Gervais, D. J. (2025, March 21). The machine as author. Vanderbilt Law Scholarship. https://scholarship.law.vanderbilt.edu/faculty-publications/1164/

Gervais, D. J. (2020a, January 4). The machine as author. *SSRN*. https://papers.ssrn.com/sol3/papers.cfm?abstract_id=3359524

Ghaiumy Anaraky, R., Lowens, B., Li, Y., Byrne, K. A., Risius, M., Page, X., Wisniewski, P., Soleimani, M., Soltani, M., & Knijnenburg, B. P. (2023). *Older and younger adults are influenced differently by dark pattern designs*. arXiv.Org, abs/2310.03830. /arxiv.2310.03830DOI: 10.48550

Ghallab, M. (2019). Responsible AI: Requirements and challenges. *AI Perspectives*, *1*, 3. DOI: 10.1186/s42467-019-0003-z

Ghani, I., & Malik, M. I. (2020). The impact of artificial intelligence on the legal profession: A review. *International Journal of Legal Information*, *48*(2), 121–138. DOI: 10.1017/jli.2020.19

Ghorayeb, A., Comber, R., & Gooberman-Hill, R. (2021). Older adults' perspectives of smart home technology: Are we developing the technology that older people want? *International Journal of Human-Computer Studies*, *147*, 102571. DOI: 10.1016/j.ijhcs.2020.102571

Giovis, R., & Rozsa, E. (2024). *Transforming customer service: How generative AI is changing the game*. IBM Artificial Intelligence.

Global Legal Insights. (2025). Artificial intelligence regulations 2025: India. Retrieved from https://www.globallegalinsights.com/practice-areas/artificial-intelligence-laws-and-regulations/india

Goel, A. (2019). Consumer protection laws in India: Current status and future directions. *Journal of Intellectual Property Rights*, *24*(2), 112–121. DOI: 10.1007/s41745-019-00117-w

Golden, T. W., Skalak, S. L., Clayton, M. M., & Pill, J. S. (2011). *A guide to forensic accounting investigation* (2nd ed.). John Wiley & Sons., https://download.e-bookshelf.de/download/0000/5848/25/L-G-0000584825-0002384529.pdf

González-Sendino, R., Serrano, E., & Bajo, J. (2024). Mitigating bias in artificial intelligence: Fair data generation via causal models for transparent and explainable decision-making. *Future Generation Computer Systems*, *155*, 384–401. DOI: 10.1016/j.future.2024.02.023

Goodall, J. R., & Hodge, G. (2020). Artificial intelligence in the legal profession: Opportunities and challenges. *Legal Technology Review, 23*(4), 34–48. DOI: 10.2139/ssrn.3504165

Google LLC v. Australian Competition and Consumer Commission, [2021] HCA 2 (High Court of Australia, 2021).

Google LLC v. Competition Commission of India. (2023). Civil Appeal No. 229 of 2023, 2023 SCC OnLine SC 88 (Supreme Court of India, Jan. 19, 2023).

Government of India. (2023). IndiaAI 2023: Expert group report – First edition. Ministry of Electronics and Information Technology. https://www.meity.gov.in/content/indiaai-2023-expert-group-report-%E2%80%93-first-editionthe-ministry-electronics-and-information

Gray, K., Yam, K. C., Zhen'An, A. E., Wilbanks, D., & Waytz, A. (2023). The psychology of robots and artificial intelligence. *The handbook of social psychology*, 1-91.

Gupta, N., Das, A. K., & Granados, C. (2026). Integrating Traditional Ecological Knowledge with Fuzzy Logic and Quantum Computing for Sustainable Agriculture in Tribal Areas of Tripura. In Horng, M., Khalaf, O., Shieh, C., & Jain, V. (Eds.), *Revolutionizing Sustainable Food Production With Quantum Computing* (pp. 177–214). IGI Global Scientific Publishing., DOI: 10.4018/979-8-3373-3957-3.ch006

Gupta, R. (2019). Role of legal system in promoting consumer protection. *Global Journal of Commerce and Business Review, 5*(1), 1–6.

Gupta, S. C. (1999). *Fundamentals of Statistics* (4th ed.). Himalaya Publishing House.

Haefner, N., Parida, V., Gassmann, O., & Wincent, J. (2023). Implementing and scaling artificial intelligence: A review, framework, and research agenda. *Technological Forecasting and Social Change, 197*, 122878. DOI: 10.1016/j.techfore.2023.122878

Hassija, V., Chamola, V., & Mahapatra, A.. (2024). Interpreting black-box models: A review on explainable artificial intelligence. *Cognitive Computation, 16*, 45–74. DOI: 10.1007/s12559-023-10179-8

Hastuti, R., & Syafruddin. (2023). Ethical considerations in the age of artificial intelligence: Balancing innovation and social values. *West Science Social and Humanities Studies, 1*(02), 76–87. DOI: 10.58812/wsshs.v1i02.191

Healy, P. M., & Palepu, K. G. (2003). The fall of Enron. *The Journal of Economic Perspectives, 17*(2), 3–26. DOI: 10.1257/089533003765888403

Henz, P. (2021). Ethical and legal responsibility for artificial intelligence. *Discover Artificial Intelligence, 1*, 2. DOI: 10.1007/s44163-021-00002-4

Herrera-Tapias, B. A., Guzmán, D. H., Zambam, N. J., Turatti, L., Rodríguez, F. A., Fröhlich, S., Staffen, M. R., Muñoz, P. C., Reyes, A. G., de la Torre, G. S., Duarte, N. R., & Ramos, E. P. (2025). Algorithmic discrimination and explainable artificial intelligence in the judiciary: A case study of the Constitutional Court of Colombia. *Procedia Computer Science*, *257*, 1227–1232. https://doi.org/https://doi.org/10.1016/j.procs.2025.03.164

Heryadi, Y. (2021). *Dasar-dasar deep learning dan implementasinya*. Gava Media.

Hildebrandt, M. (2018). Law as Computation in the Era of Artificial Legal Intelligence. *University of Toronto Law Journal*, *68*(Supplement 1), 12–35. DOI: 10.3138/utlj.2017-0044

Hofmann, F., & Keates, J. (2013). Trade marks in cyberspace: The challenges of online enforcement. *European Intellectual Property Review*, *35*(3), 129–137.

Houben, R., & Snyers, A. (2018). Cryptocurrencies and blockchain: Legal context and implications for financial crime, money laundering and tax evasion. In European Parliament's Special Committee on Financial Crimes, Tax Evasion and Tax Avoidance, *European Parliament's Special Committee on Financial Crimes, Tax Evasion and Tax Avoidance* (Report PE 619.024). https://repository.uantwerpen.be/docman/irua/80a4a6/152140.pdf

Houben, R., & Snyers, A. (2020). Crypto-assets - Key developments, regulatory concerns and responses. In European Parliament, *European Parliament* (Study PE 648.779). https://www.europarl.europa.eu/RegData/etudes/STUD/2020/648779/IPOL_STU(2020)648779_EN.pdf https://www.sciencedirect.com/

Hsueh, Y.-L., & Chou, T.-L. (2022). A Task-Oriented Chatbot Based on LSTM and Reinforcement Learning. *ACM Transactions on Asian and Low-Resource Language Information Processing*, *22*(1), 127. DOI: 10.1145/3529649

Huber, W. D. (2017). Forensic accounting, fraud theory, and the end of the fraud triangle. *Journal of Theoretical Accounting Research*, *12*(2), 28–48. https://papers.ssrn.com/sol3/papers.cfm?abstract_id=2423809

Hu, K., Chen, F., Hsu, M., & Tzeng, G. (2023). Governance of artificial intelligence applications in a business audit via a fusion fuzzy multiple rule-based decision-making model. *Financial Innovation*, *9*, 1–31. DOI: 10.1186/s40854-022-00436-4

Hung, T. W., & Yen, C. P. (2021). On the person-based predictive policing of AI. *Ethics and Information Technology*, *23*(2), 165–176. DOI: 10.1007/s10676-020-09539-x

Hu, Z., Wang, L., Lan, Y., Xu, W., Lim, E.-P., Bing, L., Xu, X., Poria, S., & Lee, R. K.-W. (2023). "LLM-adapters: An adapter family for parameter-efficient fine-tuning of large language models, arXiv:2304.01933.

IBM X-Force 2025 Threat Intelligence Index. (n.d.). IBM. https://www.ibm.com/thought-leadership/institute-business-value/en-us/report/2025-threat-intelligence-index

ICAI. (2017). *Study on forensic accounting and fraud detection.* Institute of Chartered Accountants of India. https://pqc.icai.org/assets/announcement_files/1550140046.pdf

ICAI. (2023). *Forensic accounting and investigation standards (FAIS).* Institute of Chartered Accountants of India. https://resource.cdn.icai.org/75009daab030723.pdf

ICLG. (2025). Data protection and privacy laws in India. Retrieved from https://iclg.com

IJLLR. (2025). Emerging issues in AI governance and human rights in India. International Journal of Law. *Language & Regulation, 12*(1), 55–79.

International Association of Privacy Professionals (IAPP). (2024). *AI governance in practice: Organizational approaches to responsible AI.* IAPP.

International Journal Publication | Research paper publication and Submission - IJARIIT. (2021, February 20). IJARIIT. https://www.ijariit.com/

Ioannidou, E., Promikyridis, R., & Tambouris, E. (2025). Legal and Ethical Issues Arising from the Use of Chatbots in Public Administration. *Proceedings of the 28th Pan-Hellenic Conference on Progress in Computing and Informatics*, 211–215. doi:DOI: 10.1145/3716554.3716586

IOSCO. (2020). *Issues, risks and regulatory considerations relating to crypto-asset trading platforms.* International Organization of Securities Commissions. https://www.iosco.org/library/pubdocs/pdf/IOSCOPD649.pdf

Itelman, E., Golovchiner, G., Barsheshet, A., Kornowski, R., & Erez, A. (2024, October). Balancing innovation and professionalism: The emerging role of AI-powered chatbots in medical consultation. *Heart Rhythm, 21*(10), 2037–2039. PMID: 38588991

Izacard, G., Caron, M., Hosseini, L., Riedel, S., Bojanowski, P., Joulin, A., & Grave, E. (2021). "Unsupervised dense information retrieval with contrastive learning," arXiv:2112.09118.

James, M. (2023). Blockchain and forensic accounting enhancing transparency and accountability. SSRN *Electronic Journal.* https://doi.org/DOI: 10.2139/ssrn.4642347

Janiesch, C., Zschech, P., & Heinrich, K. (2021). Machine learning and deep learning. *Electronic Markets*, *31*, 685–695. DOI: 10.1007/s12525-021-00475-2

Jayachandra Reddy, R., Reddy, G. S., & Rao, V. S. (2011). Consumer awareness and redressal mechanism: A study of Andhra Pradesh. *Indian Journal of Marketing*, *41*(6), 35–43.

Jaya, F., & Goh, W. (2021). Analisis Yuridis terhadap Kedudukan Kecerdasan Buatan atau *Artificial Intelligence* sebagai Subjek Hukum pada Hukum Positif Indonesia. *Jurnal Supremasi Hukum*, *17*(2), 1–11. DOI: 10.33592/jsh.v17i2.1287

Joachims, T., Granka, L., Pan, B., Hembrooke, H., & Gay, G. (2005). Accurately interpreting clickthrough data as implicit feedback. *Proceedings of the 28th Annual International ACM SIGIR Conference*, 154–161.

Joshi, D. (2024). AI governance in India – law, policy and political economy. *Communication Research and Practice*, *10*(3), 328–339. DOI: 10.1080/22041451.2024.2346428

Judge, B., Nitzberg, M., & Russell, S. (2025). When code isn't law: Rethinking regulation for artificial intelligence. *Policy and Society*, *44*(1), 85–97. DOI: 10.1093/polsoc/puae020

Judiciary, D. (2025). Eastern Book Company v. D.B. Modak, 2008 (36) PTC 1 (SC). Drishti Judiciary. https://www.drishtijudiciary.com/intellectual-property-rights/eastern-book-company-v-d-b-modak-2008-36-ptc-1-sc

Jui, T. D., & Rivas, P. (2024). Fairness issues, current approaches, and challenges in machine learning models. *International Journal of Machine Learning and Cybernetics*, *15*, 3095–3125. DOI: 10.1007/s13042-023-02083-2

Jumantoro, T. R. P. (2024). Menilik pro dan kontra pemanfaatan dan penetapan status hukum artificial intelligence dalam hukum Positif Indonesia. *Journal of Analytical Research. Statistics and Computing*, *3*(1), 51–70. DOI: 10.4590/jarsic.v3i1.28

Junaidi, J. (2025). Education Reform in the Application of Artificial Intelligence in Supporting Learning Media: AI and Education for Sustainable Development Goals (SDGs), *in AI, Policy, and the Future of Human-Centered Education, IGI Global Scientific Publishing,* 57-84. https://doi.org/DOI: 10.4018/979-8-3373-5781-2.ch003

Junaidi, J. (2025a). Transformation of Literary Culture in the Digital Era Through the Use of Artificial Intelligence as a Form of Copyright Protection. *in Role of AI in Producing, Evaluating, and Interpreting Literary Materials. IGI Global Scientific Publishing*, 177-204, http://dx.doi.org/DOI: 10.4018/979-8-3373-1057-2

Junaidi, J. (2020). Kajian yuridis pasal 362 Kitab Undang-Undang Hukum Pidana dan pasal 30 Undang-Undang Nomor 11 Tahun 2008 tentang Informasi dan Transaksi Elektronik terhadap pencurian internet Wi-Fi. *Jurnal Wajah Hukum*, *4*(2), 325–330. DOI: 10.33087/wjh.v4i2.190

Junaidi, J. (2023). Artificial Intelligence in The Implementation of Criminal Case Settlement Law Using Restorative Justice Based on Progressive Law. In *Proceedings of the First International Cyber Law Conference (ICL-C 2023)*, 198-204. EAI. http://dx.doi.org/DOI: 10.4108/eai.11-11-2023.2351325

Junaidi, J., & Fadzil, R. M. (2024). Urgency of legal personal data protection in e-commerce transactions involving artificial intelligence. *Walisongo Law Review (Walrev)*, *6*(2), 96–108. DOI: 10.21580/walrev.2024.6.2.25548

Junaidi, J., Pujiyono, P., & Fadzil, R. M. (2024). Legal Reform of Artificial Intelligence's Liability to Personal Data Perspectives of Progressive Legal Theory. *Journal of Law and Legal Reform*, *5*(2), 587–612. DOI: 10.15294/jllr.vol5i2.3437

Kahneman, D. (2011). *Fast and slow thinking*. Allen Lane and Penguin Books.

Kane, O., Allaya, M. M., Samb, D., & Bousso, M. (2025). An Senegalese Legal Texts Structuration Using LLM-Augmented Knowledge Graph. arXiv preprint 2510.02353.

Karapatakis, A. (2024). Metaverse crimes in virtual (Un)reality: Fraud and sexual offences under English law. *Journal of Economic Criminology*, *7*, 100118. DOI: 10.1016/j.jeconc.2024.100118

Kattnig, M., Angerschmid, A., Reichel, T., & Kern, R. (2024). Assessing trustworthy AI: Technical and legal perspectives of fairness in AI. *Computer Law & Security Review*, *55*, 106053. https://doi.org/https://doi.org/10.1016/j.clsr.2024.106053

Katyal, S. K., & Grinvald, L. C. (2018). Trademark protection and consumer search costs on the internet. *Harvard Journal of Law & Technology*, *31*(2), 555–620.

Katz, D. M., Bommarito, M. J., & Blackman, J. (2017). A General Approach for Predicting the Behavior of the Supreme Court of the United States. *PLoS One*, *12*(4), e0174698. DOI: 10.1371/journal.pone.0174698 PMID: 28403140

Kaviraj Pandit Durga Dutt Sharma v. Navaratna Pharmaceutical Laboratories, AIR 1965 SC 980 (India).

Keerthana, D., N.S., Gowda, V., & Vali, S. (2025, May 28). Ethical and legal implications of AI chatbots in legal sector. *2025 International Conference on Computational Robotics, Testing and Engineering Evaluation (ICCRTEE)*, 1–5. Presented at the 2025 International Conference on Computational Robotics, Testing and Engineering Evaluation (ICCRTEE), Virudhunagar, India. doi:DOI: 10.1109/iccrtee64519.2025.11053085

Kelly, S., Kaye, S. A., & Trespalacios, O. O. (2023). What factors contribute to the acceptance of artificial intelligence? A systematic review. *Telematics and Informatics, 77*, 101925. DOI: 10.1016/j.tele.2022.101925

Kennedy, J. F. (1962). *Special message to the Congress on protecting the consumer interest.* The White House.

Khachatryan, S. (2022). Online trademark infringement and platform liability. *Journal of Intellectual Property Law & Practice, 17*(6), 463–472.

Khanna, T., & Palepu, K. G. (2010). Winning in Emerging Markets: A Road map for Strategy and Execution. *NHRD Network Journal, 3*(3), 75. DOI: 10.1177/0974173920100316

Khatri, M., Agrawal, A., & Garg, A. (2021). PoliceBOT-An Informative RASA Powered Chatbot based Crime Registration and Crime Awareness System. International Research Journal of Engineering and Technology, 8(06).

Khurana, A., & Khurana, P. (2012). Consumer awareness and protection: An empirical study. *International Journal of Research in Commerce & Management, 3*(5), 100–104.

Khurana, H., & Khurana, N. (2012). Study of awareness among respondents towards Consumer Protection Act. [IJMASR]. *International Journal of Multidisciplinary Approach and Reviews, 1*(4), 125–132.

Kim, S., Yi, S., & Park, S. (2025). Prioritizing challenges in AI adoption for the legal domain: A systematic review and expert-driven AHP analysis. *PLoS One, 20.* Advance online publication. DOI: 10.1371/journal.pone.0326028 PMID: 40554557

Knight, D. R. T., Aakre, C. A., Anstine, C. V., Munipalli, B., Biazar, P., Mitri, G., Valery, J. R., Brigham, T., Niazi, S. K., Perlman, A. I., Halamka, J. D., & Abu Dabrh, A. M. (2023). Artificial intelligence for patient scheduling in the real-world health care setting: A metanarrative review. *Health Policy and Technology, 12*(4), 100824. DOI: 10.1016/j.hlpt.2023.100824

Kogan, A., Alles, M. G., Vasarhelyi, M. A., & Wu, J. (2014). Design and evaluation of a continuous data level auditing system. *Auditing, 33*(4), 221–245. DOI: 10.2308/ajpt-50844

Kokina, J., & Davenport, T. H. (2017). The Emergence of Artificial Intelligence: How Automation is Changing Auditing. *Journal of Emerging Technologies in Accounting, 14*(1), 115–122. DOI: 10.2308/jeta-51730

Kordzadeh, N., & Ghasemaghaei, M. (2021). Algorithmic bias: Review, synthesis, and future research directions. *European Journal of Information Systems, 31*(3), 388–409. DOI: 10.1080/0960085X.2021.1927212

Kowalczyk, M. E., Choffnes, D., Dubois, D. J., & Hartzog, W. (2023). Understanding dark patterns in home IoT devices. *International Conference on Human Factors in Computing Systems*. DOI: 10.1145/3544548.3581432

KPMG. (2017). *Global online consumer survey*. KPMG International.

Kranacher, M.-J., Riley, R. A., & Wells, J. T. (2011). *Forensic accounting and fraud examination*. John Wiley & Sons.

Krawczyk, B. (2016). Learning from imbalanced data: Open challenges and future directions. *Progress in Artificial Intelligence, 5*, 221–232. DOI: 10.1007/s13748-016-0094-0

Krestel, R., Chikkamath, R., Hewel, C., & Risch, J. (2021). A survey on deep learning for patent analysis. *World Patent Information, 65*, 102035. DOI: 10.1016/j.wpi.2021.102035

Kriebitz, R., & Lütge, C. (2020). Ethics of AI: Societal impacts and justice perspectives. *AI and Ethics, 1*, 123–135. DOI: 10.1007/s43681-020-00004-x

Kristianti, N., & Rolando, B. (2025). Pemanfaatan artificial intelligence dalam praktik hukum: Peluang dan tantangan regulasi di Indonesia. *Belom Bahadat: Jurnal Hukum Agama Hindu, 15*(1), 82–95. DOI: 10.33363/bb.v15i1.1483

Kuang, W., Qian, B., Li, Z., Chen, D., Gao, D., Pan, X., & Zhou, J. (2024, August). Federatedscope-llm: A comprehensive package for fine-tuning large language models in federated learning. In *Proceedings of the 30th ACM SIGKDD Conference on Knowledge Discovery and Data Mining* (pp. 5260-5271).

Kubat, M. (2021). *An introduction to machine learning* (3rd ed.). Springer Nature Switzerland., DOI: 10.1007/978-3-030-81935-4

Kugler, M. B., Strahilevitz, L., Chetty, M., & Mahapatra, C. (2025). *Can consumers protect themselves against privacy dark patterns?* Social Science Research Network. DOI: 10.2139/ssrn.5084827

Kulkarni, M., Tangarajan, P., Kim, K., & Trivedi, A. (2024). Reinforcement learning for optimizing rag for domain chatbots. arXiv preprint arXiv:2401.06800.

Kumar, N. (2025). From Surveillance to Sentencing: Evaluating AI's Role in Indian Criminal Justice. *Science Bulletin*, *30*, 68–78. DOI: 10.2478/bsaft-2025-0008

Kumar, S. S., Ahmed, S. T., Fathima, A. S., Nishabai, M., & Sophia, S. (2024, January). Medical ChatBot assistance for primary clinical guidance using machine learning techniques. *Procedia Computer Science*, *233*, 279–287.

L'Oréal SA v. eBay International AG, Case C-324/09, EU:C:2011:474 (Court of Justice of the European Union, 2011).

L'Oréal SA v. eBay International AG, Case C-324/09, EU:C:2011:474.

Lakatos, R., Pollner, P., Hajdu, A., & Joó, T. (2025, February). Investigating the performance of retrieval-augmented generation and domain-specific fine-tuning for the development of AI-driven knowledge-based systems. *Mach. Learn. Knowl. Extraction*, *7*(1), 15.

Latha, K. L. (2022). A study of consumer protection, rights and responsibilities in India. *Journal of Consumer Studies, 47*(1), 12–18. ISSN 0974-8946.

Laxmikant V. Patel v. Chetanbhai Shah, (2002) 3 SCC 65 (India).

Leavy, S. (2018). Gender bias in artificial intelligence: The need for diversity and gender theory in machine learning. In *2018 IEEE/ACM 1st International Workshop on Gender Equality in Software Engineering (GE)* (pp. 14–16). Gothenburg, Sweden. https://doi.org/DOI: 10.1109/GE.2018.00010

Lee, J., Yoon, W., Kim, S., Kim, D., Kim, S., So, C. H., & Kang, J. (2020). BioBERT: A pretrained biomedical language representation model for biomedical text mining. *Bioinformatics (Oxford, England)*, *36*(4), 1234–1240. PMID: 31501885

Lee, Y., Bradford, B., & Posch, K. (2024). The effectiveness of big data-driven predictive policing: Systematic review. *Justice Evaluation Journal*, *7*(2), 127–160. DOI: 10.1080/24751979.2024.2371781

Leiser, M. R. (2020). *"Dark patterns": The case for regulatory pluralism.* Social Science Research Network. DOI: 10.2139/ssrn.3625637

Levitt, T. (1960). Marketing myopia. *Harvard Business Review*, *38*(4), 45–56. PMID: 15252891

Lewis, M., Liu, Y., Goyal, N., Ghazvininejad, M., Mohamed, A., Levy, O., . . . Zettlemoyer, L. (2019). *Bart: Denoising sequence-to-sequence pre-training for natural language generation, translation, and comprehension*. arXiv preprint arXiv: 1910.13461.

Lewis, P., Perez, E., Piktus, A., Petroni, F., Karpukhin, V., Goyal, N., Küttler, H., Lewis, M., Yih, W.-T., Rocktäschel, T., Riedel, S., & Kiela, D. (2020). "Retrieval-augmented generation for knowledge-intensive NLP tasks," in Proc. *Advances in Neural Information Processing Systems*, •••, 9459–9474.

LexRAG Consortium. (2025). LexRAG: Benchmarking Retrieval-Augmented Generation in Multi-Turn Legal Consultation. arXiv preprint 2502.20640.

Liang, G., Xin, J., Wang, Q., Ni, X., Guo, X., & Chen, P. (2023). Research on metaverse security and forensics. *Computers, Materials & Continua/Computers. Materials & Continua (Print)*, *77*(1), 799–825. DOI: 10.32604/cmc.2023.038403

Lin, Z. (2024). Beyond principlism: Practical strategies for ethical AI use in research practices. *AI and Ethics*. Advance online publication. DOI: 10.1007/s43681-024-00585-5

Li, S., Hu, J., Cui, Y., & Hu, J. (2018). DeepPatent: Patent classification with convolutional neural networks and word embedding. *Scientometrics*, *117*(2), 721–744.

Li, S., & Zhang, R. (2019). Legal implications of artificial intelligence in China: A regulatory approach. *Journal of Chinese Law*, *35*(4), 75–92. DOI: 10.2139/ssrn.3384760

Li, Z. (2024). *Digital advertising and EU digital regulation.*, DOI: 10.4324/9781003168485-25

Locke, L. G., & Hodgdon, G. (2024). Gender bias in visual generative artificial intelligence systems and the socialization of AI. *AI & Society*. Advance online publication. DOI: 10.1007/s00146-024-02129-1

Lokanan, M. (2022). Predicting Money Laundering using Machine Learning and Artificial Neural Networks Algorithms in Banks. *Research Square*. https://doi.org/ DOI: 10.21203/rs.3.rs-2161095/v1

Lokanan, M. E. (2015). Challenges to the fraud triangle: Questions on its usefulness. *Accounting Forum*, *39*(3), 201–224. DOI: 10.1016/j.accfor.2015.05.002

Lokanan, M. E., & Sharma, P. (2023). Two Decades of Accounting Fraud Research: The Missing Meso-Level Analysis. *SAGE Open*, *13*(3). Advance online publication. DOI: 10.1177/21582440231197305

London. (n.d.). *Blockchain Analytics & Crypto Compliance Solutions | Elliptic*. https://www.elliptic.co/

Lu, Q., Zhu, L., Xu, X., Whittle, J., Zowghi, D., & Jacquet, A. (2022). Responsible AI Pattern Catalogue: A Collection of Best Practices for AI Governance and Engineering. *ACM Computing Surveys*, *56*, 1–35. DOI: 10.1145/3626234

Lv, K., Yang, Y., Liu, T., Guo, Q., & Qiu, X. (2024, August). Full parameter fine-tuning for large language models with limited resources. In *Proceedings of the 62nd Annual Meeting of the Association for Computational Linguistics* (Volume 1: Long Papers) (pp. 8187-8198).

Madanchian, M., & Taherdoost, H. (2025). Ethical theories, governance models, and strategic frameworks for responsible AI adoption and organizational success. *Frontiers in Artificial Intelligence*, *8*. Advance online publication. DOI: 10.3389/frai.2025.1619029 PMID: 40741285

Madaoui, N. (2024). The impact of artificial intelligence on legal systems: Challenges and opportunities. *Problems of Legality*, (164), 285–303. DOI: 10.21564/2414-990X.164.289266

Mahameru, D. E., Nurhalizah, A., Badjeber, H., Wildan, A., & Rahmadia, H. (2023). Implementasi UU Perlindungan Data Pribadi terhadap Keamanan Informasi Identitas di Indonesia. *Jurnal Esensi Hukum*, *5*(2), 115–131. DOI: 10.35586/jsh.v5i2.240

Mahmud, H., Islam, A. K. M. N., Ahmed, S. I., & Smolander, K. (2022). What influences algorithmic decision-making? A systematic literature review on algorithm aversion. *Technological Forecasting and Social Change*, *175*, 121390. DOI: 10.1016/j.techfore.2021.121390

Mahomed, S. (2019). Healthcare, artificial intelligence and the Fourth Industrial Revolution: Ethical, social and legal considerations. *South African Journal of Bioethics and Law*, *11*(2), 93–95. DOI: 10.7196/SAJBL.2018.v11i2.00664

MakeMyTrip (India) Pvt. Ltd. & Ors. v. Competition Commission of India. (2022). Competition Appeal (AT) No. 16 of 2020. National Company Law Appellate Tribunal (Dec. 23, 2022).

Malik, A., Kumar, A., Salih, S., Kim, S., Kim, N., Yaseen, Z., & Singh, V. (2020). Drought index prediction using advanced fuzzy logic model: Regional case study over Kumaon in India. *PLoS One*, *15*. Advance online publication. DOI: 10.1371/journal.pone.0233280 PMID: 32437386

Manasi, A., Panchanadeswaran, S., Sours, E., & Lee, S. J. (2022). Mirroring the bias: Gender and artificial intelligence. *Gender, Technology and Development*, *26*(3), 295–305. DOI: 10.1080/09718524.2022.2128254

Mannes, J. (2024). *Legal Aid at the Click of a Button: The Power of DoNotPay's 1,000 Bots*. https://fxis.ai/edu/legal-aid-at-the-click-of-a-button-the-power-of-donotpays-1000-bots/

Manoharan, M., & Auxcelian, M. A. (2015). Consumer dispute redressal agencies in India: A performance analysis. *International Journal of Multidisciplinary Research*, *5*(8), 112–121.

Manoharan, M., & Auxcelian, M. A. (2015). Working performance of consumer dispute redressal agencies in India. *International Journal of Innovative Research in Science, Engineering and Technology*, *4*(4), 1217–1224. https://www.ejmanager.com/files/64406/13087874584WorkingPerformaceOfConsumerDisputRedresalAgencie sinIndia.pdf

Manoj, C., & Jeevanandhan, L. (2025). *AI in Indian Governance*. Electronic Journal of Social and Strategic Studies., DOI: 10.47362/ejsss.2025.6607

Mansoor, S. I. (2026). AI and the Rule of Law in Urban Security: Upholding Police Accountability in Smart Cities. In Abdelmottlep, M. (Ed.), *AI-Driven Policing and Urban Security in Smart Cities* (pp. 55–80). IGI Global Scientific Publishing., DOI: 10.4018/979-8-3373-0245-4.ch003

Mansoor, S. I. U. (2024). Legal implications of deepfake technology: In the context of manipulation, privacy, and identity theft. *Central University of Kashmir Law Review*, *4*, 65–92.

Mansoor, S. I., & Wani, S. A. (2025). Harnessing Ethical AI: Measures of Redressing Hate Speech in the Social Media Context. In Chakraborty, S. (Ed.), *Ethical AI Solutions for Addressing Social Media Influence and Hate Speech* (pp. 37–62). IGI Global Scientific Publishing., DOI: 10.4018/979-8-3693-9904-0.ch003

Mansouri, O., Yusuf, N., & Kooli, C. (2025). Ethical frontiers and legal boundaries: Proposing a unified framework for AI regulation and accountability. *Next Research*, *2*(4), 101087. https://doi.org/https://doi.org/10.1016/j.nexres.2025.101087

Marco, A. C., Sarnoff, J. D., & deGrazia, C. A. W. (2019). Patent claims and patent scope. *Research Policy, 48*(9), 103790. DOI: 10.1016/j.respol.2019.04.014

Marey, A., Arjmand, P., & Alerab, A. D. S.. (2024). Explainability, transparency and black box challenges of AI in radiology: Impact on patient care in cardiovascular radiology. *The Egyptian Journal of Radiology and Nuclear Medicine, 55*, 183. DOI: 10.1186/s43055-024-01356-2

Marks, J. T. (2012). Fraud Pentagon: An enhancement to the fraud triangle and other models. *Crowe Horwath* white paper.

Mathews, A. (2024, July 11). The future of music is in AI; thanks to Spotify. AIM Research. https://aimresearch.co/market-industry/the-future-of-music-is-in-ai-thanks-to-spotify

Mathur, A., Mayer, J., & Kshirsagar, M. (2021). *What makes a dark pattern... dark? Design attributes, normative considerations, and measurement methods.* DOI: 10.1145/3411764.3445610

Mazer Trainer. (2024, January 9). *Metaverse scams and how to avoid them.* https://mazerspace.com/metaverse-scams-and-how-to-avoid-them/

McCrum, D. (2020). *Wirecard The Timeline. Financial Times. - References - Scientific Research Publishing.* https://www.scirp.org/reference/referencespapers?referenceid=3100404

McGinnis, J. O., & Pearce, R. G. (2014). The great disruption: How machine intelligence will transform the role of lawyers in the delivery of legal services. *Fordham Law Review, 82*, 3041–3306.

McKeown, T., Mustafina, J., Magizov, R., & Gataullina, C. (2020, December). AI in law practices. In 2020 13th International Conference on Developments in eSystems Engineering (DeSE) (pp. 27-32). IEEE.

McKinsey & Company. (2019). *Consumer data privacy and trust*. McKinsey Global Institute.

Medvedeva, M., Vols, M., & Wieling, M. (2020). Using Machine Learning to Predict Decisions of the European Court of Human Rights. *Artificial Intelligence and Law, 28*(2), 237–266. DOI: 10.1007/s10506-019-09255-y

Mehra, S. K. (2016). Antitrust and the robo-seller: Competition in the time of algorithms. *Minnesota Law Review, 103*(2), 369–430. https://www.minnesotalawreview.org/wp-content/uploads/2016/04/Mehra_ONLINEPDF1.pdf

Mehta, N., Pandit, A., & Shukla, S. (2019). Transforming healthcare with big data analytics and artificial intelligence: A systematic mapping study. *Journal of Biomedical Informatics*, *100*, 103311. DOI: 10.1016/j.jbi.2019.103311 PMID: 31629922

Metaverse and Money Laundering – How Shufti's AML Screening Helps. (2022, March 17). *Shufti Pro*. https://shuftipro.com/blog/metaverse-and-money-laundering-how-shufti-pros-aml-screening-helps/

Min, A. (2023). Artificial Intelligence and Bias: Challenges, Implications, and Remedies. *Journal of Social Research*, *2*(11). Advance online publication. DOI: 10.55324/josr.v2i11.1477

Mishra, C., & Gupta, D. L. (2016). Deep machine learning and neural networks: An overview. *International Journal of Hybrid Information Technology*, *6*(2), 66–73. DOI: 10.11591/ijai.v6.i2.pp66-73

Misra, S., Sharma, S., Gupta, S., & Das, S. (2023). A framework to overcome challenges to the adoption of artificial intelligence in Indian Government Organizations. *Technological Forecasting and Social Change*. Advance online publication. DOI: 10.1016/j.techfore.2023.122721

Mittal, S., Thakral, K., & Singh, R.. (2024). On responsible machine learning datasets emphasizing fairness, privacy, and regulatory norms with examples in biometrics and healthcare. *Nature Machine Intelligence*, *6*, 936–949. DOI: 10.1038/s42256-024-00874-y

Mohan, S., & Suganthi, V. (2017). Awareness of consumer rights among rural consumers. *International Journal of Research in Management & Business Studies*, *4*(3), 20–25.

Mozur, P. (2018, April 10). Inside China's dystopian dreams: AI, shame, and control. The New York Times. Retrieved from https://www.nytimes.com

Muhana, A. F. (2025). Legal drafting: Optimalisasi hukum melalui artificial intelligence (AI) di Indonesia. *Jurnal Hukum Ekualitas*, *1*(1), 84–94. DOI: 10.56607/9hdrcw80

Mukherjee, A., & Das, A. K. (2015b). Interval valued intuitionistic fuzzy soft multi set theoretic approach to decision making problems, 2015 International Conference on Computer, Communication and Control (IC4), Indore, India, 2015, pp. 1-5, https://doi.org/DOI: 10.1109/IC4.2015.7375640

Mukherjee, A., & Das, A. K. (2023). Essentials of fuzzy soft multisets: Theory and applications, Springer Nature Singapore Pte Ltd., 1-151. ISBN: 978-981-19-2759-1, https://doi.org/DOI: 10.1007/978-981-19-2760-7

Mukherjee, A., & Das, A. K. (2015a). Application of interval valued intuitionistic fuzzy soft set in investment decision making, *2015 Fifth International Conference on Advances in Computing and Communications (ICACC)*, Kochi, India, 2015, pp. 61-64, https://doi.org/DOI: 10.1109/ICACC.2015.37

Mukherjee, A., & Das, A. K. (2022). Einstein operations on fuzzy soft multisets and decision making. *Boletim da Sociedade Paranaense de Matematica, 40*, 1–10. DOI: 10.5269/bspm.32546

Mukherjee, A., Das, A. K., Gupta, N., Patra, S., Mahmood, T., Das, S., & Das, R. (2026). A novel generalized interval-valued neutrosophic rough soft set framework for enhanced decision-making: Application in water quality assessment. *Transactions on Fuzzy Sets and Systems*, *5*(1), 1–25. DOI: 10.71602/tfss.2026.1194037

Murugaiah, K. (2001). Consumer education through mass media. *Vikalpa*, *26*(4), 129–136. https://www.jstor.org/stable/41879966

Murugaiah, P. (2001). Consumer protection and the role of voluntary organizations. *The Indian Journal of Public Administration*, *47*(2), 289–301.

Muthuraju, V., Patnaik, S. L., Paul, G. S., & Sadhu, H. (2025, July). LexBot: AI-Powered Legal Help. In 2025 2nd International Conference on New Frontiers in Communication, Automation, Management and Security (ICCAMS) (pp. 1-4). IEEE.

Mutyala, S., Reddy, M. L., & Reddy, K. (2016). Consumer protection law in India: Some challenges and measures in the global market milieu. *International Journal of Research in IT and Management*, *x*(x), 19–27. https://www.researchgate.net/publication/386253859_CONSUMER_PROTECTION_LAW_IN_INDIA_SOME_CHALLENGES_AND_MEASURES_IN_GLOBAL_MARKET_MILIEU

N.R. Dongre v. Whirlpool Corporation, (1996) 5 SCC 714 (India).

Nagpal, S., Singh, M., Singh, R., Vatsa, M., & Ratha, N. K. (2023). In-group bias in deep learning-based face recognition models due to ethnicity and age. *IEEE Transactions on Technology and Society*, *4*(1), 54–67. DOI: 10.1109/TTS.2023.3241010

Najafli, A. (2025). The impact of artificial intelligence on the legal system: Benefits, risks, legal, and ethical challenges. *Acta Globalis Humanitatis et Linguarum*, *2*(4), 247–263. DOI: 10.69760/aghel.0250040012

Narayanan, A., Mathur, A., Chetty, M., & Kshirsagar, M. (2020). Dark Patterns: Past, Present, and Future: The evolution of tricky user interfaces. *Queue*, *18*(2), 67–92.

Neuwirth, R. (2024). The global institutional governance of AI: A four-dimensional perspective. *International Journal of Digital Law and Governance*, *1*(1), 113–153. DOI: 10.1515/ijdlg-2024-0004

Nicolau, L. (2021). Social justice and AI: Addressing inequities in algorithmic systems. *Journal of Human Rights and Technology*, *3*(2), 34–52.

Niebla, Z. J. M. (2018). Artificial Intelligence and Legal Analytics: New Tools for Law Practice in the Digital Age. *Script-ed*. Advance online publication. DOI: 10.2966/SCRIP.150118.156

Nijman, J. E. (2016). Non-state actors and the international rule of law: Revisiting the 'realist theory' of international legal personality. In *Non-state actor dynamics in international law*. Routledge.

Nikolskaia, K., & Naumov, V. (2020, October). Artificial intelligence in law. In 2020 International Multi-Conference on Industrial Engineering and Modern Technologies (FarEastCon) (pp. 1-4). IEEE.

Nishant, R., Schneckenberg, D., & Ravishankar, M. (2024). The formal rationality of artificial intelligence-based algorithms and the problem of bias. *Journal of Information Technology*, *39*(1), 19–40. DOI: 10.1177/02683962231176842

Novelli, C., Casolari, F., Hacker, P., Spedicato, G., & Floridi, L. (2024). Computer Law & Security Review : The International Journal of Technology Law and Practice Generative AI in EU law : Liability, privacy, intellectual property, and cybersecurity. *Computer Law & Security Review*, *55*(October), 106066. DOI: 10.1016/j.clsr.2024.106066

O'Neil, C. (2016). *Weapons of math destruction: How big data increases inequality and threatens democracy*. Crown Publishing.

OECD. (2017). *Trust and public policy: How better governance can help rebuild public trust*. OECD Publishing., DOI: 10.1787/9789264268920-

OECD. (2024). OECD principles on artificial intelligence. Paris: Organisation for Economic Co-operation and Development. Retrieved from https://www.oecd.org/ai

Office, U. S. C. (2021). Compendium of U.S. Copyright Office practices. U.S. Copyright Office. https://www.copyright.gov/comp3/

Online Dispute Resolution. (2021). *ODR and consumer trust in digital markets*. ODR Institute.

OPUS IP. (2025). Feilin v. Baidu: Beijing Internet Court tackles protection of AI/software-generated work and holds that copyright only vests in works by human authors. OPUS IP. https://www.opusip.co.uk/2019/11/09/feilin-v-baidu-beijing-internet-court-html/

Organisation for Economic Co-operation and Development (OECD). (2025). *Governing with artificial intelligence: Policy frameworks and institutional practices*. OECD Publishing.

Organisation for Economic Co-operation and Development. (2023). *Algorithmic competition (Background note)*. OECD Publishing. https://www.oecd.org/daf/competition/algorithmic-competition-2023.pdf

P. R. B. (2025, March 21). Artificial intelligence and intellectual property: "Artificial intelligence and intellectual property: Navigating issues of ownership and accountability". World Intellectual Property Organization. https://www.wipo.int/edocs/pubdocs/en/wipo-pub-econstat-wp-77-en-artificial-intelligence-and-intellectual-property-an-economic-perspective.pdf

Pabubung, M. R. (2023). Era Kecerdasan Buatan dan Dampak terhadap Martabat Manusia dalam Kajian Etis. *Jurnal Filsafat Indonesia*, *6*(1), 66–74. DOI: 10.23887/jfi.v6i1.49293

Pan, B., Hembrooke, H., Joachims, T., Lorigo, L., Gay, G., & Granka, L. (2007). In Google we trust: Users' decisions on rank, position, and relevance. *Journal of Computer-Mediated Communication*, *12*(3), 801–823.

Papadouli, V. (2023). Artificial intelligence's black box: Posing new ethical and legal challenges on modern societies. In A. Kornilakis, G. Nouskalis, V. Pergantis, & T. Tzimas (Eds.), *Artificial intelligence and normative challenges* (Law, Governance and Technology Series, vol. 59, pp. 67-88). Springer. https://doi.org/DOI: 10.1007/978-3-031-41081-9_4

Papagiannidis, E., Mikalef, P., & Conboy, K. (2025). Responsible artificial intelligence governance: A review and research framework. *The Journal of Strategic Information Systems*, *34*(2), 101885. DOI: 10.1016/j.jsis.2024.101885

Park, J., Hong, E., & Le, H. T. (2021). Adopting autonomous vehicles: The moderating effects of demographic variables. *Journal of Retailing and Consumer Services*, *63*, 102687. DOI: 10.1016/j.jretconser.2021.102687

Pasquale, F. (2015). *The black box society: The secret algorithms that control money and information*. Harvard University Press.

Pasquale, F. (2015). *The Black Box Society: The Secret Algorithms That Control Money and Information*. Harvard University Press., DOI: 10.4159/harvard.9780674736061

Patel Roadways Ltd. v. Birla Yamaha Ltd., (2000) 4 SCC 91 (India).

Patil, B., Alam, R., Kalal, T. V., Porwal, P., Kushwaha, N. S., & Sharma, N. (2025, April). BNS Mitra: RAG-Optimized LLM Based AI-Powered Legal Virtual Assistant. In 2025 3rd International Conference on Communication, Security, and Artificial Intelligence (ICCSAI) (Vol. 3, pp. 1501-1506). IEEE.

Periáñez, Á., Fernández Del Río, A., Nazarov, I., Jané, E., Hassan, M., Rastogi, A., & Tang, D. (2024). The digital transformation in health: How AI can improve the performance of health systems. *Health Systems and Reform*, *10*(2). Advance online publication. DOI: 10.1080/23288604.2024.2387138 PMID: 39437247

Perona, R., Carrillo, Y., & Rosa, D. (2025). Unveiling AI in the courtroom : Exploring ChatGPT ' s impact on judicial decision - making through a pilot Colombian case study. *AI & Society*, *40*(4), 2533–2540. DOI: 10.1007/s00146-024-01943-x

Peters, M. E., Ruder, S., & Smith, N. A. (2019, August). To tune or not to tune? adapting pretrained representations to diverse tasks. In Proceedings of the 4th Workshop on Representation Learning for NLP (RepL4NLP-2019) (pp. 7-14).

Peters, U. (2023). Explainable AI lacks regulative reasons: Why AI and human decision-making are not equally opaque. *AI and Ethics*, *3*(5), 963–974. DOI: 10.1007/s43681-022-00217-w

Pirmansyah, R., Junaidi, J., & Merta, M. M. (2021). *Law transformation: The law of personal data protection in the pandemic time COVID-19 on electronic system*. In *Proceedings of OSC 2021, Faculty of Law, Social and Political Sciences, Universitas Terbuka* (Theme 1). https://www.cips-indonesia.org/post/siaran-pers-kebocoran-data-ingatkan-pentingnya-legislasi-ruu-perlindungan-data-pribadi

Post, J. E., Varma, J. R., Menon, K., Desai, A., Raghavan, A., Srinivasan, V., Parekh, S. P., & Vohra, N. (2009). The Satyam Story: Many questions and a few answers. *Vikalpa*, *34*(1), 69–88. DOI: 10.1177/0256090920090106

Prakash, S., & Raju, K. S. (2018). Consumer protection in India: Contemporary issues and challenges. *International Journal of Law, Crime and Justice*, *54*, 1–11. DOI: 10.1016/j.ijlcj.2018.05.001

Praveen, S. (2009). Consumer protection as a collective responsibility. *Indian Journal of Law and Society*, *2*(1), 55–62.

Praveen, S. (2009). Consumer protection in India (with special reference to Andhra Pradesh). *International Journal of Social Science and Interdisciplinary Research, 1*(1), 1–10. https://www.researchgate.net/publication/277900279_Consumer_Protection_in_India_With_Special_Reference_to_Andhra_Pradesh

PRC. P. R. O. C. (2020). China laws portal - CJO. China Justice Observer. https://www.chinajusticeobserver.com/law/x/2019-yue-0305-min-chu-14010

PRC. P. R. O. C. (2022, April 28). Intellectual property development and protection of Fujian Province in 2020. China National Intellectual Property Administration. https://english.cnipa.gov.cn/art/2021/4/28/art_2595_158989.html

Press Information Bureau, Government of India. (2025, October 6). *Competition Commission of India releases market study on AI and competition.* https://pib.gov.in/PressReleasePage.aspx?PRID=2175607

PricewaterhouseCoopers. (2022). *PwC's global economic crime and fraud survey 2022.* PricewaterhouseCoopers. https://www.pwc.com/gx/en/services/forensics/economic-crime-survey/2022.html

Pustry, R. N., & Bardhan, R. (2025). Improving accessibility to abstract mathematical concepts us- ing generative multimodal explanations. In *Mathematics Education in the Era of Education 4.0* (Vol. 1, pp. 187–199). KBD Publication.

Putra, I. N. G. A., & Silaban, J. K. P. (2024). Penerapan Kecerdasan Artifisial dalam Pengawasan Kekuasaan Kehakiman sebagai Upaya Mereduksi Disparitas Putusan Pidana di Indonesia. *Ma'mal. Jurnal Laboratorium Syariah Dan Hukum, 5*(4), 297–320. DOI: 10.15642/mal.v5i4.382

Putri, M. C., Febyanti, A., Azzahra, S., & Putri, N. A. (2024). Pengaruh penggunaan artificial intelligence dalam pembentukan peraturan perundang-undangan. *TERANG: Jurnal Kajian Ilmu Sosial, Politik dan Hukum,* 1(2), 266-284. https://doi.org/DOI: 10.62383/terang.v1i2.235

Qian, Y., Siau, K. L., & Nah, F. F. (2024). Societal impacts of artificial intelligence: Ethical, legal, and governance issues. *Societal Impacts, 3*, 100040. DOI: 10.1016/j.socimp.2024.100040

Qin, H. X., Wang, Y., & Hui, P. (2025). Identity, crimes, and law enforcement in the Metaverse. *Humanities and Social Sciences Communications, 12*(1). *Nature.* Advance online publication. DOI: 10.1057/s41599-024-04266-w

Quteishat, E. M. A., Qtaishat, A., & Quteishat, A. M. A. (2024). Exploring the role of AI in modern legal practice: Opportunities, challenges, and ethical implications. *Journal Electrical Systems, 20*(6s), 3040–3050. DOI: 10.52783/jes.3320

Rackauckas, Z. (2024). Rag-fusion: a new take on retrieval-augmented generation. arXiv preprint arXiv:2402.03367.

Radanliev, P. (2025). Frontier AI regulation: What form should it take? *Frontiers in Political Science*. Advance online publication. DOI: 10.3389/fpos.2025.1561776

Rahardjo, S. (2004). *Hukum Progresif (Penjelajahan Suatu Gagasan).* Majalah Hukum Newsletter, 59 Jakarta: Yayasan Pusat Pengkajian Hukum.

Rahardjo, S. (2006). *Hukum Progresif sebagai Dasar Pembangunan Ilmu Hukum, dalam buku Menggagas Hukum Progresif Indonesia.* Semarang: Kerjasama Pustaka Pelajar, IAIN Walisongo dan Program Doktor Ilmu Hukum UNDIP

Rahardjo, S. (2003). *Suatu Versi Indonesia tentang Rule of Law, Sisi-sisi Lain dari Hukum Indonesia.* Kompas.

Rahardjo, S. (2006a). *Hukum dalam Jagat Ketertiban.* UKI Press.

Rahardjo, S. (2007). Arsenal Hukum Progresif. *Jurnal Hukum Progresif*, *3*(1), 1. DOI: 10.14710/hp.3.1.1

Rahardjo, S. (2007a). *Biarkan Hukum Mengalir: Catatan Kritis tentang Pergulatan Manusia dan Hukum.* Kompas.

Rahardjo, S. (2009). *Penegakan Hukum Suatu Tinjauan Sosiologis.* Genta Publishing.

Rahardjo, S. (2009a). *Hukum Progresif Sebuah Sintesa Hukum Indonesia.* Genta Publishing.

Rahardjo, S., & Dimyati, K. (2002). *Sosiologi Hukum, Perkembangan, Metode dan Pilihan Masalahnya.* Muhammadiyah University Press.

Rajamalli Keerthana, R., Fathima, G., & Florence, L. (2021). Evaluating the performance of various deep reinforcement learning algorithms for a conversational chatbot. 2021 2nd International Conference for Emerging Technology (INCET). DOI: 10.1109/incet51464.2021.9456321

Ramadhan, A., & Putri, A. (2018). *Big data, kecerdasan buatan, blockchain, dan teknologi finansial di Indonesia.* Direktorat Jenderal Aplikasi Informatika, Kementerian Komunikasi dan Informatika

Ramdhani, D. N., & Dewi, D. A. (2022). Menerapkan nilai-nilai Pancasila dalam menghadapi perkembangan ilmu pengetahuan dan teknologi. *Jurnal Kewarganegaraan*, *6*(1), 1081–1088. DOI: 10.31316/jk.v6i1.2676

Ram, O., Levine, Y., Dalmedigos, I., Muhlgay, D., Shashua, A., Leyton-Brown, K., & Shoham, Y. (2023, November). In-context retrieval-augmented language models. *Transactions of the Association for Computational Linguistics*, *11*, 1316–1331.

Raposo, V. L. (2024). When facial recognition does not 'recognise': Erroneous identifications and resulting liabilities. *AI & Society*, *39*(4), 1857–1869. DOI: 10.1007/s00146-023-01634-z

Raso, F. A.. (2018). Artificial intelligence & human rights: Opportunities and challenges. *European Journal of Risk Regulation*, *9*(2), 177–194.

Ravishankar, S. (2025). *The role of artificial intelligence in arbitration: Prospects for India*. International Journal for Multidisciplinary Research., DOI: 10.36948/ijfmr.2025.v07i02.41005

Ravizki, E. N., & Yudhantaka, L. (2022). *Artificial intelligence* sebagai subjek hukum: Tinjauan konseptual dan tantangan pengaturan di Indonesia. *Jurnal Notaire*, *5*(3), 351–376. DOI: 10.20473/ntr.v5i3.39063

Rawas, S. (2024). AI: The future of humanity. *Discover Artificial Intelligence*, *4*, 25. DOI: 10.1007/s44163-024-00118-3

Raza, A. (2025, October 20). *Top 4 Game-Changing AML Solutions in 2025*. AML Watcher. https://amlwatcher.com/blog/4-game-changing-aml-solutions-in-2025/

Re, R. M., Solow-Niederman, A., Bussel, D., Brennan-Marquez, K., Kaminski, M., Levy, K., … Volokh, E. (2019). UCLA School of Law; 2017--2019 PULSE Fellow.

Reckitt & Colman Ltd. v. Borden Inc., [1990] 1 WLR 491 (HL).

Regulation (EU) 2022/1925 of the European Parliament and of the Council of 14 September 2022 on contestable and fair markets in the digital sector (Digital Markets Act). (2022).

Regulation (EU) 2022/2065 of the European Parliament and of the Council of 19 October 2022 on a Single Market for Digital Services (Digital Services Act). (2022).

Rehman, A. & Muhammad Ali Siddiqui. (2024). Navigating Virtual Economies: Transformative Impacts and Challenges for Forensic Accounting in the Metaverse. A Conceptual overview. In *Grenze International Journal of Engineering and Technology* (Vol. 10, Issue 2, p. 916). https://thegrenze.com/pages/servej.php?fn=916.pdf&name=Navigating%20Virtual%20Economies:%20Transformative%20Impactsand%20Challenges%20for%20Forensic%20Accounting%20in%20theMetaverse.%20A%20Conceptual%20Overview&id=2932&association=GRENZE&journal=GIJET&year=2024&volume=10&issue=2

Remus, D., & Levy, F. S. (2015). Can Robots Be Lawyers? Computers, Lawyers, and the Practice of Law. SSRN *Electronic Journal*. https://doi.org/DOI: 10.2139/ssrn.2701092

Ren, Q., & Du, J. (2024). Harmonizing innovation and regulation: The EU Artificial Intelligence Act in the international trade context. *Computer Law & Security Review*, *54*, 106028. DOI: 10.1016/j.clsr.2024.106028

Rezaee, Z. (2009). *Financial statement fraud: Prevention and detection* (2nd ed.). John Wiley & Sons.

Riaz, R., Vasconcelos, A., & Pinto, P. (2024). *An overview of user psychological manipulation techniques in UI/UX web design* (pp. 1–6). DOI: 10.1109/cars61786.2024.10778887

Richmond, K. M., Muddamsetty, S. M., Gammeltoft-hansen, T., Olsen, H. P., & Moeslund, T. B. (2024). Explainable AI and Law: An Evidential Survey. In *Digital Society* (Vol. 3, Issue 1). Springer International Publishing. https://doi.org/DOI: 10.1007/s44206-023-00081-z

Rigotti, C., & Fosch-Villaronga, E. (2024). Fairness, AI & recruitment. *Computer Law & Security Review*, *53*, 105966. DOI: 10.1016/j.clsr.2024.105966

Ririh, K. R., Laili, N., Wicaksono, A., & Tsurayya, S. (2020). Studi Komparasi dan Analisis Swot pada Implementasi Kecerdasan Buatan (Artificial Intelligence) di Indonesia. *J@ti Undip. Jurnal Teknik Industri*, *15*(2), 122–133. DOI: 10.14710/jati.15.2.122-133

Risch, J., & Krestel, R. (2019). Domain-specific word embeddings for patent classification. *Data Technologies and Applications*, *53*(1), 108–122.

Rivas-Echeverría, F., Ramos, L. T., Ibarra, J. L., Zerpa-Bonillo, S., Arciniegas, S., & Asprino-Salas, M. (2025). LegalBot-EC: An LLM-Based Chatbot for Legal Assistance in Ecuadorian Law. *IEEE Access : Practical Innovations, Open Solutions*, *13*, 106817–106833. DOI: 10.1109/ACCESS.2025.3580488

Rodrigues, R. (2020). Legal and human rights issues of AI: Gaps, challenges and vulnerabilities. *Journal of Responsible Technology*, *4*, 100005. DOI: 10.1016/j.jrt.2020.100005

Ro ca, C. (2024). *Digital arms for digital consumer harms – Mapping legal and technical solutions for dark patterns in EU consumer law*. DOI: 10.26481/mup.2403

Rott, P. (2017). Data protection law as consumer law: How consumer organisations can contribute to the enforcement of data protection law. *Journal of European Consumer and Market Law*, *6*, 113–116.

Roudsari, A. H., Afshar, J., Lee, S., & Lee, W. (2021). PatentNet: Multi-label classification of patent documents using deep learning based language understanding. *Scientometrics*, *127*(1), 207–231. DOI: 10.1007/s11192-021-04179-4

Russell, S., & Norvig, P. (2016). *Artificial intelligence: A modern approach* (3rd ed.). Pearson Education Limited.

Ruzayana, Z., Hidayah, R. N., & Firsha, M. (2025). Judicial System Digitalization. *The Constitutionality of the E-Court System in Southeast Asia.*, *4*(1), 127–138. DOI: 10.57255/hakamain.v4i1.1343

S., D. (2025, March 21). Artificial intelligence and intellectual properties: Legal and ethical considerations. ResearchGate. https://www.researchgate.net/publication/376885311_Artificial_Intelligence_and_Intellectual_Properties_Legal_and_Ethical_Considerations

Salemi, A., & Zamani, H. (2024, July). Evaluating retrieval quality in retrieval-augmented generation. In *Proceedings of the 47th International ACM SIGIR Conference on Research and Development in Information Retrieval* (pp. 2395-2400).

Sane, G., & Thombre, S. (2025). Artificial Intelligence in Indian Legal Services: Challenges and a Strategic Framework. 2025 1st International Conference on AIML-Applications for Engineering & Technology (ICAET), 1-6. https://doi.org/DOI: 10.1109/icaet63349.2025.10932285

Sarabdeen, J. (2022). Protection of the rights of the individual when using facial recognition technology. *Heliyon*, *8*(3), e09086. DOI: 10.1016/j.heliyon.2022.e09086 PMID: 35309394

Sarbanes–Oxley Act of. 2002, Pub. L. No. 107–204, 116 Stat. 745 (2002). https://www.dol.gov/sites/dolgov/files/oalj/PUBLIC/WHISTLEBLOWER/REFERENCES/STATUTES/SARBANES_OXLEY_ACT_OF_2002.PDF

Sarirete, A., Balfagih, Z., & Brahimi, T.. (2022). Artificial intelligence and machine learning research: Towards digital transformation at a global scale. *Journal of Ambient Intelligence and Humanized Computing*, *13*(6), 3319–3321. DOI: 10.1007/s12652-021-03168-y

Sarkar, K., Shiuly, A., & Dhal, K. G. (2024). Revolutionizing concrete analysis: An in-depth survey of AI-powered insights with image-centric approaches on comprehensive quality control, advanced crack detection and concrete property exploration. *Construction & Building Materials*, *411*, 134212. DOI: 10.1016/j.conbuildmat.2023.134212

Sarker, I. H. (2021). Machine learning: Algorithms, real-world applications, and research directions. *SN Computer Science*, *2*(160). Advance online publication. DOI: 10.1007/s42979-021-00592-x PMID: 33778771

Sarker, I. H. (2022). AI-based modeling: Techniques, applications and research issues towards automation, intelligent and smart systems. *SN Computer Science*, *3*(2), 158. DOI: 10.1007/s42979-022-01043-x PMID: 35194580

Schäfer, R., Preuschoff, P. M., & Borchers, J. (2023). *Investigating visual countermeasures against dark patterns in user interfaces.* DOI: 10.1145/3603555.3603563

Schellekens, M. (2019). Does Regulation of Illegal Content Need Reconsideration in Light of Blockchains? *International Journal of Law and Information Technology*, *27*(3), 292–305. DOI: 10.1093/ijlit/eaz009

Schmitz, J., & Leoni, G. (2019). Accounting and Auditing at the time of Blockchain Technology: A research agenda. *Australian Accounting Review*, *29*(2), 331–342. DOI: 10.1111/auar.12286

Schuilenburg, M., & Soudijn, M. (2023). Big data policing: The use of big data and algorithms by the Netherlands Police. *Policing. Journal of Policy Practice*, *17*, paad061. Advance online publication. DOI: 10.1093/police/paad061

Schulte-Nölke, H. (2017). The brave new world of EU consumer law: Without consumers, or even without law? *Journal of European Consumer and Market Law*, *6*, 117–120.

Segev, R. (2024). Artificial intelligence, discrimination, fairness, and other moral concerns. *Minds and Machines*, *34*, 44. DOI: 10.1007/s11023-024-09702-z

Sekti, B. A. (2025a). Adversarial Machine Learning in Industrial Cybersecurity: Challenges and Solutions. In *AI-Enhanced Cybersecurity for Industrial Automation* (pp. 363–386). IGI Global Scientific Publishing. https://doi.org/DOI: 10.4018/979-8-3373-3241-3.ch018

Sekti, B. A. (2025a). AI Technology Management Concepts and Strategies. In *AI Technology Management and Value Creation* (pp. 1–32). https://doi.org/DOI: 10.4018/979-8-3373-2497-5.ch001

Sekti, B. A. (2025b). Machine Learning vs. AI: Key Concepts. In *Implementing Enterprise Cybersecurity With AI* (pp. 1–27). https://doi.org/DOI: 10.4018/979-8-3373-2252-0.ch001

Selçuk, S., Kurt Konca, N., & Kaya, S. (2025). AI-driven civil litigation: Navigating the right to a fair trial. *Computer Law & Security Review*, *57*, 106136. https://doi.org/https://doi.org/10.1016/j.clsr.2025.106136

Selvi, D., & Goele, S. *'Critical Evaluation of Awareness of Consumer Rights and Protection'* (2021) https://www.researchgate.net/publication/352704563 accessed 3rd Feb, 2026.

Seppälä, P., & Małecka, M. (2024). AI and discriminative decisions in recruitment: Challenging the core assumptions. *Big Data & Society*, *11*(1). Advance online publication. DOI: 10.1177/20539517241235872

Sergot, M., Cory, T., Hammond, P., Kowalski, R., Kriwaczek, F., & Sadri, F. (2010). Formalisation of the British nationality act. *International Review of Law Computers & Technology*, *2*(1), 40–52. DOI: 10.1080/13600869.1986.9966229

Shah, S. (2024). *Trust Dynamics in the Digital Economy: Ethical AI and Data Governance Frameworks*. Premier Journal of Artificial Intelligence., DOI: 10.70389/pjai.100005

Sharma, G. D., Yadav, A., & Chopra, R. (2020). Artificial intelligence and effective governance: A review, critique and research agenda. *Sustainable Futures: An Applied Journal of Technology, Environment and Society*, *2*, 100004. DOI: 10.1016/j.sftr.2019.100004

Sharma, M., Joshi, S., Kannan, D., Govindan, K., Singh, R., & Purohit, H. (2020). Internet of Things (IoT) adoption barriers of smart cities' waste management: An Indian context. *Journal of Cleaner Production*, *270*, 122047. DOI: 10.1016/j.jclepro.2020.122047

Shi, Y., Zi, X., Shi, Z., Zhang, H., Wu, Q., & Xu, M. (2024). Eragent: Enhancing retrieval-augmented language models with improved accuracy, efficiency, and personalization. arXiv preprint arXiv:2405.06683.

Shin, D., & Park, Y. J. (2019). Role of fairness, accountability, and transparency in algorithmic affordance. *Computers in Human Behavior*, *98*, 277–284. DOI: 10.1016/j.chb.2019.04.019

Shi, S., Tse, R., & Luo, W.. (2022). Machine learning-driven credit risk: A systemic review. *Neural Computing & Applications*, *34*, 14327–14339. DOI: 10.1007/s00521-022-07472-2

Shrestha, S., & Das, S. (2022). Exploring gender biases in ML and AI academic research through systematic literature review. *Frontiers in Artificial Intelligence*, *5*. Advance online publication. DOI: 10.3389/frai.2022.976838 PMID: 36304961

Shulner-Tal, A., Kuflik, T., Kliger, D., & Mancini, A. (2024). Who made that decision and why? Users' perceptions of human versus AI decision-making and the power of explainable-AI. *International Journal of Human-Computer Interaction*, •••, 1–18. DOI: 10.1080/10447318.2024.2348843

Silva, S., & Kenney, M. (2019). Algorithms, Platforms, And Ethnic Bias. *Communications of the ACM*, *62*(11), 37–39. DOI: 10.1145/3318157

Singh, J., & Sharma, D. (2014). Consumer Protection Act, 1986: Analysis and critique. *International Journal of Scientific Research in Management*, *5*(1), 1–5.

Singh, M., & Sodhi, P. (2025). *The role of law in the growing realm of Artificial Intelligence vis-a-vis the concern of Cyber Security*. International Journal for Multidisciplinary Research., DOI: 10.36948/ijfmr.2025.v07i02.39608

Singh, Y. (2005). Performance evaluation of district consumer forum in western Uttar Pradesh. *International Journal of Home Science*, *19*(1), 1–9. https://www.semanticscholar.org/paper/Performance-Evaluation-of-District-Consumer-Forum-Singh-Upadhyaya/09820bc0ea2c82c8a578829820a3e002c82cdaa5

Singleton, T. W., Singleton, A. J., Bologna, G. J., & Lindquist, R. J. (2010). *Fraud auditing and forensic accounting* (4th ed.). John Wiley & Sons., https://content.e-bookshelf.de/media/reading/L-580553-2336f26274.pdf

Smaili, N., & De Rancourt-Raymond, A. (2022). Metaverse: Welcome to the new fraud marketplace. *Journal of Financial Crime*, *31*(1), 188–200. DOI: 10.1108/jfc-06-2022-0124

Smaili, N., & Rancourt-Raymond, A. (2022). *We need to anticipate and address potential fraud in the metaverse*. The Conversation., DOI: 10.64628/aam.559prpde6

Snyder, H. (2019). Literature review as a research methodology: An overview and guidelines. *Journal of Business Research*, *104*, 333–339. DOI: 10.1016/j.jbusres.2019.07.039

Solove, D. J. (2006). A taxonomy of privacy. *University of Pennsylvania Law Review*, *154*(3), 477–564.

Solum, L. B. (2014). Artificial Meaning. *Washington Law Review (Seattle, Wash.)*, •••, 89.

Soysal, T. (2024). Can the right to explanation in GDPR be a remedy for algorithmic discrimination? In Kılıç, M., & Bozkuş Kahyaoğlu, S. (Eds.), *Algorithmic discrimination and ethical perspective of artificial intelligence* (pp. 57–73). Springer., DOI: 10.1007/978-981-99-6327-0_5

Staff, K. W. (2009, January 9). Scandal at Satyam: Truth, lies and corporate governance. *Knowledge at Wharton*. https://knowledge.wharton.upenn.edu/article/scandal-at-satyam-truth-lies-and-corporate-governance/

Stray, J. (2023). The AI Learns to Lie to Please You: Preventing Biased Feedback Loops in Machine-Assisted Intelligence Analysis. *Analytics*, *2*(2), 350–358. DOI: 10.3390/analytics2020020

Stucke, M. E., & Grunes, A. P. (2016). *Big data and competition policy*. Oxford University Press., https://doi.org/10.1093/law:ocl/9780198788133.001.0001

Surahmat, A., Ahmad, N., Fitri, H., Widarma, A., Ardilla, Y., Hasan. N.F., Satria, S., Army, W.L., & Wati, V. (2023). *Kecerdasan buatan dalam data mining*. Widina Bhakti Persada.

Surana, S., Chekkala, J., & Bihani, P. (2021). Chatbot based crime registration and crime awareness system using a custom named entity recognition model for extracting information from complaints. International research journal of engineering and technology, 8(04).

Surden, H., & Williams, A. (2023). Technological Opacity, Artificial Intelligence, and the Law. *Harvard Journal of Law \& Technology, 36*(2), 411–468.

Surden, H. (2014). Machine Learning and Law. *Washington Law Review (Seattle, Wash.)*, *89*(2), 87–126. DOI: 10.2139/ssrn.2410530

Surden, H. (2019). Artificial Intelligence and Law: An Overview. *Georgia State University Law Review*, *35*(4), 1306–1339. https://readingroom.law.gsu.edu/gsulr/vol35/iss4/8

Susskind, R. (2019). *Online Courts and the Future of Justice*. Oxford University Press., DOI: 10.1093/oso/9780198838364.001.0001

Susskind, R. (2023). *Tomorrow's lawyers: An introduction to your future* (3rd ed.). Oxford University Press., DOI: 10.1093/9780192864727.001.0001

Svantesson, D. J. B. (2017). Enter the quagmire: The complicated relationship between data protection law and consumer protection law. *Computer Law & Security Review*, *33*(5), 646–656. DOI: 10.1016/j.clsr.2017.07.004

Taeihagh, A. (2021). Governance of artificial intelligence. *Policy and Society*, *40*, 137–157. DOI: 10.1080/14494035.2021.1928377

Taheri, M. (2020). A comparison of Triangle, Diamond and Pentagon fraud models in fraud risk assessment. *Iranian Journal of Value and Behavioral Accounting*, *4*(8), 339–369. DOI: 10.29252/aapc.4.8.339

Tanujaya, C. N., & Sekti, B. A. (2025). Global Regulatory Landscape: The European Union Al Act Comparative International Perspectives. In *Navigating Social Trust in the AI Era* (pp. 95–121). https://doi.org/DOI: 10.4018/979-8-3373-7011-8.ch005

Tapscott, D., & Tapscott, A. (2016). *Blockchain revolution: How the technology behind bitcoin is changing money, business, and the world*. Portfolio/Penguin. https://itig-iraq.iq/wp-content/uploads/2019/05/Blockchain_Revolution.pdf

Temperman, J., & Quintavalla, L. (2023). AI, law, and human rights: Ethical implications and safeguards. *International Journal of Law and Information Technology*, *31*(1), 1–25.

The EU Declaration on Cooperation on Artificial Intelligence. (2018). *The European Parliament Resolution on Civil Law Rules on Robotics* (2015/2103 (INL)) (2018/C 252/25) 2017. https://eur-lex.europa.eu/legal-content/EN/TXT/?uri=CELEX:52018DC0237

The impact of cyber forensic accounting on quality of metaverse integrated reporting quality in metaverse local government. (2024). *Journal of Science and Technology - HaUI, 60*(11E). https://doi.org/DOI: 10.57001/huih5804.2024.341

The Rising Concern of Financial Crimes in the Metaverse – AML Screening as a Solution. (2022, November 10). *Shufti Pro*. https://shuftipro.com/blog/the-rising-concern-of-financial-crimes-in-the-metaverse-aml-screening-as-a-solution/

Thylstrup, N. B. (2019). *The Politics of Mass Digitization*. MIT Press., DOI: 10.7551/mitpress/11404.001.0001

Tiwari, N., Kumar, S., & Srivastava, V. (2023). *India's digital governance odyssey: navigating economic transformation in the digital era through prowess and legal resilience*.

Toapanta, T. M., Buenaño, J. J., Vayas, C. S., Nogales, P. R., Del Pozo, D. R., Orizaga, T. A., & Andrade, A. D. (2025). Perspectives on a Cybersecurity Governance Framework Integrating Blockchain, Artificial Intelligence, and Legal Base for one Organization. *Journal of Posthumanism*, *5*(5), 2701–2718. DOI: 10.63332/joph.v5i5.1664

Tommasetti, R., De Oliveira Leite, R., Maia, V. M., & Da Silva Macedo, M. A. (2021). Revisiting the Accounting Fraud Components: A Bottom-Up approach using the Twitter platform. *SAGE Open*, *11*(4). Advance online publication. DOI: 10.1177/21582440211058190

Touvron, H., Martin, L., Stone, K., Albert, P., Almahairi, A., Babaei, Y., . . . Scialom, T. (2023). Llama 2: Open foundation and fine-tuned chat models. arXiv preprint arXiv:2307.09288.

Trademarks Act. (1999).

Tranfield, D. R., Denyer, D., & Smart, P. (2003). Towards a methodology for developing Evidence-Informed management knowledge by means of systematic review. *British Journal of Management*, *14*(3), 207–222. DOI: 10.1111/1467-8551.00375

Trappey, A. J., Trappey, C. V., Wu, C. Y., & Lin, C. W. (2012). A patent quality analysis for innovative technology and product development. *Advanced Engineering Informatics*, *26*(1), 26–34.

Treviño, L. K., Weaver, G. R., & Reynolds, S. J. (2006). Behavioral Ethics in Organizations: A review. *Journal of Management*, *32*(6), 951–990. DOI: 10.1177/0149206306294258

Tu, S. S., Cyphert, A., & Perl, S. J. (2024). Artificial intelligence: Legal reasoning, legal research and legal writing. *Minnesota Journal of Law, Science & Technology*, *25*(2), 105–125. https://ssrn.com/abstract=4817765

Tziakouris, G. (2024, July 9). *Digital forensics for investigating the metaverse*. Cisco Blogs. Retrieved December 19, 2025, from https://blogs.cisco.com/security/digital-forensics-for-investigating-the-metaverse

UKIPO. (2020). Artificial intelligence and intellectual property: Copyright and patents: Government response to consultation. GOV.UK. https://www.gov.uk/government/consultations/artificial-intelligence-and-ip-copyright-and-patents/outcome/artificial-intelligence-and-intellectual-property-copyright-and-patents-government-response-to-consultation

UNCTAD. (2003). *E-commerce and development report*. United Nations.

UNCTAD. (2017). *Consumer protection in electronic commerce*. United Nations.

UNCTAD. (2018). *Manual on consumer protection and dispute resolution*. United Nations.

UNCTAD. *'Consumer Protection in E-Commerce'* (2016) chrome-extension://efaidnbmnnnibpcajpcglclefindmkaj/https://unctad.org/system/files/official-document/cicplpd7_en.pdf accessed 3rd Feb, 2026.

UNESCO. (2021). Recommendation on the ethics of artificial intelligence. Paris: UNESCO. Retrieved from https://unesdoc.unesco.org

Vaitkūnaitė, I., Beniušis, M., & Jurčys, P. (2021). The Lawsuit of the Decade---Google LLC v. Oracle America, Inc.: A Victory for Interoperability and the Future of Innovation. *Journal of Intellectual Property Law \& Practice, 16*(6), 463–465. https://doi.org/10.1093/jiplp/jpab089

Vaswani, A., Shazeer, N., Parmar, N., Uszkoreit, J., Jones, L., Gomez, A. N., ... (2017). Attention is all you need. In Advances in Neural Information Processing Systems 30 (pp. 5998-6008).

Venkatesh, P., Mukesh, V., Kumar, S., & Gowtham, G. (2025). Optimizing Legal Service Delivery Using AI-Based Incentives for E-Marketplaces in India. *2025 International Conference on Knowledge Engineering and Communication Systems (ICKECS)*, 1-10. https://doi.org/DOI: 10.1109/ickecs65700.2025.11035228

Vesnic-Alujevic, L., Nascimento, S., & Pólvora, A. (2020). Societal and ethical impacts of artificial intelligence: Critical notes on European policy frameworks. *Telecommunications Policy*, *44*(6), 101961. DOI: 10.1016/j.telpol.2020.101961

Vlassis, N. (2007). *A concise introduction to multiagent systems and distributed artificial intelligence*. Springer Nature., DOI: 10.2200/S00091ED1V01Y200705AIM002

Wachter, S., Mittelstadt, B., & Russell, C. (2021). Why Fairness Cannot Be Automated. *Computer Law \& Security Review, 41*, 105567. https://doi.org/DOI: 10.1016/j.clsr.2021.105567

Wahyuni, W. (2023). Praktisi hukum perlu bersiap hadapi isu hukum di era artificial intelligence. *Hukumonline.* https://www.hukumonline.com/berita/a/praktisi-hukum-perlu-bersiap-hadapi-isu-hukum-di-era-artificial-intelligence-lt652951251562f

Wang, Y., Kordi, Y., Mishra, S., Liu, A., Smith, N. A., Khashabi, D., & Hajishirzi, H. (2022). *Self-instruct: Aligning language models with self-generated instructions*. arXiv preprint arXiv: 2212.10560.

Wani, S. A., & Mansoor, S. I. (2025). Criminal Justice System in the Age of Artificial Intelligence: Exploring Rights, Risks, and Responsibilities in the Digital Era. In Kaunert, C., Raghav, A., Ravesangar, K., Singh, B., & Riswandi, B. (Eds.), *Artificial Intelligence in Peace, Justice, and Strong Institutions* (pp. 67–92). IGI Global Scientific Publishing., DOI: 10.4018/979-8-3693-9395-6.ch004

Warren, S. D., & Brandeis, L. D. (1890). The right to privacy. *Harvard Law Review*, *4*(5), 193–220.

Webb, T., Holyoak, K. J., & Lu, H. (2023). Emergent analogical reasoning in large language models. *Nature Human Behaviour*, *7*(9), 1526–1541. PMID: 37524930

Wei, J., Tay, Y., Bommasani, R., Raffel, C., Zoph, B., Borgeaud, S., . . . Fedus, W. (2022). *Emergent abilities of large language models.* arXiv preprint arXiv: 2206.07682.

Wells, J. T. (2017). *Principles of fraud examination* (4th ed.). John Wiley & Sons.

Wesche, J. S., Hennig, F., Kollhed, C. S., Quade, J., Kluge, S., & Sonderegger, A. (2024). People's reactions to decisions by human vs. algorithmic decision-makers: The role of explanations and type of selection tests. *European Journal of Work and Organizational Psychology*, *33*(2), 146–157. DOI: 10.1080/1359432X.2022.2132940

White, M. (2025, December 16). *Web3 is Going Just Great.* https://www.web3isgoinggreat.com/

Winter, J. S. (2018). Introduction to the Special Issue: Digital Inequalities and Discrimination in the Big Data Era. *Journal of Information Policy*, *8*, 1–4. DOI: 10.5325/jinfopoli.8.2018.0001

Wirtz, B. W., Weyerer, J. C., & Geyer, C. (2019). Artificial Intelligence and the Public Sector—Applications and Challenges. *International Journal of Public Administration*, *42*(7), 596–615. DOI: 10.1080/01900692.2018.1498103

Wirtz, B., Weyerer, J., & Kehl, I. (2022). Governance of artificial intelligence: A risk and guideline-based integrative framework. *Government Information Quarterly*, *39*, 101685. DOI: 10.1016/j.giq.2022.101685

Wolfe, D. T., & Hermanson, D. R. (2004). The fraud diamond: Considering the four elements of fraud. *The CPA Journal*, *74*(12), 38–42. https://digitalcommons.kennesaw.edu/cgi/viewcontent.cgi?article=2546&context=facpubs

World Intellectual Property Organization. (2023). World Intellectual Property Indicators 2023. WIPO Publication No. 941E. https://www.wipo.int/edocs/pubdocs/en/wipo-pub-941-2023-en-world-intellectual-property-indicators-2023.pdf

World Intellectual Property Organization. (2023). World intellectual property indicators report: Global patent filings reach record high in 2023. WIPO. https://www.wipo.int/pressroom/en/articles/2024/article_0015.html

Xiao, Y., Wu, J., Lin, Z., & Zhao, X. (2018). A deep learning-based multi-model ensemble method for cancer prediction. *Computer Methods and Programs in Biomedicine, 153*, 1–9. PMID: 29157442

Y Arcas, , B. A. (2022). Do large language models understand us? *Daedalus, 151*(2), 183–197.

Yesiariani, M., & Rahayu, I. (2017). Deteksi financial statement fraud: Pengujian dengan fraud diamond. *Jurnal Akuntansi & Auditing Indonesia, 21*(1), 49–60. DOI: 10.20885/jaai.vol21.iss1.art5

Yeung, K. (2018). Algorithmic regulation: A critical interrogation. *Regulation & Governance, 12*(4), 505–523.

Yip, E. (2024). The metaverse future: legal gaps in data privacy, regulation, and democracy. SSRN *Electronic Journal*. https://doi.org/DOI: 10.2139/ssrn.4908442

Zadeh, L. A. (1965). Fuzzy sets. *Information and Control, 8*(3), 338–353.

Zaidan, E., & Ibrahim, I. A. (2024). AI governance in a complex and rapidly changing regulatory landscape: A global perspective. *Humanities & Social Sciences Communications, 11*, 1121. DOI: 10.1057/s41599-024-03560-x

Zajko, M. (2021). Conservative AI and social inequality: Conceptualizing alternatives to bias through social theory. *AI & Society, 36*, 1047–1056. DOI: 10.1007/s00146-021-01153-9

Zajko, M. (2022). Artificial intelligence, algorithms, and social inequality: Sociological contributions to contemporary debates. *Sociology Compass, 16*(3), e12962. DOI: 10.1111/soc4.12962

Završnik, A. (2020). Criminal justice, artificial intelligence systems, and human rights. *ERA Forum, 20*(4), 567–583. https://doi.org/DOI: 10.1007/s12027-020-00602-0

Zhang, Y., & Wallace, B. (2017). A sensitivity analysis of (and practitioners' guide to) convolutional neural networks for sentence classification. In *Proceedings of the Eighth International Joint Conference on Natural Language Processing* (pp. 253-263).

Zhang, Z., Chen, Z., & Xu, L. (2022). Artificial intelligence and moral dilemmas: Perception of ethical decision-making in AI. *Journal of Experimental Social Psychology, 101*, 104327. DOI: 10.1016/j.jesp.2022.104327

Zhang, Z., Gu, Y., Han, X., Chen, S., Xiao, C., Sun, Z., & Sun, M. (2021). CPM-2: Large-scale cost-effective pre-trained language models. *AI Open, 2*, 216–224.

Zheng, S., Jayasumana, S., Romera-Paredes, B., Vineet, V., Su, Z., & Du, D.. (2015). Conditional random fields as recurrent neural networks. In *Proceedings of the IEEE International Conference on Computer Vision* (pp. 1529-1537).

Zhou, Z. H. (2012). Ensemble methods: foundations and algorithms. Chapman and Hall/CRC. USPTO. (2020). Manual of Patent Examining Procedure (MPEP), Ninth Edition, Revision 10, June 2020. United States Patent and Trademark Office.

Zuboff, S. (2019). *The age of surveillance capitalism: The fight for a human future at the new frontier of power*. PublicAffairs.

Zuiderveen Borgesius, F. J. (2020). Strengthening legal protection against discrimination by algorithms and artificial intelligence. *International Journal of Human Rights*, *24*(10), 1572–1593. DOI: 10.1080/13642987.2020.1743976

About the Contributors

Jerry Luftman's prominent career combines his expertise as a CIO/practitioner, management consultant, and academic leader. Renowned for his mastery of business-IT alignment and global digital trends, Dr. Luftman has authored 19 books, contributed extensively to academic research, and excelled at management consulting, coaching/mentoring, teaching, and public speaking - hallmarks of his exceptional leadership. After a distinguished 22-year career at IBM (where he was among the strategic leaders of the IBM Palisades Executive Education Center, CIO, and responsible for the successful launch of many landmark products and services), Dr. Luftman transitioned to a celebrated 20-year tenure at Stevens Institute of Technology. There, he was Professor, founder, and Associate Dean of the Information Systems programs - acknowledged as one of the largest globally.

Aditya Tomer is presently the Dean, Galgotias University, Greater Noida. He is an academician with varied and interdisciplinary interests. Dr. Tomer has to his credit more than 54 publications including Books, Monographs, Chapters, Research Papers, Articles in Magazine and Newspapers. Some of his books namely are Comparative Reflections on the Constitutional Models of India and Australia, Law Governance and Society-A Developing Socio Legal Developing Nations, Rethinking of Juvenile Perspective in Digital Age, Right to Information Act (2005), Good governance and Human rights in Developing Nations, Rethinking of juvenile Justice system in India and Gender Discourse and Legal perspectives. Dr. Tomer is a keen researcher and has supervised research leading to the award of Ph.D in Law and also LLM. He has presented more than 30 Research papers in National and International Conferences. As an editor he has improved the quality of law journal like Amity International Journal of Juridical Sciences, and Ami code e-Newsletter of Law Dr. Tomer has also contributed to the development of Law Schools by organizing many National and International Conferences, Workshops, Training programmes with NHRC,

NCW, NCPC, SCW-BPR&D etc, FDPâ€™s, Panel Discussions and Moot Court Competitions, Legal Aid Camps etc. of high repute

***

Senthil Kumar A.V. is working as Principal, Nehru Institute of Information Technology and Management, Coimbatore, India. He has worked as Professor and Director, PG and Research Department of Computer Applications, Hindusthan College of Arts & Science, Coimbatore, Tamilnadu for 15 years and as Senior Grade Lecturer in CMS College of Science and Commerce for 14 years. To his credit he has industrial experience for five years and teaching experience of 29 years. He has also received his Doctor of Science (D.Sc in Computer Science). He has to his credit 86 Book Chapters, 234 papers in International and National Journals, 85 papers in International Conferences in International and National Conferences, and edited 17 books and 3 Text books. He is as Associate Editor of IEEE Access. He is an Editor-in-Chief for many journals and Key Member for India, Machine Intelligence Research Lab (MIR Labs). He is an Editorial Board Member and Reviewer for various International Journals. He is also a Committee member for various International Conferences. He has guided 16 Ph.D scholars and guiding 3 Ph. D scholars now.

Shovonita Acharjee is an academician and researcher in the field of law, presently serving as an Associate Professor at Amity Law School, Amity University Mumbai. She has successfully completed her Doctor of Philosophy (Ph.D.) in Law from Sharda University, Greater Noida, where her doctoral thesis was titled "Juvenile Correction and Rehabilitation in Conflict with Law - With Special Reference to NCT of Delhi." With an academic career spanning nearly a decade, Dr. Acharjee has previously served as Assistant Professor of Law at reputed institutions including D.M. Harish School of Law (HSNC University, Mumbai), Thakur Ramnarayan College of Law (Mumbai University), Asian Law College (Noida), and JIMS School of Law (Greater Noida). Her teaching expertise covers a broad spectrum of subjects such as Intellectual Property Rights, Constitutional Law, Jurisprudence, Human Rights, Administrative Law, and Research Methodology. Dr. Acharjee's research interests lie in Juvenile Law, Feminist Jurisprudence, Transgender Rights, Constitutional and Human Rights, and Emerging Legal Issues in Technology and Society. She has presented papers at numerous national and international conferences, including events organized by The University of Adelaide (Australia), Lancaster University (UK), and Gujarat National Law University (India). Her scholarly contributions include several Scopus and UGC-Care indexed publications, focusing on critical socio-legal issues such as gender justice, digital privacy, juvenile rights, and transformative constitutionalism. She has also received accolades like the Best Research Paper Award at the International Conference on Law and Contemporary Trends (2023) and the Best Presenter Award at the National Conference on Criminal Justice System in India (2019). As an educator, researcher, and mentor, Dr. Shovonita Acharjee continues to contribute to legal academia through her dedication to innovative teaching, interdisciplinary research, and academic leadership.

Wesam Alkhadour holds a Ph.D. in computer science from the University of Bradford, United Kingdom. She is currently an assistant professor at the University of Petra, Jordan.

Adnan Asrar is an Assistant Professor of Law at Lloyd Law College, Greater Noida. He is engaged in teaching and academic research with a strong commitment to legal education and scholarly excellence. His academic interests include core areas of law, contemporary legal issues, and interdisciplinary perspectives on legal studies. Mr. Asrar is actively involved in mentoring students, contributing to academic discourse, and participating in institutional and professional activities aimed at advancing legal scholarship and practice.

Pankaj Chhuttani is a highly accomplished legal professional, holds a B.Com. LL.B (Hons.) degree from School of Law, UPES, Dehradun, and an LL.M. degree from Dharmashastra National Law University, Jabalpur. He has qualified the UGC-NET in Law in a first attempt, showcasing his expertise in the legal field. Presently he is an Assistant Professor of Law at National Forensic Sciences University, Gujarat, and he is also pursuing his Ph.D in law from RGNUL, Patiala. His primary interest areas include corporate law, competition law, ADR, and IBC. However, his future goal extends beyond his successful legal career. He aspires to become an academician, driven by his passion for sharing knowledge and contributing to the education of upcoming legal professionals. With his extensive knowledge, expertise, and enthusiasm, he aims to inspire and shape the minds of aspiring law students while making valuable contributions to the field of law.

Habiba Djigo is a final year Master degree student at Aivancity, La Grande Ecole De L'intelligence Artificielle Et De La Data, specializing in AI and Data Science

Rohan Rajeev Ghosh is an aspiring legal scholar hailing from Mumbai, India, currently pursuing a B.A. LL.B. (II nd Year). from Thakur Ramnarayan College of Law, affiliated with the University of Mumbai. With a deep passion for jurisprudence. Rohan has demonstrated exceptional academic performance, consistently achieving high CGPAs. His legal acumen is further evidenced by his internships at prestigious firms like NyayaSarthak and Rahul & Jayshri Associates & Co., and his contributions to various legal publications, including the IILM Law Journal. Rohan's diverse skill set spans legal research, drafting, and content writing, underpinned by strong interpersonal and critical thinking abilities. He is a published author with several articles in international journals, showcasing his commitment to legal innovation and reform. Proficient in multiple languages, including Bengali, English, and Hindi, Rohan is also deeply engaged in cause advocacy, particularly in economic empowerment, environmental sustainability, human rights, and political discourse. His achievements include top ranks in research paper competitions and moot court awards, reflecting his dedication to advancing the legal profession. Rohan's profile exemplifies a young legal mind ready to contribute meaningfully to the field of law and society at large.

Jorge Marx Gómez studied Computer Engineering and Industrial Engineering at the University of Applied Sciences Berlin (Technische Fachhochschule Berlin). He was a lecturer and researcher at the Otto-von-Guericke-Universität Magdeburg (Germany) where he also obtained a PhD degree in Business Information Systems with the work Computer-based Approaches to Forecast Returns of Scrapped Products to Recycling. From 2002 till 2003 he was a visiting professor for Business Informatics at the Technical University of Clausthal (TU Clausthal, Germany). In 2004 he received his habilitation for the work Automated Environmental Reporting through Material Flow Networks at the Otto-von-Guericke-Universität Magdeburg. In 2005 he became a full professor and chair of Business Information Systems at the Carl von Ossietzky University Oldenburg (Germany). His research interests include Very Large Business Applications, Business Information Systems, Federated ERP-Systems, Business Intelligence, Data Warehousing, Interoperability and Environmental Management Information Systems.

Junaidi, a Legal Practitioner, Writer and Lecturer at the Faculty of Law, Sjakhyakirti University Palembang. Born in 1978 in Palembang. Graduated from Muhammadiyah 9 Elementary School (1992), State Junior High School 8 (1995) and State Senior High School 7 (1998) all completed in Palembang. Bachelor of Laws completed at the Faculty of Law, Bhayangkara University, Greater Jakarta (2013) and Postgraduate Law completed at Krisnadwipayana University Jakarta (2016) with a Business Law Study Programme. Completed his Legal Auditor Education at Jimly School of Law and Government (JSLG), batch 13 (2014). The author is also a resource person in various national seminars. Active in writing scientific papers published in various national journals, national and international level proceedings and Book Chapters with various universities and research study institutions. The author is also a reviewer and editor for several national journals in the field of law.

The author is also active as a book editor in various fields, especially in the field of law

Anuradha Kar is an Associate Professor in AI and Robotics at Aivancity Paris Cachan, France, where she teaches and mentors graduate students in deep learning, AI for health, computer vision, explainable AI, and human-computer interaction. She holds a Ph.D. in Electrical Engineering from the University of Galway, Ireland. Her research interests lie at the intersection of assistive technologies, digital health, generative AI, and the ethical and fair deployment of artificial intelligence. She has conducted research at several leading institutions, including the Institut Pasteur in Paris, where she focused on deep learning applications in drug discovery, and the Paris Brain Institute in collaboration with Inria (French national institute for digital sciences), where she worked on AI-driven analysis of Alzheimer's disease biomarkers. At the École normale supérieure de Lyon, she worked in collaboration with Inria and Inrae (French national institute on agriculture and environment) developed deep learning techniques for the analysis of 3D bio-imaging datasets.

Hamza Khan (Assistant Professor Law at Symbiosis Law School Hyderabad) is a legal academic and researcher dedicated to exploring the intersection of law, technology, and policy. As a faculty member, he teaches AI & Law, and Intellectual Property Law, guiding students in understanding the legal and ethical challenges posed by emerging technologies.

Sheikh Inam Ul Mansoor (BA.LLB Hon's, LLM, CPCT WIPO, Ph.D. International Trade Law) is a highly accomplished academician presently working as an Assistant Professor Law at the Symbiosis Law School, Hyderabad, India. With a strong background in law and a passion for academia, Dr. Sheikh has made significant contributions to the field through his extensive research and publications. Pursued his BA. LLB (Hon's) from University of Kashmir, LLM from JNU Jaipur and Ph.D. International Trade Law from LPU Punjab. Prior to his academic career, Dr. Sheikh served as an Advocate and Solicitor at the Jammu and Kashmir High Court and other subordinate courts in Jammu and Kashmir. This experience as a legal practitioner has provided him with valuable insights into the practical application of law and enhanced his understanding of legal dynamics. As an Assistant Professor Law at Symbiosis Law School, Hyderabad, India, Dr. Sheikh Inam Ul Mansoor continues to make significant contributions to the legal field through his research, teaching, and involvement in various professional activities.

Tasnim Masheh is a final year Master degree student at Aivancity, La Grande Ecole De L'intelligence Artificielle Et De La Data, specializing in AI and Data Science

Jessica Mbounkap is a final year Master degree student at Aivancity, La Grande Ecole De L'intelligence Artificielle Et De La Data, specializing in AI and Data Science

Aymrick Nzooh completed his Master degree at Aivancity, La Grande Ecole De L'intelligence Artificielle Et De La Data, specializing in AI and Data Science

Khalil Omar is an assistant professor at the University of Petra in Jordan. He received his Ph.D. degree in computer science from the University of Oldenburg, Germany, in 2018. His academic focus is on distance learning and e-learning in combination with software engineering, mobile applications, usability design, adaptive interfaces, and ERP systems.

Chandika Eka Prasetya is an Information Technology professional with a strong interest in digital system development and innovative technology solutions. He focuses on the application of information systems and modern computing technologies to enhance efficiency, reliability, and operational performance. With a solid technical background and a commitment to continuous learning, Chandika actively keeps pace with emerging trends in the IT field and explores practical implementations of new technologies. His professional interests include system development, data management, and the integration of intelligent technologies to solve real-world problems. Through an adaptive, analytical, and solution-oriented approach, he aims to contribute to the development of scalable and sustainable IT solutions in both academic and professional environments.

Binastya Anggara Sekti has been a lecturer at the Faculty of Computer Science, Esa Unggul University, Jakarta, since 2016. He is actively involved in the Artificial Intelligence and Information Security Study Group. He holds a Bachelor's degree in Informatics Engineering from the Bandung Institute of Technology and a Master's degree in Information Systems Management from Trisakti University, Jakarta. Prior to entering academia, he accumulated over 25 years of professional experience as an IT practitioner in various companies across Jakarta. His work focused on developing data centers for internet service providers and delivering IT solutions for the manufacturing and oil & gas sectors. His research interests include artificial intelligence, cybersecurity, and the development of IT infrastructure.

Leny Ramadhani Setiawan is an IT professional with a strong interest in research on Artificial Intelligence (AI) and the Internet of Things (IoT). Her work focuses on exploring how intelligent systems and connected devices can be designed and integrated to support data-driven decision-making, automation, and innovative digital solutions. She is particularly interested in the practical and research-oriented application of AI and IoT in areas such as smart systems, information systems development, and emerging digital technologies. Through her professional and research activities, she aims to contribute to the advancement of intelligent and scalable IT solutions that address real-world challenges.

Devendra Singh has an impressive and diverse academic and professional background. He has an extensive and diverse educational background, including doctorate degrees in law and management & commerce, and his first Ph.D. was awarded in finance & management, and he has done a second Ph.D. in law (banking and AI laws). He has around 25 years of vast experience in teaching, academic administration, industry, consulting, and research, with an emphasis on AI and banking regulation laws, finance, and management. He has held various positions in different institutions and has made significant contributions to the field through his research, publications, and chairing many conferences.

Ankit Srivastava is currently serving as an Assistant Professor of Law at Rajiv Gandhi National University of Law (RGNUL), Punjab. He is also a distinguished Member of the Network for Indian Competition Experts at the Competition Commission of India (CCI). Dr. Srivastava holds a PhD in Law from NLU Jodhpur and an LLM from NLU Delhi. He completed his undergraduate studies in law (BA LLB) at Symbiosis Law School, Noida. With over eight years of teaching and research experience, Dr. Srivastava has previously held esteemed positions at Amity University Lucknow, National Law University (NLU) Jodhpur, and Dharmashastra National Law University (DNLU) Jabalpur. At DNLU, he notably served as the In-charge of the Moot Court Committee and the Director of the Centre for Competition Law and Policy. He has been actively involved in leading significant research projects, including an ICSSR-funded study on the Sukanya Samriddhi Yojana and a project funded by the CCI on the competition assessment of the electricity sector in India.

Showkat Wani has good publications in SAGE, IGI Global and other reputed journals like Springer. He has completed many research targets, including four PhD Research Scholars and eight P.G. Dissertations who had already completed their research and were awarded. Dr. Wani has so far written 30 Research articles and attended 48 Conferences. Dr. Wani has also edited one book.

Jamal Zraqou is an associate professor at the Department of Computer Science/Virtual and Augmented Reality, University of Petra, Jordan, where he has been a faculty member since 2022. From 2018-2029, he was also the dean of the faculty of IT at IU. His research interests include computer vision, virtual and augmented reality, internet of things (IoT), cybersecurity, and image processing.

Index

A

B

C

J

L

M

N

O

P

R

S

T

www.ingramcontent.com/pod-product-compliance
Lightning Source LLC
LaVergne TN
LVHW081319300926
849161LV00008B/1814